The People and Their Peace

The People and Their Peace

Legal Culture and the Transformation of
Inequality in the Post-Revolutionary South

LAURA F. EDWARDS

THE UNIVERSITY OF NORTH CAROLINA PRESS   CHAPEL HILL

© 2009 THE UNIVERSITY OF NORTH CAROLINA PRESS

Designed by Kimberly Bryant
Set in Arno Pro by Tseng Information Systems, Inc.
Manufactured in the United States of America

The paper in this book meets the guidelines for permanence
and durability of the Committee on Production Guidelines
for Book Longevity of the Council on Library Resources.

The University of North Carolina Press has been a member
of the Green Press Initiative since 2003.

Library of Congress Cataloging-in-Publication Data
Edwards, Laura F.
The people and their peace : legal culture and the
transformation of inequality in the post-revolutionary
south / Laura F. Edwards.
p. cm.
Includes bibliographical references and index.
ISBN 978-0-8078-3263-9 (cloth : alk. paper)
1. Law—Social aspects—Southern States—History.
2. Women—Legal status, laws, etc.—Southern States—
History—19th century. 3. Slaves—Legal status, laws, etc.—
Southern States—History—19th century. 4. Free African
Americans—Legal status, laws, etc.—Southern States—
History—19th century. 5. People with social disabilities—
Legal status, laws, etc.—Southern States—History—19th
century. I. Title.
KF366.E329 2009
340′.1150975—dc22

2008041343

13 12 11 10 09   5 4 3 2 1

FOR JOHN, *the Love of My Life*

Contents

Acknowledgments *xi*

PART I   DISTANT THUNDER *1*

1   Introduction *3*

2   All Was Chaos in Our Legal World: Excavating Localized
     Law from beneath the Layers of Southern History *26*

PART II   LOCALIZED LAW *55*

3   Keeping the Peace: People's Proximity to Law *64*

4   Bread from Chaff: Defining Offenses against the Peace *100*

5   Possession and the Personality of Property:
     The Material Basis of Authority *133*

6   Wasted Substance: The Operation and
     Regulation of Patriarchy *169*

PART III   STATE LAW *203*

7   Subjects vs. Rights-Holding Individuals *220*

8   New States: Freemen as Consistent Units of Measure *256*

Conclusion *286*

Notes *299*

Bibliography *375*

Index *411*

Maps and Illustrations

MAPS

North Carolina Counties, 1800 *17*

South Carolina Districts, 1814 *17*

ILLUSTRATIONS

Women Patriots in Edenton, Chowan County *19*

State House in Columbia, South Carolina, 1794 *33*

The first court of Spartanburg District *68*

The first courthouse in Chatham County, North Carolina *70*

Morgan Square, Spartanburg, South Carolina *76*

Bonds Conway's house, Camden, South Carolina *127*

Freedpeople, Sea Islands, South Carolina, 1862 *143*

Plantation scene in South Carolina, ca. 1860 *147*

"South Carolina Views, Going to Market, the old Ox and Cart" *148*

A street vendor and "Selling Sweet Potatoes in Charleston" *152*

A boat similar to those piloted by slaves along South Carolina's
   waterways *195*

State House, Raleigh, North Carolina, 1793–95 *206*

Capitol, Raleigh, North Carolina, remodeled 1820–24 *206*

State Capitol, Raleigh, North Carolina, 1833–40 *207*

Public Record Office in Charleston *208*

The courthouses in Union District and Kershaw Distric *216*

"South East View of Greenville, South Carolina," 1825 *217*

Camden County Courthouse, 1847, and Orange County Courthouse,
   1845 *218*

Thomas Ruffin, Anne Kirkland Ruffin, and their first house *246*

The courthouse in Marshall, the county seat of Madison County,
   North Carolina *288*

Acknowledgments

A remarkable number of people have extended their credit to me, to borrow a concept from the following pages. Their generosity and faith opened up opportunities that made it possible for me to research and write. I hope that when they read the book, they are pleased with the results. If so, that only partially covers the debts I have incurred. I look forward to repaying the balance in the years to come.

I began the research in Washington, D.C., in 1995, while I was waiting for readers' reports on my first book. I spent my days in the archives, turning over ideas for a book on domestic relations in the nineteenth-century South. I hoped the topic would provide a way to write a legal and political history centered on those people — domestic dependents — who were confined within the "private" domestic sphere and excluded from the "public" world of politics. Specifically, I wanted to explore the relationship between private and public, following the changing line that divided the two and kept domestic dependents and domestic issues outside the formal political realm. Beginning at the end of the century and moving back in time, through the Progressive Era, Reconstruction, the Civil War, the antebellum period, and the early republic, I never imagined that I would end up staying in the late eighteenth and early nineteenth centuries. But the material in that period kept calling me back. The attraction was the challenge: the more time I spent on the sources from that era, the less it seemed that I understood. The local records featuring ordinary southerners — particularly those involving slaves, free blacks, and white women — proved the most difficult and the most rewarding. Those cases then led me to state leaders, legal institutions, and the political structure. Ultimately, I found myself back at my original topic, although with a shorter timeframe. This is the book I imagined in 1995: a legal and political history constructed around ordinary people, particularly white women and African Americans.

I am extremely grateful to the many organizations that have provided financial support for this project. A postdoctoral fellowship in 1995 from the Smithsonian's National Museum of American History allowed me the time, space, and resources to lay the foundations for this project. The University of South Florida, where I taught from 1994 to 1997, gave me leave time and research funds through a summer grant and a Presidential Young Faculty

Award. At UCLA, I received a fellowship from the Center for Politics and Public Policy that provided research funds and a quarter's leave time. A postdoctoral fellowship for university professors, provided by the National Endowment for the Humanities in 1999–2000, allowed a year for research and reflection at a particularly crucial time. I am thankful to the NEH for taking a chance on this project, which was still in its early stages at the time; without that support, this book would look very different. Duke University has been particularly generous in granting leave time. In addition to two Dean's Leaves, each of which released me from teaching and other institutional commitments for a semester, the university has made it possible for me to take fellowships for two consecutive years. In 2006–2007, I spent an extremely happy and productive year at the Newberry Library in Chicago with a Mellon Postdoctoral Fellowship in the Humanities. I have a special place in my heart for the Newberry Library, where I worked on staff while I was finishing my dissertation and where I have written drafts of my dissertation and all three of my books. Jim Grossman, my former boss and now Vice-President of Research and Education at the Newberry, thinks this might be some sort of record, although he's not sure — the competition is stiff, because the Newberry is known for researchers and fellows who either refuse to leave or who keep coming back. But if one dissertation and three books do not constitute a record, they are a testament to the Newberry's superb collections and intellectual community, which have sustained, challenged, and inspired me through the years. I was then fortunate enough to spend 2007–2008 at the National Humanities Center in Research Triangle Park, North Carolina, with a Rockefeller Foundation Fellowship. This experience was an unexpected gift. The time, the incredible support from the NHC staff, and the motivation from the community there has been crucial in the final round of revision. I could not have finished the book without this fellowship, and I am grateful to the NHC and to those at Duke who made it possible, Bill Reddy, chair of the History Department, and deans Sally Deutsch and George McLendon.

This project would have been impossible without the archivists who patiently fielded numerous questions and requests, often involving obscure sources. Members of the staff at the following institutions have contributed more than they will ever know: the South Carolina Department of Archives and History; the South Caroliniana Library at the University of South Carolina; the Special Collections Library at Duke University; the North Carolina Collection and the Southern Historical Collection, both

at the University of North Carolina; the North Carolina Department of

Archives and History; the Baker Library at Harvard University; and the Library of Congress. Elizabeth Dunn, in the Special Collections Library at Duke, went above and beyond the call of duty in helping identify pertinent collections and hunting down the answers to my questions about them. I am also grateful to the library staff at the National Humanities Center. Eliza Ferguson, Jean Houston, and Josiah Drewry filled all my requests—even for nineteenth-century newspapers, which are notoriously difficult to obtain—with such speed that I began to feel slow and ineffective. Karen Carol, the house copyeditor at the National Humanities Center, entered the project during its final stages, not only rooting out errors and inconsistencies, but also serving as a much-needed pillar of efficiency and sanity in a task that tends to bring out my least efficient and sane sides.

The amount of research required for this project was truly daunting, and I could not have done it without assistance, much of which has come from people who have now gone on to successful careers of their own. I continue to be amazed by the incredible research skills of Kirsten Delegard. As a graduate student at Duke, she collected material on pardons and church records. The term "collected," though, does not begin to describe what she did: Kirsten wrung hundreds of pardons out of recalcitrant source bases and managed to identify the most interesting church records from a virtual sea of such materials. The analysis also reflects the intellectual contributions embedded in the research of Samantha Gervase, Chelsea Neal, Jessica Millward, Alisa Harrison, Kelly Kennington, Dominque Bregent-Heald, and Diana Rice.

Grey Osterud brought her editing skills to this project at a moment when I was having difficulty explaining its significance. She guided me back to firmer ground, helping me articulate the essence of the ideas, first through grant proposals and then in the book itself. Working with Grey has been pure pleasure. She has the ability to edit conceptually: to take the project on its own terms, to identify its basic intellectual structure, and to help the author build on that. She has read each chapter two and in some cases three times. To the extent that this book fulfills the goals I set out for it, it is largely because of Grey. In fact, I miss working with her so much that I am racing to find another project so that I can enlist her services again.

I am particularly grateful to the people who read the book in its entirety. It has benefited enormously from reviews by three presses, with the comments of Barbara Welke, Dylan Penningroth, Martha Jones, and two other anonymous reviewers, all of whose comments have sharpened, strengthened, and honed the analysis. Dylan also read individual chapters, providing critiques that have challenged and changed the way I saw key issues. Kate Masur, Ed Balleisen, and Dirk Hartog voluntarily and generously read from start to finish as well; their thoughts have been crucial in the process of revision. Jacquelyn Hall and Peter Coclanis, who also read drafts, must be wondering when their service as dissertation advisors will end; I am hoping that the job remains open-ended, because I so value their insights and advice. Chris Tomlins, who has been a key supporter of this project from the beginning, when the project's shape was less clear, deserves special mention. Conversations about early chapter drafts, proposals, and the first draft of the manuscript have been crucial in shaping this project and in reviving my sometimes flagging confidence.

Jacquelyn Hall has been an inspiring presence throughout the project. She has read beyond the call of duty, commenting on proposals, articles, and multiple chapter drafts. In that process of exchanging work with her, I feel as if I have relearned how to write. That experience of challenge and growth has been a treasure. I am lucky to have an incredibly creative, challenging, and supportive intellectual community in North Carolina, at Duke University and at the University of North Carolina, Chapel Hill. In addition to those I have already mentioned, other colleagues have read pieces of the work and contributed enormously to the analysis: Bob Korstad, Gunther Peck, Jolie Olcott, John French, Anne Allison, Maureen Quilligan, and Adrienne Davis. Priscilla Wald, in particular, has been an enthusiastic, insightful, and valued reader. My colleagues outside North Carolina have been equally generous with their time. Lisa Tetrault, a fellow at the Newberry Library, could be counted on to make sense of chapters when no one else could figure out what was wrong. Al Young provided incredibly helpful comments on two chapters. Ariela Gross has read so many different parts of this book as an anonymous reviewer that she deserves some kind of award or special recognition, at last, for all the work that she has done. Joe Miller, who edited an article from this project for a special edition of *Slavery & Abolition*, helped me both refine crucial aspects of the argument and see new conceptual aspects of the project. The critical eye of Mike Grossberg, who read an early proposal, set the stage for thinking about the book's basic structure. Bob Gordon, who read chapters, also played a crucial and much-appreciated role in supporting the project. Jan Reiff and Noralee Frankel lived through many aspects of the research and writing with me and offered so much support, insight, and advice along the way that I do not really know where to begin in thanking them. Glenda Gilmore provided wisdom at a particularly crucial stage of the project. That is only one of many things she has done for me over the years, and I count myself extraordinarily fortunate to have her friendship.

I have tried out much of the book at various places and have benefited from the comments I have received. Those venues include the Willard Hurst Summer Institute in Legal History, sponsored by the American Society for Legal History; the Lane Seminar series, sponsored by Northwestern University; the History Colloquium at Harvard Law School; the History Colloquium at Yale Law School; the Early American History Seminar at the University of Georgia; the conference "Making, Remaking, and Unmaking Modern Marriage," organized by the Law School, University of Southern California; a conference in United States history at LaTrobe University; a history seminar at the University of Sydney; the Legal History Seminar at the American Bar Foundation; the Labor History Seminar and the Early American History Seminar at the Newberry Library; the Political History Workshop at the University of Chicago; the Seminar in Southern History at the University of Virginia; a workshop, organized by graduate students in the History Department, for women's history month at the University of Texas, Austin; the Legal History Workshop at the University of Michigan; and the Workshop on Gender and History at the University of Minnesota.

Working with the University of North Carolina Press has been wonderful. I remember talking with Kate Torrey about the project ten years ago. Her interest in and enthusiasm for the project meant more than she can ever know. When her duties moved her away from editing, David Perry took over without missing a beat. Eric Schramm did a wonderful job with copyediting, and Ron Maner fielded all my many questions when the book was in production. It has been a pleasure working with all of them.

John McAllister read the entire manuscript, with the ear of a musician and a mind that reads both for conceptual form and rhetorical precision. He smoothed out the cadences and transitions, often explaining the problems in musical terms: the chapter was humming along in smooth 4/4, he would say, when all of a sudden it switched to 5/4 without any warning, leaving the reader with a feeling of profound disorientation. Not good. He eliminated clutter, pointed out inconsistencies, identified places where the argument had wandered out of sight, tamed unruly metaphors, and elaborated on the ones that worked. But his editing skills, while considerable, do not begin to cover his significance to this book or to me. That is why the book is for him, for everything that he has done to create the life that we have together.

Acknowledgments

PARTS OF THE FOLLOWING CHAPTERS have appeared in "Status with-out Rights: African Americans and the Tangled History of Law and Gover-nance in the Nineteenth-Century U.S. South," *American Historical Review* 112 (April 2007): 365–93; "Enslaved Women and the Law: The Paradoxes of Subordination in the Post-Revolutionary Carolinas," *Slavery & Abolition* 26 (August 2005): 305–23; "Law, Domestic Violence, and the Limits of Patri-archal Authority in the Antebellum South," *Journal of Southern History* 65, no. 4 (November 1999): 733–70; and "The Civil War and Reconstruction," in *The Cambridge History of Law in America*, vol. 2, *The Long Nineteenth Gen-eration (1789–1920)*, ed. Christopher Tomlins and Michael Grossberg (New York: Cambridge University Press, 2008), 313–44 (© 2008 Cambridge Uni-versity Press; reprinted with permission).

PART I ▪ Distant Thunder

1 Introduction

Sometimes a change in the weather announces itself. The skies darken, the wind shifts, lightning flashes, thunder rolls, and a downpour follows, washing away the dust, cleansing the air, and leaving the impression of dramatic change. Other times, the thick, cloying summer humidity turns imperceptibly into a rain shower that seems inevitable in hindsight. The subject of *The People and Their Peace* is the societal equivalent of a silent summer rain shower: changes that eased themselves into the nation's history with so little notification that, once they had been established, it appeared as if things had always been that way.

This metaphorical change in the weather involves fundamental developments in law and governance between 1787 and 1840. Here the term "law" refers to the body of ideas, customs, and practices that guided the determination of justice, broadly defined, according to the multiple, conflicting, and manifestly inequitable standards of the time. "Governance" denotes the institutional mechanisms, formal and informal, including, but not limited to, the legal system, through which decisions were made about legal cases and public issues. *The People and Their Peace* draws on detailed archival research in two slave states, North Carolina and South Carolina, to reconstruct legal culture at both the local and state levels. The state-level laws and legal institutions that so many historians assume to be authoritative emerged within the context of a profoundly decentralized system, rooted at the local level. Recovering the importance of localized law places ordinary people, rather than legal professionals and political leaders, at the center of law and governance in this period. It also recasts our understanding of key developments at the state and national levels, specifically the meaning of rights and presumption of the slave South's distinctiveness within narratives of U.S. history.

LOCALIZED LAW AND STATE LAW

Localized law and state law coexisted in two very distinct planes in the period between 1787 and 1840, operating simultaneously but largely apart. The situation was similar to the one described in Hendrik Hartog's clas- 3 sic article "Pigs and Positivism," which explores the relationship between formal law and popular legal culture through the attempted regulation of pigs, the favored livestock of many New York City residents in the early nineteenth century. Custom allowed pigs to roam free and wallow about, a practice that New Yorkers with aspirations to refinement found distasteful. Challenged in court, the pigs and their owners lost. But that outcome made no dent whatsoever in customary practice: even as the prohibition against pigs entered into the law books, pigs remained on the streets.[1] That disconnect between the law of pigs as articulated by the courts and the law of pigs as practiced in the city streets illustrates a key element of the relationship between state law and localized law in the Carolinas. Even as state law acquired institutional mass over time in the form of statutes and appellate rulings, the people who tended localized law kept to their own paths, absorbed by what they encountered there and largely oblivious to events at the state level, despite efforts to attract their attention.

While occupying legitimate spaces within the structures of government, state law and localized law were fundamentally incompatible at a basic, conceptual level. Proponents of state law, who would have sympathized with the regulatory efforts of New York City officials, aspired to create a unified body of law and a centralized institutional structure to enforce it. Localized law, by contrast, recognized multiple sources and sites of legal authority, including customary arrangements as practiced, on the ground, in local communities. Where state law protected the rights of legally recognized individuals, localized law maintained the social order — the "peace," a well-established Anglo-American concept that expressed the ideal order of the metaphorical public body. Legal professionals dominated at the state level, where they followed laws as specified in authoritative texts. Localized law depended on information conveyed orally by ordinary people — even subordinates without rights — who were all considered necessary to the legal process of maintaining the peace. When oral proceedings in localized law were reduced to writing, the resulting records did not have the authority of written legal texts produced at the state level: writing remained secondary, as a reminder of oral knowledge that had determined the process.[2]

Between 1787 and 1840, state law developed alongside the localized system, but never completely displaced it. Even as state institutions and laws assumed more importance, they did not provide the only, or even the primary, legal site or conceptual framework for addressing public matters. Although the evolution of law and legal institutions in this period has been well studied, some of the most important elements of change have gone largely unnoticed by scholars because they are so difficult to see in the sources.[3] Systemic legal change of any kind is virtually undetectable in the local court records, the body of sources on which social historians have relied, particularly for information about white women, poor whites, free blacks, and slaves. These materials mark neither the radical decentralization of government in the Revolutionary era that produced the localized system nor the later elaboration of state law. Cleaving to custom, with all the violence and inequality that pass as custom in a slave society, local proceedings convey the impression of a society stuck in the past, stubbornly resistant to change and richly deserving of its reputation for backwardness. In many ways, the processes of change are no more discernible in the materials that historians traditionally use to study law and politics. Newspapers, appellate decisions, statutes, political pamphlets, legal treatises, and the papers of the political elite actively promoted the systematization and centralization of law at the state level. But they wrapped the discussion of these "reforms" in the rhetoric of progress, with strong Whiggish undertones of inevitability. As a result, these sources read as a negation of any human agency in the conception or direction of change: law and government simply assumed the form they were always intended to have, aided by those who had access to the plan. At both state and local levels, we thus find an archival record saturated in images that obscure dynamic change — hardly an invitation for further investigation.

The images are misleading, because change marked the history of law and government at both the local and state levels between 1787 and 1840. Dismantling the centralization of imperial rule during the Revolution, white Carolinians reframed their governments to localize the most important functions, drawing on Revolutionary ideology, undercurrents of political unrest in the rural population, and established elements of Anglo-American law. These changes dramatically altered the existing structures of imperial rule by placing government business in local legal venues — not only in circuit courts, but also in magistrates' hearings, inquests, and other ad hoc forums. This localized system had no use for distinctions that would later become so important at the state level, allowing local custom, politics, and law to mingle freely and blurring the demarcation between "local administration" and "state government." In the context of post-Revolutionary government, local legal practice was not some quaint, folksy exception to a formalized, rational body of state law, as is commonly assumed. Local decisions officially shared space with legislation and appellate decisions as central components of state law, precisely because state governments were relatively weak and delegated so much authority to local jurisdictions. In fact, the state level was largely dependent on local jurisdictions.

Not all areas of law were equally localized. Even before the Revolution, professionally trained lawyers had taken control over private matters involving property—what we now know as the civil side of the system. That area of law was the first to be systematized and centralized at the state level. Local areas, though, maintained authority over public matters, which included all crimes as well as a range of ill-defined offenses that disrupted the peace.

Although many historians have associated the South with "localism," this approach to law and government was not peculiarly "southern" at the time. In this regard, the Carolinas illustrate broader trends in the legal culture of the post-Revolutionary era. As recent scholarship has emphasized, localism characterized both the theory and practice of law and government throughout the United States, even at the national level, in the post-Revolutionary period.[4] The fact that the two states were very different in matters other than law underscores the power of those legal currents. South Carolina was British North America's premier colony, with close ties to England and continental Europe and a thriving economy based in staple crop culture and slave labor. In the early nineteenth century, the cotton boom kept the state's economy buoyant. But expansion in that period masked underlying weaknesses that led to long-term economic stagnation, the effects of which became apparent in the 1830s. By contrast, colonial North Carolina was something of a backwater, with a reputation as a refuge for misfits and failures. The colony's lack of distinction in the British Empire, however, served it well later. Unfettered by dependence on staple crop production, antebellum North Carolina developed a relatively dynamic, mixed economy, in which slavery played a significant but less determinative role than it did in other slave states. Later, in the 1860s, those social and economic differences determined the two states' paths, on the way to the Civil War. South Carolina's political leaders led the Deep South out of the Union in the first wave of secession, following the election of President Abraham Lincoln. North Carolina's leaders held back, anchored by economic and political ties to the North and the presence of a large block of white voters who, while neither opposed to slavery nor even openly Unionist, had little in common with slaveholding planters in the Deep South. North Carolina finally joined the Confederacy in the second wave of secession, after Lincoln's call for troops made it clear that the federal government would use military force to resolve the crisis and that the slave states remaining in the Union would have to choose sides.[5]

But it was the fallout from the American Revolution, not the anticipation of the Civil War, that framed the development of law and government in the early republic. The localized system that emerged in the 1770s blended the new and the old, bringing Revolutionary ideals of participatory government and local control to established legal practices, namely, the multiple traditions and overlapping jurisdictions so well mapped by early modern British historians. This new, hybrid system emphasized process over principle: each jurisdiction produced inconsistent rulings aimed at restoring the peace. The peace constituted a hierarchical order that forced everyone into its patriarchal embrace and raised its collective interests over those of any given individual. Beyond that, the content of the peace remained purposefully vague, because it both governed and was constituted by relationships and practices that varied from locality to locality.

North and South Carolinians regularly called on the authority of the peace to resolve what they regarded as serious problems, drawing law into the entire range of personal conflicts and community disorders. Wandering livestock and quarrelsome neighbors shared legal quarters with gamblers, drinkers, wife beaters, and even planters who committed offenses against their slaves. Everyone participated in the identification of offenses, the resolution of conflicts, and the definition of law. Even those without rights—wives, children, servants, and slaves, all of whom were legally subordinated to their household heads, as well as free blacks, unmarried free women, and poor whites, whose race, class, and gender marked them as subordinates—had direct access to localized law. They also had some influence over it, but only through the relationships that subordinated them within families and communities, not through recognition of their individual rights. Nevertheless, it was this same subordination that gave them legal access through their specified places within the peace. Similarly, white patriarchs exercised domestic authority at the behest of the peace, not in their own right. When their actions disturbed the peace, whether through inadequate or excessive use of authority, they experienced censure. Keeping the peace meant keeping everyone—from the lowest to the highest—in their appropriate places, as defined in specific local contexts.

Local courts focused on the resolution of these highly personal, idiosyncratic disputes. Judgments rested on the situated knowledge of observers in local communities, in which an individual's "credit" (also known as character or reputation) was established through family and neighborly ties and continually assessed through gossip networks. Local officials and juries judged the reliability of testimony based on an individual's credit as well as on impersonal, prescriptive markers of status, such as gender, race, age, or class. In this system, the words of subordinates could assume considerable legal authority. A slave's well-placed remarks about his master's financial difficulties or a wife's pointed complaints to neighbors when begging for essential supplies acquired resonance as they moved through local gossip networks. Such information shaped the terms of legal matters before they even entered the system. How subordinates exercised influence in law without being able to change or even challenge their legal subordination constitutes an important strand of the analysis. Another strand considers the implications of a legal system in which any one person's experience was not transferable to another person of similar status (defined by such characteristics as gender, race, or class) or predictive of any other case's outcome. These disparate outcomes coexisted as options and alternatives, rather than contradictions requiring rationalization. The result was a legal system composed of inconsistent local rulings, which offered future courts various options rather than precedents; there was no uniform "law" to appeal to.

The importance of localized law is often overlooked, because the state leaders who opposed it have dominated the historical narrative. These white men, most of whom were professionally trained lawyers, were part of a national network that applied Revolutionary ideals to very different ends: they wished to create a rationalized body of law based on the protection of individual rights, particularly property rights, and to centralize the operations of government to regularize the creation and dissemination of that body of law. Recognizing the importance of history to that task, they compiled documentary sources and crafted narratives that cast localized law as an archaic throwback, which inevitably gave way to progressive change as laws were standardized and rights were uniformly defined and applied. Their voices acquired resonance over time, as historians relied on their archive, followed their lead, and ignored—even dismissed—legal localism.[6]

State leaders' accounts are accurate in the sense that state law became more elaborate, sophisticated, and influential between 1787 and 1840. At the end of the Revolution, there was no coherent body of law at the state level to deal with public matters. But neither was there anything inherent in the decentralized, localized system that precluded the development of such laws within state-level institutions. So reformers set about creating a body of state law based in rights. Beginning with the area of property law, they created the necessary institutional structure at the state level. By the end of the 1820s, state leaders had made considerable progress in rationalizing the legal system at the state level, even in the realm of public matters. Then they secured popular support for that project through highly visible political campaigns: the nullification campaign of 1827–32 in South Carolina and the 1835 state constitutional convention in North Carolina.

As lawmakers extended the reach of state law, they imposed the rubric of individual rights on matters formerly governed by collective conceptions of the peace, as defined in local contexts. The logic behind the developing body of state law turned white men's patriarchal authority and civic participation into individual rights, akin to their already established property rights. White men's rights expanded at this level of the legal system, increasing their claims on the legal system and to state protection of their interests. In the political rhetoric of the 1830s, they became "freemen," legally recognized individuals who were the paradigmatic citizens, at least within the realm of state law. At the same time, dependents' legal status, particularly their lack of rights, became the rationale for their exclusion from law and government. State law defined them as altogether different categories of legal persons and subordinated them according to the abstract categories of race, class, and/or gender. White women, African Americans, and the poor found it difficult to make themselves heard and their concerns visible within the body of state law, because they were excluded from the category of people with rights the state was designed to protect.

The denial of rights to the vast majority of southerners and their exclusion from the polity masked even more profound inequalities at the state level. White men were constituted as freemen through their rights *over* those without rights. In extending this legal framework, state leaders applied the precepts of liberal individualism to the patriarchal structure of localized law. They abstracted the authority white men already exercised in social context, through their obligations to the peace in localized law, and individualized both its privileges and restrictions. By the 1830s white men could claim rights not just in their property and their own labor in state law, but also in the labor and bodies of their dependents and, through the abstractions of gender and race, in the lives of other subordinate people as well. Their authority in this body of law extended over all black persons, slave or free, and no black person fully possessed his or her own body or the product of his or her labor.[7] The rhetoric of party politics construed rights broadly, linking them to freedom, liberty, and equality among white men, whether propertied or not. In practice, though, state leaders' vision of democracy did not include fundamental changes in the economic or social structure that would put all white men on equal footing. Legislators and jurists defined rights narrowly, so as to affirm existing inequalities among white men and to protect the property interests of the wealthy, particularly slavery. By the 1830s freemen could look to the state to protect their rights, defined in the limited, abstract terms of law at that level of the system. But many of the white men included in this category could not count on those rights as a means to articulate, let alone promote, their interests.[8]

State leaders were less successful in practice than either their writings or their influence on later historians suggest. State law took up more institutional space by the 1830s, but it did not triumph over localized law: the legal system, which still included localized legal practices, did *not* work as state leaders wished and represented, particularly in the broad area of public law. Localized law continued to have considerable influence in the antebellum period and long afterward, because it was embedded in the culture in ways that made it very difficult to eliminate. To further complicate matters, localized law had always accommodated multiple — even conflicting — legal traditions, so it was possible for southerners to embrace rights discourse, as developed at the state level in the 1830s, while still adhering to conflicting tenets of the local system. People might represent their interests in local courts in terms of rights, but the localized system continued to incorporate their claims just as it had always done with other claims on the peace.

The development of state law is, nonetheless, a crucial and historically neglected story. Not only did it operate by a very different logic — the logic of individual rights — than did localized law; it also cast its subjects in a different relationship to law and the government. State law would become more influential over time, as this level of government became more entrenched and more powerful. But it is not so much the relative influence of state law as the timing of its emergence that is the important story. Although scholars usually treat state law as primary, it did not emerge in the broad area of public matters until the 1820s (in appellate law and statutes) and the 1830s (in the discursive realm of politics). This periodization changes our view not only of people's influence over governance and the development of rights within the nation's political culture, but also of the relationship of slavery and the South to the rest of the nation.

THE SOUTH AND THE NATION

It is tempting to cast the narrative in terms of declension, whereby the status of marginalized southerners declined as a legal system based in rights became more influential, diluting the practices of localized law. Bad weather became worse, as intermittent rain showers turned into a flood (to continue the opening metaphor). Did the development of a legal system at the state level, based in rights, work against ordinary southerners in this period? The question does not really have enough substance to carry the analysis, because it is so easily answered in the affirmative: a legal system based in individual rights is not particularly useful to people who cannot claim them or use them. The new legal order that emerged at the state level offered possibilities that localized law did not, but only if individual rights were extended more broadly within the population and only if their meanings were defined more generously so as to address fundamental social, economic, and political inequalities. In the political context of the slave South, state law reinforced, rather than challenged, the subordination of all those who were not rights-bearing individuals and even some who were. To focus on this one question, moreover, is to miss more important points that speak to other, central historiographical issues: the privileged position of individual rights within our historical narratives, the elevation of legal professionals and printed legal materials over ordinary people and cultural currents in our conception of law, and the assumption of southern distinctiveness in all aspects of scholarship on the nineteenth-century United States.

The rights of individuals provide a poor standard by which to evaluate changes in either law or government in the period between 1787 and 1840. This measure is not only utterly inadequate, but also hopelessly anachronistic because so much legal business was conducted within a localized system that maintained the collective order of the peace, not the rights of individuals. People regularly pursued their own interests in localized law. This system, however, did not treat their claims as expressions of rights. Nor did it treat the claimants as legally recognized, autonomous individuals who exercised agency on their own behalf through the possession of rights. To the extent that individuals figured in the process at all, they did so through hierarchical family and community relationships that connected them to the peace. It was those networks, built through relations of subordination that tied southerners to one another, that brought a wide range of southerners into the dynamics of localized law. Because access depended on those social relations, even those without rights had influence within the system. To understand a localized law system in terms of individuals or individual rights is to misconstrue its most basic dynamics, stretching the standards of a single, developing area of law at the state level not only backward, but well beyond its reach.[9]

Similarly, the textual legal authorities that defined state law did not describe localized law. From the perspective of customary practice, there was no need to identify a single location of legal authority or a definitive body of texts, because the logic of localized law sanctioned the coexistence of multiple sources of legal authority. It was only in the legal framework proposed by the state elite that legal authority was located in one body of law and in one place, namely, the state. State law was the province of the few: elite, professionally trained lawyers, who divined its direction through specially designated published texts, namely, statutes, appellate decisions, and legal treatises. That law's scope was also limited, reaching only to the minority of the population that had rights.

While the admonition against relying exclusively on state-level sources might apply generally to most periods in U.S. history, it takes on particular salience in the years between 1787 and 1840. State law, as envisioned by the elite, did not yet define the system, and the legal materials generated at this level were much less authoritative than they were to become later. In the legal system as it actually existed at the time, a wide range of practices and materials, written and unwritten, informed the law: not only the legal materials produced by professional lawyers, but also religious and popular writings as well as the cultural traditions and local knowledge of southerners — men and women, black and white, rich and poor — who did not have professional training. Ordinary people, even those without rights, influenced localized law in a basic, structural sense. Indeed, these people, and the body of knowledge upon which they drew, *constituted* localized law. Its fundamental content emerged through the lives of ordinary people on the ground in local communities in ways that were not the case at the state level, where the system was based on the protection of abstract rights.

Given the centrality of people to the content of law, the topics usually relegated to social history have direct implications for the field of legal history. Relations between slaves and masters, wives and husbands, and children and parents, as well as those among neighbors and extended families, all left a direct imprint on law and legal practice. So did the conflicts and aspirations, petty and profound, of people whose names never made it into legal histories of the era. The marginality of these southerners obtained only at the state level, where it existed more in theory than in practice for much of the period.[10]

Given the dynamics of the legal system, particularly in the immediate post-Revolutionary decades, localities actually provide the best place from which to develop larger generalizations about law and government. This approach flies in the face of century-old historiographical conventions that consign local history to antiquarians, based on the assumption that provincial places were historically marginal in the past and therefore are inconsequential for understanding historical change. But the pejorative connotations so often applied to all things "local" are not applicable during the period between 1787 and 1840, particularly in legal matters. In fact, these connotations are but another legacy of the creators of state law. As part of their reform project, state leaders generated the expectation that the state would function as the final repository of legal authority. They not only separated "the state" from "the local," but also insisted on the superiority of the former to the latter. But their rhetoric, so powerfully articulated in the archival sources, has led historians to conclude that the local level actually *was* subordinate to the state in matters of law.

More important, the way state leaders pitted "the state" against "the local" presumed a conceptual framework that posits a single, controlling view of law as the only viable option. They were so successful in perpetuating these presumptions that it is now difficult for us to imagine a system in which one body of law and one institutional arena—at some level, be it local, state, or national—was not definitive. As a result, our histories of legal systems tend to be about transitions or transformations that occur as one level becomes more important than another. But the narrative that state leaders imposed does not really work for the Carolinas or anywhere else in the United States during the period from 1787 to 1840. The logic of the system, as it actually existed at the time, resolutely ignored all the presuppositions necessary to a linear narrative of a transition from one coherent legal regime to another. After the Revolution, local jurisdictions had primary control over public matters, because multiplicity was accepted as the way things were and should be, not because local jurisdictions were identified as the "top" of the judicial hierarchy. In the logic of the localized system, state laws did not necessarily control local practice, define the needs of the peace in local areas, or constitute a definitive body of law uniformly applicable throughout the state. They were just laws generated in a different place—the state level, not other, local areas. In fact, because the state was a different place, its laws might not represent the practices of a given locality particularly well. Instead of following in the path of state leaders and viewing these multiple, conflicting legal traditions as problems that required reform, we need to create new conceptual frameworks that accept these dynamics as part of the nation's past.

The emphasis on local legal arenas ultimately widens, rather than narrows, the historical lens of this study, bringing connections between the Carolinas and the nation into focus. Studying southern states to shed light on national developments, particularly in the early nineteenth century, goes against the historiographical grain in much the same way as highlighting localities does. The South has long figured as a distinctive region in the popular imagination as well as in historical writing. It is a position forged in the political crisis of secession and the Civil War, shaped in the aftermath of Confederate defeat by white southerners who created a mythical slave South to service the Cult of the Lost Cause, and buffed to a fine finish during the Jim Crow era by fiction writers and professional historians who relied on southern regionalism for vibrant characters, gothic plots, and analytical meaning. For many writers, southern exceptionalism constituted a source of pride. It demonstrated the South's continued connection with a purer era of the nation's past and its innate superiority over the rest of the country. As the civil rights, labor, and feminist movements gained ground in the twentieth century, however, southern exceptionalism underwent a critical reassessment. As early as the 1920s, activists, writers, and historians were using it to explain the South's ills, from slavery and racism to class oppression and gender inequality and the region's persistent poverty and endemic underdevelopment. Southern exceptionalism became synonymous with backwardness of all kinds — economic, social, cultural, intellectual, and political. Above all, exceptionalism separated the South from the nation. Events in the South were presumed to be unique to that region; studies of southern problems spoke to regional dynamics, not national ones. Even the boldest and most significant historical lessons about slavery and racial discrimination stopped at the Mason-Dixon Line.

Like the negative qualities attributed to the term "local," the concept of southern exceptionalism inappropriately imposes later developments on the past. In this instance, though, the elite who developed state law are not culpable. In the decades following the Revolution, they did not see themselves or their region as different or distinctive, let alone provincial or backward. South Carolina was the wealthiest state in the new nation. The state's elite moved in national and international networks, maintaining strong ties with other regions of the United States as well as the Caribbean and Europe. North Carolina's proximity to South Carolina and Virginia, two of the most influential states in the early republic, led to unflattering comparisons in which North Carolina invariably came up short. Yet even North Carolina looked outward to a wider, cosmopolitan world. The correspondence of backwoods merchants talked more of events in the commercial centers of Europe than it did of local or even state and national dynamics. Local newspapers devoted an enormous amount of space to international news with good reason, since the actions of international powers directly affected daily life. At this time, localism did not denote a provincial outlook that took no cognizance of the outside world. The region's elite was thoroughly embedded in the networks of the Atlantic world and wedded to its political and intellectual currents. And even the localism of the local legal system did not take the form of extreme provincialism, the claims of state leaders notwithstanding. Legal localism represented a different logic for resolving disputes and determining justice; it did not connote ignorance.

Moreover, the experience of the Revolution encouraged southerners, particularly those who had spearheaded the Patriot cause, to see themselves as the vanguard of progressive change. They took pride in their education, which they often received in Europe, and followed the political and intellectual currents of the Age of Reason with an enthusiasm that sometimes bordered on obsession. Moving in social networks that were not circumscribed by geography, they identified both with their states and with the new nation. They saw themselves as the architects of the new republic and its institutions, which would serve as guides for future progress. Their hubris knew no bounds; the fate of the world lay in their hands.[11]

By beginning with local areas—not with the already constituted states that would eventually form a distinct region—we can see the dynamics by which states were transformed into centralized government institutions with rationalized bodies of law. These same changes have been found elsewhere in the United States, but historians have erroneously presumed that the South formed an exception. Reform-minded southerners drew on political principles usually associated with the liberal state in the North: private property, individual rights, and a limited but theoretically democratic government that protected those rights and encouraged individual initiative.[12] In the context of a slave society, those principles resulted in extreme legal inequalities and rigid political exclusions. Although those outcomes are usually considered unrepresentative of national trends, they in fact paralleled developments in the North, where recent historiography has emphasized growing inequality, expressed in categorical terms of race, class, and gender and linked to the spread of liberal individualism. The history of these two southern states provides insights into the origins and reconstitution of inequality in the nation as a whole.

Indeed, the southern experience sheds light on national issues that still resonate today. As the history of the Carolinas indicates, the extension of rights to new portions of the population is only part of the story: the meanings given to individual rights were — and are — as important as their distribution.[13] Although rights exist as abstractions in law, they are always applied in context. Without political backing and a strong commitment to democracy and equality, a government based in the protection of individual rights can lead in profoundly oppressive directions. In the Carolinas, the same principles that we usually associate with individual liberty, democracy, and equality were mobilized in defense of slavery, the nation's most potent symbol of tyranny and repression. We usually treat slavery as an exception that can be explained by its divergence from national principles, but the system of vesting some with rights in the labor and bodies of others was far more pervasive than many Americans like to recognize. The principles of equal rights were — and still are — extended in democratic directions only by political struggle.

MAPPING THE SOURCES, PLACES, AND ANALYSIS

The People and Their Peace is based on legal records and a range of other sources from both the local and state levels between 1787 and 1840. It draws on thousands of local court records from six specific areas in the Carolinas, chosen for the quality and completeness of their records as well as the variety of their social and economic circumstances: the counties of Chowan, Orange, and Granville in North Carolina and the districts of Kershaw, Anderson-Pendleton, and Spartanburg in South Carolina. The research then extends outward to other counties and districts to include divorce, apprenticeship, poor house, and church records, as well as other local materials. At the state level, the materials cover statutes, appellate decisions, and various published legal sources; state government documents such as governors' correspondence, legislative committee reports, pardons, and petitions; newspapers; and the diaries and letters of various leaders in state law and politics.

Chowan County, the first home of North Carolina's colonial government, lies on the state's east coast. Its major city, Edenton, was a busy commercial center. The county was also a center of the Patriot movement during the Revolution, led by a tight circle of Whig lawyers, merchants, and planters, including William Hooper, Samuel Johnston, and James Iredell Sr. While these men have been largely forgotten, relegated to bit parts in most histories of the Revolution, their womenfolk are more familiar, memorialized in a widely reproduced British cartoon lampooning their boycott of

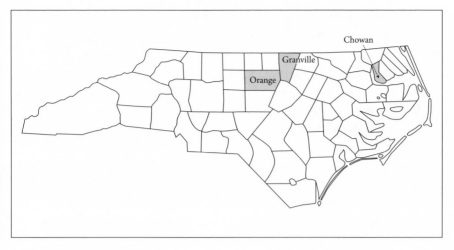

North Carolina Counties, 1800

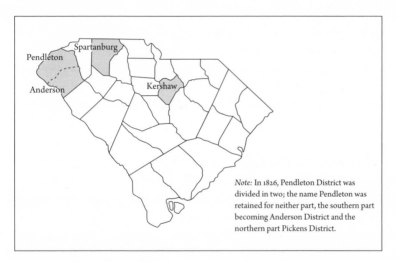

Note: In 1826, Pendleton District was divided in two; the name Pendleton was retained for neither part, the southern part becoming Anderson District and the northern part Pickens District.

South Carolina Districts, 1814

imported tea. Like Patriot leaders in other eastern port centers, the county's colonial elite were linked to the Atlantic world through family networks and economic ties, which were often one and the same. But North Carolina's elite remained on the periphery, thanks to the colony's notoriously unstable coast, which made navigation and the establishment of permanent, stable ports extremely difficult. By the early nineteenth century, though, the cotton boom had turned the coastal plain into a plantation district. In 1790 Chowan County was inhabited by 2,592 whites, 2,473 slaves, and 67 free people of color. By 1840, the enslaved population, which had grown to 3,665, outnumbered the 2,865 whites. The elite, whose fortunes rose and fell with the cotton market, worked to re-create Atlantic economic networks and threw themselves into the post-Revolutionary project of state-building, supporting education, economic development, internal improvements, and legal reform. As the cotton market softened in the 1820s and the South's economic center moved westward, Chowan County experienced economic decline, produced by the continued dependence on slavery and cotton.[14]

Located in the verdant hills of the piedmont, Orange County, North Carolina, was colonized only in the eighteenth century. Its colonial residents, yeoman farmers who had moved south from Virginia and Pennsylvania looking for land, had little in common with Chowan County's Whig planters, merchants, and lawyers. These settlers found what they came for in abundance; but to secure title to the land, they had to deal with the arcane, inefficient bureaucracy of the colonial courts. Outraged by high fees and mismanagement, many of Orange County's farmers joined the Regulator Movement in the 1760s. When the colonial government ignored their complaints, Regulators turned to force and, in Orange County, seized the court in Hillsborough. Governor Tryon responded by calling out the militia, which chased down prominent leaders and crushed the remnants of the uprising at the Battle of Alamance, also in Orange County. The Regulators' legacy did not translate into support for the Patriot cause during the Revolution. To the contrary, disgruntled farm families pitted themselves against Whig merchants, later Patriot leaders, who had moved into the backcountry in the 1760s and brought with them the economic and legal practices of the Atlantic world that Regulators had found so problematic. The county continued to be dominated by middling farm families after the Revolution. But they were unable to halt the legal and economic changes that had prompted fathers to join the Regulators. Instead, those trends intensified, turning Hillsborough into a thriving court town and home to some

Women Patriots in Edenton, Chowan County. Caricature of the Edenton Tea Party, thought to be by Philip Dawe of London, 1775. Courtesy of the North Carolina Collection, University of North Carolina Library at Chapel Hill.

of the state's most famous lawyers and leaders, including Thomas Ruffin, Archibald D. Murphey, and Duncan Cameron.[15]

Large plantations, notably the extensive holdings of the Cameron family, mushroomed amidst the county's solid family farms. But the wealth of Orange County's elite did not come only from agriculture. Many of the leading families were linked to merchants who had turned backwoods bartering into economic power. The same entrepreneurial orientation marked subsequent generations, whose interests included a wide range of capital ventures: banking, slave trading, mining, transportation, and industry. It was home to both Chapel Hill, where the state university was located, and Durham, a small country crossroads that would later become the center of tobacco manufacturing and the site of Duke University. The mix of plantations, family farms, trade, and small manufactures is evident in the population figures, which also reflect the county's relatively large geographic extent compared to eastern counties. In 1800 the county had a total population of 16,362, with 12,680 whites, 3,565 slaves, and a little over a hundred free people of color. By 1840, although the county had shrunk in size as regions to the west and south were spun off as separate counties, the population had grown to 24,356, with 16,771 whites, 6,974 slaves, and 631 free people of color.[16]

Traveling north, Orange County's green woodlands gave way to the flat, sandy scrublands of Granville County. Environmentally an extension of southern Virginia, the county was ideal for the production of bright tobacco, whose characteristic yellow color owed to the lack of nutrients in the soil. What produced excellent bright tobacco made much of the county inhospitable to yeoman farm families, who favored mixed agriculture rather than specializing in a single cash crop. Yeoman families nonetheless clustered in small communities, where they hunkered down and scratched out a living amidst the county's tobacco plantations. To grow tobacco, an incredibly labor-intensive crop, the county's planters mobilized slave labor. In 1800 the county's population was almost evenly split between free and enslaved residents, with 7,630 whites, 6,106 slaves, and 279 free people of color. By 1840 there was a slight black plurality, with 9,309 whites, 8,707 slaves, and 801 free people of color. Tobacco drew Granville County into Virginia's economic orbit. Planters marketed their crops through factors in the tobacco centers of Petersburg and Richmond, where they did their other business and maintained their social networks. Perhaps it was because the county's elite was so attached to Virginia that Granville produced fewer prominent state leaders than did other North Carolina counties.[17]

The South Carolina upcountry districts of Anderson-Pendleton and Spartanburg had more in common with North Carolina's piedmont and mountain west than they did with the eastern plantation districts in their own state. Low country planters summered in the area, drawn by the cool air and blue-green beauty of the mountains. A few planters established plantations there. But the area was dominated by middling farms and small plantations, rather than the vast operations that monopolized the low country. Those differences were apparent in the racial composition of the population. Though African Americans made up the majority of the population in the South Carolina low country, the reverse was true in the upcountry. In 1800, the recently settled Spartanburg District had 10,609 whites, only 1,467 slaves, and 46 free people of color; Pendleton District, which included the area that would later be subdivided into Anderson District, had 17,828 whites and 2,204 slaves. By 1840 Spartanburg had grown to 17,924 whites, 5,687 slaves, and 250 free people of color; Anderson District, which composed only a part of the former Pendleton District, had 12,747 whites, 5,683 slaves, and 63 free people of color. Voting tallies in the 1830s highlight the demographic differences, which also underlay upcountry whites' complaints about their lack of fair political representation in the state legislature. In Anderson District, 2,388 white men cast votes in the 1834 election; in Spartanburg, 2,715 white men voted. In the low country district of Georgetown, only 421 white men cast ballots; in nearby All Saints District, only 124 white men did. "There are several little Parishes in the lower part of this State," complained Benjamin F. Perry, the editor of Spartanburg's Unionist newspaper, the *Greenville Mountaineer*, "whose wealth and free white persons, only entitled them to one representative each, whilst they have as much influence in the Senate, as the District of Pendleton, whose property and population entitled her to seven members in the House of Representatives." Expressing the sentiments of many upcountry whites, he described the system as "entirely arbitrary."[18]

Cotton differentiated upcountry South Carolina from the counties on North Carolina's far western border. Located in the foothills, not the highlands, western South Carolina was better suited to cotton cultivation. The cotton boom in the early nineteenth century drew white families to these upcountry districts, generating wealth and, ultimately, a plantation elite. Perhaps the best known of the new gentry was John C. Calhoun, whose Anderson District plantation is now the site of Clemson University. The economic effects of the cotton boom are evident in the growth of the slave population. They also registered in the upcountry split over nullification.

While voters in some districts opposed nullification on the grounds that it advanced the interests of the low country elite, other districts supported it, precisely because they identified with those interests.

Kershaw District lay south and east of upcountry, closer to the low country in both geographic and social terms. Located just below the fall line in the piney woods, the area that became Kershaw was colonized well before the Revolution. In the colonial period, the town of Camden became a thriving commercial hub on the trade route between the low country and upcountry. The cotton boom of the early nineteenth century then turned the area into a plantation district: in 1800 the district was home to 4,706 whites, 2,530 slaves, and 104 free people of color; by 1840 there were 3,988 whites, 8,043 slaves, and 58 free people of color. The wealth of prominent Kershaw families, such as the Chesnuts, Boykins, and Blandings, rivaled that of low country dynasties. In fact, the district's elite remained tied to the low country's urban center, Charleston, a relationship solidified in the nineteenth century with canals and, later, a railroad. Yet, like the elite in Orange County, North Carolina, those in Kershaw did not depend solely on agriculture. Some planters also carried on a side business as traders, transporting crops and other goods to Charleston, selling them there, and bringing back supplies. They tended to diversify their holdings, supporting a range of economic ventures beyond agriculture.[19]

The People and Their Peace is based on extensive runs of court documents from these localities, including magistrates' trial papers, coroners' inquests, and criminal records from the circuit courts. Unlike sampling, which abstracts cases from context, this intensive approach reveals information that is essential for understanding the dynamics that shaped these conflicts and their resolutions. This approach allows insight into how people defined law on the ground. The local records do not resemble state-level legal documents that are more familiar to historians. They are written in a crabbed hand and sometimes streaked with water damage and age, on paper that is stained, torn, or just plain dirty. The researcher reads around mildew and the past depredations of large insects and small mammals, while piecing together information that creative spelling and decades of bad record keeping conspire to keep locked in the past. In North Carolina, the criminal records are collected together in a single record group that includes magistrates' trial records, coroners' inquests, and criminal records from the circuit court. They are organized by date, with the documents for any given case scattered through the files. In South Carolina, the criminal records for the circuit court tend to be grouped by case, with all the documents collected together in a single file. But the coroners' reports, magistrates' court papers, and other materials are filed in separate record groups, with minimal, if any, organization.

These records are as difficult to interpret as they are to read. Localized law valued subjectivity, not objectivity: who was involved and what others knew about them mattered more than anything else. Gossip, hearsay, and innuendo had legal standing just as information, common knowledge, and credit did. In fact, oral presentations tended to take precedence over physical evidence, because truth was thought to be established through the credit of the speaker. Testimony consisted of a narrative constructed to support one side or the other, not an objective statement of facts. The veracity of an account was only apparent to those who knew the context. Even then, veracity did not always translate into legal victory in a system that determined justice by local standards that were, at best, idiosyncratic.

The information saved for any given case varies widely. The records were created by local officials, of different degrees of literacy, who added another layer of interpretation as they wrote, when they wrote at all. Records tend to be most complete at the circuit court level, where record keeping was institutionalized in the form of an appointed clerk. Even then, cases at this level appear and then disappear without a trace, let alone an explanation. These records also tend to describe the process, not the reasoning behind it: they often include perfunctory summaries of the complaint, the charge, the outcome, and sometimes even the evidence and testimony, but not the lawyer's arguments or the judge's charge. When testimony from circuit court proceedings appears in the records, it was usually written after the fact by clerks who were preparing case summaries for appeals. The records of magistrates, coroners, and other officials, which are often attached to circuit court cases, are both more uneven and more revealing of the cases' dynamics. They are also maddeningly tantalizing, because it is impossible to know the number and type of cases local officials at other levels of the system mediated, but failed to record, making quantitative analyses of the remaining material pointless. Sometimes magistrates and other local officials simply copied out legal forms in longhand, filling in the blanks with the barest of details: the complainant's name, the accused, the offense, the location, and the date. More industrious officials took down complaints as well as other evidence and testimony in a form that approached verbatim transcription. Those records have the feel of a person speaking, with informal phrasing, graphic descriptions, obvious colloquialisms, and even noticeable accents, all written in a hurried hand.

The fact that cases are cultural artifacts rather than transparent accounts of legal proceedings is what makes them so valuable to historians. Each case, carefully constructed so as to justify its outcome, contains hidden agendas — not just those of the local officials, but also those of the people who created and presented the evidence. More often than not, those agendas remain frustratingly opaque, because what went unrecorded was usually more important than what was. Even the cases with the most voluminous documentation rest on a whole universe of unstated assumptions, the kind of everyday knowledge that was so deeply embedded in people's lives that it no longer needed to be articulated. That the woman who claimed to have been raped was the magistrate's niece and the accused man was well known for drinking and carousing, that the master accused of abusing his slave was involved in a series of conflicts with his neighbors and the slave in question was married to a slave owned by one of those neighbors — such information, usually unstated, framed local cases. The records also remain silent as to reception. What reads as powerful testimony to a modern researcher may have been laughably unbelievable to listeners then, who knew the circumstances and the people involved. Usually, the documents reveal less about the legal matter at hand than about the social relations and cultural values underlying it: they tell us about the dynamics of legal process, even as they leave us in the dark as to the reasons for the legal outcome.[20]

Given the nature of the records, volume is crucial. In any given case, it is impossible to know what went unstated, if that information was important, and why. It is impossible to discern the official's agenda, the narratives embedded within the material, or the reception of the evidence. It is also difficult to figure out whether the dynamics that structured the case were unusual or not. With thousands of cases, though, the information accumulates and forms patterns.

Localized law did not represent — or even aim to represent — a coherent, uniform view of the law, based on outcomes. The documents were authored by a range of people, with direct interests in particular conflicts, not in the concept of law as a systematic, abstract body of knowledge. Those were the interests of state leaders, and those qualities distinguish the legal sources they created: appellate decisions, statutes, and legal treatises. *The People and Their Peace* approaches these materials as ideological expressions about the form and content of law and government, rather than descriptions of the legal system. Linked together through tight social, economic, and political ties, the authors shared a common intellectual view that they hoped to impose by creating and legitimizing a coherent body of law and a centralized legal system to enforce it uniformly throughout the state.

The People and Their Peace is divided into three parts, with the first focusing on introductory material, the second on the operation of localized law, and the third on the development of state law. Chapter 2 continues the introductory material by examining the broad outlines of the legal system as it developed between 1787 and 1840, retelling the traditional narrative of state-building to include legal localism. Chapters 3 through 6, which make up part 2, explore the dynamics of localized law in the period from 1787 to 1840, beginning with the process itself and then moving to the power relations that were constituted through the system. The final two chapters, which make up the third part of the book, turn to the development of state law, with an emphasis on the period between 1820 and 1840. As the analysis shifts to the state level in these chapters, localized law moves to the background — but only in the book's discussion, not in the lives of Carolinians at the time.

The conclusion returns to the practices of legal localism, exploring how that culture and the expectations it fostered continued to shape rights and legal practice at the state level during Reconstruction. The conclusion also considers the broader implications of integrating the southern legal culture into the national narrative. The "exceptional" South has served as a useful scapegoat in the past and the present. A range of people, from popular commentators to professional historians, have used the assumed distinctiveness of the region's culture to explain some of the nation's worst features, especially racial oppression and a rapid recourse to violence. Yet this practice only distracts attention from what is a national legal culture of individual rights, a legal culture that can not only exacerbate inequalities, but diminish them as well. As *The People and Their Peace* shows, inequality is central to the conception of individual rights. That is why inequality persists throughout the United States, after emancipation and the reintegration of the Confederate states in the Union. The South's problems are, in fact, national problems. Only when the southern experience is fully admitted into the national experience is it possible to understand the dynamics that created and sustained racial, class, and gender inequalities that remain a fundamental part of the United States as a whole.

All Was Chaos in Our Legal World

2

It is easy to imagine Judge Elihu Hall Bay glaring down from the bench as he was sitting in a South Carolina district court, sometime in the early nineteenth century, listening to a case of wife beating. According to an observer who recounted the incident, the judge was not pleased with what he was hearing. The husband's lawyer, reputed to be a native of Pennsylvania and a former Lutheran minister, argued that the common law gave husbands the right to use violence to discipline their wives. Judge Bay thought otherwise. "With some emphasis, and in his slight stuttering voice," the judge announced that "there is no such law." The lawyer continued his argument and eventually returned to the same point. Judge Bay stopped him again. But the lawyer persisted. "Suppose," the lawyer asked, "when you went home, you should find your wife in an unruly mood, and she should make an attack on you." According to the observer, this last rhetorical flourish exhausted what was left of the judge's patience. "Sir," he responded, stammering more because of his anger, "if y-you make that th-that sup-po-sition a-again, I-I w- will co-commit you for a-a con-tempt." In his charge, Judge Bay informed the jurors that "the common law was the perfection of reason, and notwithstanding the loose remarks of writers, there was no such principle in that law" that would allow a husband to beat his wife. The court convicted the husband.[1]

This colloquy demonstrates how the law actually worked in criminal cases and other public offenses between 1787 and 1840 in the Carolinas. The states' Revolutionary-era constitutions decentralized the institutional structures of government, so that law was defined and applied locally, with the primary goal of resolving specific conflicts involving particular individuals. The key to this legal system was the dispersal of authority within it. When Judge Bay heard this wife-beating case in the South Carolina circuit court, there was no single directive on the legal treatment of such issues. He could not rely on particular statutes or appellate decisions, because there were none. He referred instead to the common law on this topic. But Bay did not necessarily mean Sir William Blackstone's well-known codification of English common law, which could be construed to allow for corporal punishment, even though Blackstone advised against it. While influential among professionally trained lawyers, Blackstone's *Commentaries on the Laws of England* did not define common law or occupy an officially recognized place within the laws of the state. Bay invoked common law tradition in its most expansive, archetypal form. More powerful than any treatise, decision, or statute, common law in this sense could trump any other rendering of an issue without ever settling into set patterns. In the wife-beating case, Bay used it to dismiss the "loose remarks" made by the Pennsylvania Lutheran minister turned South Carolina lawyer on a husband's disciplinary authority.[2]

Judge Bay actually dispensed "law," not "the law," which was perfectly in keeping with the requirements and expectations of the decentralized legal systems created in the Carolinas during the Revolution. The specifically singular form is inappropriate in this context, because it summons up images of a unified set of rules universally applied by robed officials in formal settings, usually in courthouses with the requisite white paint and columns. People might manipulate "the law" and even attempt to capture control over it, but they could not alter its underlying rules, which existed as a defined body of knowledge outside the context of their lives. After the Revolution, a dedicated group of professional lawyers began fashioning just such a legal system, defined at the state level, with a unified body of laws that were based on the protection of rights and were applied consistently throughout the state. Despite their efforts, though, "the law," as state leaders envisioned it, continued to share quarters with "law," a more capacious and less definitive concept, because it was more about the process than the outcome. The difference is expressed in southerners' use of the term, which sounds as awkward to modern ears as the concept is within our modern legal system: in the parlance of the time, southerners often talked about taking issues to "law," a process, not to "the law," a body of knowledge that would determine the outcome. Because it was based in process, this system accommodated not only Bay's version of law but also the Lutheran lawyer's, and those of other South Carolinians' as well. In this process-based notion of law, the basic rules were an evolving set of principles derived from a range of sources, including custom and local knowledge about the incidents in question and the persons involved in them, as well as legal treatises, case law, and statutes. As a result, its form depended on the local context in which it operated and the people who used it, and it readily incorporated inconsistencies, even contradictions. For much of the period between 1787 and 1840, the Carolinas had no institutional means for reconciling conflicting versions of law on particular issues or elevating one version over the other. Competing interpretations, produced locally, coexisted within this flexible legal system. Those inconsistencies were accepted elements of the system: they actually *constituted* law at the time; they were not deviations from it.

Even after reformers centralized institutional authority at the state level and created a unified body of state law, the culture of localism continued to influence how the legal system worked. In this regard, the situation in the Carolinas resembled that of other states at the time. To tell the story of legal localism, though, we must first peel away the layers of historical narrative and interpretation that have accumulated over two centuries. Accounts from the late eighteenth and early nineteenth centuries told a powerful story of progress that became the basis for later academic histories and continues to shape current scholarship. The key elements of this narrative were created by a group of professionally trained lawyers who were prominent in state politics, whose networks reached outward to the national level, and who sought to dismantle legal localism. This group viewed government institutions at the state level as the primary locus of power, notwithstanding actual practice; as a result, they focused their efforts on state-level reforms. The elite's prominence in the historical record, though, owes as much to their own efforts at self-preservation and -aggrandizement as it does to their political importance at the time. Their lives and work are easy to track, because they left such an impressive historical record. Joining their interest in law to a keen sense of history, infused by notions of objectivity and progress, they not only documented their own lives but also collected the documents of others and created archives with the intent of leaving the "correct" version of the past to posterity. Their version of history, which acquired more power through time, did not include the logic of legal localism, which represented what they were trying to replace.

The third part of this book returns to this group of professionally trained lawyers when their vision of law and governance began to acquire more substance and authority in the 1820s and 1830s. But, in order to excavate and appreciate legal localism, consideration of these men and the evidentiary trail they left behind is crucial at this point in the analysis. As the late Perry Miller observed, "We take the success of the courts in defending their integrity so much for granted that we forget how in the early nineteenth century their champions believed they barely survived the gale." Acknowledging the influence of these "champions" over both the archival records and the resulting historical narratives changes the analytical framework.

This perspective upends basic historiographical assumptions, revealing the artificiality of categorizing local matters in this period as historically marginal and elevating the state level. It also explains why legal localism appears as a transitory moment of little historiographical consequence, when it is acknowledged at all. To the members of that small circle of state leaders with legal training, "the state" *was* government at one, single level. They defined the concept of "the state" narrowly and horizontally in terms of the legislative, judicial, and executive branches located at the state capitols, instead of broadly and vertically in terms of all the practices and institutions that governed the public order. That conflation of "the state" with only particular parts of government, which much of the current scholarship accepts, makes it difficult to imagine it in any other way. Recognizing the emergence of that concept in the period between 1787 and 1840, the book uses the term "state law" to refer to the unified, authoritative body of law that developed at this level. In the post-Revolutionary Carolinas, however, neither the state nor the operation of law within it functioned as many of the state elite wished. Contained within their most damning comments are the most compelling insights into legal localism and the most dramatic testimony to its centrality in state government.[3]

HISTORY AND THE POST-REVOLUTIONARY LEGAL SYSTEM

As historians have rediscovered legal sources, reform-minded lawyers and jurists from the post-Revolutionary decades have renewed their grip on history. Historians of the South have deployed local legal material to great effect, using cases as a window not only on changes in the legal status of women, slaves, free blacks, and poor whites, but also on larger social and cultural currents outside the courtroom, including racial ideology, class tensions, gender relations, sectionalism, and the material circumstances of those on the social margins who otherwise left few traces of their lives.[4] For all the interest in legal sources, however, there has not been a corresponding scholarly rush to sort through the particularities of the system that produced those records. There are stellar exceptions: Ariela Gross's compelling analysis of slave law begins by walking the reader through the events of court day and makes the functioning of legal institutions central to the analysis.[5] For the most part, though, southern historians, even those who focus on legal history, tend to rely on legal sources without considering how they were created. They take the dynamics of local cases and measure them against the rules laid out in statutes and appellate decisions for insight into the past, bypassing the institutional dynamics involved in creating, disseminating, and applying the laws. Legal institutions are assumed to be a constant, unchanging background against which important, meaningful conflicts played out.

In this respect, southern historians do not differ significantly from their colleagues who study other parts of the nation. Nineteenth-century historians tend to start in the period following the Revolution, assuming that the war broke not just the nation's ties with England but its links with its early modern past more generally. As a result, questions about how the new republic made the institutional transition from a colony to a modern nation-state have not figured prominently in the historiography, even as the scholarship has relied heavily on legal materials and other government sources produced at the local, state, and national levels. Recent scholarship in legal history, which does focus on the development of law and legal institutions, suggests that nineteenth-century historians should attend more to these issues.[6]

The best place to start is with the men who produced the sources: members of the states' elite, many of whom were professionally trained lawyers, whose writings on law and government now shape the historiography. Collectively, this group has become the voice of "the law" in the post-Revolutionary South.[7] While legal reformers in the Carolinas moved in state-level networks, they were part of a regional elite with strong national ties. Their names grace many of the legal materials on which all nineteenth-century historians now rely: James Iredell Sr., Joseph Gales, Thomas Ruffin, William Gaston, and James Iredell Jr. of North Carolina; Charles Pinckney, Charles Cotesworth Pinckney, William Loughton Smith, John Faucheraud Grimké, Thomas Cooper, Langdon Cheves, David J. McCord, Henry William DeSaussure, and John Belton O'Neall of South Carolina. Many of these men were educated in the Northeast, either at law schools there or at colleges such as Princeton. A few, particularly those who grew up in colonial South Carolina, were educated in England, at the Inns of Court.[8] But even those who trained in their own states had ties beyond the region through their business, social, or political connections.

What united them was an intellectual stance, bounded by basic assumptions about law and the legal system. They all tended to see law in scientific terms as an internally consistent set of universally applicable principles, even if they often disagreed bitterly on the specifics of those principles. They also favored a hierarchical institutional structure, with authority located in trained professionals at the top of the structure to ensure uniformity, although many still thought the system should be flexible enough to allow room to achieve justice in particular circumstances at the lower levels of the system. The power of the judiciary relative to the legislature divided reformers throughout the period, particularly at the height of partisan conflict between Federalists and Jeffersonian Republicans before the War of 1812 and during the nullification crisis in South Carolina in the 1830s. So did the question of states' rights, specifically the authority of southern states relative to the nation.[9] Despite their differences, however, reformers as a group tended to support the creation of a clearly defined, definite body of state law, enforced by a strong appellate court at the apex of the judicial pyramid. That court would decide points of law in decisions that would be enforced by lower levels of the system, which fell out in orderly layers beneath, descending from district or superior courts to individual magistrates in local neighborhoods, with each level subordinate to the one above. Reformers had such confidence in this vision of the legal system that they described it in normative terms; since there was no other option, the system evolved naturally, if somewhat haltingly and fitfully, in this direction.

Reformers arrived at that conclusion by a decidedly Whiggish route. It was not always an easy road to travel. The journey began with considerable sacrifice for North Carolina printer Joseph Gales, whose publications consistently promoted legal reform throughout this period. Gales had been part of a radical group, based in Sheffield, England, that advocated constitutional reform in the 1780s and 1790s. After war broke out between France and England in 1793, his organization came under suspicion, and Gales was forced to leave the country to avoid arrest for treason. He resettled in Philadelphia, where he resumed his trade and aligned himself with the Jeffersonian Republicans. Impressed with his work, the North Carolina congressional delegation approached him in 1798, hoping to lure him to the state to promote the party's cause there. He did, setting up the *Raleigh Register*, which he eventually passed on to his youngest son, Weston. In 1833 he retired to Washington, D.C., where his eldest son, Joseph Jr., coedited the influential *National Intelligencer*. There, Gales edited a "History of the Proceedings and Debates of the Early Sessions of Congress," part of his son's project, the *Annals of Congress*. This volume epitomized the Whiggish optimism that characterized Gales's entire career. He believed that the collection and distribution of facts would achieve progressive change. One of his particular interests was the law, which he saw as the necessary foundation for the new republic. Not only did he use the *Raleigh Register* to advocate reforms to centralize and systematize state law, but he also assumed a more direct role by providing carefully rendered volumes preserving legislative proceedings, constitutional debates, statutes, and appellate decisions. His periodical, the *Carolina Law Repository*, launched in 1813, thoroughly conflated legal reform and progress, promising to keep "the Profession and the citizens in general . . . apprized of the progressive change and exposition of the law."[10]

Like Gales, other legal reformers in his circle tended to see the past as prologue to a progressive journey that culminated in a legal system defined by their principles, which formed the essential groundwork for their post-Revolutionary states. That was the Revolution's legacy, earned through sacrifice and sanctioned in blood. Relying heavily on temporal metaphors, they characterized alternate versions of law as archaic relics of an illogical and unenlightened time. Some, like North Carolina's Archibald Murphey, looked to the past as a source of building blocks for future progress. Murphey, a prominent lawyer with a plantation in Orange County who was known for his quick and creative intellect, served as a circuit court judge and a representative to the General Assembly. Like many in his cohort, he dabbled in land speculation and other moneymaking schemes, including the short-lived North Carolina gold rush, although with much less success than others. Murphey died broke, living on the charity of friends. Yet it was his ebullient — and sometimes imprudent — optimism that brought him to that end. He carried that enthusiasm into his political work, where his efforts for judicial reform, internal improvements, and education were outstripped only by his passion for history. "In no state," Murphey wrote with the expansiveness that was his hallmark, "was a more early or effectual opposition made to the encroachments of power . . . or were the principles of civil liberty better understood, more ardently cherished, or more steadily defended." Since then, "our legislature, our jurisprudence, and our institutions have kept pace with the improvements of the age." In order for the state to continue this progressive trajectory, Murphey concluded, it was imperative that the legislature provide the means to collect and preserve its historical documents. Others viewed the past warily, seeing primarily defects that subsequent progress had overcome. Both positions, however, resigned alternate versions of law to the dustbin of the past.[11]

Although evocative, reformers' temporal metaphors were inaccurate. Central elements of the decentralized legal system that they characterized as archaic had been established during the Revolution. Moreover, the remnants of "chaos" had not been banished thereafter, with Revolutionary enlightenment replacing monarchical corruption in their states' legal

The modesty of early state houses belies the grandiose visions of state leaders. In this engraving of the South Carolina state house, the tavern where legislators stayed and socialized features as prominently as the actual seat of government. State leaders later jettisoned the term "state house" for the grander term "capitol," which was meant to distinguish the site of state government from domestic residences. State House in Columbia, South Carolina, taken from Rives's Tavern, 1794, engraved by James Akin. Courtesy of South Caroliniana Library, University of South Carolina, Columbia.

systems. Reformers from this period were far more successful in imposing their vision after the fact, eventually drowning out the voices of those who saw the legal system differently. Their efforts to achieve substantive reform took decades to bear fruit. In practice, their goals were not fully realized until after the Civil War, as part of the systematic reform of the region under the terms of the congressional Reconstruction plan and the dramatic revision of state constitutions under Republican rule. The institution of capitalist labor relations and the extension of individual rights to former slaves required a hierarchical legal system that construed law as a set of universal rules, consistently applied. Most reformers who lived through the Civil War era bitterly opposed the abolition of slavery, the Fourteenth and

Fifteenth Amendments, and other changes that came with Republican rule. But their basic vision of law shared a great deal with that of Reconstruction-era Republicans. The changes to the legal system in this era instituted reforms advocated since the end of the Revolution. It is no coincidence that Democrats left them in place when they took over after Reconstruction. That outcome, in turn, lent an air of inevitability to earlier calls for reform; if secessionists and unionists, slaveholders and abolitionists, Democrats and Republicans could all agree, then surely the legal system's trajectory must have been set right from the very beginning.[12]

Judge Elihu Hall Bay's decision in the wife-beating case that opens this chapter provides an alternative to the reformers' temporal metaphors. To understand that alternative, though, it is necessary to reconsider the source of the anecdote. In the reported version, Judge Bay comes across as an eccentric relic, stuttering about the common law tradition as the pinnacle of civilization. But that impression is the invention of the man who related the story, John Belton O'Neall, who was among those who wanted to create a more centralized legal system and a systematized version of "the law." In fact, so did Elihu Hall Bay, although he was at odds with other reformers on some of the specifics, including women's property rights. Bay published the first reports on common law decisions in the state of South Carolina, which collected existing case law with the intent of identifying authoritative decisions and creating a system that would operate through precedent. "Before his reports," O'Neall effused with genuine admiration, "all was chaos in our legal world." Yet, looking back on Bay's career from the 1850s, O'Neall found it perplexing. Unable to reconcile Bay's volumes with his decisions on the bench, O'Neall expressed puzzlement: although Bay's "purposes were just," he was "often mistaken." In that one observation, O'Neall captured what he and other reformers found so unacceptable: a legal system that incorporated conflicting versions of law and left the rest to local jurisdictions.[13]

The central point is that Bay was not "mistaken," at least not in the way that O'Neall meant. The complications in Bay's decisions — or mistakes, as O'Neall would term them — were actually accepted elements within the legal system of the post-Revolutionary Carolinas. That system was not disorganized or ill conceived, struggling toward a form it was preordained to take and would eventually achieve. Nor was it a throwback to the past, stubbornly persisting in the wake of rationality's inevitable transforming power. This legal system had its own logic, which structured the operation of law so effectively that it transcended the agency of any individual judge.

Judge Bay himself may have wanted a more systematic approach, but the system was based on an open-ended conception of law and it drew him irresistibly into its logic, regardless of his avowed convictions. That logic combined elements from the English and American past with contemporary currents of political thought. This eclectic mix included Revolutionary calls for popular sovereignty, liberal notions of individual rights and limited government, republican fears of centralized authority, and early modern notions of law that encompassed popular custom as well as formal legal authorities and included public business that was later relegated to other branches of government.

This version of law is not particularly well represented in the sources. Not only were reformers who advocated change quite prolific, but they also understood the importance of history and were adept at harnessing it to serve their own ends. In this regard, legal reformers in the Carolinas shared a great deal with the other state and national leaders in their networks. As historian Joanne Freeman has argued, national leaders of the early republic developed an acute sense of the power they could wield through the historical record. Elites' interest in history was an extension of the partisan political culture of the 1790s, which conflated personal reputation with party affiliation. Through the genre of history, these men were able to justify their positions and vindicate their reputations after the fact.[14]

If anything, the interest in history became more pronounced over time. The number of reform-minded Carolina lawyers who wrote history is remarkable. Joseph Gales's "History of the Proceedings and Debates of the Early Sessions of Congress" is but one example. Like Gales, many wrote for a national, not a regional audience. John Drayton, from South Carolina, distributed his two-volume history of the Revolution widely to his friends, who included John Quincy Adams and Stephen Van Rensselaer. Thomas Jefferson was pleased to hear that U.S. Supreme Court Justice William Johnson, a South Carolina native, was nearing completion of his political history of the early republic, because "our opponents are far ahead of us in preparations for placing their cause favorably before posterity."[15]

Men in these national networks preserved their legacies by writing narratives that featured themselves, their relatives, and their friends in starring roles. In 1827, for instance, Chief Justice John Marshall wrote to Archibald Murphey praising his biographical sketches "of the eminent men of North Carolina," most of whom were lawyers or judges. "It was my happiness to be acquainted with those of whom you speak," wrote Marshall, "and I think you have given to the character of each, its true coloring." Similar concerns led to a friendly correspondence between Alexander Hamilton's son and William Gaston, who sat on the North Carolina appellate court in the 1830s and 1840s. Hamilton's son, who was collecting his father's correspondence and writing a biography, asked Gaston for documents or personal recollections as well as an account of North Carolina's credit laws, presumably for background about his father's monetary policies. Gaston was happy to comply. The lives of Archibald Murphey, William Gaston, and other leaders in both North Carolina and South Carolina were meticulously documented in turn. It is no accident that historians have more information about those involved in government at the state and national levels than they do about people who were active in local communities. Nor is it an accident that those men's confidence about the importance of their interests and accomplishments echoes through the scholarship.[16]

Legal reformers were preoccupied with collecting documents and subsequently proclaiming these collections as authoritative references on the past. Historians of Britain and Western Europe have identified similar trends, in which the development of professional history and the creation of archives were part and parcel of the liberal project of nation-building and the development of empires. Aware of the intellectual developments in Europe, reformers in North Carolina and South Carolina consciously sought to duplicate them, at the state as well as the national level. The archives and histories of European nations provided the inspiration for Archibald Murphey's plans for a state archive and an eight-volume history of North Carolina, which he grandiosely likened to Gibbon's *Decline and Fall of the Roman Empire*. "The history of each of the European nations has been long since written," he wrote in his request to the General Assembly for funding. North Carolina needed to follow their example if it hoped to keep up. In addition to collecting records from the colonial and Revolutionary eras, Murphey proposed the ongoing preservation and organization of all documents related to state business, especially those related to the legal system.[17]

Murphey's project was only the most ambitious of these efforts. Legal reformers began collecting materials immediately following the Revolution and pushed their general assemblies to revise and distribute a definitive body of state law. The North Carolina legislature provided for the printing of statutes in pamphlet form following each session, and local newspapers often reprinted the results in their columns. But these annual publications were difficult to track down and to use, creating barriers that encouraged those with less interest in these references to dispense with them altogether. So reformers produced easy-to-use, single-volume digests of the state's statutes. John Haywood's *A Manual of the Laws of North Carolina*, for instance, boasted accessibility in its subtitle, with "distinct heads in alphabetical order" and "references from one head to another." Prominent legal reformers oversaw such projects, largely because it was they who pushed for them and who had the most invested in the idea. In 1791 James Iredell Sr. put together the state's first collection. The legislature provided for new editions periodically, including a revision in 1837, prepared by a committee of three, including James Iredell Jr., who followed in his father's footsteps.[18]

North Carolina judges designated as court reporters began issuing decisions in the state's higher courts in the late 1790s, about the time that key reformers were promoting the creation of an appeals court with final authority on matters of law and equity. François Xavier Martin, one of the state's most prolific printers of legal material, published notes in 1797 on selected decisions in the state's superior courts, then the highest level of the system.[19] John L. Taylor, a superior court judge who oversaw a compilation of the revised statutes, published a series of volumes on higher-court decisions between 1798 and 1802. Between 1799 and 1806, John Haywood, another avid legal compiler, put together an additional collection. Thereafter collections appeared occasionally, often at wide intervals, when the appointed court reporters found the time to put them together.[20]

Later editing, however, created an impression of regularity and uniformity that was lacking at the time. In 1868, as part of the effort to institutionalize legal changes of the kind promoted by antebellum reformers, the North Carolina State Supreme Court renumbered all the previous volumes of reports from the higher courts consecutively. All the original records were later housed together, as a single record group, in the state archives. The results merged material from high courts that, in their various iterations, actually had different functions and powers. They also obscured differences in the authority and reach of earlier and later decisions, while creating the appearance that reports of them had been issued regularly. One edition of the volume now designated as the first in the series of North Carolina reports, for instance, is a highly edited blend of Martin's notes, Taylor's volumes, what remained of the court records, the notes of William H. Battle (who was a judge and court reporter in the 1840s), and the annotations of Walter Clark, the Progressive Era lawyer who put the volume together.[21]

South Carolina reformers encountered more difficulty in this regard.

The South Carolina legislature required appeals court judges to render their decisions in writing in 1799. Then, in 1811, it appointed a court reporter to collect those decisions into volumes for reference by the General Assembly in Columbia. The "citizens of this State" were supposed to "have access to the said books as freely as other books of record in any of the public offices of this State."[22] But the legislators did not provide for the regular dissemination of the volumes. South Carolina reporters in the appeals courts of law and equity, including Elihu Hall Bay, Joseph Brevard, and Henry William DeSaussure, published the results of their efforts. But the volumes appeared at wide and irregular intervals, usually at the initiative of the compilers. Henry William DeSaussure's volumes on equity were as much about getting himself out of debt as clarifying law in his state; he proposed the idea to the legislature and used his considerable influence to obtain funding. Not until the 1820s were reports of law and equity cases printed on a more consistent basis.[23] Other treatises and commentary in periodicals, such as John Belton O'Neall's volume on slave law or David J. McCord and Abram Blanding's *Carolina Law Journal*, stepped into the breach and summarized law in key areas in an effort to keep lawyers abreast of current trends.[24]

The effort to create a compilation of South Carolina statutes ran aground in the 1790s amidst rancorous accusations about commissioners' motives, driven by suspicions that they had chosen selectively, interpreted liberally, and imposed their own views on the results. Ultimately the legislature rejected the report it had commissioned. Despite repeated efforts to rehabilitate the project, Governor Thomas Bennett was still pleading with legislators in 1822 to revisit the task, pointing out that most of the district courts of the state did not have copies of the current state statutes, let alone guidance on which ones were in force. That request went nowhere; the first volume of revised statutes did not appear until 1836, under the auspices of a project from the nullification era spearheaded by Governor Robert Y. Hayne and undertaken by Thomas Cooper and, later, David J. McCord.[25] Until then, reformers collected material and published their own compilations privately, attaching their names to the volumes. John Faucheraud Grimké published his collection of statutes in 1790, and Joseph Brevard followed with another version in 1814. In 1831 the *Carolina Law Journal* published a list of the acts passed between 1813 and 1830, noting that "there is no digest of the acts of our legislature since Brevard's."[26] These privately issued compilations of statutes could provide suggestions for interpretation, but they did not actually have the authority to elevate one element of law over another.

All these projects of collecting and editing were labor intensive, because most of the material was in private hands. The legislatures of North Carolina and South Carolina, like most colonial legislatures, had not archived the laws they passed. Statutes had been issued in pamphlet form or printed by newspapers and were saved by interested individuals. Complete runs were rare. In Virginia, for instance, St. George Tucker failed in his efforts to obtain a full set of session laws. "Few gentlemen, even of the [legal] profession," he declared in 1803, "have ever been able to boast of possessing a complete collection of its laws." Persisting, Tucker managed to pull together an updated version of Blackstone's *Commentaries* specifically for Virginia, meshing Blackstone's version of common law with Virginia case law and statutes.[27]

This problem was not confined to the South; Samuel Alinson ran into similar difficulties when he tried to compile New Jersey's statutes in 1776. Ascertaining the current state of case law was nearly impossible. Since judges did not routinely write down their decisions or keep them when they did, opinions from the colonial as well as the post-Revolutionary courts often had to be reconstructed long after the fact. That problem continued even after legislators appointed reporters to keep track of court business. When Thomas Ruffin took over for a term as North Carolina court reporter in 1820, Archibald Murphey warned him about the difficulty of getting written opinions from judges. "I told Judge Henderson, it was essential to the Character of the Court that he should write more Opinions," chided Murphey. Unfortunately for the less-than-meticulous Leonard Henderson, Murphey had no intention of letting the matter go; he promised Ruffin to follow up and write Henderson again.[28]

The resulting volumes were not just compilations of facts. They forced existing laws into a unitary body, creating the impression of orderly progress over time — or, at least, identifying a point at which such orderly progress began, as was the case in those volumes that began by chiding their predecessors for their sloppiness. Typical were the remarks of John Faucheraud Grimké, who explained that his 1790 compilation of statutes was intended to bring order to the "profound confusion and Sibylline obscurity" of South Carolina law, the anarchy of which had lowered its citizens to "the condition of a slave." In 1836 Thomas Cooper began his volumes with similarly disparaging remarks about Grimké's work, which he thought was characterized by "a latitude" that had been "exercised too loosely" and that he "dare not follow."[29] Order had a price. These collections, even when sanctioned by the state legislatures, were all penned with a heavy editorial hand. They contained selected material and elevated certain statutes and decisions as authoritative legal guides when competing ones still existed. The selection and organization, combined with accompanying annotations, smoothed over the contradictions by presenting statutes and cases as a logical development of particular ideas over time, artificially deriving consensus and certainty from a legal culture that, in actuality, pointed in multiple, often conflicting directions.

The results conjured up order out of a past that was anything but orderly, reflecting the contemporary concerns of those who wrote the volumes. Not until legislatures made key changes in the structure of the legal system, of which these compilations were a part, did the legal systems in North Carolina and South Carolina provide a way to reconcile judges' conflicting decisions or to elevate one decision over another as *the* law that should guide future cases. These conflicts were not resolved until state legislatures revised their statutes and issued edited reports of decisions in law and equity. In fact, all the variations and conflicts that these volumes tried to explain away *were* state law. The compilations tried to create an authoritative and unified version of the law out of this patchwork of statutes and localized law.

THE LOCALIZED LEGAL SYSTEM

Compilations of what purports to be state law are better understood as attempts to change the law along those lines than as reflections of actual practice in the Carolinas at the time. Reformers' characterizations of legal localism, the system they sought to change, must not be taken at face value. In fact, after breaking with England, lawmakers in both North Carolina and South Carolina restructured the institutions of their states to place legal authority in local hands and to lodge major decisions about public governance in counties and, in some instances, even smaller jurisdictions. Both colonies kept the basic court structure that was already in place, at least on paper: tripartite systems on the British model, with magistrates serving at the first level, county courts in the middle, and circuit courts on the highest level. As in the British model, magistrates and county courts dealt with a wide range of business that was later moved to other branches of government: overseeing poor relief and other matters of social welfare; regulating issues relating to the morals of both individuals and the larger community; setting weights and measures; levying and collecting taxes; and attending to local defense. Comparing the operation of colonial courts with those in the post-Revolutionary period is a difficult undertaking. Like many things about British rule in North America, the courts in the Carolinas had not always functioned as envisaged by their imperial creators. The matter is further complicated by the fact that the courts operated even more sporadically than usual during the war.[30]

The Revolution produced radical changes in the way law operated, even though state lawmakers left the institutional structure much the same as before. In North Carolina, delegates from Orange and Mecklenburg Counties had come to the state constitutional convention with instructions to advance a more radical view of popular sovereignty: "Political power is of two kinds, one principal and superior, the other derived and inferior. . . . The principal supreme power is possessed by the people at large, the derived and inferior power by the servants which they employ." To approach power from this vantage point was to turn the institutional structure on its head. While colonial courts appeared to be without an apex, the Crown's sovereignty had always been implied, if not always asserted. By the end of the colonial period, the Crown had begun to intervene in legal matters as part of its larger effort to shore up imperial control. Revolutionaries in the Carolinas eliminated that level when they separated from Britain. As a result, judicial authority was turned upside down, in a radically decentralized system with circuit courts and local jurisdictions coequal and largely independent from one another.[31]

This devolution, which represented a major departure from the colonial period, owed a great deal to Revolutionary ideology, specifically to the notion that sovereignty no longer came from the top down. The state's Declaration of Rights placed the charge brought by the Orange and Mecklenburg County delegates—that "the principal supreme power is possessed by the people at large"—at the center of the new government. The first section announced "That all political Power is vested in and derived from the people only." The second section defined political power broadly by locating sovereignty over law and other matters of public governance in the people, who "have sole and exclusive Right of regulating the internal Government and Police thereof." Those sentiments were embodied in the state constitution, which went into great detail about the structure and responsibilities of the legislative branch but did not establish the judiciary as an independent branch of the government.[32]

Opposition to a strong, independent judiciary continued to shape political debate long after the Revolution, and not just in the Carolinas. Throughout the colonies, imperial authority appeared in the form of judges, intent on forcing compliance with the Crown's edicts. Conceptions of popular sovereignty, which were so central to Revolutionary ideology, provided the intellectual basis for this critique. If sovereignty resided in the people, then they were the ones who should have oversight, if not authority, over the legal system, instead of appointed officials with no connections to the people they judged. "It does not appear to me that the same reasons exist in this country for giving such astonishing powers to the Judges as in England," contended Charles Pinckney while he was governor of South Carolina in 1798. His explanation combined elements of republican notions of participatory government with liberal conceptions of individual sovereignty. The operation of law in a monarchical government, Pinckney elaborated, was fundamentally different than it was in a republic. The discretionary power of England's judiciary derived from the monarch's sovereign authority, which judges were bound to represent and protect. In a republic, the people delegated authority to different branches of government, but sovereignty remained with them, even in matters of law. Giving a single judge too much authority would lead inevitably to corruption within the legal system and the erosion of liberty.[33]

The Carolinas' postcolonial court systems nonetheless perpetuated certain British legal traditions, even as they departed from others. Decentralization had characterized the early modern English legal system, which provided the framework for legal institutions and legal culture in colonial North Carolina and South Carolina. Early modern England had multiple legal arenas, with their own distinct bodies of law and overlapping jurisdictions. The system was highly localized in many respects. Criminal law depended on people in local areas to identify offenses and on local officials to prosecute them, which meant that popular notions of justice and order permeated the system at its most basic level. British magistrates and county courts handled most of the business of governance. By the late 1700s political upheaval in England and changes in the intellectual climate resulted in the elevation of common law over other bodies of law, the professionalization of legal culture, and the systematization of law.[34] Those changes were evident in the Carolinas, as they were in other colonies, creating a group of lawyers who saw law and the legal system in those terms.[35] But the Revolution revived waning elements of early modern Anglo-American legal culture, providing them with a new context in which to flourish.

Colonial conflicts, particularly the Regulator Movement of the 1760s, left a visible imprint on the postcolonial legal system. In both North Carolina and South Carolina, Regulators came from middling farm families in the newly settled backcountry, the central and western areas of the colonies. Although the substantive issues were debt and the instability of land titles, those concerns involved criticisms of the legal system, which oversaw such matters. In South Carolina, Regulators protested the centralization of the courts in Charlestown, a situation that forced colonists in the backcountry to travel great distances for minor, routine legal matters or to forgo access to legal venues altogether. A central concern was the absence of legitimate legal systems within their communities, which, as they saw it, threatened to destroy the very fabric of local life. In North Carolina, centralization was also the main issue, though it pertained to the consolidation of power in certain legal officials, not in geographic jurisdictions. Yet, as in South Carolina, North Carolina Regulators did not wish to overthrow law, or even fundamentally alter it. To the contrary, law occupied a crucial place in their vision of well-ordered communities. The problem, they maintained, lay in the operation of the legal system, which made it inaccessible and unresponsive to local concerns.[36]

These issues resonated in two registers. In an immediate and material sense, the high register, the Regulators achieved recognition of their specific grievances, which included the stabilization of land titles and debt collection, more equitable representation of the backcountry in political matters, and a more accessible legal system. In the 1760s South Carolina's Regulators secured measures that created more district courts and gave western parts of the state more representation in the colonial legislature. In North Carolina, where the political distance between the Regulators and the colonial elite was more pronounced, the movement went down in bloody defeat. In the wake of that debacle, though, political leaders quietly began addressing some of the Regulators' concerns. If anything, the Revolution and its aftermath magnified both the Regulators' grievances and their political leverage. Questions about debt, in particular, continued to characterize political debate in both states, contributing to the crisis that culminated in the adoption of the U.S. Constitution.[37]

Underlying these immediate, material concerns, in the low register, were broader cultural differences regarding the operation of law. The line of cleavage was not so much between rich and poor as it was between those who looked inward to their own neighborhoods and those who looked outward across the Atlantic. Many Carolina farmers, including those who were prosperous and owned slaves, lived in communities where most of life's business was done on a face-to-face basis. Economic transactions were negotiated orally, sealed with a handshake, backed by the word of the participants, and informed more by a sense of moral order than by the calculus of capital. These agreements rested on a direct knowledge of those involved, in a culture where people expected to know one another well and to encounter one another frequently. That tangled web of social networks also secured these bargains, joining each partner to the other through their relationships with other community members. Given the circulation of notes of hand in localities (often at face value), a person's credit was a commonly understood matter in which many people, beyond just those directly involved, had investments. In that context, people measured the legal system's success in terms of its ability to respond to the particularities of each individual circumstance, valuing flexibility over consistency. For them, law was the means to a just outcome in daily life; it was a loosely defined collection of malleable principles that could guide the resolution of conflicts toward a result that best fit the circumstances of those involved and the needs of the community.[38]

This view of law was not necessarily rural. Such practices also obtained in towns and cities, which remained small enough — by modern standards — that their residents tended to know about one another. But such a localized view of law made little sense in the world of the colonial elite, whose commercial and cultural networks reached beyond their local communities to other North American colonies, the Caribbean, Africa, Britain, and the other national powers of Western Europe. Although clustered along the coast in cities such as New Bern, Edenton, and Charlestown, they had begun to move into the backcountry during the 1760s, setting up businesses and coming into conflict with other residents there. The members of this cosmopolitan colonial elite tended to define law in terms of universal, immutable principles that existed outside of social context. In their opinion, those principles should be clearly stated, in writing, and upheld consistently, regardless of the personalities involved. Their protection constituted the entire rationale of the legal system. This view of law was crucial to doing business across long distances and across cultures. The coastal elite's strong cultural and intellectual ties to Britain also disposed them to see law as a profession that required mastery of a specific body of knowledge. Many had a university education, sometimes in England, and had trained with prominent lawyers, dutifully duplicating the English experience by poring over Blackstone, Coke, and Bacon.[39] "No one," remarked North Carolina's James Iredell Sr. in his diary in 1792, "can possibly read . . . [Blackstone] . . . without infinite Pleasure & Improvement." But in his overstated certainty, this opponent of the Regulators and future U.S. Supreme Court justice misspoke.[40]

As Iredell well knew, Regulators wished to keep law out of the clutches of men like him, professionally trained lawyers who derived pleasure from reading Blackstone. Lawyers, lamented the famous North Carolina Regulator leader Hermon Husband, were the "greatest Burden and Bane of Society." They turned law into arcane rules known only to them, which they could manipulate at will to the detriment of everyone else while charging high fees for such obfuscation. "So great is the Lawyer's Art that he would Wire-draw reason from the most sacred Truth, and make a Libel of the Lord's Prayer," scoffed Husband. That made justice not only "costly" but "hard to come at." A petition signed by 250 freemen in Anson County echoed Husband's critique. "Instead of Servants for the country's use," they complained, lawyers had "become a nuisance, as the business of the people is often transacted without the least degree of fairness, the intention of the law evaded, exorbitant fees extorted, and the sufferers left to mourn under their oppression." At issue was authority over law, as Husband also made clear: "We must make these men subject to the laws or they will enslave the whole community." By "the laws," though, Husband meant something very different from Iredell's well-worn copies of Blackstone.[41]

As troubling as the Regulators' views of law were, the coastal elite found imperial efforts to centralize law even more objectionable. In addition to the well-known issues of taxation, trade, and political representation, imperial authorities began to involve themselves in other matters that colonists had come to see as their own purview. When the British Empire began to make its presence in the North American colonies known in the 1760s, it trod particularly hard on the toes of the Carolinas' colonial elite, many of whom became Revolutionary leaders. Like Patriots elsewhere, those in the Carolinas maintained that assertions of imperial authority undermined local control over law and other matters of governance. Particularly problematic to the Carolinas' elite were imperial interventions in slavery. As recent scholarship suggests, concerns about securing slavery solidified many elite southerners' support for the Patriot cause. "Our property at your disposal, our lives and liberties at your discretion, we are subject at any time to whatever arbitrary laws your Parliament may think fit to send us," wrote

Iredell in 1774, apparently oblivious to the irony that he was now making the same case for local control of law as had the Regulators, whom he had dismissed as a bunch of hooligans just a few years earlier.[42]

This conflicted backdrop shaped the decentralized legal systems that emerged from the Revolution. Those who supported the system did so for a variety of reasons, not all of which were comparable, let alone compatible. Some saw it as the realization of hard-fought claims dating back to Regulation. Some saw local control, which invested sovereignty over law in the people, as a central component of the Revolution's ideological experiment. Others saw it merely as a means of solidifying authority in their own bailiwicks, particularly their own plantations. Some saw it as the necessary cost of pacifying their political opponents and unifying support for the Revolution within their own colonies. After all, the Regulation cast a long shadow over the Revolution. As Whig leaders who had been opposed to the Regulator Movement became Revolutionary leaders in the Carolinas, many Regulators and their sympathizers thought long and hard before deciding which side to join. Although some did join the Patriots, others maintained a critical distance, as reluctant revolutionaries, if not outright loyalists during the war.[43]

Once the Revolution was over, that loose coalition fell apart. In 1798, when Governor Charles Pinckney was advocating limitations on the judiciary's power based on the sovereignty of the people, he articulated a very different vision of law than the delegates from Mecklenburg County, North Carolina, which had been a hotbed of Regulator activity. In Pinckney's view, the people might be the abstract source for the law, but the mechanics would still be handled by their chosen representatives in the legislative branch, with proper attention to established legal authorities. By contrast, the Mecklenburg delegates believed that the people should define and administer most areas of law themselves. State leaders who, like Pinckney, favored a more professional and scientific approach to law began working to realize that vision, harnessing Revolutionary rhetoric of the sovereignty of the people to a very different notion of authority.

The reformers in this group agreed on fundamental elements in the legal system, even when they disagreed about how best to realize them in practice. In practice, common assumptions about law underlay even their most bitter partisan disputes. Take the differences between North Carolina's James Iredell and South Carolina's Charles Pinckney. Iredell, a staunch Federalist, articulated his party's advocacy of an independent judiciary. "In a Republic," opined Iredell, "the Law is superior to any or all Individuals, and the Constitution, superior even to the Legislature, and of which the Judges are the guardians and protectors." Pinckney, who served his state in various capacities, including two terms as governor, was a Federalist turned Jeffersonian Republican. Espousing the position of his new party, Pinckney opposed granting unchecked authority to the judiciary. He saw the legislature, with its elected representatives, as the branch that should express the people's sovereign authority over law.[44]

Yet, despite these fundamental differences, they were united in their view of law as a consistent set of universal principles, and both men were wary of direct local control of law. As governor in 1798, for instance, Pinckney proposed changes that would have limited the legal authority of both judges *and* local communities. While a circuit court judge in North Carolina, Iredell complained constantly of those without legal training: the meddlesome demands of community members who subverted the legal process in an effort to realize their views of justice; the "silly harangues of pettifogging" lawyers who emphasized customary notions of justice and not the rules laid out in law books; and the inept judges who lacked knowledge of the appropriate legal authorities. Among the two parties' leadership, the disagreement was over the balance of powers between the judicial and legislative branches. Outside that small circle, the point of conflict was over local control of law: both Pinckney's attempt to limit the power of the judiciary and Iredell's effort to extend it removed authority over law from local areas. Within their own states, however, both men were in a decided minority on that score.[45]

THE INSTITUTIONAL PERSISTENCE OF LOCALISM

Perhaps the most dramatic evidence of the commitment to local control over law is the post-Revolutionary legal system's imperviousness to rationalization and centralization. In both North Carolina and South Carolina, the legislatures made liberal use of their authority to alter their states' legal systems, throwing them into such flux that the details can be difficult to follow, let alone fathom. Localities retained considerable authority over law, even in the face of changes that took elements of the legal system in other directions. By the 1820s legal reformers had made headway in systematizing state law and centralizing legal authority at the state level, although they did not realize the full measure of those efforts until the 1830s, which the final two chapters cover in more detail.[46]

In the decades immediately following the Revolution, the changes enacted by legislatures in both states tended to localize the legal system by widening its institutional base. South Carolina's 1785 Court Act moved jurisdiction over a broad range of civil and criminal matters from the state's six district courts to thirty-four county courts. Those changes transferred the bulk of court business to the new county courts, which oversaw all debt cases up to £20, other civil cases with damages up to £50, and criminal cases that did not involve corporal punishment. The immediate impetus for the creation of more courts was the post-Revolutionary economic crisis and escalating conflicts over debt collection. But the new system also placed magistrates, mainly local elites without legal training, at the center of the legal system, giving them extensive discretion over the interpretation and application of law. Critics singled that out as the most offensive part of what they saw as a disastrous experiment. "It was too much dependent upon ignorant and rough men for its enforcement," wrote one detractor. As a result, local justice was marked by "mistakes, prejudices and gross errors" instead of the accurate, objective, and reasoned pursuit of the law. These complaints ignored the system's popularity, particularly in the backcountry, where many appreciated a legal system that did not depend on lawyers or officials with formal legal training.[47]

The North Carolina legislature also enhanced local authority over law in the decades following the Revolution. Debate initially revolved around extending the jurisdiction of magistrates, which had been among the Regulators' key demands. These measures, known as the "ten pound law" of 1785 and the "twenty pound law" of 1787, gave magistrates jurisdiction in all civil matters with damages up to £20 and in a wide range of criminal matters, excepting the most serious offenses. Magistrates acquired significant legal discretion as a result. The process, in historian Lars C. Golumbic's apt description, allowed magistrates to "leave Blackstone and the perplexing body of common law behind and adjudicate simply, personally, and pragmatically." The legislature underscored its intent through additional measures that regulated attorneys' fees, practice, and licensing. All these laws were widely reviled by professionally trained lawyers. "My Passions," fumed James Iredell's friend William Hooper, are "agitated with the unbecoming means which had been used to cast a stigma upon the bar."[48]

The state's lawyers fought a losing battle with the legislature on the issue of magistrates' jurisdiction. Not only did the legislature slowly increase their jurisdiction after the "twenty pound law" of 1787, but it also added district courts, moving by increments toward the system that South Carolina had adopted in 1785. Then, in 1806, the legislature replaced the eight district courts with superior courts in each county. A key group of lawyers in the legislature opposed the change, because it required those who wished to practice law as their sole profession to travel to each county for court instead of having business come to them at the district courthouse. Adding insult to injury, the act also reduced the fees of the attorneys who practiced in the superior courts. "The prospect is dull to men of eminence," sulked Archibald Murphey in a letter to his mentor William Duffy, who had led the opposition to the measure in the legislature. "Under this System Genius will languish, enterprise grow feeble and Petit-fogging become fashionable." "Had not I expended so much money in making an establishment," he concluded bleakly, "I would break up and go to Nashville." According to one historian writing in the early twentieth century, the act did lead to a legal exodus from the state. Among the defectors were John Haywood, noted for his collection of statutes as well as his work on the bench and his training of a host of prominent lawyers. William Duffy apparently considered relocating as well, although he did not end up doing so.[49]

Reforms that centralized the system on paper often ran aground in practice. In 1799 the legislature overhauled South Carolina's courts, scrapping the county court system and following the advice of Aedanus Burke and John Faucheraud Grimké, two professionally trained lawyers who were avid proponents of legal reform and had been appointed to a subcommittee to revise the state's legal system after the Revolution. Yet legislators only went so far down the path laid out by the reformers. The major change was that the new district courts were run by judges who were appointed by the legislature and usually had legal training. At the same time, the legislature affirmed the basic principle of localism, replacing the thirty-four county courts with twenty-eight district courts, a difference so minor it hardly seemed worth the effort. Even this degree of centralization was not particularly popular. In 1827 the grand jurors of Kershaw District complained about the "difficulties delay and expense" of the system, which still placed minor cases in circuit courts. In matters of property, they asked that the legislature "seriously consider" extending the jurisdiction of magistrates, applying the "summary process" that existed for sums under £20 to all property matters.[50]

Although justices with legal training now had an established place in the courts, they were still working in local areas, where communities could control significant parts of the legal process. Judges operated in a setting where local people expected to participate actively in the entire system. Friends and relatives of those involved who could make their wishes known did so, mobilizing support and exerting considerable pressure on the court. Those not directly involved in a case often weighed in as well, out of a sense of proprietary interest as members of the affected community. The 1811 grand jury presentment in Greenville District, South Carolina, is suggestive of the context in which judges worked. The jurors presented to the legislature an address of thanks for having appointed the Hon. Abraham Nott, whom they commended for fulfilling "the good old maxim of common law": "It is not enough that a Judge does justice but he ought likewise to give general satisfaction." "That good old maxim," the jurors believed, had "been realized in the conduct of the honourable Judge, and witnessed by the experience of the people." Judges were expected to give satisfaction to the people; they referred to popular expectations frequently enough to indicate they were acutely aware of them. Those who failed in this respect found their terms unbearably miserable.[51]

Efforts to create more powerful appellate courts at the apex of the judicial structure had similarly mixed results. South Carolina's 1790 constitution created a Constitutional Court of Appeals that heard appeals from common law courts. There was no comparable appeals court for cases in equity until 1808. North Carolina added a similar high court in 1799 that heard cases in both law and equity. These courts, however, were extremely limited in their authority. The high courts were actually extensions of the district courts, composed of district judges who met after their circuits to discuss appeals. Although the South Carolina appeals courts did have final authority over their cases and points of law or equity, their North Carolina counterpart did not, at least initially. North Carolina's appeals court was a Court of Conference, which met after the district courts to allow judges to confer over appeals and particularly difficult cases. The Court of Conference functioned as an advisory body, making recommendations that were returned with the cases to the district courts where the final decisions were rendered. Legislators rejected other proposals to create a more powerful high court on the grounds that it would be too distant geographically from most people, too expensive for them to make use of, and too concerned with the abstractions of law to render justice.[52]

At issue were two distinct views of the legal system that echoed those from the Regulator period. Defending the unsuccessful 1799 reform measure to replace the Court of Conference with a stronger Court of Errors and Appeals, James Iredell's close associate Samuel Johnston argued that such a court was necessary to "the due execution of the laws" by which the people "hold their liberty and property." "Under our present system," he explained, "what is law at one place is not law at another. The opinions of Judges vary; and the decision of one Judge is disregarded by another." The situation made little sense to him, which was why he supported a central court "which shall govern all the varying decisions which may be given in various parts of the State." Only then would "some security . . . be had for the due administration of justice." The majority, however, saw no problem at all with the current system despite its inconsistencies. As Representative Irwin argued, the "great end of law is to obtain justice for individuals, and therefore the administration of justice ought to be made as convenient to the citizens at large as possible." For Irwin and others, the legal system was about resolving specific conflicts and achieving justice for those involved, not elaborating a uniform body of law that would hold everywhere, without attention to context. The facts of the case, not abstract points of law, were the central components of justice. Given that, he could not see "that this Judge of Appeal would be more likely to do justice than a Jury." So why have one at all?[53]

The North Carolina legislature did expand the authority of the Court of Conference, but the process was so convoluted that it is difficult to identify the decisive moment of change. In 1804 the North Carolina legislature made the Court of Conference a court of record, which turned it into something more like an appellate court in the sense that it could now render decisions instead of just dispensing advice to district courts, although it remains unclear how that worked in practice. In 1806 the legislature renamed the body the "Supreme Court," a change that some have identified as a turning point in the court's history, but it was a change with very limited results. Writing in 1912, historian William Henry Hoyt described it in this way: the court was "held twice a year at Raleigh by two or more of the Superior Court judges, to which were submitted, not appeals, but difficult or doubtful cases arising on the circuits." Those judges did not always reach consensus in each case. Even when they did, they still issued separate opinions and made no attempt to reconcile conflicting judgments on points of law. This court was supreme in name only. Some commentators identify 1810 as the key date in the court's history, for that was when the legislature approved the appointment of a chief justice to coordinate the different opinions of the justices. But the legislature neglected to specify how the chief justice would be selected; as late as 1834, it was still being done by drawing lots (that year, Thomas Ruffin won). Only in 1818 did the court become "supreme" in more than name, acquiring its own panel of judges and authority over points of law and equity. It was an unexpected victory for reformers, who seemed a little taken aback. "This will surprise you as it has every one here," wrote a delighted Archibald Murphey to Thomas Ruffin after the General Assembly's vote.[54]

South Carolina's appellate courts had more authority from the outset. But the practice of two parallel appeals courts, one for common law and one for equity, militated against the notion of an authoritative court that defined "the law" of the state. The two courts issued conflicting decisions on similar issues, a situation complicated by legal loyalties to either the common law or equity. Where equity's defenders, such as James Louis Petigru, characterized it as the very best of the English legal tradition, proponents of common law criticized equity for muddying the legal waters and undercutting the legitimacy of the entire system. Governor John Lyde Wilson once likened equity to the French Directory, calling it a five-headed monster that would destroy the state if nothing were done to stop it. In 1824 reformers finally convinced the legislature to abolish the parallel system, creating a single appeals court with its own panel of judges who heard cases in both law and equity. The number of equity judges was reduced at the same time. In 1835, at the tail end of the nullification crisis, the legislature reorganized the court system, returning to the structure that had obtained before the 1824 reforms. By this time, though, opposition to centralization was no longer the primary motivating factor for most legislators. Nullifiers, who dominated the legislature, were retaliating against two Unionist judges and trying to diffuse Unionist influence at the appellate level.[55]

In North Carolina the commitment to localized law undercut the move toward greater centralization until the 1830s. The legislature remained divided in its support for the new appellate court. So the North Carolina State Supreme Court limped along after its creation in 1818, trying to acquire institutional legitimacy in an openly hostile environment. Its critics launched measures to eviscerate it or to abolish it altogether in nearly every legislative session during the 1820s and into the 1830s. Even some of the court's justices were less than enthusiastic and could not be bothered to attend regularly. The resulting backlog of cases further tarnished the court's reputation.[56] By the 1830s the court was so unpopular that even its staunchest supporters began to doubt its efficacy. When William Gaston took the bench in 1833, the court's supporters hoped that his reputation might help repair the damage. "We think," wrote Governor David L. Swain, "*your* appointment to the Bench the only event which will preserve the Court and certainly the only event which can render it *worth* preserving." The court's unpopularity, however, gave Gaston pause. "The possibility that sooner or later these efforts of Demagogues may be successful," he wrote, made him "exceedingly loth to place himself in so precarious a situation." Yet he did place himself in this position and a few months later he was drawing lots with Thomas Ruffin to see who would become chief justice. Their compatriot, Justice Daniel, did not participate. Apparently he had no desire to take on the mantle of chief justice.[57]

■ ■ ■

BY THE 1840S the expectation in both states was that the lower levels of the court system were subordinate to the appellate courts. Reformers in North Carolina were still struggling to establish their vision of the law and the legal system during the 1830s. "Much is to be feared from the circuit court judges who act [three words illegible] against it," wrote Thomas P. Devereux in 1833 when it seemed that the court's future depended on Gaston's nomination. At the same moment when North Carolina's appellate court was finally acquiring some legitimacy in the late 1830s, South Carolina's nullifiers were carefully trying to preserve the fragile power of the judiciary while purging Unionist judges from its structure—a delicate balancing act. These courts and their decisions had authority by the 1830s. Even so, reading the legal authority that appellate courts ultimately acquired back into the historical narrative after the fact invests their decisions with far more significance than they actually had for most of the period between the Revolution and the Civil War.[58]

PART II ▪ Localized Law

I N 1796 Governor Samuel Ashe granted a pardon to Pleasant, an enslaved woman who had been convicted of arson in Granville County,
North Carolina. He did so based on the recommendation of James
Chandler, whose property Pleasant was supposed to have destroyed, the
magistrates and jurors involved in her case, and other white men of the
county. Unfortunately, their petitions did not survive. According to Governor Ashe's summary of the situation, Pleasant had confessed to the crime,
which was why she had been convicted. The petitioners nonetheless thought
her worthy of mercy, because they believed "that she had committed the
offence by coercion of a free white person." Governor Ashe failed to elaborate on that statement, leaving a host of tantalizing questions.[1] Why would
a group of white men, including the victim, rally to the defense of an enslaved woman? Who was the unnamed man? What other information did
the petitioners have? How did they obtain it? Why did Governor Ashe find
their claims credible? For this case, the questions are unanswerable. The answers would have been difficult to tease out even at the time, because they
depended on local knowledge that was circulated in specific places by the
people who lived there. Understanding one case was impossible without
understanding the entire range of relationships, past and present, in that
area. It is possible, though, to apprehend the more generalized dynamics
that shaped cases like this one: we cannot know why James Chandler and
his white neighbors petitioned to pardon Pleasant, but we can understand
the localized legal process that would produce such cases.

The four chapters in part 2 explore the operation of localized law, beginning with the institutional process of keeping the peace (chapters 3 and 4)
and then moving to the ways in which the legal mechanisms of the peace
mediated power relationships (chapters 5 and 6). In all the chapters, the
focus is on the nexus between institutions and people — white women and
children, free blacks, and slaves like Pleasant — who do not usually figure
prominently in the history of law and politics.

The analysis in these chapters builds on recent scholarship that emphasizes the importance of localism in law and government throughout the
new nation. According to William J. Novak, the historian most associated
with this argument, influential jurists, legal writers, and educators made
the principle of local self-governance central to both the theory and practice of law and government in the period between the Revolution and the
Civil War. Not only did the national level remain relatively weak, but even
state lawmakers delegated considerable legal discretion to cities, counties,
and other local jurisdictions. The result was that much of American law

was made and applied at local levels to promote the welfare of the people (*salus populi*). *The People and Their Peace*, however, argues that the localism articulated by professionally trained lawyers in written texts, while influential, was not the same thing as localized law. Localized law was more profoundly decentralized and, as a result, more deeply contextual and more variable than the legal system preferred by most professionally trained lawyers. As the second part of the book shows, southern jurists like Thomas Ruffin often invoked the concepts associated with localism—the people, their welfare, and the peace—to subvert the localized process and impose a more uniform body of state law based in rights. Many professionally trained lawyers also were critical of the role of the "people" and expressions of their "welfare" in localized law. In the localized system, law emerged from the daily lives of actual people with concrete interests in maintaining certain, often conflicting conceptions of the peace. The process was as loud, messy, and unpredictable as the communities it served, a reality far removed from the neat abstractions of written legal texts.[2]

People, even subordinates without rights, were central to localized law. White southerners used the system to regulate the behavior of people on the social margins, invoking the good order of the peace to maintain established social hierarchies. Slaves, free blacks, and poor whites appeared regularly in localized law as defendants. But these people were not just targets of social control. They also joined their higher-status neighbors in doing the basic work of the system, gathering the evidence and providing the information that decided cases. More than that, the patterns of their lives formed the customs that defined the peace in local areas and that the localized law was supposed to protect. These elements of localized law are evident in Pleasant's case. The white men of the neighborhood used the system to discipline her as an errant slave, prosecuting and convicting her of arson. Then they turned around and asked for her pardon, in recognition of the particular relationships that explained the crime she was supposed to have committed.

The prominence of people without professional training in localized law drove state leaders to distraction. They were concerned that unqualified people played such a decisive role in applying the law. But they were even more alarmed at the thought that such people determined the actual definition of the laws in their states. "The democratic power of these states is systematically organized and arrayed against the Judiciary, as a political body," wrote one irate South Carolina Federalist in 1803, in the heady aftermath of the French·Revolution and the onset of hostilities with Britain. "It may be, however," the writer continued, "that the spirit which dictates those acts of hostility to the Judiciary, extends its views still farther, and looks with jealous malignity at the laws themselves."[3] Although the editorialist missed the mark in positing a grand plot of Francophile democrats to overthrow the government, he grasped the indissoluble connection between the institutional structures of the legal system and the content of law. By allowing ordinary people a role in defining the content of the laws operative in their states, localized systems kept authority away from the judiciary.

North Carolina's William Gaston made the same connection in less conspiratorial terms when introducing the 1818 bill that would establish North Carolina's appellate court as an independent body with precedent-setting authority: "There must be in every free community some Supreme Court of Judicature to decide conclusively on every question of Law, to compel all inferior tribunals to adhere to the same exposition of the public will, and to [make] . . . Civil Conduct permanent, uniform and universal." Without such a court, "an individual can not be certain what is law to-day will be deemed law to-morrow; or that what is right in his neighbor may not be adjudged wrong in himself." Under those conditions, "property . . . [would] . . . become insecure, and liberty itself endangered by fluctuating and inconsistent adjudications." He ended with the metaphor of slavery, which had been central to the rhetoric of the Revolution and still carried considerable resonance, particularly in the slave South: "Miserable is that servitude where rights are ambiguous, and the law unknown." In this court, a select group of trained professionals would preserve liberty by tending to the abstractions of law. Thomas P. Devereux threw that same point back at Gaston in 1833, when the future of North Carolina's appellate court hung in the balance. "We never can do without a Supreme Court of some kind," wrote Devereux, hoping to convince Gaston to serve on it; "the business of the circuits in our widely extended country never can be done consistently." For lawyers like Devereux and Gaston, liberty and justice depended on consistency, uniformity, and universality within the body of state law. That required a designated court to iron out the ambiguities, clean up the mistakes, and shake out the contradictions that proliferated in the district courts to produce "the law" that applied everywhere in the state. For them, law that was only interpreted and administered locally was no law at all.[4]

What professionally trained lawyers valued was what others deplored. As the others saw it, the centralization of legal authority that reformers advocated would remove law from the people and tend toward corruption, a particularly resonant concept in this period when the possibility of oligarchy, monarchy, and the collapse of the republic was so easily invoked. Centralization would take power over law away from the very people with the knowledge necessary to make informed judgments in their communities. They saw law as principles with multiple valences. Legal principles were a means, not an end. They were valuable insofar as they helped achieve liberty, but they did not constitute liberty. Imposing inflexible rules would turn law into tyranny by privileging the abstractions of law over the practice of justice.[5]

Pardon petitions articulate that vision of law with particular clarity. Petitions expressed a view of law that merged legal principles with a particularistic view of justice. The reasons for pardons were as varied as the individuals involved: the defendant was impressionable and unduly swayed by an evil companion, as in Pleasant's case; the defendant was young, had made an unwise choice because of youthful inexperience, and should be given a second chance; the defendant was old and could not sustain the punishment; the defendant had an innocent family that depended on him and would suffer needlessly should the punishment be carried out; the offense was exceptional and would not be repeated, since the defendant had otherwise been hardworking and upstanding; the offense was mitigated by circumstances beyond the defendant's control and did not merit punishment. And so it went. Petitioners usually acknowledged the defendants' guilt: For the purposes of the petition, they also acknowledged the necessity of recognizing the offense in the abstract. But that may have been a convention for the benefit of the governor, rather than a reflection of their own views of law, because their reasoning tended to turn back on itself in ways that undercut their commitment to those abstract principles. In particular, petitioners' views of how law should be applied were linked to the circumstances and the individuals involved, which caused them to distinguish degrees of criminality and guilt that other conceptions of law did not recognize. Petitioners also assumed that their word, as people with direct knowledge of those involved, had enough legal weight to affect the outcome in the case.[6]

This highly localized view of law clashed with the version held by many professionally trained lawyers who wished to reform the legal system. Two of these reformers, North Carolina governors James Iredell Jr., who served in the late 1820s, and David L. Swain, who served in the early 1830s, took on localized law through the pardon process. Both generally refused pardons, giving lengthy rationales for their denials. Petitions, they explained, were not enough to establish the basis of a pardon, since local knowledge could never be a substitute for the objectivity of the law. Even with the appropriate evidence regarding the miscarriage of the law and legal process submitted by judges, they granted few pardons. As they maintained, justice could only be realized by maintaining the abstractions of law and applying them consistently to everyone, without exception.[7]

Both popular culture and post-Revolutionary legal institutions tended to favor localism, even after greater systematization was introduced. In this regard, reformers had a point: more than anything, ambiguity characterized both statute and case law in the decades immediately following the Revolution. By itself, legislators' acknowledgment of the reformers' point—that their state needed definite bodies of law with more cohesion and systematization—was not enough to get the job done. It took a great deal of time and effort to achieve the most limited results. Even after statutes were cleaned up and collated, they only covered a handful of legal issues. Like other states, North Carolina and South Carolina made common law operative in areas not covered by statute. Many professionally trained lawyers relied on a body of established legal authorities, including Blackstone, which many historians now identify as the recognized expression of common law. But the common law tradition was capacious enough to allow for considerable ambiguity, accentuated by the decentralized court structure that allowed for multiple interpretations of common law rules.

Slave law represents the dynamics of a system that left so much discretionary power to local officials. The legal status of slaves mirrored that of free people, to the extent that no one's status, whether slave or free, existed as a set of universally applicable principles, defined by the state. Although referred to as "codes," the slave statutes in North Carolina and South Carolina did not constitute a comprehensive and coherent body of law, as did French and Spanish slave codes. Colonial assemblies had established and defined slavery on an ad hoc basis. Neither colony had defined slaves' basic relationship to law: were they subjects within the legal order, or were they outside it? Unable to evade that question after the Revolution, state lawmakers tackled it from different directions. In North Carolina, they applied common law to slaves in all areas not covered by statute, resolving the immediate question by bringing slaves into the existing legal order and providing a body of law that could apply to them. That measure did not, however, alter the legal status of slaves relative to free people. In state law, slaves were slaves, governed by statutes that singled them out as slaves *and* by common law—in all its variability—that did not distinguish between slaves and free people. South Carolina's lawmakers determined slaves' legal position through statutes alone, which produced even more ambiguities since the statutes were not collected or widely circulated until much later.[8]

Vast areas of law fell to local forums, not just for interpretation but for their actual definition. Consider the treatment of violence against slaves in Kershaw District, South Carolina. Early South Carolina statutes did allow for the prosecution of masters and other whites for such acts, but subsequent legislation muddied the waters, and clarification did not come from either the legislature or the appellate court until late in the antebellum period. When local legal officials were faced with cases of violence against slaves, it was neither practical nor feasible for them to wait for direction from elsewhere in the legal system. Tellingly, though, they did not even bother asking. Instead, they took it upon themselves to interpret the statutes. Those interpretations resulted in the periodic prosecution of whites for violence against slaves, including assaults, manslaughter, and murder, even though historians' readings of statute and case law suggest that such cases should not exist. Kershaw District even occasionally prosecuted a master when violence resulted in a slave's death.[9]

Local officials in Kershaw District did not treat every case of violence against slaves in the same way, of course. On the contrary, the discretion allowed in legal localism resulted in various outcomes, swinging from considered mercy to arbitrary vengeance. While prosecuting some offenses against slaves as crimes and incorporating them into the public order, legal localism could likewise sanction brutal violence against slaves in the name of the public order as well. Consistency of outcome was not the point. Nor was the protection of individuals' rights, abstracted from the larger community. Every case arose from a particular incident. Legal localism did not include or exclude cases systematically, and it did not draw rigid distinctions between "the law" and the wide range of customary practices outside it. That combination of intense particularism in its approach to individual people and expansive corporatism gave people recognized places within the legal system, even though they could not claim the full range of civil and political rights in their own names.

Local jurisdictions continued to operate as if they could define law for most of the period between 1787 and 1840. They did so not from ignorance or even defiance, but from a continuing commitment to a view of law that allowed outcomes to depend on specific situations, not on abstract principles. Even after state-level institutions acquired more legal authority, they could neither represent the laws of the state nor impose a unitary definition on a set body of state law. Local jurisdictions retained considerable discretion not only because so many points of law remained unsettled at the state level, but also because so many people, including other legal officials, did not see law in the same way as state leaders. Because localized law grew out of the patterns of everyday life, it was difficult to uproot. And it is impossible to understand the nation's legal past if we separate it from these cultural patterns and the ordinary people who created them.

Keeping the Peace

3

The sun burned hot through the haze of late summer. Although the thick shade provided only the illusion of relief from the sweltering heat, a small group of people clustered under the trees near a local magistrate's house in Spartanburg District, South Carolina, in 1834. They were talking about James Woodruff, his wife and children, and his work habits. Despite the informality of the topic and the setting, they were at a formal legal hearing. Woodruff had been charged under South Carolina's 1787 vagrancy statute, based on the poor laws of early modern England but expanded to include residents who did not work their property and who failed to maintain orderly households. Those assembled at Woodruff's trial included witnesses there to testify, observers with an interest in the matter, and the panel of two magistrates and three freeholders who composed the court, listened to the information, and delivered the verdict. Witnesses had been served with written warrants. They spoke one at a time, beginning with John Ward, who had filed the initial complaint against Woodruff. One of the magistrates, pen in hand, scribbled notes that he later turned into a case summary, with a list of the participants, a transcript of each witness's testimony, and the decision. To that he added the other documents: the initial complaint by John Ward, the warrant for James Woodruff's arrest, and copies of the witnesses' warrants. Then he folded the entire bundle in thirds, tied it up with a ribbon, and gave it to the district court clerk to file.[1]

The magistrates and freeholders found James Woodruff guilty. The next chapter, which explores why offenses became crimes, will return to this case and consider why James Woodruff's behavior qualified as a criminal offense. First, though, it is necessary to step back and examine the procedural workings of localized law. The system included the informal discussions and formal entreaties involved in passing local ordinances and statutes or obtaining pardons. It also included the grand jury presentments, trials, and other business conducted at circuit courts, which were held on regular schedules in regional towns and county seats. But those elements were only the most visible part of a system that was dominated by legal proceedings like James Woodruff's trial: magistrates' hearings, inquests, and other ad hoc legal forums. It was in all these informal, nominally legal arenas that southerners did the business of "keeping the peace," a well-established concept in Anglo-American law that expressed the ideal order of the metaphorical public body, subordinating everyone (in varying ways) within a hierarchical system and emphasizing social order over individual rights.

The process defined localized law more than the verdicts. Outcomes were deeply rooted in the dynamics of local communities, which included the credit of the people involved, their families' position in the community, the social networks in which they moved, and the local customs of the area. Based in multiple variables, peculiar to specific contexts and moments in time, verdicts were so idiosyncratic that it is impossible to generalize from them. The difficulties are compounded by the distance of time and the lack of evidence to bridge the gap. Why was James Woodruff charged and convicted of vagrancy when other poor white men were not? Often, the deciding factors were so obvious to the participants that they never made their way into the court records: they were the elephant in the room that everyone saw but no one acknowledged. Nor is an analysis based in the outcomes particularly revealing, since verdicts were fleeting decisions that did not produce precedents for future cases, unlike the system that reformers hoped to build. While verdicts were unpredictable, the process was not. The formal procedures in James Woodruff's trial duplicated those of thousands of other cases conducted across the Carolinas and throughout the rest of the nation as well.[2]

The process of localized law encompassed more than formal rules. It depended on the presence and participation of people in local communities, combining popular conceptions of justice with Revolutionary ideology in a literal rendering of popular sovereignty. "The people" did not exist as the abstraction that provided the basis for government, as they did in state constitutions, statutes, appellate cases, and the U.S. Constitution. They figured as flesh-and-blood individuals, whose presence and opinions informed the entire process: people constituted the legal process, and law was what emerged through their interactions with one another. Other legal concepts that existed as abstractions elsewhere in the system—such as the people's welfare, or the good order of the peace—had concrete meanings in localized law, because they were inseparable from the people who articulated and embodied them. Conflict, not consensus, characterized these legal concepts in the localized system. The South Carolina vagrancy statute provides an excellent example. It listed some specific acts that qualified as vagrancy, such as peddling without a license. But most of the enumerated offenses trailed off into the conditional: not working diligently enough or failing to support one's family adequately. Yet vagrancy was well defined in comparison to other offenses. To enforce the statute, people in local jurisdictions had to fill in the blanks, which they did differently in each case. In this system, law flourished primarily in local contexts, tended by the people who lived there.[3]

Legal localism denotes a distinct approach to law. This culture of localism led ordinary southerners to see the legal system as something directly connected to them, and they expected it to respond as such, wherever it might be located. All kinds of people made their way to state government as well as local legal venues, sometimes pushing and shoving to get there, insistent on voicing their own conceptions of their welfare and, often, the welfare of everyone else as well. They did so because they believed the system not only should, but actually could address and resolve their concerns. Their faith was based in the popular conviction that law could keep the "peace"—a term that could accommodate idealistic, even utopian aspirations, in addition to its more prosaic duties of maintaining order and keeping people in line. Keeping the peace necessarily involved ordinary southerners, who assumed that they were part of the process. Without them, it is impossible to understand the operation and development of law in this period.[4]

THE PHYSICAL PROXIMITY OF LAW

"Law is King," announced Thomas Paine in his opening Revolutionary volley. Historian Christopher Tomlins has added meat to those bones, identifying law as the primary "modality of rule" in the early republic. Law, argues Tomlins, moved from the periphery to the center over the course of the eighteenth century to become "*the* paradigmatic discourse explaining life in America" by the end of the nineteenth century. This notion of "the rule of law" worked in two registers, one institutional and one conceptual. Institutionally, courts became the most important arena of governance in the early republic, surpassing other arenas that had once regulated society, such as churches and families. That shift gave formalized law, especially professionalized versions of common law, disproportionate authority in formulating and resolving social problems. But law had ideological power as well. People not only used its mantle to legitimize their actions but also expected it to provide answers to problems, both petty and profound. That element of Tomlins's argument echoes Alexis de Tocqueville's observations about the significance of law in the early republic. Unlike de Tocqueville, Tomlins sees the implications as unambiguously undemocratic, because the reliance on law placed major decisions about society's welfare in the hands of professionally trained lawyers and judges, who operated on the narrow, inflexible, and hierarchical terrain of formalized common law.[5]

The path that led to that result was long and uneven, given the dispersion of legal authority in early-nineteenth-century America. As Tomlins points out, the notion of a singular "rule of law" concealed deep divisions inherent in the concept, encompassing both the developments that he associates with formalized common law and Revolutionary political ideals that emphasized the people's sovereignty and their centrality to government. Those tensions occasionally surfaced in open conflict during the nineteenth century.[6] In the Carolinas, as elsewhere, they remained unresolved and influential throughout the period from 1787 to 1840. While southerners embraced law as the "modality of rule," they still saw it as *their* modality of rule, a view supported and sustained by the legal system's localized institutional structure, which kept it in close proximity to most people's lives.

In institutional terms, law in the Carolinas was everywhere and nowhere. Law took up considerable space in the two states' structures of governance. The legal system dealt with a wide variety of issues in the early national period, including poor relief, public health, and economic regulation.[7] While these matters were attended to locally, there was no single location for law. Those towns where circuit courts met were likely to have courthouses. But, since legislators kept breaking up existing districts and adding new ones to accommodate the growth of the population and its westward movement, circuit courts met in whatever buildings were large enough until courthouses were built. These early courthouses tended to be unremarkable in style. Although distinguished by their size, they blended in with the other buildings in town. Many were multipurpose public buildings used for other meetings and events when court was not in session; they lacked offices, document storerooms, and other specialized spaces that became standard in later courthouse designs. Particularly in the first few decades following the Revolution, Carolinians did not associate the legal system with courthouses or other specifically designated public structures; most legal proceedings were conducted elsewhere.[8]

The practice of law moved around promiscuously, following the officials who oversaw it and going to the people it served. Magistrates, also called justices of the peace or simply justices, occupied the first level of the legal

At the county and district level, court met in spaces where people ordinarily gathered. In Spartanburg District, the first court met at Nichols's (later Anderson's) Mill in 1785. Subsequent courts met at the homes of Thomas Williamson and John Wood, according to J.B.O. Landrum's History of Spartanburg County *(1900). Courtesy of the Spartanburg County Historical Association.*

system and did most of its work, with the help of sheriffs and constables. Appointed by the legislatures, magistrates were usually men of local standing, generally without formal legal training. Although they received fees for their services, magistrates did not take the position solely for the money or view it as a full-time occupation. It was a duty that they performed in addition to farming or other business pursuits. Magistrates relied on sheriffs and constables, who delivered warrants and made arrests. Sheriffs, who were either elected or appointed at the county or district level, delegated work to constables, who were chosen by the sheriff, the magistrates, the county commissioners, or other municipal officials. Some towns, including Camden and Charleston, had guards who served as constables. But, since designated sheriffs and constables were not always at hand when they were needed, magistrates and other officials deputized willing bystanders to perform specific duties temporarily.[9]

The legal process began with magistrates acting as gatekeepers, screening complaints. If they thought further action was necessary, they dispatched the sheriff or a constable to arrest the accused parties and to issue warrants requiring the appearance of everyone else involved, including witnesses, at a hearing or, if the offense lay within the magistrates' jurisdiction, at a trial. Depending on current statutory guidelines and the nature of the offense, trials and hearings could involve a panel of magistrates and freeholders, a group of two or three magistrates, or just a single magistrate. Trials could be indistinguishable from hearings, except that magistrates determined the outcome in trials, which in South Carolina could include a jury of freeholders, depending on the offense. In hearings, by contrast, justices considered the evidence in order to categorize the offense and to determine whether it would move on through the system. The reach of magistrates' jurisdiction was extensive and continued to expand over the period between 1787 and 1840, although the specifics shifted as legislatures tinkered with the system. In general, magistrates tried most minor criminal offenses and civil matters. South Carolina magistrates had authority over all offenses involving slaves and free people of color, including the most serious felonies.[10]

Courts literally formed around magistrates. When people had a complaint, they initiated the legal process by going to find a magistrate. Magistrates heard complaints when and where they received them, in the field where they were working or even from the bed where they had been sleeping. Then they held hearings and trials in convenient spots that would accommodate a crowd: taverns, country stores, front porches, a room in the magistrate's house, or under a canopy of trees outdoors. The proceedings could be raw and raucous, as suggested by the stream of cases involving insults to local legal officials and squabbles in their presence. Critics cringed, seeing disrespect that threatened the legitimacy of the system. "The places of trial," wrote one observer through gritted teeth, "are usually some tavern or some such place, where such scenes are sometimes exhibited, as justice never before witnessed."[11] True enough. These locations pushed law physically into the community and into the lives of the people there, much to the consternation of those reformers who wished to separate law from the community more clearly. One reason they favored greater distance was because they knew that life in rural communities was not always dignified and decorous. Ordinary southerners' failure to meet the standards of the region's elite had acquired legendary proportions by the late eighteenth

Many early courthouses did not have a distinctive style and tended to blend into their surroundings. In Chatham County, North Carolina, the first courthouse had become a garage by the 1920s, camouflaging it even more. Courtesy of the North Carolina Collection, University of North Carolina Library at Chapel Hill.

century, and they continued to live down to expectations thereafter. The subject filled the diaries and correspondence of the elite, who never tired of cataloging the sins of rural life as they traveled gingerly through the countryside. Their lists usually included inedible food, poor accommodations, abysmal manners, questionable hygiene, and wretched taste in clothes, furniture, and architecture, as well as hair-trigger tempers.[12] The tenor of local legal proceedings reflected the habits of the people involved and their emotional investment in the issues, as well as their familiarity with the officials and the legal process. Familiarity did not breed contempt so much as comfort, enough so that southerners treated local legal officials much as they would treat their neighbors — indeed, local legal officials were their neighbors.

Legal forums crystallized at community gatherings, emerging from the interactions of a range of residents: respectable and disreputable, male and female, slave and free, young and old, rich and poor, white and black and all shades in between. In this world, where social rankings were so well marked that people could mingle together, secrets were hard to keep: everyone knew everyone else's business. That was true even in cities and towns, which were built in ways that made privacy and anonymity difficult.[13]

Localized law was founded on that shared store of common knowledge, which crossed lines of race, class, and gender. Inquests provide excellent examples. When a death occurred, neighbors gathered to pay their respects, to clean and dress the body, and to grieve. That process also could reveal evidence of wrongdoing. Sometimes the signs were easily spotted by those who first saw the corpse. Sometimes they were uncovered by the women whose job it was to prepare the body for burial. And sometimes they emerged through the mourners' conversations, as information was shared and the pieces began to form ominous patterns. When doubts acquired a critical mass, the coroner or someone designated to act as coroner was called, if he was not already there. The gathering then reconstituted itself as a legal hearing: a jury was formed, often from among those in attendance, and mourners became witnesses. One by one, they offered their observations, repeating for the record what had already been said. And so law arrived at the wake, at the invitation of no one, yet at the behest of everyone.[14]

The term "community" is itself fraught, conjuring up images of bucolic hamlets governed by earnest villagers who endeavored to stave off the inhumane encroachments of the modern world with traditional notions of moral order. The slave South exposes the underside of that ideal, revealing its coercive undercurrents and making them impossible to ignore. In localized law, rural southerners acted out the extreme inequalities that defined their communities, silencing and circumscribing some while validating and elevating others. Wealthy whites had the luxury of opting out and settling their conflicts privately, instead of subjecting themselves to public display. But even the wealthiest could not distance themselves from the system entirely. Localized law tended toward inclusion of a compulsory variety that forced those at both ends of the social order into the system. Elite white men were tapped to serve as magistrates, and all the members of their families were drawn into legal conflicts when complaints were made against them or filed against their slaves. Given their standing in the community, the men and women of elite families were also expected to serve as witnesses, to testify to the physical evidence, the social background to the conflict, or the character of those involved.[15]

The compulsory nature of localized law magnified the brutalities of a social order based in stark inequalities. Legal officials scooped up slaves, free blacks, and poor whites, forcing them into the legal system whether they wanted to be there or not. The process transformed the ordinary places of daily life into menacing sites of interrogation and punishment. Slaves and free blacks, in particular, usually encountered law as raw force, when they were yanked out of their daily routines, tried, and sentenced by the same people with whom they worked and worshiped. Punishment was corporal, usually whipping, inflicted immediately and in public.[16]

Poor whites often met up with law on similar terms. Although more likely to be sentenced with fines or jail terms, white southerners also received corporal punishment, including branding, mutilation, whipping, and time in the stocks, all of which remained standard for serious crimes well into the nineteenth century. Fines, imprisonment, and court costs could have physical effects as well, forcing people into poverty and, for those without property, into involuntary labor contracts. In 1834, for example, Robert Robertson pled guilty to assault. As a result of his conviction, Robertson and his family lost most of their personal property; a horse, saddle, bridle, bed, cupboard, and chairs, as well as other furniture and household items were seized by the sheriff for sale. The fine had been only five dollars. But court costs could be much higher, even in cases that did not go to trial. With a trial, costs hovered between twenty and forty dollars, sums that few could afford to pay without sacrifice.[17]

The dynamics of localized law conformed to the social gradations that characterized local social structures. Social rankings were notoriously idiosyncratic at the local level, governed by family and community ties, personal reputation, and a host of other factors known only to those who lived there—a subject that the next chapter will discuss in more detail. The intricacies of local hierarchies mean that universal categories, such as "women" or "slaves," usually conceal as much as they reveal about the outcomes of particular cases at the local level, because there were so many modifications and exceptions. Nonetheless, the contrast between the positions of slaves and free white wives is instructive in understanding the general dynamics of the system. Although encumbered within localized law, white women had much more room to maneuver, because the terms of their subordination established strong social connections not just to their husbands but also to influential neighbors and kin. Backed by the strength of those ties, many white women wielded considerable authority within the localized system; as this and subsequent chapters show, white women's voices had particular force, clarity, and character. The dynamics of race and slavery meant that subordination took a different form for slaves, moving them to the margins of the legal system and muting their voices. A few slaves drew on their ties with whites to augment their standing within the localized legal system. Most slaves' primary social connections, though, were to other slaves, who could often provide considerable information about the system and those involved in the case, but little direct assistance in the actual process. In general, slaves' subordinate social status moved them so far to the margins that they could barely negotiate the localized legal system themselves. At the same time, slaves' subordination was so central to the maintenance of order that it resulted in stricter controls and more severe punishments.

Magistrates tended the relationship between the local social structure and the legal system. They were the ones with the power to turn ordinary conflicts into legal matters and, in the process, to transform ordinary life. But a visit to the magistrate usually began as an escalation in degree, not in kind. When confronted with threats or violence they could not handle themselves, people first sought aid from neighbors or kin. That failing, they called on local magistrates, who also could be neighbors or kin. In Charleston in 1799, for instance, Mrs. Nagle found shelter with neighbors when her husband "came home one evening very much in liquor." "As she knew his temper," Mrs. Nagle later explained, "she thought it prudent to go next door" to the Camerons. When Mrs. Nagle's husband came to find her, Mrs. Cameron refused him entry, "called him a blackguard & told him to go about his business," which sent him into a rage. At that point Mrs. Nagle and the Camerons sent another neighbor to find a city guard and a magistrate to arrest Mr. Nagle. But the conflict escalated before they arrived. Mr. Cameron shot Mr. Nagle, turning the magistrate's visit into an altogether different kind of event.[18] Of course, most disputes ended with far less drama. The patterns were nonetheless the same, with one or both aggrieved parties marching off to a magistrate when they reached an irreconcilable impasse.

The results of a trip to the magistrate often resembled the results of visits to neighbors and relatives. Only a small fraction of complaints resulted in formal charges, although the exact figures are impossible to determine. In most cases, magistrates handed out nothing more than sympathy or censure. When magistrates took action, it was usually to issue a peace warrant, labeling the actions of the perpetrator as a potential but not yet actual public offense. The errant individual then secured a bond for good behavior for a specified period of time, but did not incur any criminal penalty unless he or she broke the peace thereafter. Peace bonds threw enforcement back on the community, summoning family, friends, and neighbors to police the troublemakers. Bonds required one or more other people to put up part of the amount, making them liable if the accused broke the peace again. That economic obligation represented the signers' promise to keep the offender in line. Peace bonds put everyone else in the community on notice as well, investing them with the responsibility of policing the peace until the end of the probation period.[19]

The formal use of community policing tended to legitimize customary forms of discipline. John Clary was treated to a pointed visit from the extended family of the young woman whom he had impregnated, an action that many historians would designate as "extralegal." In fact, the difference between that action and sanctioned forms of community policing was not so clear. Although Clary prosecuted the mob and they were convicted of riot, the entire group was later pardoned by North Carolina's governor. The pardon owed partly to the nature of Clary's offense, but it also reflected the ambiguity between extralegal violence and legally sanctioned policing and the legal system's deep customary roots within local communities.[20]

The same dynamics marked the prosecution of cases. Magistrates regularly brokered settlements in conflicts, instead of treating them as criminal or civil matters. In so doing, they operated on a murky middle ground somewhere between custom and law. Arbitration was a customary resolution to conflicts that could acquire legal standing—or not. In fact, most people tried to resolve their problems or atone for damage through settlements before going to law. Negotiations operated according to unwritten but widely recognized rules. The settlements usually consisted of material compensation in goods, cash, and labor. But they could take more symbolic forms as well. Nancy Gibson, a white woman from Pendleton District, wanted personal vindication when a slave named Patt insulted her. Gibson demanded that Patt's owners apologize and inflict corporal punishment on Patt. She filed legal charges only after Patt's owners refused, apparently hoping the court would do what they would not. Magistrates often found themselves in a position to mediate disputes as part of their role in screening cases. When they did so, they were performing a customary role as third parties called in to witness or broker arbitration, to formalize whatever agreement was reached, and to ensure that its terms were observed. Yet when a magistrate was involved as the mediator, the customary settlement could ease into legal territory. This slippage happened to an overseer charged with killing a slave in Kershaw District, South Carolina. The evidence indicates that he offered to reimburse the master for the cost of the slave, instead of standing trial on criminal charges. The slave's owner refused the settlement and moved the matter into the ambit of law instead, setting the stage for criminal charges. Nonetheless, the distinction between custom and law was lost on some people, who invested out-of-court agreements with full legal authority. North Carolinian James Woods explained his failure to appear in court to stand trial for assault in those terms. "His father," he claimed, "had compromised this business with John Wallace [for] . . . the sum of thirty dollars or thereabouts in full satisfaction." Woods "therefore conceived it not to be necessary for his attendance at the last [court] term." It was a common mistake.[21]

Circuit courts were more formal and more distant from daily life, particularly the lives of women and children, slave and free, as well as enslaved men. Nevertheless, a wide range of people attended court sessions as participants and observers. The drama of court week in Laurensville, South Carolina, pushed Sarah J. Jones's other duties into the background. Recently married, Jones wrote regularly to her mother in North Carolina, but not when court was in session. "I set down to write and expect to stop before I am half done," she apologized, "for I am looking every minute for the gentlemen to come for us to go into the court house to hear a criminal tryed for murder." She returned to the letter after the conclusion of the case. "I was so interested and amused hearing the lawyers plead that I neglected to send my letter, in fact the mail had been gone 2 hours, when I returned." The combination of excitement and defensiveness that ran through Jones's description suggests that she feared her mother's disapproval. Jones made it clear that she went with male escorts and that it was customary for the women of Laurens District to attend court. According to her estimate, one-fourth of the four to five thousand people in town for court were women — "I am sorry to say," she added perfunctorily, without much conviction.[22]

People used the forum of circuit court sessions in their own ways. The courtrooms were noisy, opinionated places. Spectators packed themselves in and overflowed into the streets. When doorways were blocked by the crowd, people moved in and out through the windows, wading through onlookers perched on the sills. Not everyone's attention focused on the case being tried. Those who had legal business milled about waiting for their cases to be called, lawyers consulted with clients, and people from all over the county took the opportunity to visit when their interest in the proceedings waned. Wise judges worked with rather than against the crowd. Although they occasionally expelled inebriated or disruptive spectators,

People crowded into town for court day. Although taken much later, this photograph of Morgan Square, Spartanburg, South Carolina, is evocative of the scene on court day in the early 1800s. Courtesy of the Spartanburg County Historical Association.

judges who exerted too heavy a hand did so at their own peril. The dull roar of unrelated business being conducted in the background and the audible comments of onlookers engaged in the proceedings were expected features of courtroom culture.[23]

The proceedings spilled out into the streets, where people rehashed events and offered up their opinions. The swirl of activity surrounding court sessions constituted a popular form of entertainment. Trials spiced up the dull routines of rural life, and people followed the proceedings with the same addictive attention now reserved for television soap operas or court TV. Court provided an excuse to come to town, either to relax or to conduct business. Those who drank usually did so, often copiously. Others took the opportunity to shop or visit. Gawkers settled in around the courthouse, where there was much to see and do. Some spectators who took their revelry too far found themselves on the wrong side of the law. In one memorable event, Jeremiah Frazer was arrested when he "did so misbehave himself with a Stud Horse in the Court yard of Granville County whilst the

Court was sitting that the citizens thereof were greatly disturbed." Some cases ended outside the courthouse in physical confrontations that punctuated the legal proceedings. When the action waned, there was always conversation to be had about the cases, the guilt or innocence of the accused, the evidence presented, and the performance of the lawyers and judges. Strong opinions could provoke violence, even among those who had no direct stake in the matter, particularly when expressed by men whose attitudes had been amplified by liquor.[24]

Interest in court cases was hardly confined to the town square or the men, both white and black, who hung about the stores and streets on court day. Gossip permeated the parlors of respectable households, where white matrons entertained friends and relatives who were in town for court day. Sarah J. Jones claimed that she never would have attended the murder trial if she thought there would be a conviction, a comment revealing her involvement in the socializing that accompanied court day. Similar conversations could be overheard in the kitchens of those houses where slaves worked and visited. The discussions extended beyond the town's boundaries as well, involving people in the countryside who could not be in town for court but eagerly awaited the latest grist for the gossip mill.[25]

All that commotion served important legal purposes. Community involvement went beyond the influence of gossipy crowds on court days, although that context was significant in shaping the conduct and outcome of trials. Just as important was the way the legal process returned cases to community members for their stamp of legitimacy after the trials ended. If there was disagreement about the outcome, people had the power to modify the court's decision. The legal process officially recognized one such avenue for redress in allowing for pardons or alterations in sentencing. Pardons represented an alternative appeals process. Like those cases presented in appellate courts, pardon petitions contested a trial's outcome, although they skipped over legal points and went directly either to the facts of the case or to its social context. Petitioners constructed these appeals as if they were making extraordinary requests: they described the situations as singular, emotional, and urgent, which was why they were begging the governor to intercede with mercy. This language was intentionally misleading. Petitions circulated after every court session in a routine as predictable as clockwork. They followed specific rhetorical conventions, resulting in something akin to a handwritten legal form, in which the petitioners themselves churned out the appropriate boilerplate and then filled in the necessary details. These documents are better understood as polite demands than as submissive requests: petitioners alerted governors to local injustices with the expectation that governors would then use their authority to rectify them. The persistence of petitioners suggests these assumptions, as do the lengthy explanations offered by governors regarding their decisions when they denied pardons.[26]

Other ways of altering legal outcomes were not officially recognized, but were powerful nonetheless. Sheriffs and constables could encounter remarkable difficulties in finding defendants and bringing them to trial. They often found themselves riding around the countryside, following leads that led nowhere. Prisoners regularly escaped from custody and broke out of jail, often with the help of friends on the outside. The escapes were less surprising than the escaped prisoners' success at remaining hidden. As Constable Elijah Smith explained, it was raining hard in Pendleton District when he went to arrest Margaret Smith and her mother, Catherine Smith, both of whom had been charged with infanticide. He took the two women "into his custody but from the torrent of rain pouring down he thought it not prudent to remove them till the rain should cease." "Not thinking they would abscond at such a time," he explained somewhat sheepishly, "he did not confine them." They both escaped. One month later, he was still unable to find them.[27]

The flip side of evasion and escape was punishment outside the formal institutions of law. Defendants who escaped trial or were acquitted could face punishment outside the courtroom as debilitating as anything they would have received within it. Those who were caught inflicting extralegal punishment were likely to be acquitted, treated lightly, or pardoned, if charges were filed at all. Consider the outcome of two inquests in Pendleton District. In 1817 Jesse Corbin and George Cooley came to blows in a fight that resulted in George Cooley's death. An inquest found Corbin culpable, and murder charges were filed against him. But there is no further record of the case, suggesting that Jesse Corbin escaped conviction and punishment, at least by a court of law. He reappears in the records five years later, although this time as a dead body, the victim of what seems like an execution. Captain William Graham and all the members of his militia company road up to the door of the house where Corbin was staying, called him out, shot him through the head, and then rode off. The inquest jury found that Graham and his militia company had murdered Corbin, but there is no record that charges were filed or the case prosecuted.[28] In the localized system, legal legitimacy belonged to the people who lived with the results.

People of all kinds approached law with an air of proprietary familiarity, assuming that they could use it. They gave law respect of a particular kind, derived from close and frequent contact with a system that was integral to local culture. Respect did not take the form of blind obedience or unquestioning deference to legal authorities, whether in the form of written documents or of flesh-and-blood officials. To the contrary, southerners ignored or challenged those verdicts with which they did not agree precisely because they had enough confidence in the idea of law to believe that it could be engaged and changed. In this sense, acceptance of law represented faith in a concept that reached well beyond formal definitions or specific legal officials and institutions. Above all, ordinary people acted as if law was their "modality of rule," a system that should respond to their problems and could express their own conceptions of justice.

Established elements of the historiography have pointed in the other direction, emphasizing all southerners' distance from legal institutions and their disdain for law. Among white men, a culture of honor encouraged individual acts of retribution. The system's blatant inequalities and exclusions gave black southerners, enslaved and free, little reason to trust it. Recent scholarship, however, has underscored the importance of law and legal culture in southern society. Honor and law could comfortably coexist.[29] Nor did the denial of rights to slaves and free blacks necessarily result in their rejection of law as a conceptual system of rule. In fact, many of those on the system's margins still had faith that law could work for them under the proper circumstances. Nowhere is that more evident than during and after the Civil War, when former slaves made determined efforts to use the legal system for their benefit once they had direct access to it.[30]

Not all areas of law were equally accessible within the post-Revolutionary system. Property law, as developed in either equity or common law, had already been claimed by professional lawyers. In colonial economies that looked outward to the Atlantic world, knowledge of property law was crucial to economic success. By the time of the Revolution, links to international markets resulted in the development of relatively sophisticated financial structures to assist in property exchange, capital formation, and the management of credit and debt. That was true even in the Carolina backcountry, which lagged behind coastal areas, particularly the South Carolina low country. The influence of professionalized law was pervasive enough that even ordinary economic transactions, such as the purchase of land, required the interposition of lawyers. That was one of the primary complaints of colonial Regulators, whose target might be more accurately described as lawyers' monopoly of property law rather than either private property or law per se. Lawyers solidified their hold on economic matters in the decades following the Revolution, given the unsettled state of the economy, the scarcity of cash and credit, and the uncertainty of land titles in the Carolinas. The trend accelerated in the nineteenth century, largely because of the widespread use of notes, mortgages, and other instruments of debt as the primary means of economic exchange and capital formation. Over time, property law became even more elaborated and professionalized. The preponderance of property cases in the courts registered those trends.[31]

Other areas of law remained less professionalized longer, including those governing most crimes and other offenses against the public order. These matters were left in the realm of common law in its flexible, customary form, not its more formal variant. The legislatures dealt with minor offenses through statute on an ad hoc basis, responding to complaints from local residents. Revised codes of state law did not include these matters systematically until the 1830s. Even then, the rules were ill defined at best. The very definition of a felony, once defined as an offense punishable by death, was ambiguous. Common law definitions were short on detail. Crimes and other offenses against people and the public order had been of secondary interest to early modern common law lawyers and English common law treatise writers, with the notable exceptions of Matthew Hale, William Hawkins, and Joseph Chitty, whose volumes became staples of legal education during the nineteenth century. Blackstone, the fundamental text in post-Revolutionary legal education, had sections on crimes, but these lacked the specifics necessary to prosecute or adjudicate cases. Fines and punishments, when not established by statute, were left to the discretion of local courts and varied widely. Concerted efforts at the state level to clarify and regularize these areas of law were notably lacking, until the 1820s and 1830s, largely because they were far less lucrative for lawyers and less important to state leaders, who were often lawyers as well.[32] Lawyers and judges who might have professional training did not become involved in most offenses, even serious felonies, until the final stages, when a case went to a jury trial at the superior or district court. Only a small fraction of these matters ever went to trial in circuit courts where lawyers worked.[33]

A revolt in Kershaw District captures the difference between property law and the area of law governing public matters. In 1785, at the height of the national crisis that prompted Shays' Rebellion in western Massa-chusetts and led to the writing of the new federal Constitution, Kershaw residents effectively stopped all property suits and created their own pro-cedures for debt collections, both with the intent of cutting out lawyers. "In all probability," they announced confidently in a petition to the governor, "the Law will for some time be dormant." By "the Law" they meant prop-erty law, which they separated conceptually from matters of community policing. "We are determined to support a regular decorum on the point of Peace & good order," they explained. They would allow the court to "pro-ceed to the trial of Criminal matters alone," and "in the Execution of that Part of the Law we will give them every necessary support." Nor did they intend lawlessness when it came to property issues. Their other proposals, which carefully detailed alternative rules for the determination and col-lection of debts, were intended to bring property law closer in line with community customs. "We do form the following Resolutions" as a "means of extricating us from inevitable Ruin (in case the Law goes on) and at the same time do our Creditors every Justice that any number of reasonable Men, consistent with Reason can desire."[34]

Kershaw dissidents could allow the district court to try criminal mat-ters without surrendering control over them. Most cases were handled by magistrates, who lacked professional legal training and who turned to justices' manuals for legal guidance, when they felt the need to do so at all. Unlike other legal sources, these manuals tended to focus on crimes and other public offenses, providing descriptions and procedures. Post-Revolutionary manuals followed early modern English guides or colonial adaptations of them, which were based in common law but incorporated a range of elements within that tradition. They republished the basic defi-nitions of offenses that dated from the seventeenth and eighteenth cen-turies, appending notes to statute and case law relevant to those definitions without explaining them. They also included new sections on legal issues relating to the American experience, such as laws relating to slaves and free blacks. Although used by state officials and incorporating state law, these manuals were not issued by the states of North Carolina and South Carolina. They were compiled and issued privately—as were most legal references in this period—by the same writers responsible for other legal sources.[35]

It was to this broad, ambiguous area of law that a wide range of people turned to resolve the problems in their lives. White southerners, in particu-lar, regularly made use of the courts to solve interpersonal conflicts. Masters filed charges against slaves and hired servants whom they could not control. Families brought their feuds to court for resolution, with wives, husbands, parents, children, siblings, aunts, uncles, and cousins all lining up to air their dirty laundry. Neighbors involved legal officials in their quarrels, sometimes using the system in combination with insults, threats, and violence, as yet another weapon in an ongoing conflict. In all these instances, white people marched off to magistrates, certain that the law would back them up.

So did free blacks, despite legal barriers that limited their ability to use the system. Particularly revealing are the cases that free blacks initiated against legal officials. William Kersey's assault case against William Mallory, a Granville County constable, was not unusual, although the outcome of his suit is unknown. Elizabeth Oakley, a free black woman who also lived in Granville County, successfully prosecuted magistrate John Stephenson for assault. The case cost Stephenson, who had a history of shady dealings; in addition to paying a ten-dollar fine and court costs, he spent five days in jail. Free blacks expected the protections of law to apply to them, just as they expected law's representatives to act justly, and they went to considerable lengths to hold the system to those expectations.[36]

Although free blacks encountered difficulties, they did have the legal status to use the system. More surprising were the domestic dependents who tried to use law, even though they were unable to file legal charges or prosecute cases themselves. Free wives and children, both white and black, and even slaves occasionally appeared before magistrates to lodge complaints. It was technically possible for them to do so, although it was a different matter in practice, a topic next chapter explores in more detail. If a magistrate decided to pursue legal action, he could use the information as the basis for the charge and have someone else act as the legal agent in the proceedings.[37]

One reason southerners were willing to go to the legal system with their problems was because they approached crime as an integral part of everyday life, rather than a radical departure from it. People attached great importance and great shame to criminal behavior: that was why they made the effort to identify and prosecute offenses. But they did not always extend the same opprobrium to those who committed crimes, because they distinguished between the offenses and the offenders. Viewing crime through the lens of the Christian tradition, southerners equated criminal behavior with other kinds of misconduct, which they understood to be an inescapable aspect of the human condition. Original sin made all human beings susceptible to evil. Anyone could fall into crime, just as anyone could sin. Criminal behavior should be punished, but the commission of a crime did not necessarily make the offender a criminal. All those guilty of misconduct could be forgiven, even excused as long as they confessed and repented. Then community members could receive them back into the fold. That last step was crucial, because the remedy for individual offenders was reintegration into the community, not expulsion from it. Even capital punishment, the ultimate expulsion, did not have that intent; death was punishment for the offense, not a means of eliminating a criminal from society.[38]

This logic guided the identification and punishment of church members' transgressions in Evangelical Protestant churches. Offenses ranged widely, from dancing, drinking, and card playing to swearing, slander, and rumor mongering to fistfights. Domestic offenses included bastardy, rape, adultery, abandonment, and domestic violence. Unethical economic dealings ranged from stealing to overcharging, or withholding charity from those in need.[39] Baptists and Primitive Baptists were particularly vigilant in policing their own members. Careful scrutiny was necessary because of "mans degeneracy & impotency," as North Carolina's Bear Creek Baptist Church described it. It was the duty of all church members to watch over others in their flock and to repair rifts when they occurred. The covenant of South Carolina's Barnwell Baptist Church was typical: "As to our regard to each other in our Church communion, we feel ourselves bound to walk in all humility and brotherly love, to watch over each others conversation . . . and when cases require such measures to warn, entreat, rebuke, and admonish in the spirit of meekness . . . bearing with each others weakness and other imperfections." One member's transgression was the congregation's responsibility, a violation of the church's entire fellowship. Some Baptists prohibited congregants from initiating legal proceedings against each other because misconduct and even conflict among members represented a moral failing within the congregation that had to be resolved there.[40]

Although Baptists were the most enthusiastic in policing members' behavior, Methodists and Presbyterians across the Carolinas did the same. All denominations relied on similar, highly ritualized processes for handling such matters. At every church service, the minister or an elder asked if anyone had heard of conflicts or problems among the congregation. Church members repeated reports they had heard of wrongdoing, providing information based on firsthand knowledge or informing on themselves. If offenders were present, they were called on to explain themselves, repent, and ask forgiveness. If they were absent, the church appointed a delegation to investigate the allegations. When delegations found substance in the charges, they visited offenders and tried to convince them to confess their wrongdoing and repent. After repentance, the congregation decided whether to accept their apology. At this point, churches sometimes expelled even repentant miscreants, particularly if they did not show enough remorse, if they were repeat offenders, or if their misdeeds were serious. Usually, though, expulsion was temporary, a necessary step in bringing lost sheep back to the fold. For those who wished reconciliation, this process of public involvement and public admission was essential. Without it, offenders remained outside of the fellowship of the church, although they could always try to join other congregations, given the proliferation of small churches in rural communities.

These religious practices and the secular process of law informed one another. In fact, the line between the two was not well marked, since Anglican parishes had handled many of the issues associated with community policing before such matters were turned over to secular authorities after the Revolution. Religion's influence was particularly pronounced in pardon petitions that acknowledged the offenders' guilt but asked for leniency or a reprieve in their punishment. These requests usually began by explaining the surrender to temptation: the guilty parties had been young and lacking in experience; they had been seduced by evil-minded individuals; they had been drunk and not in possession of all their faculties; they had been inflamed by passion to the point where reason left them; they had been desperate and not in their right minds. Although convicted of particular crimes, they were not criminals and should not be marked as such. To the contrary, the guilty parties saw the error of their ways and promised to make amends. Petitioners concluded by affirming their desire to bring the offenders back into their communities: they believed in the wrongdoers' capacity to lead responsible and productive lives in the future. Moreover, they thought that society's best interests were served by forgoing further punishment, which only continued the miscreants' unnatural separation from community life and delayed reintegration into daily routines that provided essential discipline and direction. The petitioners' acceptance of the prisoners' sincerity and promise was crucial in legitimizing the grounds for pardons. These requests carried little weight when submitted by the guilty parties or their families. Only community members had the authority to forgive the offenders and to take them back. That was also why it was important to have established, well-known local leaders submitting and supporting pardons.[41]

Regardless of denominational affiliation, a broad spectrum of southern-ers subscribed to similar assumptions about misconduct and crime, which also surfaced in legislative debates over criminal punishment. In North Carolina those cultural currents routinely overwhelmed efforts to create a state penitentiary. As penitentiary opponents saw it, crime was not a so-cial crisis that required resolution; indeed, preventing crime was impos-sible. Crime was endemic, necessitating constant attention. Opponents also doubted the wisdom of separating offenders from their communities. While they could admit that new approaches to punishment might work for notorious criminals, they did not think that most offenders fell into that category. What was the point of removing those who had fallen into sin, as all mere mortals were inclined to do? Even southerners who embraced rationalized approaches to crime and punishment had not completely abandoned the logic that characterized misconduct as an inescapable part of the human condition.[42]

In this cultural milieu, what distinguished crime from other forms of misconduct was the venue in which it was handled. Misconduct became crime when it met the legal system. The bulk of magistrates' cases were similar to those offenses handled by churches: fights within families and among neighbors, or disorderly conduct that upset community relations in some way. In fact, such misconduct had long been associated with the parish system and church courts before the Revolution. Most offenses in local courts emerged out of otherwise ordinary encounters involving other-wise ordinary people who knew each other. Defendants and complainants came from a broad cross section of society, with most concentrated in its middling sections. By far the most common of criminal cases involved fights among men—white and black, slave and free—who had been so-cializing together. Fights broke out in the places where men gathered, not only in public at musters and in taverns and stores, but also in private houses where a crowd happened to gather. Men passed the time in all these spaces, sometimes just visiting and swapping stories, sometimes gambling and drinking. The combination of talk and drink was particularly volatile, often combining to produce insults and bruised egos, which led to fights. Liquor was not always implicated in these affairs, which involved verbal assault as well as physical violence. Nor was bellicose behavior confined to the ne'er-do-wells of rural communities. Otherwise reputable men—white and black, free and slave, from all parts of the economic spectrum—could be drawn into fights occasionally.

So were women of both races, although they tended to be involved in

85

cases featuring disagreements among neighbors that escalated and culminated in threats or violence. These matters tended to involve multiple household members, including children. Other women were drawn into fights when their menfolk brought their friends and their bad habits home with them. Low expectations of privacy in rural communities brought violence to women's doorsteps. For example, Deborah Cohoon was drawn into John Clayton's murder when she heard some people fighting in the road near her Tyrrell County, North Carolina, house one evening in 1813. She saw Clayton climb over her fence and stop at her well for a drink, although she did not recognize him until he walked into her house and sat down by the fire, as if he belonged there. The other man, Barney Jones, whom Cohoon also knew, followed Clayton into the house and "recommenced" the fight in Cohoon's presence. After an exchange of threats, Clayton "went into an inside room and locked himself up." Eventually they left Cohoon's house, and Jones shot and killed Clayton. Although the outcome was unusual, Deborah Cohoon's experience with violence was not. Women, both white and black, enslaved and free, often witnessed, were victimized by, or committed violent acts when everyday forms of sociability went awry or they felt the need to defend their interests and those of their families.[43]

Theft appeared more sporadically on the criminal dockets. When it did, the cases involved mundane items, such as food, livestock, tools, cloth and leather, clothing and linens, and other household goods. That was true even in cases of trading with slaves, although the rhetoric surrounding the issue emphasized slaves' propensity to appropriate their masters' cash crops. Given the court records, that concern and that characterization of slaves' participation in the market seem to have been more typical of the low country and port towns.[44]

Like other forms of misconduct, crime required public resolution. That gave a wide range of southerners direct experience with the criminal process. In fact, their position in that process was officially recognized in a legal system that gave local people the responsibility of policing their own communities. Ordinary people discovered or identified wrongdoing and initiated prosecutions by bringing complaints to their magistrates or grand jurors. They conducted the investigations, gathering the physical evidence and verbal testimony relevant to the offense. They then presented all that "information" at magistrates' hearings and trials. The term "information" covered complaints about offenses as well as facts that supported those charges, including physical evidence and other details about the crime and those involved. Because information was different from sworn testimony, people who could not legally testify could supply it, becoming active participants in the legal process. Even slaves, who were blocked from formal participation in law, participated at this level. Slaves played crucial roles in cases against other slaves, gathering physical evidence and providing background about the events and those involved. They actually testified in cases where defendants were also slaves and occasionally provided information in other cases when sworn testimony was not required.[45]

Knowledge about legal procedure was so widely diffused that ordinary people knew exactly what to do when they encountered a suspicious event. The first step was to announce the crime. When Barney McCully found his wife dead, he went immediately to Eben Smith, an Anderson District neighbor, not just to report it but also to bring him back to the house to view the scene. Joe, a slave in the same district, did the same when he found another slave, Israel, dead in a field. Joe explained at the inquest that Israel "was dead when he found him, and that he did not touch him, but went to Mr. Gordon's to give information." Joe's use of the term indicates familiarity with the legal process; he also knew to leave the body as he found it so that the coroner's jury could investigate and determine the cause of death. Barney McCully also knew not to alter the scene, for he made it a point to tell Eben Smith that he "had moved" his wife "a little from the position he found hir."[46] In cases that did not involve death, investigation was done by the people who discovered the crime. In fact, people assumed that discovery entailed the responsibility to find and evaluate evidence. They followed through, doing whatever they deemed necessary: they pursued tracks; hunted down witnesses; searched houses for stolen items; sorted through burning coals for traces of missing livestock; measured footprints against the shoes of suspects; and reconstructed fights to gauge the order, reach, and severity of participants' blows.[47]

They turned out at the next phase of the process as well, to tell everything they knew about the circumstances surrounding the crime. Sometimes people brought others with them when they filed complaints. Other cases acquired a crowd as they moved from complaint to hearing. If the magistrate acted on a complaint, he took a list of witnesses from both the complainant and the accused and then summoned them to give information on the matter. Witness lists could be extensive. But an invitation was not always necessary, because people felt a responsibility to involve themselves at all levels of the system. Their sense of responsibility ran so deep that the term "participation" does not quite capture it. People did not take time out from their daily lives to perform what they thought of as a civic duty. Rather, participation in law was an extension of the social dynamics in communities where people not only made it a point to keep tabs on everyone else but also assumed that it was their duty to do so. They showed up at hearings, whether summoned or not, expecting to have their say, even if the information was hearsay, irrelevant, or a repeat of what other witnesses had said. The repetition and accumulation of detail were central to the process, which was as much about exposing the rift in the social fabric and mending the damage as it was about establishing the facts of the event.

All the parties involved then followed through on the prosecution, a demanding process in the days before it was common to employ legal counsel. Orange County's Leonard Haze and William Marcum, for instance, became embroiled in conflict over a small quantity of corn that Haze accused Marcum of stealing. It was a typical theft case, involving people of similar economic standing; in this case, both men sat at the lower end of the economic scale. Even if they had the resources, it would have been unusual to hire a lawyer for such a minor case. A state's attorney would have overseen the prosecution of more serious criminal matters. But lawyers did not always participate in minor criminal matters, even those tried in superior or district courts, although that practice increased over time. After his conviction, however, Marcum did retain a lawyer, who had the case thrown out in a petition for arrest of judgment. To his credit, the lawyer managed to wring lofty legal principles from this insignificant matter. He argued that not only had one of the jurors not been a freeholder, but the offense had been miscategorized in the indictment as a felony, when "stealing one quart of corn is . . . too trivial . . . to fix an ignomonious [sic] corporal punishment on any person, except a notorious thief, or a person of very evil fame."[48]

While it was unusual for a lawyer to be involved in such a case, it was predictable that a lawyer's interest would take this form. Establishing a practice was extremely difficult in the late eighteenth and early nineteenth centuries, so lawyers often took high-profile criminal cases for little or nothing to obtain experience or to burnish their reputations, in hopes of using the publicity to drum up more lucrative business involving property. It appears that an enterprising lawyer saw just such an opportunity in Leonard Haze's case. Usually, though, cases of petty theft and minor violence moved through the courts with the parties themselves explaining their sides of the story and questioning witnesses.[49]

People took their knowledge of law with them when they went to other cultural, social, and religious venues. Law provided the grammar for explaining and mediating conflicts in church hearings, even in those denominations that discouraged members from using the legal system. The Abbotts Creek Primitive Baptist Church in Davidson County, North Carolina, for example, cited members for initiating civil suits against each other. At the same time, its own hearings took on a distinctly legal flavor. Consider the church minutes summarizing deliberations over Sister Sarah, or Sary, Spoolman. First there was a complaint akin to those offered to magistrates. "After divine worship" in August 1797, "the Church took under consideration the dificult circumstance of Sister Sary Spoolman leaveing her husband and taking away property and disposing of it contrary to his will for which the Church unites in suspecting her til further satisfaction." Then the church called her to answer the charges at the September meeting, in the same way that a magistrate would issue a warrant. As was often the case with warrants, the first summons was not successful. "As Sister Sarah Spoolman has failed to apear," the minutes read, "the Church has apointed Brother John Ledford to cite her to apear the next church meeting." Spoolman did respond the second time. At the October meeting the church "cald Sister Spoolman" and "on examination . . . the church removes the suspition and recieves her into the fellowship of the Church."[50]

A few decades later and a few counties over, the language that structured a report from the Cane Creek Baptist Church was even more overtly legal. It mixed religion and law more thoroughly, because it dealt with a conflict that had already been tried in court. The report began with all the legalese its writers could muster: "On the charges of Bro[ther] McCauley against Bro[ther] Oldham, touching [on] the difference in their evidence in court growing out of what is alledged to have been said by Bro Oldham to Bro McCauley at Cane Creek that Bro Oldham has by adequate testimony cleared himself from the charge of swerving from the truth in the Court House as charged by Bro McCauley." "In view to the above," the report continued, "it is the opinion of the committee that Bro McCauley should make suitable & satisfactory acknowledgments. That he was wrong in making a publick attack upon a brother because it is against the rules of the church to which he belongs." The report ended with a final flourish of lawyerly circumspection, adding that "nothing in the above report is to be so construed as to call in question the veracity of Bro. McCauley or any of the witnesses who were examined."[51]

THE IMPOSSIBILITY OF DISTINGUISHING
BETWEEN PRIVATE AND PUBLIC

What people imagined law could do was as important as what law actually did for them. They involved themselves in the legal system because they believed that law could resolve their problems. Mrs. Ritchie of Ninety-Six District, South Carolina, went to the magistrate to persuade him to show leniency to a family friend, Mr. Harris, who had been arrested for murder and denied bail. "His wife had just lain in," she later explained, and there was "no body to take care of them." Besides her concern for Mrs. Harris and the rest of the family, Mrs. Ritchie thought that justice had not been served. Her own husband, who had been arrested along with Harris, was allowed bail, and she saw no reason why Harris should not be given the same consideration. But "they refused it," she noted with obvious bitterness, and "said they would make them eat dry bread before they were done with him." Mrs. Ritchie's determination to right this wrong did not end with a plea to the magistrate. She later testified as a key witness in the case of malicious prosecution that Mr. Harris brought after he was acquitted on the murder charges.[52] Law was the arena where southerners went when they wanted to restore harmony—as they conceived of it—to the social order.

Popular expectations about law's responsiveness and effectiveness produced a never-ending stream of complaints to magistrates and grand juries about perceived threats to community health, welfare, and order. Depending on the informants' predilections, these problems ran the gamut from the serious to the absurd: gambling, fighting, fornication, drinking, poaching, pilfering, prostitution, poor work habits, dilapidated fences, blocked roads, redolent latrines, adultery, domestic violence, and infanticide. These complaints, legitimate or not, rarely led to criminal charges and trials, but instead to lesser kinds of legal actions. A peace bond was the favored remedy for minor offenses. The expectations that informed these complaints are striking. The civic-minded souls who sought legal intervention believed that law would not only respond to but actually resolve the problem. Legal action could keep a lazy man at work, a philanderer from tempting young neighborhood girls, a bully from terrorizing his neighbors, a husband from beating his wife, or a drunk from his whiskey bottle.

Those expectations extended beyond the local level into other parts of the legal system. Individual requests for private acts took up most of the state legislatures' business; in the post-Revolutionary decades, the volumes of public acts are slim by comparison. Private acts ranged as widely as complaints brought to magistrates, and included the incorporation of voluntary organizations, the chartering of businesses, grants of manumission, divorce, legitimation of children, and suspensions of existing laws in particular instances. Private acts expressed both the legislatures' sovereign authority to make or modify law and southerners' expectations that their legislatures would act on their behalf in personal matters in individualized ways. Divorce petitions occasionally appeared on South Carolina's legislative agenda, even though the state's statutes did not allow it. Petitioners were not necessarily naive or ignorant of the law; petitioners requested the legislature to use its power to make a new law specifically for them. As one man put it, "Your petitioner is well aware that your Honorable body by no means are in favor of dissolving the matrimonial tie," but he thought that his case deserved special consideration and its own private act.[53]

The demand for private acts added significantly to legislators' workloads, sometimes extending their sessions for weeks. Frustrated representatives, stuck in Raleigh or Columbia for indefinite periods of time, watched their own farms and businesses languish, while their frustrated constituents watched the costs of state government grow. The situation prompted various reform efforts. It contributed to calls for cost-cutting, which many antebellum political historians have explained in terms of a peculiarly southern hostility toward big government. It also led to measures to limit the length of legislative sessions. The rhetoric of reform, however, was stronger than the commitment to it. In the abstract, everyone could agree that legislative calendars were too long and expenses were too high. In practice, no one really wanted the legislature to ignore his requests or those of other constituents.

The line between "private acts" and "public acts" was rarely well marked. The *Raleigh Register*, which provided day-by-day reports on the General Assembly's business, only started separating out "private acts" from "public acts" around 1809. Until then, it mixed them together, even when it listed the new laws published at the end of each legislative session. It is easy to see why the *Register* did not bother to make the distinction. Many public acts were initiated in the same ways as private ones, through local initiative, usually by petitions and grand jury presentments. The difference was that the sources of public law usually came through a request authored by a group, rather than an individual, which claimed to represent the interests of a particular area or constituency. Yet many public acts, like private ones, addressed specific, highly localized problems. Typical was the 1814 grand jury presentment from Pendleton District regarding the "frequent violation of the sacredness of the divine institution of Marriage." People were living together as if they were married, but without being legally married, and then separating through customary practices and taking up new spouses. "It is conceived," wrote the grand jurors, "that the laws of the State, are not sufficient effectually to prevent such dangerous and growing evils." Apparently the available legal weapons, such as charges of vagrancy, disorderly conduct, and adultery or fornication, were insufficient. Therefore, they concluded, the legislature should pass a new law. The grand jurors' confidence in law as the best means to address this issue is remarkable. Even more striking is their assurance that the legislature would comply. They were not disappointed. The Judiciary Committee, to which the presentment was referred, reported "that a bill should be brought in to punish infractions of the same."[54] Based on a "problem" identified by twenty-four grand jurors in a sparsely settled region, the legislature moved to make a public law that could apply to everyone in the state.

Many petitions recommended changes in statutes in order to address local problems. Neither petitioners nor legislators identified this as a contradiction, let alone a problem. Local people and legislators assumed that these problems lay within the legislature's purview, and it should rally round, when called upon to do so. Moreover, people and their representatives thought it was appropriate for local issues to drive the framing of state law. "We your humble petitioners," began a missive from Orangeburg District in South Carolina, "would esteem it as a fortunate circumstance if our domestic economy was under no necessity, of legislative intervention: but this is not the case." After detailing local difficulties in regulating trade in the items that slaves produced themselves, the petitioners (not so humbly) deemed it "highly necessary" that "a law should be enacted this Session prohibiting negroes making cotton for themselves." In the next session, the South Carolina legislature raised the penalties for trading with slaves, and specifically listed cotton, rice, tobacco, and indigo as prohibited items. Hogs, cattle, and corn were the problem in Beaufort District, according to Richard Dawson and ninety-one others. More to the point, the problem was absentee owners, whose slaves "not being restrained are in the constant habit of Killing the stock of Cattle and Hogs of the Neighbors adjoining them, and also of the taking their corn from their fields before it could with safety be housed." The petitioners requested an increase in penalties for absentee owners with thirty or more slaves. The South Carolina General Assembly, whose members had to absent themselves from their planta-

92

tions to fulfill their legislative duties, declined to act in this instance.[55] The refusal of this or any other request did not signal any change in the system's underlying dynamics. Petitions continued to arrive, penned by people who expected that their concerns would be taken up by the legislature, even if these did not lead to modifications in state laws.

The labeling of statutes as "private acts" or "public acts" reflected distinctions that applied to most other legal matters. It is difficult to read through primary sources in southern history—collections of statutes and appellate decisions, the speeches and reflections of party leaders, the letters and other writings of the well-to-do, and even the information and testimony of ordinary southerners—without stumbling over the apparent distinction between "private" and "public." In legal practice and common parlance, these concepts were means rather than ends. They provided useful tools to establish and rank the seriousness of problems, determining how they would be treated within the legal process. "Private" issues either remained with those immediately involved or became civil matters; "public" matters had wider ramifications and merited collective intervention. Beyond that, the consensus broke down, because southerners invariably disagreed about what exactly should be private and public in any given situation. In legal practice and common parlance, the terms did not refer to normative principles or specific categories of people (such as domestic dependents) or places (domestic spaces) that were inherently private or public. Any given matter could be either one or the other, depending on the circumstances. A domestic issue was not, by its nature, a "private" matter. What made it private was the decision that intervention was inappropriate or unnecessary. Those determinations were part of the ongoing negotiations necessary to maintain social order. The appearance of the terms "private" and "public" indicates conflict rather than consensus. It was at moments when the distinction between private and public was most blurred that people tended to invoke the concepts most forcefully.

The way people used law, particularly at the local level, suggests that they understood private and public as a nested hierarchy rather than as two distinct spheres. They acted as if all things private were subordinated within, but connected to the public order rather than separate from it. It was possible for anyone's personal problems—even those that we would expect to be private—to emerge and assume public significance, given the right circumstances, because localized legal culture subsumed everything within the public order. That conception of private and public differs profoundly from the distinction now current in the historiography and in the U.S. legal system today. Historians of the nineteenth century no longer assume that "public" and "private" were actually separate realms, configured in a hierarchical arrangement like that posited by liberal political theorists, notably John Locke, who defined the "private" realm of the household as distinct from and subordinate to the "public" world of politics and commerce. Feminist scholars use the analytical lens of gender to explain this distinction, construing "private" and "public" as political and cultural constructs rather than expressions of nature or spatial configurations. This scholarship illuminates the ideological assumptions that underlay these concepts and the ways in which various groups of people used them. In the context of the nineteenth-century South, historians have linked the dynamics of private and public to the concept of dependency, which incorporated race and class as well as gender. Only those who could be independent—that is, white men with property sufficient to support themselves, or the capacity to acquire it—could claim the civil and political rights necessary to participate directly in public matters. Excluded from active participation in public life were all those associated with dependency, which signaled the incapacity for self-governance and, by extension, for the governance of others. This body of scholarship distinguishes between theory and practice, acknowledging the complexities and contradictions of everyday life. Yet even though these analyses illuminate how the public/private distinction worked, they still begin with the assumption that public and private delineated distinct domains.[56]

One reason for the persistence of the private/public paradigm may be that historians privilege written sources, particularly when mapping out ideas. In those texts, private and public do appear as mutually exclusive abstractions. They expressed the values of a well-ordered society and were invoked at appropriate moments to mend tears in the social fabric. The rhetoric preserved in written texts, however, cannot be separated from its dynamic use and its intended goals. Reading the sources the other way around, from action to text, allows for a different perspective. The notion of a public world that contained subordinated private elements shaped the logic of law in justices' manuals. It was most evident in the concept of the "peace." Reflecting centuries of common law practice, the "peace" was an open-ended concept that could turn virtually any act by anyone against anyone into a public offense. Typical was the definition from John Haywood's North Carolina manual, published in 1808, which identified the peace as "a quiet and harmless behavior towards the government, and all the citizens under its protection." The only deviation from English manuals was the substitution of "citizen" for "subject," which was more a post-Revolutionary flourish than a substantive change, since the manual explicitly included all domestic dependents, including free blacks and slaves, within the peace of the state: not only were they accountable to law, but they were also under its protection. Yet the assumed subject in these manuals was a free, white, adult male. Although all the entries on various crimes and procedures were written around that subject, they also listed exceptions for those categorized differently in law, especially domestic dependents. Separate entries covered every conceivable legal category of people, so as not to miss anyone: wives, widows, women, children, wards, students, free blacks, slaves, Indians, and servants. Yet those entries made the hierarchical structure particularly clear by focusing on the restrictions unique to those in each legal category. They also expressed the strong element of coercion that enforced inclusion in this system. Although everyone had a place, coercion was essential to keep people in their places.[57] The peace created a public order that extended to people and issues usually deemed private in the historiography; they were private only to the extent that private meant that they remained subordinated within the public order.

The same logic guided magistrates' classification of cases. In this context, the terms "private" and "public" did not refer to the concrete circumstances of an offense, such as the persons involved, where it took place, where it was tried, or even the issues in question. The distinction arose from the implications of an offense for the community. The law construed crimes as public offenses because they reached beyond the parties immediately involved to affect all the people of the state, a concept expressed in the denomination of such cases, as in *State v. John Smith*. The public component of an offense lay in its wider repercussions that disturbed the good order of society. Those effects justified intervention and punishment on behalf of all the people, not just the parties directly affected. By contrast, civil cases were private matters because the implications ended with complainant and defendant; thus the denomination *John Smith v. Henry Green*. Although the issues could be extremely serious, their effects did not reach outward to disturb the people or the good order of society more generally. The guilty parties owed reparations to those they had injured, not to society as a whole.[58]

For those issues handled by the courts, categorization occurred in the first stages of the legal process and was done by either the magistrates or the parties involved. Sometimes that decision was straightforward. The definition of certain kinds of offenses, particularly those involving property, had been honed to the point where neither complainants nor magistrates had to use their judgment. But other offenses against people or property could fall into several categories, depending on how the magistrate and the parties involved saw the implications. The issues in civil matters or equity suits could be exactly the same as those in criminal cases, although the basic rules and questions were different. The O. J. Simpson case provides a modern example in which a jury declared the defendant not guilty of murder in a criminal court and exempt from punishment by the state, only to have a jury in civil court decide that he was responsible enough for the offense to be liable for damages to the victim's family. Similarly, Carolinians prosecuted offenses either through common law as civil or criminal matters, or in equity, or even through a combination of both. Sometimes complainants and defendants pursued all those options, taking a case to a particular venue or from one venue to another in order to secure the outcome that they wanted.[59] Forum shopping was possible only for those who had professional legal advice and the resources to pay court costs, however. Most southerners used local courts more casually, as a means to resolve their problems and to regulate the behavior of others in their communities.

Magistrates categorized most offenses during the screening process. Those judged the most private remained outside the system altogether. Magistrates either sent the parties home or worked out a settlement with them. These conflicts were private in the sense that the magistrate did not consider them threatening enough, either to those involved or to anyone else, to warrant further intervention. In other circumstances, magistrates could label exactly the same kinds of offenses as civil matters or breaches of the peace, which made them less private and more public. Civil matters entered the legal system as serious disputes that remained private in that they were confined to those immediately involved: injured parties could obtain damages, but whatever compensation they received settled the matter. Breaches of the peace were more public, because the offenses were judged a potential threat to others in the community. Still, criminal charges did not attach until the implications were fully realized. Instead, offenders who breached the peace posted a bond, which represented their promise of good behavior to the community. If they broke that promise, they paid the bond to the public and could face criminal charges as well. Crimes were offenses that involved injury to the larger community, imagined as the "public" body. The injury could take a variety of forms. In some instances, it was the prospect of continued misconduct from the accused:

habitual lawbreakers who might continue to harass people, or evil-minded individuals who seemed incapable of controlling themselves. In other instances, it was the seriousness of the injury itself that mattered. Murder and other types of physical abuse were considered so heinous that they always affected the metaphorical public body, not just the individual physical body of the victim.

The categories seemed orderly and logical in the pages of justices' manuals. In practice, they were anything but, because every offense came attached to angry people who were determined to mobilize the legal system to its fullest extent. Those people played crucial roles in defining offenses. They contributed to the categorization of cases, in ways that suggest ordinary people's success not only in making their "private" matters into "public" concerns but also in shaping the legal process and defining the content of law. Changes in the prosecution of offenses involving physical violence provide one of the most dramatic examples.

The courts in early modern Britain handled most instances of physical violence as civil rather than criminal matters. Rules governing violence presumed that all people were subjects of the Crown, whose sovereign body represented the public order. No violent act became a "public wrong," a criminal matter that threatened the public order, unless it injured the Crown's metaphorical body by breaking the peace of the realm. The logic led Sir William Blackstone to place assault under the category of "private wrongs" in his late-eighteenth-century codification of English common law. Although that standard was subject to interpretation, the courts set the bar high in practice. As studies of prosecution patterns suggest, most assaults and other minor forms of physical violence tended to move through the courts as civil rather than criminal matters. The same logic and practices applied in the colonial South, although with slightly different outcomes. Colonial legal officials considered assault and other violent offenses on a case-by-case basis, treating some as criminal offenses, others as civil cases, and others as a combination of both. The results are probably best explained by specific local concerns and conditions that went unrecorded and are now lost to historians. Magistrates evidently considered a number of factors, including the seriousness of the offense and the social status and personal reputation of those involved, just as they did after the Revolution. A habitual rabble-rouser who inflicted random violence was different from an otherwise upstanding citizen who lost his temper in a dispute with a particularly obstreperous neighbor.[60]

Although formal laws governing violence did not change much following the Revolution, their application did. Local courts were still handling

assaults as civil offenses in the 1790s, and those cases were being appealed
through the system as civil matters as well. By the turn of the nineteenth
century, however, assault cases involving free southerners began appearing
in local courts only as criminal matters. Technically, it appears that the civil
component of the offense did not go away. Rather, it was joined to, although subordinated within, the criminal charge, which allowed victims to
obtain compensation for their injuries at the same time the perpetrator was
tried for injuring the public body. This change took place at different times
in different North Carolina and South Carolina counties, an unevenness
that suggests the localized nature of the transformation in the legal process.
Those patterns link up with general trends toward public criminal prosecution that other historians have found in the rest of the nation, although
adding an important detour. The scholarship locates the fulcrum of change
later in the antebellum period and emphasizes changes in who initiated
cases more than how cases were categorized. By mid-century, legal officials
rather than the people who witnessed it policed and prosecuted crime. The
result was to take law out of people's hands. That would ultimately happen
in the rural Carolinas, just as it happened elsewhere. But the experience of
rural southerners suggests that how cases were categorized was also important. By the first decade of the nineteenth century, the same people
who initiated prosecutions also turned their "private" injuries into "public"
crimes.[61]

The patterns follow the logic of Revolutionary ideology: once free people
replaced the Crown as sovereign members of the polity, their bodies made
up the body politic and their physical injuries became, in theory, "public wrongs." But no one described the changing patterns of prosecution in
those terms. In fact, no one described them at all. The legislatures issued
no directives, and judges made no comments. By the first decades of the
nineteenth century, justices' manuals quietly incorporated the changes
without explaining how or why they happened. The appellate courts later
registered them as well, reflecting local prosecution practices as those cases
made their way through the system. No announcement was made, but it
was official: assaults against free people were now crimes.[62]

■ ■ ■

THERE WERE LONG-TERM, wide-ranging ramifications of placing some
people, but not others, in the legal position formerly occupied by the
Crown. The recategorization of physical violence as criminal was indicative
98 of larger changes that would ultimately link free white men more directly

to the body politic, while simultaneously severing the connections of slaves and other free domestic dependents from it. Those changes would surface in state law in the 1820s and gain institutional force through political campaigns in the 1830s; they form the subject of the final two chapters of this book.

In the period between 1787 and 1820, what was clear was people's ability to change legal practice and law. Magistrates paid attention to the people who made complaints. Those people insisted that their injuries were serious. Somewhere in that exchange, those injuries became recognized as serious enough to warrant sustained public intervention and to require a public accounting, in addition to private compensation for the victims. Such a minor change in legal classification may seem like a slight form on which to hang weighty historical explanations. But that change highlights the formal power exercised by people within a legal system that was rooted in local institutions and that blended custom with formal law. Their claims mattered: they shaped not only the outcomes of local cases but also the larger structures of law. Consider the differences from the colonial period. Both before and after the Revolution, a range of people at the local level tried to use the courts to obtain redress for violence. Both before and after the Revolution, these people tried to turn their private disputes into public matters when they went to local courts. But after the Revolution, when the institutional structures explicitly blended custom and law, people's claims could change the basic mechanisms of the legal system. They expected law to respond to them — and it did.

Bread from Chaff

In James Woodruff's vagrancy case, it is difficult to say which was more withering, South Carolina's August sun or his neighbors' scrutiny. The previous chapter opened with Woodruff's trial to illustrate the operation of localized law, with its emphasis on process and people. In this chapter, his case highlights another key aspect of localized law: the time and attention allotted to matters that we might now assume to be personal or private, particularly those involving domestic issues and dependents. Like so many other cases, Woodruff's trial revolved around charges of domestic mismanagement. Neighbors claimed that Woodruff's family went hungry. Even though he had land and opportunities for paid labor, he begged rather than worked. The situation, they maintained, had degenerated to the point that his wife was forced to make bread from chaff. Other neighbors disagreed, insisting that Woodruff worked regularly and looked after his family. His neighbors told what they knew at the ad hoc Court of Magistrates and Freeholders, heedless of repetition or the possible inaccuracy of secondhand and thirdhand information. Much of that information came from women, who got the details directly from Woodruff's wife.[1]

Reading the evidence now, it is difficult to understand why the court decided to charge and convict James Woodruff. After all, the difference between begging and borrowing was one of degree in a rural economy, where the distinction lay in lenders' expectations of reciprocity. The rhythms of agricultural labor did not require constant work from sunup to sundown every day, particularly from adult white men. A lack of provisions rarely brought down the long arm of the law. Was one piece of evidence more compelling than the others? Was it a slow accretion of ill will that sealed James Woodruff's fate? Or was it just a classic example of a local court's bias or incompetence? That was exactly what district court clerk B. J. Eaton concluded when he looked over the case documents, probably before filing them in the Spartanburg courthouse. Exercising authority of dubious legitimacy, Eaton overturned the conviction, a decision that he left in the form of a scribbled note on the back of the packet of case documents: "questions whether the evidence was sufficient to convict and orders the prisoner released."[2]

Eaton's doubts and interventions were misplaced. The conviction had been by the book. South Carolina's vagrancy statute applied to residents who did not tend their land or support their families, and it affirmed local knowledge as central in identifying vagrants. Vagrancy trials turned on neighbors' suspicions, suppositions, and opinions. In this regard, they are representative of other hearings and trials in the localized legal systems of the Carolinas. B. J. Eaton's intercession does indicate the presence of countervailing trends, much in evidence by the mid-1830s when Woodruff was tried. But intervention was distinctly uncharacteristic of the legal process in the period between 1787 and 1830, when local jurisdictions retained broad discretionary authority over both the application and the interpretation of law. People in local areas had to supply their own meanings if they were to use the laws and the legal system at all.

The challenge is to understand the underlying social dynamics and cultural meanings that informed the process of interpreting and applying law locally. What made people's complaints and testimony meaningful? Who was regarded as believable, and why? The answers depend on a legal culture in which all problems could develop public significance. This journey from private to public was commonplace because the authority of localized law was comprehensive in its reach, folding everyone and everything under its patriarchal wing—though unequally so, rendering some persons subject to others. In this all-encompassing patriarchal legal order, even the most personal matters could assume broader significance, just as the domestic affairs of the Woodruff family could become fodder for a criminal investigation. At first glance, the decisions are startling in their unpredictability. But outcomes that now appear arbitrary were based in a deliberative process that determined who and what deserved public attention. These assessments reproduced carefully considered social rankings founded as much on personal reputations—credit or character in the parlance of the time—as on the external markers of status—race, class, gender, and age—that later became so important in the laws and the legal system. In this more particularistic setting, the voices of domestic dependents and other subordinates could acquire considerable legal resonance. The women in James Woodruff's case not only supplied crucial testimony but also defined the basic issues: they were in a position to pass judgment on James Woodruff because they knew his wife was forced to make bread from chaff.

The particular women involved in James Woodruff's case may have exercised such sway because of their own reputations. In local communities, individual white women, slaves, and free blacks could acquire credibility, negating elements of their subordinate status through their own actions and others' assessment of them. More often, though, these people acquired influence *because of* their subordination, which both located and connected them to the social order. The ties that bound subordinates also provided the means for collecting and transmitting information that established the credit of their husbands, fathers, owners, and other white men. The relationships that defined Mrs. Woodruff's subordination also made her a key source in her husband's trial. Women visited her as they did other wives and mothers in the neighborhood, helping one another with domestic labor, tending the ties that bound families together, and affirming the hierarchies that elevated some people over others. These entangling relationships, which pushed subordinates down the social hierarchy, also made them visible, audible, and influential within a legal system that depended on local knowledge. Mrs. Woodruff's condition, particularly her desperate efforts to make do with limited resources, testified to her integrity and her husband's indolence. Other women saw her situation, made their own judgments, and testified accordingly at the trial. In this legal culture, wives, slaves, free blacks, and other subordinates were not abstract extensions of their husbands and masters or faceless members of categorical groups, as they were defined in "the law" — statutes, appellate decisions, and legal texts that eventually codified the law at the state level. Like Mrs. Woodruff, they were distinct individuals, whose subordination took the form of relationships on which the credit of white men — and the legitimacy of localized law — were based.

THE REACH OF THE PEACE

The slave South seems an unlikely place to discover a legal culture that recognized domestic dependents and others on the social and political margins. The region has a well-deserved reputation for its profoundly hierarchical legal order. Southern states not only denied individual rights to all enslaved men and women but also restricted the civil and political rights of free black men, all free women, and white men without property. It was a legal system founded and built on inequality, fully equipped to discipline those on the margins, who also were unable to use it in their own right. Yet nineteenth-century conceptions of individual rights obscure important elements in the legal process that gave domestic dependents and other subordinated persons considerable influence in its workings. In public legal matters that involved the peace, the point was to restore order, not to protect individual rights.[3]

Slaves, free black men and women, and white women and children appeared in these cases for the same reasons that all other matters surfaced in localized law. The patriarchal legal culture subsumed all things within the "peace," a term that encompassed the entire range of interpersonal relationships in the community. Local courts routinely tried cases involving domestic dependents and other subordinate persons. The most common involved violence by husbands against wives and by whites against enslaved and free blacks. Not only were abusive husbands required to enter into bonds to keep the peace, but some were prosecuted for assault. Overseers, neighboring whites, and even masters answered criminal charges for violence against African Americans. Conversely, white southerners routinely hauled slaves into court, instead of handling such matters themselves. Slaves appeared on a wide range of relatively minor, ill-defined charges for offenses against one another, other whites, and occasionally their own masters. Local courts hosted a chaotic parade of legal matters that defy easy categorization, each case utterly unique in its specific details, yet utterly typical as part of a body of similar issues. To give just three examples: the Chowan County Superior Court prosecuted two rape cases on behalf of enslaved women, Annis and Juno, while Kershaw District tried Joseph Hodge for raping his daughter, Nancy. These cases are just the tip of a much larger legal iceberg.[4]

The presence of these cases is surprising, given the various legal disabilities that conspired to limit domestic dependents' and other subordinates' access to the system. Those barriers were on full display in statutes and appellate decisions, which imposed few legal limitations on the power of masters and husbands between 1787 and the 1820s. North Carolina and South Carolina had no statutes on wife beating; appellate courts did not take up the issue until after the Civil War. Statutes and appellate case law did not recognize either incest or the rape of enslaved women as crimes. The criminal status of other offenses against dependents was murky at best. Violence against slaves could be a crime in South Carolina, although that depended on how the statutes were interpreted, since the laws themselves were in conflict. North Carolina's reliance on common law in matters involving slaves did not produce any more clarity or consistency, since common law did not acknowledge the presence or legitimacy of slavery. Slaves' legal status either had to be extrapolated from existing common law principles or established by statute. Appellate judges and legislators in both states wrestled constantly with the issue in the decades following the Revolution, leaving such a convoluted jumble of statutes and decisions that even the most determined historians have found it difficult to impose a coherent analytical framework on them.[5]

Dependents' legal disabilities also played a leading role in Blackstone's *Commentaries*, a favored legal authority of professionally trained lawyers and historians. In fact, historians' reliance on Blackstone in matters relating to domestic authority rivals their faith in statutes and appellate decisions — with equally misleading results. The most frequently cited passage posits the wife's legal death at marriage: "By marriage the husband and wife are one person in law; that is, the very being or legal existence of the woman is suspended during the marriage; or at least is incorporated and consolidated into that of the husband; under whose wing, protection, and cover, she performs every thing."[6] Recent scholarship has extended this framework to explain other relations of domestic dependency, applying it at the level of analogy to reveal similarities in logic: just as a wife's legal existence was consolidated into her husband's, so was a slave's legal being incorporated into the master's. By exposing the nexus of race, class, and gender, this work has illuminated connections as well as parallels in the operation of inequality.[7] The emphasis on Blackstone that informs this scholarship does have a basis in history. His version of husbands' authority over their wives acquired force in legal practice after the Revolution, especially in civil matters relating to property. Ultimately, it spilled over into other areas, limiting the civil and political rights of wives, slaves, and other subordinates as well.

Yet statutes, appellate decisions, and the favored texts of professionally trained lawyers provide only a partial view of the legal landscape during the period between 1787 and 1830. The failure of statutes and appellate law to address offenses against domestic dependents is revealing, but not determinative; although these gaps reveal a great deal about the system's inequalities, they represent only one section of the available legal corpus at this time. The omissions and inconsistencies point to vast areas of law left to local initiative. When facing one of those gaps, local officials did not necessarily reach for Blackstone. In fact, southerners in the late eighteenth and early nineteenth centuries were decidedly less enthusiastic about Blackstone's version of domestic authority than later generations — and later historians. They looked to other constructions of domestic authority, common in both early modern England and the Anglo-colonial legal tradition as it developed in the British imperial context. Some historians have returned to the various elements in this broader legal tradition, exploring how they allowed dependents more leeway. Equity—a distinct body of law, which was still practiced in the early nineteenth century, but was later dropped in favor of common law—is the best known example in U.S. history, thanks to Mary Beard's classic *Women as a Force in History*. Indeed, the term "law," a shortened form of common law used frequently in the late eighteenth and early nineteenth centuries, tends to confuse modern readers, erasing the presence of equity and other bodies of law. At the time, it was assumed that "law," as practiced in a "court of law," indicated a particular body of law; today "law" refers to the entire corpus of laws. Other bodies of Anglo-American law constrained household heads' authority and recognized dependents' status as legal subjects. Interpretations of common law sometimes accomplished that end as well. Judge Elihu Hall Bay's declaration on wife beating, which opens the first chapter, provides an excellent example. Bay argued from solid legal grounding, either Blackstone's own admonition against wife beating or an interpretation of Sir Edward Coke, when he ruled that common law did not allow a husband to use force against his wife. Variant readings were very much in evidence in the late eighteenth and early nineteenth centuries.[8]

The point is not that competing legal principles negated the importance of statutes, case law, or a Blackstonian version of domestic authority. All these legal traditions coexisted as options and alternatives, rather than contradictions in need of resolution. In the decentralized legal system of the post-Revolutionary South, it was possible for legal officials to support a patriarch's domestic authority in one breath and undercut it in the next, without pause or concern. The one decision was as legally valid as the other; which interpretation to apply to any situation depended on the particular circumstances.

The legal concept of the peace made those determinations possible. In theory, the peace was both hierarchical and inclusive. While the term was common in post-Revolutionary southern legal culture, it was based in a long-standing, highly gendered construction of governmental authority that subordinated everyone to a sovereign body, just as all individual dependents were subordinated to specific male heads of household. The metaphorical public body was represented first through the king and then, after the Revolution, through "the people," via the agency of the state—although "state" authority was located at the local level between 1787 and the 1830s. The sovereign body was always a patriarch, whatever its location or physical embodiment. Its gendered authority remained the same, whether sovereignty resided in local jurisdictions or centralized institutions or whether it took the form of a male king, a female queen, or a combination of men and women from different social ranks who constituted "the people."[9]

The peace made offenses against any subject visible, not as crimes against that particular individual but as crimes against the collective public body. Although the physical injury was to the victim, the legal offense lay in the theoretical damage to the metaphorical public body. That was true even in cases involving injuries to wives, children, or slaves, where husbands, fathers, or masters were named as victims as well. Unless a local official recognized a disruption to the peace, the offense remained a private, civil matter. Local officials could invoke the patriarchal interests of the peace to trump either the authority of individual patriarchs or the inferior legal status of subordinates. Slaves, free blacks, and white wives and children who could not testify regularly gave information that initiated cases and shaped their outcomes. Even when they could not prosecute cases in their own names, they made complaints that resulted in prosecutions and convictions for their injuries. In these instances, subordinates did not use the law in their own right. Nor did their use of the legal system alter their status. Legal officials acted in the name of keeping the peace. If the peace was threatened, the source of the information and the legal status of the victim were irrelevant. Those dynamics were particularly evident in cases involving injured subordinates, whose legal status made it difficult for them to move from the passive position of victim to the active role of "prosecutor" — that is, a legally recognized individual who could act in law for themselves, who today we would call a complainant or plaintiff. For that reason, legal officials often required a domestic dependent to obtain a legal representative to assume the active role of prosecuting the case. Usually, that sponsor would be the dependent's household head, who exercised legal authority over him or her. A legal system that filtered dependents' grievances through their household heads posed difficulties. The process ran aground completely when the master, husband, or father either refused to prosecute on behalf of his dependents or used his position to evade prosecution himself. Local officials bypassed those difficulties by designating the "state" — the metaphorical public body and its "peace" — as the legal representative. The "injured" public, represented through the actions of local officials, could replace the actual victim and prosecute the case.[10]

This legal form erased injured wives, children, and slaves only in theory. In practice, dependents remained central, because the damage to the public body was done through their flesh and blood. Always present, yet unacknowledged, it was a convenient legal fiction, one of those twists for which formal law was so well known and, usually, so much despised, particularly when it came to matters involving property. In this instance, though, the law's arcane and labyrinthine logic served practical purposes, instead of confounding them.

Local officials in the Carolinas routinely invoked the peace when they confronted offenses against dependents. Or, at least, that is the best explanation for what they did, a conclusion based in the distillation of ideas from action, since magistrates, sheriffs, and circuit court judges did not stop to record what they thought. The practice of turning offenses against subordinates into offenses against the peace accounts for the mystifying array of cases that could not otherwise have been prosecuted as crimes. The logic that transformed transgressions into crimes was readily available in any number of sources: common law; legal treatises, including Blackstone; religious texts; political theory; and, most important, magistrates' guides, the legal texts local officials were most likely to own. District judges sanctioned the transformation when they tried cases. Applied to wives, the protection of the peace provided for the criminal prosecution of husbands for domestic violence. In South Carolina, the same principle filled in the gaps left by statutes in slave law, allowing for the prosecution of whites for the assault and murder of slaves. In North Carolina, where common law governed slavery, local courts went directly to the notion of slaves' connection to the peace when prosecuting violence against them. While local jurisdictions sometimes stretched the peace in unexpected directions, no one found it problematic. The South's localized legal systems were designed to accommodate just that kind of extemporization.[11]

A liberal application of the peace explains the case against Joseph Hodge for raping his daughter, Nancy. To be sure, the Kershaw District magistrate engaged in some creative legal maneuvering. In 1802, when he heard Nancy Hodge's complaint, there were no statutes or appellate decisions in South Carolina to prevent the prosecution of a father for the rape of his daughter, but there were none to authorize it either. The charge was a stretch, given that incest was a crime neither by statute nor in common law and that property law recognized a father's rights in his daughter's labor and body. Obviously aware of those hazards, the magistrate took pains to map out a clear legal course. The biggest problem was that neither the victim nor her mother could prosecute the case, because of the legal disabilities that resulted from their domestic attachments to the perpetrator. So the magistrate named them as informants, who brought a crime to his attention. Then he designated the "public" as the prosecutor, based on the fact that its peace had been disturbed. In effect, he separated the injury from Nancy Hodge, who was a precarious victim in law, and made it an offense against the social order. Nancy Hodge could not find a place in the formal mechanisms of law; but the offense against her could, because of her connections to the public peace. Joseph Hodge's case never went to trial, although that was not particularly unusual. Few criminal cases reached trial at the local level, usually for reasons that had nothing to do with the strength of the charges. Nevertheless, in Davidson County, North Carolina, a man was convicted of assault with intent to commit rape "on his own daughter", and sentenced to six months' imprisonment, a punishment that was comparable to sentences doled out to other convicted rapists.[12]

The interests of the peace rescued a host of other cases that might otherwise have fallen through the legal cracks, such as the Chowan County rape cases of the enslaved women, Annis and Juno. In the mid-1820s, when charges were filed, North Carolina statutes and case law remained silent as to the criminal status of the rape of an enslaved woman by an enslaved man, although existing elements of slave law not only militated against prosecutions but also risked recognizing slaves' rights in their own bodies. If the offense was to the public order, though, it was legally possible to prosecute rapes when enslaved women were the victims, just as it was with other criminal offenses. In this legal logic, neither Annis's and Juno's injuries nor those of their owners constituted the crime. That was why criminal prosecutions never involved compensation for the victims—with the exception of assault cases where the criminal and civil components had been explicitly joined. The criminal offenses consisted of the virtual violence to the metaphorical public body through these two women's bodies. That framework assumed these enslaved women's place within the peace and made sexual assaults on them public even as it left unaltered their legal status as slaves.[13]

No definitive statements, written or oral, tie the adjudication of specific local cases to the principle that all subjects held a place within the peace. Like most matters in the realm of common sense, this no longer needed articulation. At the local level, legal officials concerned themselves with concrete circumstances of crimes, not abstract points of law, as later appellate judges did. Their preoccupation with the particulars was apparent in the local legal records, which rarely refer to laws or legal principles but faithfully and carefully document details about the contested events. Magistrates did not record all the necessary details that we would need today to reconstruct these legal matters, but many did take extensive notes about each offense, including a description of the initial complaint as well as voluminous, sometimes verbatim summaries of the evidence offered. Then they simply noted the resulting charge, without explaining how they arrived at that conclusion. There is no way to know what a district court judge was thinking when he tried cases, because the records usually consist only of the indictment, the testimony, and the verdict. In the event of an appeal, the documents occasionally supply the judge's instructions to the jury. But the records seldom shed light on how local justices approached offenses against domestic dependents. Exceptional in this regard are the ruminations of Elihu Hall Bay, the South Carolina district judge who announced in open court that the common law allowed a husband to be convicted of assaulting his wife. That anecdote also illustrates the larger evidentiary problem. It was saved by chance, through an oral tradition that was later recorded, not in the records attached to the case. It offers no insight into how Judge Bay construed common law so as to allow this charge.[14] Yet, whatever legal officials' thinking may have been, their decisions conformed to a general pattern: local officials routinely bypassed the authority of household heads and positioned their dependents within the larger, patriarchal household of the peace.

Despite its positive connotations, the peace expressed a profoundly hierarchical order. Within the logic of the peace, which subordinated some white men to others, the concerns of individual white men were not the same as the interests of the peace, although the two could coincide. In practice, individual patriarchs wielded public authority and protected the peace, sometimes by asserting authority over other white men. But even the wealthiest, most powerful community leaders held their positions at the behest of the public order; their authority was contingent on accepting and fulfilling their own obligations within the social order. When they failed in their duties, others could invoke the interests of the peace to discipline them, just as they did with James Woodruff and James Hodge. As the operation of localized law indicates, the peace never could be defined solely in terms of individual patriarchs' interests, whatever they might be. James Woodruff might want to lie around instead of working his land. Joseph Hodge might want to have sex with his daughter. But the peace, as it was defined in Woodruff's and Hodge's communities, censured these men in their expressions of patriarchal authority: they could not exercise patriarchal authority unconditionally, because they did not yet possess it by individual right.[15]

Similarly, when legal officials recognized individual dependents, they did so without altering dependents' legal subordination to their household heads or society at large. Local officials considered complaints on a case-by-case basis, righting specific wrongs done to the metaphorical public body without extending additional rights to any category of dependents. The interests of the peace drew boundaries around each case, at least in terms of its implications for the legal status of the people involved. Acting on behalf of the peace, local officials could follow up on the complaints of one wife or one slave. They could undercut the domestic authority of one husband or one master. But those circumstantial assessments did not translate into legal statements about all wives, all slaves, all husbands, or all masters in like conditions. These cases accumulated on the books without producing any measurable movement in the hierarchical superstructure of legal doctrine. The decisions did nothing for other dependents in that same legal category, whose status neither improved nor deteriorated as a result. These cases were about the peace, not the dependents. When social order had been disrupted, dependents and subordinates could be moved out from under the legal purview of their household heads, without altering their status. But this legal logic emphasized dependents' connection to the public body through the relationships that subordinated them, not through rights that inhered to them individually.

Historians often apply a highly individualized version of patriarchy to the post-Revolutionary South, in which the personal interests of propertied white men and the goals of public order were one and the same. To be sure, many southerners at this time saw white men's authority in exactly those terms. The region's most prominent and prolific commentators expounded these views at great length. Many more southerners expressed them through their daily interactions with each other. White men habitually acted as if their domestic authority were an individual right that their government was bound to uphold. Their aspirations found support in certain areas of law and political theory. Property law, in particular, emphasized the protection of individual rights, which could be fully claimed only by those white men with the resources to maintain a large household. Revolutionary-era political principles enshrined in the Declaration of Independence, state constitutions, and the U.S. Constitution went a step further, identifying the protection of individual rights as the central purpose of law and government. From there it was a short theoretical leap to a public order defined exclusively as the collective expression of the interests of propertied white men, since they were the only ones who could claim a full range of rights as legally recognized individuals. Although that leap was not taken until later, in the 1830s and 1840s, historians often impose those political terms on the earlier period.[16]

Given the prevalence of this individualized version of patriarchy among those southerners who left most of the records, it is no wonder that historians have followed suit. But legal reformers' rhetoric and desire did not make it so, no matter how forcefully expressed. Within the institutional structures of law and government, individualized forms of patriarchy occupied only limited spaces between 1787 and 1830; rights pertained primarily to property in the realm of civil law. Later, in the 1830s, that individualistic conception of patriarchy eclipsed the alternatives in state law, achieving dominance and hegemony at that level of the system through the same mechanisms that centralized and rationalized legal authority. Between 1787 and 1830, a more encompassing form of patriarchy emphasized everyone's subordination to the peace and their place within the public body. It was also more finely graded, recognizing differences among white men as well as subordinates. In fact, those differences were crucial to social interaction in local communities and the operation of localized law.

CREDIT AND COMMON REPORT

Local determinations about the seriousness of an offense involved the shared assessments of both the victims and perpetrators, not just the disruptiveness of the act itself. An 1828 Kershaw District case involving the death of a slave, Ambrose, provides a particularly graphic example of the importance of local knowledge of both victims and perpetrators. In the first pass at the matter, a coroner's jury found Kirkland Harrison, a white man, responsible for Ambrose's death and recommended criminal charges against him. A few days later, however, the coroner reversed that decision. As he explained, the inquisition "was taken in Kershaw District where the Justice and Jurors were entire strangers to the character of Ambrose the Negro that was killed, consequently the verdict was given in as a case of murder." The coroner later found out that Ambrose "belonged to a man" in another district "where he had been a runaway for more than a year; his character was there properly known, and I am sorry to have to say was such as render him subject to be kill'd, by any person that knew him." Local knowledge transformed the meaning of Ambrose's death, turning what had been regarded as a heinous offense against the public order into an act of positive social value, at least by the standards of white officials.[17]

In many cases, knowledge about people's actions and character — or, at least, what circulated in the form of reputation — was readily available. But in some cases, both actions and character had to be investigated. Even the most gregarious, socially connected magistrates could not know everything about everybody. To ascertain the essential details about the offense and the offender, magistrates relied heavily on "information," a legal term that included physical evidence as well as verbal accounts, often presented together by informants. Above all, information was expected to be subjective and was valued for that reason. The meanings attached to information were crucial in quashing the allegation of rape brought by Lucretia Campbell, a white woman, made against a slave named Sam. The testimony reveals little about Lucretia and nothing about the circumstances in her life that prompted her to file charges. The case focused on the physical evidence, Sam, and his alibi. The physical evidence included the defendant's and the victim's clothes. But neither the magistrate nor the jury ever saw the clothing in question. It was what witnesses said about them that mattered, with some claiming they were "smutted" with signs of sexual activity and others insisting they were not. When people described the state of the clothing, they mixed those descriptions with their assessments of Sam and Lucretia Campbell. They saw the clothes differently because they saw the person who wore them differently.[18]

Magistrates did not give all information the same weight; they evaluated it through the informant's "credit" or "character," terms that were often used interchangeably. What mattered in the evaluation of testimony was the credit of the witnesses. Witnesses not only established the credibility of the victims and suspected perpetrators, but also established much of the physical evidence, which was usually described rather than produced as exhibits. Because the proceedings rested on the witnesses' credibility, their character was subject to evaluation. Credit referred broadly to a person's general reputation, not just his or her reliability in business transactions. It centered on repute: what others thought about the person, not just what the person did, although conduct and personality provided the basis for those judgments. While credit was closely related to "honor," it was not quite the same thing. Unlike honor, credit was calculated in terms that could apply to African Americans, women, and children. They could all earn it, but they did so by fulfilling their allotted roles within their families and communities. By contrast, honor tended to be a white male concern, tied up in a gendered culture of public display. Yet the distinctions often collapsed in practice. A white man's credit was inseparable from his honor, since both involved his reputation and his social status. Similarly, people often referred to the honor of white women and African Americans, referencing their credit, which was based in entirely different kinds of behaviors than the honor code of white men.[19]

Social position, which was shaped by race, gender, age, and property ownership, figured prominently in establishing credit, just as it had for centuries in the legal culture of England and continental Europe. White men with property were thought to be inherently more believable than any woman, any person of African descent, or anyone without property. The words of these men supposedly captured and conveyed truth precisely because they were independent, not subject to the pressure of superiors, landlords, or employers, and therefore free to think and speak for themselves. Acquiring weight through generations of use, these principles had solidified as the cornerstone of conventional wisdom in the post-Revolutionary Carolinas, where they structured local legal practices without having to be explained or even acknowledged. The effects were pronounced in the adjudication of local cases and magistrates' guides, both of which consistently discounted the complaints and information of domestic dependents and other subordinates.[20]

When doubts arose about testimony, they usually involved the credibility of the speakers, rather than the substance of what they said, and those questionable speakers were often white women and children, free blacks, slaves, or poor white men. For example, a key fact in one pardon request was that conviction had rested on the "uncorroborated testimony of a woman." Petitioners in another pardon request insisted on the illegitimacy of the conviction because "the most prominent witness against him was a woman . . . one of the most depraved of the human family." The language of another woman's testimony could not stand by itself, because she was "a courtezan and of course her statements [were] liable to great suspicion." A female assault victim could not be believed, because of "her extreme youth, and great liability to be influenced and imposed upon by her friends and relatives."[21] In fact, young children could be unreliable witnesses, and adults who were forced to live on society's social margins often had good reasons of their own to shade the truth. The issue of credibility captured and conveyed those structural inequalities.

The records contain fewer questions about the testimony of slaves and free blacks, but only because there were fewer cases in which they were allowed to give direct testimony. In those cases, the speakers' credibility was also an issue. A petition to set aside the conviction of two free black men, for example, alleged that "the case on behalf of the state was sustained entirely by the testimony of slaves, and free negroes, and indeed some of the principal points in the case were supported entirely by the testimony of a single slave." That was all these men's advocates felt was necessary to impugn the testimony.[22]

It was not just that the information of credible people was more believable. Those with credit could literally create truth with their words. In the largely oral culture of the post-Revolutionary Carolinas, words had concrete, material consequences, particularly when uttered by powerful people. Through the very act of speaking, credible people could elevate their accounts and opinions over other information, whether verbal statements or physical evidence. Although rarely explicated, these assumptions informed legal strategies in local courts, where hearings and trials regularly centered on information from people who had no direct knowledge of the offense in question but whose testimony was nonetheless credited. In a Kershaw District trial, for instance, a master brought in three white men as witnesses for his slave, Davey, who was charged with verbally threatening another white man. None could claim any connection to the incidents in question, but that did not matter. The men claimed Davey to be incapable of such an offense, based on what they knew about him; it could not have happened, because they did not believe it. The strategy failed in this instance, although the fault lay less with the concept than its execution: one witness waffled, admitting that Davey had once been insolent to him as well. By contrast, the strategy worked in the rape case against Sam. Two of the white men called to testify on Sam's behalf had no knowledge of any of the circumstances surrounding the alleged rape, but they claimed Sam incapable of such an offense, based on their knowledge of him. Sam simply could not have done it, whatever Lucretia Campbell, the offended woman, might claim.[23]

Words from the right people could establish criminal acts as well as efface them. In 1816 Abram Blanding of Kershaw District initiated and prosecuted criminal charges against David Carwell, a white man, for assaulting and enslaving Polly Horn, a free black woman. Nowhere in the record is there any indication that Blanding witnessed Horn's assault or abduction. But no matter: the fact that a credible white man said it made it so. Abram Blanding's credit, not his knowledge, made his testimony powerful. He had considerable property, a successful legal practice, and close ties to South Carolina's political elite. His standing made it possible for him to convince every legal official, at every level of the system, to respond to his concerns about Carwell. That Carwell was a habitual offender with numerous arrests for other petty crimes made Blanding's job easier.[24]

Despite Abram Blanding's efforts, however, Carwell was acquitted. That Blanding pursued the matter at all suggests just how dependent on local circumstances the legal process was. Blanding's prosecution of Carwell was fallout from a rumored slave conspiracy in Camden, Kershaw District's seat. On 4 July 1816, a few months before Carwell's trial, rumors of a planned slave insurrection rocked Camden. Although suspects were arrested, tried, and executed within a few days, the incident whipped up a fury of fear and suspicion that took much longer to subside. The executions, which were meant to reaffirm the racial order and calm white residents, failed to reassure them. Abram Blanding's father-in-law, Judge Henry William DeSaussure, heard the rumors in Columbia and immediately passed them along to his law partner, Timothy Ford, in Charleston. The leaders, wrote DeSaussure to Ford, "did not deny their guilt, but they disdained to implicate any others, they met death with the heroism of partners." "The tone & temper of these leaders is alarming," he continued, "as it was of a cast not suited to their condition, and shows that they have imbibed deeply the principles of liberty. . . . This is the most dangerous state of mind for slaves." "Doubtless," he concluded with more certainty than was warranted, "the detection & punishment of the leaders will repress it for a time, but I fear the spirit was sown deep into the minds of these people."[25]

With predictably stubborn silence, the court records do not connect Polly Horn, David Carwell, or Abram Blanding to the alleged Camden slave insurrection. Nonetheless, the slave insurrection reverberated in Blanding's life. Although Blanding was no critic of slavery himself, he was a native of Massachusetts, and his relatives questioned the wisdom of the slave system. His brother and sister-in-law, who had been living in Camden, moved to Indiana because of the aborted revolt. Before leaving, Blanding's sister-in-law wrote to a friend in Massachusetts expressing fears that the revolt would only make life worse for both whites and blacks, encouraging a downward spiral of violence and retaliation. If David Carwell's actions are any indication, she was right. And that may be exactly what Abram Blanding sought to forestall when he filed charges on Polly Horn's behalf. Out of context, the case looks like yet another example of a system that invariably protected the interests of white men at the expense of African Americans, like Polly Horn. But it was tied up with larger currents of political unrest, fueled by African Americans, that produced divisions among whites about the place of slaves and free blacks within the peace.[26]

In local communities, the close relationship between an informant's credit and the value of his information did not automatically exclude or discredit dependents' testimony. In fact, the emphasis placed on the identity of the current speaker, rather than the original source of the information, allowed dependents' information to enter legal deliberations through the mouths of more credible people. The dynamic was analogous to the one described by historian Ariela Gross for civil matters, in which whites turned slaves' bodies and actions into pieces of evidence. In criminal matters, whites who could testify routinely repeated information gathered from all those — white women, slaves, free blacks, children, and the propertyless — whose status cast doubt on their word. The pattern was particularly pronounced in cases involving slaves and free blacks, because their speech was the most restricted in law. Sam's wife, for instance, played a decisive role at the rape trial of her husband, although she could not be sworn in and was never even referred to by name. Sam's owner testified that it was she who had confirmed the unsoiled state of his clothes, while her owner repeated her statement that Sam had been with her all night. Even if these men embroidered the truth or attributed words to her that she had never spoken, they still had reason to think they could make this enslaved woman's information believable to the other propertied white men on the jury. That they, like so many other whites, openly attributed their information to slaves suggests their confidence in what they were doing. Information that came from slaves posed no problems as long as it was presented and validated by credible white people, preferably white men.[27]

Some cases involving serious crimes rested almost entirely on information provided by slaves. Particularly compelling are the two rape cases involving Annis and Juno, who accused enslaved men of rape. Information about the attacks had to come from them. Most suggestive of all is the fact that the offenses were prosecuted as rapes, rather than assaults or breaches of the peace. It is hard to imagine court officials leaping to this conclusion without some prompting. After all, many white southerners believed that African American women were always sexually available; only virtuous white women might experience rape. Cases involving crimes against enslaved women were not easily prosecuted within existing law. The charge itself speaks volumes about the influence of Annis's and Juno's words — although the fact that the men they accused were also black, with lower credibility than other alleged perpetrators, made these cases less racially charged and more likely to reach a public forum than others might have been.[28]

There were good reasons for whites to bring slaves' words into court. Local case records indicate that masters knew surprisingly little about the daily activities of their slaves. Other whites did not know much more, unless they were working with slaves or happened to attend gatherings with them. Since informal interracial contact so often included illicit activities such as gambling or trading, whites were not always forthcoming about those events. Other slaves were usually the only eyewitnesses, and only they could provide alibis or other exculpatory evidence in criminal matters involving slaves. That situation created obvious difficulties when slaves became enmeshed in criminal matters with whites; slaves were the ones with information, yet law restricted their testimony. Those restrictions also created difficulties for owners, who had significant financial and social capital tied up in their slaves. Masters were responsible for court costs and jail fees. Corporal punishment, such as whipping, branding, and other forms of physical mutilation, entailed a temporary loss of labor and possibly a permanent devaluation of their property. The trial of slaves also exposed the owners to a level of public scrutiny that could result in irreparable damage to their reputations; "bad masters" included those who indulged their slaves and endangered the neighborhood, as well as those who used brutal force to control them and aroused resentment. Those dynamics may explain the legal charges against the men who assaulted Annis and Juno; their owners may have pursued prosecution to protect their own reputations, not out of concern for the two women. The owners of the enslaved men charged with the rapes also acted in ways that suggest how closely their interests were tied up in those of their slaves. After the grand jury returned indictments, both of the accused men mysteriously disappeared from the jurisdiction. Apparently, their masters decided not to gamble with trials that would pit them against the owners of Annis and Juno. Given the financial costs and the cultural stakes, it was better to fold than to play their hand.[29]

What white southerners attributed to slaves did not necessarily reflect what those slaves would have said, had they been able to testify themselves. White southerners could never completely control the words of slaves or other dependents, however. That was a by-product of a legal culture in which truth depended as much on the current speaker's credit as it did on the information's original source. Slaves' words could acquire credibility beyond what their status would predict if whites repeated what slaves said. Cases of whites prosecuting slaves for slander are telling. Slaves' words mattered, because rumors started to acquire credibility as they circulated. Elizabeth Arrants, a white woman in Kershaw District, charged Elley, a slave, with slander. According to white and black witnesses, Elley repeatedly called Arrants a "blasted whore" and claimed her children were illegitimate. The insults had first circulated among slaves and then made their way to whites; Elley had even bragged that "white people had heard what she said." It was at that point that Arrants, whose position as a female head of household made her particularly vulnerable to insults of this kind, filed charges to protect her reputation. The danger for her was in white people repeating Elley's charges, spreading them and giving them credibility in the process. That happened easily and often.[30]

In fact, the mechanisms by which gossip developed credibility were so routine that they occupied an acknowledged place in localized law as "common reports"—information that was widely held to be true, even though positive proof was lacking. The mechanisms that produced common reports were so efficient and influential that Evangelical churches regularly disciplined their members for spreading false rumors. What distinguished a "true" report from a "false" one was the extent to which others believed it, not the extent to which it had a demonstrable factual basis. The true ones circulated in local information exchanges until they became common reports. In evaluating reports, courts ascertained whether they were common, not whether they were true. It was what others believed that mattered. Typical was the testimony of Bazel Compton in the 1807 vagrancy trial of William Brittain. Compton "knew nothing of his own knowledge" about Brittain, only that "common report say[s] that . . . [he] . . . is an idel disorderly person." The only way to stop the process was to discredit the sources of the information. Even that, however, was not always successful, since rumor was as much about relaying information as inventing or discovering it. Punishing the source did not always invalidate the information or stop its transmission, particularly if other people found it plausible.[31]

This ebb and flow of gossip and hearsay formed the backdrop of all legal deliberations at the local level. The reports produced and circulated through community networks became the "information" that people brought to magistrates' hearings and then offered as evidence in law. This connection drew dependents into the legal process, allowing them to influence the terms of the debate even when they could not participate directly in the institutional arenas where the conflicts were resolved. By taking advantage of the local rumor mill, Sylva managed to implicate her overseer in her own death. The conflict began when Sylva intervened to protect her son from their overseer's lash. She succeeded, but the overseer turned on her instead. Within minutes, Sylva's master had heard about the incident and called the overseer to explain himself. The only way he could have found out so quickly was through Sylva or another slave who had witnessed the incident. There were no white eyewitnesses other than the overseer. Although the overseer managed to justify his actions, the interview raised suspicions about him. Gossip spread all the more rapidly because three neighboring white men, who happened to be visiting Sylva's master at the time, witnessed the accusations and the overseer's response. Sylva, whose health declined after the whipping, kept the rumors alive. She made the seriousness of her injuries known, emphasizing the connection between her illness and the whipping. Her complaints were loud enough and frequent enough to reach beyond her plantation and into the neighborhood, where they had become "common report" by the time of her death.[32]

At the inquest, the overseer immediately and voluntarily admitted his responsibility for the beating that led to Sylva's death. He had little choice. As his statement indicates, reports of the incident from Sylva's perspective had already circulated so widely that it was impossible for him to hide or deny what he had done. He assumed that the members of the coroner's jury knew about the whipping, although he was the only white person who witnessed the incident. He also assumed that everyone believed that whipping to be the cause of Sylva's death, even though the physical evidence was less than conclusive. The jurors at the inquest accepted his responsibility for Sylva's death without question. That may be because neither the overseer nor the coroner's jury expected any legal penalty to result from the decision: a coroner's jury could find a person responsible for a death without attaching criminal charges, and that is what happened in this case. Even so, the outcome compromised the overseer. The verdict established that he had killed a slave, hardly a ringing recommendation in his line of work. He remained liable for civil charges on account of damaging his employer's property. Beyond that, the entire process opened him to public scrutiny and, ultimately, public condemnation. If the propertied white men who sat on the jury had thought that Sylva, and not the overseer, had acted inappropriately, their verdict would have been different. Her death would have been laid to "misfortune," as inquests found in the deaths of so many other slaves, even after beatings. Common report nudged the outcome in another direction, and Sylva's presence in that process is palpable. Had she not worked to publicize her version of the incident, the outcome would have been different.[33]

119

Common reports determined people's reputations for good or ill, with results that rebounded on their credit. Credit combined both personal reputation and impersonal markers of status, such as race, gender, class, and age, based in broad categorizations that applied to any number of people and were used to evaluate them in the absence of direct knowledge. Customarily, it was not enough to know that someone was white, female, and poor. To appreciate what that meant, it was also necessary to know who she was, what she did, where she came from, and with whom she kept company. Only rarely did a person's reputation trump his or her structural position in the community, although that did happen. The "most respectable citizens" of Fayetteville, North Carolina, petitioned for the manumission of Lucy, held as a slave, on those grounds. They claimed she was really the illegitimate daughter of a white woman, placed with a slave woman at birth and passed off as a slave ever since in order to spare her mother's reputation. The petitioners admitted Lucy's identity to be a matter of common report, consisting of well-known facts that could not be proved, or even directly acknowledged. That was the point: their knowledge of Lucy's reputation overrode whatever her structural status as a slave might indicate about her.[34]

What determined credit was specific knowledge or common assumptions about particular people, disseminated through the exchange of gossip among those who knew them. That was why local courts routinely included testimony about the reputations of witnesses as well as defendants and victims, if their information was crucial to the case. Character witnesses were believed necessary to establish the reliability of key accounts, a practice that suggests the personal connotations of credit; race, gender, class, age, and other impersonal markers did not provide enough information to evaluate what they said.

The practice of evaluating testimony through reputation prevailed throughout the early modern Anglo-American world. For men, the concept of credit fused personal reputation with financial standing, making it nearly impossible to separate the two.[35] The same conflation still characterized credit in the developing capitalist economy of the nineteenth-century United States. During the 1840s and 1850s, the national firm of R. G. Dun and Co. relied on local informants to establish the credit of businesses throughout the country, including those in the Carolinas. Dun's reporters relayed to the home office what they found about the owners of stores, artisan shops, hotels, farms, and plantations. The information accumulated over the years in ledgers under the name of the owner, with entries that focused as much on personal habits and domestic relations as on business practices. The first entry for Joseph Reese, of Hillsborough, North Carolina, identified him as "a sober man" who is said "to be making money." A few years later, he was still "making money." That same year, another entry described him as "a sober liquor dealer of plain & [economical habits]" with a "[very] indus. wife who is plain & econom'l . . . stands well as to [credit] . . . and is thot to be mak'g money." As these entries suggest, fact and rumor intermingled, with informants relying on what they heard from others on common report. Typical was an entry on D. R. Peebles, a Camden merchant: "conducted himself [very] correctly, have never heard anything to the contrary."[36]

The complicated local calculations of credit shaped the outcome of Sylva's case. For one, the result reflected credible white men's power to make decisions about others. In this instance, the jurors used their authority to discipline the overseer in an act that demonstrates both the contingency and contextuality of patriarchal authority in localized law: while all white men *could* have it, not all actually exercised it to the same degree. In this instance, then, the same hierarchies that subordinated enslaved women as a group made this one bondswoman, Sylva, visible and influential. It was not just his propertylessness that worked against the overseer. Nor was it just Sylva's attachment to a prominent, wealthy white man that determined the outcome. Instead, it was a complicated convergence of the overseer's reputation and Sylva's efforts within a very specific, local context. As discussions about the event circulated, community sentiment coalesced around Sylva's version of events, not the overseer's. That version then became the one validated in law.

THE ACQUISITION OF CREDIT

In a community setting where reputation was so important, the more impersonal determinants of social position, such as race, gender, class, and age, did not automatically define a person's status. Individuals had to demonstrate the attributes associated with their position in order to exercise the accustomed prerogatives, and those who earned the approbation of their superiors might enjoy privileges that others in their station did not. Status was shaped by interpersonal relationships, not just personal characteristics. Even white men, who had the greatest claim to credit because of their superior location within the social structure, had to demonstrate that they were proper patriarchs. The acquisition of credit began with their household affairs, where aspiring patriarchs gained or lost standing through their handling of domestic matters. This dynamic made dependents central in the accounting of credit.

Reports of domestic disorder routinely came back to haunt white men at the lower end of the social scale. Domestic details figured prominently in South Carolina vagrancy cases, just as they did in the trial of James Woodruff. In Anderson District, Henry Sizemore's neighbors were as concerned with his succession of "wives" as they were with his inability to support them. His most recent companion, Temperance Crow, was also charged with vagrancy. Her reputation for "parting folks as men & their wives" sealed her legal fate. What dependents did and said reflected back on heads of household, either enhancing or detracting from their status. Accusations of not keeping "good order in his family" were sufficient grounds to try James Browning, a tenant farmer in Anderson District. His wife and children pilfered from others and did not work diligently enough to suit his landlord and some of his neighbors. Where Browning did not exercise sufficient authority, Marvel Littlefield of Spartanburg District did so excessively, beating his wife and children too violently and too regularly for his neighbors to ignore.[37]

Concerns about family matters reached upward into society's highest ranks, where they tended to be expressed in polite euphemisms. No matter how tactfully or indirectly phrased, critical reports could be as ruinous as the more direct charges leveled in vagrancy cases. North Carolina's Archibald Murphey fell into despair when some of his financial backers went public about the disordered state of his affairs. "Now the Cup of my Humiliation is full to the Brim," Murphey divulged to his close friend Thomas Ruffin. It was not debt, per se, that was the problem, since dense webs of indebtedness tied together all the men in his social circle. It was that Murphey had overreached, letting his personal finances get out of hand, which impugned his business acumen, endangered friends who supported him, and failed family members and slaves who depended on him. Murphey experienced "embarrassment"—a term that underscored the social dimension of credit—for the same reasons that James Woodruff, Henry Sizemore, James Browning, and Marvel Littlefield did, although the scale of his domestic concerns was different. Murphey's embarrassment took a legal form, although his creditors sued in civil court instead of filing vagrancy charges. The worst of it, according to Murphey, was that everyone knew. "After a Life of incessant Toil and, as I hoped, of honourable exertion," sighed Murphey, he was now "degraded in the World and pointed at even by the Common Vulgar." Murphey wished to keep the details to himself, precisely because reputation was so valuable. R. G. Dun and Co. became such a successful business by specializing in the collection and sale of personal information.[38]

Credit, like honor, required an audience, as Murphey's fate suggests. Others had to acknowledge its presence for it to have currency; when they did not, it was gone. The balance was calculated through social networks of people who pierced the walls around individual households and scrutinized the conduct of both patriarchs and dependents. Those networks were made up of community members, including dependents, who watched and listened, gathering and sharing all the pieces of information that determined credit. The women who visited their neighbors' houses and passed along the details of what they saw, the slaves who chatted about their owners and the other white people in their lives, the men who swapped stories while trading at the local store, the "common vulgar" who "pointed" at Archibald Murphey—all these people contributed to the information networks that determined credit. In everyday life, it was abundantly clear that not all white men were equal, even if their maker had created them that way. They were placed along a spectrum according to their neighbors' evaluations, which explains the wide variability in how white men exercised their authority.

Wives, children, and slaves often had valuable information in this regard, because they had regular, intimate contact with their household heads. The men who testified in James Woodruff's case only knew so much. They could speak about the work they hired Woodruff to do, what they had paid him, what he obtained from them in trade, and what he grew on his own small patch of land. They suspected that Woodruff did not work enough to support his family, a key issue in South Carolina's capacious rendering of vagrancy. But the men could not speak to the conditions of Woodruff's family. They did not know whether Woodruff turned over any of his admittedly meager earnings to his family. They did not know the extent of his family's need. But their wives did. They visited Woodruff's wife regularly. They knew what the family ate, how much, and how regularly. The way they spat out the fact that Woodruff's wife made bread from chaff underscored their distaste—and that was only the symbolic starting point in the catalog of Woodruff's sins. The situation was so bad, according to one woman, that Woodruff's wife had begged her to go over her husband's head to her father, to let him know that she and her children "would starve if there was not something done." These women's voices shaped the entire case. They shifted the focus away from Woodruff's interactions with other men and defined the issues in terms of their own concerns with domestic order and their contact with his wife. The magistrates and freeholders of the jury not only allowed them to do so, but endorsed their view.[39]

Subordinates could turn the tables on the white men, using knowledge of these men's lives, their own place as dependents within households, and the importance of publicity in sustaining personal reputations. Vagrancy charges can often be traced back to the wives of the accused. The trial of Robert Mitchell, like that of James Woodruff, was largely his wife's doing. She had pointedly complained about her husband's laziness and parsimony toward others, turning niggling doubts about her husband's behavior into something more concrete. According to one witness, "Mitchell's wife complained that Mitchell allowed her to a pint of meal at a time and would quarrel with her for cutting much meat at once." Another "heard the wife of Mitchell say that Mitchell had not worked any of consequence for two or three weeks." Ultimately, Mrs. Mitchell lost the battle but won the war, which was probably her goal all along. Although her husband was acquitted, she had successfully mobilized her neighbors, turning their attention to her problematic husband. Even after the trial, those eyes would remain on her husband, providing her with moral support that she did not have before.[40]

Slaves used similar tactics, publicizing their owners' bad behavior to mobilize others and protect themselves. When slaves fled to white neighbors' houses to evade beatings or to seek shelter afterward, they expected more than a temporary haven. Exhibiting the bloody results of their masters' brutality could prompt white neighbors to intervene or plant information that could be called on later. Even if no direct action was taken at the time, these appeals set the rumor mill in motion.[41] Just as Sylva spread her version of the confrontation with her overseer, Judy, a slave in Anderson District, made her grievances about her master public. She voiced specific complaints: her owners did not give her enough to eat, and they used force too freely. Her complaints worked their way through the church membership and ultimately arrived back on her owner's doorstep, where they provoked a confrontation between her and her master. After that, Judy's master, Brother Johnson, brought her up on charges at their church, for disobedience and lying. Worst of all, according to Brother Johnson, was Judy's assertion that she had "good backers in the church to do the Evel she had done, or Else she wood not have done it." The complaint did not go the way Brother Johnson expected, because Judy had prepared the congregation to doubt what he said. The "good backers" Judy counted on required Brother and Sister Johnson to apologize for their mistreatment of Judy.

124

Ultimately Judy's recalcitrance got her excluded from the church as well. But the Johnsons' anemic apology did not satisfy the congregation either. Church members continued to investigate, subjecting the couple to regular scrutiny. Several months into the matter, Brother Johnson complained of the church "leving him behind and working over his head." The church conceded it had, and the issue cooled somewhat, but not completely. The cloud of suspicion that hung over the Johnsons remained.[42]

For dependents, the evaluation of credit was particularly capricious, fraught with all the prejudices for which the white South is so well known. People on society's margins could only shape the flow of information and the content of common report. They did not hold much power in formal legal arenas. In the case of Ambrose, the runaway South Carolina slave whose murder was excused as a public necessity, the negative evaluation provided by credible whites had predictably brutal results. But the process could also move in the other direction, emphasizing a person's good reputation and using it to cancel a misstep — to cover a debt, so to speak. North Carolina's Eliza Johnson, for example, had amassed credit enough to cancel out her conviction and punishment for infanticide. Her supporters thought a pardon "not only proper, but very desirable . . . for she had married since the birth of said illegitimate child, to a decent and industrious man, and has now a young child by her present husband." "We think that she ought not to go into gaol, as all her conduct since her former misconduct had been prudent and . . . praiseworthy." Even Governor James Iredell Jr., who was usually tightfisted with pardons, was persuaded. Other appeals came wrapped in similar logic, which had two distinctive features. First, community members claimed personal knowledge of someone in trouble and linked that person's misfortunes to their dependency, which could be the result of any number of factors, including race, enslavement, gender, youth, extreme age, or ill health. Then they elevated local knowledge over whatever might be assumed by strangers based on those external markers of dependency.[43]

It is nonetheless significant that Eliza Johnson was white. The determination of credit was blatantly racialized; all whites, regardless of gender, class, or age, were presumed to be superior to and more trustworthy than all blacks, whether enslaved or free. The ubiquity and power of whites' entrenched racial biases underscore the significance of appeals made on behalf of slaves and free blacks. The governors' papers contain many petitions for convicted blacks, supported by large numbers of whites who rallied to their cause with surprising enthusiasm and persistence. Consider the white petitioners of Bertie and Hertford Counties who requested a pardon for Jack, a slave. "Several of those whose names are undersigned have known the said Jack for many years," they wrote, and "they have never heard any thing against his character for truth & honesty before the charge of Burglary for which he has just been tried, was made against him." To the contrary, "Jack has hitherto maintained a good name in the neighbourhood where he has lived & been employed." They knew him, and that was what mattered.[44]

One of the ways white southerners recognized and communicated the credit of particular slaves was through surnames, distinct from those of their owners. It was usually men who were identified in this way, at least in the court records. In some instances, of course, second names had no significance; they simply distinguished among slaves with the same first name. Other times, though, it was clear that the second name had been earned. The fact that the name did not necessarily apply to others in the enslaved man's family underscores its use as a marker of the individual man's status. When white southerners used these second names with slaves, they were not attributing the same cultural meanings to them that they did to the family names of whites—that is, they were not identifying the enslaved man as the head of household and placing his dependents within his patriarchal purview. For instance, Sam Sinclair seems to have been one of those slaves whose last name marked his credit. He appears in the records because he was found dead under suspicious circumstances. The handling of his death then points back to the reputation implied by whites' use of a second name. Ultimately, local courts tried and convicted two white men for Sam Sinclair's murder.[45]

Some free blacks and a few slaves accumulated enough credit to claim privileges that were usually out of reach to those of their race and status. The evidence is scattered throughout the court records, manifesting distinct but irregular patterns. Consider the situation of Bonds Conway, a free black man in Camden, South Carolina. Family histories have him arriving from Virginia in 1792 or 1793, although they do not say how. He purchased his freedom soon thereafter. By the early nineteenth century, he owned a "small Charleston type house at 411 York St." and several slaves. One slave, Harriet, was his daughter by his first marriage to Ellie Coleman, an enslaved woman honored with her own last name. Conway owned at least one other slave who was not a member of his family. In addition to being a free black slave owner, which was unusual enough, Conway regularly appeared in venues that were reserved for whites only: he conducted his

Bonds Conway's house, Camden, South Carolina. Photograph by John McAllister.

legal business in the regular courts, with whites, rather than in the Court of Magistrates and Freeholders, designated for slaves and free blacks. His ability to act as if he were white was apparently understood, although not everyone shared in the knowledge. A rather surprised Nathan McGraw found this out when he tried to initiate proceedings against Conway in the Court of Magistrates and Freeholders on the charge of trading with slaves — something of a logical absurdity, given Conway's status as a free black man and the makeup of his household. The court was called, but its three members declined to prosecute, using language that managed to be simultaneously firm and impenetrable: "The Court upon due deliberation, and on examination into the Law, as to the extent of their Jurisdiction have come to the unanimous conclusion that this Court is incompetent to try the case, not possessing as they believe, authority to take cognizance of the same." The case was redirected to the Court of General Sessions, where Conway was tried like a white man. The Conway children also moved across racial categories. His daughter Harriet entered into a common law marriage with Morreau Naudin, a white man of French background, who served as the Kershaw District recorder. Essie, a daughter by his third wife, had a relationship recognized as marriage with another white man, Thomas Scanlon.[46]

Some slaves even testified in cases against whites. The slave Harriet, for instance, witnessed the event that Jacob Hammond claimed to be an assault on him by Charlotte Rogers. Although both Jacob and Charlotte were white, Harriet gave information at the magistrate's hearing. She was the most emphatic witness; where others hedged, she left no doubt as to who was at fault. She testified that she saw "Jacob strike Charlotte twice." She claimed to have rebuked Jacob Hammond at the time, a condemnation that she repeated at the magistrate's hearing. Jacob, she announced, ought "to be ashamed to strike a woman with a stick." The magistrate apparently agreed, for he did not charge Charlotte Rogers with assault. It made little sense for slaves and other people at society's margins to involve themselves where they had nothing at stake; speaking out of turn only promised trouble. Besides, subordinates often had their own secrets to hide. That may be why the other slave who was called to give information in the matter of Rogers and Hammond denied all knowledge of the event. Harriet was exceptional. She rebuked a white man to his face, in front of other white men. She gave information at a public hearing. Those exceptions are exactly the point: exceptional slaves could sometimes give information, precisely because what made them exceptional also established the credit that enabled them to do so.[47]

Like propertied white men, dependents fell along a spectrum constructed in terms of reputation. Their structural position as slaves, free blacks, children, or wives still mattered. But, within local communities, each individual acquired his or her own reputation, which distinguished that person from others in the same group. Consider the case of North Carolina's Thomas Sexton, who was accused of assaulting Patsey Allen. Sexton was a white man and a property owner, married with six children. Allen lived on her own, with her daughter whose father was not in the picture. There were no witnesses to the attack other than Sexton, Allen, and her young daughter. Ordinarily, those facts alone would predict Sexton's acquittal. But that was not the outcome in this instance, much to the consternation of Sexton and his friends. "Two respectable witnesses," they wrote with obvious outrage, "swore that . . . Allen ought not to be believed on her oath. But the Jury seemed to believe the testimony of her little daughter." Regardless of what Sexton and his friends said, the jury in Northampton County thought Allen and her daughter credible.[48] Although categorical exclusions prohibiting the testimony of children, slaves, free blacks, and wives were observed, they were less important in a system set up to evaluate truth through others' personal knowledge of the speakers. Some dependents could be believed, others could not. The process of scrutinizing the witnesses' character was about making those judgments. By modern standards, the evaluation process seems overdetermined, reproducing all the inequities of the social structure for no apparent reason other than to subject the witnesses to a humiliating examination into all their flaws and weaknesses. Why not exclude their testimony from the outset? But the point of the exercise was to see whether the dependents' character held up under fire. The negative statements of some character witnesses did not always destroy the person's credibility; that depended on the reputations of the character witnesses and of the subordinates in question. In some instances, domestic dependents and other subordinates emerged from the process as believable witnesses.

Subordinates' credit was always fragile, more prone to shatter into useless shards, more likely to evaporate into thin air leaving no trace at all. Their personal reputations rarely extended beyond the local community. The disappearance of the slave Sam Sinclair's surname is suggestive. Both the white man who reported the crime and the local magistrate who heard the complaint identified him as Sam Sinclair. Yet, as the case moved out of this local circle, Sam Sinclair became "Sam, the slave of John Chesnut."[49] The localized nature of dependents' credit also explains why communities went to such lengths to intercede on behalf of some white women, children, slaves, and free blacks; these people could not count on external markers of status to establish credibility among strangers, as white men with property could. The highly localized character of credit also explains why the damning effects of testimony so often dissipated once it left the neighborhood; in James Woodruff's case, the district court clerk was unable to fathom the reasons for his vagrancy conviction.

Reliance on personal reputation elevated the importance of the social connections required to establish and maintain credit, since everyone's credit depended on fulfilling others' expectations. For dependents, though, the expectations were more numerous and less forgiving. Subordinates' reputations were not solely the domain of powerful white men, however. As the production of common report suggests, slaves evaluated people's reputations themselves, including those of whites. White women, free blacks, and the poor of both races did the same. Although operating at society's margins, these people produced information that might make or break the   129 personal reputations of both dependents and household heads. The fact that information came from other subordinates did not necessarily limit its power to affect social superiors. Far more than white men, dependents and subordinates lived and died by the good words of others, including the words of other dependents and subordinates.

Even as social ties and expectations constrained dependents, they were also the means through which dependents became visible and influential. It was through social ties and people's knowledge of them that dependents obtained their reputations, whether for good or for ill. Their attachments to reputable white men were particularly important, because those men had credit to lend. Sam Sinclair's good name, alone, could not protect him from the predations of two white men or secure their conviction for his murder. In all likelihood, both events also had a great deal to do with his master, John Chesnut. Those kinds of social ties explain why the words of the other Sam, the slave charged with raping the white Lucretia Campbell, carried more weight than the testimony of the alleged victim. When Sam was tried, he was not alone. White witnesses entered his wife's information into the record. Other white witnesses testified to Sam's character, in order to establish the truth of his statement. One of those witnesses gave "the prisoner a remarkable civil good character and says he has been acquainted with the prisoner 25 years." H. Clinkscales "also gives the prisoner a very good civil character, they all state him to be an humble good conditiond [sic] negro as any and never heard of him being impudent to any white person." By contrast, the alleged victim, Lucretia Campbell, came to court alone. One witness testified to seeing her the morning after the alleged rape, upset and disheveled. But she needed character witnesses to back up her word, especially because of her shady reputation. By all accounts, her husband was a wastrel, and the rest of her family was no better. They were paraded in and out of court for fights, thefts, and other offenses. Lucretia herself had been involved in many incidents, through her husband and other family members. None of them showed up to back her in court in the rape case, although it was doubtful that anything they said would have established her credibility anyway. Lucretia Campbell needed people of standing behind her. She did not have them. Sam did, which gave his version the credibility it needed to materialize as truth. He was acquitted.[50]

The process folded back on itself, enveloping credible white men in their own words and binding them to the dependents for whom they spoke. Reputable men did not spend credit on behalf of dependents; they lent it with the expectation of future returns. These occasions gave them the opportunity for display, which was important because credit was a public commodity that had to be seen and acknowledged to have value. The rewards could be great, but so were the risks. White men exposed themselves to scrutiny when they exhibited their reputations, although they had less to prove than dependents. Once a man opened the door, the entire neighborhood walked in and began nosing around to see if the situation warranted the trust and authority that he claimed. In those calculations, domestic dependents mattered. It was not just that their indiscretions compromised their heads of household, although an adulterous wife, a pregnant daughter, a drunken son, or a marauding slave detracted from the balance. Dependents' good reputations reflected positively on their husbands, fathers, and masters. More than that, dependents' otherwise unacknowledged contributions to the household economy provided the material foundations on which most white men's credit rested. The productive fields, the well-tended livestock, the full larder, the clean clothes, the neighbors' good-will—all the things by which white men were judged depended on the labor of domestic dependents. Credit required an orderly household, and an orderly household required the presence and cooperation of wives, children, and slaves.

White men pegged their credit to dependents outside their households as well. In order to maintain their own standing, they needed others to accept their representations of the peace—their vision of a well-ordered community and their definition of the public interest. Those claims to represent the peace demonstrated the strength of their credit, which gave them the standing to speak for other people when they filed complaints, testified on behalf of others, or filed petitions for pardons. In all these ways, they assumed the authority to represent others and evaluate them, separating the wheat from the chaff. They demanded recognition of their decisions and acknowledgment of their authority. When white men claimed to speak for dependents and to know what was best for them, those acts were about their own reputations and their own claims to authority as well.

■ ■ ■

WHITE MEN'S EXERCISE OF DISCRETION required justification because they were subjects as well as superiors in the patriarchal order. These men invariably explained themselves in ways that gave human faces to all those involved, even to slaves. These jurors evaluated the injuries of Sylva, who was not just any slave. Because of those injuries, they held not just any white man and not just any overseer but Gabriel Coats accountable for

131

her death. Similarly, the "respectable men" of the Carolinas spoke for Jack and Sam, but not for Ambrose. They spoke for Eliza Johnson and Lucy, but not for Lucretia Campbell. Recognizing the particular character and reputation of individuals was the only way that white men could represent the patriarchal authority of the peace. Within the operation of localized law, dependents could never be the abstract extensions of their husbands, fathers, and masters that they were in legal texts. Subordinates, whether free blacks or propertyless whites, could not be faceless and silent, pushed to the margins of their communities. They had to be particular people, for good or ill, with unique identities, because the unique identities of particular people were necessary to explain white men's claims to public power. As a result, the patriarchal authority of individual white men was always partial and contingent.

5
Possession and the Personality of Property
The Material Basis of Authority

Sukey, a slave in Camden, South Carolina, was having no luck convincing the Court of Magistrates and Freeholders that the property in question belonged to her. She was on trial for stealing several items from Ignas Folmer's store on a Saturday night in 1812. Specifically, she was charged with stealing "a five dollar bill [of] the Charleston bank, one dollar and two quarter dollars in silver, three yards of bottle green . . . cloth, 2 yards cotton brown holland, one skein black silk thread, ¼ yard black satin." Martin Genley, who worked in the store, examined the five dollar bill and identified it as the one he had given Folmer to keep for him. He also heard someone, whom he identified as Sukey, enter the store on that night. Peter, a slave, testified that he had spoken to Sukey before her arrest. She had told him that she had some money and that her master had taken it from her. In order to get it back, she had asked Peter to write a letter in her husband's name, indicating that there was money in it, so that she could establish possession. But Peter had refused. Sukey's master swore that he had taken some money from her on Sunday morning, after Folmer's store was robbed. On that same morning, her master's young daughter claimed that she had seen Sukey with a bundle of three different kinds of colored cloth.[1] The odds were against Sukey; the court found her guilty and sentenced her to fifty lashes. This case also reveals the complicated nature of property in localized law: in this legal arena, the issue was Sukey's possession of *stolen* property, not her *possession* of property. A good portion of the testimony, for instance, was aimed at rebutting the unstated possibility that at least some of the property belonged to her. Genley needed to identify the five dollar bill as his, not Sukey's. Her master supported that interpretation, stating that he had not seen her with money before Sunday. If the money in question was identified and others had seen her with it, then a letter from her husband that mentioned enclosed bills could have established her claim. Likewise, no one seemed to care that Sukey had cloth in her possession until it was discovered that fabric of a similar description had been stolen.

The adjudication of crimes and other public offenses by local jurisdictions relied on common concepts of property ownership. Yet the logic of

ownership at work in localized law contrasts with conceptions of ownership in property law, as developed at the state level. The multiple, conflicting meanings of ownership make it a difficult term for this analysis, which
turns on distinctions among the conceptions of ownership operating in
different arenas, then and now. Although the term was used in both localized law and state law, it meant very different things in these two arenas.
To complicate matters, modern usage adds more layers of meaning. Historians outside legal history tend to use "ownership" to denote a form of
absolute control, formally sanctioned in law, which gives the owners unlimited authority over the property in question and reduces the property
owned to the status of a thing. That usage echoes popular conceptions that
give much wider latitude to property owners than they actually have in law.
Legal scholars are aware that this conception of property is an idealized
form that does not begin to describe the complications of legal practice.
Here, for purposes of clarity, the analysis relies on the term "possession"
to refer to various forms of ownership that appeared in public matters
within localized law and reserves "ownership" for property law in private
or civil issues that were the purview of state law. I make this distinction
with caution, aware that the terminology draws an artificially bright line
between overlapping conceptions of ownership that, in practice, often had
the same implications. These terms are intended to alert readers to the contrast between the *logic* underlying ownership in localized law versus state
law. Drawing inspiration from the colloquialism that "possession is nine-
tenths of the law," I use "possession" to refer to the practices of localized
law. In the saying, possession is a social fact that has legal standing, despite
its marginality within formal law, a usage that evokes the entire universe
of localized law, which dealt with public issues, protected the peace as defined through existing relationships, and drew on a range of legal principles,
including local custom. "Ownership" refers to the state law, compiled in
written texts and applied by professionals, which adjudicated private issues
and protected the abstract rights of individuals. This chapter is less about
ownership than possession. It focuses primarily on the dynamics of possession in localized law and relies on the extensive secondary literature for
insights into property ownership as it was developed at the state level.

Like other matters in localized law, the adjudication of property claims
elevated the maintenance of the peace over individual rights and made local
knowledge central to the legal process. As a result, possession included a
range of contingent, often ill-defined claims established through specific,
concrete circumstances, not a set of formal, legal abstractions. Individuals

like Sukey, who could not be property owners in the arena of state law, could maintain interests in property and even possess it outright in localized law. Their claims derived from the primacy of order within the legal rubric of the peace, not from the presumption of rights. The dynamics of the peace did not cast property claims in terms of absolute dominion or pit the rights of slaves and wives against those of their masters or husbands, as did concepts of ownership as developed in property law at the state level. The emphasis on order also explains why Bonds Conway, the free black man who figured in the discussion of credit in the last chapter, could hold Sukey as a slave. This anomalous situation resulted from his specific place within the town of Camden, established through years of interactions with the people there; it did not extend beyond him to frame the rights of other free blacks elsewhere.[2]

Deeply rooted in the culture of local communities, these property claims had legal resonance. They existed as acknowledged elements of the peace, formally negotiable within the bounds of localized law.[3] In fact, localized law's emphasis on order directed attention to the social context that established possession, encompassing not only the credit of the claimants but also the characteristics of the property in question. All those testifying in Sukey's case, for instance, lingered on the specific qualities of the property involved. To them, the items were as distinctive as the individuals who claimed them, and those unique attributes helped establish legal possession in the localized system. Perhaps the most interesting example is Sukey herself. When she stumbled over Martin Genley in the store on Saturday night, he did not think much of it. Feeling someone bump his cot, he asked who it was. Sukey identified herself, explaining that she was there to avoid the slave patrol. Satisfied, Genley stayed where he was and went back to sleep. Apparently, he knew Sukey well enough to conclude that nothing was seriously awry. His response is not surprising, since most Camden residents — white and black, slave and free — knew one another well enough to know who was a threat and who was not. Sukey also would have been well known because of her owner, Bonds Conway, a free black man. In Camden, Conway managed to expand the "free" part of his status to the point where it loosened the restrictions that normally would have been applied to him because of his race. Not only did he use the courts reserved for whites, but he also accumulated a significant amount of property, including slaves. All that he accomplished rested on publicity. Conway needed to make the details of his life known to others, so as to demonstrate and legitimize his various claims to property and the other privileges he enjoyed. Conway's possession of property, in particular, had to be public in order to be secure. That situation applied doubly to his claims to Sukey, because a free black man's freedom, much less the ability to own slaves, was never entirely assured. Sukey's connection to Bonds Conway then became part of her personality as property, not necessarily as she saw herself but as others saw her. She was known in Camden in terms of her connection to Bonds Conway, which also established Conway's possession of her.

White and black southerners recognized unique qualities in other forms of property as well. Clothing was different from food, which was different from tools and work animals, which were different from land. All those things were different from property that took the form of a person. These distinctions involved the recognition of property's dynamic, even animate qualities—what I will call the personality of property. In this framework, which emphasized the inherent qualities—the personality, so to speak—of property, the focus was on what particular kinds of property could do *for* the claimants, not just what claimants could do *to* or *with* property. This viewpoint structured owners' control of items such as land, livestock, tools, and slaves in which other people had interests. It also allowed a range of people to possess or control property, even though they could not own it within the rules of property law at the state level.

Legal possession, as it existed in localized law, framed the operation of patriarchal authority in the post-Revolutionary South. Property, as southern historians have argued, was inextricably linked to patriarchal authority in this period. It not only established authority, but also enabled its exercise. Property defined the physical boundaries of households over which patriarchs exercised exclusive control through their property rights. That was one reason why property, in all its various forms, generated conflicts. Regardless of the specifics, the underlying questions remained the same: Where did one individual's authority end and another's begin? Whose claims would the government support? Existing scholarship, however, has focused on just one part of the legal system, namely, the rules of property *ownership* in private matters as defined primarily in state law. This body of law focused on owners, typically free white men, and turned their specific claims into abstract statements about the rights of all owners. Emphasizing owners and characterizing all the different forms of property as things that owners controlled, state law effaced what I call the personality of property. Within this legal arena, property ownership and patriarchal authority were understood primarily as rights enjoyed by white male household heads and protected by the state.

Yet this body of law composed only part of the system. In the context of localized law, more flexible notions of legal possession proliferated alongside notions of ownership in state law, rendering patriarchal authority less absolute. In local legal culture, claims to property and authority rested as much on social context as they did on the individuals making the claims. The qualities of the property in question assumed legal meaning in ways that they did not in private matters as defined at the state level. Acknowledging the legal importance of possession at the local level and decentering state law sharpen our understanding of the development of patriarchal authority in important ways, locating legal concepts of ownership and authority in the arenas where they actually operated, historicizing their development, and revealing the pervasive influence of principles and practices not sanctioned in state law.[4] To bring those aspects of the law into focus, it is necessary to begin with the characteristics of property—the personality of property—rather than the legal rights or even the legal claims of persons. Within localized law, with its emphasis on context and social order, the personality of property was crucial in determining possession, not only what property individuals could call their own, but also how many individuals could make claims on any given piece of property.

PERSONAL PROPERTY

Professionally trained lawyers had distinct ideas about property, all of which tended to focus on its owners. These lawyers, who had taken over property law even before the Revolution, did the business of the Atlantic world's economic vanguard, overseeing the transfer of goods and capital. That business presented real challenges, because it was impersonal, conducted over long distances among parties who had no way of evaluating each other or enforcing their claims. To facilitate matters, lawyers and their clients embraced new conceptions of property. Among other things, they transformed and extended the existing category "personal property," which had applied to personal possessions, and gave owners considerable discretion to dispose of those items as they wished. Applying these principles to other forms of property, these lawyers defined ownership in terms of the person who claimed the property, not only granting owners exclusive and absolute authority over property but also turning those claims into rights that the state was bound to protect. This conception of property rights fueled the development of capitalism, by turning everything from land to people into fungible objects of exchange. The emphasis on the owner

137

tended to draw a sharp distinction between "persons" and "property," re-ducing all forms of property—including people held as property—to the status of inert "things," objects *without* rights that were owned by persons *with* rights. These trends intensified after the Revolution, as the lawyers and merchants who embraced these new visions of property emerged as political leaders in the new republic. These elites set about leveling an irregular landscape of multiple property forms and erecting a new legal structure that imposed uniformity instead.[5]

In the post-Revolutionary South, these conceptions of property rights figured most prominently in private matters, the focus of state law, where they guided property transactions of all kinds. Alternate notions of possession proliferated in the public matters adjudicated in localized law. Sprouting like weeds in untended ground beside a well-tended garden, they did not overrun private matters governed by state law, but flourished in local soil with a persistence and vigor that betrayed deep cultural roots. With property as in other matters, localized law was eclectic, drawing on a wide range of principles, incorporating professionalized property law along with everything else, to produce outcomes in accordance with the peace as it was defined in specific places. In fact, notions of possession in localized law bore a striking resemblance to the rules in law books, since ordinary southerners were no strangers to the concepts of property ownership as defined in the emerging body of state law that governed these matters. Whites and free blacks were well acquainted with the logic of these rules, because their families had to follow them in matters involving the transfer of property. The concepts were so pervasive in the post-Revolutionary period that even those who could not participate directly in this legal arena were familiar with them. A wide range of southerners embraced the same basic concepts of property ownership that legal professionals were extending beyond personal belongings to other forms of property and which entailed exclusive control, with few if any limitations on what owners could do with their property. In fact, they could be more enthusiastic in their application of the concepts than lawyers and their favored legal authorities. Southerners asserted ownership on these terms to everything from corn pone and pigs to plantations and people. Even those barred from this kind of ownership in state law, such as slaves and wives, made such claims. Southerners also embraced the notion that property ownership was politically sanctioned, although many tended to extend state protection to forms of possession not detailed in the law books. When conflicts arose, southerners expected the legal system to arbitrate.

Yet the similarities between the rules of property ownership in state law and possession in localized law went only so far. Despite a decided tendency to claim everything they could as their own, southerners did not actually treat all property in the same way. Their approaches to property reflected long-standing common law rules, in the broadest sense of the common law tradition as a reflection of local custom. Conceptions of possession in public matters that were the purview of localized law provided a range of alternatives outside the more consistent, systematic rules of ownership in private issues, as developed at the state level. These two legal practices shared space within the decentralized legal systems that characterized the Carolinas between the 1780s and the 1830s. The tensions persisted, unresolved, without forcing southerners to choose between the two. Legal possession in localized legal culture on the public side of the system ran alongside legal ownership in private matters at the state level, just as localized law formally shared space with other bodies of law in this period. The tensions evoke the deep ambiguities of a society in the throes of profound economic change. Individuals and local communities could support possession in localized law and ownership in private matters governed by state law, without any sense of contradiction. That was because possession entailed a range of alternate possibilities for negotiating property claims in distinct legal contexts. The legal implications were as valid as the more uniform rules of ownership, but different in their uses and aims. Where state law protected the legal rights of owners and the legal rules of property ownership, localized law looked after the relationships that defined the good order of the peace.[6]

Clothes, a very specific kind of property, illustrate the complicated relationship between possession in localized law and ownership in state law. Take the example of Elizabeth Billings, a widow who worked as a hired servant in South Carolina in the 1790s. During a prolonged drinking binge, which seemed to have inspired hopes of a new life and the temerity to pursue them, Billings decided to abandon servitude. Even in her state of drunken euphoria, Billings knew that leaving her employer was not enough; her status would follow her wherever she went. So she literally donned a new persona, dressing herself in clothing from her mistress's wardrobe, including a gown, petticoats, "a pair of Ladies florentine shoes," and other accessories. Unfortunately for Billings, clothing posed problems for the same reasons it was necessary: it was personal. The stolen items belonged to Billings's mistress and were identified with her. As a servant, Billings may have stood out when dressed as a mistress. Even if the clothes fit her body, she

139

might not have been able to pull off the deportment necessary to make herself believable in them. Ultimately, the disguise failed. Billings had not gotten far before someone recognized the clothes as stolen property and had her arrested.[7] Had she read published advertisements for runaway slaves, she might have altered her plan. Those advertisements identified runaways through physical characteristics and clothing, as if the two were equally expressive of individual identity. Actually, they were — and not just because most slaves had only a single suit of clothes. Slaves, like white southerners, individualized and embellished their clothing to make it their own.[8]

People treated clothing in ways that conformed to the definitions of personal property in private matters. They identified specific articles of clothing as belonging exclusively to one person. Indeed, clothes were among the personal belongings traditionally included within the formal legal category of personal property. Yet southerners applied traditional conceptions of personal property differently in the context of public matters in localized law than professionally trained lawyers did in private cases governed by state law. As lawyers extended the principles of personal property to new areas, including real estate, they also became reluctant to recognize the claims that domestic dependents had traditionally made to items, such as clothes, that fell within this category. That was because dependents' property claims had different implications in state law. New developments within property law transformed even limited claims to property into broader declarations of rights. Those rights then undermined the legal subordination of domestic dependents, an issue that was particularly fraught in a society where whites lived in fear of slave rebellions. In this legal arena, granting legal ownership of property to slaves could be construed as the first step down a road that led to abolition.

Dependents' property claims did not have broader legal ramifications in localized law, where personal property was a distinct category covering only a limited array of personal belongings. Within localized law, this claim did not imply control over other forms of property or other rights, because it rested on the specific qualities of the property, not the rights of its owners. In this legal context, the qualities of clothing made it the most personal form of property. As the extension of a particular individual, clothing was both constitutive of that person's identity and necessary to his or her social role; clothing literally identified its wearers and located them within the social structure. Given these specific qualities, southerners allowed a wide range of people to claim clothing and other items of personal

adornment as their own within the context of localized law. After Elizabeth Billings was arrested, she identified the clothing that she took as the property of her mistress, "Bridget Burns the wife of Robert Burns." Edward Calvert singled out his wife's clothing when listing stolen property to a Kershaw District magistrate. In addition to other articles, he included "one new striped homespun cotton cloth habit belonging to his wife." Similarly, Fielding Smith claimed that "a Negro man named Henry . . . did feloniously steal and carry away a Homespoun Coat the property of George Smith his son" who was "under age." In the words of a Granville County, North Carolina, magistrate, Nancy Pettiford was accused of stealing a "quantity of spun cotton and apparel of spun flax the property of Betty Chavis wife of Isaac Chavis," a free black couple. When charged with stealing dress boots from a Kershaw District store, the slave Bob defended himself by claiming that he purchased them legitimately from another slave. Localized law recognized all these people's possession of clothing. More than that, they maintained exclusive claims to the items in question, much like the ownership of personal property as defined in private matters.[9]

Like most principles in localized law, the treatment of clothing as personal property did not stand as a universal principle, clearly defined and consistently applied. Articles of clothing were not always attributed to the people who wore them. Nor did that association always imply possession, in either cultural practice or localized law. John Summerville, who filed theft charges in Kershaw District, listed a missing cambric frock as if it were his own, although if he wore it himself he would have cut a particularly striking figure in the fields behind his plow. Yet, as that image also suggests, the connection between the clothes and the wearer was both strong and evocative. Summerville charged the entire Marshall family with the crime, which included the theft of other men's and women's clothing, in addition to the cambric dress. He did not know which one of the Marshalls took the clothes, but he knew that all the Marshalls wore items that had been stolen.[10]

Claims to clothes often found their way into the account books of those local merchants who listed entries for free women and slaves. Free women usually purchased cloth and sewing notions, such as thread, ribbons, pins, and needles, as well as accessories, such as scarves, hats, and jewelry. Some of these entries reflect the fact that wives were responsible for clothing production and oversaw related transactions. Others, though, suggest that women were trading on their own account. Sometimes women paid off the debts themselves, with goods that they themselves had produced. In Camden, South Carolina, for example, Susan Blanding, the wife of lawyer and politician William Blanding, braided straw hats and traded them for fabric. Traditionally, women retained control of the proceeds from items that they produced themselves. Significantly, women traded their products for clothing materials, items over which they also could maintain control. In other instances, husbands and fathers settled the accounts recorded in their wives' and daughters' names. Regardless of who made the settlement, though, merchants maintained separate entries in women's names, linking them to particular items — usually clothing — that, presumably, the women themselves chose. These choices were theirs in a way that other household purchases were not.[11]

Clothing and related items also dominated slaves' purchases in the account books of those merchants who recorded transactions with slaves. Despite legal limitations on slaves' property ownership, some merchants did trade directly with slaves and kept accounts under the slaves' own names, although usually linking the slave to his or her owner. Among the other slaves listed on the accounts at the Kirkland store in Hillsborough, North Carolina, was Jesse, a favored slave of the famous jurist Thomas Ruffin. Like the other slaves, Jesse was identified through his master as "Jesse Mr Ruffins." But Jesse intended his purchases — linen, a vest pattern, and other sewing notions — to distinguish him as his own person. Nearby, at a store operated by the Cameron family, liquor and sugar competed in popularity with clothing among enslaved customers. Typical was the 1810 account of "Big George," who bought a "cotton bandana, 1 yard India cotton, whiskey, sugar." "Jones's Will," who bought "a hat, a cravat, 1 hank of silk," was more concerned with his appearance. Most of the entries in account books were for male slaves, many of whose names clearly represented trade for an entire family. Some entries suggest that female kinfolk also used the same accounts. Easter, the wife of "Negro Jeremiah," made purchases on her husband's account and paid on it with her labor. She bought whiskey herself, although not necessarily for herself. The buttons and two skeins of silk were probably for her own use.[12]

Why did slaves spend scarce resources on clothing? They did not receive much in the way of clothing from their masters. Beyond bare necessity, though, the value of clothing lay in its ability to express individual identity within a system that conspired to deny slaves that privilege. Buttons and silk were adornments, not necessities. Clothing was also more secure than other acquisitions. Slave owners expected that slaves would add to their meager wardrobes and were unlikely to confiscate these items for their own

This photograph of freedpeople in the Sea Islands of South Carolina in 1862 suggests the importance of clothes for slaves. Not only are all these newly freed slaves dressed differently, but many of the women are wearing beaded necklaces, which were thought to bring the wearer good luck. Group at Drayton's, #229, H. P. Moore Collection, New Hampshire Historical Society.

use. Once worn, clothing became personal in a way that other property did not. Even if it was secondhand, it quickly became associated with the current wearer as it became a means of identification and self-presentation. Clothes were among the few items that slaves could claim outright as their own. When the slave Jim paid Mary Cunningham for sewing that she had done for him, the question for the Kershaw District Court of Magistrates and Freeholders was not whether he could make the transaction, but whether the cash he had used had been stolen.[13]

Within localized law, southerners possessed currency, bank bills, and certain luxury items in the same way as clothing. The characteristics of these kinds of property linked them to specific individuals, who acquired exclusive claims as a result. Watches, china, silverware, and other decorative items were sufficiently rare and unique to be identifiable in their own right.

143

They were also readily connected to specific owners, because display was the point of possession. Currency was identifiable, not only because it was so scarce, but also because it bore the marks of the maker, distributor, or even the possessor. Spanish, Mexican, English, U.S., and French currency, as well as distinctive notes issued by specific banks, all circulated in this period, under the watchful eyes of southerners who knew their currency by sight and were alert to the possibility of fraud and counterfeiting. In 1835, for instance, the slave Bob was indicted for stealing "money amounting to between eight & nine Dollars," which his accuser carefully described as "one silver Spanish milled dollar, one silver Mexican dollar, another silver Mexican dollar, and four U.S. silver half dollars." In theft cases, neighbors lined up to give detailed genealogies of all these items, connecting them to particular people. The strength of those connections was probably why some slaves took the chance of acquiring luxury items. At the Cameron store, for instance, a handful of slaves purchased spoons, forks, and knives. It was a risk for slaves to display luxuries. But if they had the credit to take that risk, then it was possible for them to establish possession.[14]

To be safe, southerners—particularly those whose claims might be doubted—marked property to legitimize possession. Personal marks saved at least one slave from a conviction for theft. The case, tried in Anderson District in 1822, implicated both Jemima and Doctor for stealing currency. Tracing possession was complicated and involved testimony from several slaves. One slave testified that she had heard that Jemima had changed four quarters of a dollar with Doctor, who had marked each with a cross to identify them. According to another witness, that slave then passed them along to Scipio, who testified that the pieces of the dollar were all marked. From there, they went to Boatswan, who claimed to have received "4 quarters from Scipio and marked them for the purpose of a Raffle." He "returned them to Scipio last week, that same quantity . . . all marked." Other testimony muddled that chain of custody. What was clear, though, was that one of the slaves had marked the money and that the rest of them noted those marks as it passed along. But the evidence was sufficient to convince the court that only one of the slaves was guilty. Unfortunately, the records do not indicate whether it was Doctor or Jemima who was convicted, although the testimony suggests that the evidence against Jemima was stronger than that against Doctor. For the lucky party, the marks on the currency legitimized possession.[15]

In localized law, other forms of property, such as food, tools, real estate, and people, were less personal, because their different characteristics supported multiple claims to them. Possession or ownership was often lodged in certain individuals — usually, but not always, adult white men who headed their own households. But those individuals did not have exclusive claims to the items in question; other people, such as family members, maintained legal interests in the property. Unlike ownership, possession was not a zero-sum equation, with the property rights of one individual canceling out the claims of others. In fact, legal claims to possession in localized law could coexist with other legal claims to that property, even ownership that took the form of absolute property rights in state law.

Food had a distinctly communal flavor, as many historians of both Europe and America have shown. Of all forms of property, food was the most basic. Its immediate necessity justified the claims of people who did not or could not own it. That was the underlying justification of food riots: the populace insisted that markets be regulated so that food could be purchased at a "just price." Rioters' demands were based on the assumption that food, unlike other commodities, should be affordable, because it was a necessity. Sellers had a right to profit from the sale of food, but only up to a certain point, the just price. Beyond that, the claims of hungry buyers trumped those of sellers.[16]

Similar logic allowed both slaves and wives to keep what they produced. Staples and livestock, in particular, had qualities that supported multiple claims, which meant that slaves and wives could keep and control items they produced, even though it was "owned" by their masters and husbands — or by other people. This issue was at the center of a conflict between Thomas Clarkson's slaves and the overseer of Mathew Singleton, the brother of Marion Singleton Deveaux. As Clarkson explained to Singleton, his slaves had cultivated their own corn crop on land that they thought belonged to him but that actually belonged to Singleton. Singleton's overseer seized the crop for his own use, conveniently waiting until after it was ripe to do so. Because the overseer acted in Singleton's name, Clarkson had "been compelled to allow him to rob the poor creatures of their labor." But he felt it "a duty both to you & them" to bring the case to his attention, "feeling assured that . . . full justice will be given to the poor creatures who have been so unrighteously deprived of their labor." Clarkson himself

145

robbed these slaves of their labor to an even greater extent. His letter betrays no awareness of that contradiction, because the distinctive qualities of property formed such clear categories in his mind. Provisions his slaves produced on the time he allotted to them were their own, even when they were grown on someone else's land.[17]

As recent scholarship has shown, slaves accumulated a range of property through their own labor. It was common for both cotton and rice planters to set aside land for slaves to grow their own provisions and even staple crops on their own time. Clarkson's letter suggests that his slaves were extending their cultivation to additional, unused land, which they thought to be their master's, without asking his permission. Slaves also hunted, fished, and raised livestock and poultry. Some masters, like Clarkson, acknowledged slaves' claims by not inquiring too closely and granting them control of what they produced, whether they kept it or traded it for something else. Others purchased provisions from their slaves. Slaves even entered into contracts either to supply or to purchase goods. We are only beginning to appreciate slaves' role in local and regional trade networks. These patterns suggest that alternative conceptions of possession and ownership informed that trade.[18] Slaves' claims followed established rules, which white and black southerners honored, as historian Dylan Penningroth has shown. Those same practices established possession in the context of localized law. Local cases against slaves for stealing, for instance, did not begin from the presumption that possession established guilt. Rather, the testimony centered on whether the items in the slaves' possession had been stolen, which allowed for the possibility that they actually belonged to the slaves. Witnesses lined up to link the items to the purported owners. They described the physical characteristics, identified marks on livestock, and traced the lineage of possession. In defense of Caty, who was accused of theft, the slave Simon testified "respecting sugar being found in possession of the prisoner" that "he bought the sugar for Henry the prisoners husband." The chain of custody established her possession. By contrast, the slave Tate was convicted because he could not establish possession of an unmarked hog. Had the hog born his mark, the outcome might have been different. Occasionally, this logic led courts to peculiar places. The slave Milly came under suspicion because the corn in her crib was yellow, the color of Jonathan Sears's corn, not hers. In that same case, Sears's son used the tracks of Milly's horse as evidence against her. Because of the individual characteristics of the property in question and their links to certain people, it was clear that the horse was Milly's but the corn was not.[19]

A plantation scene in South Carolina. While this tableau of slaves outside their quarters was probably posed, note the table and other items in front of the cabin. People often took their possessions outside with them to be included in photographs. This stereograph is dated 1860, but was likely taken before then. Courtesy of South Caroliniana Library, University of South Carolina Library, Columbia.

Appellate courts and legislatures recognized legal practice at the local level, which allowed for slaves' possession of property but not ownership in terms of property rights in state law. Statutes restricting trade with slaves acknowledged that slaves possessed and disposed of property. So did the occasional appellate decision, when the circumstances allowed judges to distinguish possession from ownership. In 1845, for instance, the North Carolina appellate court ruled in *Waddill v. Martin* that a group of slaves in Anson County could keep the proceeds from crops they had grown on land designated by their master for their use. Questions about those claims arose when the master died and one of his executors claimed the slaves' property as part of the estate. Arguing from the framework of property 147

This stereograph, "South Carolina Views, Going to Market, the old Ox and Cart,"
portrays slaves with livestock, one form of property that they could claim as their own
in localized law. It was taken either before the Civil War or immediately afterward.
Courtesy of South Caroliniana Library, University of South Carolina, Columbia.

rights, the executor maintained that the slaves had no legally recognized
claims, because they could not own property. The particular circumstances
of this case enabled the court to uphold slaves' possession without tread-
ing on the difficult ground of property rights. It helped that the case was
tried in equity, a body of law that allowed for redress outside the rubric
of individual rights as developed in common law. Even so, the court was
careful to distinguish the slaves' claims to property from actual property
rights. Writing for the majority, Justice Thomas Ruffin emphasized that the
slaves' master had maintained ownership of whatever property he gave to
148   the slaves: "The property must be laid in the master, for the sake of the

remedy" and "the master, if he will, may take all." Ruffin nonetheless recognized the slaves' legal claims to possession, which existed outside the arena of professionalized property law. "There is an universal sense pervading the whole community of the utility, nay, unavoidable necessity, of leaving to the slave some small perquisites, which may be called his and disposed of by him as his," Ruffin concluded.[20]

Slaves' claims to property were more difficult to sustain in terms of individual rights of ownership, which implied more than simple possession. Appellate courts did not always manage to sidestep those issues, as the North Carolina State Supreme Court did in *Waddill v. Martin*. In 1845 the North Carolina court's justices stumbled in *Robert McNamara v. John Kerns et al.* At issue was an 1841 statute that empowered the wardens of the poor to confiscate slaves' property. While obviously undermining slaves' control of property, the statute did so by acknowledging slaves' possession of property, not outlawing it. But the statute explicitly framed possession as "ownership," which invoked the rubric of property rights. To uphold the statute, the court had to acknowledge that slaves owned property. The specifics of the case magnified the problem. Robert McNamara was suing the wardens of the poor in Rowan County, North Carolina, for seizing hogs that they claimed were owned by his slaves. McNamara insisted that the hogs belonged to him, since anything his slaves owned was his property. The court rejected McNamara's claim, arguing that the hogs did, in fact, belong to the slaves. When masters permitted slaves "to raise the hogs or mark them in their mark," then slaves could "exercise acts of ownership and dominion over them as if they were their own." That was the difficulty of property rights for slaves: when their property was cast in these terms, it became vulnerable, because their claims to rights were so tenuous. Possession, which could coexist with ownership within the legal bounds of the peace, was more stable.[21]

Free women also claimed provisions that they produced as their own, a point they made frequently in divorce petitions. Hannah Mitchell worried that everything she had accumulated through "her own exertions and the kindness of friends" would be taken away if her husband returned. "Believing him still unreclaimed," she feared "that his reception into the family would only bring fresh calamities and disorders against which no relief was to be expected." Bethany York put her concerns in the more formulaic language that echoed the wording of the statutes, claiming that her estranged husband was "making way with every thing she earns to the impoverishment of your petitioner and her children." These women were asking for public validation of what they knew to be true but their husbands refused to acknowledge: their claims to resources they needed to feed themselves and their families. These claims had legal resonance within the terms of localized law, even though they did not constitute grounds for a full divorce. Faced with such complaints, local courts and even legislators in North Carolina and South Carolina granted the petitioners economic independence as free traders—that is, they were allowed to manage their own economic affairs without interference from their husbands.[22]

Indigent people commonly levied claims on their neighbors' provisions. What Hannah Mitchell called the "kindness of friends" was a euphemism for those demands, gilded in the rhetoric of intimacy and voluntarism. Free white women could be aggressive in eliciting assistance. The culture of the rural South certainly supported their expectations. Women's demands fit within traditions of reciprocity, in which neighbors and kin exchanged goods and labor, without keeping exact accounts or requiring repayment within a specific time period. Women occupied particular places in these networks. Able-bodied men who could not feed themselves were offered work or, particularly in South Carolina, charged with vagrancy. But when their wives came calling, their neighbors felt obliged—although not always happy—to offer aid. At the point that wives wore out their welcome, neighbors took action against their husbands, because they were theoretically responsible for the support of their families as heads of household. Women and even indigent couples did wind up on the county dole for outdoor relief or in county poorhouses, where they were in operation. But public support, like vagrancy proceedings, required concerted, community action. Neighbors had to make complaints, supply evidence, and then see the process through in hearings with the wardens of the poor. Unless the situation reached a crisis point, it was easier to provide handouts. Even then, the effort was often for naught. Poorhouses were notoriously unpopular, and those who were committed to these institutions often refused to go. The wardens of the poor, moreover, only supported those without any other options. In 1820 the local wardens in Lincoln County, North Carolina, issued a statement to remind residents of those rules. Much to their dismay, they had discovered that "some persons have for some time been Receiving money from the Wardens . . . whose friends are well able to support them." The term "friends" referred to kin and neighbors—in fact, all those connected to the indigent person, whether by design or accident. The county, the wardens announced, would only deal with "Extreme Cases" of those without "friends."[23]

Hungry slaves also found their way to neighbors' houses, although they usually went to the cabins and quarters where other slaves lived. But whites took notice when such situations came to their attention, because the effects disrupted their control over slaves in the area. That was how the members of Bear Creek Baptist Church found themselves embroiled in the conflict—discussed in the previous chapter—between Judy, a slave, and her master and mistress. Her master charged Judy with disobedience. Judy responded by saying that she "did give ill Language to her Master & Mistress," but it was "because she had not anough to Eat—given her from them." Neighbors, white and black, felt justified in intervening because they had to take up the slack one way or another: they either provided handouts or suffered the effects of poaching and pilfering. That was how Henry Sizemore got in trouble in his neighborhood in Anderson District. His unpaid debts, erratic work habits, and languishing corn patch coincided with something of a neighborhood crime wave, and the combination developed into a vagrancy case against him. One of the questions put to the witnesses was whether Sizemore worked hard enough to support himself and his family. "I haven't seen him working on his patch," stated Mrs. White, "but I do not think [the] patch would support his family." While some of the witnesses thought he was stealing their corn to make ends meet, others doubted he was the thief. Still, they assumed that he was up to no good. "I do not know whether they got a sustenance honest or not," declared one witness, "but I cannot hear of his getting any thing to eat in the neighborhood." Evidence that Sizemore was neither producing enough food himself nor purchasing it from others was sufficient for his neighbors. They convicted him of vagrancy, which meant that they could require him to account for his labor as well as his food production and purchases for at least a year.[24]

Slaves could not file charges of theft, because they could not own anything within the terms of state-level property law, and that made their property more vulnerable to petty thefts by needy neighbors. In a particularly dramatic example, a correspondent of North Carolina planter Duncan Cameron bemoaned a rash of violence against "poor market women . . . as they move between home with their little profits, runaway negroes are supposed to be the perpetrators." Whether "runaway negroes" were to blame or not, the incidents suggest the vulnerability of slaves when it came to matters of property. That situation also makes documentation of these incidents rare. Court records indicate that violence among slaves often had its source in contested claims to property. The evidence is indirect, buried within cases of assault and murder, because slaves could not bring property

*African American market
women were a common feature
in many parts of the South.
Left: A street vendor. From
the collections of the South
Carolina Historical Society.
Below: "Selling Sweet Potatoes
in Charleston," New York
Illustrated News, 9 March 1861.
Courtesy of South Caroliniana
Library, University of South
Carolina, Columbia.*

matters to the courts for mediation. Left to resolve such matters themselves, slaves sometimes found their accusations and arguments escalating to physical violence. The source of the fight between the slave Jack and William Robertson, a free black man, was a debt that Robertson owed to Jack. Unable to collect by himself or summon the law to enforce his claim, Jack felt he had no choice but to "take it out of his hide." Because Robertson was a freeman, he had more legal leverage. He swore that Jack would "pay for it by the law" if "he struck," and he followed through on that threat. The courts only became involved at the point that violence transformed these property conflicts into a breach of the peace.[25]

Although barred from using the courts, slaves did negotiate property conflicts both informally and through more formal mechanisms in institutional arenas. The records of the Swift Creek Baptist Church of Kershaw District are suggestive. At this church, black members met separately from the white congregation to identify and adjudicate transgressions among their own. Among the charges levied by slaves against slaves was theft. While the proceedings were formalized, the mechanisms for handling these charges were similar to those used informally within the slave community, which were similar to those within localized law. The aggrieved party complained to third parties, who then acted as arbitrators. What was different was the arena, which not only lent authority to the negotiations, but also captured them for the historical record. This church, which gave slaves discretion that other churches did not, was one of the few arenas in which we can see slaves airing and resolving property conflicts that otherwise went unrecorded.[26]

Tools and work animals, such as mules and horses, had qualities that complicated questions of ownership. This property was valuable not for what it was, but for what it did: it enabled the production of everything from basic necessities to luxuries. Tools and work animals were integral to the lives of the individuals who owned them as well as the lives of all the other people with claims on the labor of the owners—family members, slave owners, employers, and creditors. Because of what they did, tools and work animals could sustain multiple claims. Use could establish an interest, even though the user could not own the item in the technical sense.

Established custom, dating back centuries, directed that workmen's tools were their own. Just as medieval journeymen carried their own tools, so did enslaved craftsmen. When Hugh McCall, a store owner in Kershaw District, accused the slave Dick of theft, the case hinged on whether Dick was seen that evening with an axe, which was used to break into the store. 153

Dick hired out his time, apparently as a carpenter. Slaves were common in this line of work in Kershaw District, so much so that other slaves were among those who hired Dick. Peter, a slave, "had hired Dick to work" on the day that he was accused of theft. When he did so, Peter "directed him to fetch his Tools." His tools included an axe. After work, according to John Cunningham, an apprentice, Dick put away his axe and "his other Tools Dick carried down [the] street himself." Other witnesses, both free and enslaved, testified that Dick had his tools with him after work, but that he did not have an axe. No one questioned whether Dick could own his tools. To the contrary, the case was dismissed, because everyone knew that he owned an axe and left it at the shop, which was left unlocked. Anyone could have taken it and used it to break into McCall's store. But that did not change the fact that it was Dick's axe. In his 1799 will, William Luten, also of Kershaw District, left his slave, John Monay, all his cabinetry tools, which were to be his "for Ever." If those were "not Sufficient" the executor was to "purchase a few more" so that Monay could pursue his trade. Not coincidentally, Luten also gave Monay all his clothing. Possession, however, did not take the form of ownership, since Luten did not free Monay. In the realm of state law, Monay's new master owned these items.[27]

Household goods were the tools of women's trades: pots, pans, and other implements used in the kitchen or dairy as well as needles, pins, cards, spinning wheels, fabric, and notions used in textile and clothing production. Long-standing custom placed these items under women's control. Whether enslaved or free, women treated them as their own, even though they belonged to their masters or husbands. As Dylan Penningroth has shown, enslaved couples recognized wives' separate interests to property that they used or produced, logic that gave wives strong claims to domestic tools. White southerners, such as the widow Jane Rowe, acknowledged those claims as well. Rowe accused the slave Caty of stealing a knife. After examining the knife in question, witnesses reached different conclusions about whether it belonged to Jane Rowe or to Caty. Ultimately, though, it was the complainant, Jane Rowe, who resolved the issue, by withdrawing her charges. The court then dismissed the case, leaving Caty in the clear and in possession of the knife.[28]

Legal officials had more opportunity to recognize the property claims of free wives, which they did routinely in divorce and separation decrees, granting wives control of domestic items. These items were often exempted from men's estates, because they were assumed to belong to the widows. In some instances, wives simply assumed control of domestic items without asking permission. In 1812 Rachel Teague was censured by her David-son County, North Carolina, church for "persuading her husband to leave home on a certain night . . . in order to get an oppertunity to elope from him and having gone away and took part of his property away with her." Was it his property or hers? Rachel Teague later apologized, but another woman in the same church who faced similar charges did not. In August 1797 Sister Sary Spoolman was excluded from her Davidson County church for "leaveing her husband and taking away property and disposing of it contrary to his will." Two months later, after hearing her side of the story, the congregation concluded that she had acted appropriately, removed "the suspition," and received "her into the fellowship of the Church." Wives had to prove their claims, but they were insistent and creative in pursuing them. When James Long was arrested for domestic violence, the magistrate who issued his warrant presented him with a deal: if he "would give her up some bed & other furniture which she claimed, she would stop the warrant."[29]

People other than the user or owner could make claims on tools and work animals, because they had an established stake in what those tools could produce. In free families, a male household head's ownership did not necessarily negate other family members' claims to these items. Wives appeared as complainants and even prosecutors in theft cases, because so many of the movable items that could be stolen — chickens, pigs, food, clothing, and linens — fell within their purview. Husbands' names often appeared on the legal forms, because they were the owners. Wives were at their sides, providing the evidence necessary for the complaint and the prosecution of the case. In some of these cases, the documentation suggests that husbands appeared only in theory, lending their names to legitimize a case that was clearly the wife's doing. Occasionally, magistrates dropped the pretense of the husbands' presence entirely. When Catherine Saunders prosecuted a neighbor woman for stealing two of her geese and selling them to another neighbor, Mrs. Warren, the indictment identifies the geese as the property of her husband, David Saunders; but he never appeared in any of the legal documents. It was Catherine who acted as the owner, filing the complaint and posting the bond necessary to prosecute. The case called the property claims of another wife, the unfortunate Mrs. Warren, into question as well.[30]

Free wives could prosecute these cases in local courts, because they were about the restoration of the peace, not competing property rights, which would have pitted wives' rights against those of their husbands. Catherine Saunders pursued the theft of "her" geese, even though the case records indicated that it was her husband who owned them. Ownership, in the technical sense of state law, was not really the issue. Catherine Saunders was demanding the return of her geese as a restoration of the peace, not recognition of her property rights. Although Saunders and other wives technically did not own the property, their claims exerted a binding force within the contours of a social order in which a husband's rights to property ownership did not negate his wife's claims to the same property or her authority over it. Catherine Oel's divorce petition expressed the sentiment well. Her husband left her, "having striped [sic] the house of the Best of our Property."[31] The property was not "his" but "ours." It was a significant difference, and a wife's claim to household possessions was widely accepted, in varying degrees, among both men and women.

REAL PROPERTY

Land did even more productive work than tools or livestock, multiplying the number of claims that could be made on it. By the late eighteenth century, land had been commodified to the point that many southerners treated it as personal property—that is, property that could be reduced to one individual's exclusive control. The attitude is best represented in land speculation, which involved virtually every member of the South's political elite and many lesser known southerners as well.[32] Even so, land retained important social and symbolic functions: it was still "real estate," immovable, productive property that supported an entire family, represented the family line, and joined past, present, and future generations. These elements pervaded the cultural view of land, even among those who also treated it as a commodity. The prominent lawyer William Gaston, for example, speculated heavily in land, accumulating tracts in Georgia and Tennessee as well as his home state of North Carolina. Yet he did not see land simply as a means to his own enrichment. He bought it to secure the future of his son and his two daughters. In 1821 he returned a certificate of deposit from rents on western land to his agent, asking him to turn it back into land. "My hope," Gaston wrote, "would be to acquire . . . something which fourteen or fifteen years hence may be useful in making provision for a child." The exchange rate made a certificate in western currency virtually worthless elsewhere. By contrast, fertile, well-situated land would continue to provide, because it could be worked for sustenance or profit and would hold its value for that reason.[33] For Gaston, the land that he had carefully acquired over time for his children became a concrete expression of the ties that bound him to past and future generations of his family. In the 1830s, when his children were grown, Gaston would not even consider a position on the North Carolina State Supreme Court until he guaranteed the protection of the land intended for them. The judgeship, which paid considerably less than his private practice, would make it impossible to pay off his debts, which could jeopardize the land he intended for his children. As he explained to his supporters, the future of his family was more important than the law or the state. "When I look back upon my culpable inattention to pecuniary matters I find it difficult to account for my folly," wrote Gaston to a close friend and political ally. "Some years have passed since I made the discovery that if I intended to leave to my children the property which I possessed, and which I had regarded as naturally coming to them at a future day, I was bound to change my course of conduct." It was only after his friends arranged alternate financing that Gaston agreed to put his name up for nomination.[34]

This vision of land applied broadly, even to white and black southerners who did not own land but aspired to ownership. That logic sanctioned Clarkson's slaves' cultivation of unused land on his plantation — or what they thought was his plantation. Their attachment to the land allowed them to use what Clarkson did not. Once their masters left, severing their connection to the land, many slaves assumed that their claims became primary, giving them control of the property, if not outright ownership. Freedpeople who did not expect to stay on their own plantations carried these conceptions with them, as their well-documented desire for land indicates. Land was not just a commodity; it was a resource necessary for the economic and political independence of families and entire communities.[35]

Family provided the means for individual patriarchs to pass on their property, as many historians have pointed out. But land's character as a collective possession and expression of lineage also supported family members' claims to it, tempering concepts of individual ownership. Who qualified as a family member varied according to the customs of particular southerners. When it came to landed estates, conceptions of family did not extend much beyond blood relatives for white southerners, particularly wealthy white southerners. Family did not include slaves in these matters. Nor did it always extend to husbands and wives who married into the family. By contrast, slaves incorporated people unrelated by blood into their families. But, regardless of how family membership was defined, land emphasized the family's collective lineage. Current family members acquired responsibilities that extended both backward and forward in time, protecting what past generations had accomplished and providing for future ones. All those acknowledged as family members could make claims on land, in addition to the male household heads who owned it. These were claims that male owners, themselves, encouraged and honored.[36]

At least some of these claims had roots in long-standing legal traditions on which state law drew, although localized law tended to reverse the logic to some degree. In these traditions, the family became a vehicle for passing along property, rather than land being a means of assuring a family's standing and future. Nonetheless, even elements of property law favored by professional lawyers characterized land as a family resource rather than as an individual possession. Common law precedents gave husbands use rights only in real estate that their wives brought into the marriage. Dower formalized the property claims of widows who had married into families and did not have the same claims to family estates that their children did. Dower gave widows use of portions of their husbands' land and the support it could provide, not rights to ownership, so that it would stay in the family line. The distinction between encumbered possession and individual ownership was also apparent in separate estates and marriage contracts, which set aside family property for female relatives who married into other families. These legal devices gave women and men access to the productive capacities of the family estate, after marriage, without necessarily giving them ownership of those resources.[37]

Primogeniture and entail kept land together in a particular family line and elevated the family's property claims over those of individual members. Primogeniture kept the family estate intact by passing it through the eldest sons, while entail limited what owners could do with the property by keeping it within a given family. Entail was widely used in the colonial South, as Holly Brewer has shown. Brewer also points out that colonial Virginia law extended the logic to slaves, defining them as real estate and subjecting them to the same rules that governed land, including entail.[38] It now seems absurdly illogical and callously inhumane to equate people with land. At the time, though, the analogy consisted in the productive capacity that distinguished both forms of property and gave them exceptional value and power. Land and slaves were animate, although in very different degrees, where other forms of property were inert. Both could provide the foundation for subsistence and for the accumulation of wealth.

These restrictions on inheritance began to disappear from property law after the Revolution. Southern state legislatures abolished both entail and primogeniture. Virginia turned slaves into personal property, a status that the Carolinas confirmed in their laws. Dower remained in the law books and on legal forms, but its meaning was eroded in practice. The logic behind these legal concepts nonetheless lingered. Free white wives often invoked the spirit of dower in divorce petitions, citing their husbands for squandering what they clearly saw as the family land. Hannah Ridge, for instance, complained that her "husband contracted habits of intemperance & sold his land for $450 & spent the money in payment of his own . . . debts."[39] As she and other wives saw it, husbands might own the family farm, but that did not negate their own claims on it. The land would provide for them and their children, even if their husbands chose not to.

In wealthier families, parents kept the spirit of familial claims to real estate alive in their wills. They set up separate estates for their daughters. They drafted marriage settlements. They also willed estates to grandchildren through their daughters, who acquired possession and use, but not ownership as an individual right. It was not that parents wished to defy patriarchal conventions by giving real estate to daughters. It was not even that they wanted to keep land out of the hands of suspect sons-in-law, although that was sometimes the case. Like William Gaston, fathers wanted to secure the future of their family line. Individual rights of property ownership were subordinate to this larger patriarchal project, in which all family members, whether male or female, tended estates that were meant to be passed along through the generations.[40] Land's patriarchal purposes sanctioned free women's possession of family estates. Not only were these women family members who needed the estate's support, but they were also essential in generating the family line and passing on its heritage. Marion Singleton Deveaux, for example, possessed and controlled two large, productive plantations without owning them outright. Her father, Richard Singleton, one of South Carolina's wealthiest planters, had carefully constructed his will to keep the land in the family. He gave Marion use of the plantations, which she managed as trustee for her father's grandchildren. They inherited as owners, although with provisions that kept the land within the family. North Carolina courts affirmed such practices in divorce judgments, some of which explicitly stated that wives would retain estates and property willed to them by their own families.[41]

For free women, this form of possession could ease into something very much like ownership, a dynamic illustrated in the 1775 will of Mary Brewton, the second wife of Miles Brewton, who made his fortune in the slave trade. Miles and Mary died at sea in 1776. Other than that, little information about Mary Brewton remains, except her will, which establishes her place within the tightly knit network of South Carolina's elite families, through which she had acquired a vast estate. It also suggests how these families routinely modified the rules of coverture. Mary's grandmother willed her an estate, which included over a thousand acres of land, in trust, intended for her and her husband's use during their marriage. Possession gave way to ownership, though, because the will allowed Mary the right to will the property to whomever she wanted, "notwithstanding coverture." Such clauses, establishing women's rights to will real estate, were standard in South Carolina marriage settlements and other legal devices. Mary's father, Joseph Izard, left her personal property in the amount of £20,000, but specified that her future husband should convert that same amount into a trust for Mary's use. She and her husband also accumulated land from other sources, much of which Mary controlled, even if she did not actually own it.[42] In her will, Mary continued the tradition, dividing the estate among female relatives if she were to die childless. Because the Brewton children died with their parents, those provisions determined the division of her estate. The language was different in regard to each woman, but the intent was clear. She gave a sizable estate to her cousin Sarah Guerard "independent of and free from the Controul or Intermedling of her Husband." She also specified that Guerard could pass along that property to whomever she chose during her lifetime or in her will. Somewhere along the line, Mary's possession of property became more like ownership as defined in state law, a privilege that she then passed along to other women. These mandates were dependent on the heiresses' husbands and male relatives, as were other women's less definitive claims to possession and use. Yet the blatant disregard of coverture underscores the fundamental ambiguity of possession, which gave women authority over the property, although not rights of ownership. But, if coverture did not prevent women from possessing and controlling family estates, then why should it prevent them from ownership? That path to ownership followed from a collective vision of land that included women within the family line.[43]

Mary Brewton's will, which was clearly written by someone with professional training, followed accepted legal practices that continued into the nineteenth century, as Marylynn Salmon's scholarship on South Carolina marriage settlements suggests. The will of Mary's sister-in-law, Rebecca Brewton Motte, was similar. Rebecca, who became famous during the Revolutionary War for refusing to hand over her house to British troops, acquired her brother Miles Brewton's property in 1776 and control over her husband Jacob Motte's estate shortly thereafter. Like her sister-in-law,

Rebecca provided legacies for her two daughters, Mary Brewton Alston and Frances Motte Pinckney, with clauses that allowed them to control the property apart from their husbands. Mary Brewton Alston, who was married to William Alston, received £2,000 "for her sole and separate use, benefit and behalf, notwithstanding her coverture, the same not to be subject to the controul of, or liable for the debts of her husband." To Frances Motte Pinckney, she gave the plantation where Frances lived with her husband, Thomas Pinckney, "for the term of her natural life." It was not that Rebecca distrusted either of her sons-in-law. She appointed Thomas Pinckney the executor of her will and gave both men the use of other property. Neither man, however, controlled the property outright. It passed through their hands to either her daughters or her daughters' children, preserving the patrimony of the Motte family through its female line for the use of future generations.[44]

Ordinary southerners acted on similar conceptions of land in their daily lives. It was no coincidence that wives filed for divorce at the moment when they were to inherit land and their families faced the prospect of what they saw as a collective resource being frittered away by dissolute husbands. Numerous legal conflicts among ordinary southerners treated land as a family rather than individual possession. In feuds between families, violence went back and forth, with one side making a raid and the other side retaliating. Women often participated alongside their menfolk, sometimes arming themselves and going on the offensive and sometimes stepping up to defend themselves and their families' property. In 1800, for instance, John Howes and his wife and Jordan Gilliam and his wife marched into Leonard Barron's house, threatened him, and then went out to the kitchen garden where Mrs. Barron was working. After driving her away, according to the complaint, "they proceeded to cut to peaces & dig up and destroy all the grothe in said garden." It was later disclosed that the source of the conflict was "the right of possession of a certain tenement," which was settled amicably through arbitration. The "certain tenement" was land, which was owned by John Howes but occupied by the Barrons—in legal terms, a tenement was real property, land, and dwellings held by an owner who did not occupy the property but rented it out or otherwise contracted its use to another. Even though the matter involved real property, it was not confined to the men who could claim ownership. All three wives were by their menfolks' sides, although they remained nameless in the documents. They also had interests in the land; after all, the main target was the Barron's kitchen garden, which was a woman's productive domain.[45]

Slaves also made claims to land in their masters' possession. Thomas Clarkson's slaves were not alone in assuming they could cultivate unused portions of their master's estate. In this instance, slaves' claims coexisted with their master's property rights. But those interests could evolve into competing claims, which surfaced during and after the Civil War. When their masters fled their plantations to escape the Union Army, slaves stayed put, certain that the land they had worked now belonged to them. As they explained to befuddled Union officials, their claims were based on their history with the land, a combination of possession, use, and the labor they had expended over the years to realize the property's value. They had developed a relationship with this unique form of property: they had made the land productive, and the land had supported them. That relationship, built up through the years alongside their masters' property rights, now placed the land in their hands.[46]

PEOPLE AS PROPERTY

People were the most complicated form of property. In the post-Revolutionary South, people's association with property fell along a continuum, which was complicated by the fact that property could have multiple meanings. To have one's value expressed in terms of property could have many connotations, not all of them negative. But the influence of state law, with its emphasis on rights, tended to make that association negative. This body of law not only expressed personal autonomy in terms of property rights but also gave property rights in some people's bodies to other people. Of all southerners, slaves were the most obviously circumscribed as property in this regard, because the property rights of masters were so extensive. The alienation of property rights also limited other southerners, although the constraints were never as complete or permanent as they were for slaves. Husbands and fathers, for instance, acquired property rights in the bodies, possessions, and labor of their wives and children. The rights of wives appeared in their most attenuated form in the pages of the legal treatises popular with reformers, such as Blackstone. But such claims also appeared regularly in practice. As the local court records indicate, free men regularly and aggressively asserted their authority with violence that reduced their wives, children, and slaves to property.[47]

Property rights even framed the lives of adult white men, although with different results, since they tended to retain control of property in themselves. Damages in private (or civil) cases, for instance, were assessed based on the status of the injured party. "In the estimation of damages," one eighteenth-century legal manual advised, "a man of honor and respectability will be entitled to much larger damages than a worthless, unfeeling fellow, because his sensibility will be much more wounded."[48] The men in this hypothetical legal example were not considered property. But property provided a metaphor to express their social value. The law assigned them different values, measured in terms usually associated with property, so as to assess damages. The man of high status possessed "sensibility" that made his life more valuable than that of a less credible, "unfeeling" man. Nonetheless, the men in both categories still retained possession and control of their bodies, their labor, and their lives.

Similar kinds of judgments followed poor men into other areas of their lives, giving others property rights in their lives. South Carolina's vagrancy laws, which applied to all "idle" and "disorderly" persons, threw those links into sharp relief. Once convicted, vagrants — even white vagrants — were "sold at publick sale . . . for a space of time not exceeding one year," if they could not post bond. If no one "purchase[d] the services of the said offender," then he or she was liable to receive up to thirty-nine lashes. White vagrants also were prosecuted in the courts designated for slaves and free blacks, the courts of magistrates and freeholders, further underscoring their proximity to the category of property. Similarly, North Carolina counties auctioned off able-bodied paupers, forcing them into labor contracts for specified periods of time to work for their support.[49]

The treatment of vagrants and paupers drew on established legal principles that applied to all menial workers in the new republic, even free white men. In the realm of labor relations — master/servant law, in legal parlance — labor was not yet separate from the body in theory or practice. Employers acquired control over workers, along with property rights in their labor. Although employers did not own their workers, their property rights translated into extensive authority over all aspects of their workers' lives, a situation similar to that which gave husbands authority over their wives. Those assumptions, which found graphic expression in the treatment of indentured servants during the colonial period, did not wither away with that institution's demise or the advent of free labor, a concept that did separate labor from the body and promise more autonomy to workers. Instead, as Christopher Tomlins has argued, post-Revolutionary jurists gave new life to legal principles that turned employers' property rights in their workers' labor into dominion over their lives, both on and off the job. Not all workers experienced their employers' authority in the same way. Skilled mechanics and artisans were subject to their masters' rule only while at work. An employers' authority over unskilled workers included the power to determine what they wore, what they ate, where they lived, what they did in their leisure time, and with whom they associated. Menial laborers subject to these restrictions were likely to be African Americans, recent immigrants, or white women. But race and gender were not the only variables in this equation. Poverty, particularly the need to labor for others, created a situation where otherwise free white men had to sell property rights in themselves to others.[50]

In general, the more property rights individuals were forced to surrender, the more complete their subordination tended to be. Slaves, who could claim no property rights, sat at the far end of this spectrum, below free wives and children. Yet the relationship was complicated, because the loss of property rights was not necessarily permanent or all-consuming. People lost and acquired them, depending on the context. The movement could result from a formal change in status. Individual women moved in and out of the status "wife," which gave white men property rights to them. Children grew up, laborers' contracts ended, and even slaves could become free. The nature of property within localized law emphasized context, not rights. Husbands, masters, or employers might assert extensive property rights in their slaves, wives, or workers, but that did not mean their claims would be recognized. These dynamics are illustrated in the experiences of white men whose lack of property placed them on the outer borders of an otherwise privileged legal status. Forced to hire out their labor to others, yet certain of the rights that came with their race and gender, they regularly collided with their employers. Many southern employers gave a broad interpretation to the property rights they acquired in their laborers, keeping track of where, when, how fast, and in what manner common laborers and even tenants and overseers performed their assigned tasks. When orders were not followed or the work was judged unsatisfactory, they summarily dismissed workers, often without pay. They expected to exert control over other aspects of their workers' lives as well: insufficiently deferential demeanor, intemperance, and even disorderly domestic habits were considered legitimate reasons for disciplinary action or dismissal. Those expectations fed more generalized claims to control over the lives of propertyless men. In South Carolina, local communities made extensive use of the vagrancy statute to discipline poor men who refused to submit to the control of an employer. W. J. McKain, of Kershaw District, became suspicious when Henry Tie, who was "idle," refused his offer of work. Another witness told a similar story, just as negative in tone. These men expected Tie to jump up and accept their "offers" with gratitude, because he was unengaged and had no resources to support himself. When Tie did not, they filed vagrancy charges against him. The excessive assertion of self-interest in bargaining for employment was also considered problematic. The general complaint against Fred Wilbanks, of Spartanburg District, was that "he wont work much unless paid first." Edmond Thacker also expected too much. When his wife died, he refused to apprentice his children, hoping instead to "keep them together a while longer." To do so, he tried to get the highest wages and the most flexibility possible from his employers. As Lewis Prichett explained, he "offered to hire [Thacker] to work" for "37 ½ cts per day." But Thacker "refused to work for that sum, he would not work for less than 50 cts." His demands angered not just Prichett but others who testified that Thacker was in no position to dictate the terms of employment and should have accepted whatever work was offered.[51]

Unlike most wives and slaves, poor white men had some leverage to evade or challenge others' demands. A number of antebellum employers recognized that situation and chose not to expend their authority. Others, in futility, sought submission to their demands, realizing too late that their own credit was insufficient to achieve their ends in this particular context. One particularly frustrated employer was Levi Davis of Anderson District, South Carolina. As Davis later explained, he hired Joseph Campbell in 1833 to cut wheat. But Campbell only worked one day and then "fooled" around and "drank up what spirits [Davis] had got for harvest." From this point on, Davis could not get rid of his troublesome worker. He hid the liquor, but Campbell found it and took it out to the woods for a drinking spree. From there, Campbell launched a series of assaults against his unfortunate employer, raiding Davis's meat house three times and stealing the cider that was stored there. Then, in the final incident, Campbell "strip[ped] himself naked and went about his house showing his nakedness particularly to [Davis's] children." Campbell's "conduct" toward Davis's niece, who was there at the time, "was very scandalous so much that she had to return home immediately to get shut of him." Although the conflict played out in particularly dramatic ways, the underlying issues were not unusual. Davis tried and failed to establish his authority over Joseph Campbell, a white man who bullied his employer into submission with tactics that would have been difficult if not impossible for either slaves or white women to use. But Campbell's victory did not invalidate the structural basis of employers' power over their laborers. Unwilling to put up with such shenanigans, Campbell's next employer had him convicted of vagrancy. Even so, Campbell and other poor white men had more credit at their disposal than slaves or white women, simply because they were white, male, and free.[52]

Localized law distinguished among property that took the form of people, just as it did with other kinds of property. The process recognized differences among those in whom others held property rights. The status of servants who were free white men was always superior to that of free wives or slaves. The localized legal process also acknowledged differences among people within those specific categories. Not all slaves were the same; neither were all wives or all servants. Individuals in these groups had personality, or credit, that not only distinguished them from others and other forms of property but also enabled and buttressed their own claims to property.

What made people desirable as property was precisely what differentiated them from other forms of property in localized law: of all property, people had the most personality. Like land and tools, people had value for what they could do. But they had more value because they did it by themselves: they provided both the labor and the knowledge necessary for production. Those qualities meant that a person's status as property did not necessarily reduce him or her to the position of an inanimate object or grant the owner absolute authority. Even as property, people remained connected to the peace precisely because their personalities made them central to the preservation of social order. Within the peace, it was possible to be both a person and property at the same time without contradiction — a striking contrast to most law books, in which these categories were distinct, and often mutually exclusive.[53]

The unique qualities of persons meant that they were the form of property that generated the most numerous and conflicting claims. As property, people came with their own desires and their own connections to families and communities. In fact, slavery and marriage, the very institutions that defined African Americans, women, and poor people as property, magnified the social effects of subordination by incorporating them into dense social networks. Husbands had property rights in their wives' bodies, land, earnings, and children. Wives, however, were more than just wives; they were also daughters, mothers, neighbors, and their own persons, with their own desires. As wives and mothers, women could claim interests in household production, family property, and the welfare of their children. As mothers, women built their own relationships with their children, which tied them to their children's families after they grew up. As daughters, they were products of existing marriages, connected to families who maintained

166

strong interests in their female relatives. As neighbors, they had their own social ties, because married women were expected to fulfill certain responsibilities to other women and families in their communities. In the lives of many women, the strength of those relationships was obvious, even to their husbands.

Unlike marriage, which solidified women's ties to others, slavery could alienate slaves from their own families and communities. But slaves' position as property also placed them firmly within existing communities of slaves and of neighboring whites, with all the attendant ties and expectations. All those people had interests in slaves, just as slaves' position of subordination within the social order gave them claims to material possessions, their own lives, and the lives of others. Those ties affirmed their subordination, as *both* property and subjects of the peace.

■ ■ ■

THE PROCESSES OF LOCALIZED LAW existed alongside state law, even in matters of property, which was the preoccupation of state leaders and state law in the decades following the Revolution. Localized law did not have its own set of principles, separate from state law, by which property cases were judged. Indeed, the notion of a definite body of principles contradicted the logic of peace as practiced in localized law. Since most property matters did not fall within the purview of the peace, they were handled as private matters, governed by the highly formalized body of law that was elaborated at the state level and overseen by professional lawyers. Property appeared in a different legal context in localized law. When property showed up in that context, it was attached to complaints about disorder and was handled according to the same logic applied to other disruptions of the peace. These separate yet coexisting approaches to property suggest how distinct localized law was from state law. In localized law, the possession of property depended on credit, not enumerated rights. Credit was not an abstraction in this context. It was locally based, built up through years of interactions with people in their communities. That was why the possession of property for slaves and wives, in particular, could seem so capricious. Just because one wife or one slave could make claims to property did not mean that any other wife or slave — either within or outside that community — could do so. The next chapter turns to that issue, exploring how the legal claims of wives and slaves fared within localized law.

Wives' and slaves' actions in law did not make the hierarchies of southern society any less rigid, the inequalities any less stark, or the experience of subordination any less brutal. But it did make for a complicated social landscape in which an array of factors located each individual in it. Slavery still confined all slaves, even though the experience of all slaves was not uniform. Similarly, marriage constrained all wives, despite the wide range of differences among them. By extension, all white men did not exercise the same authority in the same way. In the logic of localized law, uniformity was not the point. That would become the standard in state law, where reformers attempted to put all these different people into distinct, uniform legal categories — slaves, wives, and white men — just as they were doing to different forms of property.

6

Wasted Substance
The Operation and Regulation of Patriarchy

Divorce petitioners struggled to strike just the right tone of virtuous victimization in their narratives of marital strife. Very few succeeded, which is surprising, given the obvious and obviously well-known conventions of divorce petitions. Petitioners knew enough about the rules to invoke the legal causes for divorce and to cast themselves as hapless innocents in conflicts beyond their control. Invariably, they portrayed themselves as dutiful wives and husbands who had endured long years of suffering at the hands of dissolute spouses. But the devil was in the details, particularly when state legislatures handled divorces. To obtain a divorce or a legal separation, petitioners had to explain why their particular circumstances warranted the passage of their own, private act.[1] Here was where they usually stumbled, as they tried to force the unruly details of their lives into the required formula. Refusing to stay put, those details told other stories.[2]

Ambrose Dough's tale of marital woe, for instance, was revealing in ways he never intended. A sailor who lived in Currituck County on the east coast of North Carolina, Dough married Barbara Midgett in 1802. He was eighteen and she was fifteen. Soon thereafter, he went on an extended voyage and left Midgett alone on the seventy-six-acre farm that she had brought into the marriage. When he returned, he found that she was living with another man, whom she called her husband and with whom she had two children. He tried to reconcile, but she refused. She was heartless. He was devastated, and clearly deserving of a divorce.[3] Dough's interpretation did not quite hold together, however. By his own account, it would appear that Barbara Midgett had followed accepted community customs regarding remarriage. Although legal precedents required seven years' absence to establish a spouse's death, local communities could be more flexible in their accounting. Midgett was able to enter into another marriage before the prescribed waiting period expired. Two particularly telling details suggest the community's acquiescence to her new marriage: she lived openly in this second relationship, among those who knew her first husband; and she and her current husband retained possession of the farm. On his return, Dough tried to claim that property, which could have been construed as his under the rules of coverture. But Midgett and her current husband refused to surrender it. Their neighbors apparently supported that position; even if the good people of Currituck County thought coverture applied, they did not consider it sufficient to establish Dough's property rights in this instance. Dough grudgingly accepted the inevitability of that conclusion. In the divorce petition, he even used Midgett's possession of the farm as an example of the unlikelihood of reconciliation. The North Carolina legislature rejected Dough's request, leaving him in a particularly awkward situation. Dough could neither reclaim nor relinquish his position as husband.[4]

Although the voice of his one-time wife, Barbara Midgett, was not recorded in Dough's divorce petition, she loomed large in the conflict that prompted it. To see her presence, it is necessary to shift the focus from the North Carolina legislature to the localized legal system and the protection of the peace in Currituck County. After all, what did the legislature's rejection of Ambrose Dough's petition really mean? Did it mean that Barbara Midgett was still his wife? Did it compromise her new family's claim to the farm? In a word: no. Barbara Midgett never needed to obtain a legal divorce, even if she could have forced herself into one of the categories necessary to obtain one, because she already had secured public recognition of her second marriage. Acceptance located her relationship within the peace of the community, endowing it with legal legitimacy of a kind not based in coverture or the statutory causes for divorce. The outcome suggests that Barbara Midgett had more credit in the community than did Ambrose Dough. Sailors, as a group, were regarded as disreputable. Even if Dough was an exception, his local ties would have frayed during his long absence. By contrast, Barbara Midgett stayed put, cultivating community connections. She also cultivated the Midgett land, the legacy of her family, backed by Midgett patriarchs. Her credit, built through dense local networks, protected her from the harassment of a former husband, returned from a watery grave, who tried to take away her family's land and her new life. Credit was not just about the superior character of Barbara Midgett. Credit forged links between Midgett and the peace: it legitimized her new life—her husband, children, and farm—as established relationships of the kind that localized law was supposed to protect. By contrast, Ambrose Dough had spent his credit or, in a phrase that appeared later in divorce petitions, he had "wasted his substance." "Wasted substance" signaled misspent credit, not just its absence, and it compromised a man's claims both to property and to the social networks that defined the peace.[5]

As the case of Ambrose Dough and Barbara Midgett suggests, patriarchal authority was inseparable from particular people and places in localized law. Building on the analysis of property in the previous chapter, this chapter explores the dynamics of patriarchal authority, which produced dramatic variations in what local courts allowed individual patriarchs to own and to do. The range is most evident in legal matters involving wives and slaves—both in cases that they initiated and in those brought on their behalf. Departing from established conventions in the historiography, the analysis does not focus on whether such cases challenged the principles of patriarchal authority. That question not only misconstrues the legal logic that made these cases possible, but also fails to capture their importance for subordinate southerners. The issue was not *whether* they should be subordinate, but *what* their subordination should entail. Patriarchy, per se, was never in question in these cases, because it was the patriarchal construction of the peace that allowed conflicts involving wives and slaves to appear within the localized legal system. As the metaphorical source of all patriarchs' power, the peace allowed southerners to challenge the actions of individual patriarchs without undermining the principles underlying their authority. Although that rubric imposed conceptual constraints, southerners nonetheless used it to raise fundamental issues about the quality of their own lives and the character of the social order in which they lived. They questioned what forms patriarchy should take and how its authority should be exercised. Invoking the peace, legal officials handled these conflicts as individualized instances justified by the credit (or discredit) of the litigants and the conditions in which they lived. The outcomes resolved particular conflicts, maintaining the peace as it was defined in specific localities. These variations neither elevated the status of other subordinates nor undermined the authority of other white men. To the extent that dependents could exercise influence in localized law, it was because their claims did not take the form of rights that could be extended to others similarly situated or universalized to other sorts of subordinates.

Wives' and slaves' subordination within the patriarchal peace gave them legal influence, however circumscribed, by creating connections that made their presence and their problems visible within the localized system. The credit of wives and slaves, which determined their ability to mobilize those networks, was based in the fulfillment of their prescribed roles. Wives and slaves also spent credit for their own ends, including divorces and legal separations in which free women charged husbands and fathers with abuse, and cases in which slaves defended customary privileges they had negotiated. In these legal matters, subordinates leaned into the limits, working creatively within established customary practices, sometimes embroidering and embellishing them, sometimes turning them completely inside out and refashioning them to fit their own circumstances. It was difficult for wives and slaves to instigate legal suits on their own behalf, even in the localized legal system. Because of their status, free wives — even free black wives — were in a better position to do so than slaves. But the most interesting cases involving wives and slaves neither turned on their initiative nor reflected their intentions. These were cases in which subordinates fended off charges brought against them. Even well-connected wives found themselves in the middle of such legal matters. In these instances, wives and slaves did not so much pilot their social networks as get carried along in the wake, often to places they never anticipated going, let alone desired to be. Yet these cases still reveal the legal importance of the wives' and slaves' networks.

These cases shaped the legal terms of patriarchy, even though they did not alter the legal principles of subordination. Whether initiating complaints or defending themselves, wives and slaves did more than affirm existing customs within an established social order. They shaped customs, turning them into usable legal principles that defined the boundaries of patriarchal authority within the peace. That was possible because the peace was a legal process — a means, not an end — that sometimes ended up in surprising places. In the post-Revolutionary South, localized law mediated conflicts in tightly knit communities that were also heterogeneous, characterized by diversity, dissent, and dramatic social, economic, and political changes that brought the Atlantic world to the backcountry. When southerners invoked the peace, they did so with very different ideas about what maintaining order entailed. Wives and slaves, in particular, pulled at the outer edges of the peace in ways that stretched legal discourse, enveloping a much broader array of ideas than would otherwise have been the case. The results reinforced the existing order, but in a way that dispersed patriarchal authority and varied its exercise across place, over time, and among individuals. Those variations were one of the primary complaints of legal reformers, who wished to regularize the rules.

WIVES AND THE SOCIAL CONTEXT OF PROPERTY

When marriages worked, wives' property interests coexisted peacefully with those of their husbands. That balance, reached through the hard work at the root of all successful relationships, became part of the social order that the localized legal system was charged to protect. Wives' claims acquired legal legitimacy, as one of many legal principles that came into play when marriages degenerated to the point where husbands and wives sought outside intervention. For that reason, broken marriages are particularly revealing: the marital norms that most people accepted became visible at the point of dissolution, when they had been violated. At these exceptional moments, the historical documents capture what usually went unrecorded. Wives did not speak with one voice; they advocated for themselves, as distinct individuals, not as members of a group with common interests. Sometimes they did not speak at all. Instead, families, friends, or neighbors took up the cause as their own. Regardless of who spoke, though, legal matters involving wives tended to emphasize conceptions of patriarchal authority that limited husbands' individual rights by situating marriages within broader familial and community networks.

When marriages went awry, the conflicts often played out through property. Property was both necessary and symbolic; while essential for economic support, it also symbolized the balance of authority between husbands and wives. Wives who filed for divorce or separation had tolerated their husbands' bad behavior, neglect, and absence for years. It was property, in both its material and symbolic forms, that drove them to seek a formal, legal remedy. Specifically, wives petitioned when husbands appropriated property in which they also had interests. For these women, the seizure of vital resources represented abuse and betrayal of such magnitude that it foreclosed any possibility of reconciliation. The same dynamics surfaced in other legal matters involving husbands and wives. Wives expected support for their claims, because their possession of certain kinds of property had been accommodated within marriage, without negating their husbands' individual rights or patriarchal status. Even estranged husbands recognized the legitimacy of their wives' claims. As Edward Southwick informed the North Carolina legislature, his wife "took with her all the property that originally belonged to her and also a considerable part of his property."[6]

Wives' claims to property can be difficult to see, let alone interpret, because they became visible in legal contexts that also transformed them. Divorce and separation cases provide the most dramatic example. In this legal context, with deep roots in professionalized property law, it was necessary to define women's property claims in terms of individual rights, so as to separate them from those of their husbands. The legal system also categorized these matters as "private," reflecting the emphasis on individual property rights in the statutory construction of divorce and separation. Outside of the prescribed legal rules of divorce and separation, however, marital disputes were never private matters. Nor were they actually centered on the conflicting property rights of those involved. Wives, in particular, underscored that point by bringing legal claims from outside the realm of formalized property law into their petitions.

Some of the most contentious marital disputes involved resources brought into the marriage by wives. Property, particularly landed estates, symbolized women's ties to their own families. Those ties figured in the lives of husbands as well as wives, as the voluminous collections of letters in southern archives indicate. Wives were also daughters, sisters, cousins, nieces, aunts, and mothers, just as husbands were also sons, brothers, cousins, nephews, uncles, and fathers. While these networks incorporated friends and neighbors, extended family ties featured prominently. In most instances, marriage and parenthood strengthened rather than attenuated these relationships for both men and women. As men and women took on new roles as husbands and wives, they also acquired new responsibilities for their own kindred. Wives balanced their familial obligations, keeping up with their own relatives while also tending to the needs of their new households. Some husbands, however, saw the continued presence and influence of their wives' families as a challenge to their own authority. In a range of cases, from divorce and separation to incidents that ended in violence and even murder, husbands blamed meddling in-laws for the breakdown of the marriage. Thomas Chandler's response to the divorce petition of his wife, Sarah, was typical. Sarah, who filed complaints of domestic abuse against her husband on two separate occasions before petitioning for divorce, charged her husband with repeated, particularly sadistic acts of violence. Chandler responded with denial, finding fault with her family instead. "The disquiet which has existed in his family," he insisted, "and the differences existing between [him and his wife] have been principally created by the mischievous and malicious interferences of his said wife's mother & her friends."[7]

Property fueled the flames. Because so many southerners saw their property as a collective resource, they were unwilling to surrender it to their female relatives' husbands, who could take it out of the family of origin forever. Even when lineage restrictions were not outlined in formal legal instruments, they were still assumed. Husbands owned the property of their wives' families only as long as they used it for the benefit of that family's descendants — as determined by watchful relatives. One of the reasons Sarah Chandler's relatives interfered was because they did not want her husband to drink away their family's future. Concerns for their family's property interests and Sarah and her children's welfare were inseparable. Esther Preslar felt confident enough about that general principle to make the point directly to her husband. After drinking too much and working too little, he confronted her, insisting that "he wanted his land back." "He should have it," she spat back, "if he behaved himself." When he responded with violence, she left to go to her father's house, an act that underscored the source of her leverage. If the land had been his, not just his to use, he would not have needed to bully it out of her. Since it was the legacy of his wife's family, he needed to behave in order to control it — and her.[8]

Augustus Converse fell afoul of his wife's family for similar reasons. The problem was the estate of his wife, Marion Singleton Deveaux, which she controlled, through her father's will, to pass on to her children. While Marion's first husband had accepted those terms, Augustus Converse could not reconcile himself to the situation in which "all his rights as husband were subordinate to her claim." He tried everything from seduction to force to get it, but only succeeded in alienating both Marion and her relatives, whose support he needed to get around the terms of the will. Like Richard Singleton, the family patriarch, Marion and the rest of the family saw Singleton land as the Singleton legacy. Ultimately the situation deteriorated to the point where Marion filed for a separation in equity court, an action supported by her family. Opposing it, Augustus lodged charges against Marion's family for "unwarrantable interference in his domestic concerns." But he was unable to convince Marion of her "duty to him" and "the impolicy of allowing herself to be changed, and shifted in opinion by every suggestion of her relatives." What Augustus saw as a legitimate assertion of patriarchal authority, Marion and her family saw as incompetence, born of insecurity and imperiousness. In their eyes, his inability to accept Marion's responsibilities as a Singleton and his self-serving efforts to commandeer her family's property proved his failure. One of Marion's aunts referred to him as "that grasping bad evil Man."[9]

The patriarchal imperatives of wives' families confounded the construction of coverture on the professionalized side of property law, which turned family resources into the husband's private domain, defined in terms of his property rights. Marion's separation case was as much about the Singleton family's estate as it was about her welfare. In fact, the conflation of Marion's interests and those of her family was the point: she remained part of her family in a way that limited her husband's property rights and diluted his patriarchal authority. When Marion was isolated with Augustus Converse, she had no choice but to endure his psychological bullying and physical violence. Within the context of her family, though, it was Augustus who was vulnerable. Marion stayed for extended periods at the homes of her kin in New York, Philadelphia, and Virginia as well as South Carolina. When the marriage fell apart, the entire Singleton clan rallied to Marion's side. They not only encouraged Marion to file for a separation but also crafted a legal settlement, in which Augustus received a substantial settlement for relinquishing all claims on Singleton family property and leaving South Carolina. That outcome depended on the aid of influential family friends, who included such legal luminaries as Henry William DeSaussure, the executor of Marion's father's estate. Marion even dropped "Converse" from her name, which is why she appears in the archival records as Marion Singleton Deveaux—Robert Deveaux was Marion's first husband.[10] No wonder so many wives dragged their feet or remained behind when their husbands moved west. Doing so removed wives from patriarchal networks in which they had recognized claims on family resources.[11]

Wives took a similar view of property that they accumulated through their own labor. While accepting the property rights husbands acquired through coverture, wives tended to see them as a privilege contingent on the fulfillment of specific duties. Many wives assumed an ongoing role for themselves in this arrangement, allowing husbands the use of their property without surrendering all claims to it. When their husbands proved unworthy of that trust, wives expected to take the property back or, if it was gone, to be released from further obligations. That logic, which characterized many separation and divorce petitions, was particularly clear in Tabitha Fox's petition to obtain economic and bodily independence from her husband—a divorce from bed and board. Before her marriage, Fox had worked as a weaver and ran her father's household. She "applied her earnings to the purchase and raising of stock and procuring articles of furniture and utensils for house keeping." By the time of her marriage, she had amassed an impressive amount of property, including "a valuable horse, bridle and saddle, 6 head of cattle, 10 head of Hogs, 20 head of sheep, 2 excellent beds & furniture, valuable case of drawers, tables, and a very good supply of Household and kitchen furniture." While married, Fox applied "her" property to the needs of the household, subsuming it within the property that her husband "owned," although she still maintained her own sense of possession over those items she contributed to the household economy. Her willingness to do so ended when her husband abandoned his own marital obligations. Then his rights no longer applied to her property.[12]

Wives saw labor, one of the most valuable forms of property, in more expansive terms, as a family resource that never could be reduced to a personal possession. By that logic, wives maintained interests in their husbands' labor as well as their own. Those assumptions framed wives' complaints about their husbands' indolence, one of the most common of marital grievances, which ran through divorce petitions, vagrancy cases, domestic violence prosecutions, and a range of other matters. These complaints were more about husbands' waste of collective resources than their failure to provide. That was Tabitha Fox's point. Even though her husband had already run through all the property she brought into the marriage, she carefully listed all those items. Why? In the context of her petition, the list was akin to double-entry bookkeeping, with her positive balance on the one side and her husband's negative account on the other, canceling out everything she had done. Fox carefully separated her labor from that of her husband, at the same time highlighting what should have tied them together: a marriage that established the collective interests of the family. Wives like Tabitha Fox expected to contribute to the household economy. They understood that their husbands would not always be able to contribute regularly. Even so, they accepted their husbands' authority to direct the family's labor, for the benefit of the household. But they drew the line when husbands squandered that resource and the property they had accumulated. Esther Preslar captured the reasoning with stunning clarity: when husbands ceased to "behave," they lost access to family resources.[13]

Wives' views of labor were rooted in economic realities. It was impossible for most men to support their families through their labor alone, despite the rhetoric of male independence and the ideology that associated women with a domestic realm characterized by altruistic sentiment and, later, as a separate sphere unto itself.[14] The memoir of North Carolina's Edward Isham underscores the point, although from the perspective of a man who took women's labor for granted. Like other men, he seems to have transformed the masculine prerogative to direct women's labor into the right of appropriation. Just prior to his execution for murder in the 1850s, Isham recounted his life to his lawyer, a young and completely enthralled David Schenck, who later became a prominent political leader. The story has all the hallmarks of a tall tale, tracing Isham's dramatic exploits in drinking, gambling, fighting, and womanizing across the Southeast, from North Carolina to Alabama. The one thing that does ring true, largely because neither Isham nor Schenck intended to highlight it, is Isham's reliance on women. There were many women in his life, both lovers who chose his company and relatives who did not. Some women followed him, perhaps with the mistaken impression that he would settle down and support them. They did not last long, because it was usually Isham who was in need of support. As a result, he followed women himself, seeking them out when he needed shelter and sustenance. Most of these women were barely hanging on, but they were the ones with houses, food, and resources — and none of that was because of Edward Isham.[15]

While embellished to the point of fiction, Isham's account contains elements of economic truth. Cash and credit were tight for decades following the Revolutionary War. Although prosperity followed the cotton boom in the early nineteenth century, land became scarce. Prices soared in settled areas, while speculators gobbled up large tracts in the West. The volatility of the economy added a new dimension of instability, as hard-won gains disappeared in the dips of the business cycle. Even the prosperous were vulnerable. Propertyless young men had it worse, because there were few alternatives for them that did not require large initial capital outlays.[16]

Wives' economic contributions were crucial in this economic environment. They provided access to capital through their family networks. As the records of R. G. Dun and Co. indicate, kinship networks supported many a man who maintained the appearance of independence as a household head who provided for his family. Men may have managed the family resources, but the property belonged to their wives' families or their wives, who retained control through a trustee or other legal device. In some cases, the terms were dictated by the wives' families; in others, the property was in wives' names to shield it from creditors. Either way, the technicalities of ownership did not affect men's credit in the daily life of local communities. But it did matter within the increasingly formalized rules of property law on the civil side: in that legal world, husbands had no credit if their wives owned the property. That was why R. G. Dun's locally based informers spent a lot of time, with ears to the ground, trying to discern the "real" owners.[17]

Women provided crucial economic support through their labor. Domestic produce — textiles, linens, clothing, butter, eggs, poultry, fruits, and vegetables — kept families going in times of economic uncertainty. Consider the differences between Tabitha Fox and her husband. Fox described him as a "likely" man. But he had no property other than a "pretty good mare" at the time of their marriage. Landless and without kin or patronage, he had few options. By contrast, Fox could market her skills. After her husband went through all the family property and abandoned her, she gave up on farming, left the countryside, found work for her older children in a cotton mill, and "commenced weaving again" to support her family. In the account she gave, they were getting by on their own.[18] Like so many wives, Tabitha Fox stepped up when her husband stumbled. She expected to do that, as most wives did. What she and other wives could not countenance was the assertion of their husbands' interests over those of their families. According to Fox, her husband spent everything he and his family earned on himself, as if he were not married at all. The phrase "wasted his substance" communicated all the elements of that situation: a husband squandered all the family's resources that he was supposed to manage, including land, movable goods, the labor of his wife and children, his own ability to labor, and even his good name. Tabitha ran out of patience when her husband reappeared, with the intent of living off her earnings, after she had established herself on her own. She might have been able to contend with his demands, but not with those of his creditors. When dissolute husbands were distant memories, their property rights came back to haunt their wives through creditors. They arrived with lawyers and the considerable arsenal of property law, which included the force of the state, to seize wives' property in payment for their husbands' outstanding debts.[19]

The looming presence of creditors in wives' petitions indicates the pull of opposing legal trends at the state level. Later legal developments, which gave husbands absolute rights in the labor of their household dependents, are discussed in more detail in the next chapter. Acting through localized law, Fox, like other aggrieved wives, used the good order of the peace to check those developments and to constrain their husbands' prerogatives. Husbands could direct the household's labor for the interests of the family, but they could not appropriate their own or their wives' labor for their sole benefit. The clearest articulation came in the context of legal cases where wives' claims were forced into the rubric of competing property rights. The logic was nonetheless rooted in a definition of labor as a communal resource rather than private property. From that perspective, husbands' property rights in their wives' labor were always contingent, because they were based on their fulfillment of marital responsibilities in which absolute control of their wives' labor was never really a possibility.

Wives limited their husbands' rights in their bodies. The most dramatic examples involve domestic violence, a particularly extreme expression of husbands' wielding power over their wives' bodies. To challenge abuse, wives leaned on neighbors and kin, acting on a view of marriage in which married women remained connected to the social order, rather than being isolated within their husbands' households. In Spartanburg District, for instance, Mrs. Littlefield regularly sought shelter with her neighbors when her husband turned violent. Mrs. Watkins, of nearby Laurens District, did the same, spreading news in the neighborhood that her husband "whipt" her. In both instances, the women's information about their husbands featured prominently in their husbands' vagrancy trials. In these and other cases, community members had to pick up the pieces of broken domestic relations, whether they liked it or not. Churches mediated domestic disputes as part of their mission to promote harmony among all their congregants.[20] So did family members, as North Carolina's Westley Rhodes discovered. After he beat his wife "in a most cruel manner," she "fled to her father's house." Her mother came marching back to her son-in-law's house, where she "reprimanded him for his conduct" and "struck him with a tobacco stem which she had picked up on the road." Intervention required a wife's active participation; she had to make her problems known before her family and neighbors could take action.[21]

It was a short step from informal community forums to the localized legal system. Domestic violence figured in a range of legal matters, including divorce and vagrancy, and involved free women, both white and black, from varied economic backgrounds. Domestic violence also appeared as a public legal matter in its own right. The prosecution of wife beating as a breach of the peace was routine in localized law. Magistrates issued peace warrants, an action that brought husbands under public scrutiny by forcing them to post bond to keep the peace toward their wives. It is difficult to imagine that the arrest and the posting of bond did anything to improve a husband's temper. Still, peace warrants allowed wives a way out of the confines of domestic privacy, by ensuring public monitoring of the situation and promising penalties for further abuse. With this process, wives legally transformed their husbands' violence from personal conflicts into illegal acts that endangered the public order. They also affirmed a view of marriage in which their husbands' patriarchal authority did not sever wives' ties to the social order.[22]

The legal implications of wives' claims emerged in sharp relief when local officials took the next step and prosecuted husbands for assaulting their wives. To do so, officials invoked the peace, construing wives' injuries as a threat to the social order and forcing husbands to account for their actions. The South Carolina case heard by Judge Elihu Hall Bay, which opened chapter 2 of this book, is only one example. Domestic violence appeared on the court dockets as a criminal matter in both North and South Carolina throughout the entire period of this study, from 1787 into the 1840s. These cases made their way through the system with little fanfare or note, precisely because the notion that wives' injuries constituted an offense to the peace was well established within localized legal culture. They surfaced regularly, but not frequently; it is impossible to be more exact than that because of the incomplete nature of the records. Records exist for those cases that were heard by grand juries or went to trial at the district or superior court level. Those courts dealt with domestic violence cases anywhere from once a year to once a decade, depending on the county. But the existing records underestimate the number of such complaints, since many of the cases that magistrates fielded went unrecorded.[23] Indeed, the fact that the conflict had reached the district or superior court indicated that the tide of public opinion had already turned against defendants. A significant portion of defendants pled guilty. The courts took these cases seriously, issuing convictions and sentences that ranged from the symbolic to the severe. In Kershaw District, for instance, Christopher Cain was fined a dollar in 1803; Henry Butler was imprisoned for twelve months in 1824; and David Jamison was fined $20 and imprisoned for three months in 1836.[24]

That domestic violence cases appeared on court dockets at all is surprising, given the legal and cultural impediments to prosecuting husbands. Those impediments—which took the form of long-standing patriarchal principles that gave husbands the authority to discipline their wives and that discounted the credibility of wives' testimony—remained in place, despite the prosecution of domestic violence. The crime was the injury to the public body, which placed the legal emphasis on the physical act: on what abusive husbands did, not why they did it. Explanations about the cause of the conflict—from either the wife's or the husband's point of view—rarely made it into the record. Usually the documents contain only generic language indicating that the wife experienced violence that breached the peace. Typical were the case documents of Mary Jamison, which stated that her husband "did assault & beat the deponent & that he has frequently at other times beaten her & threatened her with great violence." Further explanation was unnecessary, since the physical evidence of abuse usually corroborated the complaint.[25] When officials did elaborate, they specified the weapons used, the length of the ordeal, and the severity of the blows, presumably to buttress the case. Kershaw District officials were meticulous in this regard, blazing a trail through the grisly underside of marriage. In

1807 Mary McAdams claimed that her husband assaulted her "by aiming at her head a dutch oven, which had she not warded it off by receiving the blow on her left arm, must have taken her life." He "did also some time before beat her in a cruel manner with a pair of fir[e] tongs to the danger of her life." In 1818 Mary Parker listed three incidents of violence, substantiated by her neighbors. The first time, her husband "beat hir . . . was with his fist & kicked her in the most violent manner." The second time "was with a hickery stick over the hips & loins while he held hir with hir head between his knees." The third "was with his fist, and by butting her & forcing her head against the wall with the appearant intention of braking her scull." That time, her husband also drew "his knife and swore that he would cut [her] throat, & forced her to drink ardent spirits." In 1824 Sarah Butler claimed that her husband "did shoot at the body of her the said Sarah and that she has reason to believe and does believe that it was with a premeditated intention to murder her the said Sarah." These details were crucial in cases that depended on establishing the severity of the violence wives had experienced. Brutality had to reach beyond the discretionary authority all husbands could exercise to upset the good order of the community at large.[26]

Wives' desperation is painfully audible in the documents. They begged local officials to act, corroborating their complaints with the physical evidence of their bruised and bloody bodies. But their desperation also carried a strong undertone of confidence: not the self-possession of women standing up for themselves to challenge existing norms, but the certainty of women whose lives were deeply rooted within their communities, who were familiar with local customs, and who felt entitled to support, given their particular circumstances. As these women saw it, they had experienced forms of physical violence that fell outside their husbands' patriarchal prerogatives and were certain that existing social networks should do something about it. Yet they also knew that support would not materialize without effort. They had to mobilize their own connections to neighbors and kin and push them to acknowledge the problem. Wives talked. They displayed their injuries. They appeared on doorsteps, sometimes with angry husbands on their heels. They even posted notices in newspapers advertising their husbands' bad behavior. When wives failed to create allies, they nonetheless turned reluctant bystanders into material witnesses. Those networks amplified their voices and extended the scope of the problem, transforming a marital conflict between husband and wife into a larger community concern.[27]

The work required to obtain redress was never easy. But if wives struggled to make their voices heard in domestic violence cases, they did so within a system where the logic of their subordination neither isolated them within private households nor exempted their husbands from public scrutiny. By contrast, wives ran into trouble when individual rights replaced the collective interests of the peace in the legal system. The new logic made it nearly impossible to prosecute husbands; wives' injuries could not qualify as a violation of their rights, since they were not legally recognized individuals who could claim the full array of rights in their own names. The rubric of rights also turned the cases toward the reasons for the conflict, with husbands defending their actions in terms of a violation of their rights. They made claims to their wives' services: food preparation, housekeeping, sex, child care, and emotional support as well as financial assistance in the household economy, when required. Then they stretched these expectations, turning services that wives provided within the context of a marital relationship into individual rights. When wives denied them those rights, they could retaliate, however they saw fit, to secure what was theirs. Husbands also insisted on domestic privacy, arguing that their rights as husbands turned the marriage into a private relationship. Husbands in the late eighteenth and early nineteenth centuries construed their wives' domestic services and the marital relationship in similar terms. Many may have seen themselves as "disciplining" wives who had not provided adequate domestic services, which were their due as husbands—at least as they saw it. But such views did not carry the legal weight that they later would: husbands' claims, and especially their use of violence to enforce them, did not always comport with the peace.[28]

The standard of rights, operative today, still foils the prosecution of domestic violence. Given the pervasiveness of that standard and its attendant difficulties, it is no wonder that historians have assumed that wives in the nineteenth century, who had far fewer rights than wives in the twentieth, had no legal recourse against domestic violence. Yet they did, because rights were not the basis for mounting criminal charges against husbands. Since the maintenance of quiet, orderly households was central to the community, husbands who beat their wives could be charged with disrupting the peace.[29]

Wives' domestic violence cases shared important elements with other cases of assault against women. Women, both married and unmarried, were frequent targets of violence, usually at the hands of male neighbors or kin, although some women attacked other women. Some of these acts had nothing to do with the fact that the victims were women: in a society where violence was commonplace, women were not exempt. As women, though, they were particularly vulnerable. Some men expanded patriarchal principles that established husbands' authority over their wives to make broad claims of masculine authority over all women. Women's subordinate status also lowered their credit, opening them up to scorn and abuse from men and other women. Regardless of the reasons for the violence, women fought back, using the same strategies that wives employed in domestic violence cases. If the victim was married, her husband was usually listed as the prosecutor. Not only was his presence legally necessary, but it lent credibility to his wife's claims. Generally husbands played supporting roles, particularly if the incident occurred in their absence. Their wives were the ones who initiated the process and provided all the details necessary for the case to go forward in the courts. Unmarried women prosecuted cases on their own behalf, bringing in neighbors and kin to provide statements and to testify to their good credit. Women found it easier to prosecute cases against men who were not their husbands. Even so, they still required support to amplify their voices. Through that process, they scored important legal points, placing limits on the meaning of their subordination within the patriarchal order. Their position as women did not make them equally subordinate to all men; nor did it mean that they were so degraded and isolated as to have no recourse against abuse when it occurred.[30]

Not all women could transform violence into a violation of the peace. Their ability to do so depended on credit, the assumed, unstated context that made explanations of domestic conflicts unnecessary. In 1818, for instance, fourteen men submitted a petition affirming the credit of Mary Parker, who filed charges against her husband for domestic abuse. "We the subscribers," they wrote, "do hereby certify that since Mrs. Parker . . . has lived in our neighbourhood, we have never seen any thing in her conduct, & deportment but what was fair & becoming." Because she had credit, her complaint had validity. The fact that her husband's credit was poor made her more believable. He noted as much in his own statement. "Some of those persons who signed Mrs. Parkers good character," he admitted, "did it from principles of charity & goodness." "Others," however, "did it for the purposes of gratifying their envious and malicious designs . . . to sink him in public esteem."[31]

Consider the difference between Sarah Chandler and Mary Meadows, both of whom lived in Granville County, North Carolina. In 1824 Sarah Chandler swore out two complaints against her husband. The first time, the magistrate issued a peace warrant. The second time, he charged her husband with assault and battery. Then, one year later, the Granville County Superior Court granted her a divorce, a case that featured evidence of her husband's abuse.[32] In their depositions, neighbors and kin emphasized the ways Thomas Chandler's behavior negatively affected the community. The severity of the abuse clearly transgressed community norms. He neglected his duties, as a neighbor as well as a husband. He fought constantly, introducing unnecessary conflict into the community and threatening vital social networks. He drank to excess and neglected to work his property as he should, failing to support his family and to fulfill his part in the economic web that knit rural communities together. He squandered the property that Sarah had brought into the marriage, threatening the patrimony of her family and their efforts to provide for their family's heirs, Sarah's children. The effects of Thomas Chandler's domestic abuse spun outward, affecting everyone in the community in direct, tangible ways. That was the basis of the criminal actions against him. That logic also figured into the divorce. When Sarah Chandler petitioned for divorce in 1826, cruelty was grounds for a separation. Yet the evidence of domestic abuse, established through the legal guise of the peace, buttressed her cause in a localized system where a jury decided her case.[33]

Evaluations of Thomas Chandler's credit dominate the records. Yet, in this case and others, the wives' credit was equally determinative. That Sarah Chandler was able to proceed with her legal suits indicates her credit's weight, which prompted the outpouring of community support. But the value of women's credit, which solidified their connections in their communities and established their place within the peace, is most apparent in cases where women had none. Mary Meadows's husband was as disreputable as Thomas Chandler. But so was Mary Meadows. Loud and opinionated, she was particularly vocal on the subject of her husband. As one witness later testified, Mary Meadows vowed that she "intended to have him [her husband] fixed at . . . court, so that he should not be scandalizing her." To that end, she complained about him repeatedly in the neighborhood, displaying a decided lack of skill in bringing her neighbors over to her side. Once, while grinding corn with several other women at a neighbor's house, she offered to work for the Duncan family for one year without pay if John Duncan would kill her husband. Susannah Duncan overheard a conversation between Mary Meadows and Thomas Murray, who had his own quarrel with her husband and had gone so far as to load a gun to shoot him before deciding against it. Mary Meadows reportedly said that "she wished that Murry [*sic*] had . . . blowed that load through him." She made a similar statement to Samuel Jackson, rebuking him for not "knock[ing]" her husband's "brains out" when the two men had fought earlier. When no aid was forthcoming, she felt compelled to take matters into her own hands. She told James Hobgood that she intended to have her husband beaten, boasting that he "would be the worst whiped [*sic*] man he (Hobgood) ever saw." The beating would be so severe, she claimed, that "his hide would not hold shucks." One week later, her husband was found murdered and emasculated, his severed testicles stuffed in his mouth. Mary Meadows and a slave named George were arrested for his murder. The documents do not divulge all the gossip that obviously surrounded this notorious case. Some of the statements suggest that Mary Meadows and George were involved in an illicit relationship, although the records do not establish that as a fact. Her neighbors' distaste for Mary Meadows had accumulated more slowly and less dramatically through daily interactions. Because of her own dismal credit, Mary Meadows's marital disputes, unlike Sarah Chandler's, became a public concern only when she became a defendant in her husband's murder.[34]

The concepts that wives articulated in these cases acquired legal resonance, even when they lost their suits. More to the point, women made the arguments that they did because they knew which points already had legitimacy within their local communities. Success in localized law generally depended on aligning one's cause with well-established customary arrangements, not departing from them. The inseparable relationship between custom and localized law meant that women played crucial roles in creating the customary foundation necessary for legal decisions in this system. Individual women drew on that foundation to ground their legal claims. In so doing, they also reinforced it, articulating cultural elements that usually went unsaid and obtaining communal sanction for them.

SLAVES AND THE SOCIAL CONSTRAINTS ON PROPERTY

Free wives remained solidly within the boundaries of the peace, because the terms of their subordination established strong social connections not just to their husbands, but also to influential neighbors and kin. Because of the dynamics of race and slavery, patriarchy took a different form for slaves, making them both more marginal and more central within the peace. Their subordinate status moved them so far to the margins that they were barely within the peace at all, a position that resulted in only limited access to the legal system. Unlike free wives, slaves could not prosecute cases themselves, even within the more fluid framework of localized law. A few slaves acquired the credit to evade those restrictions, but they were rare. At the same time, slaves' subordination was so central to the maintenance of order that it resulted in stricter controls and more severe punishments. Because legal inclusion was about maintaining their subordination within a hierarchical social order, it was hardly beneficial to slaves, in the sense of protecting or advancing their interests. As a result, legal cases do not provide as much information from or about slaves as they do about other groups of southerners. Slaves spoke in guarded voices, when they spoke at all. More often, their positions emerged indirectly, through others' narratives. Even then, the information was incomplete and difficult to follow: slaves' interests were rarely served by divulging the details of their lives to white southerners, regardless of their relationship to the issues at hand.

Within the rubric of the peace, slaves' subordination did not negate their status as subjects within the social order. That was true even when subordination took its most extreme form, reducing slaves to property. In matters involving the peace in localized law, the legal dichotomy between slaves' classification as property and as persons was not as important as it was in statutes, appellate decisions, legal treatises, and later histories. In fact, the distinction was largely irrelevant in a legal context where property could have personality and the individual rights accorded to legally recognized persons were just one approach to resolving conflicts. The adjudication of rights depended on an individual's relationship to abstract categories of legal personhood: as a free white man, a married woman, or a slave. Within localized law, however, it was slaves' subordination to specific people that established their connections to the "peace."[35]

White southerners figured prominently in slaves' legal cases. In fact, whites played such central roles that the cases were more about them than they were about the slaves in question. Those dynamics underscore the means by which slaves became visible within the peace. They appeared not in their own right, but through their connections with white southerners who either held authority over them or thought that they should: masters and mistresses, overseers, patrollers, and neighbors. The rubric of the peace, however, deflected the focus, shifting it from the individual rights of white southerners to the legal regulation of slavery. To be sure, regulation rarely worked in slaves' favor, given that their place within the social order was defined in terms of their subordination. The logic nonetheless acknowledged slaves' place as active subjects, in need of scrutiny to maintain the good order of the peace. The dynamics differed markedly from the model of property rights, which tended to objectify slaves, to sever their human connections, and to dissolve any constraints on white men's authority over them. Because slaves remained visible within the terms of the peace, legal matters involving them reveal a great deal about established customs, contested practices, and how slaves negotiated the outer limits of the peace.

Slaves found themselves in court when local conceptions of patriarchal authority clashed. Consider the case of Violet, a South Carolina slave who was charged and convicted of assaulting her mistress. At first glance, Violet's violent actions seem like an irrational outburst. But that is because the details come through the Burgesses, the white family in whose household she was working and who had every reason to portray Violet's actions in this way. According to the Burgesses, the incident began when Polly Burgess, the mistress, ordered Violet to stop what she was doing and perform another task instead. Violet ignored her. Polly then threatened to strike Violet if she did not obey immediately. Violet rushed at Polly. In response, Polly tried to hit Violet with some kind of kitchen implement. But Violet struck Polly first, jolting the improvised weapon from her hands and knocking her to the floor. Polly's daughters came to the rescue, helping their mother to her feet. Violet struck her down again. That brought Polly's husband into the fray, although he did not fare much better. According to the Burgesses, Violet put up such a fight that it took Thomas, Polly, and all of their daughters to subdue her. Even that was not entirely successful. After Thomas struck her ten blows with a whip, Violet escaped and stayed away for several days. Thomas Burgess filed assault charges soon thereafter. Violet ultimately was convicted of assault and sentenced to fifty lashes. That outcome sealed Violet's fate, scarring her with a public whipping. But it does not begin to describe the issues at play in this case and others like it.[36]

Like so many other cases involving slaves, Violet's legal problems resulted from differences between two white southerners — in this instance, father and son. Violet's owner was John Burgess, but at the time she was working for John's son, Thomas. John, Thomas, and Violet all seem to have understood the transfer as a limited one, moving her place of residence and giving Thomas use of her labor without granting him the same authority as her master. Their actions, at least, conform to that presumption. So do the court proceedings, which formally identify Thomas as an injured third party, not as Violet's master. Thomas also deferred to his father, although they clearly parted ways over the treatment of Violet. The documents suggest that Thomas's initial response to Violet was measured. That would explain why he and his family had so much trouble subduing her and why she escaped so easily afterward. Even more telling, however, is the fact that Thomas felt compelled to ask his father's permission to punish Violet. He whipped her ten times before he quit and went to consult his father. As he testified, he "would have been sattisfied if his father had have corected" Violet. But Thomas's father refused to let his son punish Violet further or to punish her himself, although the records do not provide any hints as to why. So Thomas followed the only remaining course, going over his father's head to file charges against Violet.[37]

Most disputes like this ended differently, with masters successfully interceding on behalf of slaves before matters degenerated to the point of litigation. They summoned their credit as white men of substance, mobilizing their reputations and their connections to defuse the conflict. Recall Thomas Clarkson's intervention on behalf of his slaves, whose corn crop Mathew Singleton's white overseer had appropriated for his own use. Clarkson bypassed the overseer to go straight to Mathew Singleton, negotiating a settlement with him directly. He penned his request with confidence, certain of his relationship and his ability to persuade his neighbor to settle in favor of his slaves.[38] The only reason why there is a record of this incident is that Clarkson wrote a letter. Conflicts were more likely to be resolved with a conversation and a handshake, which left no imprint on the historical record. What survived are the unusual cases, either unintentionally preserved or formally documented in the legal records. Those conflicts that ended up in court were particularly unusual, instances of botched mediation or inadequate credit. Either the master's credit was not enough to resolve the issue, or the master chose not to use it on the slave's behalf.

John Burgess's credit failed Violet. He was either unable to enforce his view of matters or unwilling to intervene on her behalf once the case left the family and went to the courts. He did not appear to testify at the trial. Other slaves ran up against the same problem, with results that litter the court records: convictions on the complaints of white southerners who had problems with slaves they did not own and whose owners would not give satisfaction. Eunicey Guthrie, for instance, filed assault charges against Lease after Lease's owners refused to discipline her. Eunicey, a white neighbor woman who was visiting Lease's owners, claimed that Lease had verbally threatened her when she tried to discipline Lease's children — who, like Lease, did not belong to Eunicey Guthrie. In another case, Nancy Gibson charged the slave, Patt, with slander. Although Nancy was furious at Patt for calling her a whore, she was even more outraged at Patt's owners for ignoring her demands that Patt be punished. The list could go on and on, its length a testament both to the fluidity of race relations and to the personalized nature of credit within the localized legal system. What neighboring whites deemed inexcusable breaches of racial etiquette, masters often accepted, particularly from slaves they knew well. Not all whites could muster the credit necessary to force their slaveholding neighbors to address their concerns. When masters and mistresses failed to respond, disgruntled whites pursued charges in the local courts, in hopes that their grievances would gain more purchase there.[39]

In these legal disputes, slaves found themselves caught betwixt and between the expectations of whites. That was most apparent in cases where slaves ran into trouble while doing their masters' bidding. Mary, a slave in Anderson District, found herself in court, facing charges of assault, because of an errand for her mistress. At the trial, Mary's mistress explained the nature of that errand: she had "sent the prisoner Mary to [Jane] McDowells to request [her] to make her children behave themselves." Somewhere along the way, that interaction went bad. As Jane McDowell complained, Mary did "violently assault beat & abuse" her "with a stick, at the same time making use of many threats & menacing language." The authority that Mary's mistress had tried to delegate proved impossible for her to exercise.[40]

A strong undercurrent of class runs through many of the cases involving whites and slaves. Jane McDowell resented the uninvited meddling of a slaveholding neighbor, who did not even bother to make her complaints in person, but sent a slave instead. Nancy Gibson was concerned that her reputation, and therefore credit, could be slandered with impunity by someone else's slave. Eunicey Guthrie attempted to demonstrate that she had as much authority to discipline a slave as anyone else, only to be put back in her place by that same slave. All these scenarios echo those in other complaints filed by disgruntled white overseers, patrollers, and poorer neighbors, whose fragile egos had been bruised when they did not receive the deference they expected from slaves. One is reminded of Thomas Sutpen's defining childhood moment in William Faulkner's *Absalom, Absalom!*, when he was sent to deliver a message to the master of the plantation and was told by the slave butler to never come to the front door again. For their part, slaves like Lease, Patt, Mary, and Faulkner's fictional butler were less inclined to accept the authority of whites who were not their owners, particularly if they were poor, because they were well versed in the power relationships that structured southern communities. Slaves understood that their masters' authority derived from their status as masters, not just their race, class, and gender. They also knew the calculus of credit that determined which whites, other than their masters, could command their obedience. Although slaves' actions showed them to be astute students of local culture, they nonetheless ran into trouble, because the rankings they perceived and followed offended poorer whites.[41]

Yet, as Violet's problems suggest, these cases were not just about class and race. They involved a range of problems that plagued relationships within families and among neighbors. In all these matters, slaves were only the proximate cause for the legal charges. They reminded whites of structural inequalities and the failings of human nature at inopportune moments. They underscored whites' low social status, the frustrations caused by their annoying neighbors, and the petty tyrannies of their relatives. Those problems traced back, through slaves, to masters, who cast long shadows over the proceedings, even when they did not appear directly at all. The conflict between Thomas Burgess and his father suggests enmity, likely developed through years of family history, but not elaborated in the case records. Lease's master and mistress thought that Eunicey Guthrie had no business bossing Lease and her children around. Patt's master and mistress seem to have considered Nancy Gibson's character questionable, just as Mary's mistress apparently had little respect for Jane McDowell's domestic management. Complainants prosecuted slaves because they had problems with their owners.

The same connections that made slaves legally vulnerable also defined their place within the peace. Mary, for instance, acted on her mistress's orders, which required her to confront and criticize a white neighbor. Usually a master's consent was implied. Lease's behavior did not bother her mistress. To the contrary, she ignored Lease and advised Eunicey Guthrie to do the same, "to go way & not mind a old drunken negro." Similarly, Violet's refusal to follow Polly Burgess's orders can be traced back to her past experiences with John Burgess. As one of Thomas Burgess's daughters testified, Violet had "generally done as she pleased" when she lived with John Burgess. Although she meant that as a criticism, it was also a statement of fact. Like many slaves in the area, Violet worked both on and off her master's plantation. Even while she was on loan to Thomas Burgess, she hired "out or [worked as] a field hand, but milk[ed] night & morning." Not only did she exercise discretion over her work, but she came and went with relative freedom, circulating within the neighborhood. Both Lease and Violet ended up in court because their masters had tolerated certain behavior to the point that they took it for granted. Lease might have continued to speak her mind, just as Violet might have continued to do "as she pleased," had it not been for a particular confluence of events. The problem for these slaves was that other whites did not grant them the same latitude and were not swayed by their masters' credit. Their legal defeats, though, did not erase the local context that gave rise to slaves' expectations in the first place.

The effects of such prosecutions reached beyond those immediately involved, since they reinforced community involvement in slavery and the oversight of slaves. Once the legal logic of the peace was invoked, its patriarchal interests trumped the individual rights of masters. Given their status, white southerners were in the best position to wield the peace in this way. They did so to demand more rigorous control of slavery, in the name of maintaining community order. Usually, they targeted slaves to effect discipline that owners either could not or would not exercise. The fact that slaves lost far more than white complainants gained underscores the dynamics that motivated prosecution. Punishing Lease and Patt would not repair the credit of the white women who thought themselves slandered. Punishing Mary would not end her mistress's unwelcome scrutiny of her neighbors. Violet's conviction did nothing to raise the value of Thomas Burgess's credit either. To the contrary, he had to air the details of the incident in public, which exposed both his dependence on his father and his impotence in governing his household. It was, at best, a pyrrhic victory. To the white complainants, though, these cases were not just about specific injuries done to them by specific slaves. As they saw it, their personal experiences represented deep rips in the social fabric of their communities, as they defined it. That was why they were willing to risk so much to obtain so little.

Legal officials did use the peace to address the disorder introduced by masters and nonslaveholding whites, although such efforts were grudging and sporadic. In these instances, the patriarchal interests of the community trumped the individual rights of white men. That was the legal logic that allowed prosecution of masters, overseers, and other whites for violence against slaves in North Carolina and South Carolina. Both states allowed for the criminal prosecution of masters and other whites under the guise of protecting the peace. While the logic was the same, the method was different. South Carolina based these prosecutions on statute, and North Carolina on a combination of common law and statute, although local officials in both states relied on common law to fill in where statutes failed. In South

Carolina, statutes defined excessive violence against slaves as a criminal violation of the "peace and dignity of the state." In North Carolina, local officials mounted these prosecutions under common law, which labeled all excessive violence against subjects of the state — including slaves, at least in theory — as offenses to the peace. In both instances, it was the offended interests of the peace that made the violence public and, therefore, a criminal matter rather than a private, civil issue. Statutes and common law did not criminalize all acts of violence against slaves; they only made it possible to prosecute such acts as crimes. That determination was left to local officials, as community members generated and interpreted information about the offense.[42]

The patterns of prosecution were similar to cases in which whites complained of slaves' bad behavior. Instead of informing on slaves, though, this time neighboring whites brought information about masters or other offending whites to legal officials. The documents conjure up images of tight-lipped, outraged complainants, whose patience with troublesome neighbors had finally run out. Augustus Benton feared exactly that outcome after he beat his slave Lucinda to the point of death. He called a doctor but swore him to secrecy. As the doctor later testified, Benton wished the situation of the girl kept a secret because he already had "the name of a cruel master." Given that reputation, "this circumstance if known might be magnified . . . into a crime for which he might be much persecuted." When she died, he was no longer able to keep the incident quiet. As news spread, Benton's reputation caught up with him and turned Lucinda's body into a suspicious death. All the evidence, including testimony about his past, came out at the inquest. Neighbors had been worried about Lucinda, who was still a child, for some time. They had seen her bruises and concluded that her punishment was excessive, particularly for someone so young. One neighbor had even "reproved him," extracting a promise that "he wou'd not beat her so again." Although ineffective in this instance, scrutiny did have the potential to keep men like Benton in line, not because it convinced them of the need to reform but because they cared about their reputations. It was his white neighbors' opinions that mattered, to the extent that he was concerned at all. Infusing the language of credit with particularly paranoid tones, he worried that his "enemies" could use information about Lucinda to "injure his character." The effects could be economic and legal as well as social and cultural, given the dimensions of credit in this period.[43]

The same dynamics governed cases where masters prosecuted other whites for injuries to their slaves. In 1843 James Chesnut, father-in-law of the famous Civil War diarist Mary Chesnut, sent a boat piloted by slaves to "town"—presumably Charleston—for supplies. On the way back, the crew ran into trouble while passing through the plantations of Thomas Clarkson and Richard Singleton, Marion Singleton Deveaux's father. Clarkson's and Singleton's overseers stopped the boat, claiming that the crew had stolen a hog. Then, according to Chesnut, they "committed a most violent outrage by punishing" the pilot, named Charles, "in a barbarous manner." The incident proved the truth of rumors that Chesnut had heard about the cruelty and irresponsibility of Singleton's overseer. He thought the accusation of theft was a pretext to harass his slaves, for no other reason than to "gratify a savage passion." In his opinion, such acts warranted criminal prosecution. That was why Chesnut did not take the route that Thomas Clarkson had followed, mediating a settlement personally. Nor did he seek damages through a civil suit. Instead, he wanted a public statement condemning the behavior of the two overseers. But he made it clear that his quarrel was with those two men, not the planters who hired them. The incident, wrote Chesnut to Richard Singleton, "is merely mentioned to you that in pursuing any course with them I deem proper our friendship is not to be interrupted." In selecting this course, Chesnut drew on his knowledge of those involved, the balance of credit, and the workings of social networks in his community. "Where they are known," referring to the overseers and to his slave Charles, "I suspect Charles['s] word would be credited." Chesnut's formulation limited the scope of his allegations. The problem was unreliable outliers, not two eminent slaveholders, known for their progressive plantation management and representative of all those in their class.[44]

Injured slaves faded as the conflicts among whites took over the proceedings. This predictable trajectory both reflected and reinforced slaves' connections to the legal system. While slaves' bodies represented the injured peace in such cases, it was not their plight or the plight of slaves that was at issue. For a slave's wounds to become a crime, white southerners had to take up the issue and represent it as a problem. They were not necessarily motivated by opposition to slavery, a desire to reform the institution, or even deep humanitarian sentiments. Augustus Benton's neighbors were outraged by callous behavior and excessive brutality against a child. Discipline had become sadism, of which they received frequent reminders on Lucinda's body. James Chesnut took the overseers' violence as a personal affront, seeing his slaves as innocent pawns in a conflict beyond their reckoning. In both cases, what mattered to whites were the reverberations that spread outward, not the original clash. Similarly, church disciplinary courts dealt with the abuse of slaves to preserve the peace of the congrega-

The boat that Charles piloted would have looked like these. Such boats continued to transport goods and people along South Carolina's waterways after the Civil War, when this photograph was taken. From the collections of the South Carolina Historical Society.

tion. That was also why whites occasionally prosecuted slaves for violence against other slaves. Injured slaves became ancillary in the criminal proceedings. They only appeared through the concerns of whites, affirming the hierarchies that defined slaves' subordination within and their connections to the peace.[45]

The prosecution of whites for their abuse of slaves played a faint counterpoint to the dominant themes of the South, where the social order was defined in terms of the maintenance of slaves' subordination. When white owners were convicted, they usually received minimal sentences, even for actions that others considered despicable. The experience of Warner Taylor, a particularly brutal North Carolina slaveholder, is revealing. In 1819 an inquest jury found him guilty of beating his slave Betty to death. But the grand jury did not find evidence of "wicked intent," which was necessary to prove murder, and charged him with the lesser crime of manslaughter. He was then acquitted at trial. Just six years later, Taylor admitted to beating another slave to death. This time he was convicted of manslaughter, although he still did not receive the full punishment for his crime. Instead,

195

Wasted Substance

he received "benefit of clergy," a legal loophole that allowed capital punishment to be substituted with a brand on the hand. So Taylor returned home to his unfortunate surviving slaves. It was poor punishment for a "most foul Murder," in the opinion of Archibald Murphey, the reform-minded lawyer who was involved in the case.[46]

Still, the legal rubric of the peace did provide for the possibility of raising questions about the form and content of masters' patriarchal power in legal forums, something that the rubric of property rights did not. These criminal cases depended on the physical presence of slaves. Slaves provided crucial information and evidence in many instances. In 1819 Judge Elihu Hall Bay charged John Havis for killing his slave Elsey, based on the complaint of two free white men and the evidence that Havis's "small negro boy" gave at the inquest. The two rape cases involving Annis and Juno offer another example of how evidence from slaves could help turn violence against themselves or other slaves into violations of the peace. They were crucial in identifying the actions against them as criminal violations — as rape.[47]

Examples of slaves who provided essential evidence in these cases conform to our current conceptions of legal agency, measured in terms of individuals' success in pursuing their own interests in legal venues. Yet that conception of legal agency does not fully capture slaves' role in localized legal proceedings, where adjudication was defined by a vision of the peace that prevented slaves from being legal agents in that sense. Given the logic, in which slaves' subordination also constituted their primary connection to the social order, the cases did not revolve around the interests of individuals at all, whether slave or master. Slaves mattered because their subordination was necessary to the social order. Their contributions to the proceedings were visceral, their silent but necessary bodies demonstrating a rupture in the community. The verdicts did not address their grievances. They neither compensated slaves nor prohibited future violence against them. The process nonetheless recognized slaves' place within the peace. Their bodies literally marked the outer limits of patriarchal authority, the bounds beyond which it was impermissible to go — at least not without explanation.

Customary practices that slaves negotiated with their masters and others entered into localized law. As in legal matters involving wives, custom usually appeared unannounced, as an assumed part of the process. In Violet's case, for example, the influence was so subtle yet so profound that the customary elements are now difficult to parse out from the legal process. They emerge as unidentified components in an alternative rendering of the peace that undercut Thomas Burgess's version of the conflict. From this perspective, Thomas Burgess and his wife had themselves transgressed accepted practices — perhaps even more so than Violet, although in different ways. That John Burgess refused to discipline Violet or allow his son to do so speaks volumes on this score. So does the testimony of Thomas's family, which emphasized Violet's disregard for their orders and her insistence on following John Burgess's rules. What they condemned were the arrangements that Violet carved out for herself and that John Burgess had accepted: Violet's discretion over her work, her schedule, her contacts, and the paid labor she did on her own time.[48]

This type of arrangement, which other historians have recently found across the slave South, would not have given Violet any reason to think that "she was an eaqual," as Polly Burgess claimed. In the South Carolina upcountry, as elsewhere, it was customary for slaves to leave their own plantations in the evening and on weekends to gather at the houses of their friends and kin. Masters hired out slaves, sent them to work on neighboring farms, and allowed them to hire out their own time as well. Slaves moved within an underground economy that had a definite tilt: while one end plunged deep beneath the surface, the other was clearly visible. Whites regulated what they considered to be the most disruptive of these activities, coming down brutally and decisively when they did. But they also accepted a good deal of illicit, even illegal behavior when it did not threaten open disorder. In 1828, for instance, residents of Surry County, North Carolina, petitioned the governor to pardon Thomas Gallion, who had been convicted of trading with slaves. "It is a common thing in the neighbourhood for owners of slaves to permit their slaves to raise corn & other products for sale." The petitioners did not question the legality of statutes prohibiting this trade. But, they explained, "in this section of the state there seems not to exist the same necessity for enforcing the rigid execution of this act of Assembly as in other parts, where slaves are more numerous." The customs of Surry County, which sanctioned trade with slaves, had legal force that competed with statutes, at least according to some white residents.[49]

Slaves negotiated customary arrangements of their own. Consider the experiences of Jesse, Thomas Ruffin's slave, who appeared in the previous chapter purchasing clothing at Kirkland's store in Hillsborough, North Carolina. In December 1835 Jesse left the Ruffin plantation to drive to the Hillsborough home of Paul Cameron, who was related to the Ruffins by marriage. Jesse combined his duties to Ruffin with his own business on this particular trip, bringing fifteen gallons of clover seed with him to sell to Cameron's wife. In a deal that they had struck earlier, she agreed to pay Jesse a dollar for each gallon of seed. As Paul Cameron told the story, he was less concerned about the transaction than the amount of money Jesse earned. "Upon his coming into the room to receive his pay," wrote Cameron, "I told him that $15 Dolls was too much money for him to have at one time." But Jesse prevailed, received the bulk of his earnings, and then all but disappeared for the next two days. According to Cameron, he "had his supper here on Saturday night and his breakfast on Monday morning, and I believe at no other time was he in my Kitchen while in Hillsboro." Cameron only learned about Jesse's doings after he left, through gossip in the community. Among other things, Jesse went to his favorite hangout, Kirkland's store, to purchase "a quart of Brandy and a quart of Rum." He apparently took the horses out one night as well. "This is about all that I know of him," Cameron wrote apologetically to Ruffin. He worried that Jesse might have succumbed to negative influences in the neighborhood. "I have for some time past," he wrote, "thought that the slaves over the river at Judge Norwoods were pretty much without a Master, and have forbidden my servants to visit there, or anywhere else but by my permission." But Cameron's prohibitions, like his concerns about Jesse's behavior, spoke volumes about the social practices of slavery, not just on his plantation but on surrounding ones as well. In two short days, Jesse had violated any number of laws: he purchased alcohol, he left the plantation without written permission, he sold property apparently without express permission, and he spent time in the company of other slaves unsupervised by whites. The laws regulating slavery existed alongside customary practices that did not apply uniformly to all slaves or evenly in all circumstances, but had considerable power within localized legal culture.[50]

In Violet's case, Thomas Burgess violated arrangements that she took for granted. She defended herself openly and assertively precisely because Thomas Burgess and his family were initiating change. After relocating to their farm, she had continued to act as she had when she lived with Thomas's father, John. Thomas and his family tried to change that pattern, leading to conflict on several occasions. Yet Violet remained resolute. Reading the Burgesses' testimony through this lens, Violet appears less as the strangely stubborn and capricious aggressor and more like a strong-willed woman who felt justified in her actions and who expected others to support her. She ignored Polly Burgess's interference in her work and her life. Annoyed that her new mistress persisted, Violet stood her ground, expecting that this particular confrontation would end unremarkably. She dug in her heels as the situation escalated. When it got out of hand instead, she ran from the scene, a time-honored practice among slaves to allow tempers to cool and events to sort themselves out more favorably. She appealed to her owner, John Burgess, who supported her. Then she disappeared for a week, probably seeking shelter with slaves in the area. They could harbor her because they, like Violet, had worked out customary arrangements that allowed them a certain amount of social space. To them, Violet was not an outlaw who transgressed existing social patterns to defy authority in heroic, yet ultimately self-destructive ways. She was known to them, a familiar face whose life was intertwined with their own and whose troubles echoed through the lives of all slaves in the area.[51]

The matter might have ended quietly if Thomas Burgess had accepted his father's refusal to punish Violet further. How was Violet to guess that Thomas Burgess would defy his father's wishes, question established community customs, and file charges against her? That Violet went to such lengths, with the support of others, suggests that neither she nor they anticipated that response. Violet overplayed her hand. She reached beyond what whites in her community would accept. She seems to have reached beyond what even John Burgess would accept, since he did not appear in court to defend her. But that outcome does not erase the importance of Violet's place within the peace and her conceptions of the standards that defined it, which explains why she thought that she had a hand to play in the first place.[52]

■ ■ ■

THE OUTCOMES OF THESE LEGAL MATTERS were less important than the fact that these cases were brought at all. If the cases had been about the rights of wives and slaves, the outcomes would have been crucial. In a legal milieu that privileged rights — the subject of the next two chapters — outcomes would have established larger legal points. The affirmation of the claims of one wife or one slave would have confirmed rights that, by implication, applied universally to all wives or all slaves as a group. But universalistic notions of rights were not in play in this setting; specific relationships among particular persons were at stake, and only insomuch as they threatened to disrupt the social order. Within the legal milieu of the peace, individuals were subordinated to larger questions of social order. People mattered: their possessions, their bodies, and their actions were the means of establishing order and identifying disorder. But individuals and their legal status were never the point. The point was to reinstate the peace within local communities. Because the outcomes applied only to the individuals involved, not to all wives, slaves, or masters collectively, they do not line up to reveal historical patterns in the trajectory of women's, African Americans', or even white men's legal positions, as measured in terms of the acquisition or loss of rights. Rather, it is the content and context of the case that reveals the varied definitions of patriarchal authority.

Unlike rights, the practices of the peace were deeply rooted in localities. Although the peace, as an abstraction, applied broadly and uniformly, its content had to be determined in particular places. It was about specific arrangements, confined to specific places, and linked to unique individuals. The particularity of those practices becomes more evident at the social margins. Slaves could claim few rights or privileges, because of their place at the outer edges of the peace. What they claimed, whether possession of physical property or authority over their own lives, was negotiated in context, as customs that acquired a legal legitimacy bounded by time, space, and circumstance. Slaves' claims extended only as far as local knowledge, their masters' credit, and their own connections would carry them. The arrangements that Jesse or Violet defended so assertively did not necessarily apply to other slaves, even those owned by the same masters. Although free wives had access to more resources and enjoyed greater legal legitimacy, their claims to property and authority similarly depended on their place within the social order of local communities.

The particularity of the peace produced wide variations in the exercise of patriarchal authority. Not all patriarchs exercised the same degree of authority in the same way. More to the point, not all patriarchs were allowed to exercise the same authority in the same way. By implication, some dependents — wives and slaves — could claim authority over themselves and other forms of property that would not have been possible in other areas of law, particularly in abstract forms of property law. As long as their claims were characterized as the maintenance of localized customary arrangements, they did not undermine their husbands' rights or the patriarchal order. It was only when wives' and slaves' claims were cast in terms of rights that they became problematic. That legal framework forced choices between the rights of husbands and wives and the rights of masters and slaves. When that framework was applied to the slave South, those without rights usually lost.

Within the framework of the peace, which attended to local customs and circumstances, slavery was a variable institution as well as a public one. What individual masters and individual slaves could do ranged widely. But the restraints placed on some masters and the privileges allowed some

slaves did not make slavery benign, let alone humane. Rather, they characterized the distinctive, localized dynamics of subordination, in which one
person's experience did not become a right that could be extended to an
entire group. But the variations did create legal interstices where certain
slaves could stake their own claims, not just to physical property but also
over aspects of their own lives—the most valuable property of all. While
often dismissed by historians because they did not take the form of rights,
those claims had recognized power within a localized system in which
rights were not the only means for mediating disputes. The problem was
that slaves' claims were even more variable and unstable than their masters'
claims to authority. Their tenuousness, though, did not make them any less
legal, at least within the contours of the peace.

PART III ■ State Law

I N THE 1820s North Carolina's legislators decided that they needed a new building. Proponents of the project, who included some of the most prominent legal reformers in the state, argued that the two-story brick State House, completed in 1795, was antiquated, inadequate, and altogether unbefitting as the symbolic seat of state authority. The legislature hired English architect William Nichols to turn the humble structure into a lavish Greek temple, a decision that placed North Carolina on the cutting edge of public architecture. Since the Revolution, architects had been using classical forms and motifs to express the new republic's political values, particularly the authority of law. Greek Revivalism departed from those conventions by modeling entire buildings after classical ones. Thomas Jefferson pioneered in the design with Virginia's state capitol, completed in 1789 and based on a first-century C.E. Roman temple, the Maison Carrée, in Nîmes, France. The style became the most widely used form for public buildings in the antebellum period. When North Carolina legislators adopted a Greek Revival design for the capitol, they joined the architectural vanguard and made a bold statement about state law: its location was a temple, not to be confused with the less imposing, more domestic spaces where so much legal business was still conducted at the local level.[1]

Nichols built the new state capitol around the old one, using the existing foundations but expanding them and covering them with a new façade. The building's destruction by fire in 1831 provided state leaders with an opportunity to rebuild on an even grander scale. The resulting structure exceeded its predecessor in every respect, from the stonework and porticoes of the exterior to the layout and ornamentation of the interior. Doric columns adorned the outside of the capitol, which was flanked by porticoes on the east and west and topped with a dome. Inside, in the main hall, a rotunda soared from the ground level to a skylit cupola. The two-story chambers of the House and Senate were equally impressive, with Ionic columns in the domed Senate chamber and a variation of the Corinthian order in the House chamber, which resembled an amphitheater. The North Carolina State Supreme Court and State Library resided in embellished Gothic Revival rooms on the third floor. Begun in 1833 and finished in 1840, the capitol cost over $500,000, an enormous sum for the period and much more than originally estimated. Despite complaints, the commissioners who oversaw the project refused to sacrifice quality in "an Edifice designed to last the ages." They had a point: the capitol is still in use today.[2]

Construction of North Carolina's capitol provides a fitting metaphor for the subject of part 3: the development of state law in the area of public

State House, Raleigh, North Carolina, 1793–95, Rhodham Atkins, contractor. Watercolor by J. S. Glennie, 1811. Andra De Coppet Collection, Manuscripts Division, Department of Rare Books and Special Collections, Princeton University Library.

Capitol, Raleigh, North Carolina, remodeled 1820–24. William Nichols, architect. Drawing by W. Goodacre. Courtesy of the North Carolina Collection, University of North Carolina Library at Chapel Hill.

State Capitol, Raleigh, North Carolina, 1833–40. William Nichols, Ithiel Town, Alexander Jackson Davis, and David Paton, architects. Photograph by Wharton and Tyree, 1908. Courtesy of the North Carolina Collection, University of North Carolina Library at Chapel Hill.

matters previously governed by the logic of legal localism. Greek Revival architecture and the growth of the state were even more intertwined in South Carolina. Legislators there did not decide to build their own Greek Revival capitol until the 1850s, and the project, which acquired other design elements along the way, was not completed until the twentieth century. At the same time that William Nichols was at work refashioning North Carolina's capitol, however, the noted architect Robert Mills was imposing the same Greek Revival form on public buildings across South Carolina. He did so with the blessing of the legislature, which had appointed him in 1820 to design and oversee all public construction in the state. A native South Carolinian, Mills moved in the same national circles as the leaders who hired him. He began his career working in Washington, D.C., with James Hoban on the nation's Capitol Building. He then studied with Thomas Jefferson and Benjamin Latrobe, whose influences are evident in Mills's creative use of the Greek Revival style. In addition to numerous federal buildings, he designed the Washington Monument and the Bunker

The Public Record Office in Charleston, designed by Robert Mills, is now home to the South Carolina Historical Society. From the collections of the South Carolina Historical Society.

Hill Monument. Yet throughout his career, Mills maintained his ties to his home state. His buildings for the state of South Carolina in the 1820s expressed the political vision of state leaders in the most modern, innovative forms. Mills embraced the political tenets of Greek Revivalism, particularly the sovereignty of law and the responsibility of the state to its citizens, along with the aesthetic style. He supported state leaders' projects, including internal improvements, public works, and penal reform. One of his first designs was for the Public Record Office, now home to the South Carolina Historical Society, a project designed to preserve the records so essential to state authority.[3]

Expressed in the changing form of the capitol and other public buildings, the consolidation of state authority followed similar paths and roughly the same chronology in both North Carolina and South Carolina. The 1820s remodeling of the North Carolina capitol, which draped the modest brick State House in classical robes, punctuated state leaders' first wave of institutional construction, described in chapter 2. By the 1820s, state leaders in both North and South Carolina had produced a fundamental change in the logic of law as well as the structure of legal institutions at the state level. Reformers generated a body of law, composed of statutes, appellate decisions, and legal digests, that was meant to apply uniformly and consistently throughout the state, rather than varying from place to place and case to case as localized law did. In North Carolina, reformers had convinced the legislature to organize the statutes, to issue reports of appellate cases, and to archive the materials related to state law. Although South Carolina reformers were less successful in coordinating the state's statutes, they made significant headway in designating statutes and appellate decisions as authoritative expressions of state law, reducing those materials to writing and saving them. Thanks to the prolific publishing efforts of legal reformers, the texts of state law were widely available in both states.

This same group of men laid the foundation for a centralized institutional structure to oversee state law by the 1820s. North Carolina's legal reformers turned a weak appellate court into the North Carolina State Supreme Court, perched at the top of the judicial hierarchy with precedent-setting powers that gave it the ability to define state law. In 1824 the South Carolina legislature cleaned up the institutional clutter that kept the appellate courts from defining a unified body of state law by merging its two appellate courts, one of which oversaw cases in equity and the other of which oversaw cases in common law. As outgrowths of distinct legal traditions, the two courts generated conflicts within state law by issuing competing decisions on similar issues. Like the North Carolina appellate court, South Carolina's consolidated appellate court had the authority to create a coherent body of state law. In the 1820s, though, these centralizing projects were by no means complete. Just as the old brick State House was still there beneath the façade of North Carolina's Greek Revival capitol, localized law remained at the center of the legal systems in the Carolinas, even after state institutions assumed a higher profile.

That jury-rigged capitol, with its foundation of legal localism, burned to the ground in 1831, and a new building was erected to embody the power of the state. It is tempting to reach for a literal interpretation of that event, with the fiery destruction of a building that made concessions to localized law and its subsequent replacement with a structure dedicated solely to state law. But that characterization would be reductive and inaccurate, for the situation is more complicated: rather than the state's legal order replacing or imposing its will on localized law, their relationship was reconfigured as the state extended its reach and state leaders proposed a new kind of institutional separation between "the state" and "the local." The chapters in part 3 tell this story on the state level, because that was where the relationship was imagined and remade.

Chapter 7 begins in the 1820s, when legal reformers began extending the reach of state law into areas previously left to local jurisdictions. Before then, reformers had been preoccupied with issues involving property, such as inheritance, contracts, sales, and other transfers—often referred to as private matters on what is now the civil side of the system. The legal texts of the time, produced by reformers and now used as primary sources by legal scholars, testify to those concerns. In them, property predominates, crowding out other issues. Reformers structured this emerging body of law around the logic of individual rights, drawing on the legal framework that had governed property issues even before the Revolution. Then, in the 1820s, reform-minded appellate justices and legislators in both states extended their interests beyond property and began applying the rubric of rights to criminal matters and other public issues. These new bodies of state law represented a marked departure from the states' previous handling of public issues in key ways. Before the 1820s legislatures and appellate courts had generated laws in this area sporadically and haphazardly, often in response to local concerns and not always with the expectation that state law would supersede local practice. In fact, state law recognized locally defined conceptions of the peace and incorporated localism into its approach to public matters. State law coexisted with localized law, although the two operated largely apart, with localized law occupying its own space within the legal system and operating according to its own logic. By the 1820s, however, reformers' efforts at consolidation and systematization had achieved results. Legislatures and appellate courts acted with the assumption that they should be creating a uniform body of law in public matters, applicable throughout the state and superior to local practices. Instead of conceding the importance of localism when it came to public matters, the logic of these new statutes and appellate decisions upheld abstract conceptions of individual rights created and protected at the state level. Localized law now had a competitor with aspirations to dominance.

Chapter 8 traces state leaders' efforts to legitimize the authority of state law by linking it to the rights of abstract individuals. In the late 1820s and 1830s, state leaders in both North Carolina and South Carolina mounted political campaigns that popularized the authority of the state and the rhetoric of rights—at least for adult white men. In South Carolina, the nullification movement consolidated state government more dramatically and more thoroughly than any previous reform effort. Leading nullifiers came from the same ranks as legal reformers: they moved in state and national networks, considered government at those levels to be superior to local jurisdictions, supported state-building efforts, and advocated the creation of a coherent body of state law based in individual rights. Confronted with national policies that they considered detrimental to state interests, a core group of South Carolina's leaders rallied to the state's defense. In an amazingly well-orchestrated campaign, nullifiers convinced the "freemen"—by which they meant white men—to identify with the state as the only entity that could preserve their liberty. The rhetoric of individual rights was deployed by both sides. While opposing nullification, Unionists urged freemen to support their state and protect their rights by remaining loyal to the nation. The formulation, in both its nullification and Unionist guises, placed free white men at the center of state politics and made them important in ways they never were within the political context of localism. They responded with such enthusiasm that their erstwhile leaders had difficulty controlling them.

In North Carolina, the political campaigns of the 1830s were less explosive but no less decisive. The new state constitution of 1835 popularized the rhetoric of rights and the notion that it was the state's job to protect those rights. The constitution also solidified the state legislature's authority by elevating the public business of the state government over the private matters of local jurisdictions, which involved specific individuals and communities. North Carolina's new state capitol embodied these changes in physical form. The style and location of the building set it apart as a distinct place where the most important public business was conducted. It housed all the authoritative bodies that made up the state, not just the two houses of the legislature and the appellate court, but also the texts that comprised state law. But the capitol was not public, in the sense that anyone could wander in and present their concerns. The building had no place for localized law, which was banished to localities. Also banished were the myriads of people who constituted localized law. They were replaced by the racial, class, and gendered abstractions of state law: freemen and their individual rights. The new state capitol demonstrated physically that state law, though not yet dominant, was nonetheless separate from localized law and the common people.

That separation, as imagined by state leaders and written into state government, did not mark the end of localized law, because the culture of localism did not necessarily recognize the distinctiveness, let alone the superiority, of laws generated at the state level. Localized law continued to operate in the districts and counties of the Carolinas as it always had, unless it was interrupted by officials intent on imposing the edicts of the state. It also wandered into the corridors of state government, despite efforts to keep it out. Ironically, the culture of localism, which sanctioned the review of court verdicts, provided openings for state intervention. Appeals, in particular, offered the chance for appellate courts to use their enhanced power and to impose state law on criminal matters, turning cases that involved disputed facts in local communities into broad pronouncements on points of law unrelated to the actual conflict. Increasingly, appellate courts and legislatures took an active role in public matters in a way that had a direct impact on property law, which was the conceptual foundation of state law. That is why state laws relating to divorce and slavery run through the chapters of part 3. Divorce, which disrupted the transfer of property within and among families, and slavery, which constituted a sizable portion of the region's assets, involved questions about the peace that had long been the purview of local jurisdictions.

The trajectory of divorce law in North Carolina provides an excellent example of the evolution of state law and its changing relationship to localism. Before 1814 the North Carolina legislature handed out separations and divorces "when in its judgment the cause of influence of the petitioner was sufficient to demand it." Efforts to strip the legislature of that power began in the 1790s and gathered force over time. After decades of debate, the legislature reluctantly capitulated to localism, placing jurisdiction over separations and divorces in the superior courts and giving juries discretion over material issues in these cases. Nonetheless, it was the demands of divorce petitioners, not the voices of enlightened reform, that drove the change. Petitioners overwhelmed the legislature with requests for intervention in their marital problems, extending the legislative calendar and expanding the state budget. In 1809 one proponent of reform complained that the divorces had cost the state "nearly fifty thousand Dollars" to date and "the expense is increasing every year." The legislature could not keep up with demand.[4]

Legislators wrote their distrust of localism into the new divorce statute. Where they had allowed themselves considerable discretion in granting divorces and separations, the 1814 statute limited local courts to specific causes: impotence and adultery constituted grounds for divorce, and extreme cruelty was cause for separation. Those causes reflected long-standing English precedents from chancery courts, which had informed both petitioners' requests and the legislature's decisions before 1814. In this regard, the statute did not so much create new law as affirm existing practices. Yet the legislature and petitioners always differed on matters of interpretation. While petitioners and their supporters had given creative readings to the traditional grounds for divorce and separation, the legislature had not. In enumerating specific causes for divorce before handing the matter over to the local courts, the legislature paid silent tribute to the power of petitioners to shape localized law.[5]

The power of localism also tripped up the legislature's effort to retain some control over the process. The 1814 bill required legislative approval to finalize divorces, creating a system in which the General Assembly could always trump the courts. North Carolinians seized on that loophole to bypass the courts or appeal their decisions. They continued, with the help of their representatives, to submit their petitions to the legislature.[6] In January 1827, as the 1826 session spilled over into the next year and yet another divorce petition appeared on the agenda, one tired representative could no longer contain himself. "[I] had hoped," he snapped, "that after the Legislature had passed an act on this subject, some years ago, giving the judiciary cognizance of all questions of this kind, that the House would have been no longer troubled with these applications." Yet the legislature continued to grant divorces in individual cases that had failed in court, on grounds not allowed for by statute. "The law is sufficient for the relief of all," he continued; the legislature has "no right, and of course, ought not to act on any individual case." Others shared these sentiments. In the same session another representative submitted a resolution to amend the 1814 statute. As he observed, "the law . . . giving the superior court jurisdiction in cases of Divorce and Alimony was intended to relieve the Legislature from a pressure of business with which it was then troubled at every session. But we find, notwithstanding this law, a number of cases yet find their way here." Therefore, he concluded, the law needed revision so as to "keep business of this kind from coming to the Legislature in future." The changes were passed, although they did not eliminate the legislature's authority over divorce in theory. Petitions still appeared on the agenda, presented as particularly pressing problems in need of legislative intervention.[7]

The legislature's failure to restrain petitioners and the sympathetic juries who heard their cases left an imprint on the development of statute law. Ambiguities in the causes for divorce or separation invited petitioners and local courts to interpret the statute broadly, as they did in so many other areas. Take, for instance, the definition of cruelty, which covered any situation whereby a "person shall either abandon his family or maliciously turn his wife out of doors, or by cruel or barbarous treatment endanger her life, or offer such indignities to her person as to render her condition intolerable or life burthensome." Evaluating the evidence in context, where it was impossible to separate the people involved from legal abstractions, the local courts saw cruelty more frequently than the legislature had. In 1828 the legislature acknowledged this altered legal landscape and expanded the statutes to include situations where "a man shall become an habitual drunkard or spendthrift, wasting his substance to the impoverishment of his family."[8] The phrase "wasting his substance" captured complaints that wives frequently made, not just in the context of divorce, about their husbands' misappropriation of family resources. The substance that had been wasted included a man's labor, health, guidance, and social standing as well as property, all of which should have gone for the good of the family, as wives and their supporters saw it. The phrase carried legal meaning because it expressed long-standing assumptions about marital relations, maintained within the terms of the peace, largely through the efforts of women. The 1828 statute distilled those values in stylized form, importing custom to modify a realm of law that mediated marital conflicts through the model of competing property rights.

Beginning in the 1820s, the North Carolina appellate court stepped into this amalgam of state law and persistent localism, rendering decisions intended to stabilize the meaning of the statutes and to provide a uniform interpretation applicable throughout the state. It was an uphill struggle, as the court's 1832 decision in *Scroggins v. Scroggins* suggests. Writing for the court, Thomas Ruffin overturned the divorce granted by the local court. Then he took issue with the divorce statutes, which gave superior courts "sole and original jurisdiction" and allowed them to grant divorces "upon due evidence presented, of the justice of such application." Such discretion, he argued, was so injudicious as to be legally inconceivable. It could never be "as unrestrained as the loose and general phraseology of the act would literally imply," he argued, because "then the law upon the subject would fluctuate with the varying opinions of different judges," counsel could not "advise with confidence," and the court could not "decide with certainty." For Ruffin and other state leaders, certainty in the law was paramount.[9]

Although the appellate court's decisions applied to the particular cases on which it ruled, their success in stabilizing state law was less clear. Local courts continued to decide in favor of sympathetic complainants, stretching the statutes to fit the circumstances when they wished to. If local courts did not comply, disgruntled spouses appealed to the higher courts or their state representatives, a more likely course because legislators were known to be more sympathetic than appointed appellate justices. Despite the restrictions on private matters, individual representatives knew better than to ignore constituent service, particularly when those constituents were influential and well connected. So localism not only persisted, but refused to keep to its own space and follow the dictates of state law.

In 1835 North Carolina's new constitution tried to change the relationship between state law and localism by restricting the legislature's handling of all "private legislation"—bills, including those providing divorces, that applied only to specific individuals, groups, or localities. While recognizing the authority of local jurisdictions, the amendments drew a sharp line between local issues and state issues, creating a distinct hierarchy between the two. The legislature now dealt exclusively with public issues of broad importance, which in theory affected everyone in the state. Local courts became subordinate legal bodies that specialized in the detritus of everyday life; they handled legal conflicts characterized as routine and private because they did not involve the interpretation of state law. The new state constitution shielded the state appellate court from legislative interference, ending locally minded legislators' campaigns to undermine a centralized court system that upheld state law. Before 1835 localized law had space within the state's legal system: its rulings were part of the state's body of laws, and its practices were recognized and accommodated within the state's government.[10] Although state leaders failed to eradicate localized law, they did manage to purge the logic and practices of localism from state law in theory. They rewrote the basic structures of North Carolina government in a way that not only clearly separated state law from localized law, but also established state law's superiority.

It took time for the implications of this transformation to work their way into the legal system and the practice of popular legal culture. The district courthouses that Robert Mills designed in South Carolina suggest the growing solidity and influence of state authority as well as its limits. In the 1820s Mills oversaw the design of at least fourteen district courthouses commissioned by the state legislature. All assumed the Greek Revival form, with the requisite gables, porticoes, and columns, although Mills varied it according to his own aesthetics and local building conditions. Mills tailored his courthouses to the specific requirements of state law, with offices and a fireproof storage room for documents on the first floor and the courtroom on the second floor, raised above the noise of the streets and removed from the people who milled around on court day. Because courthouses of this style now evoke nostalgia for a bygone era of small-town life, it is difficult to see them for what they were at the time: a novel vision of legal uniformity imposed by state leaders on a populace unwilling to let go of their own ways. They sat uncomfortably in local social contexts, anomalous

The courthouses in Union District (top) and Kershaw District (bottom) were both designed by Robert Mills. The legislature hired Mills to bring uniformity, in both aesthetic and functional terms, to district courthouses, the design and building of which was funded by the state initially. That building project paralleled the state leaders' efforts to systematize public law and impose consistency on its practice throughout the state. Courtesy of South Caroliniana Library, University of South Carolina, Columbia.

The new courthouses were "jewel-like temples of democracy" perched amidst the "hodgepodge hamlets" that were South Carolina's court towns. "South East View of Greenville, South Carolina," 1825, with its new courthouse, designed by Robert Mills. Abby Aldrich Rockefeller Folk Art Museum, the Colonial Williamsburg Foundation, Williamsburg, Virginia.

structures that one architectural history describes as "jewel-like temples of democracy" perched amidst the "hodgepodge hamlets" that were South Carolina's court towns.[11] The contrast with North Carolina underscores the novelty of South Carolina's courthouses. In North Carolina, where decisions about courthouse design and funding were more localized, the Greek Revival design did not make inroads until the 1840s. As products of local building campaigns, not state-sponsored efforts, North Carolina Greek Revival courthouses took more varied forms, reflecting the tastes, needs, and pocketbooks of local areas.[12]

Once erected, these temples of justice settled in and made themselves at home. The conclusion turns to the time when these new courthouses had become an accepted part of the local landscape. Their presence signified the influence of state law, which seeped into the culture to such an extent that it is now difficult to imagine the legal system in any other way. But it also represented localism's adoption and adaptation of state law. The legal logic of localism was nothing if not eclectic, with the capacity to in-

Camden County Courthouse, 1847 (top); Orange County Courthouse, 1845 (bottom). County courthouses in North Carolina were built through local initiative, which explains the greater variation in their design than in the courthouses in South Carolina, which were initially part of a state-level building project. North Carolina courthouses, though, still followed the same style. Courtesy of the North Carolina Collection, University of North Carolina Library at Chapel Hill.

corporate a wide array of conflicting concepts. Carolinians picked up the rights discourse popularized by state leaders in the 1820s and 1830s without putting down the basic principles of localized law. They walked into their new temples of justice, articulating their interests as they had always done, using the terms favored by the logic of state law as part of their rhetorical arsenal. In so doing, they gave new meanings to rights, stretching them to cover a range of circumstances never imagined by state leaders.

Subjects vs. Rights-Holding Individuals

Esther Preslar figured in the county court records—and the previous chapter—as a wronged wife insisting to her husband that the land she had brought to their marriage was a family resource, not an individual possession that he could squander. Alvin Preslar drank too much, worked too little, and found too much pleasure in abusing her. The local records suggest that she had lost confidence in his ability to manage her family's land and took control of it herself. When Esther refused to restore his power over it, he responded with such violence that she fled to her father's house, a short distance away, taking a quilt and extra clothing to keep warm in the chill November night. She never made it. The next morning her step-mother found her, barely conscious, a few hundred yards from their door. After a day of delirium and extreme pain, Esther died. The symptoms described in the testimony suggest that she sustained internal injuries that were not detectable in the medical examination and, therefore, difficult to trace back to her husband. Local officials nonetheless charged Alvin Preslar with murder, and the Union County Superior Court jury in North Carolina convicted him and sentenced him to death. To them, the case seemed clear. An injured, frightened woman died while fleeing a husband notorious for his irresponsibility and bad temper; the husband was culpable because he created the disorder that caused her death. The verdict did not end the controversy, as so often happened in localized law. People in Union County pelted the governor with petitions, basing their recommendations for pardon or punishment on their interpretations of the conflict and the events surrounding it.[1]

Up to this point, the entire process was typical of localized law, where community involvement preceded the trial and continued after the verdict. But this case was handled differently than those discussed in earlier chapters because it was tried in the 1850s. By that time the North Carolina appellate court had moved into the area of criminal law. Writing for the court in *State v. Preslar*, Justice Richmond M. Pearson overturned the verdict and ordered a new trial in a decision so acerbic that it is hard not to read it as ridicule. The jury, he thought, came to an unjustifiable conclusion on an ill-framed indictment. They convicted Alvin Preslar of murdering his wife through a combination of beating and exposure. The verdict, he claimed, implied that Esther's wounds did not directly cause her death, minimizing the effects of Alvin's violence and placing the burden of proof on the second cause. But Pearson saw no evidence that Alvin actually drove Esther from their house or forced her to remain outside. It was Esther, Pearson concluded, who made those choices, displaying extraordinarily bad judgment and needlessly placing her life in danger. By contrast, her husband operated within his rights in exercising authority over his household.[2]

This remarkable appellate decision, which blamed the victim for her own death, exemplifies the replacement of flesh-and-blood subjects of the peace at the local level by abstract rights-bearing individuals at the state level. Asserting a husband's rights as a principle that trumped his culpability for violence, the appellate court repositioned Esther Preslar as a subordinate appropriately contained within the household her husband headed. The logic was fundamentally different from that of the local court, which situated individuals within a wider set of connections and identified the main goal of law as aversion or resolution of their conflicts. As long as local arenas maintained control over public matters, state laws constituted just one of many options in a complicated legal landscape. By the end of the 1830s, though, state leaders had solidified the authority of state-level institutions and extended the reach of state law into criminal matters and other public issues previously left to local jurisdictions. The process, which began in the decades immediately following the Revolution, gained momentum in the 1820s. Localized law continued to operate, largely unchanged, within districts and counties. But it now faced powerful competition from the state level, particularly from state leaders insistent on elevating state law over localized law. By the time Alvin Preslar's case reached the North Carolina appellate court in 1856, Justice Pearson's decision figured as the definitive articulation of law in a way that appellate decisions had not done during the 1790s. Sealing Alvin Preslar's fate through abstract legal principles based in the logic of individual rights, the decision obscured all the issues that had been so important in the community: Esther's interests in family property; the importance of social and cultural networks that connected Esther's fate to the good order of the peace; and the evidentiary significance of local knowledge that allowed officials to punish Alvin without touching the authority of other patriarchs.

Violence cuts to the core of all these issues because of its disruptive power. After the Revolution, localized law regulated violence to maintain the good order of the peace. As an abstraction, the peace was notoriously difficult to define because it was purposefully flexible and adaptable. It concerned itself with the quotidian details of its subjects' lives and provided the means for adjudicating the various conflicts among them. This system dealt with particulars, not universals: the events that led up to incidents of violence, the personalities of those involved, their relationships to one another and others in the community, and the severity of the acts committed. Because the logic of localized law sought to mend tears in the social fabric, the system did not generate an elaborate body of legal principles. The primary goal, the restoration of the peace, depended on details that could never be parsed out and universalized. The rubric of rights gave violence new legal meanings. This framework reversed the logic of the peace, making individuals the basis for generalization—as rights-holders or potential rights-holders, or as subordinates over whom others legitimately held and exercised rights—and turning persons into legal abstractions. In this view, violence threatened the legal status of all rights-holding individuals. Its importance derived from how it affected the rights held by abstract individuals, not from the contours of daily life. Too much regulation could undermine rights by denying individuals the means to protect themselves. Left unregulated, violence could destroy the very basis of all rights. In the 1820s, as part of their efforts to create a unified body of law based in rights, state lawmakers turned their attention to criminal violence. By the 1830s appellate decisions and statutes turned claims to bodily integrity—to use violence and defend against it—into an individual right, held and exercised exclusively by free white men.

While dramatic in its effects, this legal transformation unfolded quietly, in language so muted as to be virtually inaudible. State laws cast their subject in terms of the abstract individual, free of race, gender, or class. They did not specify limits or explicitly exclude slaves, white women, free blacks, or impoverished white men. These qualifiers were unnecessary because the framework of individual rights restricted the laws' application to those— propertied white men—who could exercise them. White men with property in land, their own labor, and often the labor of subordinated others were the unmarked, privileged category in this new legal logic. Others were silently excluded, positioned in the body of state law as faceless dependents or subordinates over which white men exercised rights, even as they continued to resist domination and marginalization. The fact that legal reformers assumed the desirability of a system based in rights, and historians have accepted its inevitability, deepens the silence surrounding these changes.

Yet developments in the legal handling of violence were representative of national trends in this period, which expanded not only the reach of individual rights but also the authority that white men could exercise in their own lives and over others. In the South, these changes loosened the ties that connected subordinate southerners to the legal system, positioning them as subjects of individual patriarchs rather than subjects of the peace.

RIGHTS AND THE POLITICS OF VIOLENCE

Questions about individual rights frame historiographical debates about political change over the decades between the Revolution and the Civil War. Where some scholars characterize the period in terms of the expansion of civil and political rights, others identify stasis or contraction. Both sides are right: while some Americans — namely, native-born, adult white men — experienced the period as the democratic opening of law and politics, others saw those same opportunities slip beyond their grasp. Therein lies the point of historiographical disagreement: did the extension of civil and political rights to some portions of the population, but not to all, make the United States more or less democratic? Because the question itself assumes the rubric of individual rights, it cannot explain the presence of this legal framework. Viewing the period from a perspective that does not posit a legal system based in individual rights changes our analytical perspective. Rather than being contradictory trends, the simultaneous extension of civil and political rights to some and their denial to others appear as related dynamics in the institutional development of rights. Those changes were national in scope, although they unfolded differently within each state.

In the South, rights took particularly narrow forms. The resulting legal inequalities were so stark and so overt that many historians consider them to be differences in kind, not degree — the result of a distinctively southern legal and political culture. As the North embraced a legal order that recognized individual rights, the South remained mired in status relationships and other remnants of an archaic past. This contrast between northern progress and southern exceptionalism, however, is greatly overdrawn. In the decades following the Revolution, southern states led the way in applying rights to some areas of law, particularly property law. The region did lag behind later, when the engines of economic development and the concomitant need for legal innovation moved northward. Nonetheless, southern appellate courts and legislatures continued to extend the rubric of rights outward to other legal issues, including public matters formerly governed by the peace and handled at the local level.[3] The prominent place

223

of individual rights within state law did not inevitably undermine slavery. To the contrary, state lawmakers used this logic to keep slaves in subordination and to restrict free blacks, white women, and even poor white men. The expansion of rights to free white men entailed their denial to everyone else — a dynamic that breathed new life into the paradoxical pairing of slavery and freedom that, as historian Edmund S. Morgan observed, had characterized the South since Bacon's Rebellion in the 1670s.[4]

Even so, the legal trajectory of the South during the period between the Revolution and the Civil War was strikingly similar to that of other regions. Like lawmakers elsewhere in the nation, those in the South placed individual rights at the center of state law, with results that were not always egalitarian, let alone democratic. The South, with its dramatic legal extremes, complicates these historiographical issues in ways that recast our understanding of national currents.[5] Given how deeply entrenched presumptions of southern distinctiveness are in the historiography, it is useful to situate the South within those national historical currents before turning to specifics within the Carolinas.

Many scholars still identify the period between the Revolution and the Civil War as the "age of democracy," taking their cues from a venerable body of scholarship reaching back to the Progressive Era and Arthur Schlesinger's classic work. Recently Sean Wilentz has revived this argument, depicting a nation in the throes of a radical transformation that opened up government to popular participation. Beginning in the decades following the Revolution, states broadened the basis of representation in legislatures and eliminated property requirements for voting and officeholding. Voters became actively involved in party politics at the state and national levels, culminating in massive popular support for Andrew Jackson in 1828. The symbolism of his election was at least as important as his administration's policies. The political culture that mobilized around Jackson defined political rights universally, extended them to all white men, and identified the protection of rights as government's primary duty. Democratic change went only so far during this period, stopping after it reached white men who held no property in anything except their own labor. But it inspired other movements, including abolitionism and women's rights, which pushed democratic principles further to include more people.[6]

The South exemplified these national trends in key respects. Facing intense pressure from newly settled western districts, southern lawmakers adopted apportionment systems that created more equitable representation in state government and extended the vote to all white men. South

Carolina did so in 1808, and North Carolina followed suit in 1835, although property requirements for state senators remained in place there until the 1850s. These changes brought new blood to state capitals: white men whose personal style, aspirations, and place of residence made them seem fundamentally different from the low country elite that had dominated state politics in the Carolinas for so long. Their rise to political power was part of a national changing of the guard, as men such as Andrew Jackson, Henry Clay, and John C. Calhoun replaced Revolutionary leaders such as George Washington and Thomas Jefferson. Calling all free men — by which they meant white men — to the polls, these new party leaders promised a system that would uphold their rights, regardless of wealth or status. Carolina lawmakers used the same rhetoric and made the same assurances, ushering in an array of reforms in state government that included the transformation of the legal system.[7]

Other historians draw very different conclusions from the same evidence. Focusing on slaves, free blacks, white women, and poor laborers instead of free white men, they emphasize the limits of legal and political change. The pervasive, oppressive influence of race, they argue, makes it impossible to view this period as democratic. Even in the aftermath of the Revolution, the movement to abolish slavery never made much headway in the South, where most of the black population lived. Instead of freeing the region from slavery's grip, southern planters justified its continuation in terms of the preservation of Revolutionary principles. Slavery was a humanitarian necessity to keep a potentially disruptive, racially inferior, dependent population under control.[8] Similar issues as well as concerns about protecting slaveholders' property rights constrained abolition in the North, where some slaves did not obtain their freedom until the 1850s. Once free, African Americans faced the rising tide of racism, increasingly supported by legal restrictions that formally denied them civil and political rights. Racism even reached into the abolitionist movement, where many white activists opposed full civil and political equality for African Americans.[9]

Democratic rights were not extended to all white Americans either. As women's historians have shown, the gendered dimensions of post-Revolutionary political change created new barriers to white women's participation in law, politics, and the market economy. In particular, the conceptual differentiation of "feminine" domestic space from the "masculine" world of law, politics, and market relations imposed an ideological framework that devalued women's labor and made it difficult for women to claim rights in law or access to political institutions.[10] White men without property faced a combination of old and new constraints. Many states resisted proposals to eliminate property requirements for voting and officeholding and to make state government more responsive and accessible. Poor white men endured numerous legal restrictions at the local and state levels, including vagrancy laws that forced them into low-wage employment, labor laws that denied them the right to organize and subordinated them to their employers' control, and a host of other measures that kept them from exercising civil and political rights to their full extent.[11]

Similar limitations on the extension of democratic rights are visible in the South as well. State lawmakers clamped down on slavery, piling up acts that not only restricted slaves but also aimed to regulate and stabilize the institution by limiting customary privileges (such as trading, education, and mobility) that some masters allowed some slaves and by mobilizing propertyless white men to police slaves. The status of free blacks deteriorated, as legislators and appellate justices took away rights they had once exercised as free people and even questioned their place as citizens. Perhaps the most dramatic example is North Carolina's 1835 constitution, which instituted a more equitable apportionment scheme, established free white manhood suffrage, and denied free blacks the vote. State lawmakers refused to extend individual rights to white women. Instead, they insisted on women's status as dependents represented by rights-bearing male household heads, just as slaves were represented by masters. Having forged that legal link between marriage and slavery, political leaders in North and South Carolina became increasingly outspoken in their denunciations of women's rights during the second quarter of the nineteenth century.[12] Neither state led the democratic charge when it came to free white men, either. Both were known for their hierarchical governments, often referred to as oligarchies, which limited the power of poor white men and kept government in the hands of the wealthy.[13]

The proverbial glass is either half full or half empty. In fact, there is no way beyond this interpretive impasse as long as the debate is framed in terms of the distribution of rights rather than their development, definitions, and uses. When did rights begin to govern the legal issues that mattered most in ordinary people's lives? What were the implications? This chapter shifts the analytical framework by focusing on the protection of individual *life* rather than individual *rights*. To be vulnerable to physical violence without any possibility for redress—whether through individual rights or appeals to the peaceable order of the community—is to be profoundly marginalized, legally and politically. Any society's legal treatment of violence involves political decisions about the structure of the public order. Identifying which acts to censure and whom to protect determines the government's relationship to ordinary people. Analytical frameworks based in individual rights cannot adequately address this issue because they erroneously presume either that every person holds rights or that what counts as a violation of rights and which persons are protected have been mysteriously predetermined.

Between the late eighteenth and the mid-nineteenth centuries, changes in the legal treatment of violence reflected and reinforced broader changes in the political culture of the Carolinas. To understand the scope of those changes, it is necessary to pick up the threads of the analysis introduced in chapter 3, which traced the process by which assaults became public, criminal matters instead of private, civil matters. Within localized law, legal officials began treating complaints of violence as crimes against the peace rather than private matters that could be resolved through compensation to the injured party. That transformation, which was directed by the actions of ordinary southerners, exemplified people's direct relationship to the localized legal system, a political connection forged in the upheaval of the Revolution.

In the colonial South, the laws of violence underscored the relative political marginalization of all subjects. In theory, no subject's physical injuries became a "public wrong"—a criminal matter that threatened the public order—unless they also affected the king's metaphorical body by breaking the peace of his realm. Those concepts carried broader import, enabling colonial officials to control the political repercussions of violence. In most cases, violence did not pose a direct challenge either to the colonial government or to the social order it protected. Common brawlers, for instance, did not fight with the specific intent of defying their social betters, let alone challenging the political structure. For colonial officials, the problem lay in the way such acts symbolically bypassed established lines of authority. Physically defending themselves and their interests, ordinary southerners acted as sovereign individuals instead of subjects who depended on the king and his officers to represent and protect their interests. Carolina colonists—a diverse, irreverent, contentious lot—stepped over this line often, if the bellyaching of colonial officials and elite commentators is any indication. The categorization of violence as private rather than public neutralized the potential political threat, although not in the literal sense of stopping violence or even rectifying the pain and damage it caused. These

227

classifications operated more as institutional safety valves, releasing the pressure that cases of violence generated within the legal system. Labeling violent acts as private personalized them, stripping them of broader meanings so that they could not affect existing power arrangements. Men fought to maintain their reputations, neighbors came to blows over property, husbands hit their wives, masters beat their slaves, and parents whipped their children. Construed as private wrongs, none of those acts could be connected to structural problems that required sustained public attention. The dynamics affirmed the king's authority by giving his officers discretionary control in identifying which conflicts constituted public threats.

Containing the political implications of violence required constant supervision. In this period, as they did later, officials used the concepts of private and public as legal means to political ends, not as fixed categories with normative meanings. Officials shuffled different kinds of violent acts back and forth between the two designations as conditions warranted. Colonial legislatures in the Carolinas, for instance, redefined maiming—or mayhem—to include the destruction of ears and noses. Traditionally, this legal category covered only those limbs necessary for a man to fulfill his military duties to the king. The change addressed a specific problem in the colonies: ritualized fighting that involved biting off noses and ears as well as gouging eyes, which could be construed to fit within established definitions of maiming. When the lower orders used violence too freely, they not only broke the king's peace but also moved into his political territory. If unchecked, personal violence could acquire legitimacy and lead to the problematic, even subversive notion that individuals had the right to act for themselves and represent their own interests. By criminalizing these acts, lawmakers acknowledged that challenge, magnified in a colonial context where government authority was so fragile. Given the pervasiveness and predictability of ritualized fighting, it was no longer possible to defuse the political threat simply by making these offensive acts private. Colonial authorities labeled them public so as to regulate them directly.[14]

The post-Revolutionary elevation of "the people" as the metaphorical sovereign produced a seismic shift in the legal handling and political implications of physical injuries. In theory, the elimination of the king made violence to individuals—and damage to individuals' interests generally—more directly public and more obviously political. But in practice, between 1790 and 1820, those changes appeared within a notion of the peace that took what otherwise might have been egalitarian, individualistic concepts in decidedly different directions. In localized law, individuals became

legally visible as differently subordinated subjects, not rights-bearing individuals who stood in positions of abstract legal equality. The legal importance attached to individuals did establish direct connections between
these subjects and their government. But those connections preserved the
hierarchies that defined southern society, including those that subordinated all white men to the peace and made some white men subordinate
to other white men. State law tended to treat individuals as rights-holders
instead. When applied to criminal violence in the 1820s, the framework of
rights placed adult white men on theoretically equal footing, legally privileging their interests and consolidating their authority over those without
rights.[15]

INDIVIDUAL VIOLENCE AS AN OFFENSE TO
THE PEACE, FROM 1790 TO THE 1820S

Between 1790 and 1820, localized law turned injuries to individuals into
criminal matters. With their attention firmly fixed on property law, state
lawmakers left governance over most acts of violence to local jurisdictions
and their idiosyncratic interpretations of common law. Statutes and appellate decisions mirrored changes at the local level when they dealt with
violence at all. State law did address more serious offenses, such as murder,
manslaughter, rape, and maiming. But misdemeanor violence did not figure
in revised codes or appear as a topic of legislation until the late nineteenth
century. The appellate courts dealt with such matters infrequently, primarily
to sort out procedural or jurisdictional matters only tangentially related to
the crime itself. When state law made forays into criminal violence, it was
usually one step behind local jurisdictions.[16] Between 1790 and the 1820s,
state law adopted the same stance as localized law, affirming the political
emphasis on individuals but positioning them as subjects within the peace.
Only later, when state lawmakers headed more powerful institutions and
turned their attention to criminal law, would they reconceptualize those
subjects as rights-bearing individuals.

The pattern of state institutions following local practice is evident in
the published reports of appellate decisions. In these volumes, cases involving violence regularly appeared as civil matters — private wrongs — between 1790 and 1820. Increasingly, though, appellate courts reflected changing practices in local jurisdictions, where violence was being treated as a
criminal offense — a public wrong — by definition. The shift is evident in
two South Carolina appellate cases. In *State v. Wood*, heard in 1794, the

court approached violence as an act that could be a crime, but only under certain circumstances. Local authorities had charged the defendant with the criminal offense of assault, rather than treating it only as a civil matter. He took issue with the charge, arguing that he was acting in self-defense: the victim "brought this injury on herself by . . . striking the defendant first, and therefore ought to abide by the consequence." But the court agreed with the prosecutor, who maintained that the "assault was an outrageous one, committed on a woman, and out of all proportion to the nature of the injury he had received from her." Therefore, the defendant should "be considered as the aggressor" and the charges were justified. The specifics of the case, including the fact that the victim was a woman, turned this particular act of violence into a violation of the peace. Other acts of violence would not have been crimes, as the defense's arguments suggest.[17]

By 1802, in *Chanellor v. Vaughn*, the appellate court assumed that violent acts had public effects. The question was how best to deal with their disruptive implications. The presumption was particularly striking in this case because it was tried as a civil matter—still a common occurrence, even when local jurisdictions were more likely to treat a wider array of violent acts as criminal offenses. Although the case was a civil matter, the South Carolina appellate court treated the violence in question as if it were a public wrong. That presumption emerged in the court's response to the defendant's appeal, which maintained that the damages granted by the jury were excessive and should be set aside. The justices refused, arguing that high fines in cases involving violence were in the public's best interests. It was the province of the jury, the justices explained, "to assess such damages as they thought would be commensurate with the nature of the injury." The jury's responsibility in this regard extended to the community, not just the victim: "The peace and good order of the community depended very much on making proper examples of such disorderly and turbulent men as the defendant appeared to be." Given the violent nature of the offense, this private wrong contained elements of a public wrong as well. From there, it was a small leap to treating most acts of violence as public wrongs, by definition.[18]

By the 1820s, the link between violence and crime permeated appellate rulings in both North Carolina and South Carolina. Cases of violence routinely passed through these courts as crimes without the kind of discussion that marked *State v. Wood* in 1794. Occasionally questions about the legal status of violence rose as points of discussion, as they did in the North Carolina court's 1821 ruling in *Stout v. Rutherford*. The victim in this civil case was surprised to find that the public implications of violence meant he could not be awarded damages. He had appealed in order to obtain a settlement. Although the jurors decided in his favor, they had denied him damages for his injuries because he had consented to the fight. The majority opinion in the appellate court arrived at the same conclusion from a different direction: the victim could not recover damages because the primary injury was to the peace, which lifted the matter out of the hands of the two parties involved. Not all the justices were comfortable with the implications of this ruling. Justice Hall concurred with the jury: "I doubt how far a person is entitled to recover damages after having agreed to take his chance in a combat" and "after the event had proved the miscalculation he made upon his own strength." But, in testy comments that fell just short of dissent, he expressed reservations about classifying all acts of interpersonal violence as public wrongs. He was inclined to see such incidents as "merely . . . violations of . . . private rights," minimizing the legal and political importance of this kind of violence. Yet Hall agreed to abide by the new rule, which clearly marked assault as a criminal matter first and a civil matter only secondarily.[19]

The appellate courts magnified the legal importance of injuries to individuals as well. In 1794, for instance, the North Carolina court ruled in *State v. Irwin* that intent could be inferred from the context in which injuries were inflicted. In criminal matters, intent determined the severity of the charges. Malice turned an accidental death into manslaughter, and malice aforethought turned manslaughter into murder. Proving intent could be difficult, particularly if there were no witnesses to the event. Did the defendant mean to kill the victim? Or was it an accident? Those questions usually required a careful reconstruction of the entire context surrounding the incident, with testimony of witnesses who knew both parties and the nature of their relationship. In *State v. Irwin*, the North Carolina appellate court eliminated the need for evidence of intent in the criminal charge of maiming. The wording suggested a broader application to other forms of violence as well. "Malice aforethought is express or to be implied from circumstances," the court posited. Therefore "intent to maim or disfigure, may likewise be implied from circumstances; and it is not necessary to prove antecedent grudges, threatenings or an express design." The justices upheld that ruling in 1796 in *State v. Evans*: "Where an outrageous act, as a maim, is proved, the law presumes that it was done with that disposition of mind, which the law requires to constitute guilt, until the contrary is shewn." The injury to the individual, by itself, constituted proof of the crime; further evidence was unnecessary.[20]

That logic made its way into other legal categories of violence, such as affray, assault, and assault and battery. The effect was to blur traditional legal distinctions between various forms of violent offenses. Appellate courts tended to define all these crimes in terms of the individuals' injuries. In 1824 the North Carolina appellate court stretched the definition of criminal violence to cover acts that did not result in physical injury to the victim. The case involved two Granville County men convicted of affray for firing guns at a neighbor woman's house and killing her dog. Their lawyers appealed, arguing that it was a civil matter because it was carried out against a private individual in what might be construed as a private space and no public threat was implied in either the actions or the indictment. Writing for the court, Justice Taylor dismissed that argument, claiming that the acts fell under the criminal offense of affray: "It seems certain there may be an affray when there is no actual violence," but enough commotion to "cause a terror to the people." To lay that charge, though, the court substituted the offense against the individual for that done to the public: the post-Revolutionary incarnation of the king's symbolic body resided in a dead dog and a terrified woman.[21]

Another 1824 North Carolina civil suit, *White v. Fort*, underscored the legal importance of individuals' physical injuries. On appeal, the state court ruled that victims of violent felonies or their survivors could prosecute civil cases concurrently with the public prosecution of criminal charges in order to obtain compensation for their losses. In British common law the victims of such crimes could not seek redress for damages because the injury done to the king took precedence. The theoretical subordination of the individual to the king was so complete that it negated the practical possibility of a separate civil suit. The king, as prosecutor, received the convicted felon's forfeited property as compensation, leaving nothing for individual victims to claim. Although forfeiture no longer applied in North Carolina or anywhere else in the United States, the logic by which states prosecuted felonies was the same: the state's interest in controlling violence took precedence over the interest of the victim. The unresolved question, then, was the legal status of injured individuals. Did the injury to the public order trump the significance of victims' injuries to the point where they could not sue for damages? The appellate court decided to define the individual's interest as separate from that of the state and to allow concurrent civil suits in felonies. Bypassing the theoretical subordination of private to public injuries that could have prohibited concurrent civil suits, the court justified individuals' rights to bring civil suits on the more practical grounds of forfeiture. Although the justices disagreed about the details, they acknowledged that civil suits had been disallowed only because forfeiture left no property to compensate the individual and, since forfeiture had been abandoned, no basis for the prohibition remained. In fact, the justices' arguments presumed that individuals had as much right to redress as the public, granting them independent legal status that they did not previously have.[22]

The changes that linked individuals' injuries to the peace extended even to slaves, although unevenly, since slaves never shared equal or even equivalent status with other subjects. State lawmakers buttressed local practice, turning the most egregious acts of physical violence against slaves into crimes. In 1791 the North Carolina legislature made the willful killing of a slave murder unless it resulted from "moderate correction," legal discretion that was allowed household heads over all their dependents. The statute's preamble drew heavily on Revolutionary language, declaring that the previous "distinction of criminality between the murder of a white person and one who is equally a human creature, but merely of a different complexion, is disgraceful to humanity and degrading in the highest degree to the laws and principles of a free, Christian, and enlightened country." In 1817 the legislature extended the peace further, making the crime of manslaughter applicable to instances in which the victim was a slave. These statutes, however, affirmed rather than modified local practice, which already applied common law precepts—which were not always officially recognized as part of state law—to cases involving slaves. Even acts that granted slaves procedural rights tended to buttress local practice by easing the difficulties of trying slaves and cases involving slaves in a system where process was so important.[23]

In key respects the appellate court also followed local practice. The central issue in *State v. Boon*—an 1801 appellate ruling that criticized the 1791 North Carolina statute criminalizing the killing of slaves as too ambiguous to enforce—was not *whether* slaves were included in the peace, but *how* that was accomplished in the theoretical terms of law. Justice Hall argued that common law protections that applied to other subjects did not automatically extend to slaves. Drawing a connection between common law and the peace, he reasoned that slaves lived under the dominion of their masters, not under that of the peace, because slavery did not exist within common law. For slaves to be brought into the peace, common law protections had to be enacted through statute. As Hall saw it, the problem in this case was that the 1791 statute was too vague to accomplish that goal. While agreeing with Hall on the inadequacy of the statute, Justice John Louis Taylor took the opportunity to advocate the criminalization of violence against slaves in broader, more general terms. "What is the definition of murder?" he wrote, but "the unlawful killing of a reasonable creature within the peace of the State, with malice aforethought." "A slave," he continued, "is a reasonable creature, may be within the peace, and is under the protection of the State, and may become the victim of preconceived malice." Justice Samuel Johnston went further, arguing that the murder of a slave was more "atrocious and barbarous . . . than killing a person who is free, and on an equal footing." "It is an evidence of a most depraved and cruel disposition to murder one so much in your power that he is incapable of making resistance, even in his own defense." In such incidents, the legal system needed to step in, discipline the offender, and restore order. Significantly, the justices who were most outspoken in their defense of slaves' interests couched their arguments in terms of slaves' place within the peace, not their rights as individuals.[24]

The sway of the peace within localized law explains many apparent legal anomalies at the state level. Consider the 1798 case of *State v. Weaver*, which appears in John Haywood's compilation of early North Carolina appellate decisions. *Weaver* granted masters exactly the kind of latitude that judges questioned in *Boon*, although none of the opinions in *Boon* mentioned this case, even to dismiss it. The decision in *Weaver* began with an analogy between free servants and slaves: "If a free servant refuses to obey and the master endeavor[s] to exact obedience by force, and the servant offers to resist by force . . . and the master kills, it is not murder, nor even manslaughter, but justifiable." A master's use of force was "much more . . . justifiable" when directed against slaves, who were more completely subordinated than free servants.[25] The legal context of the 1790s, however, shaped the meaning and limited the applicability of this opinion. At this time the North Carolina appellate court was still a court of conference, which advised judges in local jurisdictions on especially difficult cases; it did not lay down rules that justices elsewhere were supposed to follow in other cases. Moreover, the published opinion in *Weaver* was not really a decision at all, even though it later passed as precedent. Rather, the text seems to have been the instructions given to the jury by district judge John Haywood, who later included this case in his compilation of early appellate decisions. It did not involve the rights of all masters and all slaves, as Haywood's presentation of the case implied, but the use of force by a specific master, Mr. Scott, against a specific slave, Lewis. Following Judge Haywood's advice, the jury acquitted

Scott. At the time, given the discretionary power of localized law, Scott's use of force was contingent, based in local context and exercised on behalf of the peace.[26]

South Carolina state lawmakers affirmed the power of the peace by leaving the criminal prosecution of violence against slaves to local jurisdictions, which used a combination of colonial statutes and the maxims of the peace as defined in common law. The laws passed in the wake of the Stono slave rebellion in 1740 were intended primarily to bring the institution of slavery within the bounds of the law so as to stabilize it. They codified the traditional legal practices of the peace, including its affirmation of existing social hierarchies. Predictably, the statutory burdens of legal discipline fell most heavily on slaves. But the 1740 statutes also brought white southerners under the law's control, establishing punishments for their extreme brutality against slaves as well. Local authorities in the post-Revolutionary period used the rubric of the peace to apply customary interpretations of common law—or not—as they saw fit. When such cases made it to the appellate level, the court tended to affirm local practice. In 1794, for instance, the court supported a local court's decision to include slaves among those who could commit the common law offense of riot. As late as 1825, appellate justices upheld the conviction of a white man for the murder of a slave on the basis that the charge conformed to the common law charge of manslaughter.[27]

Even when the South Carolina appellate court ruled on these matters, its decisions carried different meanings than they would later. In South Carolina, as in North Carolina, the appellate court functioned more in an advisory capacity, particularly between 1790 and the 1820s. District judges came together after completing their circuits to settle disputed or difficult cases. Not all of the cases cited in state compilations were appeals. These volumes also contain decisions that the authors thought were instructive as guides for the legal profession. Matters of interest included the facts of the case, the arguments, the instructions, and the people involved, not just the points of law addressed in the decision. The decisions that make up this early body of "appellate law" recognized local jurisdictions' creative use of the common law concept of the peace, in conjunction with statutes, to provide wider latitude in punishing whites for violence against slaves.

Historians who have searched for systematic legal patterns in these early appellate records have found them frustratingly incoherent. Some have thrown up their hands, accepting contemporary legal reformers' charges of incompetence and chaos. The most generous interpretations characterize these early appellate decisions as rendering broad interpretations of the statutes. Actually, the records say more about localized law than they do about the statutes or the direction of legal developments at the state level. These advisory opinions resulted from a system that not only allowed local jurisdictions considerable legal discretion but also subordinated the individual outcomes to the collective interests of the peace. Consider the curious arguments of Thomas Pinckney and Timothy Ford in the 1791 case of *State v. Gee*. A local jury had convicted a white man for murdering a slave and sentenced him to seven years' imprisonment, in keeping with the statutes. In their capacity as state prosecutors, Pinckney and Ford questioned the leniency of the sentence with a logic that seems bizarre for two low country Federalist luminaries who were known for their support of a centralized legal system. Applying the principles of the peace to the offense, they argued that the "atrocity" was such that it "deserved death" in this instance. The judge denied their motion. Their argument is nonetheless telling. In particular cases the common law principles of the peace regularly modified and even suspended statutes without threatening their integrity. Both bodies of law had the same goal: to maintain the peace of the state.[28]

Appellate courts did exert more authority over legal issues involving property. Professionally trained lawyers, who read appellate decisions, oversaw this area of law, and property law's close connections with economic development placed a premium on clarification and innovation so as to facilitate the exchange of goods and the accumulation of capital. Right after the Revolution, South Carolina was the wealthiest state in the union, with an economy rooted in slave labor and commodity production for an export market. The protection of property interests, which had preoccupied colonial legislators and jurists, continued to absorb lawmakers, lawyers, and compilers. South Carolina appellate judges, in particular, tended to spend their time in this area of the law. Property concerns could be heard in both law and equity courts, and judges in those two types of courts competed for personal recognition and institutional authority, making this area especially fraught with differences of opinion.[29]

State-level records of legal matters involving slaves were defined by the same preoccupation with matters of property and differences of opinion that defied systematization. Helen Tunnicliff Catterall's 1929 collection, *Judicial Cases Concerning American Slavery and the Negro*, exemplifies the problem. Catterall collected all the cases that dealt with slavery or included slaves from all the available legal compilations in both law and equity. For

South Carolina between 1784 and 1819, she lists 153 property cases and only 21 criminal cases involving slaves.[30] This source and others based on the appellate court records leave the impression that state law treated slaves primarily as property. But that was an artifact of this particular institutional arena. Not only did appellate courts deal primarily with civil matters, but those compiling appellate records were especially interested in property law. The disparity between civil and criminal cases thus tells us a great deal about appellate courts and their supporters, but not much about the full range of legal matters tried within the state. The logic of these cases, even more than their relative quantities, distinguishes localized law from law at the state level. The local counterpart to state law does not lie in a volu-minous stash of cases moldering away in the far reaches of the archives, a misplaced testament to the superior morals of a localized legal system, the homespun humanity of white southerners, or — even more problem-atically — the benevolence of slavery. The logic of the peace allowed local jurisdictions to address offenses against slaves on a case-by-case basis. While more incidents were dropped than were prosecuted, slaves occu-pied a place as subjects of the peace in local jurisdictions. By contrast, they appeared primarily as property — the subjects of rights-holders — in the de-veloping body of law at the state level.[31]

Many legal reformers sought to extend the rubric of rights beyond property matters into other areas of law, including criminal cases. Their handiwork is evident in compilations like those of North Carolina's John Haywood. In North Carolina the same sentiments resulted in statutes that extended procedural rights to slaves, including the right to trial by jury and to counsel in 1793 and the right of appeal in 1807. The rhetoric of rights figured prominently in appellate decisions. In *State v. Boon*, Judge Hall re-ferred to the common law protections of subjects as "rights," a term that neither Judge Taylor nor Judge Johnston used.[32] But when legal reformers invoked rights between 1790 and 1820, they got only so far. In localized law, assertions of slaves' humanity established their place as subordinate sub-jects within the peace, a legal framework in which rights-bearing white men were subordinated as well. Affirmation of a master's authority did not ex-tend to all masters, constituting a right that the state was bound to protect. Similarly, slaves' procedural rights recognized their place within a localized system that emphasized process over outcome. Bringing slaves into the process was necessary to maintain the peace; it did not entail recognition of their individual rights.[33]

Attempting to navigate the legal terrain of the peace with the map of

individual rights has led historians to dead ends and puzzling contradictions. Taking the ascendancy of the individualist legal paradigm for granted
and focusing on statutes and appellate decisions, they have struggled to
identify consistent patterns in the application of rights to marginalized
members of the population.[34] But those institutions and that legal framework had yet to be fully elaborated, particularly in criminal law. By the 1820s
the steady drizzle of rights rhetoric began to erode localized conceptions
of the peace at the state level, as state law expanded and spilled over onto
the terrain of localized law. But the extension of individual rights into the
legal process—the trends that scholars have observed in the development
of state law—was not the same thing as the extension of individual rights
to those individuals who made up the population as a whole.

SLAVERY AND VIOLENCE AS AN
INDIVIDUAL RIGHT, 1820–1860

By the 1820s state institutions and state law—the body of state law made
up of statutes and appellate decisions—took on new authority. At the same
time, lawmakers began importing the logic of property law into matters involving violence and other public issues. In so doing, they moved the legal
focus away from individual lives to individual rights, replacing subjects of
the peace, with their distinctive personalities and entangling relationships,
with the theoretically uniform bodies of rights-bearing individuals. Using
the rights of these abstract individuals as a reference point, they began
to redefine the peace. When reformers and state-level jurists invoked the
peace, they meant not the inclusive domain occupied by the idiosyncratic
and interconnected subjects of previous generations and localized law but
a collectivity composed of theoretically autonomous rights-bearing individuals who owned property. Property ownership was, simultaneously, the
basis for claiming rights, the model for them, and the means for mobilizing the peace. The possession of rights, construed as a form of property,
became the primary route to the legal protections of the peace. For interpersonal violence, the results were twofold. Lawmakers treated the legal
protections traditionally granted to all subjects under the peace as rights.
Once these protections were cast as rights, judges began refusing them
to domestic dependents on the basis that they would endanger husbands'
and masters' domestic authority. The legal effect was to privatize domestic relations, including slavery, by uprooting household heads' authority
238   from its place within the more expansive, localized notion of the peace and

planting it on the private property of rights-bearing individuals. All domestic dependents were repositioned as the subjects of their household heads instead of subjects of the peace. The implications were most dramatic for slaves, the most marginalized of subjects and the least able to summon the protections of the peace.

In the 1820s, when appellate courts in the Carolinas began handling more criminal matters than they had before, their decisions transformed the nature of the peace. When the peace was the guiding concept in localized law, its substance always remained plastic—and purposefully so, defined as it was in specific areas, at distinct moments in time, and through the particular relationships of the people there. Appellate courts fixed the substance of the peace by defining it primarily in terms of individual property rights. The 1823 North Carolina case of *State v. Reed*, which involved a white man convicted of manslaughter for killing a slave, captures the essence of this transition. *Reed* recapitulated the major questions in the 1801 case of *State v. Boon*: whether slaves were part of the peace and whether fatal violence against them could be tried under common law. Two of the three judges in *Reed*, John Louis Taylor and John Hall, had also issued opinions in *Boon*. In 1823, though, they sat on the newly constituted North Carolina Supreme Court, composed of three judges who only heard appeals, instead of the North Carolina Court of Conference, which had included all the judges who tried cases in district courts. Both Taylor and Hall wrote short opinions reaffirming their decisions in *Boon*, which took different positions on how to include slaves within the peace. Hall placed slaves outside the bounds of the peace and common law unless the legislature specified otherwise. Taylor, who assumed slaves' position within the peace, thought common law was applicable to them.[35]

Although Justice Leonard Henderson sided with Taylor in *Reed*, his opinion cast the issue differently by raising the question of whether slaves' position as property severed their ties to the peace and their access to the protections of the state, be it through common law or statute. "That a slave is a reasonable, or more properly a human being, is not, I suppose, denied," wrote Henderson. "But it is said that being property, he is not within the protection of the law." After stating the hypothetical that slaves' position as property excluded them from all legal protections, Henderson rejected it, but only in regard to fatal violence. No one, not even masters, had power over slaves' lives. There is no law in North Carolina, wrote Henderson, "by which the life of a slave is placed at the disposal of his master." Even so, Henderson conceded that masters' property rights shielded them from legal intervention in every other respect. The law "vested in the master, the absolute and uncontrolled right to the services of the slave, and the means of enforcing those services." In those areas, "the law has nothing to do" and will not "interfere upon the ground that the State's rights, and not the master's, have been violated." Property rights privatized the institution of slavery.[36]

In the 1820s appellate courts viewed offenses against slaves primarily through the lens of property rights. Unlike Leonard Henderson, later appellate justices saw any intervention on behalf of slaves as a violation of the masters' individual rights. In North Carolina, Justice Thomas Ruffin's decisions have provided graphic examples of this new viewpoint. Ruffin's reliance on the language of status relations has led some scholars to see him as a bulwark of tradition, a paternalist who defended slavery and marriage as organic relationships defined through the reciprocal obligations of master and slave, husband and wife. Yet Ruffin was a thoroughly modern jurist, a Whig who saw individual initiative, the unfettered control of property, and economic development as key to the nation's future and whose decisions in matters of property reflected those commitments. In his decisions on marriage and slavery, much cited by historians, Ruffin remade those status relations by infusing them with the logic of property rights.[37]

Ruffin's commitment to property rights guided his most infamous ruling. In *State v. Mann* (1829), his convictions led him to define the defendant, John Mann, as a master, even though he only hired, rather than owned, Lydia, the injured slave. As Ruffin saw it, property rights trumped status, placing hirers, whose authority over slaves was established through a contract giving them temporary property rights, in the same position as owners, whose authority could be rooted in the status relationship of master and slave. Although this aspect of the decision has received a great deal of scholarly attention, the legal practice of granting hirers the authority of masters was well established. In the 1798 case of *State v. Weaver*, for instance, both the district court and the state court of conference had treated the defendant, a slave hirer, as if he were a master. More novel was the way Ruffin departed from the logic of status, forcing the relationship between master and slave or hirer and slave into the zero-sum equation of competing individual rights. In one of his most notorious pronouncements, Ruffin declared that the "power of the master must be absolute to render the submission of the slave perfect." By making the power of a master absolute, Ruffin turned it into an individual right rather than the product of a status relationship extended at the behest of the peace with the intent of maintaining public order. In disentangling an individual master's authority from its place within the peace, Ruffin also freed it from legal contingency and regulation. It became absolute, akin to other property rights that the state was bound to protect. By implication, legal intervention on behalf of Lydia might jeopardize the rights of all masters. "The danger would be great indeed if the tribunals of justice should be called on to graduate the punishment appropriate to every temper and every dereliction of menial duty," Ruffin concluded.[38] The universality of the property rights held by masters limited the jurisdiction of the state over their conduct toward slaves.

Ten years later, in *State v. Hoover*, Ruffin seemed to backtrack from this extreme position. In his 1839 opinion, Ruffin argued that a master's authority was not so complete that he could take a slave's life at will. But he still interpreted status relations through the lens of individual rights, just as he had in *Mann*. He began by reiterating the central point in *Mann*, that a master's authority to "lawfully punish his slave" was a right that "must, in general, be left to his own judgment and humanity, and cannot be judicially questioned." The difference in the *Hoover* case, according to Ruffin, was that violence had become so chronic and so brutal that it ceased to be punishment. "They are barbarities" that "do not belong to a state of civilization," so they "cannot be fairly attributed to an intention to correct or to chastise." Ruffin did not need to appeal to the peace to justify legal intervention; rather, his argument hinged on the contention that because of his behavior, John Hoover had ceased to act as a master in his relationship with the slave Mira. Therefore, his authority over Mira was no longer a right that the law was bound to protect. The court could punish him as a man who committed murder, rather than a master whose rights the court compromised. That ruling applied to other masters only when their exercise of authority took on the character of torture and placed them outside the category of master. Otherwise, the state would protect property rights by staying out of the master/slave relation.[39]

South Carolina lawmakers followed the same path. In 1821 the state legislature buttressed masters' property interests by increasing the criminal penalties for deadly violence against slaves, making murder by a third party a capital offense and fixing a relatively stiff penalty—a $500 fine and six months' imprisonment—for killing in "sudden heat and passion." In 1825 the appellate court ruled that the statute allowed for common law prosecutions of manslaughter, thereby affirming local practices that treated slaves as subjects of the peace. But subsequent rulings interpreted the new statute so as to limit the criminal responsibility of masters for the deaths of their slaves. The effect was to remove slaves from the protection of the peace and to turn their masters' authority into a right.[40]

The transformation began in 1826 with *State v. Raines*. Raines, who was not the dead slave's master, faced two charges: murder and the lesser count of killing in "sudden heat and passion." The district court jury placed their own interpretation on the statute and found Raines guilty of manslaughter instead. Apparently jury members took sudden heat and passion to be the same thing as manslaughter, a reasonable conclusion, since the common law definition of manslaughter was killing that resulted from anger without the specific intent to kill. Writing for the appellate court, Judge Charles Colcock overturned that decision, giving the 1821 statute both a narrow interpretation and an expansive application. That statute, Colcock insisted, replaced previous statutes and practices based in common law at the local level. While gesturing toward a unified body of state law, Colcock's decision underscored the distance between that legal vision and actual conditions. In 1821 South Carolina had no official collections of current statutes and no mechanisms in place to reconcile conflicting statutes, unless one specifically repealed another, which was not the case in this instance. Nor did statutes and appellate decisions constitute the only body of law operative in the state. Common law, in both its professional and customary forms, guided local proceedings, as the district court's handling of *Raines* indicates. Colcock nonetheless construed the 1821 statute as definitive. Since the statute only criminalized killing a slave "in the heat of passion" and not manslaughter, he reasoned, the jury's finding was impossible. Manslaughter was an offense in common law "between men standing on equal footing in society." That charge and, by extension, other common law protections did not apply to slaves. Neither did the existing statutory charge of homicide by "undue correction," which local courts used to prosecute masters.[41]

Later decisions placed masters' authority further beyond the reach of the peace. The court did backtrack in 1839 in *State v. Gaffney*, ruling that South Carolina law recognized killing by undue correction as a criminal offense. *Gaffney*, which affirmed the continued viability of earlier statutes, suggests the limited effect of *Raines* when appellate courts still shared space with other legal venues. The self-referential character of the appellate court's decisions also limited their implications. The court looked only at law made at the state level and excluded local practice, where customary renderings of common law often informed the application of statutes. In *Raines*, the jury filtered the statutory charge of killing by sudden heat and passion through the common law form of manslaughter. In 1848 the appellate court disavowed local jurisdictions' use of common law altogether. *State v. Fleming* was similar to *Raines*, except it was the slave's master who was convicted of manslaughter. Jurors faced two choices on the indictment: murder, or killing in sudden heat and passion. They decided on the second, and the verdict was recorded as manslaughter. The court overturned that decision on the ground that the 1821 statute did not provide for manslaughter, a charge in common law, but only for murder. The justices did extend the statute, arguing that killing by undue correction was included within the statutory charge of killing in sudden heat and passion. But masters could only be tried on that charge. Murder, manslaughter, and by extension other charges in common law did not extend to acts that resulted in the deaths of slaves. Only the statutes, limited as they were, applied. That decision refuted longstanding legal practices at the local level, which placed slaves within the peace of the state. The most telling evidence came in the dissent of Justices John Belton O'Neall and John Smith Richardson to *State v. Fleming*. O'Neall and Richardson argued that common law was in force—in fact, had been in force—until the passage of statutes.[42]

The 1849 case of *State v. Bowen* pushed a master's authority closer to the status of a right. A local jury had found the defendant guilty of denying his slaves sufficient food and clothing, a criminal offense by statute. While the court upheld that conviction, it also removed masters from legal scrutiny. "Instances do sometimes, though rarely, occur, in which it is necessary to interfere in behalf of the slave against the avarice of his master," the court acknowledged. But "the law should interpose its authority" only when the neighbors' property interests were involved, when neglect reached the point that it became "necessary to protect property from the depredation of famishing slaves." The court gestured to the peace, invoking "public sentiment." But it defined the peace—that the state would protect—purely in terms of property rights. The master's rights, firmly based on his domestic authority, were limited only insomuch as they infringed on the property rights of his neighbors.[43]

Appellate judges in both North and South Carolina then extended these principles to cases where the parties were not in the same household, explicitly turning a prerogative of status into a right possessed by all white men. In case after case, judges gave wide latitude to white men who used force against slaves. These decisions all turned on the rights of the white male defendants and focused on the provocation offered by the enslaved victim. If those actions were sufficiently damaging, then the defendant had the right to respond with violence without incurring criminal liability.

The standard was very different in cases involving free white men, where provocation consisted only in actual threats of violence, such as drawing a knife within striking range. For slaves, appellate courts defined provocation broadly: insults, disobedience, or threatening gestures proved sufficient to justify free white men's use of physical force. The North Carolina court laid out the standard in *State v. Tackett* in 1820: "It exists in the very nature of slavery, that the relation between a white and a slave is different from that between free persons, and, therefore, many acts will extenuate the homicide of a slave which would not constitute a legal provocation if done by a white person." This same standard also applied to assault, as the court explained in *State v. Hale* in 1823: "*Every* battery on a slave is not indictable, because the person making it may have matter of excuse or justification, which would be no defense for committing a battery on a free person. Each case of this sort must, in a great degree, depend on its own circumstances." *Hale* affirmed local practice that allowed assaults against slaves to be tried as criminal offenses to the peace. Yet here, as elsewhere, the court invoked the peace to limit the conduct of slaves and to protect the rights of white men who might be accused of criminal offenses for battering slaves.[44]

Not only was this vision of the peace narrower and more rigid than those that preceded it, but it defined the interests of the peace purely in terms of the interests of property owners. Defined primarily as property, slaves no longer figured as subjects of the peace unless explicitly included by the legislators and jurists who created this body of state law. Even then, they were liable to be ignored because the legal focus invariably shifted to the protection of their owners' property rights. Conceived in terms of property rights, the peace rested on exclusion, not inclusion; it cast slaves outside its borders instead of subordinating them within its dominion. That same logic applied, with lesser severity, to other domestic dependents.

THE PRIVATIZATION OF MARRIAGE, 1820–1860

As subjects who could not own property, wives found their access to the peace limited. At the state level, the treatment of divorce marked the way. The South Carolina legislature refused to deal with divorce at all, effectively removing regulation of the marital relationship from the body of state law. Beginning in the 1820s, the North Carolina appellate court set off in the same direction, amassing an impressively restrictive set of rulings in divorce cases. The justices draped their decisions in the rhetoric of the peace, linking the sanctity of marriage to the maintenance of social order.

But, in abstracting marriage from social context and advancing a rigid set of rules that applied universally, these rulings departed dramatically from legal practice at the local level. Where local courts were interested in maintaining marriages that contributed to the social order, the appellate court was interested in maintaining order by establishing abstract rules and protecting property rights.[45]

The North Carolina appellate court embraced a decidedly Blackstonian view of coverture, applying a strictly contractual characterization of marriage and an extreme view of wives' subordination and husbands' rights. Justices gave narrow interpretations to the statutory causes for dissolving the marriage contract, which led to a domestic version of *caveat emptor*. One of the most notorious decisions was the racially charged denial of Marville Scroggins's appeal for a divorce, a case decided in 1832 that has fascinated historians concerned with the legal meanings of race, sex, and gender. Scroggins sued for divorce on the grounds that his wife, who was white, had married him without disclosing that she was pregnant by a black man, even though none of her alleged actions — fornication, fraudulently representing herself as chaste at the time she married, and bearing a child of visibly mixed parentage — were among the causes for divorce specified by statute. Despite white society's unconditional condemnation of sexual contact between white women and black men, the North Carolina State Supreme Court joined the local court in ruling against the aggrieved husband. On first glance, that outcome seems to undermine the authority of husbands. But that seeming contradiction is what makes this case such a compelling example of the court's commitment to privatizing marriage. The appellate justices were was so committed to that position that they were willing to discipline individual husbands in order to free marital relations from legal intervention, which had the effect of ensuring the principle of all husbands' rights to govern their wives and their households. By vacating its space in domestic matters, the court created room for the expansion of household heads' rights.[46]

Those principles took precedence over the problems of any individual husband. According to Justice Ruffin, Scroggins was the author of "his own dishonor, in marrying a woman whom he knew to be lewd." He should take his wife as he found her. The good order of society, as Ruffin saw it, was served by maintaining uniform legal rules regarding marriage. Although in this instance the local jury came to the same decision, perhaps because it did not find Scroggins's story credible, juries often disregarded Ruffin's narrow interpretation of the divorce statutes. Because they placed less em-

Thomas Ruffin, Anne Kirkland Ruffin, and the house (given to the couple by her father) where they set up housekeeping after their marriage. Courtesy of the Southern Historical Collection, Wilson Library, the University of North Carolina at Chapel Hill.

phasis on abstract rules and more on the regulation of marriages as social institutions that served concrete purposes within communities, local juries were more willing to dissolve marriages that had ceased to function, especially if they had become a source of disorder. In fact, many couples separated without seeking divorces, and local communities regularly accepted informal dissolutions.[47]

The appellate court's refusal to intervene in this contractual relationship constituted judicial activism. The justices admitted as much in the text of their ruling, which not only denied Marville Scroggins a divorce but also limited the discretion of the superior courts in marital disputes. This case was discussed in the introduction to part 2, in which Ruffin took issue with the statutes for granting too much discretion to local jurisdictions. The results, as Ruffin argued, unsettled the law, which had the effect of impairing "the sanctity of the marriage compact . . . and the morals of society." Preserving social order, as Ruffin and the North Carolina appellate court defined it, consisted in the articulation and application of universal legal rules to abstract individuals. They maintained their commitment to those rules even when marriages unraveled in ways that threatened the social fabric of local communities.[48]

By placing all marital issues outside the bounds of law, the North Carolina appellate court followed the South Carolina state legislature in blocking wives' access to the legal system. Even when the North Carolina court refused the pleas of aggrieved husbands, as it did with Marville Scroggins, the legal result was the same. The failure of particular husbands' grievances supported the authority and the property rights of all husbands. Wives became yet another possession within their husbands' households, the borders of which were defined by property rights. Their husbands' authority became more absolute, and wives' connections outside their households had less power within the legal system than they once did.[49]

The logic of rights inevitably undermined the wives' claims to property that they possessed but did not own as individuals. Consider the experience of Mary Polk Badger, the daughter of William Polk, a Revolutionary War colonel who became prominent in North Carolina state politics. Like other fathers of his generation, William Polk had tried to look after the interests of his children and to keep his property within his family line. When Mary married George E. Badger, Polk set them up with land and slaves. At his death in 1834, he split his considerable estate among his children. Mary Polk Badger received her portion in the form of a separate estate, overseen by Thomas P. Devereux, a family friend and prominent legal reformer at the state level. The separate estate kept the property in Mary's hands, through her trustee, but gave her husband use of the estate during his lifetime and designated that it would pass to Mary's children at her death. Use of his wife's family property was not enough for Badger; he wanted something closer to absolute ownership. That was hard to accomplish, given the terms of William Polk's will. But in 1835 Badger came about as close as he possibly could. Devereux deeded Mary's separate estate to Badger, making Badger the trustee, giving him exclusive rights to the property, and allowing Mary use of it only should he die first. The property still passed to the children of Mary and George Badger, should they have any; if not, it reverted to George Badger and his heirs, not to Mary Polk's relatives, the family from whom the property came. Justice Thomas Ruffin, a friend of Badger and Devereux, witnessed and approved the transfer. When Mary died soon thereafter, the Polk family property moved permanently and absolutely into Badger's hands.[50]

Charity Cain Mangum, a younger woman in the same social circles as the Badgers, Devereuxs, and Ruffins, articulated the sentiments about marriage that underlay the modification of the separate estate set up under the will of Mary Polk Badger's father. Charity's husband, Willie P. Mangum, was a prominent Democrat and political rival of Badger, Devereux, and Ruffin, who were all allied with the Whig Party, but their opposing partisan allegiances did not entail social antagonism or indicate divergent views about property. The significant shift was generational. Charity Mangum's father died in the same year as Mary Badger's father and structured his will similarly, leaving Charity her portion in a separate estate. She was furious when she found out. Not realizing that these terms had been conventional in wealthy families in previous generations, Charity interpreted the will as an unusually outrageous public insult to her husband by implying that he could not be trusted with her property. She blamed her sister, whom she suspected of supporting women's rights, for exerting undue influence over their elderly father. In a particularly uncharitable letter, she threatened to break off all communication. "I care nothing for property," wrote Charity, "except as it would add to the comfort of my husband & children." In keeping with her conception of the marital union, her share of the estate should have gone directly to her husband. "I would prefer to work as long as my strength will hold out," she continued, with rising drama, "rather than do or consent to anything to hurt my husbands honor or character. For I have not learned & hope I never may to feel that my husband's lot is not mine."

To the contrary, "I . . . feel . . . his dependence more sorely than my own." Given the terms, she and her husband considered her legacy so tainted as to be utterly unacceptable. They refused to touch it, and planned to give all the proceeds to support free schools for poor children. Charity's outburst had little practical effect on her sister; when she remarried in 1839, she set up a separate estate to maintain possession of her property.[51]

These family dramas illustrate fundamental changes occurring throughout the country that have been well documented by historians. By the 1830s conceptions of absolute ownership were shouldering out other forms of legal possession in North Carolina and almost everywhere else, starting among the dominant middle class.[52] That transformation has structured classic debates in legal history, which explore the legal processes in the nineteenth century that gave individuals freedom to use their property and pursue their interests without the encumbrances that had restricted property owners' actions in the past. The same dynamics lie at the center of Mary Ritter Beard's 1946 classic study, *Women as a Force in History*. In this critique of liberal individualist versions of feminism, Beard argues that nineteenth-century advocates purposefully downplayed other legal forms of property possession in their single-minded pursuit of individual rights.[53] This preoccupation with rights was deeply rooted in the broader culture, she notes, connecting proponents of women's rights to larger shifts in the political economy. The evidence from the South conforms to the patterns Beard outlines. It was not just the upcoming generation of Mangums, Badgers, Devereuxs, and Ruffins who saw property in these terms. So did proslavery ideologues, who linked both slaves' and wives' control of property to radical social movements—abolition and feminism—that sought to extend rights to these groups more generally. An absolute individual right to property, whether restricted to white men or extended universally to women and nonwhite persons, was neither a self-evident truth nor a welcome outcome of economic development in a milieu in which it was possible to possess property, in forms ranging from landed estates to enslaved laborers, without claiming ownership in terms of rights. By the 1830s, though, it was already difficult to imagine how anyone might control property without also claiming a full array of rights. Those presumptions remain entrenched in scholarship, lingering with particular force in the literature on slavery. Careful, painstaking research has established that slaves controlled property and traded with masters, in defiance of conceptions that masters owned their bodies and appropriated all the products of their labor. Even now, many who think in liberal individualist terms find it difficult to fathom how slaves could actually possess property when they were themselves property and had no rights.

The conflation of husbands' authority with their property rights shaped criminal matters as well. The North Carolina appellate court's ruling in *State v. Preslar*, which acquitted the husband of murdering his wife because she fled the house after he beat her and died before reaching her parents' door, characterized a husband's authority as a right by limiting legal intervention in it. At the same time, the appellate court expanded husbands' rights to use force in the protection of their authority. In 1844 Justice Thomas Ruffin ruled in *State v. Craton* that "a husband has a right to use compulsion, if necessary, to enable him to regain the possession of his wife." In this instance, that right excused John Craton's killing of his wife's lover. It also had the effect of reducing wives to the position of property, which their husbands had the right to protect as they did other property, by force if necessary. The court pushed the logic further in *State v. Hussey* in 1852, reversing decades of local practice that allowed wives to contest their husbands' authority in law. Faced with legal issues that involved domestic violence, Justice Frederick Nash allowed wives to testify against their husbands only if they had "lasting injuries" and gave husbands the right to use physical force as long as they were not motivated by "mere wantonness and wickedness." The principle that husbands could compel their wives' obedience was not new. Localized law had applied this concept, in the name of the peace, to excuse many a husband's violent behavior against his wife or his wife's lover. The difference was the institutional context: the appellate courts of the 1820s redefined a husband's use of force through a uniform legal rule as a right that applied to all husbands in the state, whereas the rubric of the peace had been used to regulate and limit domestic violence at the same time that it allowed it.[54]

The courts granted those same patriarchal rights to white men in relation to women who were not their wives and to slaves they did not own as well. Mrs. Allison, who acted according to older expectations in a fight with a neighbor in 1821, unexpectedly found herself blamed when the neighbor killed her husband. Her husband and a man named Roberts were gambling at the Allisons' house. Fed up with the situation, Mrs. Allison ordered Roberts to leave. Perhaps she was intervening in an argument between the two. Perhaps she had grown tired of her husband gambling away the family resources. Perhaps they were just in her way. Whatever the reason, the argument escalated. When Roberts refused to go, Mrs. Allison threw water on Roberts and then knocked off his hat, a symbolic offense to his honor and, admittedly, a rather gutsy move on Mrs. Allison's part. In response, Roberts whacked her with a rifle, knocking her to the ground. Mrs. Allison's husband then advanced on Roberts and was killed in the ensuing fight. The Supreme Court of North Carolina refused to charge Roberts with murder, arguing that Mrs. Allison "certainly commenced" the fight "by her rudeness." None of Mrs. Allison's actions would have constituted legal provocation had she been a man. But since she was a woman, "rudeness" alone was sufficient justification for Roberts's assault on her and, consequently, the death of her husband by Roberts's hand.[55]

Appellate justices' dedication to a unified body of law based in rights was so strong that they protected its abstract rules even when they benefited such unlikely defendants as slaves, free blacks, disreputable white women, and propertyless white men. The case law is filled with instances, usually centered on procedural points, in which appellate courts overturned local convictions on legal technicalities. Historians have puzzled over these rulings, particularly those that benefited slaves, trying to figure out why legal officials so committed to the maintenance of slavery would undermine the system by extending what seemed like rights to slaves.[56] The perspective of the peace casts those rulings in a different light. Appellate courts were careful not to turn procedural rights into broader claims to individual rights when it came to slaves, wives, and other domestic dependents — or, later, to African Americans and white women in general, a topic introduced in the first section of this chapter and examined in the next. The justices' commitment to legal rules did not challenge, let alone displace, their racial, gender, and class biases. To the contrary, they believed that uniform legal rules, consistently applied, provided the best method of securing the hierarchies that defined southern society. As Eugene Genovese argued in *Roll, Jordan, Roll*, exceptions that favored individual slaves affirmed the underlying logic of the system. But that logic, which based the patriarchal order on uniform rules and individual rights, was not the last gasp of an organic society hanging onto the past, but the creation of modern jurists, with their feet planted firmly in a post-Revolutionary republic.[57]

■ ■ ■

TAPPING REEVE WAS SOMETHING OF A CELEBRITY in the decades after the Revolution, when common law traditions and colonial statutes were being remolded into a legal system suitable for a republic. His law school in Litchfield, Connecticut, trained some of the nation's foremost lawyers, including John C. Calhoun. Aspiring southerners coveted places at the school, eager for the prestige and social connections that would lead to financial and political success. The trip to Litchfield functioned as a rite of passage into the legal profession. William Dickinson Martin, of South Carolina, described every detail of his 1809 journey in a diary that, unfortunately, fell short of its author's literary aspirations. Arriving in Litchfield, Martin judged it to be "one of the most beautiful country towns in the world." He then turned his attention to the people, attempting to summarize their physical and cultural characteristics. Martin found the men "remarkably healthy," but "homely." The women, by contrast, "possess very great beauty." After finding no satisfying explanation for this aesthetic disparity between the sexes, he moved on to their behavior. He thought the manners of people in Connecticut were the same as those in South Carolina but was struck by the difference in customs. He noted that Connecticut was "the land of steady habits," echoing what had become a common cliché of the time and implying that the South was not.[58]

The law was among the fundamental things that South Carolina and Connecticut shared. All the students studied from the same legal authorities, which drew no sectional differences. "Many of the young men here are from the southern states," wrote North Carolina's Robert McCauley in 1820, "and when one comes from there they treat him with great regard and attention." No wonder, then, that the logic of Reeve's most important treatise, *The Law of Baron and Feme*, echoes through the legal opinions of state leaders during the early nineteenth century. Despite its seemingly narrow and archaic title, *The Law of Baron and Feme* covered the law of domestic relations, including the relations of husband and wife, parent and child, and master and servant, although not master and slave. First published in 1816, it went through numerous editions to become one of the standard legal references of the nineteenth century, in the South as well as elsewhere in the nation.

The passage on domestic violence, based in established common law principles, survived the revisions. As Reeve explained, household heads were supposed to prevent the development of "vicious habits" in their dependents that might prove "a nuisance to the community." As long as they acted "from motives of duty" in pursuit of that goal, then "no verdict ought to be found against" them. Although Reeve was writing about children and free servants, the point applied generally to all domestic dependents—

which, in the South, included slaves. The logic cast almost any act of defiance on the part of a dependent as provocation and made it difficult to prove "wicked intent" on the part of household heads, particularly masters of slaves.[59] The hierarchies of domestic authority determined who could use force and under what circumstances—issues known in the professional idiom of law as "intent" and "provocation," the catalysts that turned violent acts into crimes. Both intent and provocation acted as interpretive filters that fixed legal meaning to violent acts. Intent ratcheted up criminal penalties, while provocation had the opposite effect, erasing criminal responsibility. With sufficient intent, killing became murder; with sufficient provocation, the same act became justifiable homicide. Legally, both intent and provocation operated differently within domestic institutions than outside them because household heads' authority could be extended to justify the use of force to discipline their dependents.

The institutional context was crucial in determining how these principles would be applied. In localized law, household heads derived their authority from the peace. The power they could legitimately exercise was contingent, based in the circumstances of their lives and other people's assessments of them. Reeve's principles took on very different meanings in a legal system that applied universal rules, based in individual rights, to criminal issues—which was exactly the kind of system that treatises like *The Law of Baron and Feme* helped bring into being. Justice Ruffin's 1849 discussion of the legal limits of self-defense in *State v. Caesar* is particularly suggestive. Caesar was charged with killing a white man in a situation that would have been construed as self-defense if Caesar had been white. The victim was part of a gang that misrepresented themselves as patrollers and then assaulted Caesar and his two companions for no apparent reason. Was Caesar's act murder or justifiable self-defense? Ruffin argued that violence, in the form of corporal punishment, was integral to all domestic dependents' subordination. By extension, he reasoned, the law assumed that domestic dependents responded to violence differently than did free white men. It also judged their violent acts by different standards. A child who killed a parent while being punished, for instance, was guilty of murder because the act could be seen only as "a malignant and diabolical spirit of vengeance." Ruffin then extended this logic to cover slaves' dealings with all free people. "It is a just conclusion of reason when a slave kills a white man . . . that the act did not flow from . . . uncontrollable resentment, but from a bad heart." Then Ruffin revealed how dangerous domestic dependents' violent acts were to his understanding of public order. In his words, slaves with "bad hearts" were "intent upon the assertion of an equality, social and personal, with the white, and bent on mortal mischief in support of the assertion." Wives, whose domestic status also followed them beyond the household, could be substituted for slaves. Their evil intent would be the "assertion of an equality, social and personal" with men. If the court sanctioned their use of violence, that would grant them equality and the rights that status implied.[60]

Wrestling with the moral and ethical dimensions of placing slaves' lives in masters' hands, Ruffin sanctioned Caesar's act of self-defense against a white man. Dissenting from the majority and going against the grain of his own rulings, Ruffin felt compelled to explain why his decision did not endanger masters' property rights or extend rights to slaves. He did so by describing slaves' acts of self-defense as "natural" responses exhibited by all animals when their lives were endangered, not the expression of rights granted to legally empowered individuals.[61]

The cumulative effect was to erase violence involving domestic dependents from the texts that defined state law and, to a certain extent, from the historical record. State law, as it emerged in the decades after 1820, confined the political implications of slaves' and wives' complaints about their patriarchs' exercise of unlimited, arbitrary power by categorizing their violence as "private" and "personal," outside the purview of the state. The law also privatized violence committed by domestic dependents against their household heads, casting these acts as isolated incidents, the product of evil and demented minds, not of legitimate complaints or systemic problems with the South's social structure. Free white men's relationship to violence was legally different. When white men fought with women, African Americans, and even other white men, the state intervened to uphold their rights and to set precedents involving other citizens' rights as well. In the process, the law made some kinds of violence more visible, more legitimate, and more political than other kinds.

As the youthful ruminations of William Dickinson Martin and Robert McCauley suggest, professionally trained southern lawyers had more in common with their northern counterparts than with the people who carried on the customs of localized law in their own backyards. Changes in the legal handling of violence connect the South to national currents. Like the North, the South created a legal system based around rights and extended them broadly among white men. Those rights, newly enshrined in the legal system in the 1820s, sanctioned white men's use of violence by freeing it from the legal oversight of the peace. The presence of slavery shaped the definition and use of rights. In this regard, southern distinctiveness actually sheds light beyond the region. In the South, as elsewhere, the political context shaped the meanings given to rights — and those meanings mattered as much as people's access to rights.

8

New States

Thomas Cooper went from the French Revolution to nullification without missing a beat. Born in London, England, in 1759 and trained as a barrister, Cooper embraced the principles of the Age of Revolution, espousing scientific reason and "the rights of man." He defended the Jacobins when they first came to power, a position that thrust him onto the center stage of English politics, elicited a public denunciation from Edmund Burke, and signaled the combative tenor of his entire career. When the Jacobins turned violent and the English repressed radicals, Cooper lost his political footing. In 1794, accompanying Joseph Priestley, a fellow radical and religious dissenter as well as a brilliant natural scientist, he immigrated to the United States and settled in Pennsylvania, where he immediately entered the bar. By 1799 Cooper counted himself among the friends of Thomas Jefferson and championed the anti-Federalist cause, defending freedom of speech with such vehemence in the newspaper he edited that he was jailed briefly under the Sedition Act. In 1804 the triumphant Jeffersonians appointed him to the judiciary. But Cooper's embrace of the Democratic-Republican Party did not make him a democrat. His elitism, expressed in imperiousness and pomposity, combined with his later alignment with those who advocated a centralized judiciary, earned him the enmity of reform-minded Pennsylvanians who advocated changes that would have restored local control of the legal system. In 1811 he was forced off the bench by a legislative censure from his own party's liberal faction for "arbitrary conduct." Cooper then turned his long-standing interest in science into a profession, teaching at Dickinson College and the University of Pennsylvania before taking a position in chemistry at South Carolina College in 1820. Chosen as president of the college in 1821, he integrated courses ranging from natural philosophy to the applied sciences into the classical curriculum. Cooper continued to be politically active in his second adopted state. A staunch advocate of free trade and limited government, he attached himself to the cause of nullification. With characteristic zeal, he produced a small mountain of propaganda depicting the tariff as the unlawful seizure of property, a violation of individual rights, and an indefensible usurpation of authority by the federal government.[1]

Through it all, Cooper counted and classified, reducing everything to consistent units of measure. In this respect, he was very much like his friend Jefferson. Using scientific methods, Cooper grouped like items together according to their fundamental characteristics, organized them into a structured taxonomy, and generalized from the results. As part of his studies in chemistry and geology, for example, Cooper assembled a collection of minerals that was reputed to be one of the best in the United States. He applied the same systematic, categorical methods to his other endeavors. One of the most striking examples is his 1794 informational pamphlet on the United States, which took the same form as Hector Crèvecoeur's *Letters from an American Farmer*, but with the tone and content of Jefferson's *Notes on the State of Virginia*. It laid out the climate, geography, prices, products, laws, and customs in great detail, state by state, to attract and advise immigrants. Other pamphlets—including *Letters on the Slave Trade, Propositions Respecting the Foundations of Civil Government, A Manual of Political Economy*, and *A Practical Treatise on Dyeing, and Callicoe Printing*—featured equally meticulous lists. As Cooper saw it, the collection and organization of facts created knowledge, which was essential to human progress. And so he surveyed the world, cataloging its every aspect in hopes of discovering and controlling its mysteries. While this approach found a receptive audience in South Carolina when it came to education and politics, it was far less popular when Cooper applied the same methods to religion and found Christianity wanting. In 1831 complaints about his atheism and his refusal to allow religious instruction resulted in an investigation into his conduct as college president. After being exonerated, he resigned. Cooper's career as a cataloger of knowledge, however, continued. In 1835, out of respect for his work during the nullification crisis, he was awarded the task of organizing South Carolina's statutes. Picking up the threads of his abandoned legal career, he completed five volumes before his death in 1839. The great advocate of states' rights became the great compiler of state law; his collections are still used today as the authoritative edition of South Carolina law in the period before the Civil War.[2]

Nullification is usually seen as entirely distinct from contemporaneous political movements in other states. But the nullification movement's prominence in Cooper's ideological trajectory was not a mere accident of geography. Nullification rode the larger political currents of the 1830s, as the Second Party System—defined by the rivalry between Whigs and Democrats—took shape and political reform movements to expand the rights of adult white men gained momentum throughout the United States.

Concerns about slavery, sharpened by Nat Turner's aborted revolt in 1831, drove politics in South Carolina and the rest of the slaveholding South in ways they did not elsewhere. However, like political leaders in other parts of the nation, South Carolina nullifiers employed the rhetoric and organizational tactics characteristic of 1830s party politics, and they did so with particularly stunning success. They sought out ordinary white men, united with them under the banner of "freemen," and made them central to state politics. Even the racial issues, so politically prominent in nullification, paralleled trends elsewhere in the nation, where the extension of rights to white men was accompanied by greater restrictions on free people of color, virulently racist rhetoric, and often violence. North Carolina's political leaders, while not so flamboyant as nullifiers, relied on similar tactics. In fact, that state's 1835 constitution perfectly captures the common combination of democracy and exclusion: it simultaneously extended adult white men's political power and disfranchised free blacks.[3]

Professionally trained lawyers left their imprint on these political conflicts. As party leaders, they shaped the substance and tone of political campaigns, popularizing the esoteric logic of rights that had been driving legal change at the state level. In so doing, they legitimized the centralization of legal authority in the state, the systematization of law, and the elevation of rights over the peace as the rubric through which to resolve most legal issues, not just those involving property. These moves fundamentally transformed the basic institutions of governance. Unlike the peace, which was inclusive and hierarchical in structure, the legal order that emerged at the state level in the 1830s was both exclusive and democratic; it included only freemen—adult white men who could claim the full range of individual rights, not only political and property rights, but rights over other people as well. This dynamic was about the formation of a new kind of political subject—what we refer to as citizens today. Freemen, the paradigmatic citizens, were constituted through their holding of rights, conceived as property in themselves, and, to varying degrees, power over others. Those rights then became the basis for inclusion within the polity as political subjects.

Freemen's rights depended on consistent units of measure. The "state," the "rights" it protected, and the "freemen" who owned them were all abstractions, unlike the idiosyncratic subjects and conflicts of localized law. The state existed as a distant political entity that managed the interests of freemen even though few of those men had direct contact with it. It did so, primarily, by protecting rights. Those rights existed outside the context of everyday life and applied to all those who could claim them. Freemen included all rights-bearing individuals but referred to no one in particular. In this political context, the categories "wives," "slaves," "children," "free blacks," and "women" functioned similarly, but in reverse. They encompassed those who were not rights-bearing individuals, distinguishing one group from the other without allowing for variations among the people within these groups. As the idiom of rights gained ground, political rhetoric and legal practice relied on race and gender to explain the denial of rights, conflating women with wives and free blacks with slaves. These universalizing conceptions of rights stripped away not only social, economic, and cultural differences but also personality, family connections, and social networks so as to create faceless, interchangeable units. Decisions about the rights of one freeman applied to all freemen. Decisions about the denial of rights to one slave or one wife extended to all black persons or to all women.

The political context of the slave South blunted the progressive potential of rights, even for freemen. This system created obvious inequities for those without rights—the vast majority of the population. In theory, rights can be liberating and empowering for marginalized and oppressed persons, who would otherwise experience discrimination and arbitrary treatment. But rights accomplish nothing until people can actually claim them. White women and African Americans found themselves blocked from participation in this system. White men enjoyed access to rights, which state law expanded to give them more authority over their property and their dependents as well as all white women and African Americans more generally. New political rights also increased their participation in state government. Nevertheless, those rights had definite limits within the context of state law, which defined them so narrowly that they served primarily to buttress existing inequalities. Appellate courts, in particular, emphasized the protection of property in ways that not only implicitly privileged the wealthy but also defined the public good in terms of their interests. The political rhetoric of the period magnified the implications of those trends by legitimating the state's monopoly on legal authority. At the state level, all people—even freemen—existed as consistent units of measure to be slotted into universalizing legal categories. That system protected rights, not people. And rights, particularly in the political context of the slave South, did not always provide an effective method for addressing the problems in most people's lives.

"THE PICTURE OF A MAGNIFICENT GOVERNMENT"

South Carolina figures in the historiography as the state most at odds with the ideological and institutional underpinnings of the modern nation-state. The nullification crisis marks an important juncture in its slow but steady march away from the rest of the nation. During nullification, state leaders attacked the federal tariff with a brilliant political campaign that featured a militant doctrine of states' rights, paired with a shrill defense of slavery. Nullifiers were so persuasive that they succeeded in calling a state constitutional convention that affirmed the principle of state sovereignty and annulled the tariff. This vision of states' rights entailed a rejection of federal authority. Its support for slavery was equally clear, given nullifiers' insistence that unchecked federal power would inevitably lead to abolition. It is understandable, then, that historians have extended the analysis by identifying South Carolina's brand of states' rights as evidence of the state's embrace of localism, small government, and a legal system rooted in early modern conceptions of status. Considering what we know about subsequent events, namely, secession and the Civil War, these retrospective characterizations seem reasonable. More than any other southern state, South Carolina forged an oppositional, regional political identity based in chattel slavery. Its distinctiveness is regarded as representative: by standing apart from the rest of the nation, it foreshadows the South that was to emerge in the crisis of sectional upheaval.[4]

Although historical hindsight can provide remarkable clarity, its inescapable teleology can also distort our perspective. In the case of South Carolina, the view from the Civil War has obscured connections between it and other states, both within and outside the South. During the nullification crisis, South Carolina's political course owed as much to its acceptance as to its rejection of national trends. The doctrine of states' rights popularized during the nullification crisis posited a unified, centralized state charged with the protection of rights—not only states' rights, but the rights of legally recognized individuals as well. What distinguished this vision was its application within the context of a slave society. Political leaders solidified the institutional base of the state and then harnessed its authority to the service of profoundly undemocratic ends.[5]

The nullification crisis began with a controversy over the protective tariff, which southern planters had always opposed. They did not necessarily object to the tariff itself, which was nothing more than a tax schedule on imports revised regularly by the U.S. Congress to fund the federal government. What riled them were high duties imposed on manufactured goods, with the goal of protecting domestic manufacturers and raising revenues. By the nineteenth century, "the tariff" became synonymous with those protective duties, which many southern farmers saw as a double tax. The tariff not only increased the price of items that farmers needed to purchase but also lowered the relative value of agricultural products, especially cotton, that they sold in an international market. As a means for debating the direction of the nation and the extent of federal power, the tariff had deep political resonance. It became a charged issue in George Washington's second presidential term, when Thomas Jefferson faced off against Alexander Hamilton. Hamilton's protective tariff symbolized the entire range of political differences in this conflict: agriculture vs. manufacture; rural vs. urban; South vs. North; Francophiles vs. Anglophiles; democracy vs. elite rule; states' rights vs. a strong, centralized federal government. The battle between Hamilton and Jefferson resulted in the first significant constitutional challenge when Jefferson maintained that states retained the right to reject federal legislation. His views found forceful expression in the *Virginia and Kentucky Resolutions*, early briefs for states' rights that also broached the issue of nullification. Although tensions never escalated to the point of national disunion in the 1790s, they did split the national leadership into distinct parties, the Federalists and Jeffersonian Republicans. Thereafter, the tariff remained a volatile issue. It figured in policy debates of all kinds, from the War of 1812 to the settlement of western land.

Controversy over the tariff intensified in the late 1820s, just as the Second Party System was taking shape and the cotton boom was collapsing. On one side of the new political divide were the Jacksonian Democrats, suspicious of all concentrations of power, particularly at the federal level. On the other side were the Whigs, who advocated a unified national economy, fueled by geographic expansion, commercial exchange, and industrial development to be directed by a federal system of transportation, regulation, and taxation. Democrats pioneered in the creation of modern political parties, tight organizations that disseminated a well-honed, consistent message and kept the rank and file engaged. The Whigs followed suit, after the election of Andrew Jackson in 1828 demonstrated the effectiveness of these strategies and heightened the importance of party identification as a factor in elections.[6]

The subsequent political realignment coincided with a downward spiral in the cotton market that hit South Carolina particularly hard. Planters there had hitched their futures to cotton more completely than their 261 counterparts in other southern seaboard states. By the 1820s they faced stiff competition from producers in the new Southwest and other parts of the globe. In this oversaturated market, South Carolina planters were at a distinct disadvantage; their depleted soil produced low yields of inferior cotton that brought disappointing prices.[7] In 1828, when Congress passed higher duties, South Carolina planters howled in protest. Blaming the tariff for the state's economic and political woes, influential political leaders asserted states' rights over national authority and, eventually, threatened to nullify the tariff. The national dynamics of the Second Party System framed the ensuing political conflict in significant ways. The crisis involved key issues — the tariff and federalism — that the architects of partisan politics used adroitly not only as an organizational tool but also to define the parties' platforms. Adding fuel to the fire were the ambitions of career politicians hungry for power, most notably John C. Calhoun. But the notion of a singular crisis — *the* nullification crisis — is a reflection of the attention that scholars have paid to national party politics: the debates in Congress over the tariff; the tensions between President Jackson and Vice President Calhoun during the first administration; and the president's showdown with Calhoun and South Carolina nullifiers after his reelection in 1832. From this perspective, the crisis peaked when South Carolina passed the Nullification Ordinance in 1832 and Jackson declared it void, threatening to use force to keep the state in line. It dissipated soon thereafter when the president tempered his position and appeased nullifiers by supporting the reduction of protective duties, which Congress passed in the Compromise Tariff. In March 1833 another South Carolina constitutional convention rescinded the Nullification Ordinance.[8]

The contours of national party politics, however, do not contain the dynamics of nullification as a political movement. Nullifiers' position on states' rights was so extreme that it placed them outside the orbit even of the Democratic Party, the party critical of centralized federal authority. Significantly, South Carolina Unionists did not align themselves with the Whigs, the party of nationalism, but with Jackson's Democrats. Leading nullifiers and Unionists came from the same political circles and tended to agree on most issues except nullification.[9] Within the state, the movement unfolded over several years. From 1827 to 1832, leading nullifiers built an extraordinarily effective statewide political network, utilizing the new methods of political mobilization to popularize the issue of states' rights. After a contentious, often violent campaign, they seized the state legislature in 1832 and called for a constitutional convention to pass a nullification ordinance. Meeting soon thereafter, the convention fulfilled its duty, provoking another storm of unrest that kept attention riveted on states' rights until 1835.[10]

Although nullifiers focused on the federal government, their cause involved innovative conceptions of "the state" as the center of South Carolina government. They offered a distinctive vision and succeeded where previous advocates of state centralization had failed; they made the state, an altogether abstract entity, so compelling a concept that ordinary white South Carolinians could identify with it. Nullifiers constructed the state in opposition to the federal government, directing their ire against political leaders in Washington and homegrown Unionists who refused to surrender their national loyalties. That strategy carried implications for national party politics, whose outcomes — secession and war — lay much further down the road. In the meantime, nullifiers' efforts had more immediate and profound implications within South Carolina, by elevating the state as a primary locus of law and government. In this way, nullifiers built the scaffolding for the legal culture they shared with their sworn enemies, both South Carolina Unionists and reform-minded political leaders elsewhere.

The logic of states' rights betrayed nullifiers' nationalist roots. The most famous example is John C. Calhoun, who made his reputation as a war hawk by advocating a strong military response to British attacks on American commerce. But Calhoun's nationalism was common among South Carolina's political elite, many of whom identified closely with the effort to create a new nation and assumed that they were central to that project — sometimes more central than they actually were. In 1830, as tensions over nullification mounted, fellow nationalist-turned-nullifier James Hamilton remembered those earlier political loyalties with fondness. "There was something in the picture of a magnificent government," he reminisced, "invincible in war, beneficent in peace, holding in exact equipoise the scales of justice, presiding over all, sustaining all, protecting all, with neither the power nor inclination to do injury to any, well calculated to fascinate the imagination." In its basic outlines, this "magnificent government" bore a striking resemblance to the peace as practiced in localized law. Unlike the localized peace, though, Hamilton's version existed as an abstraction, national in scale and purposefully removed from people's daily lives. In his description, the government was so distant that it was not even represented by the blindfolded, toga-draped woman who so often held the scales of justice in the imagery of the early republic. It existed only as the scales, held by unseen, disembodied hands. The political order implied by such abstract conceptions appealed to South Carolina's political elite, who were raised in the afterglow of the Revolution and schooled in the principles of the Enlightenment. The nation did not seem distant to them because they moved in national circles, not local ones. As a clique within a tightly connected yet geographically dispersed political class, they saw the nation as their own: they were the ones who held the scales.[11]

South Carolina's political elite applied this same expansive vision to the state level. During the first decades of the nineteenth century, state legislators compiled a record that bore an uncanny resemblance to the later agenda of the Whig Party, although the emphasis was on state rather than national development. In 1801 the legislature established South Carolina College to train a new generation of state leaders. There, as one of the college's professors explained, the "youths of all sections, all classes, and all creeds should meet as sons of a common mother." College graduates who identified with that "common mother," the state of South Carolina, would govern it wisely. Legislators also spent liberally on transportation to bring different parts of the state together so as to encourage commercial development. The same goals led to tight centralized control and fiscal conservatism in the state banks—policies that mirrored those of the Bank of the United States under Nicholas Biddle, the Jacksonians' nemesis. Legal reforms featured prominently in the agenda of state building. Legislators and jurists of varying political stripes concurred in their support for the centralization of the legal system and the creation of a uniform body of law based in individual rights, even when they were divided over the best means of achieving those ends.[12]

This concept of a unified state animated the nullification movement. Particularly revealing is the transformation of George McDuffie, who became the nullifiers' orator. Despite his humble background, McDuffie acquired impeccable credentials as Calhoun's protégé. A South Carolina College graduate, McDuffie built a successful career in law before being elected in 1820 to the U.S. Congress, where he established himself as a staunch nationalist. "Few congressmen," writes historian William Freehling of McDuffie's early political career, "favored a more expansive view of federal power, and no one else so effectively challenged the extreme versions of the states' rights creed." By 1828, however, McDuffie had changed sides. Furious at the passage of higher import duties, McDuffie converted to nullification with a sense of bitterness and betrayal that was as much personal as political. The federal government, he raged to a Charleston crowd in 1831, had become a "system of stupendous oppression" intent on destroying South Carolinians: "We are steadily and rapidly sinking into utter and hopeless ruin." Although he had fought against this turn of events, all his efforts had "proved utterly impotent and unavailing."[13] When the national government that McDuffie had supported so faithfully for so long turned against him, he transferred his faith to the state of South Carolina.

The success of leading nullifiers in spreading the gospel of states' rights drew charges of Jacobinism from irate Unionists, echoing the charges that had been leveled at Thomas Cooper in England and Pennsylvania. Like Thomas Cooper, though, nullifiers did not advocate radical democracy or extreme localism. At the core of their political vision lay a single, coherent political entity, the state of South Carolina, with a monopoly on legal authority. "In all governments there must be some *one* supreme power," McDuffie argued in the early 1820s while defending federal authority on the floor of the U.S. Congress. "Every [constitutional] question must be susceptible of a legal and peaceable determination by some tribunal of acknowledged authority, or force must be the inevitable consequence." That principle applied at the state level as well. In 1824 leading nullifiers participated in the restructuring of the state court system, an effort that not only centralized legal authority over state law in a single appeals court for law and equity but also introduced systematization to reconcile what had been parallel, competing bodies of law. Governor Stephen D. Miller, an ardent nullifier, declared those changes a success in his annual address to the legislature in 1829. In fact, nullifiers' constitutional arguments assumed this kind of legal structure. To them, constitutional principles were sacrosanct, like other natural rights. Neither legislatures nor courts could alter them. To protect them, the state needed that "*one* supreme power," a strong, centralized court system, designed to define and extend a unified body of law.[14]

"THE PEOPLE'S MOST VALUABLE GIFT"

The nullifiers' conception of governance was distinctly at odds with the decentralized structures in which localized law flourished. That centralizing vision of the state was widely shared, even by those who opposed nullification. South Carolina Unionists made the same assumptions about law and the state, as did politicians and jurists elsewhere in the nation. In 1833 the North Carolina legislature rejected South Carolina's plea for support and voted down a resolution condemning federal force. North Carolina Democrats, suspicious of federal authority, found the bombast of the nullification campaign, as well as its denunciations of President Andrew Jackson, difficult to swallow. North Carolina Whigs, many of whom opposed the tariff, could barely contain their disdain. Nullification, wrote Congressman Lewis Williams, would "inevitably lead to monarchy, or the right of a single individual to govern the whole nation." William Lenoir, a Revolutionary hero and anti-Federalist who ended up in the Whig Party, likened nullifiers to devils, who were once "Angels of light" peculiarly favored by God but had conspired against "the Creator by nullifying his edicts and assuming prerogatives against his divine purpose in their creation, for which they were hurled down to perdition." The issue so dispirited William Gaston, a Whig who took a seat on the North Carolina Supreme Court in 1835, that he could barely summon the energy for outrage. "It grieves me to see such happy prospects blasted or threatened to be blasted by Pride Ambition Perverted Ingenuity and sickened Selfishness," he wrote to his daughter in 1833; "I sometimes wish that I could withdraw my mind entirely from the consideration of all public concerns."[15] Like nullifiers, though, North Carolina Whigs envisioned a state that subordinated local jurisdictions to its workings. During the 1830s state lawmakers moved both North Carolina and South Carolina closer to that ideal.

Political battles following the passage and withdrawal of the Nullification Ordinance underscore nullifiers' commitment to legal centralization. After the crisis, state leaders generally put aside their differences to pursue legal reform. Indeed, a legal conflict between the nullification movement and the Unionists that *threatened* centralization actually ended up rallying state leaders to the cause of legal reform. Crucial in the postordinance political fallout was a loyalty oath, referred to as the test oath, which required civil and military officials to swear primary allegiance to the state. The oath particularly riled Unionists. Not only did it require a personal renunciation of the federal government, but it could be used to eliminate everyone but extreme states' rights proponents from office, effectively disfranchising Unionists. The oath, which was part of the original Nullification Ordinance, was resuscitated by the 1833 convention. The legislature then substituted a watered-down version. Some leading Unionists advised compliance, seeing no harm in affirming loyalty to the state as long as that did not entail renunciation of the nation. Other Unionists, sensing coercion and conspiracy, promised armed revolt. Despite threats of violence, the crisis took a decidedly legal turn, with the most significant challenges unfolding in court.[16] In 1834 the South Carolina appellate court found the test oath unconstitutional, unleashing a stream of vitriol from nullifiers and a new round of political conflict within the state. Nullifiers, united as the State Rights Party now that nullification was no longer an issue, lost their cherished oath. Worse, the system in which they placed such faith had turned against them. How could the court abandon its duty and undermine the constitutional principles it was supposed to protect? Unable to let go of their core beliefs, nullifiers blamed the two Unionist justices, John Belton O'Neall and David Johnston, who were responsible for the ruling. They threatened impeachment, floated a bill to enable prosecutions for treason, and initiated measures that would have banished the two judicial miscreants by abolishing the appellate court on which they sat.[17]

One particularly extreme proposal, which would have taken out the entire court system along with the appellate court, served as a political wake-up call, bringing legislators on both sides of the aisle to the legal system's defense. The negotiations fell to James Hamilton and James Louis Petigru, an outspoken, low country Unionist. In the midst of the crisis, Petigru acknowledged the cooperation of his political adversaries. "The influence of [William Campbell] Preston," a longtime proponent of nullification, "has been exerted to prevent any assault on the Judiciary," wrote a beleaguered Petigru to his friend Hugh S. Legaré; "How far he has succeeded God only knows." According to Unionist Abram Blanding, however, the threat to the judiciary had never been all that serious. The "bill could gain no support," he wrote a friend during the legislative session, "except among the most violent, who constituted less than a third of the nullification party." A correspondent for the *Charleston Mercury*, an advocate of states' rights, concurred, "I do not believe the entire State Rights Party are unanimous on the subject, and although there may be a version of the Judiciary System required, yet there are some not prepared for this measure, which cuts at the root of the whole system."[18] The speed with which legislators agreed to the compromise affirmed this assessment.

The bipartisan defense of the legal system owed to a common legal culture that pervaded politics at the state level. Many state-level leaders were professionally trained lawyers, whose education in formal precepts of property law disposed them toward a hierarchical legal system. Whatever their opinions about nullification, they could agree on the necessity for a unified body of state law, a centralized state that exercised legal authority over local jurisdictions, and an independent appellate court that served as the final arbiter of state law. This common political and intellectual culture, when translated into the practice of law, forged social and economic bonds as well. James Petigru and James Hamilton had been law partners. Petigru still looked after the interests of many of the state's leading families; indeed, historians have identified Petigru's law practice, reputed to be one of the most lucrative in South Carolina, as a distraction that kept him from being a more effective politician. Neither Unionists nor nullifiers could do business without lawyers whom they trusted and a legal system that upheld the rights of property according to uniform rules applicable across the state. Petigru, like other Unionist leaders, never opposed the new oath of 1834. He felt comfortable with it because he agreed with the principle of a unified state that functioned as the primary locus of governance and commanded its citizens' loyalties. What divided nullifiers and Unionists were the state's relation to the federal government and personal rivalries over who would control the state. The legal system became bound up in those issues because of the appellate court's decisions, but it did not figure as the primary point of contention.[19]

The 1834 compromise included an agreement to postpone action on the court system until the next legislative session. The debates that took place in the fall of 1835 reveal the political ground that Unionists and nullifiers shared. Legislators focused not on the legal system but on the judges, who had come to represent the issues that divided nullifiers and Unionists. The nullifiers on the Judiciary Committee advocated changes that would remove the offending justices but maintain or strengthen the structure of the legal system. David J. McCord ridiculed the justices in a speech bursting with examples of incompetent record keeping, hopelessly bungled legal logic, and ignorance of established authorities, including the state's own statutes and appellate rulings — in other words, the practices of a decentralized system in which localized law played an important role. "Mr. McCord's array of practical cases," wrote the correspondent for the *Charleston Mercury*, "were so numerous, so grave, of such solemn consequence to the general liberties of the country," and "in such flagrant violation of rules the plainest and the most indispensable to security of property and even of person" as to inspire revolt against the system.[20]

McCord's critique aimed to discredit the sitting justices, not the system. He assumed that the legal system would produce a coherent set of universally applicable precedents, developed logically over time and applied consistently across the state. If it did not, it must be because of incompetent judges. But the standards McCord employed did not yet match legal practice. The appellate justices could not have achieved the logical, consistent outcomes that he wanted because decentralization and localism continued to occupy considerable institutional space. McCord's comments read like a condemnation of localized law, implying the need for greater centralization and systemization.[21] James J. Caldwell, the nullifier who chaired the Judiciary Committee, underscored the commitment to centralized legal authority. He emphasized "the importance, under all systems, of the Appellate power." If "wisdom, learning, strength, integrity, were to adorn, to elevate, to invigorate any part of your Judicial administration of the laws, they must be concentrated here," Caldwell opined. Only this "high power" was "capable, for good or for ill, of a general control of the entire justice of the country." The problem, as he described it, lay in "the practical operation of the system," which rendered "the law uncertain." The appellate court needed modification, but only because its personnel were failing in their duties.[22]

The resulting legislative compromise preserved the existing, hard-fought gains of legal centralization, established in 1824, while diluting Unionists' political influence at the appellate level. Nullifiers instituted a legislative suspension so as to reach into the court system and make the necessary changes before setting the whole judicial mechanism back in motion. First they abolished the appellate court. From that point, they proceeded carefully in order to preserve the principle of judicial independence. The compromise bill did not banish the current appellate justices completely, much to the disappointment of the *Charleston Mercury*'s correspondent and other nullifiers for whom political victory took precedence over the integrity of legal institutions. The final bill incorporated the Unionists' proposal to reassign the displaced appellate justices to three new positions in the courts of common law and equity. The legislation replaced the current appeals court with two separate appeals courts, one for common law and the other for equity, formed from the judges who heard cases on the circuit. This measure, which returned to the structure that existed before the 1824 reforms, might seem like a decentralizing move intended to restore popular control of the law. Yet the intent was less to democratize the courts than to dilute the power of Unionists by elevating nullifiers in the circuit courts to the appellate level. Leading nullifiers had no intention of abandoning the principle of hierarchical legal authority—that "one supreme power" at the apex of court structure, responsible for defining state law. To those ends, they created a Court of Errors to oversee "all constitutional questions arising out of the constitution of this State, or the United States." That court, which included all common law and equity judges, also ensured the presence of nullifiers in the state's supreme court. The legislature even rejected a last-minute proposal for the legislative review of judges. Straining to achieve political compromise while preserving the structures of legal centralization, the architects of the revised court system managed to secure bipartisan support for their plan.[23]

In the midst of the crisis over the test oath and the court system, nullifiers initiated a project, long advocated by legal reformers, to create a unified body of state law. Governor Robert Y. Hayne saw the project as part of his legacy to the state. He envisioned the state, consolidated as a distinct political entity, with a commitment to the protection of rights. "My heart," he concluded in his address to the South Carolina legislature in 1834, is "filled with gratitude to Almighty God, that while the peace of the Country has been preserved, YOUR RIGHTS AND LIBERTIES HAVE SUFFERED NO DETRIMENT IN MY HANDS."[24] During his last days as governor in 1834, Hayne proposed the drafting of a digest of state law as a way to secure those rights and liberties. As he explained, the goal of the digest was not to democratize the law. Hayne did not think "that 'every man' can be made 'his own lawyer,'" and he was "still less inclined to believe that any individual can be safely trusted to prepare a CODE OF LAWS." He nonetheless thought that the state's laws could "be greatly simplified, by digesting them under proper heads, and stating in the fewest possible words, the provisions of existing statutes, and the decisions of the Courts thereon." Hayne had previously commissioned a digest of militia and patrol laws, which directed the same white men who made up militias to police slaves. He now directed legislators to that recently completed volume, explaining its organization with undisguised enthusiasm. The new digest would include only statutes and appellate decisions, which constituted "state law," the only body of law that the "free and enlightened people" of South Carolina had any need to know. "A Digest of the whole Statute Law of this State made on such principles, with the Statutes at large annexed thereto," he concluded, "would certainly be one of the most valuable gifts that could be made to the people of South Carolina."[25]

Hayne was well aware of the contentious history that surrounded proposals for a compilation of state laws. Immediately following the Revolution, the legislature had directed three of the state's eminent jurists to collect and coordinate the statutes. But the project had fallen victim to legal localism, expressed as doubts about the need for a digest and suspicions about the intent of those proposing it. Subsequent efforts had run aground as well. By 1834, however, the nullification campaign had generated new attachments to the state, dissipating concerns about systematizing law and centralizing it at the state level. The legislature passed Hayne's recommendation and gave authority over the project to the incoming governor, George McDuffie. In 1835 McDuffie announced the appointment of Thomas Cooper, who promptly took over the project and began reducing South Carolina law to consistent units of measure. David J. McCord, the nullifier who led state judicial reform in 1835, took over after Cooper's death in 1839.[26]

North Carolina arrived at the same destination by a different political route. There, the 1835 constitutional convention marked a crucial turning point in solidifying the authority of state institutions. Proponents of localism, whose attempts to gut the appeals court had been something of an annual ritual in the 1820s, still wielded considerable influence. They expressed their antipathy toward centralized state power at the convention with proposals for biennial (rather than annual) meetings of the state legislature and for the impeachment of judges.[27] Although both measures entered the new constitution, the amendments actually tended to affirm and amplify currents that favored consolidation. Convention delegates balanced judicial impeachment with a measure that insulated the courts from legislative control in a more crucial area. They made it impossible for legislators to reduce judges' salaries during their tenure, effectively closing off the primary means that proponents of localism had used to undercut the appellate court and, more important, the legal authority and the unified body of law it represented. Constant legislative bickering over salaries turned judicial posts into insecure, altogether unattractive positions. Many potential nominees could not afford to give up lucrative law practices for the bench. William Gaston, who almost turned down a position on the state appellate court because of low pay and the constant threat of further salary reductions, was elated by the amendment. "The public liberty," he wrote to Robert Moore, editor of the *New Bern Spectator*, will be "materially secured" with these changes.[28]

Gaston spoke even more enthusiastically about the amendments restricting the legislature's handling of "private legislation" that applied to specific individuals, groups, or localities. "The mischiefs of private legislation were immense," he told Moore, "the time of the General Assembly wasted and a vast public expenditure annually incurred by preparing amending enacting and repealing local regulation not worth the paper upon which they were written." The amendments kept these issues out of state government by clearly separating the "local" from the "state" through a specific conceptualization of "private" and "public." The state government now dealt exclusively with public issues, defined as matters of broad importance that theoretically applied to everyone throughout North Carolina, not as issues involving the maintenance of the peace in local areas. In practice, though, the legislature and appellate court primarily handled issues involving the rights of freemen, which put distinct limits on the meaning of the term "public" and the reach of state law. In this schema, local courts became subordinate legal bodies that specialized in the detritus of everyday life; they handled legal conflicts characterized as routine and private because they did not involve the interpretation of state law.[29]

During the debates over the new constitution, the North Carolina legislature launched a project, strikingly similar to the one initiated by South Carolina nullifiers, to digest the statutes. "It is believed that complete copies of these enactments are not to be found in half a dozen libraries in the State," noted Governor David Swain, the Whig who spearheaded the initiative in 1833. "A part of those in force" were "published in Newbern, thirty years since, but the work did not equal public expectation and is now out of print. The legislation of nearly five centuries is a sealed book to the great body of the community, and in some degree even to the profession, whose interest and duty render the study of the Law the business of life." Like nullifiers in South Carolina, Swain painted a picture of legal chaos, with examples of ludicrously outdated statutes and farcical proceedings caused by incomplete information. "The truth is that not only the source but the very existence of our statute law, is . . . 'as undiscoverable as the sources of the Nile.'" As he saw it, the situation was unconscionable. To protect "the lives, the liberty and property of our citizens," it was essential to create a definitive digest of current statutes.[30]

Governor Swain followed up in 1835 with a companion project for appellate decisions. As he explained, the need for the project presented itself when the governors of Kentucky and Maryland solicited "an exchange of law reports" with North Carolina. The state had already received "reports of the decisions of the Supreme Courts of Maryland, Kentucky, Indiana, Illinois and Missouri." "An interchange of the Statute Laws of all the States, has existed, perhaps from the foundation of the government and seems indeed to be essential to enlightened legislation," Swain observed. The "reported decisions of the Supreme Courts of the several states" were now equally valuable to governance, as the exchange among states indicated. Unfortunately, North Carolina's laws were in no condition to be shared. The volumes read like lists, incomplete, laden with errors, and lacking indexes, summaries, or marginal notes. Swain recommended additional funding so that appellate decisions could assume their proper place as part of state law. Not only would other states learn from North Carolina, but the state would benefit by solidifying the body of state law and elevating it over the law as practiced in the courts at the local level.[31]

"AS A BAND OF BROTHERS JOINED"

In both North and South Carolina, state lawmakers popularized the consolidation of legal authority at the state level by adopting and disseminating the discourse of rights. The idiom encouraged "freemen," who by definition were adult, white, and male, to identify with the state as the political entity charged with defending their rights. Henry L. Pinckney, an outspoken nullifier and editor of the partisan *Charleston Mercury*, made that connection particularly clear. "We are contending for our rights as freemen, and for the protection of our properties from the iron grasp of avarice and extortion," he lectured a crowd in 1830. "Our object is to support the sovereignty of our State, and the liberties of our people." "Should we fail," he concluded, "we will at least be able to tell our Parent State how many of her sons are true to her in Charleston, and what she may expect, in the prosecution of her rights, from her chief city and commercial metropolis." At the North Carolina constitutional convention, James W. Bryan disclosed the racial subtext in this obviously gendered discourse. Arguing for the disfranchisement of free blacks, Bryan insisted that free blacks "are *not freemen*": "the [state] Constitution was *not* framed with an eye to their rights and privileges, and they were not regarded at that time, as composing a part even of the *freemen* of North Carolina."[32] Both men followed the chain of associations linking adult white men directly to the state through their possession of individual rights: rights established liberty, the highest political principle; only freemen possessed rights; the state's duty was to protect those rights so as to secure freemen's liberty; therefore the state was defined in terms of the interests of freemen. The logic was tight and tautological.

Rights discourse offered an empowering, compelling message for adult white men. It singled them out, emphasizing the authority they held in the form of rights, promising them a privileged place within the governing order, and making them important in ways that they never were in the dynamics of localized law. No wonder it succeeded in rallying so many to the cause of South Carolina during the nullification movement. While politically persuasive, rights discourse was also deeply rooted in the logic of law as it was defined and exercised at the state level. By the 1830s, in both North and South Carolina, state law pivoted around the precepts of liberal individualism and focused on the protection of individual rights, the full complement of which only adult white men could claim. Rights discourse was inevitably linked to the state, the level of government where questions about rights took precedence.

The political appeal of rights discourse is evident in the nullification campaign. The arguments, which appeared in different political contexts in North Carolina and other states, built on the legal framework of rights that was emerging at the state level in the 1820s. Nullifiers harnessed those concepts to a particular political end: luring white male voters into their party. The sheer volume of printed material, which barely skims the surface of the campaign's deep propaganda well, attests to the magnitude of the effort. As professionally trained lawyers known for their oratorical skills, nullifiers translated esoteric legal principles into the idiom of popular politics. They spoke in CAPITAL LETTERS and exclamation points!!! They also spoke plainly. Combining republican forms with Lockean substance, nullifiers appealed to the virtues of "liberty," the dangers of "tyranny," and the need for collective political action. But, like the state appellate court judges who routinely invoked the interests of the peace while reshaping it, they defined liberty and tyranny through the protection of individual rights. In 1828 South Carolina voters were not inclined to support the Nullification Party. By 1832 they were convinced.[33]

Nullifiers studded their pamphlets and speeches with references to rights that invariably led back to property. "One of our noblest rights, the right of property, has been invaded," wrote "Unticensis" in the *Charleston Mercury*. Robert Turnbull made the connection explicit. Nullification, he maintained, was about "liberty": "the liberty of regulating his own industry in the manner that shall seem to himself most proper, and of having the fruits and earnings of that industry secured from the grasp of unjust and exorbitant taxation." Labor was important only insofar as it produced property, which the federal government was stealing through the tariff. "The General Government," fumed Turnbull, "is about to dry up, by the scorching fires of construction, all those sources of our prosperity, which, under any other system, would make us a flourishing, a great, and a happy State." "Our trade is diminished," he elaborated, "real property is depreciated; our mechanics are without employment. . . . Confidence is lost, and despondency and gloom universally prevail." With the tariff, the federal government sucked wealth out of South Carolina and gave it to other parts of the country. If the state emerged at all, it would be as an impoverished shell of its former self. As went the state, so went its freemen.[34]

Rights figured as a form of property. Elaborating on existing conceptions of property rights in state law, nullifiers extended the logic. Where appellate courts used rights as the means to protect property and gestured toward the possession of rights as a form of property, political leaders turned rights *into* property; rights became possessions that freemen controlled absolutely, just as they did other forms of property. They posited the archetypical freeman as an adult white man who owned his body and his labor, and who properly should own or at least control the product of his labor and skill. The sovereign self existed not as an abstraction, but in specific economic and political terms. Rights then drew all freemen into nullification's fold by focusing on abstract property, in the form of rights, that all white men owned, rather than physical property, namely, slaves and plantations, owned only by the wealthy. Rights leveled the economic differences among men. Historian Stephanie McCurry makes a similar point, emphasizing the racial and gendered underpinnings of this framework. Nullifiers invoked an audience of white men, who exercised dominion over households that included dependent wives, slaves, and children as well as land and material possessions. Even the poorest white men were "masters of small worlds" because of their gender and race.[35] That scenario, which linked white men together on the basis of shared identity and position based in gender and race, was possible because of individual rights, modeled on property rights. All adult white men could claim rights and the authority that came with them, even if they did not own property.

Rights discourse turned an unlikely enemy, the tariff, into an immediate, ominous threat. Unattached to rights, the tariff remained conceptually elusive. It did not knock down the door and hold its victims captive at gunpoint, while stealing their possessions out from under their noses. It took the form of duties, the actual economic effect of which was difficult to establish, let alone see. Casting the tariff in terms of the degradation of their rights gave white men a way to connect it to their own lives. It was the theft of their property, even if that property was an intangible construct. South Carolina, wailed George McDuffie, would not be "taunted with the charge of treason and rebellion, because she has the intelligence to understand her rights, and the spirit to maintain them." The *Charleston Mercury* editorialist "Unticensis" finished off the argument, claiming that the tariff threatened "a right that freemen can never relinquish without ignominy and disgrace — 'twas in defense of this right that our fathers raised the standard of opposition to Great Britain, exhibiting the sublime spectacle of 275 freemen bleeding in the sacred cause of Liberty." "The attempted violation of this right," he concluded, "has caused even despots to tremble on their thrones."[36]

Rights talk gave the tariff ominous overtones that resonated well beyond the immediate issue. As an isolated instance of plunder, the tariff was an irritant, but not necessarily a symptom of systemic pathology. As a violation of rights, by contrast, the tariff threatened all freemen; rights turned this issue into a larger system of oppression. In this regard, nullifiers argued like the lawyers that they were, applying individual rights as they were construed in property law and generalizing from particular determinations to establish broad-reaching precedents. Their client was the hypothetical white male planter, whose property the tariff destroyed. The offense perpetuated by the federal government violated the planter's rights. But the effects did not stop there, since the violation of that man's rights represented a threat to all men's property, including slaves and, by extension, slavery itself. "The Constitution," roared one nullifier, "was not framed to enable a set of northern speculators to commit plunder and robbery on the Southern planters, and having done so for a dozen years together, to claim the right of robbery as a vested interest!"[37] The threat implicated all rights holders, not just property holders. If unchecked, the violations perpetrated by the tariff would assume their own authority within the nation's laws and lead to tyranny.

The nullifiers' ubiquitous references to slavery tended to conflate the ownership of abstract property, in the form of rights, with the ownership of physical property. Throughout the campaign, abolition loomed as the inevitable consequence should the tariff go unchallenged. The tariff, nullifiers insisted, laid the groundwork for federal interference in South Carolina planters' slave property. As evidence, they cited proposals for federal funding of the American Colonization Society, which aimed to resettle blacks in Africa, as the first step on the road to abolition. Colonization, according to nullifiers, would raise doubts about slavery's permanence, undermine the value of slaves, and send South Carolina's economy into a downward spiral that would end in either forced emancipation or slave revolt. A blow to slavery would affect all white men in the state, even those without slaves. What made the hyperbole convincing was the way nullifiers incorporated the symbolic meanings of slavery. Building on ideological currents dating back at least to the Revolution, nullifiers positioned slaves and slavery as the opposites of freemen and liberty. "Thus the naked question is now submitted to the southern people," exhorted one pamphlet: "SUBMISSION to

the manufacturers, or RESISTANCE? SLAVERY, or FREEDOM?" "Absolute
submission and passive obedience, to every extreme of tyranny are the
characteristics of slaves only," declared George McDuffie. While drawing
on concepts deeply rooted in American political culture, nullifiers mapped
the rubric of rights directly onto these notions, creating a particular kind
of dichotomy between freemen, who owned rights, and slaves, who did
not.[38] This distinction cut two ways, marking slaves as property without
legal rights or political standing *and* defining freemen as rights-bearing
individuals with direct connections to the state. To be a freeman entailed
the possession of rights and loyalty to the state that defended them. To
accept any other political identity was to become a slave — an unthinkable
position for a white man.

The discourse of rights intensified white southerners' fears of slave revolts. In the nullifiers' conception of the polity, with its stark dichotomy between those with rights and those without, there was no middle ground for
embattled freemen. Without rights, freemen became slaves and the South
descended into chaos. Any threat to rights, whether real or perceived, constituted an assault on slavery. Those rhetorical connections played on white
southerners' deepest fears about their personal safety in a slave society,
which rose to the level of panic with Nat Turner's revolt in 1831. In this
context, anything vaguely critical became a generalized attack not just on
slavery, but on the lives of all white southerners. The nullifiers' obsession
with the American Colonization Society provides an excellent example;
they saw its mission to resettle free blacks as the first step in the planned destruction of the South. Abolitionist literature presented an equally serious
threat. The fact that there was no evidence of these destructive designs mattered not at all. Within the rubric of rights as formulated by the nullifiers,
anything that questioned the status quo, especially slavery, constituted a
threat to all freemen and, through them, to the entire region.[39]

The regulation of slavery topped South Carolina's legislative agenda in
the 1830s. The legislature enacted strict penalties for the distribution of in-
cendiary literature, which they defined broadly to include almost anything
that was the least bit critical of slavery or cast doubt on the notion that
the institution was under assault. Legislators passed new restrictions on
slaves, limiting their mobility, literacy, and trading. Significantly, Thomas
Cooper recommended a separate section on "law relating to the *Colored
Population*" in the introduction to the multivolume digest of statutes that,
otherwise, was organized chronologically. Folding free blacks in with slaves
in the language of race that was becoming so prominent in law and politi-

cal rhetoric at the state level, Cooper explained the necessity for a separate section in terms of expediency. There were so many laws that they would be "dispersed through the volumes chronologically," making "reference to them, even with the aid of an index . . . extremely troublesome and laborious." Grouping those laws together, though, also provided a solid foundation so that the state could better regulate slavery — and race relations — in the interests of protecting freemen's rights.[40]

The only way freemen could avoid becoming enslaved, nullifiers argued, was for them to stand behind the state, the only political entity that would protect their rights. "Remember," bellowed one nullifier in a speech right before the crucial election in 1832, "our allegiance is due at home . . . to OUR OWN STATE." Nullifiers rhetorically invested the state with interests, agency, and even a personality with which their audience could identify. "With united counsels, the State cannot fail to be triumphant," declared George McDuffie in 1832; "If the State so wills it we are free." While protecting their freedom, the state would create community among its adherents "as a band of brothers joined." Robert Y. Hayne used the same imagery to naturalize the state as the primary object of loyalty and the only locus of political action. "It is the soil of CAROLINA," Hayne declared, "which has been enriched by the precious blood of our ancestors, shed in defense of those rights and liberties, which we are bound, by every tie divine and human, to transmit unimpaired to our posterity." As Stephanie McCurry has argued, invocations of "Carolina" often took gendered forms, with the state portrayed as a cherished female relative deserving of masculine loyalty and protection. In fact, the state took many familiar forms — as home, family, community, and the sole source of white men's identity. Wielding Carolina in this way, nullifiers encouraged white men to identify with the state, not the federal government or local jurisdictions.[41]

The same process unfolded, although less fractiously, in North Carolina, where political leaders in the late 1820s and 1830s also addressed their audiences as "freemen." Debates at the 1835 constitutional convention relied on that concept, defining freemen in terms of the possession of individual rights and identifying the protection of those rights as the state's primary obligation. The resulting constitutional changes placed those principles at the center of state governance, providing white men new ways of connecting with the state and dissipating opposition to centralization. Perhaps the most important was the amendment making representation in the House of Commons proportional to the population rather than to the value of property, an apportionment system that had long given wealthier plantation districts in the east more seats in the legislature than western districts with more free people but less property and fewer slaves. Convention delegates retained limits on universal white manhood suffrage, leaving property qualifications in place for presidential electors as well as candidates for the state senate and keeping that body firmly in the hands of eastern slaveholders. The new apportionment scheme still favored eastern slaveholding districts by implementing the federal method of counting slaves on a three-fifths ratio for purposes of representation. Overall, though, the new apportionment system gave more adult white men greater say in state government. "If any qualification is necessary," argued delegate Nathaniel Macon, he "would prefer age; it is age that makes the man." The electoral system positioned freemen as the basic components of state government: only they could exercise the right to vote for state officeholders.[42] The direct election of the governor, too, turned the selection of a relatively unimportant official into an important public ritual that directed attention to the state government. William Gaston admitted as much in his comments on gubernatorial elections, although he cast the point in the more familiar language of sectionalism. The elections, he predicted, would become sectional contests that pitted the eastern part of the state against the west, with the west invariably coming out on top. In his explanation, Gaston slipped into the new idiom, which emphasized the role of adult white men in state government. He concluded that the west would be victorious because that region had a majority of the "white population."[43]

The amendment disfranchising free blacks accomplished similar ends. Nathaniel Macon did not believe that free blacks "had any right to vote." Indeed, one reason he opposed property qualifications was that they served as a means of enfranchising free blacks along with white men. Concerns about free blacks' political power did not drive the movement to disfranchise them; they were never numerous enough to determine electoral outcomes, even though they formed significant voting blocks in some counties. Their votes worried white delegates for reasons that had to do with white men's position within state government. Political leaders of all stripes saw free blacks' voting rights as an insult to freemen and a perversion of the state's mission. Hostility was fueled by rising concerns about abolition, propagated by the nullifiers' publicity machine, and by widespread fears of slave rebellion, confirmed by Nat Turner's revolt. As proponents of disfranchisement argued, free blacks were nothing more than freed slaves. They never had the full array of rights that defined the status of freemen. So why should they vote? More to the point, why had they ever been allowed to vote in the first place? The most ardent framed their arguments in terms of rededicating the state to its original mission, as they saw it, to look after the rights of freemen—that is, adult white men.[44]

Rights framed the entire debate about free blacks' exercise of the vote. William Gaston was among the few who took an expansive view of rights, emphasizing their universalizing qualities and severing them from race by locating them in practice, not nature: free blacks had exercised the right to vote and, therefore, should continue to do so. That position gained few adherents. The only politically viable option was the preservation of the vote for free black property owners, and even that failed. Opponents emphasized race, arguing that African descent kept both free blacks and slaves from claiming rights. Those who argued in favor of allowing property-owning black men to vote did not seek to sever the link between race and rights. Instead, they maintained that culture could sometimes overcome nature. Some free blacks, they insisted, had earned the right of suffrage by demonstrating the character and commitment to work that was required to acquire property. Some of these delegates also favored the concept of property qualifications more generally, hoping to keep them in place for whites as well. John Branch "was willing to keep the door open to the most intelligent and deserving of the free men of color" because he was "unwilling to part with the freehold qualification." Jesse Wilson articulated the common response, asserting the power of race to erase rights. "However much colored persons might be elevated," he claimed, "their color alone would prove a barrier to keep them in a degraded state."[45] Wilson's position carried the day. In disfranchising free blacks, North Carolina convention delegates affirmed that rights were the possession of white men.

White women rarely appeared in the discourse of rights at all. At the North Carolina constitutional convention, the delegates briefly discussed whether to open up space on the floor for them: since the galleries were overflowing and could not accommodate everyone, female spectators were either uncomfortably crowded in with the men or unable to gain admission at all. The resulting debate bordered on the farcical, with delegates rushing to defend women's interests as it pertained to their accommodation in the chamber, only to drop all references to women thereafter, never broaching the issue of women's rights, political or otherwise. The always practical William Gaston pointed out that the whole question about opening the convention floor to women was pointless anyway, since the delegates had already decided to exclude male spectators from the floor. "Ladies," he insisted, "would feel a delicacy in coming here unattended by their beaux."[46]

For nullifiers, white women figured as faceless extensions of their menfolk, just as they did in William Gaston's formulation. Nullifiers invoked women, along with "Carolina," to mobilize white men. "Have we," asked James Hamilton, "the poorest and humblest among us, no hostages to give for our loyalty to our country?" "Yes," he vowed, "if not alone in the life-blood that gushes from our hearts, in our wives and our children, whom the love of manhood has made us swear to protect, and the very sacrament of nature leads us to love, honor, and obey." In this formulation, Hamilton linked poor white men's wives and children to wealthy white men's plantations and slaves; all were the "hostages" threatened by the tariff. From this perspective, free women had no interests of their own. Their fates depended on the defense of freemen's rights, and they embraced that cause enthusiastically—or so these men proclaimed. Carolina women, bragged Turnbull, "will be the Spartan mothers, ready to give to each of their sons a shield with the sacred injunction, 'to return with it or to return upon it.'" Free women were so completely subsumed into the households of their husbands and fathers that they occasionally appeared as a species of property. "What property I have, my wife and children, are the capital—my stock in trade—which I will confide to the honor and moral sense of South Carolina," announced Governor Stephen D. Miller in 1830, in a transparent attempt to make common cause among white men across class lines. Miller spoke the truth, in the sense that white men held property in the labor of their wives and children. But, like other wealthy slaveholders, Miller's slaves, not his wife and children, constituted his capital and his stock in trade. Within the discursive framework of nullification, anyone who did not have rights ran the risk of being controlled by those who did. Following the path forged by the state appellate court in the 1820s, nullifiers locked women within the households of free men, their husbands and fathers, who could claim control over every aspect of their domestic space as a right.[47] In this respect, they resembled their counterparts in other factions and parties, and in other states and regions, though perhaps they stated the assumptions and arguments of this position more explicitly than men elsewhere.

Elite white women—and the enslaved African Americans who attended them at these political forums—watched and listened. Although women were refused seating on the floor of the North Carolina convention, they continued to ascend to the galleries, just as they did to hear legislative debates. White women with ties to the state's political elite followed the nullification movement closely, as their correspondence indicates. They attended legislative sessions so regularly that their absence provoked comment. Covering the debates over the test oath in 1834, the *Charleston Mercury* correspondent observed that a "profound silence ... reigned in the hall and in the gallery, which was crowded by our fellow citizens (only three ladies being present, as it happened to-day)." The formulation of this observation also indicates the ladies' political positions: they were not among the "fellow citizens" who crowded the hall and gallery.[48]

A wider range of southerners heard the speeches at political rallies and campaigns. Electioneering was a decidedly white male affair, conducted at militia musters and other exclusive gatherings. Even so, campaigning was less restrictive than the actual elections. Candidates spoke outside, in open forums that brought work to a halt and drew people together. Oratory, a valued form of entertainment, was sure to attract a crowd regardless of the topic—be it law, current events, drama, religion, or politics. A few wives stood by their menfolk's sides. Some slaves attended their masters, while others hung around the edges, listening in so as to catch useful information and relay it to others. Afterward, everyone talked about what had been said and done, just as they did following local court sessions, spreading the news more broadly in the process. The presence of wives and slaves in these forums, though, took a very different form than it did within localized law: at the state level, they were bystanders in the process instead of participants.

■ ■ ■

THE STATE ERECTED IN THE 1830s represented a radical departure from the past, despite the historical claims of its architects. The rhetoric and concepts—freemen, rights, and allegiance to the polity charged with protecting those rights—had featured prominently in the Revolution. But the historical narrative to which legal reformers appealed was manufactured. Conjuring up images of patriotic soldiers fighting for liberty, it conveniently ignored the fact that many Carolinians had been Loyalists. The Revolutionary generation had passed away, and the political milieu that gave meaning to their ideas had been transformed. In the 1830s centralized legal systems competed with localized processes for keeping the peace. In this political context, encomiums to freemen's rights legitimized the concentration of authority in the state. In the wake of the Revolution, the government at the state level had appeared as a distant, almost foreign political body, dominated by a small clique drawn exclusively from the elite, conducting public business with little relevance to most people's lives: efforts to enlarge its domain had provoked considerable controversy. By the 1830s, however, the state appeared as white men's closest ally, protecting their most valuable possessions — the rights that made them freemen. This notion of the state, popularized in the campaigns that became the hallmark of party politics during the Jacksonian period, became so common as to be unremarkable, its novelty cloaked in familiar rhetorical flourishes and its naked power shrouded in abstract conceptions of justice.

The political discourse of rights found an appreciative audience among the adult white men who qualified as freemen and who constituted the voting population. But the extension of political rights and the construction of state-level legal institutions did not necessarily make governance more accessible or responsive to ordinary white men than it had been before, although these changes did connect them more directly to the state. The problem lay in consistent units of measure, which erased all the differences that shaped white men's lives. Those differences were as profound as the economic gulf between South Carolina's low country elite and the propertyless young men who pieced together a living catch-as-catch-can, and as idiosyncratic as the personality traits and interpersonal connections that were so central in evaluating character and reputation at the local level. All these diverse people now occupied a single category, with a single, defining characteristic: the possession of rights. As freemen, they were all alike. As particular men who occupied distinct social positions, they were not. The problems of small farmers, who struggled on a few acres of land, were not those of George McDuffie, James Hamilton, or William Gaston. Access to state government and the legal system depended on a white man's social location — a matter of connections and character as well as wealth. The meaning of rights remained deeply contextual, embedded in family ties, religious affiliations, ethnicity, and social networks. Adult white men were equal only in theory. As labor historians have pointed out, that framework provided little space for articulating, let alone addressing, the structural inequalities that characterized white men's lives.[49]

Moreover, the dichotomy between freemen and everyone else was legally unstable. As feminist scholars have pointed out, the universalizing logic that constituted freemen as rights-bearing individuals also raised questions about the limitations of rights in practice. Why could only adult white men claim them? What if any position did women occupy in the polity? What duties did freemen owe to the state, and what obligations did the state have to protect their individual interests? Those questions lurked between the lines of the appellate rulings in cases involving family property, spousal violence, and disorder arising from interpersonal conflict. They could not be resolved simply by ignoring them, treating them as private rather than public matters. No wonder state leaders drained their ink wells explaining the reasons for the limitations of white women's rights.

Similar questions about the rights of African Americans haunted the consciences of the most committed supporters of rights. The contradictions involved in defining relationships of domination and subordination through the model of property law were intensified rather than resolved by early-nineteenth-century legal developments. Although state law placed slaves under their masters' exclusive control instead of positioning them as subjects of the peace, issues of rights could not be entirely avoided in cases of severe violence against slaves perpetrated by white men who proved themselves unable or even unfit to exercise mastery. Confronted with the tortuous logic inherent in cases involving slaves' self-defense against whites' murderous violence, Thomas Ruffin finally flinched. William Gaston's faith in rights led him to defend the suffrage of free black men and even, toward the end of his life, to question slavery itself. When the antithesis to a rights-bearing individual was a position so abject that it reduced people to the status of inanimate objects, the moral implications of supporting slavery and other institutions that denied rights were impossible to ignore. Despite the misgivings of a few influential jurists, the explanations that circulated in law and politics increasingly utilized existing concepts of race and sex to explain the denial of rights: rights were natural to freemen but unnatural to white women and African Americans.

Legal language hid those innovations in logic. Jurists used existing terms to express new concepts and legitimate new social structures, as was the practice in law. "Wives" and "slaves," categories based in status, still appeared in court decisions as the appendages of "freemen." In the new institutional context of the state, however, those categories reduced amazingly diverse groups of people to the singular, universalizing attributes of race and gender that also encompassed free blacks and unmarried women. Of course, wives and slaves had difficulties claiming rights before the consolidation of state power. But the limitations mattered less in localized law, where rights provided only one point of entry into the process of adjudication, and patriarchs, too, were subject to the peace. In a system of governance based primarily in rights, the inability to claim rights resulted in a new kind of subordination, characterized by exclusion instead of inclusion.

Exclusion revealed even more profound inequalities by placing patriarchal authority among the individual rights that distinguished freemen and that the state was bound to protect. In localized law, white men's exercise of patriarchal authority was a proper subject for legal intervention and government regulation because every white man exercised it at the behest of the peace. In the newly organized states of the 1830s, freemen's patriarchal authority became unconditional and absolute, like other rights that the state protected. The dynamics did not just exclude wives and slaves and, by extension, women and free blacks, from the institutions of state government; they also excluded concerns unique to them, given their legal status of subordination, particularly those involving white men's exercise of power over them. The inequalities that grounded freemen's status are most apparent in the southern context, where rights were the most capacious and the least regulated. But the rights southern freemen held over slaves were but an extreme form of rights that freemen elsewhere in the new republic held, in lesser degrees, over other people — women, free blacks, and even poor white men. The subsequent extension of rights to women and African Americans would produce vicious, violent conflict as some freemen realized that the extension of rights to others entailed a loss of rights for them — a loss that they were primed to interpret as a threat to their very status as citizens.

Conclusion

In 1869 Maria Mitchell, an African American woman in Edgecombe County, North Carolina, did something that she could not have done before emancipation: she "talked for her rights." As her son later explained in his testimony, Mitchell had a complaint against B. D. Armstrong, a white landowner who may have been her employer. Mitchell expressed her anger with eloquent words, using a highly stylized, customary attack that took the form of a loud, verbal barrage, designed to draw attention to the situation and to shame the intended target. As her son described it, "his Mama was talking loud." Caught out by this stream of invective, Armstrong demanded to know what all the "fuss" was about. Weaving her explanation into the performance, Mitchell responded that "she was talking for her rights and would as much as she pleased and as loud as she pleased." Obviously irritated, Armstrong issued a threat: "If she did not hush he would make her hush." When the words continued unabated, he "struck her in the face five licks and broke out a piece of her tooth." Not so easily silenced, Mitchell kept "talking for her rights," filed charges of assault against Armstrong, and succeeded in obtaining an indictment against him.[1]

Maria Mitchell's words and actions signaled dramatic changes in law and the legal system. Generally, historians place African Americans' claims of rights within the context of emancipation and Reconstruction: the abolition of slavery, the extension of civil and political rights with the Fourteenth and Fifteenth Amendments, and the democratization of southern state governments. Yet public policy changes, while dramatic, constitute only part of the story when it comes to understanding African Americans' legal actions in the post-emancipation period. Maria Mitchell's case also reflects the mingling of the culture of localized law with rights discourse generated at the state level before the Civil War and, afterward, at the national level. Joining rights to the principles of localized law, with its emphasis on social order, African Americans extended rights in directions never imagined by its pre–Civil War advocates. The rubric of rights, as developed in state law before the Civil War, also changed localized legal practices. During Reconstruction, federal and state policies extended and solidified that legal framework, embedding it firmly within the institutional structures of government — and not just within the South. This body of law then expanded,

286

gobbling up institutional space and acquiring legitimacy as it did.[2] Its growing size did not entail the eradication, let alone the transformation, of localized law; these practices continued in the institutional spaces allotted to
them well into the present, as Michael Willrich's brilliant analysis of courts
in Progressive Era Chicago shows. But the increasing size and prominence
of a body of law based in rights did result in the subordination of localized
law within the structures of government. While the practices and principles
that characterized localized law continued, they did so largely in the realm
of legal culture, not as defining aspects of the law—within either states or
the nation—in the same way that they had done during the first decades of
the nineteenth century.[3]

The legacy of rights in the post-emancipation United States was decidedly mixed. Individual rights both enabled and limited efforts to define
civil and political rights beyond their central concern with property and
to extend them more widely through the population. In the South, rights
gave African Americans new access to the legal system and authority within
it for a brief moment. Yet rights only took them so far. Ultimately state
and national leaders imposed a narrow version of rights more akin to the
framework of state law before the Civil War. Rights became the vehicle
for exclusion once again, not only marginalizing but also silencing African
Americans, white women, and the poor. Even so, the culture of localized
law and the expansive view of rights that it encouraged continue into the
present, animating efforts to widen the political base of the polity, to bring
those on the outside into the national political culture, and to transform the
principles underlying that culture.[4]

During the Civil War and Reconstruction, black southerners regularly
made claims through formal legal channels. In wartime, refugees and black
soldiers fired off letters and complaints to federal officers and agencies.
Afterward, freedpeople brought complaints to federal Freedmen's Bureau
officials, turning them into legal intermediaries. Following passage of the
Fourteenth Amendment and the democratic restructuring of southern
state governments, freedpeople made valiant efforts to use all the new legal
and political arenas open to them, at the local, state, and federal levels. They
turned to the legal system because Reconstruction's policy changes not
only granted them individual rights that allowed new kinds of access but
also encouraged them to think that the system could be a reliable ally.[5]

Existing legal currents within the South shaped African Americans' expectations just as profoundly as top-down policy change. Freedpeople saw
the courts as a likely venue for redress because of their familiarity with the

The development of state law did not mean the end of localized practices. In this late-nineteenth-century stereograph of Marshall, the county seat of Madison County, North Carolina, the courthouse is indistinguishable from the other buildings, just as early courthouses had been. Courtesy of the North Carolina Collection, University of North Carolina Library at Chapel Hill.

process of localized law. They had experienced law as a system designed to protect the peace and to achieve order. They viewed the legal system as a means for achieving substantive social, economic, and political goals, not just protecting individual rights, whether defined narrowly in terms of property within state law before the Civil War or in their broader incarnations in the Reconstruction Acts and the Fourteenth Amendment. After emancipation, black southerners had reason to think that they could assume more active roles in defining the public order, even when their claims to individual rights were still tenuous.

288   While firmly rooted in localized law, African Americans' legal claims

registered changes resulting from the development of state law within southern states between the 1830s and 1860, as the logic and rhetoric of rights began working its way into localized legal culture. That idiom, however, could not dominate within the context of localized law, given its capaciousness, its emphasis on process, and its concern with social order. It is likely that rights discourse, as it developed in the period between the 1830s and the Civil War, did alter the way some individuals—most likely the adult white men who were included among the freemen whose rights the state protected—conceived of the peace and made their claims on it. Like state leaders, they may have begun to see the peace as a social order based in the protection of property, not the maintenance of relations established through custom in specific communities. But those invocations of rights posed no challenge to the logic or practices of localized law. The logic of localized law meant that it could protect the rights of property holders, as elements of the peace, without altering the conceptual framework of the system. Localized law incorporated elements of state law as yet another set of useful legal principles, directed toward the larger goal of protecting the peace. The fact that so few people used "rights" within the context of criminal cases and other public matters in localized law between 1787 and the 1830s underscores the distinctiveness of this legal context. When the term appeared, it was either in the context of property rights or it was introduced by lawyers. In localized law, North and South Carolinians used "right" to mean "correct," the opposite of "left," or as an intensifier, as in she's "right smart." The introduction of rights discourse into this system would take time. Even after the Civil War, few people used the idiom in their own statements in local courts unless they were talking about property.[6]

The institutional structure of the legal system did nothing to hasten state law's transformation of localized law. Between 1830 and 1860, state law and localized law continued to operate largely apart, as separate systems occasionally joined when circuit court judges imposed new statutes and appellate decisions. Although many state leaders would have liked to subordinate localized law to state law more completely, it would have been impossible—in both political and institutional terms—for the state level to assume control of all issues relating to public order. State leaders did try to exert more control over public matters related to state security, as they saw it. In particular, legislatures and appellate courts took a more active role in regulating slavery and the status of slaves. Historians usually attribute the proliferation of slave law in the antebellum period to white southerners' growing concerns about slave uprisings. Nat Turner's revolt in 1831, which followed on the heels of Denmark Vesey's alleged conspiracy in 1822, sent white southerners into hysteria about the potential for slave violence. Other political currents—including the emancipation of slaves in the British Caribbean, the circulation of abolitionist literature, and the nullifiers' reliance on race and slavery to solidify their political position—only magnified those fears. That anxiety, however, does not explain legal action at the *state* level. Usually local communities acted to regulate slavery when faced with a crisis. As late as 1822, after Denmark Vesey's alleged conspiracy, the Charleston city government took the initiative, passing a host of new regulations in the name of public safety. State efforts were fairly minimal by comparison. It was the consolidation of legal authority at the state level in the 1830s and the state law's new conception of the public interest, based on the protection of property, that explains why *state* lawmakers began intervening so systematically and decisively in an area previously left to local control. They sought to protect property and property owners, which defined the public interest in state law. Given the political context, with emancipation in the British colonies and abolitionists building strength within the United States, state leaders were unwilling to leave the regulation of this form of property to individuals and the idiosyncratic logic of localized law.[7]

Maria Mitchell's retort—that she was "talking for her rights"—underscores both the novelty of that discourse within localized law and southerners' familiarity with it. Southerners of both races were fluent in the idiom of rights, which were pervasive in the South before the Civil War even though it did not feature prominently within localized law. Most notably, the calls to protect the rights of white men rallied white southerners to the cause of the Confederacy. The aggressive assertions of white men's rights underscored the importance of their denial to slaves and free blacks. It would have been difficult for African Americans to miss this discourse and its implications. Rights not only defined white southerners' freedom but also served as the symbolic badge of their own association with slavery. Abolitionist literature and the rhetoric of the Republican Party during the Civil War reinforced those messages. Then Reconstruction placed civil and political rights at the center of major policy changes and made the federal government responsible for protecting them. As Maria Mitchell's claims suggest, the rubric of rights had migrated from state law and party politics into popular discourse and even localized law by the 1860s.[8]

Localized law's inherent flexibility provided people with the space to transform the meaning of rights. Not all southerners attached the same legal and political meanings to rights that state leaders did. These alternative visions emerged with particular force and clarity during and after the Civil War in the claims of freedpeople like Maria Mitchell, who used rights discourse to articulate their hopes for the peace. Instead of cleaving to the practices established by white leaders, though, freedpeople asserted their own customary ideals of economic justice, racial equality, and political democracy. African Americans not only used the rhetoric of rights in their political statements, but also stretched the rubric of rights to accomplish their own goals within the legal system: to legalize their marriages; to prevent children from being apprenticed to white masters; to keep family members at home instead of being forced to work for white employers; to obtain pay for the work that they did; to congregate for religious services, social gatherings, and political meetings; to speak their minds; to conduct themselves with dignity without overt displays of deference; to educate themselves; and to defend themselves and their families from physical attack. Rights provided a powerful idiom. Articulated in terms of rights, freedpeople's concerns rose to new levels of importance as legal universals that required state protection and, barring that, federal action—at least in the period of Republican control over Reconstruction. But these conceptions of rights were also traceable to a localized system in which individuals' concerns—about their own lives, the actions of their neighbors, and the future of the social order—had actual legal standing as elements of the peace.[9]

African Americans' expansive conception of rights ultimately failed to transform state law or federal law. Their claims made inroads, but state and national political leaders eventually reverted to a narrow definition of rights and a constricted view of the public interest more in line with conceptions operative in state law before the Civil War. In this regard, there were distinct parallels between former slave states in the South and the rest of the nation. The legal handling of race relations within the states of the former Confederacy laid the groundwork for an emerging nationwide legal order that enabled many Americans to see all people of color as marginal, to countenance extreme inequalities in economic status, to exclude women from the rights that supposedly were extended to all citizens, and to characterize legal change in the Reconstruction period to achieve civil and political rights for African Americans as the "excesses" of radicals.

In 1867, congressional Republicans seized control over Reconstruction from President Johnson, divided the former Confederacy into military districts, and placed them under federal authority. Confederate states would be reconstituted and readmitted to the Union only if they accepted major changes in their legal order, as mandated by congressional Republicans. Specifically, the former Confederate states had to ratify the Fourteenth Amendment, which prohibited legal distinctions on the basis of race, religion, or previous servitude and, thus, extended civil and political rights to African American men. Then these states had to square their constitutions and their laws with those principles. The delegates charged with making these changes to their state constitutions had to be selected by an electorate that included African American men, excluded all high-ranking Confederate officials, and required everyone else involved in the Confederacy to take loyalty oaths. The Fifteenth Amendment, which more specifically protected political rights, was ratified in 1868, when the newly reconstructed states were part of the Union.

At the constitutional conventions mandated under congressional Reconstruction, delegates created some of the most democratic state governments in the nation. Besides extending full civil and political rights to African American men, they opened up the legal system and government at both the state and local levels to whites of poor and moderate means as well. Over the next few years, the dynamics of governance were literally upended in the states of the former Confederacy as African Americans used their rights to extend legal and political change. African Americans participated directly in formal legal arenas, although black women experienced the same restrictions as white women. African American men voted for local officials, such as sheriffs and magistrates, who played crucial roles in the administration of law. They selected representatives to their legislatures, which solidified and built on the democratic changes in their states' constitutions. The extension of suffrage to African American men turned former Confederate states with large black populations into Republican strongholds, supporting further legal change at the state and federal levels in keeping with the spirit of congressional Reconstruction—sometimes more so than many states that had remained in the Union.

Many congressional Republicans were reluctant to follow through on federal enforcement of laws protecting this expansive definition of rights because they were unwilling to take that much authority away from the states. They were willing to extend federal power to reconstruct the states of the former Confederacy, but after that, many Republicans and their northern constituents began to question the further use of federal authority. One reason for foot-dragging was that the legal changes of the Reconstruction era did not affect the former Confederacy alone. The Fourteenth and Fifteenth Amendments, at least in theory, altered the legal status of everyone in the Union and moved questions about the rights of citizens from the states to the federal government. They negated legal restrictions on free blacks in northern states, just as they did in southern states. Beyond that, these amendments opened up a series of troubling questions about the extent of federal authority over state laws regulating civil and political rights as well as individuals' ability to appeal to the federal government to protect their rights. Additional legislation to extend the federal government's ability to apply and enforce those measures was unpopular among white northerners who were more interested in punishing Confederates than they were in remaking the nation's legal order. In fact, the Fourteenth and Fifteenth Amendments might never have been approved had not Congress required former Confederate states to adopt the Fourteenth and had not Republican-dominated southern states led approval of the Fifteenth. When Congress and the federal courts gave up on enforcement of the Reconstruction amendments, they gave conservative Democrats in the South the chance to seize control of southern state governments and then enact legislation that restricted African Americans' civil and political rights. In so doing, they also abandoned federal support for an expansive vision of rights for all Americans, white and black, North and South.[10]

The commitment to property rights—as defined at the state level both within and outside the South before the Civil War—limited the reach of legal change during Reconstruction. The principle that freemen's rights included authority over their dependents, for instance, made it difficult to extend full civil and political rights to women. Women's rights activists did argue for inclusion, hoping to extend the Fourteenth Amendment to women as well as African American men. Many had been active in the abolition movement and brought a similar critique to the status of women. After the Civil War, they hoped that the nation would address gender as well as racial inequality. Yet despite their involvement in the Union war effort, close ties to Republican legislators, and active lobbying on behalf of both women and African Americans, they were disappointed. Congressional Republicans refused to include women in the Reconstruction amendments, arguing that the extension of civil and political rights to them was politically impossible and would only undermine efforts to obtain those rights for African American men.[11]

Granting rights to women also would have undermined the logic, as articulated by the Republican Party, of extending them to African Americans. African American men had used their new rights as husbands, fathers, and heads of household to gain a purchase on other rights as well. Using fathers' parental rights, they reclaimed children who had been apprenticed to local planters and put to agricultural labor in the fields. They also found husbands' legal rights useful in shielding women, as wives, from the abuse of employers and other whites. Republicans drew on that same logic, emphasizing men's differences from women and their responsibilities for their families in justifying the extension of rights to African American men. Like white men, African American men served in the military, demonstrating their fitness for freedom. Now that African Americans were free and expected to take care of their families and represent their interests, they needed the civil and political rights to do so.[12]

The decision to extend rights to men only turned the traditional legal relationship between household position and rights into a wholly gendered relationship: all men could, at least in theory, claim those rights, but no woman of any race could. The denial of rights to women became a "natural" result of their very being, rather than a consequence of their structural position within society. Arguing in a neat circle, the U.S. Supreme Court upheld the denial of civil rights to women in *Bradwell v. The State of Illinois* (1873) on that basis: women were different by nature than men; men were citizens with claims to full civil and political rights; therefore, the rights guaranteed to all citizens by the Fourteenth Amendment did not extend to women. This decision and others limited the implications of the Fourteenth Amendment, excluding half of the nation's citizens from its protections. Legitimating women's inequality through nature also conveniently placed the issue beyond the control of society and made the possibility of change that much more remote.[13]

Property rights also constrained the legal status of wage laborers, constituting another link between North and South. During presidential Reconstruction, in the period after the Confederate surrender and before congressional Reconstruction, southern Democrats passed the infamous Black Codes that framed these restrictions in terms of race, with the intent of forcing free African Americans into agricultural wage labor supervised by whites. Contemporary critics and later historians rightly saw these laws as creating a labor relation akin to slavery. To be sure, the restrictions on black workers moved them very close to the position of slaves. They also faced constraints that white workers did not. Yet the laws were not just a throwback to slavery. In many instances, they restated existing state laws that already applied to free white laborers in the South—and in the North as well. Like the Black Codes, those laws cast the labor relationship as an unequal relationship between "master" and "servant." Employees surrendered rights by entering into the wage contract: they could not leave until the end of the contract, they could forfeit all their wages and face criminal penalties if they left, and they had virtually no legal recourse in conflicts with their employers. The terms of the contract could limit workers' rights even further. Employers wrote in all sorts of restrictions regulating their employees' dress, place of residence, hours of labor, recreation, and demeanor. Other than refusing to work, which carried the possibility of vagrancy charges, there was nothing workers could do about the terms demanded by their employers. Some states intentionally extended the application of labor legislation beyond African Americans by passing a separate set of laws that applied to all wage workers.[14]

Subsequent federal policies, most notably the Fourteenth Amendment, prohibited restrictions that applied only to African Americans. But the inequalities in the labor relation never drew the fire or the attention that racial inequalities did. In fact, the elimination of racial distinctions had the effect of extending those inequalities in labor law to all workers, regardless of race. Nor was the situation much different elsewhere in the nation. Regardless of political affiliation or place of residence, many of the nation's leaders believed those kinds of laws to be necessary. As they saw it, people should be able to enter into contracts to sell their labor and should receive compensation for it. All propertyless people, though, needed some coercion to direct them into steady labor and to keep them working to support themselves. At the very end of the Civil War, some Republicans did advocate the confiscation and redistribution of plantations, with the goal of turning former slaves into the kinds of independent producers who occupied such a central place in the party's rhetoric and who would not need to work for wages at all. Those proposals foundered on the shoals of property rights, which were also central to Republican political rhetoric and the legal foundation of independent production. Even so, these proposals completely sidestepped the problematic place of wage laborers in the legal order.[15]

The emphasis on employers' property rights continued under Republican regimes in the South, although Republicans did infuse the labor relationship with some progressive aspects of northern free labor ideology when they were in power. Most states, for instance, strengthened workers' ability to collect their wages through laborers' lien laws. But Republicans did not change the hierarchical structure of the labor relationship. Quite the opposite. Laborers' lien laws generally restrained workers' mobility and their right to determine the terms of the labor relationship by specifying that the lien applied only if the laborer had worked the contract's full term and fulfilled its other specifications. A few states, South Carolina among them, granted laborers' liens without such restrictions and established procedures for mediating contract disputes. This legislation allowed workers to bring their complaints to mediators who could force employers to meet contractual obligations and made labor-related issues a matter of public debate. Even more than laborers' liens, contract mediation held the potential for remaking labor relations by allowing workers legal recourse. Still, the effects were limited because the mediation process affirmed the very inequalities that had subordinated laborers as domestic dependents. Laborers brought themselves to elite white mediators at great personal risk, facing fines and imprisonment if they were judged to have broken their contracts' provisions. At a time when contracts regularly demanded such things as obedience and respect from workers, the burden of proof clearly rested with the workers.[16]

Under Republican rule, the states of the former Confederacy expanded the category of common labor to include sharecroppers. During the antebellum period, no southern state except North Carolina recognized a distinction between sharecroppers and renters. All were tenants, who retained legal rights over their labor and its products when they rented land. Even in North Carolina, where the law placed sharecroppers under the direct supervision of their landlords and denied them property rights in the goods they produced, the legal definition was not always observed in practice. But this modicum of independence, whether legal or customary, became problematic for landlords after emancipation. White planters first assumed that former slaves would work for them as wage laborers. Then credit shortages, poor crops, and the resistance of freedpersons themselves closed off this possibility. As African American laborers began to work for a share of the crop on specific plots of land, the courts denied them the legal rights granted tenants, turned them into sharecroppers, and lumped them into the same category as common laborers. Although sharecroppers might exercise some authority over their labor and its products in practice, they had no legally established rights to either.[17]

The restrictions in southern labor law were extreme, but in line with the direction of change in labor relations across the nation. Throughout the United States, more people entered the ranks of wage labor. They sold their labor and received wages for it, but had no claim on the products of their labor. With few options, they were forced to sign contracts that demanded the surrender of a range of rights to their employers and to work in dangerous conditions over which they had little control. Northern workers registered their dissatisfaction in a series of strikes that rocked the North and Midwest during the last decades of the nineteenth century. Beginning in the late 1870s, labor unrest not only overlapped with Reconstruction in the South but also picked up on issues central to the process of change there. Workers also resorted to legal appeals, trying to use Fourteenth Amendment rights to alter the balance of power at the workplace. But the courts consistently used the Fourteenth Amendment against them, maintaining that the ability to contract was a protected right. Any measure that undercut it by dictating the contracts' terms and taking the decision out of individuals' hands was a violation of the Fourteenth Amendment. At the same time, the courts recognized corporations as legal persons and extended Fourteenth Amendment rights to them. The results only magnified workers' inequality, making them merely theoretically equal to corporations that grew in size and power as the century wore on and refusing intervention that might equalize that situation.

The failure of rights in state and federal law was a failure of political will. Yet there is another legacy of this era, one rooted in the cultural power of legal localism, carried on by those who used to be subordinated within localized law and who were now marginalized within the rubric of rights in state and federal law. The persistence of legal localism is evident in the actions not only of African Americans but also of white southerners during and after the Civil War. Local court records indicate that many white southerners approached the legal system and other institutions of state and federal government with similar expectations as black southerners. White women marched off to local officials to demand redress for the various problems in their lives. During the Civil War, they sent off missives to state leaders and Confederate officials, with every expectation that the government would deal with their personal problems. White men did so as well, requesting favors, transfers, and leaves as if the war should accommodate their desires. Even though white men could rely on their individual rights and could assume that their interests were central in defining the social order, they were accustomed to operating in a legal system in which individual rights were not the only way to define justice. Of course, white southerners' conceptions of that public order were very different from those of African Americans. But the way they viewed the process of achieving that order — however it might be defined — was strikingly similar. All these people drew on a common legal culture in which citizenship and participation in governance were not defined exclusively in terms of individual rights, particularly as they were defined at the state and federal levels in the nineteenth century. These claims provide an important historical counternarrative, in which individual rights provide only one way to imagine and produce claims on the state. Turning our attention to people at these local levels provides a different understanding of legal and political history. In this history, ordinary men and women without civil and political rights have more substantive roles. This history also would be based in a different narrative of political development, defined through expansive historical contests over the content of the public order instead of the acquisition of individual rights.

Notes

ABBREVIATIONS

APS	American Periodical Series Online
DNCB	Powell, ed., *Dictionary of North Carolina Biography*
DU	Special Collections, Duke University, Durham, N.C.
GLB	Governors' Letter Books
GP	Governors' Papers
HCB	2004, Historical Census Browser, University of Virginia, Geospatial and Statistical Data Center, http://fisher.lib .virginia.edu/collections/stats/histcensus/index.html (accessed 2 December 2007)
LC	Library of Congress, Washington, D.C.
NCDAH	North Carolina Department of Archives and History, Raleigh
R. G. Dun & Co.	R. G. Dun & Co. Collection, Baker Library, Harvard Business School, Boston, Mass.
SCDAH	South Carolina Department of Archives and History, Columbia
SCE	Edgar, ed., *South Carolina Encyclopedia*
SCHS	South Carolina Historical Society, Charleston
SCL	South Caroliniana Library, University of South Carolina, Columbia
SHC	Southern Historical Collection, University of North Carolina, Chapel Hill

CHAPTER 1

1. Hartog, "Pigs and Positivism."

2. See Hartog, "Public Law of a County Court," for a particularly apt description of local courts' approach to governance. Localized law echoes what Tomlins refers to as a broad-based understanding of "police" in *Law, Labor, and Ideology* and the practices that Herrup describes in *Common Peace*.

3. The issues are of central importance for legal historians, with debates tending to focus on the centralization of law and government and the displacement of localized practices, the timing of that change, and the extent to which such changes fueled capitalist development and subverted more democratic—because more

localized—governing practices. For the range of debate on these issues, see Horwitz, *Transformation of American Law*; Hulsebosch, *Constituting Empire*; Hurst, *Law and the Conditions of Freedom*; Kramer, *People Themselves*; Nelson, *Americanization of Common Law*; Novak, *People's Welfare*; and Tomlins, *Law, Labor, and Ideology*.

4. The authority of local courts in Massachusetts was similar. See Hartog, "Public Law of a County Court." Although Hartog argues that structural changes transformed the local courts and eroded localism in Massachusetts as early 1803, recent scholarship in the early national and antebellum periods has emphasized the continued importance of localities and personal networks rather than the state or nation. See Freeman, *Affairs of Honor*; Jacobs, Novak, and Zelizer, *Democratic Experiment*; Gross, *Double Character*; Hartog, *Man and Wife in America*; Kramer, *People Themselves*; Novak, *People's Welfare*; Pasley, Robertson, and Waldstreicher, *Beyond the Founders*; Penningroth, *Claims of Kinfolk*; Tomlins, *Law, Labor, and Ideology*; and Waldstreicher, *In the Midst of Perpetual Fetes*. The historiographical presumption has been that southern states lagged behind in strong, centralized governing institutions. But recent scholarship has suggested that southern states were not as undeveloped or as distinctive as previously thought. See Bardaglio, *Reconstructing the Household*; Escott, *Many Excellent People*; and Huebner, *Southern Judicial Tradition*.

5. For South Carolina, see Coclanis, *Shadow of a Dream*; Ford, *Origins of Southern Radicalism*; Klein, *Unification of a Slave State*; and McCurry, *Masters of Small Worlds*. For North Carolina, see Censer, *North Carolina Planters and Their Children*; Escott, *Many Excellent People*; Fischer, *Suspect Relations*; Cecil-Fronsman, *Common Whites*; Kay and Cary, *Slavery in North Carolina*; and Lefler and Powell, *Colonial North Carolina*.

6. Following the conceptual framework created by state leaders, nineteenth-century historians tend to assume that the local level of the legal system was subordinate to the state level. As such, legal historians tend to ignore local materials and use sources generated at the state level to define legal trends. Two of the most influential examples are Horwitz, *Transformation of American Law*, and Hurst, *Law and the Conditions of Freedom*. See also Bardaglio, *Reconstructing the Household*; Grossberg, *Governing the Hearth*; Morris, *Southern Slavery and the Law*; Salmon, *Women and the Law of Property*; and Steinfeld, *Invention of Free Labor*. Although social and political historians have mined local court records for information about the lives of ordinary southerners, they also tend to see state-level materials as definitive expressions of the law. See, for instance, Bynum, *Unruly Women*; Edwards, *Gendered Strife and Confusion*; Hodes, *White Women, Black Men*; Rothman, *Notorious in the Neighborhood*; and Sommerville, *Rape and Race in the Nineteenth-Century South*.

7. Recent scholarship, influenced by feminist theory and critical race theory, has focused on the gendered and racialized nature of citizenship within emerging, modern nation-states and the resulting difficulties in extending individual rights to all those on the social margins. See especially Pateman, *Sexual Contract*; and

P. Williams, *Alchemy of Race and Rights.* Feminist historians of the United States have taken up these insights, although with differing assessments of the possibilities that liberal individualist conceptions of citizenship held for women. See Cott, *Public Vows*; Kerber, *No Constitutional Right to Be Ladies*; and Kessler-Harris, *In Pursuit of Equity.* Fields, "Slavery, Race and Ideology," links modern conceptions of race in the United States to the new nation's embrace of liberal individualism in the post-Revolutionary period. The critical assessment of race and rights is particularly pronounced in the context of emancipation. See Foner, *Nothing but Freedom*; T. Holt, *Problem of Freedom*; and Saville, *Work of Reconstruction.* In the history of the U.S. South, scholars have combined race and gender with class in their analyses. See Bercaw, *Gendered Freedoms*; Dailey, *Before Jim Crow*; Edwards, *Gendered Strife and Confusion*; Schwalm, *Hard Fight for We*; and Stanley, *From Bondage to Contract.*

8. The analysis builds on Tomlins, *Law, Labor, and Ideology*, which makes a similar argument, although basing it in the development of labor law in this period.

9. For a brilliant discussion of these issues, see W. Johnson, "On Agency." Recent scholarship in legal history has taken up similar questions, exploring the ways that people who did not have formally recognized individual rights nonetheless influenced legal proceedings and the content of law. See Gross, *Double Character*; Gross, "Beyond Black and White"; Hartog, *Man and Wife in America*; and Penningroth, *Claims of Kinfolk.* For an analysis of similar dynamics within the context of market transactions, see W. Johnson, *Soul by Soul.* The analysis also builds on literature that explores the political agency of African Americans, even when they did not have civil and political rights. See E. Brown, "Negotiating and Transforming the Public Sphere"; Camp, *Closer to Freedom*; Hahn, *Nation under Our Feet*; Link, *Roots of Secession*; and H. Williams, *Self-Taught.* See also Kelley, "'We Are Not What We Seem,'" and Gilmore, *Gender and Jim Crow.*

10. Although much of the literature in legal history has focused on statutes and appellate decisions, recent scholarship in social history has turned to local records. See note 6 above. While building on this literature, I use local legal sources in a fundamentally different way. Because of the institutional structure of the legal system, I use them not just for information about social dynamics but also as central components of state law in the period before legal authority was centralized.

11. For the importance of intellectualism and cosmopolitanism to elite southerners, see McInnis, *Politics of Taste*, and M. O'Brien, *Conjectures of Order.*

12. See Boydston, *Home and Work*; Cott, *Bonds of Womanhood*; Melish, *Disowning Slavery*; Montgomery, *Beyond Equality*; Montgomery, *Citizen Worker*; Roediger, *Wages of Whiteness*; Saxton, *Rise and Fall of the White Republic*; Stanley, *From Bondage to Contract*; Steinfeld, *Coercion, Contract, and Free Labor*; and Tomlins, *Law, Labor, and Ideology.*

13. One of the best examples of the scholarship that emphasizes the spread of rights, rather than their meanings, is R. Smith, *Civic Ideals*, which pits inherently progressive liberal principles against inherently oppressive traditional principles

and then charts the extension of liberal principles; the analytical focus is always on the extension of rights, not their meanings, which are presumed at the outset.

14. Population figures from HCB. Harriet Jacobs's narrative is set in Edenton; see *Incidents in the Life of a Slave Girl*.

15. Kars, *Breaking Loose Together*.

16. Population figures from HCB. Censer, *North Carolina Planters and Their Children*; Kenzer, *Kinship and Community*.

17. Population figures from HCB. Carlson, "Homeplace and Tobaccoland"; Robert, *Tobacco Kingdom*; and Tilley, *Bright Tobacco Industry, 1860–1929*, 3–88.

18. For 1834 voting results, see *Greenville Mountaineer*, 1 November 1834. Pendleton was divided into two judicial districts, Anderson and Pickens, in 1826, but it remained an electoral district. The *Greenville Mountaineer* broke down the votes from Pendleton to reflect the new judicial district. Population figures from HCB. See also Ford, *Origins of Southern Radicalism*; and Klein, *Unification of a Slave State*.

19. Kershaw County, formed in 1791, had originally been part of Camden District. Between 1785 and 1800, districts (judicial and electoral areas) were composed of several counties. The county became Kershaw District in 1800, when most of the state's counties were formed into districts. Population figures from HCB. Ernst and Merrens, "'Camden's Turrets Pierce the Skies!'"; and Klein, *Unification of a Slave State*.

20. For an excellent discussion of these issues, in relation to the interpretation of local records, see M. Johnson, "Denmark Vesey and His Co-Conspirators."

CHAPTER 2

1. O'Neall, *Biographical Sketches of the Bench and Bar*.

2. Bay may have had Blackstone in mind, although his general understanding of women's legal status was very different. Blackstone, *Commentaries on the Laws of England*, 1:432–33, condemns husbands' use of violence against their wives and notes that a wife can have "security of the peace against her husband" or peace bonds, which gave abused wives protection by forcing husbands to post bond on the promise of future good behavior. That logic was also articulated in justices' manuals, one of the primary legal sources at the local level. But this case took the logic a step farther by charging the husband with an actual crime. Moreover, Blackstone subordinated wives so thoroughly to their husbands that his legal conception of marriage was used to shield husbands from legal regulation of their authority. By contrast, Bay also was known for his rulings that supported wives' independent control of property, apart from their husbands' authority. See O'Neall, *Biographical Sketches of the Bench and Bar*, 1:56–57.

3. P. Miller, *Life of the Mind in America*, 236. The analysis in this chapter also is informed by various different strands of scholarship that address state formation and historical practice. It takes seriously Benedict Anderson's notion of the na-

tion as an "imagined" community, in the sense that the concept of a nation and attachment to it needs to be created, and argues that nationalism is facilitated by histories that take the nation as its subject. See Anderson, *Imagined Communities*. Those insights apply to individual states within the United States, particularly in the post-Revolutionary period. The process of naturalizing the work of state-building in North Carolina and South Carolina is similar to that described by political theorist Etienne Balibar, "Nation Form: History and Ideology." As he argues, nations require a history that obscures the work that went into creating them by making them appear rooted in nature. Although Balibar emphasizes ethnicity and race, the larger point is that historical narratives make nations appear as inevitable formations that arise naturally from dynamics that may, in fact, have had nothing to do with their development. This chapter also relies on the work of James Vernon and others in nineteenth-century British political history who explain exactly how those processes of nation-building were obscured. In particular, this scholarship suggests the importance of exploring the broader cultural work accomplished through the political process. Those debates and conflicts not only had immediate material effects but also created powerful narratives that legitimated particular political formations and shaped how people understood what politics was. See, for instance, Vernon, *Politics and the People* and *Re-Reading the Constitution*. Bonnie Smith, in *Gender of History*, argues that the historical narratives linked to nation-building were deeply gendered, in ways that marginalized not only women but also particular topics and methods associated with them. Those gendered structures are still evident in the dismissal of local history as "particular" rather than "general" and "representative," the realm of "amateurs" and "antiquarians" rather than "professionals." Scholarship in Latin American history that explores alternate visions of "the state" and "the nation" provides the final element in this analysis. Focusing primarily on peasants in the postcolonial period, this work shifts the perspective away from political differences within and between Western nations. In so doing, this work establishes an important corrective, reminding scholars of the United States and western Europe that the liberal state, in the forms that it took in those nations, was not the only available alternative. See, for instance, Mallon, *Peasant and Nation*, and Joseph and Nugent, *Everyday Forms of State Formation*.

4. See, for instance, Baptist, *Creating an Old South*; Bardaglio, *Reconstructing the Household*; Block, *Rape and Sexual Power*; K. Brown, *Good Wives, "Nasty Wenches," and Anxious Patriarchs*; Bynum, *Unruly Women*; Fischer, *Suspect Relations*; Hodes, *White Women, Black Men*; W. Johnson, *Soul by Soul*; C. Morris, *Becoming Southern*; Rothman, *Notorious in the Neighborhood*; and Sommerville, *Rape and Race*. I drew heavily on legal sources in my first book, *Gendered Strife and Confusion*, but it never occurred to me to consider how the legal system worked.

5. Gross, *Double Character*. See also F. Miller, *Juries and Judges*; Curtis, "Jefferson's Chosen People." In a particularly insightful article on the recent use of legal sources by southern historians, Ariela Gross argues that a cultural approach can

result in a very different view of law and other structures of power; see "Beyond Black and White."

6. This body of legal history, influenced by work in critical legal studies, approaches law as a distinct arena governed by a series of powerful practices and assumptions interior to the system itself. This view of law is not instrumentalist; neither the rules nor the institutions are tools that one group can capture and use to achieve a particular end. Rather, law plays an independent role, generating contradictions and complications for those who try to use it. Yet law is still connected to the society in which it operates, shaping the terms of debate over key issues and taking them in directions that even the most powerful could not have predicted. This critical perspective has not yet made its way into the mainstream of nineteenth-century history. As a result, southern historians tend to assume that the legal system worked as this group of men said it should, not as it actually did. Ariela Gross's focus on legal institutions is a reflection of her training as both a legal historian and a southern historian. For other analyses, see Dayton, *Women before the Bar*; Grossberg, *Judgment for Solomon*; Mann, *Neighbors and Strangers*; Novak, *People's Welfare*; Tomlins, *Law, Labor, and Ideology*.

7. Duplicating these reformers' criticisms, historians once routinely dismissed law and the legal process in the region as dysfunctional, backward, or both. Southern legal historians have devoted a great deal of space to rehabilitating the reputation of southern law and legal practitioners, beginning with Sydnor, "Southerner and the Laws." The issue is still an undercurrent in the scholarship. Many southern legal historians have focused on materials authored by reformers that portray the law as an orderly system with an intellectually consistent body of principles. The resulting work moved the field in important directions, establishing southern law as a legitimate topic in its own right. Yet, in responding to past debates, this work has also duplicated some of its underlying assumptions. See Bardaglio, *Reconstructing the Household*, esp. 5–23; Bodenhamer and Ely, *Ambivalent Legacy*; Huebner, *Southern Judicial Tradition*; T. Morris, *Southern Slavery and the Law*; Schafer, *Slavery, Civil Law and the Supreme Court of Louisiana*; Tushnet, *American Law of Slavery*; and Waldrep, *Roots of Disorder*. The presumption, long held in southern history, that most matters involving slaves and, by extension, other domestic dependents were resolved on the plantation or within the household accentuated this tendency. As a result, many southern historians looked everywhere but the legal system for answers to basic questions about power and inequality in the region. See, for example, Ayers, *Vengeance and Justice*; Hindus, *Prison and Plantation*; Kolchin, *American Slavery*; and Wyatt-Brown, *Southern Honor*.

8. Duncan Cameron studied law with Paul Carrington of Virginia; see Powell, *DNCB*, 1:311. James Iredell Sr., who was appointed to the U.S. Supreme Court by President George Washington, studied with Samuel Johnston, a Patriot leader; Powell, *DNCB*, 3:253–54. François Xavier Martin, a French émigré and legal publicist in North Carolina, later moved to Louisiana, where he served as state attorney

general and as a justice and chief justice of the state appellate court; *DNCB*, 4:225. Joseph Gales was part of a reform group in Sheffield, England, and identified with the political radical Thomas Paine and the religious freethinker Joseph Priestley; *DNCB*, 2:267–69. William Gaston went to Georgetown, then Princeton, studied law with François Xavier Martin in Edenton, and took over John Louis Taylor's Edenton law practice when Taylor gave it up to take a position as circuit court judge; *DNCB*, 2:283–85. John Haywood, who was self-taught, served on the North Carolina and Tennessee appellate courts and compiled legal materials and histories of both states; *DNCB*, 3:87. William Hooper, signer of the Declaration of Independence, was the son of Rev. William Hooper, rector of Trinity Episcopal Church in Boston, attended Harvard University, and studied with James Otis; *DNCB*, 4:199–202. Archibald D. Murphey went to the University of North Carolina and studied law with William Duffy in Hillsborough; *DNCB*, 4:345–46. Thomas Ruffin went to Princeton and studied law with Archibald D. Murphey in Hillsborough; *DNCB*, 5:266–68. James Iredell Jr. went to Princeton; *DNCB*, 3:255. David Lowry Swain went to the University of North Carolina and studied law with John Louis Taylor; *DNCB*, 5:482–86. John Louis Taylor was born in London of Irish parents, emigrated to America with his older brother after he was orphaned at age twelve, attended William and Mary, studied law on his own, and went on to become one of the most influential law teachers in North Carolina; *DNCB*, 6:11–12. William Drayton, John Faucheraud Grimké, John Laurens, Gabriel Manigault II, Peter Manigault, Arthur Middleton, Alexander Moultrie, James Moultrie, Charles Pinckney, Charles Cotesworth Pinckney, Thomas Pinckney, John Julius Pringle, Jacob Read, Edward Rutledge, Hugh Rutledge, John Rutledge, and William Loughton Smith are among the many South Carolina colonial elite to enroll in the Inns of Court; see Canady, *Gentlemen of the Bar*. Thomas Cooper, who was born and educated in England, emigrated to the United States because of his support for the French Revolution and, like Joseph Gales, identified with Joseph Priestley; Edgar, *SCE*, 224–25; Malone, *Public Life of Thomas Cooper*. Langdon Cheves, who did not attend college, studied with William Johnson (who later sat on the U.S. Supreme Court) in Charleston, acquired ties to Patriot elite during the Revolution, and served in the U.S. Congress and as president of the Bank of the United States from 1819 to 1822; Edgar, *SCE*, 168–69, and Huff, *Langdon Cheves*. David J. McCord attended South Carolina College, practiced law and published sources on state law, and later edited the *Columbia Telescope*; see Malone, *Dictionary of American Biography*, 11:604–5. Henry William DeSaussure went to Princeton, studied law with Jared Ingersoll (a Philadelphia attorney who played a leading role at the U.S. Constitutional Convention and who would become an influential Federalist), and served as director of the U.S. Mint under George Washington before returning to South Carolina; Edgar, *SCE*, 260–61. John Belton O'Neall attended South Carolina College; Edgar, *SCE*, 683–84.

9. Nullification in South Carolina provides the most interesting example of how

agreement about law underlay bitter partisan differences, an issue that the final chapter explores in more detail. Nullifiers and Unionists disagreed over the state's relation to the nation, but both defined "the state" in terms of one level of government. Thomas Cooper and David J. McCord, nullifiers who worked on the digest of statutes, advocated both states' rights *and* the greater systematization of state law, particularly in matters involving slavery; in their minds, the two projects were conjoined.

10. *Raleigh Register and North Carolina Weekly Advertiser*, 29 January 1813. Gales supported a range of other causes, including libraries, internal improvements, education, penal reform, and the American Colonization Society. Although opposed to slavery, he never openly supported abolition while he lived in the South. For Gales, see Armytage, "Editorial Experience of Joseph Gales"; Cotlar, "Joseph Gales and the Making of the Jeffersonian Middle Class"; Eaton, "Winifred and Joseph Gales"; *DNCB*, 2:265–67.

11. A. D. Murphey, Memorial to the General Assembly of North Carolina, Regarding his Projected History of North Carolina, 1 January 1827, folder 6, Archibald D. Murphey Papers, #533, SHC. For Murphey's life, see Connor, *Ante-Bellum Builders of North Carolina*, 34–62; Hoyt, *Papers of Archibald D. Murphey*; H. Turner, *The Dreamer Archibald DeBow Murphey*. For a more wary view of the past, see O'Neall, *Biographical Sketches of the Bench and Bar*.

12. Those accounts focusing on the development of the courts in both states usually note the trend toward centralization, with consolidation occurring during Reconstruction. See, for instance, Senese, "Building the Pyramid"; Adams, "Evolution of Law in North Carolina"; McIntosh, "Jurisdiction of the North Carolina Supreme Court"; Orth, "North Carolina Constitutional History"; and Stacy, "Brief Review of the Supreme Court of North Carolina." For a fascinating account of conflicts over centralization during Reconstruction, see Powell, "Centralization and Its Discontents."

13. O'Neall, *Biographical Sketches of the Bench and Bar*, 1:54.

14. Freeman, *Affairs of Honor*, 263–88.

15. John Drayton to John Quincy Adams, 8 August 1821, and John Drayton to Stephen Van Rensselaer, 31 July 1821; both in John Drayton Papers, SCL. Thomas Jefferson, Monticello, to Judge Johnson, Charleston, S.C., 12 June 1823 (43/521), SCHS. These men wrote state and local as well as national histories. In addition to his *Biographical Sketches of the Bench and Bar*, O'Neall published *Annals of Newberry*. See also Swain, *Early Times in Raleigh*; Swain, *British Invasion of North Carolina in 1776*; Martin, *History of North Carolina from the Earliest Time*; and W. Smith, *Comparative View of the Constitutions*. John Haywood, a prominent North Carolina lawyer and legal writer who relocated to Tennessee, wrote *Civil and Political History of the State of Tennessee*.

16. Quotations from Chief Justice John Marshall to Archibald D. Murphey, 6 October 1827, in Hoyt, *Papers of Archibald D. Murphey*, 1:365. William Gaston

to John C. Hamilton, 1 August 1833, folder 57; William Gaston to John C. Hamilton, 30 August 1833, folder 58; John C. Hamilton to William Gaston, 27 September 1834, folder 64; all in box 4, William Gaston Papers, #272, SHC. William Gaston's son-in-law, Robert Donaldson, wanted to collect and publish Gaston's correspondence and writings while he was still alive, but Gaston declined. William Gaston to Robert Donaldson, 5 November 1832, folder 54, box 4, William Gaston Papers, #272, SHC. Gaston family members, though, did preserve their father's papers, as did the friends and relatives of others in this group. For other correspondence concerning the collection of documents and historical information, see Archibald D. Murphey to William Polk, 16 July 1819; Archibald D. Murphey to General Joseph Graham, 10 January 1821; Archibald D. Murphey to Colonel Ransom Sutherland, 8 March 1821; Archibald D. Murphey to General Joseph Graham, 20 July 1821; Allen J. Davie to Archibald D. Murphey, 17 January 1826; all in Hoyt, *Papers of Archibald D. Murphey*, 1:147–48, 191–94, 194–97, 211–13, 327–29. This material, which was housed in state and university archives that these same men and their families also supported, became the basis for later published collections, many of which are cited in this chapter.

17. A. D. Murphey, His Memorial to the General Assembly of North Carolina, Regarding his Projected History of North Carolina, 1 January 1827, folder 6, Archibald D. Murphey Papers, #533, SHC. William Gaston was a "counsellor" in the American Antiquarian Society; American Antiquarian Society to William Gaston, 4 February 1824, folder 35, box 3, William Gaston Papers, #272, SHC. He also corresponded with George Bancroft about their mutual interest in history; George Bancroft to William Gaston, 9 October 1837, folder 77, box 5, William Gaston Papers, #272, SHC. David L. Swain, who served as governor and president of the University of North Carolina, followed up on Murphey's archival project; see Swain, *Report of the Hon. David L. Swain*. For links between the interest of European nations and their leaders in creating—and, in some cases, capturing—existing archives and larger expressions of national power, see B. Smith, *Gender of History*, 116–28; and Vernon, "Narrating the Constitution," in *Re-Reading the Constitution*, 204–29.

18. After James Iredell's 1791 digest, John Haywood published an edition in 1801, which was updated in 1808, 1814, and 1819. The legislature provided for a new revisal in 1821, which was updated by John L. Taylor in 1827. See Iredell, *Laws of the State of North-Carolina*. Haywood, *A Manual of the Laws of North Carolina* (1801); the second, updated edition appeared in 1808, a third edition in 1814, and a fourth edition in 1819. See also Henry Potter et al., *Laws of the State of North Carolina* (1821); J. Taylor, *A Revisal of the Laws of the State of North Carolina* (1827); Nash, Iredell, and Battle, *Revised Statutes of the State of North Carolina* (1837). Subsequently, James Iredell Jr. oversaw another updated digest as well: *A New Digested Manual of the Acts of the General Assembly of North Carolina* (1851).

19. Martin, *Notes of a Few Decisions in the Superior Courts of the State of North Carolina* (1797). The enthusiasm and reach of François Xavier Martin's efforts were

typical. A printer, lawyer, and French émigré, Martin published the *North Carolina Gazette* and augmented collections issued by the legislature with his own compilations. An ad in his *North Carolina Gazette*, 8 February 1794, announced the publication of his collection of private acts, which had been left out of Iredell's 1791 collection of statutes; Martin thought these too valuable to be lost. For the results of his work, see *Collection of the Private Acts of the General Assembly of the State of North Carolina: From the Year 1715 to the Year 1790* (1794); *Acts of the General Assembly of the State of North Carolina: Passed During the Sessions Held in the Years 1791, 1792, 1793, and 1794* (1795); *Public Acts of the General Assembly of North Carolina, Revised and Published Under the Authority of the Legislature, by James Iredell; and Now Revised by François-Xavier Martin* (1804). Joseph Gales Sr. of the *Raleigh Register* took over when Martin left for New Orleans — where he turned to the systematization of Louisiana's law.

20. J. Taylor, *Cases Determined in the Superior Courts of Law and Equity of the State of North Carolina [1796–1802]* (1802); Haywood, *Reports of Cases Adjudged in the Superior Courts of Law and Equity of the State of North Carolina: From the Year 1789 to the Year [1806]* (1799–1806), 2 vols. Thereafter, reports appeared regularly, but at inconsistent intervals. Cameron and Norwood, *Reports of Cases Ruled and Determined by the Court of Conference of North Carolina* (1805); Murphey, *Reports of Cases Argued and Adjudged in the Supreme Court of North Carolina* (1821–26), 3 vols.; Taylor, *Cases Adjudged in the Supreme Court of North Carolina from July Term 1816 to January Term 1818, Inclusive* (1818); Ruffin and Hawks, *Reports of Cases Argued and Adjudged in the Supreme Court of North Carolina: During the Years 1820 & 1821 [December Term 1825 & June Term 1826]* (1823–28), 4 vols.; Devereux, *Cases Argued and Determined in the Supreme Court of North Carolina: From December Term 1826, to June Term [1834]* (1829–36), 4 vols.; Devereux, *Equity Cases Argued and Determined in the Supreme Court of North-Carolina* (1831–36), 2 vols.; and Devereux and Battle, *Reports of Cases at Law Argued and Determined in the Supreme Court of North Carolina* (1837–40), 4 vols.

21. The change is referred to in Soule, *Lawyer's Reference Manual of Law Books and Citations* (1883): "By order of the Supreme Court, the reports from the adoption of the new constitution of 1868 (which abolished the distinction between actions at law and suits in equity) have been entitled simply 'North Carolina reports.' In calculating the number [63] of the first volume issued under this name, the latest edition of the early reports and of Winston have been taken as the standard, and the volumes have been counted as now bound, and not as originally published." It is also clearly stated in the edited volumes; see, for instance, 1 N.C. (1778–1804).

22. Cooper and McCord, *Statutes at Large of South Carolina*, 7:295, 312.

23. For DeSaussure's reports, see Henry William DeSaussure to Timothy Ford, 15 November 1815, 11/131/27; Henry William DeSaussure to Timothy Ford, 31 March 1817, 11/131/27; Henry William DeSaussure to Timothy Ford, 16 August 1817, 11/131/27; Henry William DeSaussure to Timothy Ford, May 1818, 11/131/27; Henry

William DeSaussure to Timothy Ford, 14 May 1822, 11/131/28; all in Timothy Ford Papers, 1776–1830 (1027.03.01), SCHS. Reports of law cases first appeared in 1798 and then at irregular intervals: Bay, *Reports of Cases Argued and Determined in the Superior Courts of Law, in the State of South Carolina, Since the Revolution* (1798), 2 vols.; Bay, *Reports of Cases Argued and Determined in the Superior Courts of Law in the State of South Carolina, Since the Revolution [1783–1804]* (1809–11), 2 vols.; and Brevard, *Reports of Judicial Decisions in the State of South Carolina, from 1793 to 1816* (1839–40), 3 vols. There were no reports on equity cases, until Henry William De-Saussure's volumes, published between 1817 and 1819: DeSaussure, *Reports of Cases Argued and Determined in the Court of Chancery of the State of South Carolina* (1817–19), 4 vols. (covering cases from the Revolution to 1817). For the regularization of the publication of decisions in law and equity, see *Reports of Cases Determined in the Constitutional Court of South-Carolina / By the State Reporter* (1824); *Reports of Equity Cases, Determined in the Court of Appeals, of the State of South Carolina, By the State Reporter* (1825); *Reports of Cases: Argued and Determined in the Court of Appeals of South Carolina: on Appeal from the Courts of Law, 1828–1832 By H. Bailey* (1833–34).

24. O'Neall, *Negro Law of South Carolina*. The *Carolina Law Journal* (1830–1831), APS, published key decisions in the state appellate courts as well as essays that read like short treatises on particular legal questions.

25. For post-Revolutionary attempts to coordinate the statutes, see O'Neall, *Biographical Sketches of the Bench and Bar*, 1:31–42; *Pennsylvania Packet and Daily Advertiser*, 23 June 1789, Aedanus Burke Papers, SCL. For Governor Bennett's plea, see *Charleston Courier*, 30 November 1822. The act authorizing the digest of statutes was passed in 1835; see Thomas Cooper's preface to Cooper and McCord, *Statutes at Large of South Carolina*, 1:iii–xiii. The digest was completed and then updated annually by the secretaries of state.

26. Quotations from "Digested Index of the Acts of Assembly from 1813 to 1830 Inclusive," *Carolina Law Journal* (1830–31); April 1831:1, 4; APS, 461 (for the list, see 461–92); Grimké, *Public Laws of the State of South-Carolina: From Its First Establishment as a British Province Down to the Year 1790, Inclusive* (1790); and Brevard, *Alphabetical Digest of the Public Statute Law of South-Carolina* (1814), 3 vols.

27. For references to Tucker, see Cook, *American Codification Movement*, 6. The quotation about Tucker's frustrations with cataloging Virginia law is from the introduction to his version of Blackstone; see Tucker, *Blackstone's Commentaries*, 1:iv.

28. Archibald D. Murphey to Thomas Ruffin, 4 August 1820, in Hoyt, *Papers of Archibald D. Murphey*, 1:169–70; quotation from 170. For Alinson, see Cook, *American Codification Movement*, 6.

29. Quotations from Cook, *American Codification Movement*, 5 (original in Grimké, *Public Laws of the State of South Carolina*, 1:1); Cooper and McCord, *Statutes at Large of South Carolina*, 1:iv.

30. Stevenson, "Higher Court Records," 331–44; Senese, "Building the Pyramid."

For the complications in the courts in these two colonies, see, for instance, Fischer, *Suspect Relations*; Kars, *Breaking Loose Together*; Klein, *Unification of a Slave State*; and Spindel, *Crime and Society in North Carolina*.

31. Quoted in Golumbic, "Who Shall Dictate the Law?"; original in Saunders, ed., *Colonial Records of North Carolina*, 10:870a–b.

32. Quoted from the Declaration of Rights, passed on 17 December 1776, in Powell, Huhta, and Farnham, *Regulators in North Carolina: A Documentary History, 1759–1776*, 552; see 555–62 for the 1776 state constitution.

33. Quoted in Senese, "Building the Pyramid," 357–59; quotation from 357, original in Governor Charles Pinckney, Message of 26 November 1798, SCDAH. Debates about the authority of the federal judiciary figured in the framing and passage of the U.S. Constitution, conflicts between Federalists and Jeffersonian Republicans, and questions about slavery and territorial expansion in the years leading up to the Civil War. They continued through the post–Civil War era and into the present day. For a study that highlights conceptions of law within the political debates of the new republic, see Cornell, *Other Founders*.

34. The literature on early modern English law is vast. For these points in particular, see Baker, *Law's Two Bodies*; Erickson, *Women and Property in Early Modern England*; Gowing, *Domestic Dangers*; Herrup, *Common Peace*; B. Shapiro, *"Beyond Reasonable Doubt" and "Probable Cause"*; Wrightson, "Two Concepts of Order."

35. For discussions of parallels between the colonies and England in legal matters, particularly the professionalization of its practice and systematization of its content, see Chapin, *Criminal Justice in Colonial America*; Dayton, *Women before the Bar*; Mann, *Neighbors and Strangers*; Friedman, *Crime and Punishment in American History*, 19–58; and Roeber, *Faithful Magistrates and Republican Lawyers*. Although the bulk of the literature emphasizes those changes, other work points out the importance of continuity in the conception of law and its application; see Horn, *Adapting to a New World*, and J. Nelson, *Blessed Company*.

36. For analyses that emphasize the centrality of law to the Regulators' demands, see Klein, *Unification of a Slave State*, 47–77, and Whittenburg, "Planters, Merchants, and Lawyers." See also Jones, "Herman Husband"; Kars, *Breaking Loose Together*; and Kay, "North Carolina Regulation, 1766–1776."

37. For the continuation of the issues that had characterized the Regulation in the Carolinas, see Golumbic, "Who Shall Dictate the Law?," and Klein, *Unification of a Slave State*. The issues in the Carolinas were similar to those elsewhere, including Shays' Rebellion in Massachusetts, leading many national leaders to support the creation of a stronger national government with the U.S. Constitution.

38. These differences are identified as one of the underlying issues in the North Carolina Regulation by Whittenburg, "Planters, Merchants, and Lawyers"; see also Kars, *Breaking Loose Together*. For the economic context of these local communities, see Mann, *Neighbors and Strangers*; and Ulrich, *Midwife's Tale*.

39. Whittenburg, "Planters, Merchants, and Lawyers." His observations with

regard to the cosmopolitan elite's version of law are also noted in Roeber, *Faithful Magistrates and Republican Lawyers*; Miller, *Juries and Judges versus the Law*; and Curtis, "Jefferson's Chosen People."

40. Higginbotham, *Papers of James Iredell*, 1:194. For the range of Iredell's reading in law, see 1:56; Iredell embarked on his second reading of Blackstone in 1772, 1:220n35. Like many lawyers of his generation, he saw Blackstone as the stylistic representation of order, not just a reference for the content of law. For this point, see P. Miller, *Life of the Mind in America*, 117–55.

41. Quotes from Whittenburg, "Planters, Merchants, and Lawyers," 236. Originals in Boyd, *Some Eighteenth Century Tracts Concerning North Carolina*, 291; Henderson, "Hermon Husband's Continuation of the Impartial Relation"; and Boyd, *Eighteenth Century Tracts*, 417, 343.

42. Quotation from Higginbotham, *Papers of James Iredell*, 1:254. Although Britain never tried to include slaves as subjects within the empire as comprehensively as either the French or the Spanish, it did try to do so in the late colonial period, as part of the effort to consolidate the empire. That produced conflict between British officials and colonists, who were unwilling to cede de facto authority over their slaves to the Crown's representatives. See C. Brown, "Empire without Slaves"; Young, *Domesticating Slavery*; and Holton, *Forced Founders*. For similar conflicts elsewhere in the British Empire, see T. Holt, *Problem of Freedom*.

43. Kars, *Breaking Loose Together*, 206–14; Klein, *Unification of a Slave State*, 78–108.

44. Quoted in Higginbotham, *Papers of James Iredell*, 1:xc.

45. After first extolling the power of juries over judges as the sovereign expression of the people's control over law, Pinckney then advised the legislature to establish criminal penalties. Such a measure would limit not only judges but also juries, which often made recommendations about punishments. See Senese, "Building the Pyramid," 357–59; original in Governor Charles Pinckney, message dated 28 November 1798, SCDAH. For the role of juries in sentencing, see John Drayton to the Judges of the Courts of Law in South Carolina, 1 February 1800, John Drayton Papers, SCL. For Iredell, see Higginbotham, *Papers of James Iredell*, 1:lxxviii–lxxix; quotation in 2:115–17.

46. In both North Carolina and South Carolina, the courts had been created through statute, not the state constitutions. Although the principle of judicial independence obtained in theory, the courts were dependent on the legislatures in practice.

47. Quotation from Gibbes, "Early History of the Judiciary of South Carolina," in O'Neall, *Biographical Sketches of the Bench and Bar*, 1:x. For the changes, see Cooper and McCord, *Statutes of South Carolina*, 7:211–42. See also Klein, *Unification of a Slave State*, 135–42.

48. Quotation from Golumbic, "Who Shall Dictate the Law?" 74, 78; originals in McRee, *Life and Correspondence of James Iredell*, 2:132–33.

49. Quotation from Archibald D. Murphey to William Duffy, 6 January 1806, in Hoyt, *Papers of Archibald D. Murphey*, 1:8; for discussion of the effects of the law, see 7–9n2.

50. Grand Jury Presentment, 1827, Court of General Sessions, Journals, Kershaw District, SCDAH. Senese, "Building the Pyramid"; Cooper and McCord, *Statutes of South Carolina*, 7:290–300.

51. *Charleston Courier*, 29 May 1811.

52. For South Carolina, see Senese, "Building the Pyramid." For North Carolina, see Adams, "Evolution of Law in North Carolina"; McIntosh, "Jurisdiction of the North Carolina Supreme Court"; Orth, "North Carolina Constitutional History"; Stacy, "Brief Review of the Supreme Court of North Carolina"; and Stevenson, "Higher Court Records."

53. Quoted from *Raleigh Register and North Carolina Weekly Advertiser*, 10 December 1799. The debate was closely followed elsewhere in the state; see, for instance, *North Carolina Mercury and Salisbury Advertiser*, 26 December 1799.

54. Quotations from Hoyt, *Papers of Archibald D. Murphey*, 1:7n2; William Gaston to Robert Donaldson, 3 January 1834, folder 61, box 4, William Gaston Papers, #272, SHC; Archibald D. Murphey to Thomas Ruffin, 3 December 1818, in Hamilton, *Papers of Thomas Ruffin*, 1:211. The change provoked a flurry of correspondence: Romulus M. Saunders to Thomas Ruffin, 17 December 1818, 1:212; James Mebane to Thomas Ruffin, 18 December 1818, 1:212–13; George E. Badger to Thomas Ruffin, 18 December 1818, 1:213; Duncan Cameron to Thomas Ruffin, 25 December 1822, 1:273; all in Hamilton, *Papers of Thomas Ruffin*. For these changes, see Adams, "Evolution of Law in North Carolina"; McIntosh, "Jurisdiction of the North Carolina Supreme Court"; Orth, "North Carolina Constitutional History"; Stacy, "Brief Review of the Supreme Court of North Carolina"; and Stevenson, "Higher Court Records."

55. Senese, "Building the Pyramid"; the references to Petigru and Wilson are on 365. Public criticisms of equity and its judges in the 1829 legislative session so offended Henry William DeSaussure's son that it nearly led to a duel. Excerpt of J. E. Holmes's Letter to John Gadsden, Esq., Columbia, 5 December 1829, 11/121/10, Henry William DeSaussure Papers, 1795–1838 (1022.02.02), SCHS. For the changes in 1835, see Cooper and McCord, *Statutes at Large of South Carolina*, 7:163–342. For a critique of the court system as it was established in 1835, see "PART. VII.— THE JUDICIARY SYSTEM OF SOUTH-CAROLINA," The *Southern Quarterly Review* (1842–1857), 1 November 1850, 464, http://www.proquest.com/ (accessed 10 March 2008).

56. The North Carolina State Supreme Court only barely survived repeated efforts to dismantle it; see *Raleigh Register*, 17 December 1819 (a bill to reduce the salaries of state supreme court judges, a recurring effort meant to discourage the centralization and professionalization of the judiciary); 8 December 1820 (to reduce the salaries of state supreme court judges and to abolish the state supreme

court); 30 November 1821 (to limit the meetings of the supreme court to once a year, thereby limiting the authority of the court); 26 December 1823 (to reduce the salaries of the state supreme court judges); 26 November 1824, 17 December 1824, and 24 December 1824 (to abolish the state supreme court); 2 January 1829 (to establish an extra term to meet in Salisbury and other places throughout the state, which were efforts to re-create the old district system); 23 January 1829 (to reduce judges' salaries); 26 November 1829 (to abolish the supreme court and reestablish the conference court); 25 November 1830 (to have the court meet in other parts of the state); 6 January 1831 (to reduce judges' salaries); 18 January 1833 and 25 January 1833 (to reduce judges' salaries); 26 November 1833 (to abolish the court); 3 December 1833 (to replace the court with the old district system and a conference court); 17 December 1833 (to reduce judges' salaries). See also Holt and Perry, "Writs and Rights, 'Clashings and Animosities'"; Pratt, "Struggle for Judicial Independence."

57. Quotation from David Swain to William Gaston, 3 September 1833, folder 59, box 4; William Gaston to Thomas Ruffin, 25 August 1833, folder 58, box 4; William Gaston to Robert Donaldson, 3 January 1834, folder 61, box 4; all in William Gaston Papers, #272, SHC. Supporters of a strong appellate court saw the appointment of Gaston as key and the resulting correspondence reveals a great deal about the problems they sought to resolve; see William Gaston to Hannah Manly, 31 December 1832, folder 54, box 4; T. P. Devereux to William Gaston, 15 August 1833, folder 57, box 4; William Gaston to T. P. Devereux, 19 August 1833, folder 57, box 4; Thomas Ruffin to William Gaston, 21 August 1833, folder 58, box 4; T. P. Devereux to William Gaston, 21 August 1833, folder 58, box 4; William Gaston to T. P. Devereux, 26 August 1833, folder 58, box 4; David Swain to William Gaston, 27 August 1833, folder 58, box 4; T. P. Devereux to William Gaston, 30 August 1833, folder 58, box 4; "Attempt to Destroy Supreme Court," 26 November 1833, from the *Raleigh Register*, folder 60, box 4; "Attempt to Destroy Supreme Court," 10 December 1833, from the *Raleigh Register*, folder 60, box 4; Joseph Hopkinson to William Gaston, 28 December 1834, folder 67, box 5 (this letter refers to events in South Carolina as well); B. F. Perry to William Gaston, 10 July 1836, folder 73, box 5 (this letter actually refers to South Carolina as well); all in William Gaston Papers, #272, SHC. Thomas Ruffin to William Gaston, 25 August 1833, in Hamilton, *Papers of Thomas Ruffin*, 2:92–96.

58. Quotation from T. P. Devereux to William Gaston, 21 August 1833, box 4, folder 58, William Gaston Papers, #272, SHC.

PART II

1. Pardon, Samuel Ashe, May 1796, p. 36, vol. 12, GLB, NCDAH. Pleasant's master was Thomas Pool, a prominent planter in Granville County. Ashe's pardon does not mention whether he was among the petitioners; he may well have been the white man who exerted such influence over Pleasant.

2. Novak, *People's Welfare*. Even Novak misses how profoundly local the resulting legal order was. Intent on demonstrating the extent of public regulation in a period long assumed to be the peak of laissez faire, he turns the analysis to the legal out-comes — ordinances, statutes, and appellate decisions — and not the institutional process that produced them. In those outcomes, "the people" and "their welfare" became abstractions, invoked to explain the necessity for a particular decision or law. See also Freeman, *Affairs of Honor*; Jacobs, Novak, and Zelizer, *Democratic Experiment*; Kramer, *People Themselves*; Waldstreicher, *In the Midst of Perpetual Fetes*.

3. *Charleston Courier*, 18 June 1803.

4. Quotes from *Raleigh Register*, 4 December 1818 (report by the legislature subcommittee, chaired by William Gaston, on creating a separate appellate court with authority over law); and T. P. Devereux to William Gaston, 21 August 1833, folder 58, box 4, William Gaston Papers, #272, SHC. This same argument linking the need for uniformity in law to liberty appeared repeatedly in reformers' efforts to centralize and systematize law in the post-Revolutionary period. Joseph Gales, editor of the *Raleigh Register*, tended to print articles and series promoting such a view of law; see 3 September 1804, 24 September 1804, and 1 October 1804 (a series of articles advocating, among other things, the rationalization of property law and the criminal code); 13 December 1810 (address of Governor John Tyler of Virginia critiquing the judicial system in that state); 21 November 1817 (Governor John Branch's address to the legislature); 5 December 1817 (report of the legislative subcommittee, chaired by Bartlett Yancey, on creating a separate appellate court); 19 December 1817 (speech by Abner Nash advocating reform of the criminal code and the creation of a penitentiary); 6 March 1818 (an article critical of the inconsistencies resulting from current common law practices); 24 December 1824 (speech by J. A. Hill against the act to abolish the state supreme court).

5. In *Law, Labor, and Ideology*, Christopher Tomlins makes the same point relative to laborers and the development of labor law. Invoking the notion of "police," which located legal authority within the community, some labor leaders argued that decisions about the economic development and the distribution of resources and labor should be openly debated and determined through democratic means that included a range of community members. They opposed the notion that such matters belong in the courts, where judges interpreted the issues through contract law and imposed decisions from above.

6. This analysis is based on about 650 letters and petitions related to pardon requests to North Carolina governors, from 1787 through 1845. This correspondence is in two different record groups, Governors' Papers and the Governors' Letter Books, vols. 6–36, NCDAH. Although only governors had pardoning power, many petitions were directed to the General Assembly as well. Although I did not make a thorough search for these records, they can be found scattered among the petitions in Session Records of the General Assembly, NCDAH. Thanks to Kirsten Delegard for finding this information.

7. For Iredell, see, for example, Denial of Pardon for Thomas Denby, 3 March 1828, pp. 28–29; Denial of Pardon for Nathaniel Clark, 19 May 1828, p. 63; Denial of Pardon for James Cotton, 19 May 1828, p. 64; Denial of Pardon for Henry Hedgepeth, 20 May 1828, p. 67; all in vol. 27, GLB, NCDAH. For Swain, see, for example, Denial of Pardon for Robert Potter, 1 May 1833, pp. 64–65; David Swain to Henry Potter, Regarding the Denial of Pardon for Benjamin Seaborn, May 1834, pp. 204–5; David Swain to J. W. Capers and others, Regarding the Pardon for Benjamin Seaborn, 30 May 1834, pp. 208–10; all in vol. 30, GLB, NCDAH. In an effort to control the pardoning process, Governor John Drayton made a similar appeal for requests to be documented, although he allowed more latitude for juries to recommend sentencing; John Drayton to the Judges of the Courts of Law in South Carolina, 1 February 1800, John Drayton Papers, SCL.

8. Colonial slave "codes" were simply collections of statutes thought necessary for the governance of slaves at that time; they did not attempt to control all aspects of the master/slave relation. For analyses that emphasize the ad hoc, incomplete nature of colonial statutes relating to slavery, see C. Brown, "Empire without Slaves"; Bush, "Free to Enslave"; Watson, *Slave Law in the Americas*; and Wiecek, "Statutory Law of Slavery." For an example of the ambiguity of these statutes in a common law regime, see Higginbotham and Price, "Was It Murder for a White Man to Kill a Slave?" For further discussion about the development of slave law at the state level, see chapter 7.

9. For a discussion of these cases, see chapter 6. The treatment of slave killings at the local level was distinctly at odds with the trajectory of the issue in the statutes and appellate courts.

CHAPTER 3

1. *State v. James Woodruff*, 1834, Spartanburg County, Magistrates and Freeholders Court, SCDAH. The vagrancy statute, passed in 1787, was one in a series of acts supported by upcountry farmers who wished to discourage herding and other less intensive uses of the land; see Klein, *Unification of a Slave State*, 51–61, 119–20.

2. Other historians have also emphasized the importance of process in legal proceedings in both England and English settlements in North America. While usually associated with the early modern period, recent work stresses its continued importance in the early nineteenth century. See Block, *Rape and Sexual Power*; Rice, "Criminal Trial before and after the Lawyers."

3. The statute, adopted in 1787, offered no guidance in determining what amount of work was enough or what level of support was adequate. See James, *Digest of the Laws of South Carolina*, chap. 80. In 1836 the legislature added several new classes of vagrants, but the treatment of vagrants remained essentially the same. The constitutionality of the law was challenged but upheld by the state supreme court in 1837; see *State v. Maxcy, Arthur, et al.*, 1 McMullen S.C. 501 (1840). The records include

numerous examples of people in the same area who committed offenses that were also leveled at vagrants but got off on lesser charges; see Vagrancy Trials, Magistrates and Freeholders Court, Anderson District, Camden District, Kershaw District, Laurens District, Pendleton District, Spartanburg District, SCDAH. See also R. Morris, "White Bondage in Ante-Bellum South Carolina." Churches dealt with similar kinds of offenses in their disciplinary hearings, without resorting to such extreme forms of punishment.

4. The blending of local custom and formal law characterized local court proceedings throughout the nineteenth century and into the present. See Willrich, *City of Courts*. The implications for law's content, however, were different in the late nineteenth and early twentieth centuries, because local courts occupied a different place within the institutional structures of law and exercised much more authority within the system. Recent scholarship on the nineteenth-century South has emphasized the importance of local custom in the legal process. See Block, *Rape and Sexual Power*; Gross, *Double Character*; Hodes, *White Women, Black Men*; Rothman, *Notorious in the Neighborhood*; and Sommerville, *Rape and Race in the Nineteenth-Century South*. The dynamics also conform to those described by Hartog, "Public Law of a County Court."

5. Tomlins, *Law, Labor, and Ideology*, quotation on 21; see 19–34 for his discussion of law as "the modality of rule" in the nineteenth century. For Alexis de Tocqueville's discussion of law, see *Democracy in America*, 262–76. The discussion of the localized legal process in this section draws on Edwards, "Enslaved Women and the Law," and Edwards, "Status without Rights."

6. Tomlins, *Law, Labor, and Ideology*, 33–34; see also 35–97.

7. With the disestablishment of the Anglican Church, local courts also took over duties that used to lie in the purview of the parish; see J. Nelson, *A Blessed Company*.

8. For the evolution of courthouses and the cultural implications of their architectural design, see Lounsbury, *Courthouses of Early Virginia*, and McNamara, *From Tavern to Courthouse*. Vernon, *Politics and the People*, notes that town halls and other government buildings were linked to changes that formalized the political process, even as it was democratized. The evidence suggests that the Carolinas followed similar patterns. John Faucheraud Grimké noted the lack of courthouses in South Carolina, as new districts were being formed. See J. F. Grimké, Rough Draft of Address on the European Situation and Fear of Slave Revolt due to French Intervention, 11/172/33, Grimké Family Papers, 1761–1866 (1040.00), SCHS. See also William Drayton, Remarks in a Tour through the Back Country of the State of South Carolina, 1784–89 (34/630), SCHS, 41–52, which includes notes on his trip through the northern circuit courts as judge in 1789. Even when there were courthouses, they were not always in the best condition and grand juries routinely issued demands to the state legislature for funds to remedy the situation. See Kershaw County, Grand Jury Presentments, April 1805, SCL; Charleston, Grand Jury Presentment, in *South-*

Carolina State-Gazette, and Timothy and Mason's Daily Advertiser, 5 February 1794; and List of Statutes, *South-Carolina State-Gazette, and Timothy and Mason's Daily Advertiser,* 12 June 1794. There are few pictures of these early courthouses, but given the complaints, it is difficult to imagine that these structures were the imposing symbols of state authority that they later came to be.

9. Comparing successive collections of statutes and codes of both states demonstrates how frequently the legislatures modified the duties of local legal officials. The office of sheriff provides a good example. In South Carolina, sheriffs were appointed by the legislature between 1776 and 1800. In 1810, the new state constitution made the office elective. In North Carolina, sheriffs were appointed by the county court until the 1830s, when the office became elective. For South Carolina, see Cooper and McCord, *Statutes at Large of South Carolina,* vol. 7, which lists significant legislative changes in the structure of the courts from the colonial period to 1840. For relevant changes to law courts between 1785 and 1840, see 211–41, 243–45, 245–46, 247–49, 253–57, 260–70, 283–89, 290–93, 293–300, 300–303, 325–28, 334–37, 339–41. For North Carolina, see the appropriate headings in Potter et al., *Laws of the State of North Carolina,* and Nash, Iredell, and Battle, *Revised Statutes of the State of North Carolina.*

10. See note 9. For North Carolina, see the appropriate headings in Potter et al., *Laws of the State of North Carolina;* and Nash, Iredell, and Battle, *Revised Statutes of the State of North Carolina.* The descriptions of local courts in the following paragraphs are drawn from the following records. Criminal Action Papers, Granville County, 1790–1840; Criminal Actions Concerning Slaves and Free Persons of Color, Granville County, 1800–1839; Superior Court Minutes, Granville County, 1790–1840; Criminal Action Papers, Orange County, 1787–1808; Superior Court Minutes, Orange County, 1787–1840; all in NCDAH. Sessions Docket, County and Intermediate Court, Kershaw District; Dockets, County and Intermediate Court, Common Pleas, Kershaw District; Indictments, County and Intermediate Court, Kershaw District; Trial Papers, Court of Magistrates and Freeholders, Kershaw District; Indictments, Court of General Sessions, Kershaw District; Journal, Court of General Sessions, Kershaw District; Coroner's Inquisitions, Court of General Sessions, Kershaw District; all in SCDAH. Trial Papers, Court of Magistrates and Freeholders, Anderson/Pendleton District; Indictments, Court of General Sessions, Anderson County; Peace Bonds, Court of General Sessions, Anderson County; Coroner's Inquisitions, Court of General Sessions, Pendleton District; Coroner's Inquisitions, Court of General Sessions, Anderson District; Vagrancy Trials, Court of Magistrates and Freeholders, Anderson District; Indictments, County and Intermediate Court, Pendleton District; Pleadings and Judgments, Court of Common Pleas, Pendleton District; Coroner's Inquisitions, Court of General Sessions, Pendleton District; Indictments, Court of General Sessions, Pendleton District; Journals of the County and Intermediate Court, Pendleton District; Peace Bonds, County and Intermediate Court, Pendleton District; Peace Bonds, Court of Gen-

eral Sessions, Pendleton District; Vagrancy Trials, Court of Magistrates and Free-holders, Pendleton County; all in SCDAH.

11. Quotation from *Raleigh Register*, 25 October 1822. For examples of disturbances involving magistrates and other local officers, which usually took place while making an arrest or execution of property or during the hearing or trial, see *State v. Andrew Burke*, 1789; *State v. John Parkes*, 1789; *State v. Robert Ferguson*, 1791; *State v. Samuel Benton*, 1791; *State v. Alexander Duncan*, 1791; *State v. William Nash*, 1792; *State v. George Watson*, 1796; *State v. William Lister, Jr., and John McDade*, 1797; *State v. Armon King*, 1800; *State v. Robert Duke*, 1800; *State v. Samuel Shaw and William Mebane*, 1800; *State v. James Ray*, 1800–1801 (in boxes 5 and 6); *State v. Vernon King*, 1800; *State v. Robert Duke*, 1800; *State v. John Carrington*, 1801; *State v. Thomas Thomas*, 1801; *State v. William Brown Mebane*, 1804; *State v. Isaac Bracken, Jr.*, 1804; *State v. James Carroll*, 1808; all in Criminal Action Papers, Orange County, NCDAH. *State v. John Morris*, 1807; *State v. Mary Hester, Nancy H. Pullam and Rachel Hester*, 1813; *State v. Martin Rear*, 1818; *State v. Isaac Hester*, 1813–14; *State v. Ezekiel Bonner*, 1820; *State v. Thomas Morris*, 1820; *State v. John Creath, Jr.*, 1823; *State v. John Stephenson*, 1828; *State v. Samuel Forsythe*, 1828; *State v. Thomas Jones*, 1835; all in Criminal Action Papers, Granville County, NCDAH. *State v. John Duncan, John Brackenridge, Elson Burgan, Peter McPhail, and Samuel Brown*, Spring Term 1835, #3; *State v. Alfred Barkley*, Fall Term 1834, #2; *State v. Hugh Rains*, Fall Term 1835, #18; *State v. John Wardlaw*, Fall Term 1838, #10; all in Indictments, Court of General Sessions, Anderson County, SCDAH. *State v. Jacob Cherry, Jr.*, 1816; *State v. Starling Johnston*, 1817; *State v. Joseph McAdams*, 1800; *State v. Thomas McCown*, 1827; *State v. George McIntosh*, 1839; all in Indictments, Court of General Sessions, Kershaw District, SCDAH.

12. See, for instance, Woodmason, *Carolina Backcountry on the Eve of the Revolution*; Higginbotham, *Papers of James Iredell*, 2:5–9, 11; Hamilton, *Papers of Thomas Ruffin*, 1:355–57. By contrast, William Drayton, in Remarks in a Tour Through the Back Country of the State of South Carolina, 1784–89 (34/630), SCHS, characterized the South Carolina backcountry as a thriving place and generally had few complaints, although he seemed concerned primarily with the economic potential of the region.

13. Even larger cities, like Charleston, which were built to create privacy around the domestic spaces of their wealthy white residents, facilitated the surveillance of slaves and the poor as well as the creation of dense social networks of various kinds. See McInnis, *Politics of Taste*. See also Tolbert, *Constructing Townscapes*.

14. These patterns are drawn from Coroner's Inquisitions, Court of General Sessions, Kershaw District; Coroner's Inquisitions, Court of General Session, Pendleton District; Coroner's Inquisitions, Court of General Session, Anderson District; all in SCDAH.

15. For the tendency of elites in the eighteenth and early nineteenth centuries to take certain issues—particularly those involving family relations—out of public

legal forums and settle them privately, see Dayton, "Turning Points and the Relevance of Colonial Legal History"; Dayton, *Women Before the Bar*; and Wall, *Fierce Communion*. Ford, *Origins of Southern Radicalism*, 67, also suggests that elite whites avoided court as a means for dispute settlement with poorer neighbors.

16. The compulsory and brutal qualities of law are obvious in cases with slave defendants. See Criminal Actions Concerning Slaves and Free Persons of Color, Granville County, 1800–1839, NCDAH; Trial Papers, Court of Magistrates and Freeholders, Anderson/Pendleton District, SCDAH; Trial Papers, Court of Magistrates and Freeholders, Kershaw District, SCDAH; Trial Papers, Court of Magistrates and Freeholders, Spartanburg District, SCDAH. Those inequalities are well documented in the scholarship as well. See, for instance, Ayers, *Vengeance and Justice*; Hindus, *Prison and Plantation*; T. Morris, *Southern Slavery and the Law*; and Waldrep, *Roots of Disorder*.

17. *State v. Robert Robertson*, Spring Term 1834, #27, Indictments, Court of General Sessions, Anderson County, SCDAH. The following records from South Carolina occasionally provide information about court costs, fines, and punishments: Indictments, Court of General Sessions, Anderson County; Indictments, Court of General Sessions, Kershaw District; Indictments, Court of General Sessions, Pendleton District; all in SCDAH. In the North Carolina records, court costs often appear on documents, such as warrants and executions, related to efforts to obtain payment. See Criminal Action Papers, Orange County; Criminal Action Papers, Granville County; both in NCDAH. Punishments appear in the Superior Court Minutes for Orange County and Granville County; both in NCDAH.

18. Thomas Waties Papers, *State v. Alexander Cameron*, January 1799, 86, ser. I: 1–265, microfilm, SCL.

19. For South Carolina, see County and Intermediate Court, Peace Bonds, Pendleton District, 1792–97; Court of General Sessions, Peace Bonds, Anderson County, 1828–1905; both in SCDAH. In North Carolina, peace bonds are mixed in with the other court documents: Criminal Action Papers, Orange County; Criminal Action Papers, Granville County; Criminal Actions Concerning Slaves and Free Persons of Color, Granville County; all in NCDAH.

20. David Stone, Pardon of Nixon, White, Copeland, Copeland, Townsend, and Jordan, 31 October 1809, p. 115, vol. 17, GLB, NCDAH. The point is similar, but not the same as the one made by Wyatt-Brown, *Southern Honor*, 366, that extralegal sanctions replaced legal punishments within the southern criminal justice system, without undermining the integrity of law. In contrast to Wyatt-Brown, I am arguing that the distinction between "legal" and "extralegal" was less meaningful because of the institutional structures of law.

21. *State v. Patt*, 1825, #14, reel 2916, Trial Papers, Court of Magistrates and Freeholders, Anderson/Pendleton District, SCDAH. *State v. Robert Thompson*, 1818, Indictments, Court of General Sessions, Kershaw District, SCDAH. *State v. James Wood*, 1800, Criminal Action Papers, Orange County, NCDAH. Occasionally cases

would indicate that they had been settled out of court. The following are examples: *State v. Isham Elrod*, Spring Term 1835, #5; *State v. Ambrose Jones*, Spring Term 1836, #4B; Indictments, Court of General Sessions, Anderson County, SCDAH. *State v. Jacob Shiver*, 1808; *State v. Samuel Jones*, 1812; *State v. James Gee*, 1821; *State v. John Lowry, John Irvin, and Reuben Lowry*, 1824; *State v. Powell McRa*, 1826; *State v. John Johnson*, 1830; *State v. Isaac Mothershed*, 1834; all in Indictments, Court of General Sessions, Kershaw District, SCDAH. *State v. Jordan Gilliam*, 1800, Criminal Action Papers, Orange County, NCDAH.

22. Sarah J. Jones to Mira E. Lenoir, 16 April 1818, folder 26, subseries 1.1, Lenoir Family Papers, #426, SHC. See also Lounsbury, *Courthouses of Early Virginia*, 3–8.

23. O'Neall, *Annals of Newberry*, 17–22. Diaries of David Schenck and William D. Valentine, both of North Carolina, also contain descriptions of trials and courtrooms. See diaries, series 1, folder 2, vol. 1, David Schenck Papers, #652, SHC, particularly 7–8, 33, 80–82, 137–40, 151; William D. Valentine Diaries, #2148, SHC, 14 April 1837, 16 August 1837, 21 September 1837, 23 March 1838, 16 May 1838, and 21 September 1838. The patterns echo those in colonial Virginia described so well by Roeber, "Authority, Law, and Custom," although early national and antebellum courts seemed to be less decorous. See also Gross, *Double Character*, 22–46; and Isaac, *Transformation of Virginia*.

24. *State v. Jeremiah Frazer*, 1802, Criminal Action Papers, Granville County, NCDAH. In Granville County and Anderson County, the convention was to indicate the location of a fight, if it took place at court. The numbers in those two counties suggest that such incidents were common on court day. *State v. Daniel Tucker*, 1808; *State v. Willie Parham, John Walker, and Dawson McLaughlin*, 1816; *State v. John Frazier, Thomas Ricks, and David Graves*, 1808; *State v. John Morris*, 1800; all in Criminal Action Papers, Granville County, NCDAH. *State v. Martha Skelton and Richard Skelton*, Spring Term 1830, #17; *State v. Jedithan Cason*, Fall Term 1831, #2; *State v. Nimrod Smith*, Spring Term 1832, #13; *State v. David Gortney*, Spring Term 1836, #4A; *State v. Robert Jolley*, Spring Term 1836, #5; *State v. John Smith*, Spring Term 1836, #9; *State v. David Crawford*, Fall Term 1839, #2; *State v. James E. Hall*, Fall Term 1839, #5; *State v. Polly May, Elizabeth May and Sarah May*, Fall Term 1839, #14, and Fall Term 1839, #16; *State v. Samuel Richardson*, 1837; all in Indictments, Court of General Sessions, Anderson County, SCDAH. For an excellent description of all the activities associated with court day, see Lounsbury, *Courthouses of Early Virginia*, 3–8, 28–38.

25. For court day as a place to exchange gossip and for gossip about court cases and court officials, see John Hill Wheeler to David S. Reid, in Butler, *Papers of David Settle Reid*, 1:207–10, 222–24, 229–30. Hoyt, *Papers of Archibald D. Murphey*, 1:93–95, 168–70. David Schenck Diary, p. 151, folder 2, vol. 1, ser. 1, David Schenck Papers, #652, SHC. *Raleigh Register*, 14 July 1808, contains a suggestive article regarding the governor's attempts to gauge public opinion through circuit judges and their contact with people and gossip at court. The *Raleigh Register* also reported on notorious

cases in a way that suggested the larger swirl of gossip that surrounded them: 12 July 1810, 11 October 1810, 22 February 1822, 9 April 1824, 12 April 1825, 12 November 1829, 8 April 1830, 20 May 1830, 7 October 1830. William Valentine's evaluations of judges' and lawyers' abilities are also suggestive; see, for instance, 16 August 1837, 21 September 1837, 18 August 1837, 16 May 1838, 21 September 1838, 29 October 1841, 27 September 1845, 18 March 1846, 12 October 1846, 26 March 1847, 1 June 1848, 6 June 1848, 20 December 1848; all in William D. Valentine Diaries, #2148, SHC.

26. This analysis is based on about 650 letters and petitions related to pardon requests to North Carolina governors from 1787 through 1845. See notes 6 and 7 in chapter 1 for a description of the records and examples of denials from Governor James Iredell Jr. and Governor David Swain. As converts to modern ideas about punishment, they did not think it appropriate to grant pardons, but both went to great lengths to explain their denials to petitioners.

27. Inquest of the Infant of Margret Wright, 1814, folder 1 and folder 3, Court of General Session, Coroner's Inquisitions, Pendleton District, SCDAH. The large number of outstanding warrants is also suggestive. For escapes, see *State v. William Norris*, 1793, Sessions Docket, County and Intermediate Court, Kershaw District, SCDAH. *State v. William Norris*, 1792–93, Indictments, County and Intermediate Court, Kershaw District, SCDAH. *State v. John Parker*, 1816; *State v. John Shiver and James Shiver*, 1817–21; *State v. Isaac Mothershed and William Mothershed*, 1837, Indictments, Court of General Sessions, Kershaw District, SCDAH. *State v. John Beeson*, 1834, Indictments, Court of General Sessions, Anderson County, SCDAH. *State v. Ezekiel Hayes*, 1794; *State v. Jeremiah Hester and others*, 1824; *State v. Parker F. Stone*, 1829; *State v. Washington Taborn*, 1832; *State v. Lyman Latham*, 1833; *State v. Leslie Gilliam*, 1833; all in Criminal Action Papers, Granville County, NCDAH. *State v. John Allison, Henry McCollum, James McCawly*, 1795; *State v. William McCulloch*, 1801; *State v. Henry Bracken*, 1803; *State v. Ezekiel Brewer and Thomas Lloyd*, 1808; all in Criminal Action Papers, Orange County, NCDAH.

28. Inquest of George Cooley, 1817, folder 3; Inquest of Jesse Corbin, 1822, folder 5; both in Coroner's Inquisitions, Court of General Session, Pendleton District, SCDAH.

29. For the South, see Gross, *Double Character*, esp. 53–57, and Wyatt-Brown, *Southern Honor*, 401. For the compatibility of honor with law as well as with other institutions and cultural practices associated with a more "modern," liberal state, see also Reddy, *Invisible Code*; Freeman, *Affairs of Honor*. For work in southern history that proceeds with the assumption that honor and law were compatible, see Rothman, *Notorious in the Neighborhood*, and Sommerville, *Rape and Race in the Nineteenth-Century South*. Traditionally, though, southern historians have tended to posit a conflict between honor and law, with honor winning out. See Ayers, *Vengeance and Justice*; Hindus, *Prison and Plantation*; Waldrep, *Roots of Disorder*; and Kolchin, *American Slavery*.

30. Freedpeople's determination to use the courts is a common theme in the

literature on Reconstruction. The series, *Freedom: A Documentary History of Emancipation, 1861–1867*, emphasizes African Americans' involvement with various government institutions and legal forums at the federal, state, and local levels. See, for instance, Berlin, Reidy, and Rowland, *Black Military Experience*; Berlin, Fields, Glymph, Reidy, and Rowland, *Destruction of Slavery*; Berlin, Miller, and Rowland, "Afro-American Families in the Transition from Slavery to Freedom." Subsequent scholarship has relied extensively on legal materials, produced at various levels of government. See, for instance, Bercaw, *Gendered Freedoms*; Bryant, "'We Have No Chance of Justice before the Courts'"; Edwards, *Gendered Strife and Confusion*; Fields, *Slavery and Freedom on the Middle Ground*; Frankel, *Freedom's Women*; Hodes, *White Women, Black Men*; Penningroth, *Claims of Kinfolk*; Rosen, "'Not That Sort of Woman'"; Rodrigue, *Reconstruction in the Cane Fields*; Saville, *Work of Reconstruction*; Sommerville, *Rape and Race in the Nineteenth-Century South*, 147–75; Schwalm, *A Hard Fight for We*, 147–268; and Waldrep, "Substituting Law for the Lash."

31. Eastern North Carolina and the South Carolina low country were successful economies based in exports and international trade by the time of the Revolution, and growth continued for the next few decades, although at a slower pace. See Coclanis, *Shadow of a Dream*, and Keith, "John Gray and Thomas Blount, Merchants." Similar economic trends marked the backcountry by the 1760s and intensified thereafter; see Ernst and Merrens, "'Camden's Turrets Pierce the Skies!'"; Ford, *Origins of Southern Radicalism*, 6–19; Klein, *Unification of a Slave State*. Whittenburg, "Planters, Merchants, and Lawyers," explicitly links those economic patterns to law and lawyers, particularly civil law. Civil suits constituted the great bulk of court business in most southern jurisdictions. In *Vengeance and Justice*, Ayers estimates that there were about three or four civil cases for every criminal case in a typical southern court (32). See also Gross, *Double Character*, 23. Those patterns characterized the courts in Granville County, Orange County, Kershaw District, and Anderson/Pendleton District. At that time, civil suits over financial and property transactions predominated throughout the United States. The place of law in a wide range of economic exchange is also apparent in lawyers' practices, which are composed largely of property matters. See DeSaussure and Ford Day Book, 1790–92, Timothy Ford Papers, 1776–1830 (1027.03.01); Abstract of Cases Determined in the Constitutional Courts at Charleston & Columbia, 1795–1805, William Loughton Smith Papers, 1774–1834 (1119.00); Oliver M. Smith, Docket Book, 1834–39 (34/305); all in SCHS. John Wrought Mitchell, Receipt Book, 1817–35; Henry William DeSaussure and Timothy Ford, Record Book, 1786–92; both in SCL. Letter Book, William Gaston Papers, #272, box 7; the business-related correspondence in subser. 1.2, boxes 4–28, Cameron Family Papers, #133; both in SHC.

32. For books used by law students at the University of South Carolina, see John Phillips, "Book of Precedents and Other Legal Documents," ca. 1788–1839

(34/400), SCHS. For books used in legal education, see Tod R. Caldwell to Thomas

Ruffin, 9 January 1840, in Hamilton, *Papers of Thomas Ruffin*, 2:180–81. John Bynum to William Gaston, 9 July 1834, box 4, folder 63, William Gaston Papers, #272; William B. Rodman to William Gaston, 6 July 1837, box 5, folder 76; William Gaston Papers, #272; both in SHC. Robert Williams to William Lenoir, 30 July 1799, folder 9, subser. 1.1, Lenoir Family Papers, #426, SHC. The guidelines in Blackstone are representative of the lack of details in governing legal authorities read by aspiring lawyers. See Blackstone, *Commentaries on the Laws of England*, vol. 3 on private wrongs and vol. 4 on public wrongs.

33. For the infrequency of minor criminal matters in circuit courts, see 27 May 1839, William D. Valentine Diaries, #2148, SHC. J. F. Grimké, Draft Address to the Grand Juries of the Western Division, 11/172/32, Grimké Family Papers, 1761–1866 (1040.00), SCHS. William Drayton, Remarks in a Tour through the Back Country of the State of South Carolina, 1784–89 (34/630), SCHS. The difference is also apparent in comparing cases actually tried in the court minutes against the records in the Criminal Action Papers series in North Carolina and the Indictments series in South Carolina, which contain the documentation of cases that came from magistrates and lower courts but that did not always appear in circuit courts; there are far fewer cases in the minutes than there are in the other series.

34. Quotations from Copy, Resolutions to the Governor regarding the District Court at Camden and Payment of debts, unsigned, 23 April 1785; see also Rough Draft of a Report on the description of proceedings of the Court of Common Pleas at Camden [J. F. Grimké], 18 May 1785; both in 11/172/12, Grimké Family Papers, 1761–1866 (1040.00), SCHS. Such actions were common in this period; in addition to Shays' Rebellion, see Bouton, "Road Closed."

35. The standard manual in North Carolina was written by Haywood, *Duty and Office of Justices of the Peace*; one of the most popular manuals in South Carolina was by Grimké, *South Carolina Justice of the Peace*. The manuals were usually based on either Michael Dalton, *Countrey Justice*, or Richard Burn, *Justice of the Peace, and Parish Officer*. They also duplicated earlier colonial guides; see Simpson, *Practical Justice of the Peace*. To that base, the authors added statutes, legal decisions, and practices particular to the individual states.

36. *State v. William Mallory*, 1816, and *State v. John Stephenson*, 1820; both in Criminal Action Papers, Granville County, NCDAH. In North Carolina, cases involving free blacks and slaves went to the regular courts, while in South Carolina they went to the magistrates' and freeholders' courts. But even in South Carolina, free blacks prosecuted cases against whites, sometimes in the regular courts, where they technically were not supposed to appear.

37. For the guidelines, see Haywood, *Duty and Office of Justices of the Peace*; Grimké, *South Carolina Justice of the Peace*.

38. These ideas were reinforced in the religious revivals that spread across the South in the 1790s and early 1800s and that led to the more general movement, the Second Great Awakening. See Boles, *Great Revival, 1787–1805*; Mathews, *Religion in*

the Old South; Friedman, *Enclosed Garden*, esp. 14–20; Klein, *Unification of a Slave State*, 269–302; Ford, *Origins of Southern Radicalism*, 19–43.

39. This analysis is based on the minutes of about forty-five Evangelical churches in North Carolina and South Carolina, from the collections at the SCL, SHC, and NCDAH. They include Baptist, Primitive Baptist, Methodist, and Presbyterian, although Baptist and Primitive Baptist comprise the majority. These patterns are also described in Mathews, *Religion in the Old South*; Friedman, *Enclosed Garden*, 14–20; Klein, *Unification of a Slave State*, 294–98; and Ford, *Origins of Southern Radicalism*, 33–36.

40. Quotations from Bear Creek Church Records, 1805 entry, #M-3124, SHC; Minutes, First Baptist Church, Barnwell County, p. 1, SCL.

41. This analysis is based on about 650 letters and petitions related to pardon requests to North Carolina governors, from 1787 through 1845; see GP and GLB, vols. 6–36, NCDAH.

42. For the process by which the handling of misconduct was secularized, see Nelson, *Blessed Company*, 273–81. For debates about the penitentiary, a reform particularly dear to editor Joseph Gales's heart, see *Raleigh Register*, 31 March 1801, 11 July 1803, 1 October 1804, 13 December 1810, 16 August 1811, 23 August 1811, 30 August 1811, 6 September 1811, 13 September 1811, 6 December 1811, 8 December 1815, 22 December 1815, 27 December 1816, 3 January 1817, 10 January 1817, 17 January 1817, 12 December 1817, 19 December 1817, 26 December 1817, 25 January 1818, 6 November 1818, 22 December 1823, 2 September 1825, 9 September 1825, 27 April 1827, 29 October 1829, 12 November 1829, 17 December 1829, 28 October 1830, and 23 December 1834. For North Carolina, see also Ayers, *Vengeance and Justice*, 49–51, 188–89. For debates about the establishment of penitentiaries, see Meranze, *Laboratories of Virtue*. Despite their support for reforms that suggest a different view of vice and crime, elite parents' letters to their adolescent children drew on views similar to those operative in localized law, focusing on the cultivation of individual character so as to overcome the innate tendency toward vice. See William Gaston Papers, #272, SHC, particularly Gaston's letters to his children in box 1. The advice given by the Camerons and Ruffins of North Carolina and the Singletons of South Carolina was similar; see Cameron Family Papers, ser. 1.2, #133, SHC; Hamilton, *Papers of Thomas Ruffin*, vol. 1; Singleton Family Papers, LC.

43. Duncan Cameron to William Hawkins, 9 November 1814, 20:435–38, GLB, NCDAH. See also Edwards, "Law, Domestic Violence, and the Limits of Patriarchal Authority."

44. The unimportance of theft relative to assaults and other forms of physical violence is born out by reports submitted by South Carolina districts in response to the state attorney general's 1835 request for summaries of court business since the end of the Revolution. See Samuel M. Stevenson (Horry District) to R. B. Smith, Attorney General, 18 September 1835; W. McWhorter (York District) to R. B. Smith, 18 November 1835; both in South Carolina Attorney General Papers, SCL.

45. Grand juries in both states also identified community problems that required legal action based on "information" that had been given to them. Providing information was one of the ways to establish a criminal charge in British law. In its strict sense, information was the charge brought by one individual against another. That information was then investigated by the magistrate, who determined whether the case would go forward. In practice, in post-Revolutionary North Carolina and South Carolina, information acquired a broader definition, encompassing all the evidence given at the investigatory hearing. See A. P. Scott, *Criminal Law in Colonial Virginia*, 72–75.

46. Inquest of Israel, slave of James Gordon, 1845; Inquest of Sarah McCulley, 1841; both in Court of General Session, Coroner's Inquisitions, Anderson County, SCDAH.

47. The process of private detection was similar to that described by Herrup, *Common Peace*, 67–92.

48. *State v. Leonard Haze*, 1788, box 2, Criminal Action Papers, Orange County, NCDAH. Neither appears in the 1790 census, suggesting a few possibilities, all of which indicate their marginal position in the community: either the men did not own real estate, or they did not head up their own households, and/or they did not have roots or prospects in the area and had moved on by that time. For the place of lawyers in the process, see also Rice, "Criminal Trial before and after the Lawyers."

49. In his diaries, William D. Valentine discusses the difficulties of establishing a practice; see William D. Valentine Diaries, #2148, SHC. He took on criminal cases for indigent clients in order to build up his reputation; see, in particular, 16 May 1838. Similar complaints were common. See W. Norwood to William Lenoir, 26 November 1791, folder 3, subser. 1.1; Robert Williams to William Lenoir, 30 July 1799, folder 9, subser. 1.1; both in Lenoir Family Papers, #426, SHC. Louisa Susanna Cheves McCord, 1810–79, Notes and Letters on Langdon Cheves, ca. 1876 (1167.03.03), SCHS. Gabriel Ford to Timothy Ford, 4 December 1808, 11/131/15, Timothy Ford Papers, 1776–1830 (1027.03.01), SCHS. Archibald D. Murphey to William Duffy, 6 January 1806, in Hoyt, *Papers of Archibald D. Murphey*, 1:6–9.

50. Abbott's Creek Primitive Baptist Church, Minutes, 1783–1879, Davidson County, NCDAH; for entries on Sarah Spoolman, see August, September, and October 1797; for citations against those using the courts, see July 1824. Church members also settled property claims against one another through the church rather than using law; see September 1801.

51. Cane Creek Baptist Church, Minutes and Membership Roll, 1829–1941, Orange County, North Carolina, NCDAH; see entry for October 1843.

52. Thomas Waties Papers, *Harris v. Campbell and Anderson*, April 1793, 22, ser. I: 1–265, microfilm, SCL. This section draws on points developed in Edwards, "Status without Rights."

53. Quote from Curtis Winget, Petition for Divorce, 1830, General Assembly   325

Records, SCDAH. Other petitions for divorce or arrangements that approximated divorce came in at regular intervals: Rachel Teakle, Petition for Divorce, 1802; Henry Gable and Nancy Gable, Petition for Divorce, 1810; Richard Hembree Hughes, Petition for Divorce, 1818; Mary Wilson, Petition for Divorce, 1821; Elizabeth Hamilton, Petition for Annulment and Exoneration from her Husband's Debts, 1813; William Chick, Petition for Divorce, 1821; Thomas Miller, Petition for Divorce, 1841; Wilson Bartlett, Petition for Divorce, 1844; Marmaduke James, Petition for Divorce, 1847; all in General Assembly Records, SCDAH.

54. Pendleton District, Grand Jury Presentment, 1814, General Assembly Records, SCDAH.

55. For the petition from Orangeburg District, see Schweninger, *Southern Debate over Slavery*, 55–56; 47–58 for Richard Dawson. Schweninger's collection of petitions, from all southern states, suggests that these expectations were common; this collection is particularly revealing, because it indicates whether and what action was taken on petitions. For other petitions in North Carolina and South Carolina in which local problems resulted in new statutes, see Schweninger, *Petitions to Southern Legislatures*, 62–63, 117–22, 134–35, 148–50, 152–54.

56. The trajectory of southern historiography reflects the private/public distinction. The traditional focus on political history and the men who figured in law and party politics emphasized the public side of the equation. Later work on social history moved in the other direction back toward the private sphere, although it was broadly conceived to include such matters as economic production, labor, and the slave system as well as the daily lives of all those enmeshed in that system, particularly slaves and their white mistresses. Recent work, including my own, has used gender as an analytical lens to explore the construction and implications of private and public. Much of this work has been in the field of southern history, largely because the presence of slavery provides the opportunity for joining gender with race and class; see Bardaglio, *Reconstructing the Household*; Bercaw, *Gendered Freedoms*; K. Brown, *Good Wives, "Nasty Wenches," and Anxious Patriarchs*; Bynum, *Unruly Women*; Dailey, *Before Jim Crow*; Edwards, *Gendered Strife and Confusion*; Fox-Genovese, *Within the Plantation Household*; Frankel, *Freedom's Women*; Gilmore, *Gender and Jim Crow*; McCurry, *Masters of Small Worlds*; O'Donovan, *Becoming Free in the Cotton South*; Schwalm, *A Hard Fight for We*; Stanley, *From Bondage to Contract*; and Whites, *Civil War as a Crisis in Gender*.

57. Quoted from Haywood, *Duty and Office of Justices of the Peace*, 191. See also Grimké, *South Carolina Justice of the Peace*.

58. Magistrates' manuals explain the logic clearly; see Haywood, *Duty and Office of Justices of the Peace*; Grimké, *South Carolina Justice of the Peace*. The manuals echo other English authorities. Only if "the Kings people were disturbed," Robert Kitchin wrote, did the assaults become "more than particular" matters. Quoted in Chapin, *Criminal Justice in Colonial America*, 131. The difference between assault and other criminal categories of violence underscores the logic that determined whether vio-

lent acts were private wrongs or public wrongs. Murder, rape, and mayhem (maiming) were always criminal acts. The seriousness of the injuries gave these offenses public implications. As Blackstone explained, they violated "the laws of nature . . . the moral as well as political rules of right," they always included a "breach of the peace," and they "threaten[ed] and endanger[ed] the subversion of all civil society" by "their example and evil tendency." But it was not the individual's suffering per se that made murder, mayhem, and rape criminal acts. Were any of "these injuries . . . confined to individuals only, and did they affect none but their immediate objects, they would fall absolutely under the notion of private wrongs." By implication, it was the extent to which these offenses infringed on the king's sovereign power over his realm and his subjects' lives that made them public wrongs. Blackstone, *Commentaries on the Laws of England*, 4:176.

59. For forum shopping, see Hartog, *Man and Wife in America*; Grossberg, *Judgment for Solomon*.

60. For the legal handling of assault in colonial North Carolina, see Spindel, *Crime and Society in North Carolina*, 46, 49–50, 52, 55–59, 93–94, 135–37. In colonial South Carolina, the routine handling of assault cases is less clear because the centralization of the court system meant that minor criminal matters remained in the hands of magistrates, who left few records. See also Chapin, *Criminal Justice in Colonial America*; A. P. Scott, *Criminal Law in Colonial Virginia*, 176–78. Chapter 4 explores the role of status and reputation in more detail.

61. Court minutes from across North Carolina and South Carolina follow the general pattern: Superior Court Minutes, Randolph County; Superior Court Minutes, Granville County; Superior Court Minutes, Orange County; all in NCDAH. For South Carolina, see Holcomb, *Edgefield County, South Carolina, Minutes of the County Court*; Holcomb, *Winton (Barnwell) County, South Carolina: Minutes of County Court and Will Book 1*; Wells, *York County, South Carolina, Minutes of the County Court*; *Newberry County, South Carolina, Minutes of the Country Court, 1785–1798*; Journals of the County and Intermediate Court, 1790–93, Pendleton District, SCDAH; Indictments, County and Intermediate Court, Pendleton District, SCDAH. For similar patterns elsewhere, see Steinberg, *Transformation of Criminal Justice*. See also Meranze, *Laboratories of Virtue*.

62. Local officials seem to have consolidated the civil and criminal component of assault cases, prosecuting them under the single criminal offense of "trespass, assault, and battery." This form of prosecution had always been an option; what changed was the frequency with which it was used. The changes were reflected in justices' manuals. For instance, Grimké, in *South Carolina Justice of the Peace*, 23, still separated the injury to the individual from the injury to the state. Assault, he claimed, is "an action, at the suit of the party, wherein he shall render damages, and also to an indictment, at the suit of the State, wherein he shall be fined, according to the heinousness of the offence." But by 1808 Haywood, *Duty and Office of Justices of the Peace*, 16, no longer made this distinction. Assaults were "breaches of the peace,

an affront to the government and a damage to the citizens—they are indictable and punishable by fine and imprisonment in the county court." The appellate courts also registered the changes, as cases filtered up to them; see chapter 7 for further discussion.

CHAPTER 4

1. *State v. James Woodruff*, 1834, Magistrates and Freeholders Court, Spartanburg County, SCDAH.

2. Ibid.

3. My analysis dovetails with W. Johnson's recent critique of slavery, "On Agency," although my analysis emphasizes the importance of the legal system where rights— and associated notion of individual agency—were not particularly relevant for anyone. For these points, see Edwards, "Enslaved Women and the Law" and "Status without Rights." The analysis also builds on recent work that emphasizes slaves' indirect influence over the legal process. See, in particular, Gross, *Double Character*; Gross, "Beyond Black and White." Generally, though, legal studies of slaves, free blacks, and white women have tended to emphasize what the law did to them, not how they acted in law. Historians defined status in terms of individual rights, compared the rights of these groups of people to those of free white men, and considered the extent to which the legal system recognized and upheld or denied and circumscribed the rights of these groups. Recent scholarship includes both slaves and white women under the rubric of domestic relations. See Bardaglio, *Reconstructing the Household*; Bynum, *Unruly Women*; and Fox-Genovese, *Within the Plantation Household*. Previously, historians considered white women, slaves, and free blacks separately, following the development of laws that distinguished these groups. The scholarship on white women often folded legal status into broader analyses; see Clinton, *Plantation Mistress*; A. F. Scott, *Southern Lady*; and Wyatt-Brown, *Southern Honor*. The scholarship on slaves and free blacks focused more exclusively on legal status. For slaves, see Hadden, *Slave Patrols*; Hindus, *Prison and Plantation*; T. Morris, *Southern Slavery and the Law*; Tushnet, *American Law of Slavery*; and Waldrep, *Roots of Disorder*. For free blacks, see Franklin, *Free Negro in North Carolina*, and Schweninger, *Black Property Owners in the South*.

4. *State v. Joseph Hodge*, 1802, Indictments, Court of General Sessions, Kershaw District, SCDAH. For other, similar cases, see the following: *State v. Martin Bear*, 1814, Criminal Action Papers, Granville County, NCDAH. *State v. George*, 1826; *State v. Tom*, 1824; both in Criminal Action Papers, Chowan County, NCDAH. *State v. William Pettifoot*, 1840, #83, Trial Papers, Court of Magistrates and Freeholders, Kershaw District, SCDAH. For a case brought against a father for beating his children, see *State v. Johnson Clement*, Spring Term 1839, #1, Indictments, Court of General Sessions, Anderson County, SCDAH.

5. See chapter 5 for further discussion.

6. Quotation from Blackstone, *Commentaries on the Laws of England*, 1:430. It is difficult to overstate the influence of Blackstone's *Commentaries* in the realm of property law, particularly on women's property rights and, by implication, their civil and political status. Women's rights activists emphasized those links in the nineteenth century. So have generations of later historians, whose scholarship reveals new aspects of nineteenth-century activists' critiques as well as new elements in the gendered logic that denied women both economic independence and civil and political rights. See Isenberg, *Sex and Citizenship*; Kerber, *No Constitutional Right to Be Ladies*; and Kessler-Harris, *Woman's Wage* and *In Pursuit of Equity*.

7. Recent feminist scholarship focuses on the structure of domestic authority, recognizing that it took different forms depending on the specific relationship; masters exercised far more discretionary force than husbands or fathers. Feminist historians first linked the logic of racial and gender oppression, particularly in the context of the U.S. South. In particular, see Hall, "'The Mind That Burns in Each Body.'" Fox-Genovese, *Within the Plantation Household*, made the argument more specific to the institutions of slavery and marriage in the antebellum South, connecting them through household heads' domestic authority. The idea of a common foundation for all domestic relationships is now established in the scholarship. In addition to Bardaglio, *Reconstructing the Household*, and Bynum, *Unruly Women*, see Bercaw, *Gendered Freedoms*, Edwards, *Gendered Strife and Confusion*, McCurry, *Masters of Small Worlds*, and Stanley, *From Bondage to Contract*.

8. In *Women as Force in History*, Mary Ritter Beard argued that the elevation of common law over other legal traditions, first by nineteenth-century lawyers and then by feminist reformers and professional historians, erased the importance of equity, which had allowed wives a different legal status and gave them much more leverage in law. Lebsock, *Free Women of Petersburg*, demonstrated the importance of equity not only for individual women's control of property but also in southern culture more generally. Hartog, *Man and Wife in America*, makes a similar point about women's legal options, not just through equity but also within the Anglo-American legal tradition more generally. Holly Brewer recently demonstrated the presence and power of a less absolute conception of domestic authority in legal practice in the North American colonies. According to Brewer, eighteenth-century interpreters of common law, such as Sir Edward Coke, allowed for much greater legal leeway for wives, children, and servants. Those elements of the common law past were later buried by Blackstone and his version of the common law tradition. See Brewer, "Domestic Relations and the Law" and *By Birth or Consent*. See also Sturtz, *Within Her Power*. Early modern English historians have questioned the emphasis placed on certain elements of common law and highlighted women's active use of other bodies of law and other legal arenas. See Amussen, "'Being Stirred to Much Unquietness'"; Erickson, *Women and Property in Early Modern England*; Gowing, *Domestic Dangers*; and Stretton, *Women Waging Law*.

9. This summary draws on the scholarship that uses gender to illuminate women's

status and their relation to government in the early modern period and the age of revolution. See, for instance, Amussen, *Ordered Society*; Brown, *Good Wives, "Nasty Wenches," and Anxious Patriarchs*; Fraser and Gordon, "Genealogy of Dependency"; Kerber, *Women of the Republic*; and Landes, *Women and the Public Sphere*.

10. Edwards, "Law, Domestic Violence, and the Limits of Patriarchal Authority." The household head's consent to prosecution was registered by joining his name to cases, although his actual participation could be nominal. These rules are outlined in the states' magistrates' manuals: Haywood, *Duty and Office of Justices of the Peace*, and Grimké, *South Carolina Justice of the Peace*. Blackstone echoed the same logic in his volume entitled "Of Public Wrongs," in *Commentaries on the Laws of England*, vol. 4.

11. This framework for prosecution is more common in scholarship on British history and the Commonwealth than it is in the histories of the post-Revolutionary United States, although the United States continued to draw primarily on English legal traditions after its formal separation from Britain. The reasons for this difference seem to lie in a distinct historiographical tradition in the United States, which has tended to assume national exceptionalism and to define national character in terms of individual liberty.

12. *State v. Joseph Hodge*, 1802, Indictments, Court of General Sessions, Kershaw District, SCDAH. In this case, the magistrate also included information that the abuse had started when Nancy Hodge was underage, a fact that negated the issue of consent and made the sexual act itself a crime, whether coerced or not. Although age of consent did not apply when the accused was the victim's father, it suggests that the magistrate was thinking around all the various legal barriers. David Swain, Pardon of David Owens, 7 January 1834, pp. 165–66, vol. 30, GLB, NCDAH. Stevenson, *Life in Black and White*, 108, also notes incest cases in early-nineteenth-century Virginia. For the development of incest statutes that positioned the violated child as the injured party, see Bardaglio, "'An Outrage upon Nature.'"

13. *State v. George*, 1826; *State v. Tom*, 1824; both in Criminal Action Papers, Chowan County, NCDAH. T. Morris, *Southern Slavery and the Law*, 305–7, notes the loopholes in rape laws and discusses several cases: two Virginia cases from the 1780s, where enslaved men were tried for raping enslaved women; an 1859 Mississippi case, in which the Mississippi State Supreme Court overturned a local judge's ruling that allowed for the trial and conviction of an enslaved man for the rape of an enslaved child under ten years old on the basis that statute and common law did not apply to slaves; and six Virginia cases, between 1790 and 1833, in which enslaved men were tried for raping free black women. Morris characterizes all the Virginia cases as exceptions and the Mississippi State Supreme Court decision as the rule. Given the changes in the court structure, however, another interpretation would be that local jurisdictions retained the ability to define and prosecute such incidents as rapes, until the appellate courts acquired the power to say they could not, and heard cases relating to the matter and rendered decisions that specifi-

cally disallowed prosecution. Within a year after the Mississippi court's decision, the legislature passed a statute that established the rape of any African American female under twelve by an African American man as a crime. Given their assumptions about the structure and logic of the legal system, Morris and other historians concluded that this statute extended new rights. For a discussion of the Mississippi statute, see Bardaglio, *Reconstructing the Household*, 67–68. But that statute may have been reinstating practices that were assumed at the local level but not named at the state level. Sommerville, *Rape and Race*, 64–68, notes rape cases involving African American females, although she emphasizes the age of the victims and attributes prosecution to social proscriptions that categorized the rape of children as a distinct, particularly heinous offense.

14. For Bay, see O'Neall, *Biographical Sketches of the Bench and Bar*, 1:56–57.

15. See chapter 6 for further discussion of this issue.

16. Historical debates about post-Revolutionary political ideology once focused on the relative influence of liberal individualism vs. republicanism characterized by a more corporate sensibility. The residue of those debates still shapes current scholarship, although recent work is less likely to accept the dichotomy between liberalism and republicanism. These bodies of political thought were less distinct in practice than in theory. Moreover, as scholarship on gender suggests, both liberalism and republicanism tended to affirm the individual rights of male household heads and their authority over both private property and household dependents. See Bercaw, *Gendered Freedoms*; Boydston, *Home and Work*; Edwards, *Gendered Strife and Confusion*; Kerber, *No Constitutional Right to Be Ladies*; MacLean, *Behind the Mask of Chivalry*; McCurry, *Masters of Small Worlds*; Stanley, *From Bondage to Contract*; Stansell, *City of Women*. The historical scholarship follows feminist theory that emphasized the gendered subtexts in both liberalism and republicanism; see, for instance, Pateman, *Sexual Contract*, and Pitkin, *Fortune Is a Woman*. Previous scholarship reached different conclusions because the work tended to assume a male subject; recent work compares those male subjects to other subordinate groups, primarily white women, free blacks, and slaves. See Appleby, *Capitalism and the New Social Order*; Diggins, *Lost Soul of American Politics*; Bailyn, *Ideological Origins of the American Revolution*; Handlin and Handlin, *Commonwealth*; Pocock, *Machiavellian Moment*; Wood, *Creation of the American Republic*; and Wood, *Radicalism of the American Revolution*.

17. "Inquest on the body of a negro man, Ambrose, slave property of Berryman Burge," Court of General Sessions, Coroner's Inquisitions, Kershaw District, SCDAH. This section draws on Edwards, "Enslaved Women and the Law."

18. *State v. Sam*, 1830, #50, reel 2916, Trial Papers, Court of Magistrates and Freeholders, Anderson/Pendleton District, SCDAH.

19. For honor in the South, see Greenberg, *Honor and Slavery*, and Wyatt-Brown, *Southern Honor*.

20. For the importance of status in establishing truth within Western legal cul-

ture, see especially B. Shapiro, *Beyond "Reasonable Doubt" and "Probable Cause,"* 6–12, 114–85.

21. Petition for the Pardon of James Cotton, to James Iredell, 26 April 1828, pp. 36–37, vol. 27, GLB, NCDAH. Petition for the Pardon of William Blankenship, to James Iredell, n.d. [1828], p. 143, vol. 27, GLB, NCDAH. For Mary Dodd, see David Swain to Henry Potter, Regarding the Pardon of Benjamin Seaborn, 26 May 1834, pp. 206–7, vol. 30, GLB, NCDAH. For Edney Grise, see Petition for Henry Hedgepeth, to James Iredell, 16 April 1828, pp. 39–40, vol. 27, GLB, NCDAH. Brewer, *By Birth or Consent*, traces the development of a legal concept of childhood in the eighteenth century and the resulting restrictions placed on children's testimony. In practice, though, local courts still allowed children to testify, because of the mechanisms in place to evaluate their speech.

22. Petition for Pardon of Frank Key and Offa Cautank, Robert Strange to James Iredell, 3 May 1828, pp. 41–42, vol. 27, GLB, NCDAH.

23. *State v. Davey*, 1839, #77, #79, Trial Papers, Court of Magistrates and Freeholders, Kershaw District, SCDAH; Davey was convicted and sentenced to twenty-five lashes. *State v. Sam*, 1830, #50, reel 2916, Trial Papers, Court of Magistrates and Freeholders, Anderson/Pendleton District, SCDAH. Cases involving slander, which were often tried as criminal matters, indicate the power of words. The handling of slander in this period still bears resemblance to such cases in the early modern period, in both the colonies and England. See Gowing, *Domestic Dangers*; Kamensky, *Governing the Tongue*; and Norton, "Gender and Defamation in Seventeenth-Century Maryland." See also Bailey, *Gifts and Poison*.

24. *State v. David Carwell*, 1816, Indictments, Court of General Sessions, Kershaw District, SCDAH; the jury acquitted David Carwell, and the records leave no trace of Polly Horn's fate. For Abram Blanding, see O'Neall, *Biographical Sketches of the Bench and Bar*, 2:236–46. Third parties who had the legal status to do so could bring criminal charges on behalf of another who could not, whether through a temporary incapacity (such as a debilitating injury) or a permanent one (such as a subordinate status, like that of slaves, that resulted in the denial of certain legal rights). Legally, they could do so as members of the injured public, as Abram Blanding did on behalf of Polly Horn. Men and sometimes women of standing (who were usually white) initiated legal proceedings and prosecuted crimes committed against those who could not or would not do so themselves: not only slaves and free blacks, but also wives and children in neighboring households. See, for instance, the cases from Granville County. *State v. Abner Gordon*, 1816 (the case is from 1815 although it is in the 1816 folder); *State v. John Baileys (sometimes Bailis or Baylis) and John Walker*, 1819; *State v. John Allen*, 1821; *State v. John Wood*, 1822; *State v. James Blackwell and Joseph Bragg*, 1825; *State v. Francis Robinson*, 1826; *State v. Eldridge Mayo, Samuel Richardson, John Mitchell, and Betsey Oakley*, 1834; *State v. William Meadows Sr. and William Meadows Jr.*, 1836; *State v. Anthony, a slave*, 1837; *State v. John Hutchinson*, 1838; *State v. John McGrath*, 1839; Criminal Action Papers, Granville County, NCDAH. *State v.*

Robert Chambliss, 1817–18; *Regarding Elizabeth Willis and Delilia Willis,* 1819; *State v. Nelson Duke (sometimes Burke),* 1825; Criminal Actions Concerning Slaves and Free Persons of Color, Granville County, NCDAH. Early modern British legal historians have emphasized the importance of laypeople defining crimes in similar ways; see Herrup, *Common Peace,* and Wrightson, "Two Concepts of Order."

25. Henry William DeSaussure to Timothy Ford, 9 July 1816, 11/131/27, Timothy Ford Papers, 1776–1830 (1027.03.01), SCHS. For the Camden slave insurrection, see Inabinet, "'The July Fourth Incident' of 1816."

26. Rachel Blanding to Hannah Lewis, 25 July 1816, folder 1, William Blanding Papers, SCL. See also Rachel Blanding to Hannah Lewis, 4 July 1816, folder 1, William Blanding Papers, SCL.

27. *State v. Sam,* 1830, #50, reel 2916, Trial Papers, Court of Magistrates and Freeholders, Anderson/Pendleton District, SCDAH. See also Gross, *Double Character.*

28. *State v. George,* 1826; *State v. Tom,* 1824; both in Criminal Action Papers, Chowan County, NCDAH. Many scholars have noted whites' acceptance of the idea that black women were sexually available to white men. Recently, however, historians have shown its place within the basic structures of power within the slave South. See Baptist, "'Cuffy,' 'Fancy Maids,' and 'One-Eyed Men'"; Brown, *Good Wives, "Nasty Wenches," and Anxious Patriarchs;* A. D. Davis, "Private Law of Race and Sex"; Fischer, *Suspect Relations.* For African American women and coerced sex, see A. Alexander, *Ambiguous Lives;* A. Davis, "Reflections on the Black Woman's Role in the Community of Slaves"; Jacobs, *Incidents in the Life of a Slave Girl;* Jennings, "'Us Colored Women Had to Go Through a Plenty'"; Stevenson, *Life in Black and White,* 236–38; and D. White, *Ar'n't I a Woman,* 27–46.

29. For the connection between the status of masters and their slaves' behavior, see Gross, *Double Character,* 89–92.

30. *State v. Elley,* 1807, #6, Trial Papers, Court of Magistrates and Freeholders, Kershaw District, SCDAH. For similar cases, see *State v. Peter and Demce,* 1815–16; *State v. Nowell,* 1810–12; both in Criminal Actions Concerning Slaves and Free Persons of Color, Granville County, NCDAH. *State v. Patt,* 1825, #14; *State v. Fed,* 1828, #37; *State v. Cain,* 1835, #75; *State v. Toney,* 1838, #97; *State v. Spencer,* 1839, #106; *State v. Fanny and Richmond,* 1839, #109; *State v. Margret,* 1840, #115; all in reel 2916, Trial Papers, Court of Magistrates and Freeholders, Anderson/Pendleton District, SCDAH. *State v. Titus,* 1833, #8; *State v. Chang,* 1835, #13; *State v. Jacob,* 1835, #15; *State v. Tom,* 1841, #35; all in reel 2920, Trial Papers, Court of Magistrates and Freeholders, Spartanburg District, SCDAH. See also the example of slaves in Mississippi who waged a war of rumor to get their overseer fired; Kaye, *Joining Places,* 103–18. Also revealing are William Valentine's fears, after a fight with his landlady, of how she would publicize the incident and what that would do to his reputation; see 4 June 1842, vol. 6, William D. Valentine Diaries, #2148, SHC.

31. Quotation from *State v. William Brittain,* 1807, Vagrancy Trials, Magistrates and Freeholders Court, Spartanburg County, SCDAH. The term "report" appeared

frequently in church hearings. Members reported on themselves and others, investigated those reports to find out whether they were true or false, and charged people with false reports or false swearing. For particularly illustrative examples, see New Hope Baptist Church Minutes, Purleer, Wilkes County; Cane Creek Baptist Church, Minutes and Membership Roll, Orange County; Brassfield Baptist Church, History and Minutes, Creedmore, Granville County; Wheeley's Primitive Baptist Church, Session Minutes and Roll Book, Roxboro, Person County; all in NCDAH. First Baptist Church, Minutes, Barnwell County; Cashaway Baptist Church, Record Book, Darlington [Craven] County; Methodist Church, Darlington County and Florence County, Darlington Circuit; Big Creek Baptist Church, Williamston, Anderson County, Records; Methodist Church, Florence County, Lynch's Creek Circuit; Thomas Memorial Baptist Church, Church Book, Marlboro County, Bennettsville; all in SCL.

32. Inquest on negro Sylva, the property of John Brown, 1822, Court of General Sessions, Coroner's Inquisitions, Kershaw District, SCDAH.

33. Inquest on negro Sylva, the property of John Brown, 1822, Court of General Sessions, Coroner's Inquisitions, Kershaw District, SCDAH. See, by contrast, Inquest of Jack, slave of W. Williams, 1835; Inquest of Moses, slave of Clayton Webb, 1844; Coroner's Inquisitions, Court of General Sessions, Anderson County, SCDAH.

34. The petition was for the manumission of Lucy and her daughter; see Schweninger, *Petitions to Southern Legislatures*, 18–20.

35. See Muldrew, *Economy of Obligation*. Credit carried over into the legal evaluation of other kinds of information; see Gowing, *Domestic Dangers*, 50–52, 232–62; and Herrup, *House in Gross Disorder*.

36. North Carolina, vol. 19, p. 232; South Carolina, vol. 11, p. 42; both in R. G. Dun & Co. For the symbiosis of credit and reputation within the legal system of the new republic, see Mann, *Republic of Debtors*. For the importance of individual character in the assessment of financial matters, see also Balleisen, *Navigating Failure*; and Hilkey, *Character Is Capital*.

37. *State v. Henry Sizemore*, 1841; *State v. Temperance Sizemore or Temperance Crow*, 1841; *State v. James Browning*, 1841; all in Vagrancy Trials, Magistrates and Freeholders Court, Anderson District, SCDAH. *State v. Marvel Littlefield*, 1841, Vagrancy Trials, Magistrates and Freeholders Court, Spartanburg District, SCDAH.

38. Archibald D. Murphey to Thomas Ruffin, 18 August 1820, in Hoyt, *The Papers of Archibald D. Murphey*, 1:173–74. For the importance of personal ties in credit and economic networks, see Balleisen, *Navigating Failure*; and Lamoreaux, *Insider Lending*.

39. *State v. James Woodruff*, 1834, Vagrancy Trials, Magistrates and Freeholders Court, Spartanburg District, SCDAH.

40. *State v. Robert Mitchell*, 1844, Vagrancy Trials, Magistrates and Freeholders Court, Spartanburg District, SCDAH.

41. See, for instance, *State v. Jim*, 1849, #109, reel 2920; *State v. Patsy*, 1854, #165, reel 2921; both in Trial Papers, Magistrates and Freeholders Court, Spartanburg District, SCDAH. For other examples of slaves complaining to powerful neighbors, see Doyle, "Lord, Master, and Patriot," 111–13, 151.

42. For the dispute between Brother Johnson and Judy, see 10, 16, and 17 September and 4 October 1824, and 5 January 1827, Big Creek Baptist Church, Anderson District, SCL. For a similar analysis of African Americans' use of church disciplinary hearings, see B. Wood, "'For Their Satisfaction or Redress.'"

43. Petition for the Pardon of Eliza Johnson, to James Iredell, [1828], pp. 29–30, vol. 27, GLB, NCDAH; James Iredell, Pardon of Eliza Johnson, 24 March 1828, p. 30, vol. 27, GLB, NCDAH. For other pardon petitions, see Pardon, Samuel Ashe, 14 December 1795, p. 35, vol. 12, GLB, NCDAH; Pardon, Samuel Ashe, May 1796, p. 36, vol. 12, GLB, NCDAH.

44. Petition for the Pardon of Jack, to James Iredell, [1828], pp. 133–35, vol. 27, GLB, NCDAH.

45. Inquest on the body of Sam, property of John Chesnut, Coroner's Inquisitions, Court of General Sessions, Kershaw District, SCDAH; *State v. Ephraim Stratford, Joiner Middleton, and Douglas Minton*, Indictments, Court of General Sessions, Kershaw District, SCDAH. For other cases in Kershaw District of slaves with two names, see the following cases: *State v. John Bull*, 1815, #14; *State v. George and David*, 1831, #46; *State v. John*, 1831, #48; *State v. Charles*, 1832, #53; all in Trial Papers, Court of Magistrates and Freeholders, Kershaw District, SCDAH. *State v. James Edmonds*, 1818; *State v. James Johnson*, 1817; both in Indictments, Court of General Sessions, Kershaw District, SCDAH.

46. I would like to thank Lisa Lindsay for sharing with me the information about the Conway family. For Bonds Conway's slave, see *State v. Sukey*, 1812, #8–1, #9, Trial Papers, Court of Magistrates and Freeholders, Kershaw District, SCDAH. For biographical information, see Kershaw County census compilation, 1810, p. ii. For the case that was moved out of the Magistrates and Freeholders Court to the Court of General Sessions, see *State v. Bonds Conway*, 1826, Indictments, Court of General Sessions, Kershaw District, SCDAH. For a related case against the slave who supposedly traded with Conway, see *State v. Tom*, 1826, #34, Trial Papers, Court of Magistrates and Freeholders, Kershaw District, SCDAH. For cases prosecuted by Bonds Conway and his wife Dorcas, see *State v. Thomas McCown*, 1820–21 (although Bonds and Dorcas Conway filed the complaint, William Rhodes became the named prosecutor); *State v. Jesse Havis*, 1821; *State v. James Roberts*, 1826; all in Indictments, Court of General Sessions, Kershaw District, SCDAH. For similar experiences among free blacks in Virginia, see Rothman, *Notorious in the Neighborhood*, 53–87.

47. *State v. Charlotte Rogers*, n.d. [1800–1839], Indictments, Court of General Sessions, Kershaw District, SCDAH. In some instances, it appears that slaves gave information at magistrates' hearings because they could do so without giving an oath; information, in other words, could be different from sworn testimony.

48. Petition for the Pardon of Thomas Sexton, to James Iredell, [1828], pp. 68–69, vol. 27, GLB, NCDAH.

49. Inquest on the body of Sam, property of John Chesnut, Coroner's Inquisitions, Court of General Sessions, Kershaw District, SCDAH. Kaye, *Joining Places*, esp. 119–76, makes a similar point in relation to slaves. As he argues, neighborhoods played a significant role in defining slaves' lives, because they had established ties there that they could depend on and influence, to a certain extent.

50. *State v. Sam*, 1830, #50, reel 2916, Trial Papers, Court of Magistrates and Freeholders, Anderson/Pendleton District, SCDAH.

CHAPTER 5

1. *State v. Sukey*, 1812, #8–1, #9, Trial Papers, Court of Magistrates and Freeholders, Kershaw District, SCDAH.

2. For similar dynamics that allowed specific free blacks privileges in specific local areas, see M. Johnson and Roark, *Black Masters*; and Rothman, *Notorious in the Neighborhood*.

3. My analysis builds on scholarship on slaves' possession of property, but departs from it by characterizing such claims as legal, not just cultural and, therefore, not departures from or exceptions to the formal rules. See especially Penningroth, *Claims of Kinfolk* and "Claims of Slaves and Ex-Slaves." See also Berlin and Morgan, *Slaves' Economy*; Campbell, "As 'A Kind of Freeman'?"; Forret, "Slaves, Poor Whites, and the Underground Economy"; Kaye, *Joining Places*, 103–18; P. Morgan, "Ownership of Property by Slaves"; Olwell, *Masters, Slaves, and Subjects*, 141–80; Penningroth, "Slavery, Freedom, and Social Claims to Property"; Reidy, *From Slavery to Agrarian Capitalism*, 58–81; Saville, *Work of Reconstruction*, 5–11; Schwalm, *Hard Fight for We*, 57–71; Schweninger, *Black Property Owners in the South*, 29–60; R. Scott and Zeuske, "Property in Writing, Property on the Ground"; B. Wood, *Women's Work, Men's Work*; and B. Wood, "'Never on a Sunday.'"

4. The logic of possession and authority in localized law alters, rather than negates, the importance of scholarship based on the legal rules of ownership on the civil side of the system. In fact, much of the current scholarship on the nineteenth-century South frames discussions of patriarchal authority in terms of legal conceptions of property ownership taken from the professionalized rules of property law on the civil side. In *Masters of Small Worlds*, McCurry begins with a particularly evocative case that uses property rights as a metaphor for patriarchal authority. See also Bardaglio, *Reconstructing the Household*; Bynum, *Unruly Women*; Edwards, *Gendered Strife and Confusion*; Fox-Genovese, *Within the Plantation Household*; Hodes, *White Women, Black Men*; and Whites, *Civil War as a Crisis in Gender*.

5. As the scholarship on the Anglicization of American law indicates, those trends were particularly evident in the area of property, although they also extended to other areas as well. See, in particular, Dayton, *Women before the Bar*; Mann, *Neigh-*

bors and Strangers; W. Nelson, *Americanization of Common Law*; and Sturtz, *Within Her Power*. In the nineteenth century, the literature in legal history has emphasized the transformation of all forms of property into personal property, which conferred more authority to the owner, specifically the ability to alienate it at will — although the scholarship also emphasizes that the transition was long and complicated. See Horwitz, *Transformation of American Law*. For the economic context that fueled these changes, see, in particular, Coclanis, *Shadow of a Dream*.

6. The classic work on property in U.S. legal history is Horwitz, *Transformation of American Law*. Some strands of legal history underscore the continued presence of competing visions of property well into the nineteenth century. See G. Alexander, *Commodity and Propriety*; Hartog, "Pigs and Positivism"; McCurdy, *Anti-Rent Era in New York Law and Politics*; and Novak, *People's Welfare*. Work in rural history emphasizes the continuation of communal forms of property, but tends to characterize them as evidence of resistance to capitalist development. See Hahn, "Common Right and Commonwealth"; Hahn, *Roots of Southern Populism*; Hahn and Prude, *Countryside in the Age of Capitalist Transformation*; Huston, *Land and Freedom*; Jacoby, *Crimes against Nature*; Kulikoff, *Agrarian Origins of American Capitalism*; Taylor, *Liberty Men and Great Proprietors*. Fence laws, in particular, have inspired heated debates among southern historians over the survival of customary notions of the commons that rejected individual ownership of land.

7. *State v. Elizabeth Billings*, 1795, Indictments, County and Intermediate Court, Kershaw District, SCDAH. Henry, a slave in Anderson District, suffered a similar problem; the dress he stole for a woman friend was identified and returned to its owner. *State v. Henry*, 1833, #65, reel 2916, Trial Papers, Court of Magistrates and Freeholders, Anderson/Pendleton District, SCDAH. For similar cases involving distinctive clothing, see *State v. John Evans*, 1817; *State v. John Marshall, Sr., Agnes Marshall, John Marshall, Jr., and Mary Marshall*, 1820; *State v. Jiney Cunningham, John Parrish, Lithy Murphy*, 1826; Indictments, Court of General Sessions, Kershaw District, SCDAH. *State v. Walker Ballard*, 1795; *State v. Louis and Basil*, 1808; *State v. John Thomason*, 1817; *State v. George Cozens*, 1817; *Major, slave of Mrs. William Gooch*, 1818; *State v. Washington Taborn*, 1825; *State v. Mary May*, 1827 (two separate cases); *State v. Martha Smith*, 1833; *State v. Betsy Bush*, 1834; *State v. Hawkins Fuller*, 1837; Criminal Action Papers, Granville County, NCDAH. *State v. Granville*, 1819; *State v. Washington Taborn*, 1832; Criminal Actions Concerning Slaves and Free Persons of Color, Granville County, NCDAH. *State v. Mary Madden*, 1788; *State v. Katharine Brown*, 1790; *State v. Mary Anderson*, 1790; *State v. Rutha Booth*, 1792; *State v. Elizabeth Castlebury*, 1792; Criminal Action Papers, Orange County, NCDAH.

8. Examples of such ads are in the following newspapers: *State Gazette of South-Carolina*, 31 January 1788, 2 February 1790, 25 February 1790, 4 March 1790, 10 March 1790, 5 April 1790, 9 January 1792, 12 January 1792, 23 February 1792, 28 May 1792, and 28 June 1792; *South-Carolina State-Gazette, and Timothy and Mason's Daily Advertiser*, 30 January 1794, 8 March 1794, 14 May 1794, and 25 June 1794; *South-*

Carolina State Gazette and Columbia Advertiser, 26 May 1827. For similar points about the significance and possession of clothing, see Prude, "To Look Upon the 'Lower Sort.'" For the importance of clothes to slaves and freedpeople, see Camp, *Closer to Freedom*, 78–87; Foster, *"New Raiments of Self,"* 137–223; Hunter, *To 'Joy My Freedom,'* 4–5, 182–83; Starke, "Nineteenth-Century African-American Dress"; Starke, Holloman, and Nordquist, *African American Dress and Adornment*; and White and White, *Stylin'*, 5–36.

9. *State v. Susannah Mills, Burwell Mills, and William Mills*, 1797, Indictments, County and Intermediate Court, Kershaw District, SCDAH; *State v. Henry*, 1828, #45, reel 2916, Trial Papers, Court of Magistrates and Freeholders, Anderson/Pendleton District, SCDAH; *State v. Nancy Pettiford*, 1814, Criminal Action Papers, Granville County, NCDAH; *State v. Bob and Bill*, 1805, #3 and #4, Trial Papers, Court of Magistrates and Freeholders, Kershaw District, SCDAH. For other cases in which clothing and items of personal adornment are attributed to free women and children, see the following records: *State v. Sherwood Laughon and Valentine Parrish*, 1795; *State v. John Thomason*, 1817; *State v. George Cozens*, 1817 (he stole property from Polly Harris, who lived with Moody Fowler, although they were not married); *State v. Martha Smith*, 1833; *State v. Hawkins Fuller*, 1837; Criminal Action Papers, Granville County, NCDAH. *State v. Elizabeth Smith*, 1800–1808, Criminal Actions Concerning Slaves and Free Persons of Color, Granville County, NCDAH. *State v. Henry*, 1833, #65, reel 2916, Trial Papers, Court of Magistrates and Freeholders, Anderson/Pendleton District, SCDAH. In *State v. James Campbell*, 1826, Indictments, Court of General Sessions, Kershaw District, SCDAH, the testimony indicates that it was Campbell's wife who was trading homespun cloth that she made with a slave, although it was her husband who was prosecuted. For slaves' possession of that kind of property, see note 13 below.

10. *State v. John Marshall, Sr., Agnes Marshall, John Marshall, Jr., and Mary Marshall*, 1820, Indictments, Court of General Sessions, Kershaw District, SCDAH.

11. For merchants who kept separate entries for slaves and free women, while still attaching them to their masters, husbands, and fathers, see vol. 1, John U. Kirkland Account Books, #405, SHC; vol. 73, subser. 6.5.1, 1792–1812, Cameron Family Papers, #133, SHC; John W. Harris Papers, Special Collections, DU. Clothing featured prominently in the accounts of free women and slaves. Although the reference to Susan Blanding is in private correspondence, it suggests the separate trading patterns in which married women engaged; see Susan Blanding to Elizabeth Carpenter, 29 September 1808, William Blanding Papers, unmarked folder, SCL. The patterns resemble those described by other historians in the colonial period and the new republic. See Boydston, *Home and Work*; C. Clark, *Roots of Rural Capitalism*; Sturtz, *Within Her Power*, 111–40; and Ulrich, *A Midwife's Tale*.

12. Vol. 1, John U. Kirkland Account Books, #405, SHC. Cameron Family Papers, #133, subser. 6.5.1, vol. 73, 1792–1812, SHC. Also revealing is the response of the

First Baptist Church in Columbia, South Carolina, to the charge against Brother

Wilkins for "selling some Dry goods to a negro." Brother Wilkins responded that such dealings were "the general or universal practice of all merchants, who were all equally exposed to be prosecuted by any ill natured or mallicious [*sic*] person, almost every day; and also as he did not consider it as an offense against any law of God." The congregation was divided in its opinion as to whether such practices were censurable; Wilkins ultimately agreed not to sell to slaves who did not have permission from their owners to trade, underscoring the widespread acceptance of slaves' possession of such items, as long as slaves used their own resources to obtain them. See 24 March 1816, First Columbia Baptist Church, Richland County, SCL.

13. *State v. Jim*, #30, Trial Papers, Court of Magistrates and Freeholders, Kershaw District, SCDAH. Jim was convicted of burglary and sentenced to death. For other cases in which clothing and other items of personal adornment were attributed to slaves, as their possessions, see *State v. Bob and Bill*, 1805, #3 and #4; *State v. Sukey*, 1812, #8–1, #9; both in Trial Papers, Court of Magistrates and Freeholders, Kershaw District, SCDAH. *State v. Ben and Levi*, 1825, #16, reel 2916, Trial Papers, Court of Magistrates and Freeholders, Anderson/Pendleton District, SCDAH. *State v. Elizabeth Smith*, 1800–1808; *State v. William Frasier*, 1813–14; *State v. Abner Gordon*, 1830–32; all in Criminal Actions Concerning Slaves and Free Persons of Color, Granville County, NCDAH. In *State v. Negro Granville, William Hunt, Thomas B. Lewis*, 1820, Criminal Action Papers, Granville County, NCDAH, Hunt and Lewis claimed innocence, because they did not know the dry goods they received from Granville were stolen; by implication, his possession would have negated the charges. Advertisements for runaway slaves suggest recognition of their possession of clothes. In one, a slave owner indicated that he could not describe the runaway's clothes, "as he carried off all his cloaths, having several suits of them"; see *State Gazette of South-Carolina*, 26 March 1792. Similarly, one runaway female slave had "a number of clothes which she may disguise herself with"; *South-Carolina State-Gazette, and Timothy and Mason's Daily Advertiser*, 10 April 1794. McInnis, *Politics of Taste*, 240–42, 255–58, notes that slaves in that city acquired clothing, recognized as their own, beyond what their masters gave them. See also Prude, "To Look Upon the 'Lower Sort.'"

14. *State v. Bob, slave of James Downey*, 1835–37, Criminal Actions Concerning Slaves and Free Persons of Color, Granville County, NCDAH. For additional examples, see the following cases: *State v. Harriet*, 1820–22, Criminal Actions Concerning Slaves and Free Persons of Color, Granville County, NCDAH. *State v. Isham Powell*, 1795; *State v. Susannah Mills, Burwell Mills, and William Mills*, 1797; both in Indictments, County and Intermediate Court, Kershaw District, SCDAH. *State v. Doctor and Jemima*, 1822, # 3; *State v. Jack*, 1828, #40; and *State v. Tony*, 1836, #81; all in reel 2916, Trial Papers, Court of Magistrates and Freeholders, Anderson/Pendleton District, SCDAH. One of the strongest indications of slaves' possession of household goods and other items is the fact that such property did not appear in their owners' inventories; see McInnis, *Politics of Taste*, 269–76, for that point and

slaves' possession of such property more generally. For cases describing currency, bank bills, and luxury items in ways that suggest their distinctiveness, see the following records: *State v. James Daniel*, 1805; *State v. William Lancaster*, 1815; *State v. John Davison*, 1817; *State v. William Bradley*, 1819; *State v. Barnard Brady and Anne Brady*, 1827; *State v. William Bartlet*, 1829; *State v. Squire McDonald*, 1829–30; all in Indictments, Court of General Sessions, Kershaw District, SCDAH. *State v. Sherwood Lawhorn*, 1796; *State v. Jeremiah Moore*, 1796; *State v. Washington Taborn*, 1825; all in Criminal Action Papers, Granville County, NCDAH. *State v. Leonard Duger*, 1792; *State v. Rhody Dugar*, 1792; all in Criminal Action Papers, Orange County, NCDAH. People who had been robbed also advertised in newspapers, describing exactly what had been stolen and asking people to be on the lookout for those goods. See *State Gazette of South-Carolina*, 30 August 1792; *South-Carolina State-Gazette, and Timothy and Mason's Daily Advertiser*, 26 April 1794, 17 May 1794; *South-Carolina State Gazette and Columbia Advertiser*, 25 August 1827.

15. *State v. Doctor and Jemima*, 1822, # 3, reel 2916, Trial Papers, Court of Magistrates and Freeholders, Anderson/Pendleton District, SCDAH. Although the index indicates a verdict of not guilty, there are actually two outcomes attached to the records, one indicating a guilty verdict and another indicating an acquittal, suggesting a split decision, with only one of the defendants found guilty. Unfortunately, the verdicts do not give the slaves' names. For slaves marking and otherwise keeping track of money, see Penningroth, *Claims of Kinfolk*, 97–98. For the practice of marking money more generally, see V. Zelizer, *Social Meaning of Money*. There was good reason for such practices, since passing counterfeit bills and forging promissory notes and other mediums of exchange were common crimes; see *State v. James Barker and wife*, 1792; *State v. Gabriel Dunn*, 1793; *State v. Joseph McAdams*, 1797; *State v. David Meyers and Thomas Daniel*, 1798; all in Indictments, County and Intermediate Court, Kershaw District, SCDAH. *State v. Jim*, 1822, #30, Trial Papers, Court of Magistrates and Freeholders, Kershaw District, SCDAH. *State v. Joseph J. Martin*, 1800; *State v. Joseph McAdams*, 1800; *State v. William Lowden*, 1801; *State v. William Davis*, 1804; *State v. William Linton and John J. Robinson*, 1812–14; *State v. William Linton, Newman Robinson, and William Bragg*, 1813; *State v. Mary Cunningham*, 1818; all in Indictments, Court of General Sessions, Kershaw District, SCDAH. *State v. William Frazier*, 1812; *State v. Squire Shearmon*, 1812; both in Criminal Action Papers, Granville County, NCDAH.

16. For the South, see Bynum, *Unruly Women*, 111–50, and Escott, "Moral Economy of the Crowd."

17. Thomas B. Clarkson to M. R. Singleton, 3 August 1852, Singleton Family Papers, SCL. In addition to cases involving clothing (see note 9 above), divorce and separation cases provide the most dramatic illustrations of legal matters in which wives were either connected with property they produced or allowed possession of it. See chapter 6 for a more detailed discussion. For slaves, see *State v. Jacob*, 1835, #15, reel 2920, Trial Papers, Court of Magistrates and Freeholders, Spartanburg

District, SCDAH; *State v. Nathan Hawley*, 1817, Criminal Action Papers, Granville County, NCDAH. Although the evidence indicates that Hawley was trading with slaves, the charge was for stealing or receiving bank notes. In *State v. William Scott, Elizabeth Nunnery, Charles Stephens*, 1821, Indictments, Court of General Sessions, Kershaw District, SCDAH, Stephens pleaded for mercy from the charge of trading with slaves, because he did not know that the ham he purchased had been stolen; by implication, there would have been no crime if the slave had possessed the property. Other cases made the same distinction. *State v. William Huddleston and Dicey Huddleston*, 1823, Criminal Action Papers, Granville County, NCDAH. *State v. Wyatt Roberts*, 1817–18; *State v. Betsey Landers*, 1819; *State v. Benjamin Wingfield*, 1830–32; Criminal Actions Concerning Slaves and Free Persons of Color, Granville County, NCDAH. *State v. Thomas Crabtree and Elizabeth Crabtree*, 1805, Criminal Action Papers, Orange County, NCDAH.

18. Recent work suggests the prevalence of property ownership in both the colonial and antebellum South; see note 3 above.

19. *State v. Lewis, Henry, and Caty*, 1837, #73; *State v. Tate*, 1838, #75; both in Trial Papers, Court of Magistrates and Freeholders, Kershaw District, SCDAH. *State v. Milly, belonging to Banks estate*, 1815–16; *State v. Jonathan Dew*, 1815–16; both in Criminal Actions Concerning Slaves and Free Persons of Color, Granville County, NCDAH. Penningroth, in *Claims of Kinfolk*, 91–108, discusses similar dynamics, although locating them in culture, as distinct from law. See also Kaye, *Joining Places*, 103–18, and T. Morris, *Southern Slavery and the Law*, 350–51, 352.

20. *Thomas Waddill v. Charlotte D. Martin*, 1845 N.C. LEXIS 194. The case is discussed in Penningroth, *Claims of Kinfolk*, 94–95.

21. *Robert McNamara v. John Kerns et al.*, 1841 N.C. LEXIS 53. The case is discussed in Penningroth, *Claims of Kinfolk*, 94–95. See also T. Morris, *Southern Slavery and the Law*, 348–53.

22. *Hannah Mitchell v. Robert B. Mitchell*, 1831, Divorce Records, Granville County; *Bethany York v. Seymore York*, [1844], Divorce Records, Randolph County; both in NCDAH. Establishing a wife's economic independence was usually done through a divorce from bed and board (which allowed the couple to live separately and severed economic ties between them) instead of a complete divorce (which severed the marital relationship and allowed the innocent party to remarry). Some women may have preferred a divorce from bed and board, since that option allowed for alimony. Of the 35 divorce petitions in Granville County between 1819 and 1860, for instance, the court granted 8 divorces from bed and board and 3 complete divorces. In the remaining 24 cases, there is no indication of a decision; often the initial complaint ended the matter because the defendant could not be found to respond. In the 42 cases in Randolph County between 1815 and 1860, the court granted 11 divorces from bed and board and 7 complete divorces; there was no indication of a decision in 21 cases. In one the court decreed a marriage had not existed, and another ended in a separation agreement.

23. October Session 1820, Minutes of the Wardens of the Poor, 1820–68, Lincoln County, NCDAH. For vagrancy cases where women were active in soliciting material support, see the following cases: *State v. William Brittain*, 1807; *State v. James Woodruff*, 1834; *State v. Marvel Littlefield*, 1841; *State v. Robert Mitchell*, 1844; *State v. Stephen Bass*, 1847; *State v. John Quinn*, 1852; all in Vagrancy Trials, Court of Magistrates and Freeholders, Spartanburg County, SCDAH. *State v. William McElvaney*, 1806; *State v. James Hunnicutt*, 1816; *State v. Thomas Watkins*, 1819; *State v. John Griswell*, 1825; *State v. John Thomason*, 1826; all in Vagrancy Trials, Court of Magistrates and Freeholders, Pendleton County, SCDAH. *State v. Elias Ross*, 1830; Grand Jury Presentment (regarding Polley Dear), February 1832; both in Criminal Action Papers, Granville County, NCDAH. *State v. Joseph Bennett*, 1792, Criminal Action Papers, Orange County, NCDAH. Cases involving the theft of food sometimes suggest the "thief's" sense of entitlement; in *State v. James Campbell*, 1825, Indictments, Court of General Sessions, Kershaw District, SCDAH, the complainant claimed that Campbell "turned around and looked at him while he was carrying them [two shocks of oats] towards home." It is clear from the records of the wardens of the poor in North Carolina that outdoor relief, forced labor, or committal to the poorhouse, where available, took concerted community action. Minutes and Accounts, Wardens of the Poor, 1832–55, Ashe County; Minutes, Wardens of the Poor, 1838–51, Bertie County; Minutes of the Wardens of the Poor, 1844–66, Carteret County; Minutes of the Wardens of the Poor, 1837–71, Craven County; Records, Wardens of the Poor, Granville County; Minutes of the Wardens of the Poor, 1820–68, Lincoln County; all in NCDAH. Wardens of the Poor, Records, Person County, SHC. See also Klebaner, "Some Aspects of North Carolina Public Poor Relief."

24. Big Creek Baptist Church, Records, Williamston, Anderson County, 10, 16, and 17 September and 4 October 1824, and 5 January 1827, SCL. *Isaac Sizemore and Henry Sizemore*, 1841, Vagrancy Trials, Court of Magistrates and Freeholders, Anderson District, SCDAH. For cases in which accusations of vagrancy were also linked to charges of theft, see *State v. Lot Cragg*, n.d., Indictments, Court of General Sessions, Kershaw District, SCDAH.

25. *State v. Jack*, 1828, #40, reel 2916, Trial Papers, Court of Magistrates and Freeholders, Anderson/Pendleton District, SCDAH. See also Mary Anderson to Duncan Cameron, 22 August 1798, subser. 2, box 3, folder 71, Cameron Family Papers, #133, SHC.

26. Swift Creek Baptist Church, 1827–68, Kershaw District, South Carolina, SCL, p. 11, 5 June 1830. The black members of the Thomas Memorial Baptist Church, in Marlboro District, South Carolina, also met separately from the white congregation. In this church, it seems that some theft charges against blacks were initiated by whites for stealing their property. In 1841, for instance, Plato was excluded for stealing cotton from the gin house of W. S. Sparks. But given this context, where slaves could and did make complaints against each other and usually went unnamed un-

less they were accused, other cases that did not identify the accusers or the victims may well have involved slaves who stole from other slaves. Thomas Memorial Baptist Church, Marlboro County, SCL; for Plato, see January 1842 and March 1842; for other cases, see July 1838, December 1841, February 1844, January 1845. For slaves settling disputes in church courts and other community forums, see Penningroth, *Claims of Kinfolk*, 100–101, 117–20, and B. Wood, "'For Their Satisfaction or Redress.'"

27. *State v. Frank, Dick, and Milton*, #15, #16, 1816, Trial Papers, Court of Magistrates and Freeholders, Kershaw District, SCDAH. Will of William Luyten, 27 February 1799, Will Transcripts of Kershaw County, vol. 1, reel 14, p. 37, SCDAH. Such forms of possession were contested. *State v. Booker and Phil*, 1819, Criminal Actions Concerning Slaves and Free Persons of Color, Granville County, NCDAH, was initiated by a grand jury presentment charging that the two slaves kept a horse "acknowledged by their master to be their own property." Carolina Raoul was one of those slaveholders who allowed slaves to possess horses, although her concern was making sure that the proceeds of the sale of a deceased slave's horse went to his children rather than his wife's new husband, and she was considering legal action to ensure that outcome; Caroline Raoul to James Henry Hammond, 26 December 1829, James Henry Hammond Papers, LC. Slaves' possession of firearms, which some owners allowed, was not sanctioned by localized law, as the following cases indicate. *State v. George*, 1831, #44; *State v. Eli*, 1831, #50; both in Trial Papers, Court of Magistrates and Freeholders, Kershaw District, SCDAH. *State v. Samuel Shannon*, 1838, Indictments, Court of General Sessions, Kershaw District, SCDAH.

28. *State v. Lewis, Henry, and Caty*, 1837, #73, Trial Papers, Court of Magistrates and Freeholders, Kershaw District, SCDAH; although the complaint charged the three with stealing cash from Jane Rowe, the testimony focused on the provenance of the knife and the stolen sugar. Penningroth, *Claims of Kinfolk*, 103–8. See also Kaye, *Joining Places*, 111–12.

29. Abbott's Creek Primitive Baptist Church, Minutes, 1783–1879, Davidson County, NCDAH. *State v. James Long*, 1828 (box 10, containing cases not filed by date), Indictments, Court of General Sessions, Anderson County, SCDAH. Divorce judgments occasionally indicated that wives would retain certain domestic items, presumably because there had been some contention over possession. See, for instance, *Sarah Chandler v. Thomas Chandler*, 1826, Divorce Records, Granville County, NCDAH; *Lydia Hussey v. Jesse Hussey*, 1854, Divorce Records, Randolph County, NCDAH.

30. *State v. Mary McAfee*, 1804, Indictments, Court of General Sessions, Kershaw District, SCDAH. For similar cases, with women prosecuting or identified as the possessors of property, see the following records: *State v. James Day*, 1825; *State v. Katherine Walls and Burgess Walls*, 1831; *State v. William Bailey*, 1834; all in Criminal Action Papers, Granville County, NCDAH. *State v. Phebe Anderson*, 1830–32; *State v. Burton Cozens and Lucy Cozens*, 1833–34; both in Criminal Actions Concern-

343

ing Slaves and Free Persons of Color, Granville County, NCDAH. *State v. Thomas Castles*, 1787 (although it is likely that the complainant, Mary Patterson, was either unmarried or widowed); *State v. Elias Pettiford*, 1792; both in Criminal Action Papers, Orange County, NCDAH. *State v. Eben*, 1811, #7, Trial Papers, Court of Magistrates and Freeholders, Kershaw District, SCDAH. *State v. Owen Coffee*, 1803, Indictments, Court of General Sessions, Kershaw District, SCDAH. In *State v. Zachariah Bowen*, 1824, Indictments, Court of General Sessions, Kershaw District, SCDAH, Bowen entered into a contract with Mary Milton, the wife of Miles Milton, to provide food for him and "his people." Mary Cunningham, wife of William Cunningham, was charged frequently in relation to property she possessed, which was related to her business activities. She was prosecuted for selling liquor without a license (1818), for passing counterfeit money (1818), for keeping a disorderly house (1818), and for trading with slaves (1832–33); all in Indictments, Court of General Sessions, Kershaw District, SCDAH. *State v. Alfred Tucker*, Fall Term 1829, #22; *State v. John Flowers*, Spring Term 1830, #10; *State v. Sylvanus Prince, Washington Scroggins, Hesnon Posey, Patsy Dove, and Fanny Davis*, Fall Term 1834, #17A; Indictments, Court of General Sessions, Anderson County, SCDAH.

31. Catherine Oel, 1809, Petitions, General Assembly, Sessions Records, NCDAH.

32. The subject dominates the correspondence of the political elite to such an extent that it is easy to see why Charles Beard saw it as the primary force in state and national policy in the new republic.

33. 22 September 1821, Letter Book, box 7, William Gaston Papers, #272, SHC.

34. Quotation from William Gaston to T. P. Devereux, 19 August 1833. For Gaston's view of the land, see William Gaston to Robert Donaldson, 27 December 1832. For the barriers this posed when he was asked to serve on the state appellate court, see also William Gaston to Thomas Ruffin, 25 August 1833; T. P. Devereux to William Gaston, 21 August 1833; William Gaston to T. P. Devereux, 26 August 1833; T. P. Devereux to William Gaston, 30 August 1833; Thomas Ruffin to William Gaston, 31 August 1833; William Gaston to Thomas P. Devereux, 9 September 1833; William Gaston to Thomas Ruffin, 9 September 1833; Thomas P. Devereux to William Gaston, 12 September 1833; all in box 4, folder 54, William Gaston Papers, #272, SHC.

35. See Penningroth, *Claims of Kinfolk*, 47–49, 158–61; and Saville, *Work of Reconstruction*, 15–20.

36. These values were clearly visible in individual wills, where fathers tried to keep land within the family line. South Carolina, in particular, was known for this tradition. See Salmon, "Women and Property in South Carolina." The enactment of early women's property rights statutes provides one of the most dramatic illustrations of the familial vision of land. Intended to protect family land from creditors, those statutes undermined the treatment of land as solely a commodity. See

Basch, *In the Eyes of the Law*, 113–35; Chused, "Married Women's Property Law"; Lebsock, *Free Women of Petersburg*, 84–86; Lebsock, "Radical Reconstruction and the Property Rights of Southern Women"; and Warbasse, "Changing Legal Rights of Married Women," 143–50, 203–5.

37. Recent scholarship in British history emphasizes women's control of land through such devices. See, for instance, Erickson, *Women and Property in Early Modern England*. Recent work on colonial British North America and the early republic has found similar patterns. See Alexander, *Commodity and Propriety*, 158–84; Cara Anzilotti, "Autonomy and the Female Planter in Colonial South Carolina"; Brewer, "Entailing Aristocracy in Colonial Virginia"; Lebsock, *Free Women of Petersburg*, 54–86; Lee, "Land and Labor"; Salmon, "Women and Property in South Carolina"; Sturtz, *Within Her Power*, 19–70. The classic statement is M. Beard, *Women as Force in History*, although Beard argues for the superiority of the equity tradition over the common law tradition by giving women control over property, in their own names.

38. Brewer, "Power and Authority in the Colonial South" and "Entailing Aristocracy in Colonial Virginia."

39. *Hannah Ridge v. Meredith Ridge*, 1849, Divorce Records, Randolph County, NCDAH.

40. Bardaglio, *Reconstructing the Household*, 31–32; Bynum, *Unruly Women*, 64–68; Lebsock, *Free Women of Petersburg*, 54–86; Salmon, *Women and the Law of Property*, 90–116, 168–72; Salmon, "Women and Property in South Carolina."

41. For the will, see Will, Richard Singleton, 22 July 1848, Richard Singleton Papers, SCL; *Marion Converse v. Augustus L. Converse*, Equity Court Records, Sumter District, 1854, roll 227, SCDAH. Singleton, *Singletons of South Carolina*, explains the terms of the will and notes that the trust set up was not broken until the 1870s. Richard Singleton did not die until 1852; apparently, he gave over control of the estate to Marion earlier. For divorce cases where wives were granted estates willed to them from their families, see the following: *Sarah Chandler v. Thomas Chandler*, 1826; *Susan Phillips v. Nelson Phillips*, 1837; *Margaret Strother v. Christopher Strother*, 1837; all in Divorce Records, Granville County, NCDAH. *Sally Wilson v. Benjamin Wilson*, 1831; *Haley Morgan v. Prudence B. Morgan*, 1839; *William Larence v. Mary Larence*, 1840; *Sarah Latham v. William Latham*, 1848; Divorce Records, Randolph County, NCDAH. Wives also retained possession of slaves; see *State v. Patrick McKenna*, 1820, Indictments, Court of General Sessions, Kershaw District, SCDAH.

42. Mary Brewton's Will, 1775, Richard Singleton Papers, DU. The will is filed in the Singleton family papers for reasons that have long since been forgotten and are now lost; the archivists and I were unable to reconstruct the logic of that decision. There is no evidence that I could find that Mary Brewton was actually related to the Singletons. Similar distributions reflected common practice in South Carolina, which allowed families considerable discretion in preserving estates through female

relatives. See Salmon, "Women and Property in South Carolina," 655–85; see 677 for clauses that allowed women to will real estate. See also Anzilotti, "Autonomy and the Female Planter."

43. Mary Brewton's Will, 1775, Richard Singleton Papers, DU.

44. Will of Rebecca Motte, Thomas Pinckney Papers, LC. The date of Jacob Motte's death is unclear; some sources indicate the date as 1776, others 1781. Rebecca Motte's will is somewhat difficult to follow because Thomas Pinckney's first wife, Elizabeth, was also Motte's daughter. The first version, written after Elizabeth died, gave Pinckney oversight of Motte property that was intended for Elizabeth's children; later revisions gave Frances Motte Pinckney use of the property for life. For discussion of the will, see also E. W. Weyman to Rebecca Motte, 1 November 1809; William Drayton to Joseph Gist, 27 March 1812; Mary Brewton Alston to the Sheriff, 7 April 1816; all in Thomas Pinckney Papers, LC.

45. *State v. John Howes and wife and Jordan Gilliam and wife*, 1800, Criminal Action Papers, Orange County, NCDAH. *State v. Rachel Campbell*, Fall Term 1829, #7 (Campbell assaulted a constable who was trying to seize family property in payment for a debt); *State v. Willard Watson, Maria Watson, James Brownlow, Hezekiah Kelly, and Sidney Brownlow*, Spring Term 1831, #12 (Maria Watson was instrumental in the attempt to repossess land from which her family seems to have been evicted); all in Indictments, Court of General Sessions, Anderson County, SCDAH.

46. See, for instance, Litwack, *Been in the Storm So Long*; Mohr, *On the Threshold of Freedom*; Rose, *Rehearsal for Reconstruction*; Saville, *Work of Reconstruction*, esp. 15–20; and R. Scott and Zeuske, "Property in Writing, Property on the Ground."

47. Recent work in southern history has used the concept of dependency to highlight connections among axes of power, particularly those of gender, race, and class, that were once considered separately. The result has been to connect the status of women to that of other subordinate groups, including slaves and, after emancipation, working-class people more generally. See Bardaglio, *Reconstructing the Household*; Bercaw, *Gendered Freedoms*; Brown, *Good Wives, "Nasty Wenches," and Anxious Patriarchs*; Bynum, *Unruly Women*; Edwards, *Gendered Strife and Confusion*; Fox-Genovese, *Within the Plantation Household*; McCurry, *Masters of Small Worlds*; Schwalm, *Hard Fight for We*; Stanley, *From Bondage to Contract*. See also Stanley, "Conjugal Bonds and Wage Labor."

48. Swift, *System of Laws of the State of Connecticut*, 2:36.

49. R. Morris, "White Bondage in Ante-Bellum South Carolina," chronicles the ways in which others' property rights in poor white men, wives, and children limited their rights to the point of bondage. The South Carolina vagrancy statute was adopted in 1787; see James, *Digest of the Laws of South Carolina*, chap. 80. In 1836 several new classes of vagrants were added, but the treatment of vagrants remained essentially the same. See Vagrancy Trials, Court of Magistrates and Freeholders, in Pendleton District, Anderson District, Spartanburg District, and Kershaw District; all in SCDAH. For North Carolina poor relief, see Klebaner, "Some Aspects of

North Carolina Public Poor Relief." The state also forcibly institutionalized paupers in county poorhouses, where they were forced to labor for their living. See also Edwards, "Problem of Dependency."

50. Tomlins, *Law, Labor, and Ideology*. Restrictions were based on traditional practices that characterized everyone as a "servant," dependent on a master; see Fraser and Gordon, "Genealogy of Dependency." For work that discusses limitations on laborers that restricted their legal rights as "people" in ways that gave others property rights in their labor and lives, see Forbath, "Ambiguities of Free Labor"; Hahamovitch, *Fruits of Their Labor*; Lichtenstein, *Twice the Work of Free Labor*; Peck, *Reinventing Free Labor*; Stanley, "Beggars Can't Be Choosers"; Steinfeld, *Invention of Free Labor* and *Coercion, Contract, and Free Labor*; and Woodman, *New South, New Law*.

51. *State v. Henry Tie*, 1855, Vagrancy Trials, Court of Magistrates and Freeholders, Kershaw District, SCDAH. *State v. Fred Wilbanks*, 1851; *State v. Marvel Littlefield*, 1841; both in Vagrancy Trials, Court of Magistrates and Freeholders, Spartanburg District, SCDAH. *State v. Edmond Thacker*, 1852, Vagrancy Trials, Court of Magistrates and Freeholders, Anderson District, SCDAH.

52. *State v. Joseph Campbell*, 1833, Vagrancy Trials, Court of Magistrates and Freeholders, Anderson District, SCDAH.

53. See, for instance, Blackstone, *Commentaries on the Laws of England*. See also Cobb, *Inquiry into the Law of Negro Slavery*; and O'Neall, *Negro Law of South Carolina*.

CHAPTER 6

1. Although the South Carolina legislature received petitions, it never granted a private bill for divorce. As a result, South Carolinians pursued legal separations through equity courts and customary arrangements (which were facilitated by the fact that the state neither required the registration of marriages nor criminalized fornication and adultery). In North Carolina, statutes directed the legislature to grant private acts of divorce. Before 1814 the legislature fielded petitions for divorce and separation, granting them "when in its judgment the cause or influence of the petitioner was sufficient to demand it." In 1814 jurisdiction was moved from the legislature to the superior courts, where the material facts were heard by a jury. But between 1814 and 1827, the North Carolina legislature continued to hear and grant divorce petitions, in particular instances, as it had done before. Only in 1835, through an amendment to the constitution, did the legislature relinquish control over questions of divorce and separation. See G. Johnson, *Ante-Bellum North Carolina*, 217–23; Stevenson, "Marriage and Divorce Records," 305–6.

2. N. Davis, *Fiction in the Archives*. For the importance of narrative in divorce cases, see also Censer, "'Smiling through Her Tears'"; Grossberg, *Judgment for Solomon*; Hartog, *Man and Wife in America*.

3. Ambrose Dough, 1809, Petitions, General Assembly, Sessions Records, NCDAH.

4. Ibid. Although some couples colluded in divorce petitions, that is an unlikely scenario in this case. Many white southerners followed cultural rules, rather than legal forms, for establishing and severing marriage that were similar to those of slaves. See Edwards, *Gendered Strife and Confusion*, 60–62. For the marital customs of slaves, see Bercaw, *Gendered Freedoms*, 99–116; Frankel, *Freedom's Women*, 79–159; Kaye, *Joining Places*, 51–82.

5. The changes to the divorce statutes were added in 1828; G. Johnson, *Ante-Bellum North Carolina*, 222–23.

6. Mary Southwick, 1810, Petitions, General Assembly, Sessions Records, NCDAH. Edward Southwick submitted a competing petition, which is attached to his wife's petition.

7. *Sarah Chandler v. Thomas Chandler*, 1826, Divorce Papers, Granville County, NCDAH. Husbands often blamed in-laws for their marital troubles. See, for instance, Inquest of Elizabeth Martin, 1820, folder 1 and folder 4, Coroner's Inquisitions, Court of General Session, Pendleton District, SCDAH.

8. *Sarah Chandler v. Thomas Chandler*, 1826, Divorce Papers, Granville County, NCDAH. *State v. Alvin Preslar*, 1856, #5626, Supreme Court Original Cases, NCDAH. Sometimes women made direct claims to their husbands' property, usually in the context of alimony, indicating that they saw it as a family possession. *Lydia Hussey v. Jesse Hussey*, 1854; *Margaret Johnston v. Andrew Johnston*, 1843; *Nancy Pugh v. Jesse E. Pugh*, 1836; all in Divorce Records, Randolph County, NCDAH. Patience Dollar, 1808; Catherine Oel, 1809; both in Petitions, General Assembly, Sessions Records, NCDAH. Usually, though, they claimed property that came from their own families. See *Susan Phillips v. Nelson Phillips*, 1837; *Margaret Strother v. Christopher Strother*, 1837; *Elizabeth Wheeler v. Moses Wheeler*, 1831; all in Divorce Records, Granville County, NCDAH. *Mary Baldwin v. Osborn Baldwin*, 1856; *Emeline Finch v. Samuel J. Finch*, 1848; *Jane Hicks v. Willis Hicks*, 1834; *Sally Jackson v. George Jackson*, 1819; *Hannah Ridge v. Meredith Ridge*, 1849; *Deborah Vuncannon v. Kenneth Vuncannon*, 1845; *Sally Wilson v. Benjamin Wilson*, 1831; all in Divorce Records, Randolph County, NCDAH. Ann Tillery, 1803; Amelia Harris, 1803; James Hoffler, 1803; Elizabeth Davis, 1808; Lucy Self, 1808; Phebe McKaughan, 1810; Susan P. Davis, 1821–22; Jane Welborn, 1823–24; Sarah McCully, 1825–26; Eliza Bevins, 1825–26; Eliza Dowling, 1826–27; Eliza Simmons, 1827–28; Rachel Hamblet, 1827–28; Frances H. Dilliard, 1828–29; all in Petitions, General Assembly, Sessions Records, NCDAH.

9. Quotations from Answer of Augustus L. Converse in *Marion Converse v. Augustus L. Converse*, Sumter District Equity Court Records, 1854, roll 227, SCDAH; and [illegible; probably her mother's sister, Betty Coles] to Marion Deveaux Converse, Charlottesville, 11 January 1858, Singleton-Deveaux Family Papers, SCL.

10. Marion's petition in the separation suit reveals how she involved her family

during her marriage; see *Marion Converse v. Augustus L. Converse,* Sumter District Equity Court Records, 1854, roll 227, SCDAH. See also Marion Converse to Matt Singleton, 20 December 1853; Marion Converse to Matt Singleton, 25 December 1853, both in Singleton Family Papers, SCL. For the extended family's and friends' response, see, for instance; Betty Coles to Marion Deveaux, 19 February 1854; Betty Coles to Marion Deveaux, 1 April 1854; Betty Coles to Marion Deveaux, 11 April 1854; Betty Coles to Marion Deveaux, 16 May 1854; Betty Coles to Marion Deveaux, 31 July 1854; Betty Coles to Marion Deveaux, 15 January 1855; Betty Coles to Marion Deveaux, 5 June 1856; Betty Coles to Marion Deveaux, 28 June 1856; Betty Coles to Marion Deveaux, 17 September 1856; Betty Coles to Marion Deveaux, 11 January 1857; Sally W. Taylor to Marion Converse, 11 March [1850–55]; all in Singleton Family Papers, LC. J. Hamilton to Marion Converse, 22 November 1853; [illegible] to Marion Deveaux Converse, Charlottesville, 11 January 1858; both in Singleton-Deveaux Family Papers, SCL. For the final cash settlement with Augustus Converse, see Agreement, 20 February 1857, Singleton-Deveaux Family Papers, SCL. The rest of the family correspondence, particularly the Singleton-Deveaux Family Papers, SCL, and the Singleton Family Papers, LC, indicates that Marion lived as if the marriage had never happened. She even dropped the Converse name after the case. See Marion Deveaux to Sissie, 8 February 1858; V. M. Deveaux to Sissie, 3 April 1858; John B. Moore to Marion Deveaux, 6 August 1858; all in Singleton-Deveaux Family Papers, SCL. One family history, which indicates that Marion was unsuccessful in her suit, may be referring to the fact that the Singletons were unable to get some of the property back and had to pay Augustus Converse a sizable settlement; see Cassie Nicholes Papers, SCL.

11. Cashin, *Family Venture,* 44–49; Baptist, *Creating an Old South,* 25–26. Billingsley, *Communities of Kinship,* maintains that extended kin networks supported western migration in the South and that, therefore, the isolation of women has been overstated.

12. *Tabitha Fox v. John Fox,* 1840, Divorce Records, Randolph County, NCDAH. For petitions in which women or other deponents refer to "their" property, either property women produced or property they brought into the marriage, see *Mary W. Green v. Joseph Green,* 1847; *Hannah Mitchell v. Robert B. Mitchell,* 1831; *Eli Ann Royster v. William Royster,* 1853; *Patty Scott v. Harvey Scott,* 1824; *Susan Yarborough v. Thomas Yarborough,* 1832; all in Divorce Records, Granville County, NCDAH. *Andrew Arwick v. Susannah Arwick,* 1850; *Elizabeth Brower v. Christian Brower,* 1833; *Lydia Hussey v. Jesse Hussey,* 1854; *Sally Jackson v. George Jackson,* 1819; *Susannah Lamb v. Nathan Lamb,* 1850; *Mary Moffitt v. Samuel Moffitt,* 1841; *Susannah Presnell v. Randal Presnell,* 1855; *Bethany York v. Seymore York,* [1844]; *Tabitha York v. Jabez York,* 1837; all in Divorce Records, Randolph County, NCDAH. Elizabeth Sumner, 1801; Drusella Byars, 1808; Mary Gregory, 1808; Hanna Gunter, 1808; Lucy Crockett, 1808; Rebecca Kinster, 1809; Frances Murden, 1809; Mary Warren, 1809; Bond V. Brown, 1809; Mary Scott, 1809; Mary Southwick, 1810; Margaret Jackson, 1825–26; Mary

Turner, 1826–27; Elizabeth Dare, 1826–27; Frances H. Dilliard, 1828–29; all in Petitions, General Assembly, Sessions Records, NCDAH.

13. *Tabitha Fox v. John Fox*, 1840, Divorce Records, Randolph County, NCDAH. *State v. Alvin Preslar*, 1856, #5626, Supreme Court Original Cases, NCDAH. Women's divorce petitions often contained formulaic language about their husbands' refusal of support in order to establish abandonment, which was one of the statutory grounds for divorce. In some petitions, however, women elaborated on this theme, revealing a clear sense of labor—their own, their children's, and their husbands'— as being a family resource. *Martha Meacham v. Samuel Meacham*, 1839; *Lucy Minor v. John Minor*, 1834; *Eli Ann Royster v. William Royster*, 1853; *Susan A. Satterwhite v. James A. Satterwhite*, 1859; *Mary Stanfield v. John A. Stanfield*, 1839; *Amanda Walker v. William Walker*, 1847 (she is also referring to his appropriation of slaves' labor); *Elizabeth Wheeler v. Moses Wheeler*, 1831; all in Divorce Records, Granville County, NCDAH. *Jane Hicks v. Willis Hicks*, 1834; *Susannah Lamb v. Nathan Lamb*, 1850; *Nancy Pugh v. Jesse E. Pugh*, 1836; *Hannah Ridge v. Meredith Ridge*, 1849; all in Divorce Records, Randolph County, NCDAH. Elizabeth Stevens, 1808; Sally Hampton, 1823–24; Jane Welborn, 1823–24; all in Petitions, General Assembly, Sessions Records, NCDAH.

14. In the post-Revolutionary period, as Ruth H. Bloch has argued, the domestic sphere was distinctive, although not separate, associated with sentiment. See "American Female Ideals in Transition" and "Gendered Meanings of Virtue in Revolutionary America." By the 1820s and 1830s, domesticity was construed as a separate sphere, although the ideology did not reflect actual, material changes in the construction of domestic space. See Cott, *Bonds of Womanhood*; Kerber, "Separate Spheres, Female Worlds, Woman's Place"; and Ryan, *Cradle of the Middle Class*. For the influence of domestic ideology in the South, see Bynum, *Unruly Women*, 47–58, and McMillen, *Motherhood in the Old South*.

15. Biography of Edward Isham alias Hardaway Bone, Notebook of David Schenck, David Schenck Papers, NCDAH. See also the transcription of his narrative and interpretive essays in Bolton and Culclasure, *Confessions of Edward Isham*. On the economic volatility that prevailed during this period, see P. Johnson, "Modernization of Mayo Greenleaf Patch."

16. For the difficulties presented by economic change in this period, see, in particular, Balleisen, *Navigating Failure*, and Sandage, *Born Losers*. Concerns about economic volatility are apparent in much of the scholarship on the South in the period between 1787 and 1860. See Bolton, *Poor Whites*; Coclanis, *Shadow of a Dream*; Escott, *Many Excellent People*; Hahn, *Roots of Southern Populism*; and McCurry, *Masters of Small Worlds*.

17. See, for instance, William I. Leary, North Carolina, vol. 5, p. 237; James D. Williams, North Carolina, vol. 5, p. 234A; Dr. W. I. McKain, South Carolina, vol. 11, p. 42; all in R. G. Dun & Co.

18. Women supporting themselves was unusual, but not uncommon; the same

skills that women contributed to the household economy also had value outside it. See G. Johnson, *Ante-Bellum North Carolina*, 245–50. Recent scholarship has stressed the value of women's labor on the market. Most of that work focuses on the North, but the same trends were evident, although to a lesser degree, in the South. See Boydston, *Home and Work*; C. Clark, *Roots of Rural Capitalism*; Dublin, *Women at Work*; P. Johnson, "Modernization of Mayo Greenleaf Patch"; and McCurry, *Masters of Small Worlds*.

19. For petitions that identify husbands' debts and creditors as the reason for obtaining a divorce or separation, see the following records: *Susan Yarborough v. Thomas Yarborough*, 1832, Divorce Records, Granville County, NCDAH. *Christiana Deving v. Thomas Deving*, 1821; *Susannah Lamb v. Nathan Lamb*, 1850; *Even Lane v. John Lane*, 1829; *Mary Moffitt v. Samuel Moffitt*, 1841; *Susannah Presnell v. Randal Presnell*, 1855; *Nancy Pugh v. Jesse E. Pugh*, 1836; *Hannah Ridge v. Meredith Ridge*, 1849; *Eltha Vuncannon v. John Vuncannon*, 1841; *Tabitha York v. Jabez York*, 1837; all in Divorce Records, Randolph County, NCDAH. Susannah Query, 1801; Mildred Wills, 1801; A. E. Barbara Elrod, 1803; Elizabeth Davis, 1808; Lucy Crockett, 1808; Jane O'Briant, 1808; Catherine Oel, 1809; Mary Warren, 1809; Nancy Johnson, 1809; Phebe McKaughan, 1810; Susan P. Davis, 1821–22; Levice Pennington, 1821–22; Jane Welborn, 1823–24; Margaret Jackson, 1825–26; Sarah McCully, 1825–26; Mildred McLilley, 1826–27; Elizabeth Dare, 1826–27; Nancy McKinney, 1826–27; all in Petitions, General Assembly, Sessions Records, NCDAH.

20. Churches regularly mediated domestic conflicts. For records where such cases were particularly prominent, see Abbott's Creek Primitive Baptist Church, Minutes, 1783–1879, Davidson County; Bush Arbor Primitive Baptist Church, Minutes, 1806–1919, Anderson Township; Caswell County and Bush Arbor Primitive Baptist Church, Minutes, 1807–1960, Anderson Township, Caswell County; Red Banks Primitive Baptist Church, Minutes, 1791–1904, Pitt County; Three Forks Baptist Church, Minutes, 1790–1895, Wilkes County; Wheeley's Primitive Baptist Church, Roxboro, Minutes and Roll Book, 1790–1898, Person County; all in NCDAH. Methodist Church, Horry County, Waccamaw Circuit and Conwayborough Circuit; Bethabara Baptist Church, Laurens County; Thomas Memorial Baptist Church, Marlboro County; Bethesda Baptist Church (Primitive), Church Book, 1823–1905, Kershaw District; all in SCL. Fall Creek Baptist Church Records, 1819–90, Chatham County, #4418, SHC. See also Ford, *Origins of Southern Radicalism*, 33–36, and J. Friedman, *Enclosed Garden*, esp. 14–20.

21. *State v. Marvel Littlefield*, 1841, Vagrancy Trials, Court of Magistrates and Freeholders, Spartanburg District, SCDAH. *State v. Thomas Watkins*, 1819, Vagrancy Trials, Court of Magistrates and Freeholders, Laurens District, SCDAH. The account of Westley Rhodes appears in Cecil-Fronsman, *Common Whites*, 133; see also 156–64. Women often mention fleeing to neighbors or relatives in divorce petitions that allege physical abuse. See also Edwards, "Law, Domestic Violence, and the Limits of Patriarchal Authority." For women in similar social contexts, although

very different time periods, mobilizing community ties to protect themselves against violence by their husbands, see also Amussen, "'Being Stirred to Much Unquietness'"; D'Cruze, *Crimes of Outrage*; and Haag, "'Ill-Use of a Wife.'"

22. Manuals for justices of the peace dating from the early part of the century clearly stated that wives could swear out peace warrants against their husbands. In law, the offense acquired the status of a public crime because it was a breach of the public peace. There was no clear legal line between peace warrants and other crimes involving violence. By this logic, local officials could charge abusive husbands with the crime of assault either in addition to or as a component of the peace warrant. See Haywood, *Duty and Office of Justices of the Peace*, 6–7, 15–16, 28–32, 191; and Grimké, *South Carolina Justice of the Peace*, 7–9, 23–32, 450–68. Between 1800 and 1840, for instance, there were twenty-five peace warrants that were saved in the Granville County Criminal Action Papers, NCDAH; but that figure does not represent all the peace warrants, let alone all the complaints, since not all of the magistrates' papers were saved. The peace bonds for Anderson District and Pendleton District in South Carolina are separated from the other court records, unsorted, and voluminous. A sampling of these records indicates that magistrates routinely swore out bonds against husbands on complaints of their wives and daughters. See Peace Bonds, 1828–1905, Court of General Sessions, Anderson County, SCDAH. For similar patterns, see Cole, "Keeping the Peace."

23. There were twelve recorded assault cases in Granville County between 1800 and 1840. See *State v. Thomas Banner*, 1813; *State v. Solomon Bobbitt*, 1817; *State v. Solomon Bobbitt*, 1817 (a separate case); *State v. William Hickman*, 1818; *State v. Samuel Cauthon*, 1819; *State v. Evan Ragland*, 1822; *State v. Charles Bearden*, 1823; *State v. Barnett Eakes*, 1824; *State v. Thomas Chandler*, 1825; *State v. William Hickman*, 1828; *State v. John Hutchinson*, 1838 (although this indictment was for the murder of his wife's unborn child; she miscarried after the beating); *State v. William Jeffreys*, 1839; all in Criminal Action Papers, Granville County, NCDAH. Barnett Eakes and Evan Ragland apparently disappeared after their indictments; for Ragland's disappearance, see *State v. Evan Ragland*, 1824, Criminal Action Papers, Granville County, NCDAH. Although there is no record that his wife brought the charge, Willie Parham gave bond to answer "the State for a nuisance and great violence committed on his wife"; *State v. Willie Parham*, 1816, Criminal Action Papers, Granville County, NCDAH. There are fourteen assault cases in the records for Kershaw District between 1795 and 1840. See *State v. Henry Rattenburg*, 1795, Sessions Docket, County and Intermediate Court, and Indictments, County and Intermediate Court, Kershaw District, SCDAH. *State v. Christopher Cain*, 1803; *State v. Joseph McAdams*, 1807; *State v. Samuel Thompson*, 1813; *State v. Samuel Thompson*, 1814 (this appears to be a separate case); *State v. Joseph McAdams*, 1814; *State v. Benjamin Grant*, 1815; *State v. John Parker*, 1818; *State v. Patrick McKenna*, 1820 (nol pros); *State v. Henry L. Butler*, 1824; *State v. Isaac Jones*, 1835; *State v. David Jamison*, 1836; *State v. Pleasant Purdee*, 1838; all in Indictments, Court of General Sessions, Kershaw District,

SCDAH. *State v. John Duncan*, 1824, Journals, Court of General Sessions, Kershaw District, SCDAH. The cases against Christopher Cain, Samuel Thompson, Joseph McAdams, and Henry Butler appear in the Journals as well as the Indictments, Court of General Sessions, Kershaw District, SCDAH. There is only one recorded assault case in Anderson District, *State v. Andrew Oliver*, Spring Term 1839, #6, Indictments, Court of General Sessions, Anderson District, SCDAH. For similar patterns, see Cole, "Keeping the Peace."

24. *State v. Christopher Cain*, 1803, Indictments; *State v. Henry L. Butler*, 1824, Journal and Indictments; *State v. David Jamison*, 1836, Indictments; all in Court of General Sessions, Kershaw District, SCDAH.

25. *State v. David Jamison*, 1836, Indictments, Court of General Sessions, Kershaw District, SCDAH.

26. *State v. Joseph McAdams*, 1807; *State v. John Parker*, 1818; *State v. Henry L. Butler*, 1824; all in Indictments, Court of General Sessions, Kershaw District, SCDAH.

27. The cases from Kershaw District are particularly revealing of wives' strategies in mobilizing community support. Wives' advertisements, which included abandonment and adultery as well as abuse, established a paper trail that legitimized further action against their husbands; for such advertisements, see G. Johnson, *Ante-Bellum North Carolina*, 244–45. For wives' strategies in publicizing cases, see Edwards, "Women and the Law."

28. After the Civil War, the records were more likely to include husbands' explanations, which emphasized wives' failure to provide domestic services as a violation of their rights; see Edwards, "Women and the Law." In the late eighteenth and early nineteenth centuries, by contrast, the records tended to omit such explanations, largely because they were irrelevant to the proceedings. When they were included, husbands usually cited their wives' alienation of affection or adultery as the reason for their violence.

29. Existing scholarship in southern history focuses on the courts' refusal to deal with wife-beating, child abuse, and other forms of violence by household heads against domestic dependents. See Bardaglio, *Reconstructing the Household*, 33–34; Bynum, *Unruly Women*, 70–72; and Edwards, "Women and the Law." Work on violence by husbands against wives in the nineteenth century generally also tends to emphasize community controls over legal ones, affirming the idea that the issue remained outside official structures of governance. See Peterson del Mar, *What Trouble I Have Seen*; Gordon, *Heroes of Their Own Lives*; Haag, "'Ill-Use of a Wife'"; Nadelhaft, "Wife Torture"; Pleck, *Domestic Tyranny*; and Stansell, *City of Women*, 78–83.

30. Assaults against women and prosecuted by women—or women and their husbands or fathers—were common in the local court records. See Edwards, "Law, Domestic Violence, and the Limits of Patriarchal Authority."

31. *State v. John Parker*, 1818, Indictments, Court of General Sessions, Kershaw District, SCDAH.

32. *State v. Thomas Chandler*, 1825, Criminal Action Papers, Granville County, NCDAH. *Sarah Chandler v. Thomas Chandler*, 1826, Divorce Papers, Granville County, NCDAH.

33. Thomas Chandler had a history of violence in the neighborhood that continued after his separation from Sarah. See *State v. Thomas Chandler*, 1825 (for the assault of Henry Yancey); *State v. Thomas Chandler and Polly Cutts*, 1829 (for fornication and adultery); both in Criminal Action Papers, Granville County, NCDAH. In 1823 he was pardoned for the maiming of Henry Yancey; see Gabriel Holmes, Pardon of Thomas Chandler, 11 September 1823, p. 111, vol. 25, GLB, NCDAH.

34. *State v. George and Mary Meadows*, 1847, Criminal Actions Concerning Slaves and Free Persons of Color, Granville County, NCDAH. For a more detailed discussion of this case, see Edwards, "Law, Domestic Violence, and the Limits of Patriarchal Authority." See also Bynum, *Unruly Women*, 85–87.

35. Slaves' status as property and the presumed contradiction between that status and the rights of the individual assumed more importance in appellate cases and statutes, beginning in the 1820s; see chapter 7.

36. *State v. Violet*, 1854, #160, reel 2921, Trial Records, Court of Magistrates and Freeholders, Spartanburg District, SCDAH.

37. Ibid.

38. Thomas B. Clarkson to M. R. Singleton, 3 August 1852, Singleton Family Papers, SCL.

39. *State v. Lease*, 1841, #37, reel 2920, Trial Records, Court of Magistrates and Freeholders, Spartanburg District, SCDAH. *State v. Patt*, 1825, #14, reel 2916, Trial Papers, Court of Magistrates and Freeholders, Anderson/Pendleton District, SCDAH. For similar cases, see the following records: *State v. Mary*, 1826, #26; *State v. Jack*, 1828, #40; *State v. Anthony*, 1834, #73; *State v. Jordan*, 1828, #42; *State v. Smart and Sealy*, 1831, #57; *State v. David, Adam, and Dick*, 1834, #72; *State v. Anthony*, 1834, #73; *State v. Cain*, 1835, #75; *State v. Tony*, 1836, #81; *State v. Big Dave, Frank, Tom, and Nero*, 1838, #95; *State v. Toney*, 1838, #97; *State v. Will*, 1839, #100; *State v. Spencer*, 1839, #106; *State v. Margret*, 1840, #115; all in reel 2916, Trial Papers, Court of Magistrates and Freeholders, Anderson/Pendleton District, SCDAH. *State v. Dick*, 1824, #4; *State v. Moses*, 1832, #6; *State v. Titus*, 1833, #8; *State v. Saul*, 1833, #9; *State v. Edmund*, 1835, #12; *State v. Phil*, 1837, #19; *State v. Alfred*, 1838, #23; *State v. Cornelius*, 1838, #26; *State v. Joe*, 1841, #34; all in reel 2920, Trial Papers, Court of Magistrates and Freeholders, Spartanburg District, SCDAH; *State v. Eben*, 1811, #7; *State v. Dick, Lisbon, and March*, 1815, #12; *State v. Abraham*, 1816, #17; *State v. Sam*, 1822, #25; *State v. Jim*, 1822, #30; *State v. Phil*, 1825, #33; *State v. Burke*, 1829, #37; *State v. Nathan*, 1829, #38; *State v. Jeff*, 1829, #69; *State v. Samuel*, 1830, #41; *State v. Dublin*, 1831, #45; *State v. Henry*, 1831, #47; *State v. John*, 1831, #48; *State v. Walt*, 1831, #49; *State v. Mose*, 1832, #51; *State v. Jack*, 1832, #52; *State v. Charles*, 1832, #53; *State v. Charity*, 1832, #54; *State v. Jarrett*, 1832, #55; *State v. Mary*, 1832, #56, #57, #58, #59, and #63; *State v. Harriet*, 1832, #60; *State v. Isaac*, 1832, #61; *State v. Lynda*, 1832, #62; *State v. Titus*, 1832, #64; *State v. Lewis*,

Henry, and Caty, 1837, #73; *State v. Isaac Mothershed and William Mothershed*, 1837; *State v. Tate*, 1838, #75; *State v. Matt*, 1838, #76; *State v. Davey*, 1839, #77, #79; *State v. Ben and Friday*, 1839, #39; all in Trial Papers, Court of Magistrates and Freeholders, Kershaw District, SCDAH. *State v. Nowell*, 1810–12; *State v. Bob*, 1815–16; *State v. Jack*, 1827–29; *State v. Edward*, 1827–29; *State v. Gilbert*, 1830–32; all in Criminal Actions Concerning Slaves and Free People of Color, Granville County, NCDAH. *State v. William Pannell*, 1807 and 1808 (it was alleged that Pannell had his slave, Moses, set fire to a neighbor's house); *State v. William Brinkley*, 1838 (Brinkley threatened a slave — presumably Moses — belonging to William Pannell); all in Criminal Action Papers, Granville County, NCDAH. *State v. Gray, a slave*, 1795; *State v. Ben, a slave*, 1795; both in Criminal Actions, Orange County, NCDAH.

40. *State v. Mary*, 1826, #26, reel 2916, Trial Papers, Court of Magistrates and Freeholders, Anderson/Pendleton District, SCDAH.

41. The tensions between slaves and patrollers are evident in Hadden, *Slave Patrols*, and Wyatt-Brown, "Community, Class, and Snopesian Crime."

42. For cases from two counties/districts, see the following records: *State v. Samuel Nettles*, 1806 (assault by a master); *State v. Davis Cooper*, 1808 (murder by a third party); *State v. Thomas English and William Hammonds*, 1808–9 (murder by a master and another third party); *State v. Samuel Coates*, 1809 (murder by a third party); *State v. John Havis*, 1819 (murder by a master); *State v. Robert Thompson*, 1818 (murder by a third party); *State v. James Barfield, Jr., and James Barfield, Sr.*, 1818 (murder by third parties); *State v. Ephraim Stratford, Joiner Middleton, and Douglas Minton*, 1820 (murder by third parties); *State v. Robert Bell, John Bell, and Andrew Hood*, 1821 (murder by third parties); all in Indictments, Court of General Sessions, Kershaw District, SCDAH. *State v. John Brown*, 1797 (assault; whether Brown is the master or a third party is not stated), Sessions Docket, County and Intermediate Court, Kershaw District, SCDAH. *State v. Sherwood Larhorn, Cloe Larhorn, Humphrey Haines, Molly Haines, and Jane Haines*, 1791 (assault by third parties); *State v. Willie Howington*, 1802 (assault by a third party); *State v. Joseph Crews*, 1818 (assault and attempted murder by a third party); *State v. Vincent Day*, 1818 (assault by a third party); *State v. Charles Robertson*, 1825 (assault by a third party); *State v. John Prewett and John Jenkins*, 1828 (assault by third parties); *State v. William Brinkley*, 1838 (assault, ultimately handled as a peace bond); *State v. Gulielmus Wiggins*, 1839 (assault by a constable); all in Criminal Action Papers, Granville County, NCDAH. *State v. William Ball*, 1808–10 (murder by a third party); *State v. Abington Kimbel*, 1815–16 (assault by a third party); *State v. Bannister Yancey*, 1817–18 (assault by a third party); *State v. Warner Taylor*, 1819 (murder by a master); *State v. Wilkens Stovall, James Nunn, Elijah Wilkerson*, 1820–22 (assault by a third party); *State v. Thomas Huff and Warner Taylor*, 1825 (murder by a master and a third party); *State v. Nelson Duke*, 1825 (assault by a third party); *State v. Benjamin Williams*, 1827–29 (assault by a third party); *State v. Michael Beck*, 1830–32 (assault by a third party); *State v. James Brinkley*, 1833–34 (assault by a third party); *State v. Irby Creath*, 1833–34 (assault by a

third party); *State v. Thomas Neal*, 1833–34 (assault by a third party); *State v. Beverly Eakes*, 1833–34 (assault by a third party); *State v. Cephus Daniel*, 1833–34 (threats by a third party related to the complainant); *State v. William Huddleston*, 1835–37 (assault by a third party, although Huddleston may be a free black man); *State v. Osborn Ball*, 1835–37 (assault by a third party with intent to kill); *State v. Moses Winston*, 1835–37 (assault by a third party); *State v. Simmon Clark*, 1838–39 (threats by a third party); all in Criminal Actions Concerning Slaves and Free Persons of Color, Granville County, NCDAH. The list of cases from Granville County include white-on-black violence (although there may be some free black defendants in the list whose race I was unable to identify); there are other cases in which free blacks were prosecuted for violence against slaves.

43. *State v. Augustus Benton*, 1806, Criminal Action Papers, Orange County, NCDAH.

44. James Chesnut to Richard Singleton, 17 July 1834, James Chesnut Papers, SCL. There is no indication that this case ended up in court. But fourteen years earlier, a similar case from the Chesnut plantation did. In 1820 John Chesnut prosecuted three men for killing his slave, Sam Sinclair. The complaint suggests that the men were part of a slave patrol, which, finding Sam outside at night, beat him to death. Two of the defendants were convicted, although the records do not indicate whether they were convicted of killing a slave or the lesser count of killing a slave in the heat of passion while in the act of discipline. *State v. Ephraim Stratford, Joiner Middleton, and Douglas Minton*, 1820, Indictments, Court of General Sessions; Inquest on the body of Sam, property of John Chesnut, 1820, Coroner's Inquisitions, Court of General Sessions; both in Kershaw District, SCDAH.

45. December 1828, Bush Arbor Primitive Baptist Church, Minutes 1806–1919, Anderson Township, Caswell County, NCDAH: "Report was Sister Gregory for barbarous treatment to one of her servants such that the church thought advisable she be delt with"; when she appeared, she did not repent and was excommunicated in 1829. Other churches investigated similar conflicts, although not always siding with slaves. See 10, 16, and 17 September 1824, 4 October 1824, and 5 January 1827, Big Creek Baptist Church, Anderson District; 6 July 1859, Records, Bethesda Presbyterian Church, Camden, Kershaw County; 4 September 1830, 1 January 1831, 5 March 1831, 4 June 1831, 2 July 1831, 6 August 1831, 1 October 1831, First Baptist Church, Barnwell County; 22 September 1837, Bethabara Baptist Church, Laurens County; February 1820, William Swamp Baptist Church, Orangeburg County; all in SCL. B. Wood, "'For Their Satisfaction or Redress.'"

46. *State v. Warner Taylor*, 1819; *State v. Thomas Huff and Warner Taylor*, 1825; both in Criminal Actions Concerning Slaves and Free Persons of Color, Granville County, NCDAH. Archibald D. Murphey to Thomas Ruffin, 9 October 1825, in Hoyt, *Papers of Archibald D. Murphey*, 1:317–18. Taylor asked for the benefit of clergy, a privilege of free people that waived the death sentence in capital offenses if granted. Use of the benefit of clergy was increasingly rare during the antebellum

period, suggesting that Taylor probably would not have been allowed it had the victim been free and white. For Taylor, see also T. Morris, *Southern Slavery and the Law*, 180, 477n95.

47. *State v. John Havis*, 1819, Indictments, Court of General Sessions, Kershaw District, SCDAH. For Annis and Juno, see *State v. George*, 1826; *State v. Tom*, 1824; both in Criminal Action Papers, Chowan County, NCDAH. See also chapter 3. The legal dynamics, which required the presence of slaves, are analogous to those described for civil cases in Gross, *Double Character*.

48. *State v. Violet*, 1854, #160, reel 2921, Trial Records, Court of Magistrates and Freeholders, Spartanburg District, SCDAH.

49. Petition for the Pardon of Thomas Gallion, to James Iredell, 3 August 1828, pp. 117–18, vol. 27, GLB, NCDAH. Slave ledger, subser. 6.5.1, vol. 73, 1792–1812, Cameron Family Papers, #133, SHC. The court records in Anderson, Pendleton, Spartanburg, and Kershaw Districts all contain numerous references to these patterns. In cases where criminal charges were filed, the witnesses often made distinctions between legal and illegal trading or made statements indicating that such trading was less the exception than the rule. *State v. Caesar*, 1832, #7; *State v. Wyatt Harris*, 1842, #48; *State v. Daniel*, 1842, #49; all in reel 2920, Trial Papers, Court of Magistrates and Freeholders, Spartanburg District, SCDAH. *State v. Ben*, 1824, #6; *State v. Ishmael Shavis*, 1827, #34; *State v. Washington*, 1830, #52; *State v. Henry*, 1833, #65; all in reel 2916, Trial Papers, Court of Magistrates and Freeholders, Anderson/Pendleton District, SCDAH. The references to trading in cases involving other, unrelated issues are numerous. For examples, see the following records: *State v. Doctor and Jemima*, 1822, # 3; *State v. Ben and Levi*, 1825, #16; both in reel 2916, Trial Papers, Court of Magistrates and Freeholders, Anderson/Pendleton District, SCDAH. *State v. Jacob*, 1835, #15, reel 2920, Trial Papers, Court of Magistrates and Freeholders, Anderson/Pendleton District, SCDAH.

50. Paul C. Cameron to Thomas Ruffin, 1 December 1835, in Hamilton, *Papers of Thomas Ruffin*, 2:150–51.

51. Kaye, *Joining Places*, 132–36, makes the point that slaves supported other runaways they knew, trusted, and respected from their own neighborhoods; they were much less supportive of runaways they did not know from outside the neighborhood and of those within the neighborhood who had strained social ties.

52. *State v. Violet*, 1854, #160, reel 2921, Trial Records, Court of Magistrates and Freeholders, Spartanburg District, SCDAH.

PART III

1. Although its membership changed over the course of construction, the board of commissioners included legal reformers Duncan Cameron, Henry Seawell, R. M. Saunders, and W. R. Gales, the son of Joseph Gales who had taken over editorship of the *Raleigh Register*. William Gaston also had strong interests in the building;

some sources credit his son-in-law, the New York–based Robert Donaldson, with the choice of the New York architectural firm of Town and Davis. For the North Carolina capitol, see Bishir and Southern, *Guide to the Historic Architecture of Piedmont, North Carolina*, 104, 107–8, and Bishir, *North Carolina Architecture*, 196–206; Elliot, "North Carolina State Capitol"; Sanders, "North Carolina State House and Capitol" and "'This Political Temple, the Capitol of North Carolina.'" For the influence of the Virginia state capitol, see Lounsbury, *Courthouses of Early Virginia*, 127–28. Other states built similar capitols in this period, but North Carolina's is one of the best exemplars of the style; see Hitchcock and Seale, *Temples of Democracy*, 64–120.

2. See note 1. Quotation from Bishir and Southern, *Guide to the Historic Architecture of Piedmont North Carolina*, 108.

3. Bryan, *Robert Mills Architect, 1781–1855*; Lane, *Architecture of the Old South*, 157–84. Mills's career, particularly his work in South Carolina, underscores the argument that the professionalization of law and architecture went hand in hand. See McNamara, *From Tavern to Courthouse*, esp. 81–102. Mills's South Carolina plans incorporated local design elements into the Greek Revival form.

4. First quotation from G. Johnson, *Ante-Bellum North Carolina*, 217; second quotation in *Raleigh Register*, 8 June 1809 (also quoted in G. Johnson, *Ante-Bellum North Carolina*, 218).

5. For the changes in divorce laws, see G. Johnson, *Ante-Bellum North Carolina*, 217–23; and Stevenson, "Marriage and Divorce Records," 305–6. According to Bynum, *Unruly Women*, 72–75, decisions in superior courts often ran counter to the state's strict statutes and the edicts issued by the state supreme court. With greater personal knowledge of the couples, judges and juries at the local level were also far more sympathetic to their difficulties and thus more willing to bend the abstractions of the law to fit the complex reality of individual cases. See also Bardaglio, *Reconstructing the Household*, 32–34, 134; Censer, "'Smiling through Her Tears'"; Clinton, *Plantation Mistress*, 79–85; Wyatt-Brown, *Southern Honor*, 242–47, 283–91, 300–307.

6. G. Johnson, *Ante-Bellum North Carolina*, 217–23.

7. Quotations from *Raleigh Register*, 5 January 1827, and 12 January 1827. Many more petitions were submitted in the session, following the 1827 statute, apparently before it went into effect; see *Raleigh Register*, 7 December 1827. *Raleigh Register*, 9 December 1834, indicates several petitions for divorce in the state senate in that session. There were, predictably, several attempts to bring divorces back into the purview of the legislature after the 1827 statute; see *Raleigh Register*, 30 December 1830 and 23 December 1834.

8. G. Johnson, *Ante-Bellum North Carolina*, 217–23.

9. *Marville Scroggins v. Lucretia Scroggins*, 1832 N.C. LEXIS 97.

10. Counihan, "North Carolina Constitutional Convention," 359.

11. Hired as a paid member of the Board of Public Works in 1820, Mills was re-

sponsible for designing and overseeing the construction of the state's public buildings. In that capacity, he took over the project of building district courthouses. Originally, the state legislature had imagined even more uniformity for district courthouses, approving a plan for identical courthouses in each district; those plans had been drawn up for the state by the English architect, William Jay, in 1819. Mills modified those plans, keeping the Greek Revival style but elaborating on it and varying it for each district. His design remained influential, even after the state legislature abolished his position. The legislature continued to contract with him for projects on an ad hoc basis. So did the local commissioners (who were often part of the state elite) who were now charged with coming up with their own designs for public buildings within their districts. He achieved the original goal of creating a uniform expression of state law in each district. See Waddell and Liscombe, *Robert Mills's Courthouses and Jails*; and Lane, *Architecture of the Old South*, 171–72.

12. For local courthouses in North Carolina, see Bishir, *North Carolina Architecture*, 206–13.

CHAPTER 7

1. *State v. Alvin Preslar*, 1856, #5626, Supreme Court Original Cases, NCDAH; *State v. Alvin Preslar*, 1856 N.C. LEXIS 122. For a discussion, see Bynum, *Unruly Women*, 82–83.

2. *State v. Alvin Preslar*, 1856, #5626, Supreme Court Original Cases, NCDAH; *State v. Alvin Preslar*, 1856 N.C. LEXIS 122. The reasoning duplicated one of the petitions sympathetic to Alvin Preslar that also blamed his wife for exposing herself when she was unwell; see Bynum, *Unruly Women*, 83.

3. The scholarship on southern distinctiveness is vast, reaching back to the late nineteenth century when southern writers began popularizing the notion of a unique regional culture influenced by archaic values more than modern ones. For discussions of this literature, see Gardner, *Blood Irony*; Murphey, *Rebuke of History*; and Oakes, "Present Becomes the Past." Historian Eugene D. Genovese analyzed the South as a prebourgeois region, *in* but not *of* the capitalist world. See Genovese, *World the Slaveholders Made*; Genovese, *Roll, Jordan, Roll*; and Genovese and Fox-Genovese, *Fruits of Merchant Capital*. Recent refutations of southern distinctiveness underscore the importance of rights within the South's legal system. See Coclanis, *Shadow of a Dream*, and Oakes, *Slavery and Freedom*. See also Oakes, *Ruling Race*.

4. E. Morgan, *American Slavery, American Freedom*. See also Brown, *Good Wives, "Nasty Wenches," and Anxious Patriarchs*; Greene, "Slavery or Independence"; Lockridge, *On the Sources of Patriarchal Rage*; Parent, *Formation of a Slave Society in Virginia*.

5. Much of the literature in legal history, particularly the work on aspects of property law, tends to treat the South less as distinctive than as backward. See,

for instance, Horwitz, *Transformation of American Law*; and Friedman, *History of American Law*. Huebner, *Southern Judicial Tradition*, emphasizes legal parallels between North and South, particularly in the realm of property law. The literature on slave law also emphasizes regional difference, since there was no comparable body of law elsewhere in the nation, where slavery had been abolished.

6. For key works in the historiography, see Beard and Beard, *Rise of American Civilization*; Schlesinger, *Age of Jackson*; F. Turner, *United States, 1830–1860*; Hofstadter, *Idea of a Party System*; Wiebe, *Opening of American Society*; G. Wood, *Radicalism of the American Revolution*; and Wilentz, *Rise of American Democracy*.

7. Departing from earlier scholarship, recent work on the Carolinas tends to place democratizing tendencies in the context of hierarchical governing structures, following historiographical trends that emphasize political and/or social and cultural ties among white men and the consequent racial inequalities. For the classic statement of racial solidarity, see Fredrickson, *Black Image in the White Mind*. Recent scholarship identifies different foundations for solidarity — race, slavery, republican independence, and gender — and assigns different meanings to the resulting political ties. See Ford, *Origins of Southern Radicalism*, 106–8; Klein, *Unification of a Slave State*; McCurry, *Masters of Small Worlds*; and H. Watson, *Jacksonian Politics and Community Conflict*.

8. For the retrenchment of slavery after the Revolution, see Berlin, *Many Thousands Gone*; P. Morgan, *Slave Counterpoint*; Frey, *Water from the Rock*; Olwell, *Masters, Slaves, and Subjects*; Sinha, *Counter-Revolution of Slavery*; and Young, *Domesticating Slavery*. The literature on paternalism, best exemplified by Genovese's *Roll, Jordan, Roll*, maintains that slaveholders recast slavery in positive terms, as a humane institution that protected slaves' interests.

9. Fields, "Slavery, Race and Ideology in the United States of America," argues that the Revolution engendered a racial justification of slavery that also buttressed the subordination of free blacks. On abolition in the North, see Berlin, *Many Thousands Gone*, 228–55; Harris, *In the Shadow of Slavery*; Melish, *Disowning Slavery*; Nash and Soderlund, *Freedom by Degrees*; Painter, *Sojourner Truth*; and S. White, *Somewhat More Independent*. Radicals pushed for a more egalitarian racial politics within the abolition movement; see Stauffer, *Black Hearts of Men*. For endemic racism in the political culture, see Roediger, *Wages of Whiteness*, and Saxton, *Rise and Fall of the White Republic*.

10. Recent scholarship is critical of domestic ideology — commonly called "separate spheres" — emphasizing its political and cultural power rather than its value as a social description. Separate spheres belied the actual conditions of most women, but the ideology had a powerful influence on the possibilities open to them in this period by devaluing their labor and severing them from public matters. See, for instance, Boydston, *Home and Work*; Boydston, Kelley, and Margolis, *Limits of Sisterhood*; Cott, *Bonds of Womanhood*; Ryan, *Cradle of the Middle Class*; and Sklar, *Catharine Beecher*. For women's rights and political activism, see DuBois, *Feminism*

and Suffrage; Kerber, *No Constitutional Right to Be Ladies*; and Isenberg, *Sex and Citizenship*. For the gendered context of political discourse, see Smith-Rosenberg, "Dis-Covering the Subject"; and Ryan, *Civic Wars*.

11. On legal changes for working people, particularly working men, see Tomlins, *Law, Labor, and Ideology*. By contrast, Steinfeld, *Invention of Free Labor*, emphasizes the opening up of labor relations over the nineteenth century. See also Steinfeld, *Coercion, Contract, and Free Labor*.

12. On slave laws, see T. Morris, *Southern Slavery and the Law*, and Hadden, *Slave Patrols*. For the deterioration in the status of free blacks, see Franklin, *Free Negro in North Carolina*; and M. Johnson and Roark, *Black Masters*. In *Masters of Small Worlds*, Stephanie McCurry argues that men's gendered role as household heads provided the logic for linking the expansion of free white men's rights to the denial of rights to slaves and women. See also Bardaglio, *Reconstructing the Household*; Bercaw, *Gendered Freedoms*; Bynum, *Unruly Women*; and Fox-Genovese, *Within the Plantation Household*.

13. Bynum, *Unruly Women*; Escott, *Many Excellent People*; G. O'Brien, *Legal Fraternity*; and Sinha, *Counter-Revolution of Slavery*. See also Thornton, *Politics and Power*.

14. For maiming, see *Laws of North Carolina, 1754*, chap. 15, in W. Clark, *State Records of North Carolina*, 23:420. The penalties were later downgraded; see Act of 1791, Rev., chap. 339. Swift, *System of Laws*, 178–79, explains the connection between mayhem and fitness for military duties. On the prevalence of this ritualized violence, see Gorn, "'Gouge and Bite, Pull Hair and Scratch.'"

15. These changes in the legal handling of violence do not figure in the historiography, largely because the presumption of southern distinctiveness has led historians to view violence as part of a unique regional culture of honor that tolerated, even encouraged, these acts in white men. In this literature, white men's violence and their privileged positions in the social order fit together as expressions of an archaic social order that rejected national principles of democracy, equality, and individual rights. The dynamics that historians tend to characterize as backward, however, actually represented radical changes in the legal system and people's relationship to it. For violence and honor, see Ayers, *Vengeance and Justice*, esp. 132–36; Greenberg, *Masters and Statesmen* and *Honor and Slavery*; Ownby, *Subduing Satan*; Stowe, *Intimacy and Power*; and Wyatt-Brown, *Southern Honor*.

16. The dearth of laws at the state level has reinforced historians' characterizations of the South's legal system as unconcerned with violence and driven, instead, by a code of honor that emphasized personal retribution.

17. *State v. Wood*, 1 Bay, 351 (S.C., 1794). The line of causation in this case is difficult to follow. According to Wood, the defendant, the prosecutrix, Mrs. Rouple, first struck him with a cowskin. Mrs. Rouple justified her actions on the grounds that she had been provoked by "words spoken by the defendant, injurious to her character." The judges rejected that justification, ruling that "no words will justify

an assault." They also refused Wood's claim that he acted in self-defense, arguing that the "degree of resistance ought to be in proportion to the nature of the injury received." Because the victim was a woman and the nature of the violence was so severe, Wood was culpable of criminal assault, affirming the local jurisdiction's handling of the case, which identified Wood's actions as a public offense.

18. *Chanellor v. Vaughn*, 2 Bay, 416 (S.C., 1802). In *Dodd v. Hamilton and Hamilton*, 1816 N.C. LEXIS 48, the North Carolina court also refused to grant a new trial because of excessive damages. See also *Barry v. Inglis et al.*, 1799 N.C. LEXIS 35, which ruled out previous provocation to mitigate damages; and *Sledge v. Pope*, 1806 N.C. LEXIS 26, which allowed previous threats (as opposed to provocation) to increase damages.

19. *Stout v. Rutherford*, 1821 N.C. LEXIS 36.

20. *State v. Irwin*, 2 N.C. 151 (1794); *State v. Evans*, 2 N.C. 368 (1796).

21. *State v. Langford*, 10 N.C. 381 (1824). See also *Barry v. Inglis et al.*, 1 N.C. 147 (1799); although a civil case, it ruled out extenuating circumstances to focus on the injury alone.

22. *White v. Fort*, 10 N.C. 251 (1824).

23. Haywood, *Manual of the Laws of North Carolina*, 4th ed.; for the 1791 statute, 530–31; and for the 1801 statute rectifying the original, 543. *Session Laws of North Carolina, 1817*, 18–19.

24. *State v. Boon*, 1802 N.C. LEXIS 2 (the case was actually tried in 1801). In response to this ruling the legislature quickly amended the law to clarify the crime against slaves, making no substantive change in its provisions or procedures.

25. *State v. Weaver*, 1798 N.C. LEXIS 28.

26. Ibid. For a different discussion of this case, see T. Morris, *Southern Slavery and the Law*, 161–81.

27. *State v. Thackam and Mayson*, 1 Bay, 358 (S.C., 1794); the decision was upheld in *State v. William Calder*, 2 McCord, 462 (S.C., 1823). *State v. Thomas Wimberly*, 3 McCord, 190 (S.C., 1825). The prosecution of violence against slaves as criminal matters in the local courts is discussed in chapters 1 and 4. For the 1740 statutes, see P. Wood, *Black Majority*, and Olwell, *Masters, Slaves, and Subjects*, 57–101.

28. *State v. Gee*, 1 Bay, 163 (S.C., Spring 1791). See also *State v. Welch*, 1 Bay, 172 (S.C., May 1791), in which the court affirmed the distinctive authority of masters and, by extension, overseers and others who were delegated that authority and then affirmed the defendant's conviction for manslaughter, a common law charge that was not explicitly named in the statutes and later became a point of contention.

29. The economic interests of the state elite, which extended across their state, national, and international boundaries, contextualize and explain these concerns; for two revealing examples, see the John Chesnutt Papers, LC, and the Levinus Clarkson Papers, LC. The South Carolina legislature's decision to consolidate the

appellate courts of law and equity was tied up in rivalries among judges in common law (or law) and equity. Henry William DeSaussure, a noted equity judge, found the entire debate and its outcome particularly insulting. Henry William DeSaussure to Timothy Ford, 18 December 1829, 11/131/28, Timothy Ford Papers, 1776–1830 (1027.03.01), SCHS. For similar conflicts in Virginia, see Huebner, *Southern Judicial Tradition*, 10–39.

30. Catterall, *Judicial Cases*, 2:271–314. Although Catterall's collection is not definitive, it has provided the starting point for many scholars of slave law. Historians have also interpreted the fines mandated by South Carolina statutes for criminal violence against slaves as evidence of slaves' position as property. The difference between punishments for whites and blacks was more complicated, however. In the colonial period, fines were the traditional punishment for criminal violence, while corporal punishment usually applied to property crimes. Those patterns persisted into the nineteenth century, when courts still punished a range of criminal violence, even white-on-white violence, with fines.

31. Quantity has been an issue in discussions about the relationship between appellate and local prosecutions, with the underlying point of contention being whether local courts were more protective of slaves' rights than otherwise thought. In his analysis of appellate decisions that protected slaves' interests, A. Nash, "A More Equitable Past?" suggests that the existence of those cases represent a large stash of undiscovered local cases. In *Southern Slavery and the Law*, T. Morris disagrees, characterizing the local record as "uninspiring" (181).

32. *State v. Boon*, 1802 N.C. LEXIS 2.

33. North Carolina, in particular, is noted for statutes that extended procedural rights to slaves. See A. Nash, "More Equitable Past?" and T. Morris, *Southern Slavery and the Law*, 209–48.

34. The difficulties, which are particularly evident in the scholarship on slave law, are summed up in the title of Walter Johnson's review essay, "Inconsistency, Contradiction, and Complete Confusion." In general, the literature continues to use rights as the standard to determine changes in slaves' status over time. See Fede, *People without Rights*; Flanigan, "Criminal Procedure"; Genovese, *Roll, Jordan, Roll*, 25–49; Hindus, *Prison and Plantation*, 125–61; T. Morris, *Southern Slavery and the Law*; A. Nash, "Negro Rights and Judicial Behavior"; Schwarz, *Twice Condemned*; Waldrep, *Roots of Disorder*, 15–58; and Tushnet, *American Law of Slavery*.

35. *State v. Reed*, 1823 N.C. LEXIS 37. *State v. Boon*, 1802 N.C. LEXIS 2.

36. *State v. Reed*, 1823 N.C. LEXIS 37. *State v. Boon*, 1802 N.C. LEXIS 2.

37. Huebner, *Southern Judicial Tradition*, 130–59. Ruffin's political positions are apparent in his published, collected correspondence; see Hamilton, *Papers of Thomas Ruffin*. For the group of lawyers, planters, and businessmen in Ruffin's circle, see G. O'Brien, *Legal Fraternity and the Making of a New South Community*.

38. See *State v. Mann*, 13 N.C. 263 (1829).

39. See *State v. Hoover,* 1839 N.C. LEXIS 92. See also *State v. Weaver,* 3 N.C. 77 (1798); *State v. Walker,* 4 N.C. 662 (1817); and *State v. Mann,* 13 N.C. 263 (1829). T. Morris, *Southern Slavery and the Law,* 174–79, offers an alternative interpretation of these cases. The racial ideology of elite white southerners, some of whom were certain that African Americans' racial makeup prevented them from feeling pain in the same way as whites, reinforced legal practice. E. Clark, "'Sacred Rights of the Weak.'"

40. O'Neall, *Negro Law of South Carolina,* 19. *State v. Thomas Wimberly,* 3 Mc-Cord, 190 (S.C., 1825).

41. *State v. Raines,* 3 McCord, 533 (S.C., May 1826).

42. *State v. Gaffney,* Rice, 431 (S.C., 1839); *State v. Fleming,* 2 Strob., 464 (S.C., 1848); and *State v. Motley et al.,* 7 Rich., 327 (S.C., 1854). See also O'Neall, *Negro Law of South Carolina,* 19. For a discussion of the cases, see T. Morris, *Southern Slavery and the Law,* 174–79.

43. *State v. Bowen,* 3 Strob., 574 (S.C., 1849). See also Cobb, *Law of Negro Slavery,* 84–96, 98–99.

44. *State v. Tackett,* 8 N.C. 210 (1820); and *State v. Hale,* 9 N.C. 582 (1823). The results of *State v. Raines,* 3 McCord, 315 (S.C., 1826), made it nearly impossible to secure a conviction against any white for killing a slave. But the court later allowed for more flexibility, including "undue correction" within "heat of passion," the 1821 statute. See *State v. Gaffney,* Rice, 431 (S.C., 1839); *State v. Fleming,* 2 Strob., 464 (S.C., 1848); and *State v. Motley et al.,* 7 Rich., 327 (S.C., 1854). See also Edwards, "Law, Domestic Violence, and the Limits of Patriarchal Authority."

45. For the North Carolina appellate court's record on divorce, see Bynum, *Unruly Women,* 68–75.

46. *Marville Scroggins v. Lucretia Scroggins,* 1832 N.C. LEXIS 97.

47. Ibid. Notably, Ruffin was forced to back off from this position in *Barden v. Barden,* 14 N.C. 538 (1832), a similar case involving miscegenation. Outraged by the circumstances and inclined to uphold the local court's decision, the other justices overruled Ruffin, who nonetheless made it clear that his position had not changed. See also *Long v. Long,* 1822 N.C. LEXIS 41; *Frederick H. Collier v. Lucretia W. Collier,* 1829 N.C. LEXIS 17; *Andrew Whittington v. Lucy Whittington,* 1836 N.C. LEXIS 40; *William B. Moss v. Nicey Moss,* 1841 N.C. LEXIS 50; *Rebecca J. Wood v. Lorenzo Wood,* 1845 N.C. LEXIS 176; *Nancy Harrison v. Nathaniel Harrison,* 1847 N.C. LEXIS 85; *Ruthey Ann Hansley v. Samuel G. Hansley,* 1849 N.C. LEXIS 153. Historians have tended to see *Scroggins* as exemplary of Ruffin's paternalism and his embrace of an organic view of marriage based in status rather than contract. See Bardaglio, *Reconstructing the Household,* 63–64, and Bynum, *Unruly Women,* 69–70.

48. *Marville Scroggins v. Lucretia Scroggins,* 1832 N.C. LEXIS 97.

49. *State v. Alvin Preslar,* 48 N.C. 421 (1856).

50. Indenture, George E. Badger and Mary Badger to Thomas P. Devereux, 25 December 1834; Deed of Conveyance, Thomas P. Devereux to George E. Badger, 12

November 1835; Mortgage Deed, George E. Badger and John C. Rogers, 3 July 1839; all in folder 2, George E. Badger Papers, #37-Z, SHC.

51. Charity Cain Mangum to Mary Cain Sutherland, 5 November 1834, folder 2, Mangum Family Papers, #483, SHC. Though signed in Charity's name, the hand-writing of the letter is the same as that in letters written by Willie P. Mangum in the 1840s. Indenture, Mary Cain Sutherland, Willie N. White, and William M. Green, 28 December 1839, folder 2, Mangum Family Papers, #483, SHC.

52. For North Carolina, see Bynum, *Unruly Women*, 59–87. For national patterns, see Salmon, *Women and the Law of Property*.

53. M. Beard, *Women as Force in History*. Other scholars have made similar ob-servations in different contexts. See Hurst, *Law and the Conditions of Freedom*, and P. Miller, *Life of the Mind in America*, 99–265.

54. *State v. Craton*, 1845 N.C. LEXIS 44; and *State v. Hussey*, 44 N.C. 124 (1852). See also Bynum, *Unruly Women*, 70. *State v. John*, 1848 N.C. LEXIS 81, moderated these principles somewhat, limiting the force that husbands could use against their wives' seducers; but this case also involved slaves, not whites. See Hartog, "Lawyer-ing, Husbands' Rights, and 'the Unwritten Law,'" for the broader recognition of a husband's right to use force to regain custody of his wife or in retaliation against a man who seduced her, particularly when caught in the act.

55. *State v. Roberts*, 8 N.C. 349 (1821). For similar dynamics, see Bynum, *Unruly Women*, and Stansell, *City of Women*.

56. In particular, see A. Nash, "More Equitable Past?" The same questions also underlie recent work on the treatment of slave defendants in rape cases. See Bar-daglio, "Rape and the Law in the Old South," and Sommerville, *Rape and Race*.

57. Genovese, *Roll, Jordan, Roll*, 25–49.

58. From 25 May 1809, William Dickinson Martin, Diary, SCL. For a similar ac-count, see Robert McCauley to John McCauley, 16 December 1819; Robert McCau-ley to John McCauley, 1 January 1820; both in Andrew McCauley Papers, #4059z, SHC.

59. Robert McCauley to John McCauley, 1 January 1820, Andrew McCauley Papers, #4059z, SHC. Quotation from Reeve, *Law of Baron and Femme*, 420. In this passage, Reeve is actually talking about a parent's disciplinary authority, but that power also extended to masters and servants; see 535.

60. *State v. Caesar*, 31 N.C. 391 (1849). Ruffin was dissenting from the majority opinion as stated by Justice Richmond Pearson, but his point was that the "rule" Pearson laid out in this instance was unnecessary because the common law already allowed for the resolution of such cases. *State v. Will*, 18 N.C. 121 (1834), although exceptional in many respects, also conforms to the general rule of self-defense as a "natural" reaction. The same logic shaped the adjudication of slave violence in South Carolina; see Edwards, "Law, Domestic Violence, and the Limits of Patriar-chal Authority."

61. *State v. Caesar*, 31 N.C. 391 (1849).

CHAPTER 8

1. Malone, *Public Life of Thomas Cooper*, and Freehling, *Prelude to Civil War*, 128–31. For a sample of Cooper's nullification propaganda, see Cooper, *Consolidation*; Cooper, *Two essays*; and Cooper's "Value of the Union" speech. Cooper was credited with exercising considerable editorial authority in the strongest states' rights newspaper, the *Columbia Telescope*, through his close ties to editor David J. McCord; see Malone, *Public Life of Thomas Cooper*, 326–36.

2. E. Green, *History of the University of South Carolina*, 34–43. Cooper, *Some Information Respecting America*; Cooper, *Supplement to Mr. Cooper's Letters on the Slave Trade*; Cooper, *Propositions Respecting the Foundations of Civil Government*; Cooper, *Practical Treatise on Dyeing, and Callicoe Printing*; Cooper, *Manual of Political Economy*. For the religious claims that his opponents found most troubling, see Cooper, *On the Connection between Geology and the Pentateuch*.

3. There was a nationwide wave of constitutional conventions in the 1830s, with common goals and similar results; states that did not have conventions accomplished the same ends through the legislative process. See F. Green, *Constitutional Development in the South Atlantic States*. For the racist rhetoric of Jacksonians, see Saxton, *Rise and Fall of the White Republic*.

4. The scholarship on South Carolina tends to use the state as a means of explaining the coming of the Civil War. See Banner, "Problem of South Carolina"; Freehling, *Prelude to Civil War*; Ford, *Origins of Southern Radicalism*; and Sinha, *Counter-Revolution of Slavery*.

5. For a similar perspective, although emphasizing economic rather than political development, see Coclanis, *Shadow of a Dream*. McCurry, *Masters of Small Worlds*, argues that the gendered basis of republicanism — with its simultaneous emphasis on the independence of white men and dependence of everyone else — explains the state's distinctiveness from and its connection to national political currents.

6. For the Second Party System, see McCormick, *Second American Party System*, and Wilentz, *Rise of American Democracy*.

7. Coclanis, *Shadow of a Dream*, 111–58; Freehling, *Prelude to Civil War*, 25–48, 126–33, 136–44; and Ford, *Origins of Southern Radicalism*, 6–19, 99–141.

8. Freehling, *Prelude to Civil War*, esp. 260–97. For nullification as a crisis of national party politics, see Ellis, *Union at Risk*; Peterson, *Olive Branch and Sword*; Schlesinger, *Age of Jackson*; and Wilentz, *Rise of American Democracy*, 374–89.

9. The scholarship emphasizes common political ground between nullifiers and Unionists, many of whom opposed the tariff and embraced milder forms of states' rights as well as supporting centralized visions of state government. See Freehling, *Prelude to Civil War*, 241–44; Ford, *Origins of Southern Radicalism*, 145–82; and Sinha, *Counter-Revolution of Slavery*, 33–61. Those ties are also evident in the personal papers of political leaders. The correspondents of nullifier Waddy Thompson included Unionists Hugh Legaré and James Louis Petigru; Thompson also wrote

a laudatory biography of Unionist James Louis Petigru; see Waddy Thompson Papers, LC, and Waddy Thompson Papers, SCL. See Edward Frost Papers, LC, for an attempt to navigate the polarized politics of the time.

10. For the organization of nullifiers, see Freehling, *Prelude to Civil War*, 149–52, 219–59; Ford, *Origins of Southern Radicalism*, 130–41; McCurry, *Masters of Small Worlds*, 265–76; Sinha, *Counter-Revolution of Slavery*, 36–44; and Stewart, "'Great Talking and Eating Machine.'" Revealing also are the James Henry Hammond Papers, LC, particularly the correspondence from 1830; for examples and further discussion, see note 33.

11. Quoted in Freehling, *Prelude to Civil War*, 96–97; from *Southern Patriot*, 9 July 1830. See also Freehling, *Nullification Era*, 1–9; Freehling, *Prelude to Civil War*, 89–133; and Ford, *Origins of Southern Radicalism*, 103–14. After the War of 1812, Calhoun and other state representatives backed internal improvements and commercial development as part of an agenda of national economic growth. The national connections of leading nullifiers are evident in their papers and those of their families, which focus on national political issues and posts. See, for instance, William Lowndes Papers, LC; Thomas Pinckney Papers, LC; and Charles Cotesworth Pinckney Papers, SCL.

12. Quoted in E. Green, *History of the University of South Carolina*, 10. For state-building policies, see Freehling, *Prelude to Civil War*, 89–133; Klein, *Unification of a Slave State*, 239–46; and Ford, *Origins of Southern Radicalism*, 15–19, 105–6.

13. Quotations from Freehling, *Prelude to Civil War*, 145, and *Nullification Era*, 105; original in George McDuffie, *Speech ... at ... Charleston May 19, 1831* (Charleston, S.C., 1831). As late as 1827, McDuffie still opposed nullification, a position that made him a political target for nullifiers like Thomas Cooper. McDuffie was married to Mary Rebecca Singleton, Marion Singleton Deveaux's older half-sister, although Mary died after the birth of their first daughter, Mary McDuffie, who later married Wade Hampton.

14. Quoted in Freehling, *Nullification Era*, 6; original in McDuffie, *National and State Rights*. For charges of Jacobinism, see James L. Petigru to Hugh S. Legaré, 29 October 1832; James L. Petigru to Hugh S. Legaré, 15 July 1833; both in James Louis Petigru Papers, SCL. For a response, see Hamilton, *Introductory Address of Governor Hamilton*. For the centralization of the state legal system and Hayne's support thereof, see Senese, "Building the Pyramid." Nullifiers made a point of upholding the concept of judicial authority in their critique of the federal courts; see Turnbull, *Crisis*.

15. For the North Carolina legislature's response, see *Raleigh Register*, 14 December 1832, and 11 January 1833. See also H. Watson, *Jacksonian Politics and Community Conflict*, 153–54, 177. For Williams, see *Carolina Watchman*, 2 March 1833. Address Opposing Nullification, William Lenoir's Speeches, Writings, and Notes [1831], folder 243, subser. 2.2.1, Lenoir Family Papers, #426, SHC. William Gaston to Hannah Manly, 31 December 1832, box 4, folder 54, William Gaston Papers, #272, SHC.

16. For an account of the conflict, see Freehling, *Prelude to Civil War*, 309–21.

17. For the cases declaring the test oath unconstitutional, see *The State ex relatione Ed. M'Cready v. B. F. Hunt, Col. 16th Regt. So. Ca. Militia* and *The State ex relatione James M'Daniel v. Thos. M'Meekin, Brig. Gen. 6th Brigade So. Ca. Militia*, 1834 WL 1462 (S.C. App.). For coverage of the conflict, see *Charleston Mercury*, particularly November and December 1834. See also Freehling, *Prelude to Civil War*, 319–21.

18. Quotations from James L. Petigru to Hugh S. Legaré, 29 November 1834, James Louis Petigru Papers, SCL; Abram Blanding to Henry Alexander DeSaussure, 18 December 1834, 11/121/11, Henry William DeSaussure Papers, 1795–1838 (1022.02.02), SCHS; and *Charleston Mercury*, 11 December 1834. Legaré repeated the information, including that phrase, in his correspondence. See Hugh S. Legaré to Alfred Huger, 15 December 1834, Hugh Swinton Legaré Papers, SCL. For the compromise, see Carson, *Life Letters and Speeches of James Louis Petigru*, 157–71; and *Charleston Mercury*, 27 November 1834, and 5, 6, 8, 11, 13, 18, 24 December 1834. See also Freehling, *Prelude to Civil War*, 319–20.

19. For Petigru's position on the 1834 oath, see James L. Petigru to Hugh S. Legaré, 29 November 1834, James Louis Petigru Papers, SCL; Freehling, *Prelude to Civil War*, 319–20. For his stance on loyalty to the state, see Carson, *Life, Letters, and Speeches of James Louis Petigru*, 130–37, 142–53; and Freehling, *Prelude to Civil War*, 314–15. The connections forged through legal education and professional practice among the state-level elites in both South Carolina and North Carolina are evident in their correspondence and personal papers. Young men studied in the law offices of their fathers' friends. Their connections then sustained their legal practices, which focused on the various economic interests of the states' elite families. Wealthy planters who had no legal training still needed lawyers to conduct their affairs.

20. For McCord's speech, see *Charleston Mercury*, 8 December 1835. For the commentary on it, see *Charleston Mercury*, 9 December 1835. The editor of the *Charleston Mercury*, which was aligned with the Nullification Party, made it clear that the main concern was with punishing the Unionist appellate justice and limiting the political influence of Unionism on the bench. See, for instance, *Charleston Mercury*, 30 November 1835 and 17 December 1835. The issue acquired new political overtones in 1835, after the appeals court ruled against states' rights again, upholding a congressional act that allowed state courts to prosecute anyone interfering with the U.S. post. Anger at that decision translated into opposition to the judges and the appellate court, although it was expressed as hostility toward the court system more generally.

21. *Charleston Mercury*, 8 December 1835 and 9 December 1835.

22. *Charleston Mercury*, 10 December 1835 and 4 December 1835.

23. For debate about the judiciary bill, see *Charleston Mercury*, 30 November; and 3, 4, 7, 8, 9, 10, 14, 17, 21, 22, 23, 24 December 1835. See also Freehling, *Prelude to*

Civil War, 260–339; Ford, *Origins of Southern Radicalism*, 119–53; and Senese, "Building the Pyramid," 365–69.

24. *Charleston Mercury*, 27 November 1834.

25. *Charleston Mercury*, 10 December 1834.

26. The *Charleston Mercury*, which rarely withheld commentary on issues of interest to its partisan states' rights readers, reprinted the Hayne proposal and reported the legislature's passage of the resulting resolution without comment: 10, 18, and 19 December 1834. For Cooper's appointment and McCord's subsequent assumption of the project, see Malone, *Public Life of Thomas Cooper*, 370–73. For earlier calls for such a project, see the governors' messages in *Charleston Courier*, 30 November 1822 and 28 November 1826. Hayne was referring to proposals to create a code. See T. Grimké, *Oration*.

27. Counihan, "The North Carolina Constitutional Convention of 1835." *Proceedings and Debates of the Convention of North Carolina*, 163–78, 366–68.

28. William Gaston to Robert Moore, 16 August 1835, folder 70, box 5, William Gaston Papers, #272, SHC. *Proceedings and Debates of the Convention of North Carolina*, 422–23 (for amendment), 377–82 (for debate). Counihan, "North Carolina Constitutional Convention of 1835," 360.

29. William Gaston to Robert Moore, 16 August 1835, folder 70, box 5, William Gaston Papers, #272, SHC. *Proceedings and Debates of the Convention of North Carolina*. Counihan, "North Carolina Constitutional Convention of 1835," 359.

30. *Raleigh Register*, 26 November 1833. For the revised statutes, see Nash, Iredell, and Battle, *Revised Statutes of North Carolina, 1836–37*.

31. *Raleigh Register*, 24 November 1835.

32. *Charleston Mercury*, 11 September 1830; *Proceedings and Debates of the Convention of North Carolina*, 65.

33. The volume of published literature relating to nullification in South Carolina is astounding; the quantity of political pamphlets and like materials in other states pales in comparison. The studied, constructed nature of the campaign is particularly evident in the correspondence of James Henry Hammond, who wrote extensively on behalf of nullification and edited the newspaper the *Southern Times*. See, for instance, Robert Y. Hayne to James Henry Hammond, 25 February 1830; Eldred Simkins to James Henry Hammond, 6 March 1830; William D. Martin to James Henry Hammond, 10 March 1830; F. N. Pickens to James Henry Hammond, 13 March 1830; Robert Y. Hayne to James Henry Hammond, 29 March 1830; A. H. Pemberton to James Henry Hammond, 1 April 1830; James D. Cork to James Henry Hammond, 11 May 1830; F. N. Pickens to James Henry Hammond, 26 June 1830; Syd P. Saxon to James Henry Hammond, 6 July 1830; J. M. Joby to James Henry Hammond, 6 July 1830; Bird M. Pearson to James Henry Hammond, 13 July 1830; F. M. Pickens to James Henry Hammond, 14 July 1830; F. M. Pickens to James Henry Hammond, 21 July 1830; D. Wardlaw to James Henry Hammond, 24 July 1830; Benjamin F. Whitmer to James Henry Hammond, 11 September 1830; Bird M.

Pearson to James Henry Hammond, 1 October 1830; all in James Henry Hammond Papers, LC. Historians have emphasized the republican strains of nullification, South Carolina politics, and southern political culture more generally. For South Carolina, see Ford, *Origins of Southern Radicalism*, and McCurry, *Masters of Small Worlds*. For the South, see M. Holt, *Political Crisis of the 1850s*.

34. *Charleston Mercury*, 25 June 1830; Turnbull, *Crisis*. For a concise statement of this argument, which was common in the nullification literature, see "Report of the Committee of Twenty-One," in *Report, Ordinance, and Addresses of the Convention of the People of South Carolina*, 3–21.

35. McCurry, *Masters of Small Worlds*, esp. 239–76.

36. *Charleston Mercury*, 5 and 25 June 1830. The language is duplicated in other statements; nullification literature routinely recycled successful stock phrases.

37. *Appeal to the People on the Question What Shall We Do Next*, 6.

38. Ibid., 10; *Charleston Mercury*, 5 June 1830.

39. For examples, see *Charleston Mercury*, 17 June 1830; 18 September 1830; 1, 2, and 13 October 1835; 26 November 1835; and 19 December 1835. See also Cooper, untitled ("Value of the Union"); Turnbull, *Crisis*. For the connection between nullification and proslavery ideology, see Freehling, *Prelude to Civil War*, esp. 49–86, 327–39; McCurry, *Masters of Small Worlds*, esp. 208–38; and Sinha, *Counter-Revolution of Slavery*, 33–61.

40. Cooper, *Statutes at Large of South Carolina*, 1:xii. Cooper also suggested separate sections on the militia and the courts—both of which had played key roles during nullification—as well as internal improvements, the city of Charleston, the Incorporated Societies, topics about which there had been significant legislation, but that were more like private acts, in that they often had specific, not statewide, application. The legislature approved his recommendation. Volume 7, published in 1840, when David J. McCord took over the series, contains topical groups of all the laws in each of four areas: Slaves, Charleston, the Courts, and Rivers. Either McCord or the legislature amended Cooper's call for a section on the "coloured population" to one on "slaves." For legal restrictions on slaves in this period, see Freehling, *Prelude to Civil War*, 334–36; T. Morris, *Southern Slavery and the Law*, 337–53. Abolitionists were sending literature south; the fact that other states and the federal government also acted decisively to stop its circulation suggests the broader reach of these political currents. Wyatt-Brown, "Abolitionists' Postal Campaign of 1835"; John, *Spreading the News*, 257–83; and Wilentz, *Rise of American Democracy*, 340, 410–12.

41. *Appeal to the People on the Question What Shall We Do Next*, 6; McDuffie quoted in Freehling, *Nullification Era*, 119 (original in McDuffie, *Speech . . . at . . . Charleston May 19, 1831*); and Freehling, *Prelude to Civil War*, 264 (original in *Pendleton Messenger*, 26 December 1832). For other examples of the personification of the state, see *Catechism on the Tariff, for the Use of Plain People of Common Sense*; McCurry, *Masters of Small Worlds*, 260–61.

42. *Proceedings and Debates of the Convention of North Carolina*, 70 (for quota-

tion), 126–62 (for debates on representation). Counihan, "North Carolina Constitutional Convention of 1835." See also H. Watson, *Jacksonian Politics and Community Conflict*, 198–202. Pratt, "Struggle for Judicial Independence," notes that opposition to North Carolina's appellate court, the symbol of legal centralization, dissipated in the 1830s, after the 1835 constitutional convention.

43. William Gaston to Robert Moore, 16 August 1835, folder 70, box 5, William Gaston Papers, #272, SHC. See *Proceedings and Debates of the Convention of North Carolina*, 332–40, for debate on the popular election of the governor.

44. *Proceedings and Debates of the Convention of North Carolina*, 60–81, 351–58. James W. Bryan made a strong link between the disfranchisement of free blacks and the state's mission to protect freemen's rights (62–69).

45. *Proceedings and Debates of the Convention of North Carolina*, 70, 71.

46. Ibid., 20–21.

47. Quoted in McCurry, *Masters of Small Worlds*, 259; original in *Charleston Mercury*, 18 September 1830.

48. *Charleston Mercury*, 13 December 1834.

49. Tomlins, *Law, Labor, and Ideology*. The literature on the post-emancipation period is particularly critical of the inequalities produced by narrow visions of rights. See Fields, *Slavery and Freedom on the Middle Ground*; Forbath, "Ambiguities of Free Labor"; T. Holt, *Problem of Freedom*; Scully, *Liberating the Family?*; Scott, *Slave Emancipation in Cuba*; and Stanley, *From Bondage to Contract*.

CONCLUSION

1. *State v. B. D. Armstrong*, 1870, Criminal Action Papers, Edgecombe County, NCDAH; the records do not reveal the outcome of the case. There is no evidence in the court records to suggest why Mitchell was so angry. She may have been involved in the protests against white landowners that African Americans organized in Edgecombe County during this period. Or she may have acted on her own, after a particularly difficult day. For similar cases, see *State v. Lazina Sherond*, 1868; *State v. Nero Jones alias John Jones, 1881*; both in Criminal Action Papers, Edgecombe County, NCDAH. For political action in Edgecombe County and the surrounding area, see Hinton, *Politics of Agricultural Labor*. For further discussion of Maria Mitchell's case, see Edwards, "Captives of Wilmington."

2. Accounts focusing on the development of the state's courts usually note this point. See, for instance, Adams, "Evolution of Law in North Carolina"; McIntosh, "Jurisdiction of the North Carolina Supreme Court"; Orth, "North Carolina Constitutional History"; and Senese, "Building the Pyramid."

3. Willrich, *City of Courts*. See also Dorr, *White Women, Rape, and the Power of Race*, and K. Shapiro, *New South Rebellion*, 58–63.

4. The analysis in the conclusion draws on two previously published pieces: Edwards, "Status without Rights," and Edwards, "Civil War and Reconstruction."

5. The resulting documentary record, which is voluminous at the federal, state, and local levels, has inspired a new generation of scholarship that explores how former slaves used the legal system to express and pursue their goals as free people. See chapter 3, note 30.

6. The local court records used for this study reveal only a few references to rights in the period between 1787 and 1840. In Granville County and Edgecombe County, North Carolina, references to rights were more common in the 1860s, 1870s, and 1880s, but were still relatively rare and tended to involve property. In addition to the cases cited in note 1 above, see also, for instance, *Jane Williams v. Margaret Hughie*, 1870, and *State v. Robert Kirkland*, 1872; both in Criminal Action Papers, Granville County, NCDAH. I do not know if North and South Carolinians used rights discourse more extensively in the 1840s and 1850s, because I did not extend my research into that period; but it seems unlikely, given the records from the post–Civil War era. Moreover, the system maintained integrity, apart from state law, which would shape how such claims were received.

7. For Denmark Vesey and the aftermath, see Egerton, *He Shall Go Out Free*; Freehling, *Prelude to Civil War*, 53–65; McInnis, *Politics of Taste*, 66–89; Pearson, *Designs against Charleston*; M. Johnson, "Denmark Vesey and His Co-Conspirators"; and Robertson, *Denmark Vesey*. Michael P. Johnson has critiqued Pearson's, Egerton's, and Robertson's readings of the records, arguing—among other things—that the conspiracy may have been more a product of white Charlestonians' imaginations than an actual plot. Nonetheless, the documentary record, however presented or interpreted, does underscore white Charlestonians' fears and their efforts to regulate slavery more effectively within the city.

8. For the circulation of broader political currents, including rights discourse, among slaves, even before the Civil War, see Camp, *Closer to Freedom*, 93–116; M. Johnson, "Denmark Vesey and His Co-Conspirators"; Hahn, *Nation under Our Feet*; Link, *Roots of Secession*; Reidy, *From Slavery to Agrarian Capitalism*; and H. Williams, *Self-Taught*.

9. The literature emphasizes that freedpeople valued collective goals that were often at odds with the liberal agenda of many Republicans. Perhaps the most influential statements of this view are the introductory essays in Berlin et al., *Black Military Experience*; *The Destruction of Slavery*; and *Wartime Genesis of Free Labor: The Lower South*. See also Bercaw, *Gendered Freedoms*; Edwards, *Gendered Strife and Confusion*; Fields, *Slavery and Freedom on the Middle Ground*; Foner, *Nothing But Freedom*; Frankel, *Freedom's Women*; Hahn, *Nation under Our Feet*; T. Holt, *Black over White*; Penningroth, *Claims of Kinfolk*; Reidy, *From Slavery to Agrarian Capitalism*; Rodrigue, *Reconstruction in the Cane Fields*; Saville, *Work of Reconstruction*; and Schwalm, *Hard Fight for We*.

10. The best overview of this narrative is Foner, *Reconstruction*. For scholarship that deals with questions about the balance between federal and state power, see Belz, *Abraham Lincoln, Constitutionalism, and Equal Rights*; Benedict, *Compromise*

of Principle; Bensel, *Yankee Leviathan*; Cox and Cox, *Politics, Principle, and Prejudice*; Hyman, *More Perfect Union*; Kyvig, *Explicit and Authentic Acts*; W. Nelson, *Fourteenth Amendment*; and Paludan, *Covenant with Death*. While focusing on the same issues, recent work has rooted legal and political debates in social context, revealing new complexities and contingencies. See, for instance, Vorenberg, *Final Freedom*.

11. The classic work on women's efforts for inclusion in the Fourteenth Amendment, which emphasizes the reformers' focus on civil and political rights and the subsequent split in the movement along racial lines, is DuBois, *Feminism and Suffrage*. See also Newman, *White Women's Rights*. For a different interpretation that emphasizes the broader vision of some women activists, which included economic issues and racial justice within the rubric of rights, see Faulkner, *Women's Radical Reconstruction*.

12. See Cott, *Public Vows*; Dailey, *Before Jim Crow*; Edwards, *Gendered Strife and Confusion*; Bercaw, *Gendered Freedoms*; Stanley, "Conjugal Bonds and Wage Labor"; and Stanley, *From Bondage to Contract*.

13. For particularly good analyses of the gendered implications of rights, see Boris, *Home to Work*; Cott, *Public Vows*; Kerber, *No Constitutional Right to Be Ladies*; Kessler-Harris, *Woman's Wage*; Kessler-Harris, *In Pursuit of Equity*; and Stanley, *From Bondage to Contract*.

14. Tomlins, *Law, Labor, and Ideology*; Stanley, "Beggars Can't Be Choosers" and *From Bondage to Contract*. Also see Eric Foner, *Free Soil, Free Labor, Free Men*, for the ways that free labor ideology did not necessarily include propertyless workers. For the relationship between free labor ideology and race, see T. Holt, "'An Empire over the Mind'"; and Richardson, *Death of Reconstruction*. For a different perspective that emphasizes the liberalization of labor arrangements, see Steinfeld, *Invention of Free Labor*.

15. Montgomery, *Beyond Equality*. Recent work in labor history has highlighted the inequalities inherent within the concept of free labor before and after the Civil War. The emphasis on the limitations of laborers' legal rights also suggests the parallels between the legal status of working-class men and other subordinated groups, namely African Americans and women. See Forbath, "Ambiguities of Free Labor"; Hahamovitch, *Fruits of Their Labor*; Lichtenstein, *Twice the Work of Free Labor*; Montgomery, *Citizen Worker*; Peck, *Reinventing Free Labor*; and Steinfeld, *Coercion, Contract, and Free Labor*.

16. Woodman, *New South, New Law*. See also Edwards, "Problem of Dependency"; Reidy, *From Slavery to Agrarian Capitalism*.

17. See note 16.

Bibliography

MANUSCRIPTS

Boston, Mass.
    Baker Library, Graduate School of Business Administration, Harvard
        University
    R. G. Dun and Company Collection
Chapel Hill, N.C.
    Southern Historical Collection, University of North Carolina
        George E. Badger Papers, #37-Z
        Bear Creek Church Records, #M-3124
        Bullock and Hamilton Family Papers, #101
        Hutchins Gordon Burton Papers, #110
        Burwell Family Papers, #112
        Cameron Family Papers, #133
        Richard Caswell Papers, #145
        Fall Creek Baptist Church Records, Chatham County, #4418
        Peter Gaillard Plantation Records, #2435
        William Gaston Papers, #272
        John Berkeley Grimball Diary, #970
        Peter Wilson Hairston Papers, #229
        James Hogg Papers, #341
        John U. Kirkland Account Books, vol. 1, #405
        Lenoir Family Papers, #426
        Mangum Family Papers, #483
        Matrimony Creek Baptist Church, Records, Rockingham County, #1825
        Andrew McCauley Papers, #4059z
        Archibald D. Murphey Papers, #533
        David Schenck Papers, #652
        Silver Creek Primitive Baptist Association Minutes, Burke and Caldwell
            Counties, #3473
        Robert Strange Papers, #M-1296
        Wardens of the Poor, Records, Person County
        William D. Valentine Diaries, #2148
Charleston, S.C.
    South Carolina Historical Society
        Cheves, Langdon, 1848–1939. Historical and Genealogical Research Papers,
            1860–ca. 1934 (1167.01.01)

Cheves, Langdon, 1776–1857. Legal Papers, 1795–1836 (1166.01.03)

Cheves, Langdon, 1776–1857. Personal and Business Papers, 1777–1861 (1166.01.01)

DeSaussure, Henry William, 1763–1839. Henry William DeSaussure Papers, 1795–1838 (1022.02.02)

Drayton, William. Legal Notebook, 1784 (53–1, 34/0632)

Drayton, William, 1732–90. Remarks in a Tour Through the Back Country of the State of South Carolina, 1784–89 (34/630)

Ford, Timothy, 1762–1830. Timothy Ford Papers, 1776–1830 (1027.03.01)

Grimké family. Grimké Family Papers, 1761–1866 (1040.00)

Jefferson, Thomas, 1743–1826. Letter: Monticello, to Judge Johnson, Charleston, S.C., 12 June 1823 (43/521)

McCord, Louisa Susanna Cheves, 1810–1879. Notes and Letters on Langdon Cheves, ca. 1876 (1167.03.03)

Nott, Abraham, 1768–1830. Letter: Columbia, [S.C.], to Judge Johnston, Charleston, [S.C.], 15 March 1830 (43/524)

Phillips, John, fl. 1839. Book of Precedents and Other Legal Documents, ca. 1788–1839 (34/400)

Smith, Oliver M. Docket Book of Oliver M. Smith, 1834–1839 (34/305)

Smith, William Loughton, 1758–1812. William Loughton Smith Papers, 1774–1834 (1119.00)

Washington, George, 1732–1799. Letters to Thomas Pinckney, 1789–1792 (43/67)

Columbia, S.C.

South Carolina Department of Archives and History

Anderson/Pendleton District

County and Intermediate Court, Indictments, Pendleton District

County and Intermediate Court, Journals, Pendleton District

County and Intermediate Court, Peace Bonds, Pendleton District

Court of Common Pleas, Pleadings and Judgments, Pendleton District

Court of General Sessions, Coroner's Inquisitions, Anderson County

Court of General Sessions, Coroner's Inquisitions, Pendleton District

Court of General Sessions, Indictments, Anderson County

Court of General Sessions, Indictments, Pendleton District

Court of General Sessions, Peace Bonds, Anderson County

Court of General Sessions, Peace Bonds, Pendleton District

Court of Magistrates and Freeholders, Trial Papers, Anderson County/ Pendleton District

Court of Magistrates and Freeholders, Vagrancy Trials, Anderson District

Court of Magistrates and Freeholders, Vagrancy Trials, Pendleton District

Kershaw District

County and Intermediate Court, Common Pleas Docket

County and Intermediate Court, Indictments
County and Intermediate Court, Sessions Docket
Court of General Sessions, Coroner's Inquisitions
Court of General Sessions, Indictments
Court of General Sessions, Journal
Court of Magistrates and Freeholders, Trial Papers
Court of Magistrates and Freeholders, Vagrancy Trials
Will Transcripts
Other
Court of Magistrates and Freeholders, Vagrancy Trials, Camden District
Court of Magistrates and Freeholders, Vagrancy Trials, Spartanburg
County
Equity Court Records, Sumter District
General Assembly Records
South Caroliniana Library, University of South Carolina
Anonymous, Law Notebook, Charleston, 1796
Aveleigh Presbyterian Church, Records, Newberry County
Bennettsville Presbyterian Church, Records, Marlboro County
Bethabara Baptist Church, Records, Laurens County
Bethel Baptist Church, Records, Newberry County
Bethesda Baptist Church (Primitive), Church Book, Kershaw District
Bethesda Presbyterian Church, Records, Camden, Kershaw County
Big Creek Baptist Church, Records, Williamston, Anderson County
Black Creek Primitive Baptist Church, Church Book, Beaufort County
William Blanding Papers
George Bowie, Lawyer's Precedent Book, 1796
Aedanus Burke Papers
Cashaway Baptist Church, Record Book, Darlington [Craven] County
James Chesnut Papers
Henry William DeSaussure Papers
Henry William DeSaussure and Timothy Ford, Record Book, 1786–92
John Drayton Papers
First Baptist Church, Minutes, Barnwell County
First Columbia Baptist Church, Records, Richland County
First Presbyterian Church, Records, Columbia, Richland County
Flint Hill Baptist Church, Records, York County
John Faucheraud Grimké Papers
William Francis Baker Haynsworth Papers
Holy Cross Protestant Episcopal Church, Records, Claremont Parish,
Statesburg, Sumter County
Kershaw County, Grand Jury Presentments
Hugh Swinton Legaré Papers

William Dickinson Martin Diary
Mechanicsville Baptist Church, Records, Darlington County
Methodist Church, Records, Darlington County and Florence County,
    Darlington Circuit
Methodist Church, Records, Florence County, Lynch's Creek Circuit
Methodist Church, Records, Horry County, Waccamaw Circuit and
    Conwayborough Circuit
John Wrought Mitchell, Receipt Book, 1817–35
Mountain Creek Baptist Church (formerly Bethesda), Minutes, Anderson
    County
Mount Aron Baptist Church, Church Book, Allendale County
Neal's Creek Baptist Church, Journal, Anderson County
Cassie Nicholes Papers
John Belton O'Neall Papers
James Louis Petigru Papers
Charles Cotesworth Pinckney Papers
Richard Singleton Papers
Singleton Family Papers
Singleton-Deveaux Papers
Smyrna, Great Pee Dee, and Blenheim Presbyterian Church, Church Book,
    Marlboro County
South Carolina Attorney General Papers
St. Phillips Protestant Episcopal Church, Records, Charleston County
Swift Creek Baptist Church, Church Book, Kershaw District
Taylor Family Papers
Thomas Memorial Baptist Church, Church Book, Marlboro County,
    Bennettsville
Waddy Thompson Papers
Thomas Waties Papers
William Swamp Baptist Church, Records, Orangeburg County
Durham, N.C.
Special Collections, Perkins Library, Duke University
J. Eli Gregg Papers
Grimké Family Papers
John W. Harris Papers
Ralph Izard Papers
Hugh Swinton Legaré Papers
Thomas Legaré Papers
George McDuffie Papers
Mary Singleton McDuffie Papers
Stephen Decatur Miller Papers
John Rutledge Papers

Richard Singleton Papers

Augustin L. Taveau Papers

Raleigh, N.C.

North Carolina Department of Archives and History

Abbott's Creek Primitive Baptist Church, Minutes, Davidson County

Brassfield Baptist Church, History and Minutes, Creedmore, Granville County

Bush Arbor Primitive Baptist Church, Minutes, Anderson Township, Caswell County

Cane Creek Baptist Church, Minutes and Membership Roll, Orange County

Criminal Action Papers, Chowan County

Criminal Action Papers, Granville County

Criminal Action Papers, Orange County

Criminal Actions Concerning Slaves and Free Persons of Color, Chowan County

Criminal Actions Concerning Slaves and Free Persons of Color, Granville County

Criminal Actions Concerning Slaves and Free Persons of Color, Orange County

Divorce Records, Granville County

Divorce Records, Haywood County

Divorce Records, Randolph County

General Assembly, Sessions Records

Governors' Letter Books

Governors' Papers

Lickfork Primitive Baptist Church, Minutes, Rockingham County

Methodist Church, Records, Wilkes Circuit, North Wilkesboro District, Western Carolina Conference

Mt. Herman Baptist Church, Register and Minutes, Orange County

Mt. Zion Christian Church, Minutes, Orange County

New Hope Baptist Church, Minutes, Purleer, Wilkes County

Oxford Presbyterian Church, Session Minutes, Oxford, Granville County

Providence Presbyterian Church, Session Minutes, Providence, Granville County

Red Banks Primitive Baptist Church, Minutes, Pitt County

Spring Grove Presbyterian Church, Session Book, Granville County

State Supreme Court, Original Records

Tar River Primitive Baptist Church, Records, Granville County

Three Forks Baptist Church, Minutes, Wilkes County

Tosneot Baptist Church, Minute Book, Edgecombe County

Wardens of the Poor, Minutes and Accounts, Ashe County

Wardens of the Poor, Minutes, Bertie County
Wardens of the Poor, Minutes, Carteret County
Wardens of the Poor, Minutes, Craven County
Wardens of the Poor, Records, Granville County
Wardens of the Poor, Minutes, Lincoln County
Wheeley's Primitive Baptist Church, Session Minutes and Roll Book,
    Roxboro, Person County
Washington, D.C.
    Manuscript Division, Library of Congress
        John Chesnut Papers
        Levinus Clarkson Papers
        Richard K. Crallé Papers
        Edward Frost Papers
        James Henry Hammond Papers
        George Frederick Holmes Papers
        William Lowndes Papers
        Thomas Pinckney Papers
        Singleton Family Papers
        Waddy Thompson Papers

NEWSPAPERS AND PERIODICALS

American Weekly (Fayetteville, N.C.)
Camden Journal (S.C.)
Carolina Federal Republican (New Bern, N.C.)
Carolina Gazette (Charleston, S.C.)
Carolina Law Journal (Charleston, S.C.)
Carolina Watchman (Salisbury, N.C.)
Charleston Courier (S.C.)
Charleston Mercury (S.C.)
City Gazette and Daily Advertiser (Raleigh, N.C.)
Edenton Gazette (N.C.)
Fayetteville Gazette Weekly (N.C.)
Halifax Weekly (N.C.)
Herald of the Times (Elizabeth City, N.C.)
Morning Herald (New Bern, N.C.)
Mountaineer (Greenville, S.C.)
New Bern Spectator (N.C.)
North Carolina Chronicle (Fayetteville, N.C.)
North Carolina Intelligencer (Fayetteville, N.C.)
North Carolina Journal (Fayetteville, N.C.)
North Carolina Mercury (Salisbury, N.C.)

Raleigh Register (N.C.)

Republican Weekly (Washington, N.C.)

South-Carolina State Gazette and Columbia Advertiser (S.C.)

South-Carolina State-Gazette, and Timothy and Mason's Daily Advertiser (Charleston, S.C.)

Southern Quarterly Review

Southern Times and State Gazette (Columbia, S.C.)

State Gazette of North Carolina (Fayetteville, N.C.)

State Gazette of South Carolina (Charleston, S.C.)

Tarborough Free Press (N.C.)

Tarborough Press (N.C.)

True Republican and Newbern Weekly Advertiser (New Bern, N.C.)

Western Carolinian (Salisbury, N.C.)

Yadkin and Catawba Journal (N.C.)

PUBLISHED PRIMARY SOURCES

An Appeal to the People on the Question What Shall We Do Next: Political Tract, No. 12, July 1, 1832. Columbia: The Free Trade and State Rights Association, 1832.

Bay, Elihu Hall. *Reports of Cases Argued and Determined in the Superior Courts of Law, in the State of South Carolina, Since the Revolution.* 2 vols. Charleston, S.C.: Elliott & Burd, 1798.

Blackstone, William. *Commentaries on the Laws of England.* 4 vols. London, 1765–69; reprint, Chicago: University of Chicago Press, 1979.

Boyd, William K. *Some Eighteenth Century Tracts Concerning North Carolina.* Raleigh, N.C.: Edwards and Broughton, 1927.

Brevard, Joseph. *An Alphabetical Digest of the Public Statute Law of South-Carolina.* 3 vols. Charleston, S.C.: J. Hoff, 1814.

————. *Reports of Judicial Decisions in the State of South Carolina, from 1793 to 1816.* 3 vols. Charleston, S.C.: W. Riley, 1839–40.

Butler, Lindley S., ed. *The Papers of David Settle Reid.* 2 vols. Raleigh, N.C.: Division of Archives and History, 1993.

Cameron, Duncan, and William Norwood. *Reports of Cases Ruled and Determined by the Court of Conference of North Carolina.* Raleigh, N.C.: J. Gales, 1805.

Carson, James Petigru. *Life, Letters, and Speeches of James Louis Petigru: The Union Man of South Carolina.* Washington, D.C.: W. H. Lowdermilk, 1920.

A Catechism on the Tariff, for the Use of Plain People of Common Sense. Charleston, S.C.: The State Rights and Free Trade Association, 1831.

Catterall, Helen Tunnicliff. *Judicial Cases Concerning American Slavery and the Negro.* 5 vols. Washington, D.C.: Carnegie Institute of Washington, 1926–37.

Clark, Walter, ed. *The State Records of North Carolina.* 16 vols. Goldsboro, N.C., 1904.

Cobb, Thomas Reade Roots. *An Inquiry into the Law of Negro Slavery in the United States of America.* Philadelphia: T. & J. W. Johnson; Savannah: W. T. Williams, 1858.

Cooper, Thomas. *Consolidation, An Account of Parties in the United States from the Convention of 1787, to the Present Period.* 2 vols. Columbia, S.C.: Printed by Black & Sweeney, 1824–34.

———. *A Manual of Political Economy.* Washington, D.C.: D. Green, 1833.

———. *On the Connection between Geology and the Pentateuch: In a Letter to Professor Silliman, from Thomas Cooper, M.D.: To Which is Added the Defence of Dr. Cooper Before the Trustees of the South Carolina College.* Columbia, S.C.: Printed at the Times and Gazette Office, 1833.

———. *A Practical Treatise on Dyeing, and Callicoe Printing: Exhibiting the Processes in the French, German, English, and American Practice of Fixing Colours on Woollen, Cotton, Silk, and Linen.* Philadelphia: Thomas Dobson, 1815.

———. *Propositions Respecting the Foundations of Civil Government.* London, [18??].

———. *Some Information Respecting America.* Dublin: P. Wogan, 1794.

———. *Supplement to Mr. Cooper's Letters on the Slave Trade.* Warrington [Eng.]: W. Eyres, 1788.

———. *Two essays: 1. On the Foundation of Civil Government, 2. On the Constitution of the United States.* Columbia, S.C.: Printed by D. & J. M. Faust, 1826.

———. Untitled article (known as the "Value of the Union" speech). *Niles Weekly Register,* 8 September 1827, 28–32.

Cooper, Thomas, and David J. McCord, eds. *The Statutes at Large of South Carolina, Edited, Under Authority of the Legislature.* 10 vols. Columbia, S.C.: A. S. Johnson, 1836–41.

DeSaussure, Henry William. *Answer to a Dialogue between a Federalist and a Republican: First Inserted in the News-Papers in Charleston, and Now Republished at the Desire of a Number of Citizens.* Charleston, S.C.: W. P. Young, [1800].

———. *Equity Cases Argued and Determined in the Supreme Court of North-Carolina.* 2 vols. Raleigh, N.C.: J. Gales and Son, 1831–36.

———. *An Oration, Prepared, To Be Delivered in St. Phillip's Church, Before the Inhabitants of Charleston, South-Carolina, on the Fourth of July 1798. In Commemoration of the American Independence. By Appointment of the American Revolution Society. Published at the Request of That Society, and also of the South-Carolina State Society of Cincinnati.* Charleston, S.C.: W. P. Young, 1798.

———. *Reports of Cases Argued and Determined in the Court of Chancery of the State of South Carolina.* 4 vols. Columbia, S.C.: Cline & Hines, 1817–19.

Devereux, Thomas P. *Cases Argued and Determined in the Supreme Court of North Carolina: From December Term 1826, to June Term [1834].* 4 vols. Raleigh, N.C.: J. Gales and Son, 1829–36.

Devereux, Thomas P., and William H. Battle. *Reports of Cases at Law Argued*

and Determined in the Supreme Court of North Carolina. 4 vols. Raleigh, N.C.:
Turner & Hughes; Philadelphia: P. H. Nicklin & T. Johnson, 1837–40.

Ford, Timothy. *An Enquiry into the Constitutional Authority of the Supreme Federal
Court, Over the Several States, in Their Political Capacity: Being an Answer to
Observations Upon the Government of the United States of America, by James
Sullivan, Esq., Attorney General of the State of Massachusetts, by a Citizen of South
Carolina.* Charleston, S.C.: W. P. Young, 1792.

[Ford, Timothy]. *The Constitutionalist; or, An Enquiry How Far It Is Expedient
and Proper to Alter the Constitution of South Carolina: Published Originally in
Numbers, in the City Gazette and Daily Advertiser.* Charleston, S.C.: Markland,
M'I'ver, 1794.

Freehling, William W. *The Nullification Era: A Documentary Record.* New York:
Harper Torchbooks, 1967.

Grimké, John Faucheraud. *The Public Laws of the State of South-Carolina: From
Its First Establishment as a British Province Down to the Year 1790, Inclusive. . . .*
Philadelphia: R. Aitken & Son, 1790.

———. *The South Carolina Justice of the Peace.* Philadelphia, 1788.

Grimké, Thomas. *An Oration on the Practicability and Expediency of Reducing the
Whole Body of the Law to the Simplicity and Order of a Code.* Charleston, S.C.,
1827.

Hamilton, J. G. de Roulhac, ed. *The Papers of Thomas Ruffin.* 2 vols. Raleigh, N.C.:
Edwards and Broughton, 1918.

———. *The Papers of William Alexander Graham.* 6 vols. Raleigh, N.C.: State
Department of Archives and History, 1961.

Hamilton, James. *The Introductory Address of Governor Hamilton, at the First
Meeting of the Charleston State Rights and Free Trade Association of South-
Carolina, Held at Lege's Long Room, on August 1, 1831.* Charleston, S.C.: E. J. Van
Brunt, 1831.

Haywood, John. *The Civil and Political History of the State of Tennessee: From Its
Earliest Settlement up to 1796, Including the Boundaries of the State.* Knoxville,
Tenn.: Heiskell & Brown, 1823.

———. *The Duty and Office of Justices of the Peace, Sheriffs, Coroners, Constables,
&c. According to the Laws of the State of North Carolina.* Raleigh, N.C., 1808.

———. *A Manual of the Laws of North Carolina.* Raleigh, N.C.: J. Gales, Printer
to the State, 1801.

———. *A Manual of the Laws of North Carolina.* 2nd ed. Raleigh, N.C.: J. Gales
and W. Boylan, 1808.

———. *A Manual of the Laws of North Carolina.* 3rd ed. Raleigh, N.C.: J. Gales,
1814.

———. *A Manual of the Laws of North Carolina.* 4th ed. Raleigh, N.C.: J. Gales,
1819.

———. *Reports of Cases Adjudged in the Superior Courts of Law and Equity of the*

383

State of North Carolina: From the Year 1789 to the Year [1806]. 2 vols. Halifax,
    N.C.: Abraham Hodge, 1799–1806.

Higginbotham, Don, ed. *The Papers of James Iredell*. 2 vols. Raleigh, N.C.: Division
    of Archives and History, 1976.

Holcomb, Brent H., comp. *Edgefield County, South Carolina, Minutes of the County
    Court, 1785–1795*. Easley, S.C., 1979.

———. *Winton (Barnwell) County, South Carolina: Minutes of County Court and
    Will Book 1*. Easley, S.C., 1978.

Hoyt, William Henry, ed. *The Papers of Archibald D. Murphey*. 2 vols. Raleigh,
    N.C.: Publications of the North Carolina Historical Commission, 1914.

*The Independent Citizen: Or, the Majesty of the People Asserted Against the
    Usurpation of the Legislature of North-Carolina, in Several Acts of Assembly,
    Passed in the Years 1783, 1785, 1786, and 1787*. New Bern, N.C.: François Xavier
    Martin, 1787.

Iredell, James. *Laws of the State of North-Carolina: Published, According to Act of
    Assembly*. Edenton, N.C.: Hodge and Willis, Printers to the State, 1791.

———. *A New Digested Manual of the Acts of the General Assembly of North
    Carolina*. Raleigh: Seaton Gales, 1851.

James, Benjamin. *A Digest of the Laws of South Carolina*. Columbia, S.C., 1814.

Martin, François Xavier. *The Acts of the General Assembly of the State of North
    Carolina: Passed During the Sessions Held in the Years 1791, 1792, 1793, and 1794*.
    Newbern, N.C.: F. X. Martin, 1795.

———. *A Collection of the Private Acts of the General Assembly of the State of North
    Carolina: From the Year 1715 to the year 1790*. New Bern, N.C.: F. X. Martin, 1794.

———. *The History of North Carolina from the Earliest Time*. New Orleans: A. T.
    Penniman, 1829.

———. *Notes of a Few Decisions in the Superior Courts of the State of North
    Carolina: And in the Circuit Court of the United States: for North-Carolina
    District*. New Bern, N.C.: François Xavier Martin, 1797.

———. *Public Acts of the General Assembly of North Carolina, Revised and
    Published Under the Authority of the Legislature, by James Iredell; and Now
    Revised by François-Xavier Martin*. New Bern, N.C.: Martin & Ogden, 1804.

McDuffie, George. *National and State Rights, Considered by the Hon. George
    M'Duffie, Under The Signature of One of the People, in Reply to the "Trio," with the
    Advertisement Prefixed to it, Generally Attributed to Major James Hamilton, Jr.
    When Published in 1821*. Charleston, S.C.: Printed and published by W. S. Blain,
    1830.

McRee, Griffith J. *Life and Correspondence of James Iredell*. 2 vols. New York:
    D. Appleton, 1857–58.

Murphey, Archibald D. *Reports of Cases Argued and Adjudged in the Supreme
    Court of North Carolina: From the Year 1804 to the Year 1819 . . . Inclusive*. 3 vols.
       Raleigh, N.C.: J. Gales & Son, 1821–26.

Nash, Frederick, James Iredell, and William H. Battle. *The Revised Statutes of the State of North Carolina*. 2 vols. Raleigh, N.C.: Turner and Hughes, 1837.

Newberry County, South Carolina, Minutes of the County Court, 1785–1798. Easley, S.C., n.d.

O'Neall, John Belton. *The Annals of Newberry, Historical, Biographical, and Anecdotal*. Charleston: S. G. Courtenay, 1859.

———. *Biographical Sketches of the Bench and Bar of South Carolina*. 2 vols. Charleston: S. G. Courtenay, 1859.

———. *The Negro Law of South Carolina*. Columbia, S.C.: J. G. Bowman, 1848.

Potter, Henry, et al. *Laws of the State of North Carolina: Including the Titles of Such Statutes and Parts of Statutes of Great Britain as Are in Force in the Said State*. Raleigh, N.C.: J. Gales, 1821.

Powell, William S., Mes K. Huhta, and Thomas J. Farnham, eds. *The Regulators in North Carolina: A Documentary History, 1759–1776*. Raleigh, N.C.: State Department of Archives and History, 1971.

Proceedings and Debates of the Convention of North Carolina, Called to Amend the Constitution of the State; Which Assembled at Raleigh, June 4, 1835. Raleigh, N.C.: Joseph Gales and Son, 1836.

Reeve, Tapping. *Law of Baron and Femme, of Parent and Child, of Guardian and Ward, of Master and Servant: and of the Powers of Courts of Chancery: with an Essay on the Terms, Heir, Heirs, and Heirs of the Body*. New Haven: Oliver Steele, 1815.

The Report, Ordinance, and Addresses of the Convention of the People of South Carolina: Adopted, November 24th 1832. Columbia, S.C.: A. S. Johnston, 1832.

Reports of Cases: Argued and Determined in the Court of Appeals of South Carolina: on Appeal from the Courts of Law, 1828–1832/ By H. Bailey. Charleston, S.C.: A. E. Miller, 1833–34.

Reports of Cases Determined in the Constitutional Court of South-Carolina/ By the State Reporter. Columbia, S.C.: Black & Sweeney, 1824.

Reports of Equity Cases, Determined in the Court of Appeals, of the State of South Carolina, By the State Reporter. Columbia, S.C.: Black & Sweeney, 1825.

Ruffin, Thomas, and Francis L. Hawks. *Reports of Cases Argued and Adjudged in the Supreme Court of North Carolina: During the Years 1820 & 1821 [December Term 1825 & June Term 1826]*. 4 vols. Raleigh, N.C.: J. Gales & Son, 1823–28.

Saunders, William L., ed. *The Colonial Records of North Carolina*. 10 vols. Raleigh, N.C.: State of North Carolina, 1886–90.

Schweninger, Loren, ed. *Petitions to Southern Legislatures*. Vol. 1 of *The Southern Debate Over Slavery*. Urbana: University of Illinois Press, 2001.

Simpson, William. *The Practical Justice of the Peace and Parish-Officer, of His Majesty's Province of South-Carolina*. Charleston, S.C., 1761.

Singleton, Virginia Eliza. *The Singletons of South Carolina*. Columbia, S.C., 1914.

Smith, William Loughton. *A Comparative View of the Constitutions of the Several*

States with Each Other, and with that of the United States.* Philadelphia: John
Thompson, 1796.

Soule, Charles C. *The Lawyer's Reference Manual of Law Books and Citations.*
Boston: Soule and Bugbee, 1883.

Swain, David L. *British Invasion of North Carolina in 1776, Delivered Before the
Historical Society of the University of North Carolina.* N.p., [1853?].

——. *Early Times in Raleigh: Addresses Delivered by the Hon. David L. Swain.*
Raleigh: Walters, Hughes, 1867.

——. *Report of the Hon. David L. Swain: On the Historical Agency for Procuring
Documentary Evidence of the History of North-Carolina.* Raleigh, N.C.: Holden
and Wilson, Printers to the State, 1858.

Swift, Zephaniah. *A System of Laws of the State of Connecticut.* 2 vols. Windham,
Conn.: Printed by John Byrne, for the Author, 1795–96.

Taylor, John Louis. *Cases Adjudged in the Supreme Court of North Carolina from
July Term 1816 to January Term 1818, Inclusive.* Raleigh: J. Gales, 1818.

——. *Cases Determined in the Superior Courts of Law and Equity of the State of
North Carolina [1796–1802].* New Bern, N.C.: Martin & Ogden, 1802.

——. *A Revisal of the Laws of the State of North Carolina: Passed from 1821–1825.*
Raleigh, N.C.: J. Gales, 1827.

Tocqueville, Alexis de. *Democracy in America.* Ed. J. P. Mayer. New York: Harper
and Row, 1969.

Tucker, St. George. *Blackstone's Commentaries: With Notes of References to the
Constitution and Laws, of the Federal Government of the United States, and of the
Commonwealth of Virginia.* 5 vols. Philadelphia: William Young and Abraham
Small, 1803.

Turnbull, Robert J. *The Crisis.* Charleston: A. E. Miller, 1827.

Wells, Laurence K., comp. *York County, South Carolina, Minutes of the County
Court, 1786–1797.* N.p., 1981.

Woodmason, Charles. *The Carolina Backcountry on the Eve of the Revolution:
The Journal and Other Writings of Charles Woodmason, Anglican Itinerant,* ed.
Richard J. Hooker. Chapel Hill: University of North Carolina Press, 1953.

SECONDARY SOURCES

Adams, William J. "Evolution of Law in North Carolina." *North Carolina Law
Review* 2 (1923–24): 133–45.

Alexander, Adele Logan. *Ambiguous Lives: Free Women of Color in Rural Georgia,
1789–1879.* Fayetteville: University of Arkansas Press, 1991.

Alexander, Gregory S. *Commodity and Propriety: Competing Visions of Property in
American Legal Thought, 1776–1970.* Chicago: University of Chicago Press, 1997.

Amussen, Susan Dwyer. "'Being Stirred to Much Unquietness': Violence and

Domestic Violence in Early Modern England." *Journal of Women's History* 6 (Summer 1994): 70–89.

———. *An Ordered Society: Gender and Class in Early Modern England.* Oxford: Blackwell, 1988.

Anderson, Benedict. *Imagined Communities: Reflections on the Origins and Spread of Nationalism.* London: Verso, 1983.

Anzilotti, Cara. "Autonomy and the Female Planter in Colonial South Carolina." *Journal of Southern History* 63 (May 1997): 239–68.

Appleby, Joyce. *Capitalism and the New Social Order: The Republican Vision of the 1790s.* New York: New York University Press, 1984.

Armytage, W. H. G. "The Editorial Experience of Joseph Gales, 1786–1794." *North Carolina Historical Review* 28 (July 1951): 332–61.

Ayers, Edward L. *Vengeance and Justice: Crime and Punishment in the Nineteenth-Century American South.* New York: Oxford University Press, 1984.

Bailey, F. G. *Gifts and Poison: The Politics of Reputation.* New York: Schocken Books, 1971.

Bailyn, Bernard. *The Ideological Origins of the American Revolution.* Cambridge, Mass.: Belknap Press, Harvard University Press, 1967.

Baker, J. H. *The Law's Two Bodies: Some Evidential Problems in English Legal History.* New York: Oxford University Press, 2001.

Balibar, Etienne. "The Nation Form: History and Ideology." In *Race, Nation, Class: Ambiguous Identities,* ed. Etienne Balibar and Immanuel Wallerstein, 86–106. London: Verso, 1991.

Balleisen, Edward J. *Navigating Failure: Bankruptcy and Commercial Society in Antebellum America.* Chapel Hill: University of North Carolina Press, 2001.

Banner, James M. "The Problem of South Carolina." In *The Hofstadter Aegis: A Memorial,* ed. Stanley Elkins and Eric McKitrick, 60–93. New York: Alfred A. Knopf, 1974.

Baptist, Edward E. *Creating an Old South: Middle Florida's Plantation Frontier before the Civil War.* Chapel Hill: University of North Carolina Press, 2002.

———. "'Cuffy,' 'Fancy Maids,' and 'One-Eyed Men': Rape, Commodification, and the Domestic Slave Trade in the United States." *American Historical Review* 106 (December 2001): 1619–50.

Bardaglio, Peter. "'An Outrage upon Nature': Incest and the Law in the Nineteenth-Century South." In *In Joy and in Sorrow: Women, Family, and Marriage in the Victorian South, 1830–1900,* ed. Carol Bleser, 32–51. New York: Oxford University Press, 1991.

———. "Rape and the Law in the Old South: 'Calculated to excite indignation in every heart.'" *Journal of Southern History* 60 (November 1994): 749–72.

———. *Reconstructing the Household: Families, Sex, and the Law in the Nineteenth-Century South.* Chapel Hill: University of North Carolina Press, 1995.

Basch, Norma. *In the Eyes of the Law: Marriage and Property in Nineteenth-Century New York.* Ithaca: Cornell University Press, 1982.

Beard, Charles A., and Mary R. Beard. *The Rise of American Civilization.* 2 vols. New York: Macmillan, 1927.

Beard, Mary Ritter. *Women as Force in History: A Study of Traditions and Realities.* New York: Macmillan, 1946.

Belz, Herman. *Abraham Lincoln, Constitutionalism, and Equal Rights in the Civil War.* New York: Fordham University Press, 1998.

Benedict, Michael Les. *A Compromise of Principle: Congressional Republicans and Reconstruction, 1863–1869.* New York: W. W. Norton, 1974.

Bensel, Richard Franklin. *Yankee Leviathan: The Origins of Central State Authority in America, 1859–1877.* New York: Cambridge University Press, 1990.

Bercaw, Nancy D. *Gendered Freedoms: Race, Rights, and the Politics of Household in the Delta, 1861–1875.* Gainesville: University Press of Florida, 2003.

Berlin, Ira. *Many Thousands Gone: The First Two Centuries of Slavery in North America.* Cambridge, Mass.: Belknap Press, Harvard University Press, 1998.

Berlin, Ira, Barbara J. Fields, Thavolia Glymph, Joseph P. Reidy, and Leslie S. Rowland, eds. *Freedom: A Documentary History of Emancipation, 1861–1867.* Series 1, vol. 1: *The Destruction of Slavery.* New York: Cambridge University Press, 1985.

Berlin, Ira, Thavolia Glymph, Steven F. Miller, Joseph P. Reidy, Leslie S. Rowland, and Julie Saville, eds. *Freedom: A Documentary History of Emancipation, 1861–1867.* Series 1, vol. 3: *The Wartime Genesis of Free Labor: The Lower South.* New York: Cambridge University Press, 1990.

Berlin, Ira, Stephen F. Miller, and Leslie S. Rowland, eds. "Afro-American Families in the Transition from Slavery to Freedom." *Radical History Review* 42 (1988): 89–121.

Berlin, Ira, and Philip D. Morgan, eds. *Slaves' Economy: Independent Production by Slaves in the Americas.* London: Frank Cass, 1991.

Berlin, Ira, Joseph P. Reidy, and Leslie S. Rowland, eds. *Freedom: A Documentary History of Emancipation, 1861–1867.* Series 2: *The Black Military Experience.* New York: Cambridge University Press, 1982.

Billingsley, Carolyn Earle. *Communities of Kinship: Antebellum Families and the Settlement of the Cotton Frontier.* Athens: University of Georgia Press, 2004.

Bishir, Catherine W. *North Carolina Architecture.* 1990. Reprint, Chapel Hill: University of North Carolina Press, 2005.

Bishir, Catherine W., and Michael T. Southern. *A Guide to the Historical Architecture of Piedmont, North Carolina.* Chapel Hill: University of North Carolina Press, 2003.

Bloch, Ruth H. "American Female Ideals in Transition: The Rise of the Moral Mother." *Signs* 4 (Winter 1978): 237–52.

———. "The Gendered Meanings of Virtue in Revolutionary America." *Signs* 13 (Autumn 1987): 37–58.

Block, Sharon. *Rape and Sexual Power in Early America*. Chapel Hill: University of North Carolina Press, 2006.

Bodenhamer, David J., and James W. Ely Jr., eds. *Ambivalent Legacy: A Legal History of the South*. Jackson: University Press of Mississippi, 1984.

Boles, John B. *The Great Revival, 1787–1805*. Lexington: University Press of Kentucky, 1972.

Bolton, Charles C. *Poor Whites of the Antebellum South: Tenants and Laborers in Central North Carolina and Northeast Mississippi*. Durham, N.C.: Duke University Press, 1994.

Bolton, Charles C., and Scott P. Culclasure, eds. "The Autobiography of Edward Isham, Alias 'Hardaway Bone.'" In *The Confessions of Edward Isham: A Poor White Life of the Old South*, ed. Charles C. Bolton and Scott P. Culclasure, 1–18. Athens: University of Georgia Press, 1998.

Boris, Eileen. *Home to Work: Motherhood and the Politics of Industrial Homework in the United States*. New York: Cambridge University Press, 1994.

Bouton, Terry. "A Road Closed: Rural Insurgency in Post-Independence Pennsylvania." *Journal of American History* 87 (December 2000): 855–88.

Boydston, Jeanne. *Home and Work: Housework, Wages, and the Ideology of Labor in the Early Republic*. New York: Oxford University Press, 1990.

Boydston, Jeanne, Mary Kelley, and Anne Margolis. *The Limits of Sisterhood: The Beecher Sisters on Women's Rights and Woman's Sphere*. Chapel Hill: University of North Carolina Press, 1988.

Brewer, Holly. *By Birth or Consent: Children, Law, and the Anglo-American Revolution in Authority*. Chapel Hill: University of North Carolina Press, 2005.

———. "Domestic Relations and the Law." In *Cambridge History of Law in America*, vol. 1, *Early America (1580–1815)*, ed. Christopher L. Tomlins and Michael Grossberg, 288–323. New York: Cambridge University Press, 2008.

———. "Entailing Aristocracy in Colonial Virginia: 'Ancient Feudal Restraints' and Revolutionary Reforms." *William and Mary Quarterly* 54 (1997): 307–46.

———. "Power and Authority in the Colonial South: The English Legacy and Its Contradictions." In *Britain and the American South: From Colonialism to Rock and Roll*, ed. Joseph P. Ward, 27–51. Jackson: University Press of Mississippi, 2003.

Brown, Christopher L. "Empire without Slaves: British Concepts of Emancipation in the Age of the American Revolution." *William and Mary Quarterly* 56 (April 1999): 273–306.

Brown, Elsa Barkley. "Negotiating and Transforming the Public Sphere: African American Political Life in the Transition from Slavery to Freedom." *Public Culture* 7 (Fall 1994): 107–26.

Brown, Kathleen M. *Good Wives, "Nasty Wenches," and Anxious Patriarchs: Gender, Race, and Power in Colonial Virginia.* Chapel Hill: University of North Carolina Press, 1996.

Bryan, John Morrill. *Robert Mills, Architect, 1781–1855.* Columbia, S.C.: Columbia Museum of Art, 1976.

Bryant, Jonathan M. "'We Have No Chance of Justice before the Courts': The Freedmen's Struggle for Power in Greene County, Georgia, 1865–1874." In *Georgia in Black and White: Explorations in the Race Relations of a Southern State, 1865–1950,* ed. John C. Inscoe, 13–37. Athens: University of Georgia Press, 1994.

Buckley, Thomas E. *The Great Catastrophe of My Life: Divorce in the Old Dominion.* Chapel Hill: University of North Carolina Press, 2002.

Burns, Robert Paschal. *100 Courthouses: A Report on North Carolina Judicial Facilities.* 2 vols. Raleigh, N.C., 1978.

Bush, Jonathan. "Free to Enslave: The Foundations of Colonial American Slave Law." *Yale Journal of Law and the Humanities* 5 (1993): 417–70.

Bynum, Victoria. *Unruly Women: The Politics of Social and Sexual Control in the Old South.* Chapel Hill: University of North Carolina Press, 1992.

Camp, Stephanie M. H. *Closer to Freedom: Enslaved Women and Everyday Resistance in the Plantation South.* Chapel Hill: University of North Carolina Press, 2004.

Campbell, John. "As 'A Kind of Freeman'? Slaves' Market-Related Activities in the South Carolina Upcountry, 1800–1860." *Slavery and Abolition* 12 (May 1991): 131–69.

Canady, Hoyt P. *Gentlemen of the Bar: Lawyers in Colonial South Carolina.* New York: Garland, 1987.

Carlson, Andrew J. "Homeplace and Tobaccoland: A History of Granville County." In *Heritage and Homesteads: The History and Architecture of Granville County, North Carolina.* [Granville County, N.C.]: The Granville Historical Society, 1988.

Cashin, Joan. *Family Venture: Men and Women on the Southern Frontier.* New York: Oxford University Press, 1991.

Cecil-Fronsman, Bill. *Common Whites: Class and Culture in Antebellum North Carolina.* Lexington: University Press of Kentucky, 1992.

Censer, Jane Turner. *North Carolina Planters and Their Children, 1800–1860.* Baton Rouge: Louisiana State University Press, 1984.

——. "'Smiling through Her Tears': Ante-Bellum Southern Women and Divorce." *American Journal of Legal History* 25 (January 1982): 114–34.

Chapin, Bradley. *Criminal Justice in Colonial America, 1606–1660.* Athens: University of Georgia Press, 1983.

Chused, Richard H. "Married Women's Property Law: 1800–1850." *Georgetown Law Journal* 71 (1983): 1359–1425.

Clark, Christopher. *The Roots of Rural Capitalism: Western Massachusetts, 1780–1860*. Ithaca, N.Y.: Cornell University Press, 1990.

Clark, Elizabeth B. "'The Sacred Rights of the Weak': Pain, Sympathy, and the Culture of Individual Rights in Antebellum America." *Journal of American History* 82 (September 1995): 463–93.

Clinton, Catherine. *The Plantation Mistress: Woman's World in the Old South*. New York: Pantheon Books, 1982.

Coclanis, Peter A. *The Shadow of a Dream: Economic Life and Death in the South Carolina Low Country, 1670–1920*. New York: Oxford University Press, 1989.

Cole, Stephanie. "Keeping the Peace: Domestic Assault and Private Prosecution in Antebellum Baltimore." In *Over the Threshold: Intimate Violence in Early America*, ed. Christine Daniels and Michael V. Kennedy, 148–69. New York: Routledge, 1999.

Connor, R. D. W. *Ante-Bellum Builders of North Carolina*. Studies in North Carolina History, no. 3. Greensboro: North Carolina College for Women, 1923.

Cook, Charles M. *The American Codification Movement: A Study of Antebellum Legal Reform*. Westport, Conn.: Greenwood Press, 1981.

Cornell, Saul. *The Other Founders: Anti-Federalism and the Dissenting Tradition in America, 1788–1828*. Chapel Hill: University of North Carolina Press, 1999.

Cotlar, Seth. "Joseph Gales and the Making of the Jeffersonian Middle Class." In *The Revolution of 1800: Democracy, Race, and the New Republic*, ed. James Horn, Jan Ellen Lewis, and Peter S. Onuf, 331–59. Charlottesville: University of Virginia Press, 2002.

Cott, Nancy F. *The Bonds of Womanhood: "Women's Sphere" in New England, 1780–1835*. New Haven: Yale University Press, 1977.

———. *Public Vows: A History of Marriage and the Nation*. Cambridge, Mass.: Harvard University Press, 2000.

Counihans, Harold J. "The North Carolina Constitutional Convention of 1835: A Study in Jacksonian Democracy." *North Carolina Historical Review* 46 (Autumn 1969): 335–64.

Cox, LaWanda, and John H. Cox. *Politics, Principle, and Prejudice, 1865–1866: Dilemma of Reconstruction America*. New York: Free Press, 1963.

Curtis, Christopher M. "Jefferson's Chosen People: Legal and Political Conceptions of the Freehold in the Old Dominion from Revolution to Reform." Ph.D. diss., Emory University, 2002.

Dailey, Jane. *Before Jim Crow: The Politics of Race in Postemancipation Virginia*. Chapel Hill: University of North Carolina Press, 2000.

Davis, Adrienne D. "The Private Law of Race and Sex: An Antebellum Perspective." *Stanford Law Review* 51 (January 1999): 221–88.

Davis, Angela. "Reflections on the Black Woman's Role in the Community of Slaves." *Black Scholar* 3 (December 1981): 3–15.

Davis, Natalie Zemon. *Fiction in the Archives: Pardon Tales and Their Tellers in Sixteenth-Century France.* Stanford: Stanford University Press, 1987.

Dayton, Cornelia Hughes. "Turning Points and the Relevance of Colonial Legal History." *William and Mary Quarterly* 50 (January 1993): 7–17.

———. *Women before the Bar: Gender, Law, and Society in Connecticut, 1639–1789.* Chapel Hill: University of North Carolina Press, 1995.

D'Cruze, Shani. *Crimes of Outrage: Sex, Violence and Victorian Working Women.* DeKalb: Northern Illinois University Press, 1998.

Diggins, John P. *The Lost Soul of American Politics: Virtue, Self-Interest, and the Foundations of Liberalism.* New York: Basic Books, 1984.

Dorr, Lisa Lindquist. *White Women, Rape, and the Power of Race in Virginia, 1900–1960.* Chapel Hill: University of North Carolina Press, 2004.

Doyle, Christopher Leonard. "Lord, Master, and Patriot: St. George Tucker and Patriarchy in Republican Virginia, 1772–1851." Ph.D. diss., University of Connecticut, 1996.

Dublin, Thomas. *Women at Work: The Transformation of Work and Community in Lowell, Massachusetts, 1826–1860.* New York: Columbia University Press, 1979.

DuBois, Ellen Carol. *Feminism and Suffrage: The Emergence of an Independent Women's Movement in America, 1848–1869.* Ithaca: Cornell University Press, 1978.

Eaton, Clement. "Winifred and Joseph Gales: Liberals in the Old South." *Journal of Southern History* 10 (November 1944): 461–74.

Edgar, Walter, ed. *The South Carolina Encyclopedia.* Columbia: University of South Carolina Press, 2006.

Edwards, Laura F. "Captives of Wilmington: The Riot and Historical Memories of Political Conflict, 1865–1898." In *Democracy Betrayed: The Wilmington Race Riot of 1898 and Its Legacy*, ed. Timothy B. Tyson and David S. Cecelski, 113–41. Chapel Hill: University of North Carolina Press, 1998.

———. "The Civil War and Reconstruction." In *The Cambridge History of Law in America*, vol. 2, *The Long Nineteenth Century (1789–1920)*, ed. Christopher Tomlins and Michael Grossberg, 313–44. New York: Cambridge University Press, 2008.

———. "Enslaved Women and the Law: The Paradoxes of Subordination in the Post-Revolutionary Carolinas." *Slavery & Abolition* 26 (August 2005): 305–23.

———. *Gendered Strife and Confusion: The Political Culture of Reconstruction.* Urbana: University of Illinois Press, 1997.

———. "Law, Domestic Violence, and the Limits of Patriarchal Authority in the Antebellum South." *Journal of Southern History* 65 (November 1999): 733–70.

———. "The Problem of Dependency: African Americans, Labor Relations, and the Law in the Nineteenth-Century South." *Agricultural History* 72 (Spring 1998): 313–40.

———. "Status without Rights: African Americans and the Tangled History of Law and Governance in the Nineteenth-Century U.S. South." *American Historical Review* 112 (April 2007): 365–93.

———. "Women and the Law: Domestic Discord in North Carolina after the Civil War." In *Local Matters: Race, Crime, and Justice in the American South*, ed. Donald Nieman and Christopher Waldrep, 125–54. Athens: University of Georgia Press, 2000.

Egerton, Douglas R. *He Shall Go Out Free: The Lives of Denmark Vesey.* Rev. ed. Lanham, Md.: Rowan and Littlefield, 2004.

Elliot, Cecil D. "The North Carolina State Capitol." *Southern Architect* 5 (May 1958): 12–33; 5 (June 1958): 23–26; 5 (July 1958): 24–27.

Ellis, Richard E. *The Union at Risk: Jacksonian Democracy, States' Rights, and the Nullification Crisis.* New York: Oxford University Press, 1987.

Erickson, Amy Louise. *Women and Property in Early Modern England.* New York: Routledge, 1993.

Ernst, Joseph A., and H. Roy Merrens. "'Camden's Turrets Pierce the Skies!': The Urban Process in the Southern Colonies during the Eighteenth Century." *William and Mary Quarterly* 30 (October 1973): 549–74.

Escott, Paul D. *Many Excellent People: Power and Privilege in North Carolina, 1850–1900.* Chapel Hill: University of North Carolina Press, 1985.

———. "The Moral Economy of the Crowd in Confederate North Carolina." *The Maryland Historian* 13 (Spring/Summer 1982): 1–18.

Faulkner, Carol. *Women's Radical Reconstruction: The Freedmen's Aid Movement.* Philadelphia: University of Pennsylvania Press, 2003.

Fede, Andrew. *People without Rights: An Interpretation of the Fundamentals of the Law of Slavery in the U.S. South.* New York: Garland, 1992.

Fields, Barbara J. *Slavery and Freedom on the Middle Ground: Maryland during the Nineteenth Century.* New Haven: Yale University Press, 1985.

———. "Slavery, Race and Ideology in the United States of America." *New Left Review*, no. 181 (May–June 1990): 95–118.

Fischer, Kirsten. *Suspect Relations: Sex, Race, and Resistance in Colonial North Carolina.* Ithaca: Cornell University Press, 2001.

Flanigan, Daniel J. "Criminal Procedure in Slave Trials in the Antebellum South." *Journal of Southern History* 40 (November 1974): 537–64.

Foner, Eric. *Nothing But Freedom: Emancipation and Its Legacy.* Baton Rouge: Louisiana State University Press, 1983.

———. *Reconstruction: America's Unfinished Revolution.* New York: Harper and Row, 1988.

Forbath, William E. "The Ambiguities of Free Labor: Labor and the Law in the Gilded Age." *Wisconsin Law Review* 4 (July 1985): 767–817.

Ford, Lacy K., Jr. *Origins of Southern Radicalism: The South Carolina Upcountry, 1800–1860.* New York: Oxford University Press, 1988.

Forret, Jeff. "Slaves, Poor Whites, and the Underground Economy of the Rural Carolinas." *Journal of Southern History* 70 (November 2004): 783–824.

Foster, Helen Bradley. *"New Raiments of Self": African American Clothing in the Antebellum Period.* Oxford and New York: Berg, 1997.

Fox-Genovese, Elizabeth. *Within the Plantation Household: Women in the Old South.* Chapel Hill: University of North Carolina Press, 1988.

Frankel, Noralee. *Freedom's Women: Black Women and Families in Civil War Era Mississippi.* Bloomington: Indiana University Press, 1999.

Franklin, John Hope. *The Free Negro in North Carolina, 1790–1860.* Chapel Hill: University of North Carolina Press, 1943. Reprint, New York: Russell and Russell, 1969.

Fraser, Nancy, and Linda Gordon. "A Genealogy of Dependency: Tracing a Keyword of the U.S. Welfare State." *Signs* 19 (December 1994): 309–36.

Fredrickson, George M. *The Black Image in the White Mind: The Debate on Afro-American Character and Destiny, 1817–1914.* New York: Harper and Row, 1971.

Freehling, William W. *Prelude to Civil War: The Nullification Controversy in South Carolina, 1816–1836.* New York: Harper & Row, 1966.

Freeman, Joanne B. *Affairs of Honor: National Politics in the New Republic.* New Haven: Yale University Press, 2001.

Frey, Sylvia R. *Water from the Rock: Black Resistance in a Revolutionary Age.* Princeton: Princeton University Press, 1991.

Friedman, Jean E. *The Enclosed Garden: Women and Community in the Evangelical South, 1830–1900.* Chapel Hill: University of North Carolina Press, 1985.

Friedman, Lawrence M. *Crime and Punishment in American History.* New York: Basic Books, 1993.

———. *A History of American Law.* 2nd ed. New York: Simon and Schuster, 1985.

Gardner, Sarah. *Blood Irony: Southern White Women's Narratives of the Civil War, 1861.* Chapel Hill: University of North Carolina Press, 2004.

Genovese, Eugene D. *Roll, Jordan, Roll: The World the Slaves Made.* New York: Vintage Books, 1976.

———. *The World the Slaveholders Made: Two Essays in Interpretation.* New York: Pantheon Books, 1969.

Genovese, Eugene D., and Elizabeth Fox-Genovese. *Fruits of Merchant Capital: Slavery and Bourgeois Property in the Rise and Expansion of Capitalism.* New York: Oxford University Press, 1983.

Gilmore, Glenda Elizabeth. *Gender and Jim Crow: Women and the Politics of White Supremacy in North Carolina, 1896–1920.* Chapel Hill: University of North Carolina Press, 1996.

Golumbic, Lars C. "Who Shall Dictate the Law? Political Wrangling Between 'Whig' Lawyers and Backcountry Farmers in Revolutionary Era North Carolina." *North Carolina Historical Review* 73 (1996): 56–82.

Gordon, Linda. *Heroes of Their Own Lives: The Politics and History of Family Violence*. New York: Viking Press, 1988.

Gorn, Elliott J. "'Gouge and Bite, Pull Hair and Scratch': The Social Significance of Fighting in the Southern Backcountry." *American Historical Review* 90 (February 1985): 18–43.

Gowing, Laura. *Domestic Dangers: Women, Words, and Sex in Early Modern London*. Oxford: Clarendon Press, 1996.

Green, Edwin L. *A History of the University of South Carolina*. Columbia, S.C.: The State Company, 1916.

Green, Fletcher. *Constitutional Development in the South Atlantic States, 1776–1860*. New York: W. W. Norton, 1966.

Greenberg, Kenneth. *Honor and Slavery: Lies, Duels, Noses, Masks, Dressing as a Woman, Gifts, Strangers, Humanitarianism, Death, Slave Rebellions, the Proslavery Argument, Baseball, Hunting, and Gambling in the Old South*. Princeton: Princeton University Press, 1996.

———. *Masters and Statesmen: The Political Culture of American Slavery*. Baltimore: Johns Hopkins University Press, 1985.

Greene, Jack P. "Slavery or Independence: Some Reflections on the Relationship Among Liberty, Black Bondage, and Equality in Revolutionary South Carolina." *South Carolina Historical Magazine* 80 (1979): 193–214.

Gross, Ariela. "Beyond Black and White: Cultural Approaches to Race and Slavery." *Columbia Law Review* 101 (April 2001): 640–82.

———. *Double Character: Slavery and Mastery in the Antebellum Southern Courtroom*. Princeton: Princeton University Press, 2000.

Grossberg, Michael. *Governing the Hearth: Law and the Family in Nineteenth-Century America*. Chapel Hill: University of North Carolina Press, 1985.

———. *A Judgment for Solomon: The d'Hauteville Case and Legal Experience in Antebellum America*. Cambridge: Cambridge University Press, 1996.

Haag, Pamela. "The 'Ill-Use of a Wife': Patterns of Working-Class Violence in Domestic and Public New York City, 1860–1880." *Journal of Social History* 25 (Spring 1992): 447–77.

Hadden, Sally E. *Slave Patrols: Law and Violence in Virginia and the Carolinas*. Cambridge, Mass.: Harvard University Press, 2001.

Hahamovitch, Cindy. *The Fruits of Their Labor: Atlantic Coast Farmworkers and the Making of Migrant Poverty, 1870–1945*. Chapel Hill: University of North Carolina Press, 1997.

Hahn, Steven. "Common Right and Commonwealth: The Stock-Law Struggle and the Roots of Southern Populism." In *Region, Race, and Reconstruction: Essays in Honor of C. Vann Woodward*, ed. J. Morgan Kousser and James M. McPherson, 51–88. New York: Oxford University Press, 1982.

———. *A Nation under Our Feet: Black Political Struggles in the Rural South from*

Slavery to the Great Migration. Cambridge, Mass.: Harvard University Press, 2003.

———. *The Roots of Southern Populism: Yeoman Farmers and the Transformation of the Georgia Upcountry, 1850–1890.* New York: Oxford University Press, 1983.

Hahn, Steven, and Jonathan Prude, eds. *The Countryside in the Age of Capitalist Transformation: Essays in the Social History of Rural America.* Chapel Hill: University of North Carolina Press, 1985.

Hall, Jacquelyn Dowd. "'The Mind That Burns in Each Body': Women, Rape, and Racial Violence." In *Powers of Desire: The Politics of Sexuality,* ed. Ann Snitow, Christine Stansell, and Sharon Thompson, 328–49. New York: Monthly Review Press, 1983.

Handlin, Oscar, and Mary Flug Handlin. *Commonwealth: A Study of the Role of Government in the American Economy: Massachusetts, 1774–1861.* New York: New York University Press, 1947.

Harris, Leslie M. *In the Shadow of Slavery: African Americans in New York City, 1626–1863.* Chicago: University of Chicago Press, 2003.

Hartog, Hendrik. "Lawyering, Husbands' Rights, and 'the Unwritten Law' in Nineteenth-Century America." *Journal of American History* 84 (June 1997): 67–96.

———. *Man and Wife in America: A History.* Cambridge, Mass.: Harvard University Press, 2000.

———. "Pigs and Positivism." *Wisconsin Law Review* 4 (July 1985): 899–935.

———. "The Public Law of a County Court: Judicial Government in Eighteenth-Century Massachusetts." *American Journal of Legal History* 20 (1976): 282–329.

Henderson, Archibald. "Hermon Husband's Continuation of the Impartial Relation." *North Carolina Historical Review* 18 (1941): 282–329.

Herrup, Cynthia B. *The Common Peace: Participation and the Criminal Law in Seventeenth-Century England.* New York: Cambridge University Press, 1987.

———. *A House in Gross Disorder: Sex, Law, and the 2nd Earl of Castlehaven.* New York: Oxford University Press, 1999.

Higginbotham, Don, and William S. Price Jr. "Was It Murder for a White Man to Kill a Slave? Chief Justice Martin Howard Condemns the Peculiar Institution in North Carolina." *William and Mary Quarterly* 36 (October 1979): 593–601.

Hilkey, Judy. *Character Is Capital: Success Manuals and Manhood in Gilded Age America.* Chapel Hill: University of North Carolina Press, 1997.

Hindus, Michael S. *Prison and Plantation: Crime, Justice and Authority in Massachusetts and South Carolina, 1767–1878.* Chapel Hill: University of North Carolina Press, 1980.

Hinton, Robert. *The Politics of Agricultural Labor: From Slavery to Freedom in a Cotton Culture, 1862–1902.* New York: Garland Press, 1997.

Hitchcock, Henry Russell, and William Seale. *Temples of Democracy: State Capitols of the U.S.A.* New York: Harcourt, Brace, and Jovanovich, 1976.

Hodes, Martha. *White Women, Black Men: Illicit Sex in the Nineteenth Century South.* New Haven: Yale University Press, 1997.

Hofstadter, Richard. *The Idea of a Party System: The Rise of Legitimate Opposition in the United States, 1780–1840.* Berkeley: University of California Press, 1969.

Holt, Michael F. *The Political Crisis of the 1850s.* New York: Wiley, 1978.

Holt, Thomas C. *Black over White: Negro Political Leadership in South Carolina during Reconstruction.* Urbana: University of Illinois Press, 1977.

———. "'An Empire over the Mind': Emancipation, Race, and Ideology in the British West Indies and the American South." In *Region, Race, and Reconstruction: Essays in Honor of C. Vann Woodward,* ed. J. Morgan Kousser and James McPherson, 283–331. New York: Oxford University Press, 1982.

———. *The Problem of Freedom: Race, Labor, and Politics in Jamaica and Britain, 1832 to 1938.* Baltimore: Johns Hopkins University Press, 1992.

Holt, Wythe, and James R. Perry. "Writs and Rights, 'Clashings and Animosities': The First Confrontation Between Federal and State Jurisdictions." *Law and History Review* 7 (1989): 89–120.

Holton, Woody. *Forced Founders: Indians, Debtors, Slaves, and the Making of the American Revolution in Virginia.* Chapel Hill: University of North Carolina Press, 1999.

Horn, James. *Adapting to a New World: English Society in the Seventeenth-Century Chesapeake.* Chapel Hill: University of North Carolina Press, 1994.

Horwitz, Morton. *The Transformation of American Law, 1780–1860.* Cambridge, Mass.: Harvard University Press, 1977.

Huebner, Timothy S. *The Southern Judicial Tradition: State Judges and Sectional Distinctiveness, 1790–1890.* Athens: University of Georgia Press, 1999.

Huff, Archie Vernon. *Langdon Cheves of South Carolina.* Columbia: University of South Carolina Press, 1977.

Hulsebosch, Daniel Joseph. *Constituting Empire: New York and the Transformation of Constitutionalism in the Atlantic World, 1664–1830.* Chapel Hill: University of North Carolina Press, 2005.

Hunter, Tera W. *To 'Joy My Freedom': Southern Black Women's Lives and Labors after the Civil War.* Cambridge, Mass.: Harvard University Press, 1997.

Hurst, James Willard. *Law and the Conditions of Freedom: In the Nineteenth-Century United States.* Madison: University of Wisconsin Press, 1956.

Huston, Reeve. *Land and Freedom: Rural Society, Popular Protest, and Party Politics in Antebellum New York.* New York: Oxford University Press, 2000.

Hyman, Harold. *A More Perfect Union: The Impact of the Civil War and Reconstruction on the Constitution.* New York: Alfred A. Knopf, 1973.

Inabinet, L. Glen. "'The July Fourth Incident' of 1816: An Insurrection Plotted by Slaves in Camden, South Carolina." In *South Carolina Legal History*, ed. Herbert A. Johnson. Spartanburg, S.C.: Reprint Company, 1980.

Isaac, Rhys. *The Transformation of Virginia, 1740–1790*. Chapel Hill: University of North Carolina Press, 1982.

Isenberg, Nancy. *Sex and Citizenship in Antebellum America*. Chapel Hill: University of North Carolina Press, 1998.

Jacobs, Harriet. *Incidents in the Life of a Slave Girl, Written by Herself*. Ed. Jean Fagan Yellin. Cambridge, Mass.: Harvard University Press, 1987.

Jacobs, Meg, William J. Novak, and Julian E. Zelizer, eds. *The Democratic Experiment: New Directions in American Political History*. Princeton: Princeton University Press, 2003.

Jacoby, Karl. *Crimes Against Nature: Squatters, Poachers, Thieves, and the Hidden History of American Conservation*. Berkeley: University of California Press, 2001.

Jennings, Thelma. "'Us Colored Women Had to Go Through a Plenty': Sexual Exploitation of African American Slave Women." *Journal of Women's History* 1 (Winter 1990): 45–74.

John, Richard R. *Spreading the News: The American Postal Service from Franklin to Morse*. Cambridge, Mass.: Harvard University Press, 1995.

Johnson, Guion Griffis. *Ante-bellum North Carolina: A Social History*. Chapel Hill: University of North Carolina Press, 1937.

Johnson, Michael P. "Denmark Vesey and His Co-Conspirators." *William and Mary Quarterly* 58 (October 2001): 915–76.

Johnson, Michael P., and James L. Roark. *Black Masters: A Free Family of Color in the Old South*. New York: W. W. Norton, 1984.

Johnson, Paul E. "The Modernization of Mayo Greenleaf Patch: Land, Family, and Marginality in New England, 1766–1816." *New England Quarterly* 55 (December 1982): 488–516.

Johnson, Walter. "Inconsistency, Contradiction, and Complete Confusion: The Everyday Life of the Law of Slavery." *Law and Social Inquiry* 22 (Spring 1997): 405–34.

———. "On Agency." *Journal of Social History* 37 (Fall 2003): 113–25.

———. *Soul by Soul: Life Inside the Antebellum Slave Market*. Cambridge, Mass.: Harvard University Press, 1999.

Jones, Mark Haddon. "Herman Husband: Millenarian, Carolina Regulator, and Whiskey Rebel." Ph.D. diss., Northern Illinois University, 1983.

Joseph, Gilbert M., and Daniel Nugent, eds. *Everyday Forms of State Formation: Revolution and the Negotiation of Rule in Modern Mexico*. Durham, N.C.: Duke University Press, 1994.

Kamensky, Jane. *Governing the Tongue: The Politics of Speech in Early New England*. New York: Oxford University Press, 1997.

Kars, Marjoleine. *Breaking Loose Together: The Regulator Rebellion in Pre-*

Revolutionary North Carolina. Chapel Hill: University of North Carolina Press, 2002.

Kay, Marvin L. Michael. "The North Carolina Regulation, 1766–1776: A Class Conflict." In *The American Revolution,* ed. Alfred F. Young, 71–123. DeKalb: Northern Illinois University Press, 1976.

Kay, Marvin L. Michael, and Lorin Lee Cary. *Slavery in North Carolina, 1748–1775.* Chapel Hill: University of North Carolina Press, 1995.

Kaye, Anthony E. *Joining Places: Slave Neighborhoods in the Old South.* Chapel Hill: University of North Carolina Press, 2007.

Keith, Alice Barnwell. "John Gray and Thomas Blount, Merchants, 1783–1800." *North Carolina Historical Review* 25 (April 1948): 195–205.

Kelley, Robin D. G. "'We Are Not What We Seem': Rethinking Black Working-Class Opposition in the Jim Crow South." *Journal of American History* 80 (June 1993): 75–112.

Kenzer, Robert C. *Kinship and Community in a Southern Community: Orange County, North Carolina, 1849–1881.* Knoxville: University of Tennessee Press, 1987.

Kerber, Linda K. *No Constitutional Right to Be Ladies: Women and the Obligations of Citizenship.* New York: Hill and Wang, 1998.

———. "Separate Spheres, Female Worlds, Woman's Place: The Rhetoric of Women's History." *Journal of American History* 75 (June 1988): 9–39.

———. *Women of the Republic: Intellect and Ideology in Revolutionary America.* Chapel Hill: University of North Carolina Press, 1980.

Kessler-Harris, Alice. *In Pursuit of Equity: Women, Men, and the Quest for Economic Citizenship in 20th-Century America.* New York: Oxford University Press, 2001.

———. *A Woman's Wage: Historical Meanings and Social Consequences.* Lexington: University Press of Kentucky, 1990.

Klebaner, Benjamin Joseph. "Some Aspects of North Carolina Public Poor Relief, 1700–1860." *North Carolina Historical Review* 31 (October 1954): 479–92.

Klein, Rachel N. *Unification of a Slave State: The Rise of the Planter Class in the South Carolina Backcountry, 1760–1808.* Chapel Hill: University of North Carolina Press, 1990.

Kolchin, Peter. *American Slavery, 1619–1877.* New York: Hill and Wang, 1993.

Kramer, Larry D. *The People Themselves: Popular Constitutionalism and Judicial Review.* New York: Oxford University Press, 2004.

Kulikoff, Allan. *The Agrarian Origins of American Capitalism.* Charlottesville: University of Virginia Press, 1992.

Kyvig, David E. *Explicit and Authentic Acts: Amending the U.S. Constitution, 1776–1995.* Lawrence: University of Kansas Press, 1996.

Lamoreaux, Naomi R. *Insider Lending: Banks, Personal Connections, and Economic Development in Industrial New England.* New York: Cambridge University Press, 1994.

Landes, Joan B. *Women and the Public Sphere in the Age of the French Revolution.* Ithaca: Cornell University Press, 1988.

Lane, Mills. *Architecture of the Old South: South Carolina.* Savannah, Ga.: The Beehive Press, 1984.

Leary, Helen F. M., ed. *North Carolina Research: Genealogy and Local History.* Raleigh: North Carolina Genealogical Society, 1996.

Lebsock, Suzanne. *The Free Women of Petersburg: Status and Culture in a Southern Town, 1784–1860.* New York: W. W. Norton, 1984.

———. "Radical Reconstruction and the Property Rights of Southern Women." *Journal of Southern History* 43 (May 1977): 195–216.

Lee, Jean Butenhoff. "Land and Labor: Parental Bequest Practices in Charles County, Maryland, 1732–1738." In *Colonial Chesapeake Society,* ed. Lois Green Carr, Philip D. Morgan, and Jean B. Russom, 306–41. Chapel Hill: University of North Carolina Press, 1988.

Lefler, Hugh T., and William S. Powell. *Colonial North Carolina: A History.* New York: Charles Scribner and Sons, 1973.

Lichtenstein, Alex. *Twice the Work of Free Labor: The Political Economy of Convict Labor in the New South.* New York: Verso, 1996.

Link, William A. *Roots of Secession: Slavery and Politics in Antebellum Virginia.* Chapel Hill: University of North Carolina Press, 2003.

Litwack, Leon. *Been in the Storm So Long: The Aftermath of Slavery.* New York: Alfred A. Knopf, 1979.

Lockridge, Kenneth A. *On the Sources of Patriarchal Rage: The Commonplace Books of William Byrd and Thomas Jefferson and the Gendering of Power in the Eighteenth Century.* New York: New York University Press, 1992.

Lounsbury, Carl R. *The Courthouses of Early Virginia: An Architectural History.* Charlottesville: University of Virginia Press, 2005.

MacLean, Nancy. *Behind the Mask of Chivalry: The Making of the Second Ku Klux Klan.* New York: Oxford University Press, 1994.

Mallon, Florencia E. *Peasant and Nation: The Making of Postcolonial Mexico and Peru.* Berkeley: University of California Press, 1995.

Malone, Dumas. *Dictionary of American Biography.* 20 vols. New York: Charles Scribner's Sons, 1928–36.

———. *The Public Life of Thomas Cooper, 1783–1839.* New Haven: Yale University Press; London: H. Milford, Oxford University Press, 1926.

Mann, Bruce H. *Neighbors and Strangers: Law and Community in Early Connecticut.* Chapel Hill: University of North Carolina Press, 1987.

———. *Republic of Debtors: Bankruptcy in the Age of American Independence.* Cambridge, Mass.: Harvard University Press, 2002.

Mathews, Donald G. *Religion in the Old South.* Chicago: University of Chicago Press, 1977.

McCormick, Richard P. *The Second Party System: Party Formation in the Jacksonian Era.*

McCurdy, Charles W. *The Anti-Rent Era in New York Law and Politics, 1839–1865.* Chapel Hill: University of North Carolina Press, 2001.

McCurry, Stephanie. *Masters of Small Worlds: Yeoman Households, Gender Relations, and the Political Culture of the Antebellum South Carolina Low Country.* New York: Oxford University Press, 1995.

McInnis, Maurie D. *The Politics of Taste in Antebellum Charleston.* Chapel Hill: University of North Carolina Press, 2005.

McIntosh, Atwell Campbell. "The Jurisdiction of the North Carolina Supreme Court." *North Carolina Law Review* 5 (1926–27): 5–29.

McLaurin, Melton. *Celia, A Slave.* Athens: University of Georgia Press, 1991.

McMillen, Sally G. *Motherhood in the Old South: Pregnancy, Childbirth, and Infant Rearing.* Baton Rouge: Louisiana State University Press, 1990.

McNamara, Martha J. *From Tavern to Courthouse: Architecture and Ritual in American Law, 1658–1860.* Baltimore: Johns Hopkins University Press, 2004.

Melish, Joanne Pope. *Disowning Slavery: Gradual Emancipation and "Race" in New England, 1780–1860.* Ithaca: Cornell University Press, 1998.

Meranze, Michael. *Laboratories of Virtue: Punishment, Revolution, and Authority in Philadelphia, 1760–1835.* Chapel Hill: University of North Carolina Press, 1996.

Miller, F. Thornton. *Juries and Judges versus the Law: Virginia's Provincial Legal Perspective, 1783–1829.* Charlottesville: University of Virginia Press, 1994.

Miller, Perry. *The Life of the Mind in America: From the Revolution to the Civil War.* New York: Harcourt, Brace, and World, 1965.

Mohr, Clarence. *On the Threshold of Freedom: Masters and Slaves in Civil War Georgia.* Athens: University of Georgia Press, 1986.

Montgomery, David. *Beyond Equality: Labor and the Radical Republicans, 1862–1872.* New York: Alfred A. Knopf, 1967.

———. *Citizen Worker: The Experience of Workers in the United States with Democracy and the Free Market during the Nineteenth Century.* New York: Cambridge University Press, 1993.

Morgan, Edmund S. *American Slavery, American Freedom: The Ordeal of Colonial Virginia.* New York: W. W. Norton, 1975.

Morgan, Philip D. "The Ownership of Property by Slaves in the Mid-Nineteenth Century Low Country." *Journal of Southern History* 49 (August 1983): 399–420.

———. *Slave Counterpoint: Black Culture in the Eighteenth-Century Chesapeake and Lowcountry.* Chapel Hill: University of North Carolina Press, 1998.

Morris, Christopher. *Becoming Southern: The Evolution of a Way of Life, Warren County and Vicksburg, Mississippi, 1770–1860.* New York: Oxford University Press, 1995.

Morris, Richard B. "White Bondage in Ante-Bellum South Carolina." *South Carolina Historical and Genealogical Magazine* 49 (1948): 191–207.

Morris, Thomas D. *Southern Slavery and the Law, 1619–1860*. Chapel Hill: University of North Carolina Press, 1996.

Muldrew, Craig. *The Economy of Obligation: The Culture of Credit and Social Relations in Early Modern England*. New York: St. Martin's Press, 1998.

Murphey, Paul V. *The Rebuke of History: The Southern Agrarians and American Conservative Thought*. Chapel Hill: University of North Carolina Press, 2001.

Murrin, John M. "The Legal Transformation: The Bench and Bar of Eighteenth-Century Massachusetts." In *Colonial America: Essays in Politics and Social Development*, ed. Stanley N. Katz and John M. Murrin, 540–72. 3rd ed. New York: Alfred A. Knopf, 1983.

Nadelhaft, Jerome. "Wife Torture: A Known Phenomenon in Nineteenth-Century America." *Journal of American Culture* 10 (Fall 1987): 39–59.

Nash, A. E. Keir. "A More Equitable Past? Southern Supreme Courts and the Protection of the Antebellum Negro." *North Carolina Historical Review* 48 (1970): 197–241.

———. "Negro Rights and Judicial Behavior in the Old South." Ph.D. diss., Harvard University, 1967.

Nash, Gary, and Jean R. Soderlund. *Freedom by Degrees: Emancipation in Pennsylvania and Its Aftermath*. New York: Oxford University Press, 1991.

Nelson, John K. *A Blessed Company: Parishes, Parsons, and Parishioners in Anglican Virginia, 1690–1776*. Chapel Hill: University of North Carolina Press, 2001.

Nelson, William E. *Americanization of Common Law: The Impact of Legal Change on Massachusetts Society, 1760–1830*. Cambridge, Mass.: Harvard University Press, 1975.

———. *The Fourteenth Amendment: From Political Principle to Judicial Doctrine*. Cambridge, Mass.: Harvard University Press, 1988.

Newman, Louise Michele. *White Women's Rights: The Racial Origins of Feminism in the United States*. New York: Oxford University Press, 1999.

Norton, Mary Beth. "Gender and Defamation in Seventeenth-Century Maryland." *William and Mary Quarterly* 44 (January 1987): 3–39.

Novak, William J. *The People's Welfare: Law and Regulation in Nineteenth-Century America*. Chapel Hill: University of North Carolina Press, 1996.

Oakes, James. "The Political Significance of Slave Resistance." *History Workshop* 22 (Autumn 1986): 89–107.

———. "The Present Becomes the Past: The Planter Class in the Postbellum South." In *New Perspectives on Race and Slavery in America*, ed. Robert H. Abzug and Stephen E. Maizlish, 149–63. Lexington: University Press of Kentucky, 1986.

———. *The Ruling Race: A History of American Slaveholders*. New York: Alfred A. Knopf, 1982.

———. *Slavery and Freedom: An Interpretation of the Old South*. New York: Alfred A. Knopf, 1990.

O'Brien, Gail Williams. *The Legal Fraternity and the Making of a New South Community*. Athens: University of Georgia Press, 1986.

O'Brien, Michael. *Conjectures of Order: Intellectual Life and the American South, 1810–1860*. 2 vols. Chapel Hill: University of North Carolina Press, 2004.

O'Donovan, Susan E. *Becoming Free in the Cotton South*. Cambridge, Mass.: Harvard University Press, 2007.

Olwell, Robert. *Masters, Slaves, and Subjects: The Culture of Power in the South Carolina Low Country, 1740–1790*. Ithaca: Cornell University Press, 1998.

Orth, John V. "North Carolina Constitutional History." *North Carolina Law Review* 70 (1991–92): 1759–87.

Ownby, Ted. *Subduing Satan: Religion, Recreation, and Manhood in the Rural South, 1865–1920*. Chapel Hill: University of North Carolina Press, 1990.

Painter, Nell Irvin. *Sojourner Truth: A Life, a Symbol*. New York: W. W. Norton, 1996.

Paludan, Phillip S. *A Covenant with Death: The Constitution, Law, and Equality in the Civil War Era*. Urbana: University of Illinois Press, 1975.

Parent, Anthony S., Jr. *The Formation of a Slave Society in Virginia, 1660–1740*. Chapel Hill: University of North Carolina Press, 2003.

Pasley, Jeffrey L., Andrew W. Robertson, and David Waldstreicher, eds. *Beyond the Founders: New Approaches to the Political History of the Early American Republic*. Chapel Hill: University of North Carolina Press, 2004.

Pateman, Carole. *The Sexual Contract*. Stanford: Stanford University Press, 1988.

Pearson, Edward A., ed. *Designs against Charleston: The Trial Record of the Denmark Vesey Slave Conspiracy of 1822*. Chapel Hill: University of North Carolina Press, 1999.

Peck, Gunther. *Reinventing Free Labor: Padrones and Immigrant Workers in the North American West, 1880–1930*. Cambridge: Cambridge University Press, 2000.

Penningroth, Dylan C. *The Claims of Kinfolk: African American Property and Community in the Nineteenth-Century South*. Chapel Hill: University of North Carolina Press, 2003.

———. "The Claims of Slaves and Ex-Slaves to Family and Property: A Transatlantic Comparison." *American Historical Review* 112 (October 2007): 1039–69.

———. "Slavery, Freedom, and Social Claims to Property among African Americans in Liberty County, Georgia, 1850–1880." *Journal of American History* 84 (September 1997): 405–35.

Peterson, Merrill D. *Olive Branch and Sword: The Compromise of 1833*. Baton Rouge: Louisiana State University Press, 1982.

Peterson del Mar, David. *What Trouble I Have Seen: A History of Violence Against Wives*. Cambridge, Mass.: Harvard University Press, 1996.

Pitkin, Hanna Fenichel. *Fortune Is a Woman: Gender and Politics in the Thought of Niccolo Machiavelli*. Berkeley: University of California Press, 1984.

Pleck, Elizabeth. *Domestic Tyranny: The Making of Social Policy Against Family Violence from Colonial Times to the Present*. New York: Oxford University Press, 1987.

Pocock, J. G. A. *The Machiavellian Moment: Florentine Political Thought and the Atlantic Republican Tradition*. Princeton: Princeton University Press, 1975.

Powell, Lawrence. "Centralization and Its Discontents in Reconstruction Louisiana." *Studies in American Political Development* 20 (Fall 2006): 105–31.

Powell, William S. *Dictionary of North Carolina Biography*. 6 vols. Chapel Hill: University of North Carolina Press, 1979.

Pratt, Walter F., Jr. "The Struggle for Judicial Independence in Antebellum North Carolina: The Story of Two Judges." *Law and History Review* 4 (1986): 129–59.

Prude, Jonathan. "To Look Upon the 'Lower Sort': Runaway Ads and the Appearance of Unfree Laborers in America, 1750–1800." *Journal of American History* 78 (June 1991): 124–59.

Reddy, William M. *The Invisible Code: Honor and Sentiment in Postrevolutionary France, 1814–1848*. Berkeley: University of California Press, 1997.

Regosin, Elizabeth. *Freedom's Promise: Ex-Slave Families and Citizenship in the Age of Emancipation*. Charlottesville: University of Virginia Press, 2002.

Reidy, Joseph P. *From Slavery to Agrarian Capitalism in the Cotton Plantation South: Central Georgia, 1800–1880*. Chapel Hill: University of North Carolina Press, 1992.

Rice, James D. "The Criminal Trial before and after the Lawyers: Authority, Law, and Culture in Maryland Jury Trials, 1681–1837." *American Journal of Legal History* 40 (Fall 1996): 454–75.

Richardson, Heather Cox. *The Death of Reconstruction: Race, Labor and Politics in the Post–Civil War South, 1865–1901*. Cambridge, Mass.: Harvard University Press, 2001.

Robert, Joseph C. *The Tobacco Kingdom: Plantation, Market and Factory in Virginia and North Carolina, 1800–1860*. Durham, N.C.: Duke University Press, 1938.

Robertson, David. *Denmark Vesey*. New York: Alfred A. Knopf, 1999.

Rodrigue, John C. *Reconstruction in the Cane Fields: From Slavery to Free Labor in Louisiana's Sugar Parishes, 1862–1880*. Baton Rouge: Louisiana State University Press, 2001.

Roeber, A. G. "Authority, Law, and Custom: The Rituals of Court Day in Tidewater Virginia, 1720–1750." *William and Mary Quarterly* 37 (January 1980): 29–52.

———. *Faithful Magistrates and Republican Lawyers: Creators of Virginia Legal Culture, 1680–1810*. Chapel Hill: University of North Carolina Press, 1981.

Roediger, David R. *The Wages of Whiteness: Race and the Making of the American Working Class*. London: Verso, 1991.

Rose, Willie Lee. *Rehearsal for Reconstruction: The Port Royal Experiment.* New York: Alfred A. Knopf, 1964.

Rosen, Hannah. "'Not That Sort of Woman': Race, Gender, and Sexual Violence during the Memphis Riot of 1866." In *Sex, Love, Race: Crossing Boundaries in North American History*, ed. Martha Hodes, 267–93. New York: New York University Press, 1999.

Rothman, Joshua D. *Notorious in the Neighborhood: Sex and Families across the Color Line in Virginia, 1787–1867.* Chapel Hill: University of North Carolina Press, 2003.

Ryan, Mary. *Civic Wars: Democracy and Public Life in the American City during the Nineteenth Century.* Berkeley: University of California Press, 1997.

———. *Cradle of the Middle Class: The Family in Oneida County, New York, 1790– 1865.* New York: Cambridge University Press, 1981.

Salmon, Marylynn. "Women and Property in South Carolina: The Evidence from Marriage Settlements, 1730–1830." *William and Mary Quarterly* 39 (October 1982): 655–85.

———. *Women and the Law of Property in Early America.* Chapel Hill: University of North Carolina Press, 1986.

Sandage, Scott A. *Born Losers: A History of Failure in America.* Cambridge, Mass.: Harvard University Press, 2005.

Sanders, John L. "The North Carolina State House and Capitol, 1792–1872." *Magazine of Antiques* (September 1985): 474–84.

———. "'This Political Temple, the Capitol of North Carolina.'" *Popular Government* 43 (Fall 1977): 1–10.

Saville, Julie. *The Work of Reconstruction: From Slave to Wage Laborer in South Carolina, 1860–1870.* New York: Cambridge University Press, 1994.

Saxton, Alexander. *The Rise and Fall of the White Republic: Class, Politics, and Mass Culture in Nineteenth-Century America.* London: Verso, 1990.

Schafer, Judith Kelleher. *Slavery, Civil Law, and the Supreme Court of Louisiana.* Baton Rouge: Louisiana State University Press, 1994.

Schauinger, Joseph H. "William Gaston: Southern Statesman." *North Carolina Historical Review* 18 (1941): 99–132.

———. "William Gaston and the Supreme Court of North Carolina." *North Carolina Historical Review* 21 (1944): 97–117.

Schlesinger, Arthur M., Jr. *The Age of Jackson.* Boston: Little, Brown, 1945.

Schwalm, Leslie A. *A Hard Fight for We: Women's Transition from Slavery to Freedom in South Carolina.* Urbana: University of Illinois Press, 1997.

Schwarz, Philip J. *Twice Condemned: Slaves and the Criminal Laws of Virginia, 1705–1865.* Baton Rouge: Louisiana State University Press, 1988.

Schweninger, Loren. *Black Property Owners in the South, 1790–1915.* Urbana: University of Illinois Press, 1990.

Scott, Anne Firor. *The Southern Lady: From Pedestal to Politics, 1830–1930.* Chicago: University of Chicago Press, 1970.

Scott, Arthur P. *Criminal Law in Colonial Virginia*. Chicago: University of Chicago Press, 1930.

Scott, Rebecca J. *Slave Emancipation in Cuba: The Transition to Free Labor, 1860–1899*. Princeton: Princeton University Press, 1985.

Scott, Rebecca J., and Michael Zeuske. "Property in Writing, Property on the Ground: Pigs, Horses, Land, and Citizenship in the Aftermath of Slavery, Cuba, 1880–1909." *Comparative Studies in Society and History* 44:4 (2002): 669–99.

Scully, Pamela. *Liberating the Family? Gender and British Slave Emancipation in the Rural Western Cape, South Africa, 1823–1853*. Portsmouth, N.H.: Heinemann; Oxford: James Currey; Cape Town: David Philip, 1997.

Senese, Donald. "Building the Pyramid: The Growth and Development of the State Courts System of Antebellum South Carolina, 1800–1860." *South Carolina Law Review* 24 (1972): 357–89.

Shapiro, Barbara. *"Beyond Reasonable Doubt" and "Probable Cause": Historical Perspectives on the Anglo-American Law of Evidence*. Berkeley: University of California Press, 1991.

Shapiro, Karin A. *A New South Rebellion: The Battle against Convict Labor in the Tennessee Coalfields, 1871–1896*. Chapel Hill: University of North Carolina Press, 1998.

Sinha, Manisha. *The Counter-Revolution of Slavery: Politics and Ideology in Antebellum South Carolina*. Chapel Hill: University of North Carolina Press, 2000.

Sklar, Kathryn Kish. *Catharine Beecher: A Study in American Domesticity*. New Haven: Yale University Press, 1973.

Smith, Bonnie. *The Gender of History: Men, Women, and Historical Practice*. Cambridge, Mass.: Harvard University Press, 1998.

Smith, Rogers M. *Civic Ideals: Conflicting Visions of Citizenship in U.S. History*. New Haven: Yale University Press, 1997.

Smith-Rosenberg, Carol. "Dis-Covering the Subject of the 'Great Constitutional Discussion,' 1786–1789." *Journal of American History* 79 (December 1992): 841–73.

Sommerville, Diane Miller. *Rape and Race in the Nineteenth-Century South*. Chapel Hill: University of North Carolina Press, 2004.

Spindel, Donna J. *Crime and Society in North Carolina, 1663–1776*. Baton Rouge: Louisiana State University Press, 1989.

Stacy, Walter Parker. "Brief Review of the Supreme Court of North Carolina." *North Carolina Law Review* 4 (1925–26): 115–17.

Stanley, Amy Dru. "Beggars Can't Be Choosers: Compulsion and Contract in Postbellum America." *Journal of American History* 78 (March 1992): 1265–93.

———. "Conjugal Bonds and Wage Labor: Rights of Contract in the Age of Emancipation." *Journal of American History* 75 (September 1988): 471–500.

―――. *From Bondage to Contract: Wage Labor, Marriage, and the Market in the Age of Slave Emancipation.* New York: Cambridge University Press, 1998.

Stansell, Christine. *City of Women: Sex and Class in New York, 1789–1860.* Urbana: University of Illinois Press, 1987.

Starke, Barbara M. "Nineteenth-Century African-American Dress." In *Dress in American Culture,* ed. Patricia A. Cunningham and Susan Vaso Lab, 66–79. Bowling Green, Ohio: Bowling Green State University Popular Press, 1993.

Starke, Barbara M., Lillian O. Holloman, and Barbara K. Nordquist. *African American Dress and Adornment: A Cultural Perspective.* Dubuque, Iowa: Kendall/Hunt, 1990.

Stauffer, John. *The Black Hearts of Men: Radical Abolitionists and the Transformation of Race.* Cambridge, Mass.: Harvard University Press, 2003.

Steinberg, Allen. *The Transformation of Criminal Justice: Philadelphia, 1800–1880.* Chapel Hill: University of North Carolina Press, 1989.

Steinfeld, Robert J. *Coercion, Contract, and Free Labor in the Nineteenth Century.* New York: Cambridge University Press, 2001.

―――. *The Invention of Free Labor: The Employment Relation in English and American Law and Culture, 1350–1870.* Chapel Hill: University of North Carolina Press, 1991.

Stevenson, Brenda E. *Life in Black and White: Family and Community in the Slave South.* New York: Oxford University Press, 1996.

Stevenson, George. "Higher Court Records." In *North Carolina Research: Genealogy and Local History,* ed. Helen F. M. Leary, 331–44. Raleigh: North Carolina Genealogical Society, 1996.

―――. "Marriage and Divorce Records." In *North Carolina Research: Genealogy and Local History,* ed. Helen F. M. Leary, 305–6. Raleigh: North Carolina Genealogical Society, 1996.

Stewart, James Brewer. "'Great Talking and Eating Machine': Patriarchy, Mobilization, and the Dynamics of Nullification in South Carolina." *Civil War History* 27 (1981): 197–220.

Stowe, Steven. *Intimacy and Power in the Old South: Ritual in the Lives of Planters.* Baltimore: Johns Hopkins University Press, 1989.

Stretton, Tim. *Women Waging Law in Elizabethan England.* New York: Cambridge University Press, 1998.

Sturtz, Linda L. *Within Her Power: Propertied Women in Colonial Virginia.* New York: Routledge, 2002.

Sydnor, Charles S. "The Southerner and the Laws." *Journal of Southern History* 6 (February 1940): 3–23.

Taylor, Alan. *Liberty Men and Great Proprietors: The Revolutionary Settlement on the Maine Frontier, 1760–1820.* Chapel Hill: University of North Carolina Press, 1990.

Thornton, J. Mills, III. *Politics and Power in a Slave Society: Alabama, 1800–1860*. Baton Rouge: Louisiana State University Press, 1978.

Tilley, Nannie May. *The Bright Tobacco Industry, 1860–1929*. Chapel Hill: University of North Carolina Press, 1967.

Tolbert, Lisa C. *Constructing Townscapes: Space and Society in Antebellum Tennessee*. Chapel Hill: University of North Carolina Press, 1999.

Tomlins, Christopher L. *Law, Labor, and Ideology in the Early American Republic*. New York: Cambridge University Press, 1993.

Turner, Frederick Jackson. *The United States, 1830–1860: The Nation and Its Sections*. New York: H. Holt, 1935.

Turner, Herbert Snipes. *The Dreamer Archibald DeBow Murphey, 1777–1832*. Verona, Va.: McClure Press, 1971.

Tushnet, Mark V. *The American Law of Slavery, 1810–1860: Consideration of Humanity and Interest*. Princeton: Princeton University Press, 1981.

Ulrich, Laurel Thatcher. *A Midwife's Tale: The Life of Martha Ballard, Based on Her Diary, 1785–1812*. New York: Alfred A. Knopf, 1990.

Vernon, James. *Politics and the People: A Study in English Political Culture, c. 1815–1867*. Cambridge: Cambridge University Press, 1993.

———. *Re-Reading the Constitution: New Narratives in the Political History of England's Long Nineteenth Century*. Cambridge: Cambridge University Press, 1996.

Vorenberg, Michael. *Final Freedom: The Civil War, the Abolition of Slavery, and the Thirteenth Amendment*. New York: Cambridge University Press, 2001.

Waddell, Gene, and Rhodri Windsor Liscombe. *Robert Mills's Courthouses and Jails*. Easley, S.C.: Southern Historical Press, 1981.

Waldrep, Christopher. *Roots of Disorder: Race and Criminal Justice in the American South, 1817–80*. Urbana: University of Illinois Press, 1998.

———. "Substituting Law for the Lash: Emancipation and Legal Formalism in a Mississippi County Court." *Journal of American History* 82 (March 1996): 1425–51.

Waldstreicher, David. *In the Midst of Perpetual Fetes: The Making of American Nationalism, 1776–1820*. Chapel Hill: University of North Carolina Press, 1997.

Wall, Helena M. *Fierce Communion: Family and Community in Early America*. Cambridge, Mass.: Harvard University Press, 1990.

Warbasse, Elizabeth Bowles. "The Changing Legal Rights of Married Women, 1800–1861." Ph.D. diss., Radcliffe College, 1966.

Watson, Alan. *Slave Law in the Americas*. Athens: University of Georgia Press, 1989.

Watson, Harry L. *Jacksonian Politics and Community Conflict: The Emergence of the Second American Party System in Cumberland County, North Carolina*. Baton Rouge: Louisiana State University Press, 1981.

White, Deborah Gray. *Ar'n't I a Woman: Female Slaves in the Plantation South*. New York: W. W. Norton, 1985.

White, Shane. *Somewhat More Independent: The End of Slavery in New York City, 1770–1810*. Athens: University of Georgia Press, 1991.

White, Shane, and Graham White. *Stylin': African American Expressive Culture from Its Beginnings to the Zoot Suit*. Ithaca: Cornell University Press, 1998.

Whites, LeeAnn. *The Civil War as a Crisis in Gender: Augusta, Georgia, 1860–1890*. Athens: University of Georgia Press, 1995.

Whittenburg, James P. "Planters, Merchants, and Lawyers: Social Change and the Origins of the North Carolina Regulation." *William and Mary Quarterly* 34 (April 1977): 215–38.

Wiebe, Robert H. *The Opening of American Society: From the Adoption of the Constitution to the Eve of Disunion*. New York: Alfred A. Knopf, 1984.

Wiecek, William M. "The Statutory Law of Slavery and Race in the Thirteen Mainland Colonies of British America." *William and Mary Quarterly* 34 (April 1977): 258–80.

Wilentz, Sean. *The Rise of American Democracy: Jefferson to Lincoln*. New York: W. W. Norton, 2005.

Williams, Heather. *Self-Taught: African American Education in Slavery and Freedom*. Chapel Hill: University of North Carolina Press, 2005.

Williams, Patricia J. *The Alchemy of Race and Rights*. Cambridge, Mass.: Harvard University Press, 1991.

Willrich, Michael. *City of Courts: Socializing Justice in Progressive Era Chicago*. New York: Cambridge University Press, 2003.

Wood, Betty. "'For Their Satisfaction or Redress': African Americans and Church Discipline in the Early South." In *The Devil's Lane: Sex and Race in the Early South*, ed. Catherine Clinton and Michele Gillespie, 109–23. New York: Oxford University Press, 1997.

———. "'Never on a Sunday': Slavery and the Sabbath in Lowcountry Georgia, 1750–1830." In *From Chattel Slaves to Wage Slaves: The Dynamics of Labour Bargaining in the Americas*, ed. Marty Turner, 79–96. Bloomington: Indiana University Press, 1995.

———. *Women's Work, Men's Work: The Informal Slave Economies of Lowcountry Georgia*. Athens: University of Georgia Press, 1995.

Wood, Gordon S. *The Creation of the American Republic, 1776–1787*. Chapel Hill: University of North Carolina Press, 1969.

———. *The Radicalism of the American Revolution*. New York: Alfred A. Knopf, 1992.

Wood, Peter. *Black Majority: Negroes in Colonial South Carolina from 1670 through the Stono Rebellion*. New York: Alfred A. Knopf, 1974.

Woodman, Harold D. *New South, New Law: The Legal Foundations of Credit and*

Labor Relations in the Postbellum Agricultural South. Baton Rouge: Louisiana State University Press, 1995.

Wrightson, Keith. "Two Concepts of Order: Justices, Constables, and Jurymen in Seventeenth-Century England." In *An Ungovernable People: The English and Their Law in the Seventeenth and Eighteenth Centuries,* ed. John Brewer and John Styles, 21–46. New Brunswick, N.J.: Rutgers University Press, 1980.

Wyatt-Brown, Bertram. "The Abolitionists' Postal Campaign of 1835." *Journal of Negro History* 50 (1965): 22–38.

———. "Community, Class, and Snopesian Crime." In *Class, Conflict and Consensus: Antebellum Southern Community Studies,* ed. Orville V. Burton and Robert C. McMath Jr., 171–206. Westport, Conn.: Greenwood Press, 1982.

———. *Southern Honor: Ethics and Behavior in the Old South.* New York: Oxford University Press, 1982.

Young, Jeffrey Robert. *Domesticating Slavery: The Master Class in Georgia and South Carolina, 1670–1837.* Chapel Hill: University of North Carolina Press, 1999.

Zelizer, Viviana A. *The Social Meaning of Money: Pin Money, Paychecks, Poor Relief, and Other Currencies.* Princeton: Princeton University Press, 1997.

Index

Abolition: state leaders' opposition to, 33–34; slaves' property rights leading to, 140, 249; and Jackson's political culture, 224; and slaveholders' property rights, 225; nullifiers' apprehensions about, 260, 276, 279; literature of, 277, 290, 370 (n. 40); and emancipation, 286

Absentee owners, 92–93

Adams, John Quincy, 35

Ad hoc legal forums, 5, 65, 70–71

African Americans: lack of possession of own body and products of labor, 9; restricted rights of, 9, 259, 280, 293; trust in law, 79; credit of, 112; pardon petitions for, 125–26; and property rights in body, 164; and procedural rights, 251; rights claimed by, 286, 287, 291; legal claims of, 288–89; men's civil and political rights, 292, 293. *See also* Free blacks; Slavery; Slaves

African American women: use of law, 82, 328 (n. 3); rape cases concerning, 116, 333 (n. 28); restricted rights of, 292, 293

Age, 8, 120, 121

Age of Reason, 15

Alamance, Battle of, 18

Alimony, 341 (n. 22), 348 (n. 8)

Alinson, Samuel, 39

American Colonization Society, 276, 277

Anderson, Benedict, 302–3 (n. 3)

Anderson-Pendleton District, S.C., 16, 21, 92

Anglican Church, 84, 316 (n. 7)

Appellate courts: and state law, 37, 38, 209, 212, 214, 271, 309 (n. 24); creation of, 50–52, 53; and the people as abstraction, 65; and contesting trials' outcome, 77; and private/public acts, 98, 328 (n. 62); barriers to access to legal system, 103;

and dependents, 104; and abstract points of law, 108; and slaves' possession of property, 147, 149; and violence as crime, 229–35; and property, 236, 237; and individual rights, 239, 251; and property rights, 240, 259; and violence against slaves, 242–44; and divorce, 244, 247; and domestic violence, 250; and test oath, 266, 267; justices of, 268–69; and regulation of slavery, 289; and rape cases, 330–31 (n. 13); and states' rights, 368 (n. 20)

Appellate law: and state law, 10, 12, 24, 31, 208; and dependents, 104

Arbitration, and customary arrangements, 74–75

Armstrong, B. D., 286

Ashe, Samuel, 57, 313 (n. 1)

Atlantic economic networks, 18, 43, 44, 79, 137

Ayers, Edward L., 322 (n. 31)

Bacon's Rebellion, 224

Balance of powers, 31, 47, 311 (n. 46)

Balibar, Etienne, 303 (n. 3)

Baptists, 83, 89

Barden v. Barden (1832), 364 (n. 47)

Battle, William H., 37

Bay, Elihu Hall: and common law, 26–27, 34, 105, 109, 302 (n. 2); and domestic violence cases, 26–27, 180–81; and logic of localized law, 34–35; and higher court records, 38; and slaves' testimony, 196

Beard, Charles, 344 (n. 32)

Beard, Mary Ritter, 105, 249, 329 (n. 8)

Bennett, Thomas, 38

Biddle, Nicholas, 264

Billings, Elizabeth, 139–41

Black Codes, 294–95

Blacks. *See* African Americans; Free blacks; Slaves

Blackstone, William: and common law, 26–27, 39, 48, 61, 80, 329 (n. 8); and professional legal training, 45, 311 (n. 40); and criminal law, 80, 323 (n. 32); and private/public acts, 97, 327 (n. 58); and dependents, 104; on women's property rights, 104, 162, 329 (n. 6); and property law, 104, 329 (n. 6); and domestic violence, 105, 302 (n. 2)

Blanding, Abram, 38, 114–15, 267

Blanding, Susan, 141–42

Blanding, William, 142

Blanding family, 22

Bloch, Ruth H., 350 (n. 14)

Boykin family, 22

Bradwell v. The State of Illinois (1873), 294

Branch, John, 280

Brevard, Joseph, 38

Brewer, Holly, 158, 329 (n. 8), 332 (n. 21)

Brewton, Mary, 159–60, 345–46 (n. 42)

Britain: and historical narratives, 36; decentralization characterizing legal system, 42; and private/public acts, 97, 326–27 (n. 58); legal culture of, 113, 212; and victims of violent felonies, 232; emancipation of slaves in Caribbean, 290; and prosecution for violations of peace, 330 (n. 11)

Bryan, James W., 273, 371 (n. 44)

Burgess, John, 188–89, 191, 197, 198, 199

Burgess, Polly, 188, 191, 197, 198

Burgess, Thomas, 188–89, 191, 192, 196–97, 198, 199

Burke, Aedanus, 49

Burke, Edmund, 256

Caldwell, James J., 269

Calhoun, John C., 21, 225, 252, 262, 263, 264, 367 (n. 11)

Cameron, Duncan, 20, 151, 304 (n. 8), 357 (n. 1)

Cameron, Paul, 197–98

Cameron family, 20, 142

Campbell, Lucretia, 112, 114, 130, 132

Capitalism: and labor relations, 33; and property rights, 137, 337 (n. 6)

Carolina Law Journal, 38, 309 (n. 24)

Carolina Law Repository, 32

Carwell, David, 114–15, 332 (n. 24)

Case law, 27, 34, 38, 39, 61, 62, 309 (n. 23)

Catterall, Helen Tunnicliff, 236–37, 363 (n. 30)

Chancery courts, 212

Chandler, James, 57

Chandler, Sarah, 174–75, 184–85

Chandler, Thomas, 174, 185, 354 (n. 33)

Chanellor v. Vaughn (1802), 230

Character. *See* Individuals' credit

Charleston Mercury, 267, 268, 273, 274, 275, 282, 368 (n. 20), 369 (n. 26)

Chesnut, James, 193–94

Chesnut, John, 130, 356 (n. 44)

Chesnut family, 22

Cheves, Langdon, 30, 305 (n. 8)

Children: use of law, 82; testimony of, 106, 113, 129, 332 (n. 21); fathers' property rights in bodies of, 107, 162, 166; credit of, 112, 113, 128; information on individuals' credit, 123

Chitty, Joseph, 80

Chowan County, N.C., 16, 18

Christian tradition, and criminal behavior, 82–84, 85, 323 (n. 38)

Churches: and conflict resolution, 83–84, 89; transgressions of members, 83–84, 85, 89, 118; and individuals' credit, 124–25; and property claims, 153, 155, 325 (n. 50), 342–43 (n. 26); and domestic violence, 180; and violence against slaves, 194–95, 356 (n. 45)

Circuit courts: and decentralization, 5; and conflict resolution, 22; completeness of records, 23; and tripartite court structure, 40; business conducted by, 64; location of, 67; attendance of spectators, 75–77; formality of, 75; and criminal law, 80

Citizenship: gendered and racialized nature

of, 300–301 (n. 7). *See also* Civil rights; Political rights

Civil law, 96, 97, 98, 322 (n. 31), 327 (n. 62)

Civil rights: restrictions on, 102, 223, 226, 293; of white women, 102, 329 (n. 6); and race, 225, 286; extension of, 287, 292; and Reconstruction, 290; and federal government, 293

Civil rights movement, 14

Civil War: and North Carolina's ties to North, 6; and South Carolina's secession, 6, 263; and freedpeople's use of legal system, 79; and land claims, 162; and claims of African Americans, 287

Clark, Walter, 37

Clarkson, Thomas, 145–46, 162, 189, 194

Class: legal subordination based on, 7, 9, 25, 104; and legal authority in gossip networks, 8; and liberal individualism, 15; and local legal material, 29; local knowledge crossing lines of, 71; and private/public acts, 94; and individuals' credit, 120; and social ranking, 121; and domestic violence, 180; and slaves, 190, 191; and property ownership, 249. *See also* Poor whites; Wealthy whites

Clay, Henry, 225

Clothes, as property, 136, 139–43

Coke, Edward, 45, 105, 329 (n. 8)

Colcock, Charles, 242

Colonial courts, 41

Common law: and Blackstone, 26–27, 39, 48, 61, 80, 329 (n. 8); and localized law, 26–27, 61, 80, 229; and domestic violence, 26–27, 105, 109, 252–53; elevation of, 42, 105, 329 (n. 8); and magistrates' discretion, 48; appeals courts for, 50, 52, 209, 269; ambiguity in, 61; and slaves, 61, 103–4, 107; professionalized versions of, 66–67, 79–80; and criminal law, 80; and dependents, 105, 329 (n. 8); equity law dropped in favor of, 105, 329 (n. 8); and property, 139; and real property, 158; and violence against slaves, 192, 193, 233, 235, 239, 242, 243; and violence, 232

Common reports, 118–20, 122, 125, 129

Commons, 337 (n. 6)

Community dynamics, 65, 69, 77–78, 88

Community policing, 74, 84, 86–88

Community relationships. *See* Social relations

Complaints, 87, 90, 91, 106

Compromise Tariff, 262

Conflict resolution, 7, 22, 26, 81–82, 83–84, 89, 221–22, 304 (n. 7)

Constables, 68–69, 78

Constitutional Court of Appeals, 50

Conway, Bonds, 126–28, 135–36

Cooper, Thomas: education of, 30, 256, 305 (n. 8); on statutes, 38, 39–40, 257, 271, 306 (n. 9), 370 (n. 40); on federal government, 256; on legal authority, 265; on regulation of slavery, 277–78; on states' rights, 366 (n. 1); and McDuffie, 367 (n. 13)

Coroners, 71, 87, 111

Corporatism, 62

Cotton cultivation, 18, 21, 22, 261–62

County courts, 40, 48

Court Act of 1785, 48

Court costs, 72

Courthouses, 67, 215, 217, 316–17 (n. 8), 359 (n. 11)

Court of Conference, 50, 51, 234, 239

Court of Errors, 269

Court of General Sessions, 127

Court of Magistrates and Freeholders, 127, 133, 143

Court structure, 40–42, 47–53, 61, 269

Coverture, 160, 161, 170, 175, 176, 245

Crèvecoeur, Hector, 257

Criminal behavior, 82–84, 85, 86–87, 323 (n. 38)

Criminal law: and localized law, 42, 48, 80, 229, 323 (n. 32); and misconduct cases, 85; and legal professionals, 88; and private/public acts, 95–99, 327–28 (n. 62); and appellate courts, 220, 221; and individual rights, 237, 238, 289

Critical legal studies, 304 (n. 6)

Critical race theory, 300–301 (n. 7)

Cult of the Lost Cause, 14

Culture: localized law embedded in, 10, 63, 79, 287; as defining law, 12; and local court records, 24; and economic transactions, 44; misconduct distinguished from crime, 85; and property claims, 135, 138; and land, 156; and women's legal claims, 186; and divorce, 348 (n. 4). *See also* Legal culture

Currency: as personal property, 143, 144, 340 (n. 15); value of, 156

Custom: and localized law, 5, 27, 35, 65, 99, 186, 316 (n. 4); and property law, 81, 139; and women's domestic tools, 154; legal subordinates' shaping of, 172

Customary arrangements: and localized law, 4, 12, 47, 62, 74; and arbitration, 74–75; law distinguished from, 75; and divorce, 169, 247, 347 (n. 1); and slaves, 171–72, 196–99, 200, 201, 226; and patriarchal authority, 172; and women's legal claims, 186, 200

Debt collection, 43, 48, 81

Declaration of Independence, 110

Democratic Party, 34, 261, 262, 265, 293, 294

Democratic-Republican Party, 256

Dependents: legal status of, 9, 104, 105, 110; use of law, 82, 328 (n. 3); and private/public acts, 94, 95; connection to body politic, 99; and localized law, 100; exercise of influence in law, 102, 171; access to localized law, 103; criminal status of offenses against, 103; offenses against, 103, 107, 109; legal representatives for, 106, 332 (n. 24); and damage to public body, 106–7, 181; discounting complaints and information of, 113; and accounting of credit, 122, 123; evaluation of credit of, 125; credit of, 128–31; property claims of, 140; as property, 162, 346 (n. 47); and state law, 222; lack of individual rights for, 238–39; and authority of household heads, 253; plantation as center of con-

flict resolution, 304 (n. 7). *See also* Legal subordinates

DeSaussure, Henry William, 30, 38, 115, 176, 305 (n. 8), 309 (n. 23), 363 (n. 29)

Deveaux, Marion Singleton, 145, 159, 175–76

Devereux, Thomas P., 53, 59, 248

Discipline: customary forms of, 74; and interests of the peace, 190. *See also* Punishment

District courts, 43, 48–49, 50, 59, 107, 129

Divorce: legal rules for, 91, 174, 347 (n. 1); and women's rights to provisions produced as own, 149–50, 176–77; and property claims of domestic items, 154–55, 156, 176, 340 (n. 17); and real property, 159, 161, 173–76, 185, 220, 345 (n. 41), 349 (n. 10); granting of, 169, 347 (n. 1); narratives of, 169–70; and women's credit, 171; and patriarchal authority, 173; and domestic violence, 174, 180, 185, 220, 351–52 (n. 21); and women's labor, 177, 179, 350 (n. 13); and creditors, 179; and state law, 212, 244; grounds for, 212–14, 245; and definition of cruelty, 213; types of, 341 (n. 22)

Domestic ideology, 225, 350 (n. 14), 360 (n. 10)

Domestic issues: and localized law, 100, 101, 104–5, 253; and incest cases, 103, 107–8; and domestic disorder, 122; and individuals' credit, 122–24, 131; and privatizing domestic relations, 238; law of, 252–53. *See also* Divorce; Marriage

Domestic violence cases: and common law, 26–27, 105, 109, 252–53; and peace bonds, 103, 180, 184–85, 302 (n. 2), 352 (n. 22); and peace, 107, 180–81; and common reports, 122; and women's credit, 171; and divorce, 174, 180, 185, 220, 351–52 (n. 21); and kin, 176, 180, 182; and complaints about husbands' indolence, 177; and women limiting husbands' right in bodies, 179–80; and patriarchal authority, 181–82; and women's mobilization of community support, 182, 353

(n. 27); husbands' claims in, 183, 250, 353 (n. 28)

Donaldson, Robert, 307 (n. 16), 358 (n. 1)

Dower, 158, 159

Drayton, John, 35, 315 (n. 7)

Drayton, William, 305 (n. 8), 318 (n. 12)

Duffy, William, 49, 305 (n. 8)

Dun, R. G. and Co., 120–21, 123, 178

Eaton, B. J., 100–101

Economic issues: North and South Carolina, compared, 6; and operation of law, 43–44; and rule of law, 67; and international markets, 79, 322 (n. 31); and professionalization of law, 79–80; trade networks, 146, 147, 150, 197, 249, 277, 357 (n. 49); independence of women, 150, 341 (n. 22); in post-Revolutionary period, 178; and property law, 236, 362–63 (n. 29); and tariffs, 275; and inequalities, 291. *See also* Class

Edenton, N.C., 16

Elites: and state law, 12; and historical narratives, 35; and Atlantic economic networks, 44; on rural life, 69–70; as magistrates, 71; and uniformity of property, 138; and land speculation, 156–57; and Revolutionary ideology, 264; and white women, 281–82; letters to adolescent children on vice, 324 (n. 42); connections among, 368 (n. 19). *See also* State leaders; Wealthy whites

Emancipation, and conception of race and rights, 286, 288, 301 (n. 7)

Enslaved men, and rape cases, 103, 108, 116–17, 330 (n. 13)

Enslaved women: rape of, 103, 108, 116–17, 330 (n. 13); domestic tools of, 154

Entail, 158

Equity: DeSaussure's volumes on, 38; appeals court for, 50, 52, 209, 269, 363 (n. 29); and property law, 79, 148, 236; and private/public acts, 96; and dependents, 105, 329 (n. 8); and divorce, 175, 347 (n. 1)

European nations, 36

Evangelical Protestant churches, 83–84, 118

Evidence: ordinary people's responsibility for providing, 86–87; slaves' providing of, 87, 196, 335 (n. 47); witnesses establishing, 112; whites using slaves' bodies and actions as, 116; information as, 118, 119

Faulkner, William, 190

Federal government: and historical narratives, 36; and the people as abstraction, 65; and South Carolina nullification campaign, 263, 264–65, 266, 268, 274; role of, 292–93

Federalists, 31, 46, 58–59, 261, 310 (n. 33)

Federal judiciary, authority of, 310 (n. 33)

Feminism, 14, 249. *See also* Women's rights

Feminist theory, 94, 283, 300–301 (n. 7), 331 (n. 16)

Fence laws, 337 (n. 6)

Fifteenth Amendment, 34, 286, 292–93

Fines, 72, 80

Food, as property, 145–48

Ford, Timothy, 115, 236

Former Confederate states, 291–92, 296

Forum shopping, 96

Fourteenth Amendment, 33–34, 286, 287, 288, 292–93, 294, 295, 297, 373 (n. 11)

Fox, Tabitha, 176–79

Free blacks: and local court records, 5; as defendants, 58; and slaves' legal status, 61; localized law experienced by, 72; and rule of law, 79; laws relating to, 81; and protections of law, 82; and private/public acts, 95; credibility of, 101, 113; men's restricted rights, 102; restrictions on, 102, 258, 259, 277–78, 285, 290; violence of whites toward, 103; testimony of, 106, 113–14, 116, 129; individual credit of, 126–27, 128, 135; as slave owners, 126–27, 135–36; and property transfer, 138; clothing of, 141, 338 (n. 9); as legal subordinates, 224, 360 (n. 9); legal status of, 226; disenfranchisement of, 258, 273,

279, 371 (n. 44); expansion of rights, 293.
See also Freedpeople
Free black women: use of law, 82, 172, 328
(n. 3); restricted rights of, 102; clothing
of, 141–42, 338 (n. 11); possession of
food produced by, 149–50; and domestic
violence, 180
Freedmen's Bureau, 287
Freedpeople: legal system used by, 79,
287–88, 291, 321–22 (n. 30), 372 (n. 5);
and land, 157
Freehling, William, 264
Freeman, Joanne, 35
Freemen, as paradigmatic citizens under
state law, 9, 10, 211, 258–59, 272, 273, 274,
275–80, 283–85
French Directory, 52
French Revolution, 58

Gales, Joseph, Jr., 31
Gales, Joseph, Sr., 30, 31–32, 35, 305 (n. 8),
306 (n. 10), 308 (n. 19), 314 (n. 4), 357
(n. 1)
Gales, W. R., 357 (n. 1)
Gales, Weston, 31
Gaston, William: education of, 30, 305
(n. 8); and appellate court, 36, 59, 271,
313 (n. 57); and North Carolina State
Supreme Court, 52–53; and land speculation, 156–57, 159; and South Carolina
nullification, 266; and private legislation,
271; on gubernatorial elections, 279; on
free blacks, 280, 284; on women's rights,
280–81; and American Antiquarian
Society, 307 (n. 17); correspondence of,
307 (n. 16); and North Carolina capitol
building, 357 (n. 1)
Gender: legal subordination based on, 7,
9, 25, 104; and legal authority in gossip
networks, 8; and liberal individualism, 15;
and local legal material, 29; local knowledge crossing lines of, 71; and private/
public acts, 94, 326 (n. 56); and individuals' credit, 120; and social ranking,
121; and denial of rights, 259, 284, 294;

and citizenship, 300–301 (n. 7); and his-
torical narratives on nation building, 303
(n. 3); and liberalism and republicanism,
331 (n. 16)
Genovese, Eugene D., 251, 359 (n. 3), 360
(n. 8)
Gibbon, Edward, 36
Gibson, Nancy, 74, 189–90, 191
Golumbic, Lars C., 48
Gossip networks, 7–8, 23, 77, 118–21, 124,
186, 198, 320–21 (n. 25)
Governance, 3, 4, 5, 7, 8, 10, 26, 66, 299
(nn. 2, 3)
Grand juries, 90, 91–92
Granville County, N.C., 16, 20
Greek Revivalism, 205, 207, 208, 215, 359
(n. 11)
Greenville District, S.C., 50
Greenville Mountaineer, 21
Grimké, John Faucheraud: education of,
30, 305 (n. 8); compilation of statutes,
38, 39–40; reform of legal system, 49; on
courthouses, 316 (n. 8); and magistrates'
manuals, 323 (n. 35); and private/public
acts, 327 (n. 62)
Gross, Ariela, 29, 116, 303–4 (n. 5), 304
(n. 6)
Guthrie, Eunicey, 189, 190, 191

Hale, Matthew, 80
Hall, John, 231, 233–34, 237, 239
Hamilton, Alexander, 36, 261
Hamilton, James, 263, 267, 281
Hammond, James Henry, 369–70 (n. 33)
Hartog, Hendrik, 3–4, 299 (n. 2), 300
(n. 4), 329 (n. 8), 365 (n. 54)
Hawkins, William, 80
Hayne, Robert Y., 38, 270, 278, 369 (n. 26)
Haywood, John: compilation of statutes, 37,
49, 305 (n. 8), 307 (n. 18); and education
of lawyers, 49; and magistrates' manu-
als, 94, 323 (n. 35); and violence against
slaves, 234–35; and criminal cases, 237;
and private/public acts, 327–28 (n. 62)
Henderson, Leonard, 39, 239–40

Herrup, Cynthia B., 299 (n. 2)

Hillsborough, N.C., 18, 20

Historical narratives: and state leaders' narratives of law, 8, 10; and individual rights, 11; and local history, 12–13, 303 (n. 3); and transitions, 13; and distinctiveness of South, 14; and rhetoric of progress, 28; and local legal material, 29, 303–4 (n. 5); on southerners' disdain for law, 79, 321 (n. 29); and private/public acts, 93–94, 326 (n. 56); and dependents, 104; and conception of ownership, 134; on nation, 303 (n. 3)

Hoban, James, 207

Hodge, Joseph, 103, 107–8, 109

Hodge, Nancy, 103, 107–8, 330 (n. 12)

Honor: law's compatibility with, 79, 321 (n. 29); individuals' credit distinguished from, 112–13; audience for, 123; and personal retribution, 361 (n. 16); and toleration of violent acts, 361 (n. 15)

Hooper, William, 16, 48, 305 (n. 8)

Horn, Polly, 114, 115–16, 332 (n. 24)

Horwitz, Morton, 337 (n. 6)

Household heads: authority of, 105, 110, 238–39, 247, 253; as legal representatives of dependents, 106; prosecution of, 106, 109, 330 (n. 10); dependents' activities reflecting on, 122, 131; dependents' knowledge of, 123; credit of, 130; and property ownership, 136; and possession of property, 145, 155; and land, 158; women as subordinates of, 226, 361 (n. 12); and violence against slaves, 233; property rights of, 245, 247; African American men as, 293–94

Hoyt, William Henry, 51

Human agency, 5, 11, 301 (n. 9)

Husband, Herman, 45

Immigrants, 164

Imperial rule: dismantling centralization of, 5; as undermining localized law, 45; and slavery, 45–46, 311 (n. 42); and sovereign body, 105–6; and violence, 227–28

Imprisonment, 72, 78

Incest cases, 103, 107–8, 330 (n. 12)

Independent judiciary, 46–47, 311 (n. 46)

Individual rights: lack of, for legally subordinated individuals, 7, 9, 11, 102, 171, 200, 300 (n. 7); protection of, 8; state law based on, 8, 9–10, 11, 12, 27, 33, 58, 162, 210, 219, 221, 222, 224, 229, 238, 258–59, 264, 273–76; and party politics, 9; and inequalities, 9–10, 11, 25, 102, 224, 259, 283, 285, 291; and localized law, 11, 35, 140; meanings given to, 16, 283, 301–2 (n. 13); social order emphasized over, 65; conceptions of, 102, 110–11, 222, 291, 298; of white men, 110–11, 210, 222, 224, 229, 243–44, 254–55, 257, 258, 259, 273, 274, 275, 280, 283, 289, 290, 297, 366 (n. 5); and property claims, 140; and women's property rights, 173; and domestic violence cases, 183; universalistic notions of, 199; and South Carolina nullification, 210–11, 273–77; and violence, 222–23, 226–27, 238–44; and property law, 223, 276, 284; political context of, 255; expansionist view of, 287, 288, 292–93

Individuals' credit: gossip networks assessing, 7–8, 118–21, 124; and oral presentations, 23; and process of localized law, 65; and social ranking, 101; and local knowledge, 111–12; and testimony, 113–15, 116, 120; determination of, 120; acquisition of, 121–31; social dimension of, 122, 129–30; and domestic issues, 122–24, 131; audience for, 123; localized nature of, 129; and property claims, 135, 167; and divorce, 170; personalized nature of, 190

Inequalities: in state law, 9–10, 11, 15; and individual rights, 9–10, 11, 25, 102, 224, 259, 283, 285, 291; in localized law, 71, 79; and gender, 294; in labor law, 295–97, 373 (n. 15)

Ingersoll, Jared, 305 (n. 8)

Inns of Court, 30, 305 (n. 8)

Innuendo, 23

Inquests, 5, 22–23, 64, 71, 78

Iredell, James, Jr., 30, 37, 60, 125, 305 (n. 8), 307 (n. 18)
Iredell, James, Sr.: and Patriot movement, 16; as state leader, 30; and publishing statutes, 37, 307 (n. 18), 308 (n. 19); on Blackstone, 45, 311 (n. 40); on localized law, 46, 47; on independent judiciary, 46–47; legal studies of, 304 (n. 8)
Isham, Edward, 177–78

Jackson, Andrew, 224, 225, 261, 262, 265
Jay, William, 359 (n. 11)
Jefferson, Thomas, 35, 205, 207, 225, 256, 257, 261
Jeffersonian Republicans, 31, 47, 261, 310 (n. 33)
Jim Crow era, and mythical slave South, 14
Johnson, Andrew, 291
Johnson, Eliza, 125, 132
Johnson, Michael P., 372 (n. 7)
Johnson, Walter, 328 (n. 3), 363 (n. 34)
Johnson, William, 35, 305 (n. 8)
Johnston, David, 267
Johnston, Samuel, 16, 50–51, 234, 237, 304 (n. 8)
Judicial authority: role of, 41–42, 46, 47; localized law undermining, 59
Judicial hierarchy, 13, 41
Judicial independence, 269
Juries: and individuals' credit, 7–8, 119, 124; and trials, 69; and domestic violence cases, 185; and divorce, 212, 245, 247; and murder cases, 220–21; and violence against slaves, 242–43; and popular sovereignty, 311 (n. 45)
Justice: role of law in determination of, 3; popular notions of, 42, 65, 79; particularistic view of, 60; abstract conceptions of, 283; economic justice, 291
Justices of the peace. See Magistrates

Kentucky, 272
Kershaw District, S.C., 16, 22, 49, 62, 80–81
Kin: and social relations, 72, 174, 175, 176; and conflict resolution, 73–74; and assistance for poor, 150; and domestic violence cases, 176, 180, 182; and violence against women, 184
Kitchin, Robert, 326 (n. 58)

Labor: white men's rights over, 9; and southern exceptionalism, 14; inequalities in, 16; and property rights in body, 163–66, 347 (n. 50); as family resource in divorce petitions, 177, 350 (n. 13); as communal resource, 179; husbands' rights to labor of dependents, 179; slaves' paid labor, 197; devaluing of women's labor, 225–26, 360 (n. 10); and freeman, 275; and strikes, 297
Labor contracts: involuntary, 72; and poor whites, 163, 347 (n. 49); and African Americans, 294–97
Labor law: and subordination of poor whites, 226; inequalities in, 295–97, 373 (n. 15); development of, 314 (n. 5)
Land: titles, 43, 80; as real property, 156–62, 173–76; speculation in, 156–57; and family, 157–62, 174–76, 185, 344 (n. 36), 348 (n. 8)
Latin American history, 303 (n. 3)
Latrobe, Benjamin, 207
Laurens, John, 305 (n. 8)
Law: definition of, 3, 7, 12, 22, 27, 44, 45, 46, 52, 58, 59, 62, 105; relationship with popular legal culture, 4; unified body of, 4; evolution of, 4–5, 299–300 (n. 3); centralization of, 5, 8, 299 (n. 3); controlling view of, 13; rule of, 66–67, 79; physical proximity of, 66–78; conceptual proximity of, 79–89; authority of, 205; sovereignty of, 208; labor law, 226, 295–97, 314 (n. 5), 373 (n. 15). See also Localized law; Slave law; State law
Lebsock, Suzanne, 329 (n. 8)
Legal authority: of state law versus localized law, 4, 11, 13, 29, 40, 47, 210, 238, 259, 265, 282–83, 290; of subordinates within

gossip networks, 8; dispersal of, 26, 67; and localism, 40; legal professionals on, 59–60, 61, 258; and ordinary people, 79; and court structure, 269

Legal change, and state law/localized law relationship, 4–5, 299–300 (n. 3)

Legal culture: of South Carolina, 3, 6, 13, 27–28, 47, 263, 311 (n. 46); of North Carolina, 3, 6, 13, 27–28, 47, 311 (n. 46); popular legal culture, 4, 61, 215; and legal professionals, 42, 44–45, 47; and social relations, 103; of Britain, 113, 212

Legal history, 12–13, 29–30, 301 (n. 10), 304 (n. 6)

Legal institutions: evolution of, 4–5, 289; and property law, 8; historical assumptions of, 30; state leaders' conceptions of, 30–32, 46, 59, 208–9, 221, 283; and localism, 61, 67; legal authority of, 62–63; and rule of law, 66; role of local courts in, 316 (n. 4)

Legal procedure, knowledge of, 87

Legal proceedings, location of, 67, 69, 205, 316–17 (n. 8)

Legal professionals: and state law, 3, 8, 12, 27, 267; and property law, 6, 8, 79–80, 88, 137, 158, 167, 236, 267, 322 (n. 31); elevation over ordinary people, 11; and historical narratives, 28, 30; and legal culture, 42, 44–45, 47; Regulator Movement on, 45; magistrates compared to, 48; on court structure, 48–49; on legal authority, 59–60, 61, 258; and rule of law, 67; and criminal law, 88; establishment of practice, 88, 325 (n. 49); and forum shopping, 96; and Blackstone, 104; and property ownership, 137–38; and individual rights, 258

Legal subordinates: lack of rights under state law, 7, 9, 11, 102, 300 (n. 7); and access to localized law, 7, 11, 103, 186–87; legal authority of, 8; exercise of influence in law, 8, 102, 171–72; white men's rights over, 9; as central to localized law, 58;

and social order, 102, 110, 172; lack of civil and political rights, 102, 329 (n. 6); and local courts, 103; complaints of, 106; and patriarchal interest of the peace, 106, 186–87, 199–200; discounting complaints and information of, 113; and individuals' credit, 124, 130; testimony of, 128; credit of, 129, 130; unique identities of, 132; and property rights in body, 164, 166, 167; and patriarchal authority, 171, 183, 184, 285; defense against charges, 172; and individual rights, 221; and state law, 222, 224; legal representatives for, 332 (n. 24). *See also* Dependents

Legal treatises, 12, 24, 27, 38, 162, 208, 210, 309 (n. 24)

Legaré, Hugh S., 267, 366 (n. 9)

Lenoir, William, 266

Liberal individualism, 9, 15, 249–50, 273, 301 (n. 7), 331 (n. 16)

Lincoln, Abraham, 6

Lindsay, Lisa, 335 (n. 46)

Local administration, and state government, 5–6

Local courts: records of, 5, 16, 22–24, 297, 300 (n. 6), 372 (n. 6); and dispute resolution, 7–8; inconsistency in rulings, 8; and rights-based interests, 10; and fines and punishments, 80; and misconduct cases, 85; and private/public acts, 97–98, 327–28 (n. 62); and dependents, 103; legal strategies of testimony in, 114; and testimony of individuals' credit, 120; and patriarchal authority, 171; subordination of, 215, 272; and marriage, 245; and localism, 300 (n. 4); and disestablishment of Anglican Church, 316 (n. 7); role in legal institutions, 316 (n. 4); and rape cases, 330 (n. 13)

Local history, and historical narratives, 12–13, 303 (n. 3)

Localism: in theory and practice of law, 6–7; lack of provincial outlook in, 15; traditional narrative of state building in,

25; culture of, 28, 66, 211–12; and legal authority, 40; institutional persistence of, 47–53, 297–98; legal professionals' articulation of, 58; and violence against slaves, 62; and state law, 210, 211, 270, 271; and divorce, 213, 214, 215, 358 (n. 5); and South Carolina's nullification, 260; and local courts, 300 (n. 4)

Localized law: state law's relationship to, 3–10, 13, 22, 28–29, 40, 209–10, 212, 215, 221, 236, 237, 238, 266, 272–73, 287, 289, 300 (n. 6); and governance, 4, 7, 299 (n. 2); and custom, 5, 27, 35, 65, 99, 186, 316 (n. 4); and decentralization, 5, 27, 40, 58, 105, 265, 268; access to, 7, 11, 43, 51, 103, 284; overlooking importance of, 8; legal professionals' view of, 8, 28–29, 47, 58, 60; patriarchal structure of, 9; accommodation of multiple legal traditions, 10, 12, 13, 35, 107, 138, 139; legal business conducted under, 11; subjectivity valued by, 23; dynamics of, 25, 72–73; inconsistencies and contradictions in, 27–28, 34, 51, 58, 209, 258; logic of, 34–35, 217, 219, 222, 289; and popular sovereignty, 35, 41, 46; and economic transactions, 43–44; and postcolonial legal system, 47–53; widening institutional base of, 48; operation of, 57; context of, 58, 65, 66, 77, 137, 164, 167, 289; and specific situations, 62; discretion of, 63, 101, 236; procedural workings of, 64–65; compulsory nature of, 71–72, 319 (n. 16); and slaves, 72, 73, 237, 363 (n. 31); and private/public acts, 93–94, 98; and domestic issues, 100, 101, 104–5, 253; legitimacy of, 102; and unique identities of dependents, 132; property ownership in, 133–37, 167, 289; and personal property, 140; and people as property, 166; and divorce, 170, 220; and domestic violence, 180, 181, 250; and rights of African Americans, 286, 289; African Americans' familiarity with, 287–88; and rights discourse, 290–91; displacement of, 299 (n. 3)

Local knowledge: as defining law, 12, 24, 27, 60–61; and outcome of cases, 57; as basis of localized law, 71; and legal subordinates, 102; and determination of seriousness of offenses, 111–12; and gossip networks, 118; and individuals' credit, 125; and property claims, 134

Local newspapers: and international news, 15. *See also specific newspapers*

Local officials: and individuals' credit, 7–8; duties of, 68–69, 317 (n. 9); southerners' treatment of, 70; and inequalities, 72; respect for, 79; free blacks' cases against, 82; policing and prosecution of crime, 98; and dependents, 104; and "injured" public, 106; and offenses against dependents, 107, 110; and concrete circumstances of crimes, 108–9, 110

Locke, John, 94

Lost Cause, Cult of the, 14

Loyalty oaths, 292

Macon, Nathaniel, 279

Magistrates: trial records, 22–23; and tripartite court systems, 40; discretion of, 48; jurisdiction of, 48, 49, 69; case summaries of, 64; and practice of law, 67–68; lack of legal training, 68, 81; and screening process, 69, 74, 96; and categorization of cases, 69, 95–96, 97, 98; elite white men as, 71; and social ranking, 73; and peace bonds, 73–74; settlements brokered by, 74; manuals used by, 81, 94–95, 97, 98, 107, 113, 302 (n. 2), 326 (n. 58), 327–28 (n. 62), 352 (n. 22); and misconduct cases, 85; and community policing, 86; popular expectations of, 90; and private/public acts, 95, 96, 99; notes on offenses, 109; reliance on information, 112–13, 118–19, 124; and domestic violence cases, 181; African Americans electing of, 292

Magistrate's hearings: and decentralization of imperial rule, 5; informality of, 64; trials compared to, 69; location of, 69,

71; ordinary people's involvement in, 86–88; information as evidence in, 118, 335 (n. 47)

Manigault, Gabriel, II, 305 (n. 8)

Manigault, Peter, 305 (n. 8)

Marriage: wife's legal death at, 104; and women's property rights, 172–73; privatization of, 244–45, 247–51. *See also* Divorce

Marshall, John, 35

Martin, François Xavier, 37, 304–5 (n. 8), 307–8 (n. 19)

Martin, William Dickinson, 252, 254

Maryland, 272

Massachusetts, 300 (n. 4)

McCauley, Robert, 252, 254

McCord, David J., 30, 38, 268–69, 271, 305 (n. 8), 306 (n. 9), 366 (n. 1), 370 (n. 40)

McCurry, Stephanie, 275, 278, 336 (n. 4), 361 (n. 12)

McDuffie, George, 264–65, 271, 275, 277, 278, 367 (n. 13)

McGraw, Nathan, 127

Meadows, Mary, 184, 185–86

Mecklenburg County, N.C., 41, 46

Men: fights among, 85; free black men's restricted rights, 102; and individuals' credit conflated with financial standing, 120–21; and individuals' credit, 123. *See also* Enslaved men, and rape cases; White men

Methodists, 83

Middleton, Arthur, 305 (n. 8)

Miller, Perry, 28

Miller, Stephen D., 265, 281

Mills, Robert, 207–8, 215, 358 (n. 3), 358–59 (n. 11)

Mississippi, 330–31 (n. 13)

Mitchell, Maria, 286, 290, 291, 371 (n. 1)

Moore, Robert, 271

Morgan, Edmund S., 224

Morris, T., 330–31 (n. 13), 363 (n. 31), 364 (n. 39)

Moultrie, Alexander, 305 (n. 8)

Moultrie, James, 305 (n. 8)

Murphey, Archibald D., 20, 32, 35, 36, 39, 49, 51, 122–23, 196, 305 (n. 8)

Nash, A., 363 (n. 31)

Nash, Frederick, 250

Nation: South's relationship to, 10–16, 25; and South Carolina's nullification campaign, 260, 264; as imagined community, 302–3 (n. 3). *See also* Federal government

National exceptionalism, 330 (n. 11)

National Intelligencer, 31

Nationalism, 263, 264, 367 (n. 11)

Neighbors: and social relations, 72; and conflict resolution, 73–74; and individuals' credit, 124, 131; and theft cases, 144; and assistance for poor, 150, 151; and domestic violence cases, 180, 182, 185, 186; and violence against women, 184; and violence against slaves, 193

New Jersey, 39

Nichols, William, 205, 207

North: North Carolina's ties to, 6; inequality in, 15; and statutes, 39; and individual rights, 223, 254; legal parallels with South, 360 (n. 5)

North Carolina: legal culture of, 3, 6, 13, 27–28, 47, 311 (n. 46); state law/localized law relationship, 4, 211; South Carolina distinguished from, 6; state constitution of, 9, 41, 215, 226, 258, 271, 278–79, 280; connection to nation, 14; in post-Revolutionary era, 14; local court records of, 16; decentralization of governance in, 26, 27, 40–41, 139; and historical narratives, 35–36; higher court records, 37; and Regular Movement, 43; slave law in, 61, 107; legal institutions of, 67; land titles in, 80; and opponents to state penitentiary, 85; and violence against slaves, 192, 193; public architecture of, 205, 208, 211, 217, 357–58 (n. 1); and consolidation of state authority, 208; voting rights for white men, 225; democratizing tendencies in, 225, 360 (n. 7); and appeals courts, 235; and international trade, 322 (n. 31); free blacks' cases in, 323 (n. 26)

North Carolina legislature: and localized law, 48, 52; and Court of Conference, 50, 51; and appeals court, 59; and divorce, 170, 212, 213, 214–15, 347 (n. 1), 358 (n. 7); and public architecture, 205

North Carolina State Supreme Court: and reports from higher courts, 37; establishment of, 51–52, 209, 239; efforts to dismantle, 52–53, 59, 312–13 (n. 56); and property cases, 149; in state capitol building, 205; support for, 313 (n. 57)

Nott, Abraham, 50

Novak, William J., 57, 314 (n. 2)

Nullification Party, 274, 368 (n. 20)

Offenses: and authority of the peace, 7, 106, 107–8; conditional enumeration of, 66; magistrates' categorization of, 69, 95–96, 97, 98; and magistrates' manuals, 81; people's role in identification of, 97; against dependents, 103, 107; determinations of seriousness of, 111

Oligarchies, 226

O'Neall, John Belton, 30, 34, 38, 243, 267, 305 (n. 8)

Oral knowledge, 4

Oral presentations, and individuals' credit, 23

Orange County, N.C., 16, 18, 20, 41

Ordinary people: and localized law, 3, 4, 12, 59, 63, 99; and state law, 11; and keeping the peace, 66; and conceptual proximity of law, 79; and community policing, 86–88; and private/public acts, 97, 98; and legal treatment of violence, 227; and local court records, 300 (n. 6)

Otis, James, 305 (n. 8)

Overseers, 103, 118–19, 145, 189, 190, 194

Paine, Thomas, 66, 305 (n. 8)

Pardon petitions: and local knowledge, 57, 60–61; and particularistic view of justice, 60; governors' reaction to, 60–61, 78, 315

(n. 7); as alternate appeals process, 77; rhetorical conventions of, 77; religion's influence in, 84; and testimony, 113, 114; and individuals' credit, 125; for African Americans, 125–26

Party politics, 9, 35, 224, 225, 261, 263, 283

Paternalism, 360 (n. 8)

Patriarchal authority: limits to exercise of, 109–10, 172, 284, 285; of white men, 110; contingency and contextuality of, 121, 132; and acquisition of credit, 121–23, 132; and legal possession, 136, 137; development of, 137; and wives, children, and slaves as property, 162; dynamics of, 171; dispersal of, 172; women's families as challenge to, 174; and women's ties to social order, 180; and domestic violence cases, 181–82, 221; and violence against women, 184; and slaves, 186, 188–92; varied definitions of, 200; and property rights, 249, 250; and individual rights, 251; of freemen, 285; and property ownership, 336 (n. 4)

Patriarchy: of hierarchical order of peace, 7, 103, 131–32; and structure of localized law, 9, 101, 103; of sovereign body, 105–6; interests of the peace, 106, 109–10, 111, 171; individualized version of, 110–11; and land as expression of lineage, 157–58, 159; legal terms of, 172

Patriot movement, 16, 18, 45

Peace: localized law maintaining, 4, 6, 7, 9, 10, 11, 57, 64–65, 66, 109, 222, 234, 239, 263, 289; hierarchical order of, 7, 11, 103, 105, 109–10, 258; collective conceptions of, 9, 11, 106, 108, 210, 289; conflicting conceptions of, 58, 221–22; and social order, 65, 103, 108; concept of, 94–95; and private/public acts, 96, 97; and incest cases, 103, 107–8; inclusive order of, 105; legal concept of, 105; disruptions to, 106; and state as legal representative for dependents, 106; patriarchal interests of, 106, 109–10, 171, 192; and offenses against dependents, 107; and domestic violence,

107, 180–81, 183, 185; slaves' connection to, 107, 186–88, 191–96, 199, 200, 201, 233–34, 235, 237, 239, 244; and individuals' credit, 131; and property claims, 134–35, 138, 139, 153, 155–56, 167; and people as property, 166; and divorce, 170, 214, 244; as legal process, 172; violence as crime against, 227, 229–38; redefining of, 238, 244; and individual rights, 239

Peace bonds: magistrates' issuing of, 73–74; for minor offenses, 90; function of, 96; and domestic violence cases, 103, 180, 184–85, 302 (n. 2), 352 (n. 22)

Pearson, Richmond M., 220–21, 365 (n. 60)

Penningroth, Dylan, 146, 154

People, the: in localized law, 65; and metaphorical public body, 65, 105–7, 108, 110, 181, 228, 332 (n. 24)

Perry, Benjamin F., 21

Personal conflicts, and authority of the peace, 7

Personal property, 137–44, 156, 337 (n. 5)

Petigru, James Louis, 52, 267–68, 366–67 (n. 9)

Pinckney, Charles, 30, 42, 46, 47, 305 (n. 8), 311 (n. 45)

Pinckney, Charles Cotesworth, 30, 305 (n. 8)

Pinckney, Henry L., 273

Pinckney, Thomas, 161, 236, 305 (n. 8), 346 (n. 44)

Political rights: restrictions on, 102, 223, 226, 293; of white women, 102, 329 (n. 6); of white men, 224, 258, 259; and race, 225, 286; extension of, 287, 292; and Reconstruction, 290; and federal government, 293

Polk, William, 247–48

Pool, Thomas, 313 (n. 1)

Poorhouses, 150, 342 (n. 23)

Poor relief, and rule of law, 67

Poor whites: and local court records, 5; rights under state law, 9, 226, 285, 292; as defendants, 58; localized law experienced by, 72; testimony of, 113; and claims on

neighbors' provisions, 150, 342 (n. 23); property rights in lives of, 163–64, 165, 346–47 (n. 49); and respect from slaves, 190, 191; as legal subordinates, 224, 226; surveillance of, 318 (n. 13)

Popular legal culture, 4, 61, 215

Popular sovereignty: and localized law, 35, 41, 46; and Revolutionary ideology, 41, 42, 46, 65, 67; and juries, 311 (n. 45)

Popular writings, as informing law, 12

Possession: in localized law, 134, 136, 137, 138, 139, 167, 336 (n. 4); and negotiating property claims, 139; and personal property, 140–44; and lack of exclusive claims to property, 145, 155; legal claims to, 145–46; ambiguity in, 160

Postcolonial legal system: development of, 40–47; and localized law, 47–53

Post-Revolutionary era: and dismantling of centralization of imperial rule, 5; trends in legal culture of, 6–7; and textual legal authorities defining state law, 12; political ideology of, 110–11, 331 (n. 16); as age of democracy, 224

Power relations: and localized law, 25, 41; and popular sovereignty, 41, 46; and legal mechanisms of the peace, 57; in southern communities, 190

Presbyterians, 83

Prescriptive status markers, 8

Preslar, Alvin, 220–21

Preslar, Esther, 175, 177, 220–21

Preston, William Campbell, 267

Priestley, Joseph, 256, 305 (n. 8)

Primitive Baptists, 83, 89

Primogeniture, 158

Pringle, John Julius, 305 (n. 8)

Private/public acts: distinguishing between, 90–98, 101, 326 (n. 56); and gender, 94, 326 (n. 56); and criminal law, 95–99, 327–28 (n. 62); and civil law, 96, 97, 98, 327 (n. 62); and violence, 97–98, 227–28, 230, 232, 326–27 (n. 58), 327–28 (n. 62)

Process-based law: in post-Revolutionary

legal culture, 7; local court records describing, 23; localized law as, 27, 57, 65–66, 172; role of the people in, 65, 66; and community dynamics, 65, 69, 77–78; importance in early nineteenth century, 315 (n. 2)

Progress, rhetoric of, 5, 28, 31–32, 39

Progressive Era, 224, 287

Property: concepts of ownership, 133–34; personality of, 136, 137, 166, 187; forms of, 136, 137–43, 168, 337 (n. 5); personal, 137–44, 337 (n. 5); transfer of, 138, 212; real, 156–62; people as, 162–67; and divorce, 173–74; and voting rights, 279, 280

Property law: and legal professionals, 6, 8, 79–80, 88, 236, 322 (n. 31); public law compared to, 80–81; and father's rights to daughter's labor and body, 107; and white men's individual rights, 110; conceptions of ownership in, 134, 136; and land as family resource, 158; and coverture, 160, 161, 170, 175; and women's property rights, 173, 174; and individual rights, 223, 276, 284; and appeals courts, 236

Property ownership: conceptions of, 133–34, 249; in localized law, 133–37, 167, 289; in state law, 134, 135, 136, 137, 138–39, 145, 147, 167, 168, 209–10, 212, 336 (n. 4); and legal professionals, 137–38; and personal property, 140; of slaves, 149; and women's property rights, 160; and individual rights, 238

Property rights: protection of, 8; of white patriarchs, 9, 10, 110–11; and slavery, 10, 240–41, 244; and categorization of cases, 96; of slaves, 133, 148; and legal professionals, 137–38; undermining legal subordination, 140; and possession, 145; alienation of, 162; and divorce, 214; and marriage, 245; of white men, 258; and state law, 275; and Reconstruction, 293

Prosecution, process of, 88

Public health, and rule of law, 67

Public law: and state law versus localized law, 10, 13, 80; property law compared to, 80–81; and conflict resolution, 81–82; private acts distinguished from, 90–98

Punishment: as corporal, 72; and social ranking of slaves, 73; extralegal sanctions vs. legal, 74, 78, 319 (n. 20); discretionary use of, 80; capital punishment, 83; and church members' transgressions, 83–84; criminal punishment, 85; and private/public acts, 95; of slaves, 117, 187, 193; of dependents, 253

Race: legal subordination based on, 7, 9, 25, 72–73, 104; and legal authority in gossip networks, 8; and liberal individualism, 15; racial ideology, 29; local knowledge crossing lines of, 71; and private/public acts, 94; and individuals' credit, 120, 125–26; and social ranking, 121; and limits of democratizing tendencies, 225; and denial of rights, 259, 277–78, 280, 284; legal handling of race relations, 291; and citizenship, 300–301 (n. 7)

Raleigh Register, 31, 91, 320–21 (n. 25), 357 (n. 1)

Rape cases, 103, 108, 112, 114, 116–17, 130, 196, 330–31 (n. 13)

Read, Jacob, 305 (n. 8)

Real estate, 140, 156, 158

Real property, 140, 156–62, 173–76

Reconstruction: and localized law, 25; and systematization of state law, 33–34; and rights of African Americans, 286, 287, 288, 290; characterization of, 291; and Confederate states' readmission to Union, 291–92; and Black Codes, 294; and labor unrest, 297

Reeve, Tapping, 251–53

Regulator Movement, 18, 43, 45, 46, 48, 50, 80

Religious writings, as informing law, 12

Republicanism, 331 (n. 16), 366 (n. 5)

Republican Party, 33–34, 290, 291–96, 372 (n. 9)

Republics, monarchies contrasted with, 42

Revolutionary ideology: and decentralization of governance, 5, 32, 41; application of, 8; and state leaders, 32; and localized law, 35; and popular sovereignty, 41, 42, 46, 65, 67; and slavery, 59; and private/public acts, 98; and individual rights, 110–11; and elites, 264

Richardson, John Smith, 243

Robert McNamara v. John Kerns et al. (1841), 149

Ruffin, Thomas: and Hillsborough, 20; education of, 30, 305 (n. 8); as court reporter, 39; and North Carolina State Supreme Court, 51, 52, 53; and localism, 58; and Murphey, 122; and slaves' property, 148–49; and divorce, 214, 245, 247, 364 (n. 47); and property rights, 240–41; and women's property rights, 248; and husbands' rights, 250; and legal limits of self-defense, 253–54, 284, 365 (n. 60)

Rule of law, conceptual notion of, 66–67, 79

Runaway slaves, 140, 151, 199, 339 (n. 13), 357 (n. 51)

Rural life, 76, 86, 98, 150, 337 (n. 6)

Rural population, 5, 69–70, 318 (n. 12)

Rutledge, Edward, 305 (n. 8)

Rutledge, Hugh, 305 (n. 8)

Rutledge, John, 305 (n. 8)

Salmon, Marylynn, 160

Saunders, R. M., 357 (n. 1)

Schenck, David, 177–78

Schlesinger, Arthur, 224

Scroggins v. Scroggins (1832), 214, 245, 247

Seawall, Henry, 357 (n. 1)

Secession, 6, 14, 260, 263

Second Party System, 257, 261, 262

Sedition Act, 256

Sentencing, alterations in, 77

Sharecroppers, 296

Shays' Rebellion, 81

Sheriffs, 68–69, 78, 292, 317 (n. 9)

Simpson, O. J., 96

Sinclair, Sam, 126, 129, 130, 356 (n. 44)

Singleton, Mathew, 145, 189

Singleton, Richard, 159, 175, 194, 345 (n. 41)

Sizemore, Henry, 122, 151

Slander cases, 117–18, 189, 332 (n. 23)

Slave law: treatises and commentary on, 38; and localized law, 61; colonial, 61–62, 315 (n. 8); and magistrates' manuals, 81; and slaves' rights in their own bodies, 108; and Catterall, 236–37, 363 (n. 30); and application of rights, 238, 363 (n. 34); proliferation of, 289; Black Codes, 294–95

Slave revolts, 115–16, 140, 277, 279, 289–90

Slavery: North and South Carolina, compared, 6; relationship to rest of nation, 10; and property rights, 10, 240–41, 244; liberal principles used in defense of, 16, 225; and tobacco production, 20; and imperial rule, 45; definition of, 61; legal regulation of, 187–88, 192, 200, 235, 277, 289, 290; and state law, 212, 306 (n. 9); and individual rights, 224, 255, 276, 284; privatizing of, 238, 240; and South Carolina nullification, 258, 260

Slaves: and local court records, 5; legal authority of, 8; as defendants, 58, 87, 319 (n. 16); legal status of, 61–62, 103–4, 108; and social rankings, 72, 73; localized law experienced by, 72, 73, 237, 363 (n. 31); and rule of law, 79; use of law, 82, 328 (n. 3); and theft, 86; evidence supplied by, 87, 196, 335 (n. 47); trading with, 92; and private/public acts, 95; connection to body politic, 99; credibility of, 101, 113; criminal charges against, 103; violence of whites toward, 103, 107, 192–96, 233–36, 240–44, 284, 362 (n. 27), 364 (n. 44); testimony of, 106, 113–14, 116, 117, 128, 129, 144, 146, 196; and slander cases, 117–18; and gossip networks, 118–21; and individuals' credit, 123, 124–26, 131; credit of, 126–27, 128, 171, 187, 190; property of, 133, 135, 138, 140, 142, 144, 146–49, 151, 153, 167, 249, 250, 336 (n. 3), 338–39 (n. 12), 339–40 (n. 14), 343 (n. 27); clothing of, 140, 141, 142–43, 338 (n. 11), 339 (n. 13);

cultivation of unused land, 145–46, 157, 162, 197; and possession of produced food, 145–48; theft from, 151, 153; tools of, 153–54; concept of family, 157, 167; as real estate, 158; as personal property, 158–59; land claims of, 162; as property, 162–63, 164, 165, 166, 167, 187, 237, 239–40, 244, 354 (n. 35); lack of uniform experiences, 168; and patriarchal authority, 171, 186; and customary arrangements, 171–72, 196–99, 200, 201, 226; and expectations of whites, 190; as legal subordinates, 224, 226; and procedural rights, 237, 251, 363 (n. 33); dichotomy with freeman, 277; restrictions on, 277, 285, 290; plantation as center of conflict resolution for, 304 (n. 7); surveillance of, 318 (n. 13). *See also* Enslaved men, and rape cases; Enslaved women

Slave society: distinctiveness within narratives of U.S. history, 3, 11, 14, 300 (n. 4); inequalities in, 5, 15, 25; violence in customs of, 5, 25; and state law, 11; and Cult of the Lost Cause, 14; coercive undercurrents of, 71; hierarchical legal order of, 102; political context of, 259

Smith, Bonnie, 303 (n. 3)

Smith, Elijah, 78

Smith, R., 301–2 (n. 13)

Smith, William Loughton, 30, 305 (n. 8)

Social order: and keeping the peace, 65, 66, 103, 110; inequalities in, 71–72; restoring harmony to, 90; and private/public acts, 93–94, 95, 97; and legal subordinates, 102, 110, 172; offenses against, 108; and localized law, 135, 137, 289; and people as property, 166, 167; and patriarchal authority, 171; and domestic violence cases, 180, 182; and slave as subjects in, 187, 195, 196; and violence, 227; and sanctity of marriage, 244; conceptions of, 297–98

Social rankings: marking of, 70–71; idiosyncratic nature of, 72–73; coercion involved in, 95; and private/public acts, 97; and individuals' credit, 113

Social relations: and access to localized law, 11; hierarchy of, 11, 65, 70–73; as influence on law, 12; and local court records, 24; and economic transactions, 44; localized law used to maintain, 58, 65; and ad hoc legal forums, 70–71; inequalities defining, 71; reintegration of criminals into, 83; and participation in law, 88; and legitimacy of localized law, 102; and patriarchal legal culture, 103; dependents' connection to public body, 110, 181; and social ranking, 121; and individuals' credit, 123; and dependents' credit, 130; and divorce, 170

Sommerville, Diane Miller, 331 (n. 13)

Soule, Charles C., 308 (n. 21)

South: assumption of distinctiveness of, 3, 11, 14, 15, 25, 223, 255, 300 (n. 4), 359 (n. 3), 361 (n. 15); localism associated with, 6, 300 (n. 4); relationship to rest of nation, 10–16, 25; liberal principles used in, 15–16; decentralized legal system of, 105, 139; individualized version of patriarchy applied to, 110–11; and property rights, 138; legal history of, 224, 304 (n. 7), 359 (n. 5); as exemplary of national trends, 224–25; and individual rights, 254; legal parallels with North, 360 (n. 5). *See also* Slave society

South Carolina: legal culture of, 3, 6, 13, 27–28, 47, 263, 311 (n. 46); state law/localized law relationship, 4; North Carolina distinguished from, 6; connection to nation, 14; in post-Revolutionary era, 14; local court records of, 16; criminal records of, 22–23; decentralization of governance in, 26, 27, 40–41, 139; and historical narratives, 36; higher court records, 38; and Regular Movement, 43; and slave law, 61–62, 107; vagrancy statute of, 64, 65, 100, 101, 122–24, 150, 151, 163, 164–66, 315 (n. 1), 315–16 (n. 3), 346–47 (n. 49); legal institutions of, 67; land titles in, 80; and violence against slaves, 192–93; public architecture of,

207, 215, 217, 359 (n. 11); and consolidation of state authority, 208; and appeals court, 209, 235; democratizing tendencies in, 224–25, 360 (n. 7); voting rights for white men, 224–25; free blacks' cases in, 323 (n. 36); and international trade, 322 (n. 31)

South Carolina College, 264

South Carolina legislature: and balance of powers, 31; and legal system reform, 49, 52; and divorce petitions, 91, 347 (n. 1); and private acts, 91–93; and public architecture, 207; and test oath, 266

South Carolina nullification campaign of 1827–32: and rationalization of state law, 9; upcountry split over, 21–22; and power of judiciary relative to legislature, 31; and reorganization of court system, 52; and power of judiciary, 53, 367 (n. 14); and individual rights, 210–11, 273–77; and tariffs, 256, 260–61, 262, 274, 275–76, 366 (n. 9); and Second Party System, 257; and relationship to nation, 260; and states' rights, 262–63; and agreement about law, 305–6 (n. 9)

Southern exceptionalism, 14, 25, 223

Spartanburg District, S.C., 16, 21

Spoolman, Sary, 89, 155

State government: and local administration, 5–6; entrenchment of, 10; transformation into centralized government, 15, 263; defining of, 29; and the people as abstraction, 65; and peoples' concerns, 66; white men's participation in, 259, 283; democratization of, 286, 287, 292

State law: localized law's relationship to, 3–10, 13, 22, 28–29, 40, 209–10, 212, 215, 221, 236, 237, 238, 266, 272–73, 287, 289, 300 (n. 6); decentralization of, 5; elaboration of, 5, 8; systematization and centralization of, 5, 24–25, 28, 29, 31–34, 36–40, 47, 59–60, 61, 209, 210, 258, 264, 265, 266, 268–69, 282–83, 304 (n. 7), 305–6 (n. 9), 314 (n. 4); rationalization of, 8–9; inequalities in, 9–10, 11, 15; limited, abstract

terms of, 10, 12, 24, 60, 61, 210, 221; textual legal authorities defining, 12; local issues influencing, 92; property ownership in, 134, 135, 136, 137, 138–39, 167, 168, 212, 336 (n. 4); and property rights, 138; and legal categories of people, 168, 187, 259, 283, 284–85; and public architecture, 205; jurisdiction of, 209–10

State leaders: and state law, 3, 8, 300 (n. 6); localized law characterized by, 8, 32, 58, 300 (n. 6); and rationalization of state-level legal system, 8–9; inequalities maintained by, 9–10; and controlling view of law, 13; and legal authority of state law, 13, 24, 36–38, 40, 266; and historical narratives, 28, 30, 35–36; conceptions of legal institutions, 30–32, 46, 59, 208–9; characterization of alternate versions of law, 32–33, 34; temporal metaphors of, 32–33, 34; opposition to abolition of slavery, 33–34; separation of law from community, 69–70; and criminal law, 80; and property rights, 138; and property law, 167; and public architecture, 205, 208

State Rights Party, 267

States' rights: state leaders on, 31, 305–6 (n. 9); and South Carolina nullification, 260, 261, 262, 263, 264, 266, 366 (n. 9)

State v. Boon (1801), 233–34, 237, 239

State v. Bowen (1849), 243

State v. Caesar (1849), 253–54

State v. Craton (1844), 250

State v. Evans (1796), 231

State v. Fleming (1848), 243

State v. Gaffney (1839), 242

State v. Gee (1791), 236

State v. Hale (1823), 244

State v. Hoover (1839), 241

State v. Hussey (1852), 250

State v. Irwin (1794), 231

State v. Mann (1829), 240

State v. Preslar (1856), 220, 250

State v. Raines (1826), 242

State v. Reed (1823), 239

State v. Tackett (1820), 244

State v. Weaver (1798), 234, 240

State v. Welch (1791), 362 (n. 28)

State v. Will (1834), 365 (n. 60)

State v. Wood (1794), 229–30, 361–62 (n. 17)

Statutes: and state law, 10, 12, 24, 36–39, 208, 307 (n. 18), 309 (n. 25); and process-based law, 27; publishing of, 37, 209, 307 (n. 18), 308 (n. 19); Cooper's organization of, 38, 39–40, 257, 271, 306 (n. 9), 370 (n. 40); ambiguity in, 61, 62; and violence against slaves, 62, 192, 193, 237, 241–43, 363 (n. 30); vagrancy statute, 64, 65–66, 100, 101, 122–24, 150, 151, 163, 164–66, 315 (n. 1), 315–16 (n. 3), 346–47 (n. 49); and the people as abstraction, 65; and criminal law, 80; and private/public acts, 90–98; and barriers to access legal system, 103; and slaves, 103–4; and dependents, 104; and divorce, 212, 213, 214; and violence, 229; digest of, 270, 272

Stono slave rebellion, 235

Stout v. Rutherford (1821), 230–31

Superior courts: published decisions from, 37, 308 (n. 21); and district courts, 49; and divorce, 212, 213, 214, 247

Surnames, and slaves' credit, 126

Swain, David Lowry, 52, 60, 272–73, 305 (n. 8), 307 (n. 17)

Taylor, John Louis, 37, 232, 234, 237, 239, 305 (n. 8)

Taylor, Warner, 195–96, 356–57 (n. 46)

Ten pound law of 1785, 48

Testimony: legal requirements for, 87; of dependents, 106, 113–14; of slaves, 106, 113–14, 116, 117, 128, 144, 146; and individuals' credit, 113–15, 116, 120; and property cases, 133

Test oath, 266–67, 268, 270, 282

Theft cases, 86, 88, 139–41, 144, 146, 151, 153–56, 324 (n. 44), 340 (n. 15)

Thompson, Waddy, 366–67 (n. 9)

Tocqueville, Alexis de, 67

Tomlins, Christopher, 66–67, 163, 299 (n. 2), 301 (n. 8), 314 (n. 5)

Trade networks: slaves' role in, 146, 147, 197, 249, 277, 357 (n. 49); free black women's role in, 150

Trials, 69, 77–78

Truth: and individuals' credit, 23, 113–14, 117, 129, 130; and gossip networks, 118

Tryon, William, 18

Tucker, St. George, 39

Turnbull, Robert, 274, 281

Turner, Nat, 258, 277, 279, 289–90

Twenty pound law of 1787, 48

Unionists, 262, 263, 265, 266, 268, 269, 366 (n. 9), 368 (n. 20)

U.S. Constitution, 43, 65, 81, 110, 310 (nn. 33, 37)

U.S. Supreme Court, 294, 304 (n. 8)

Vagrancy cases: and process of localized law, 64, 65; and private/public acts, 100, 101; and common reports, 122; and women's testimony, 123–24; and neighbors, 150, 151; punishment in, 163; and labor, 164–66, 177; and domestic violence, 180; and labor contracts, 295; and discouragement of herding, 315 (n. 1); determination of vagrancy, 315–16 (n. 3); treatment of vagrants, 346–47 (n. 49)

Valentine, William D., 325 (n. 49), 333 (n. 30)

Van Rensselaer, Stephen, 35

Vernon, James, 303, 316 (n. 8)

Vesey, Denmark, 290, 372 (n. 7)

Violence: against slaves, 62, 103, 107, 192–96, 233–36, 240–44, 284, 362 (n. 27), 364 (n. 44); ambiguity between legal sanctions and extralegal, 74; and circuit court sessions, 77; women's experience of, 85–86; and criminal cases, 85–86, 88, 324 (n. 44); and private/public acts, 97–98, 227–28, 230, 232, 326–27 (n. 58), 327–28 (n. 62); of whites toward free blacks,

103; among slaves, 151, 153, 195; of slaves toward masters, 188–89; and localized law, 221–22, 227, 228–29; and individual rights, 222–23, 226–27, 238–44; and social order, 227; political implications of, 227–28; and appeals courts, 229–35; as crime against the peace, 229–38; legal categories of, 232; privatizing of, 254. *See also* Domestic violence cases

Virginia, 20, 39, 158–59

Virginia and Kentucky Resolutions, 261

Voting rights: and white men, 224, 279; and free blacks, 226, 279–80

Waddill v. Martin (1845), 147, 149

Warrants, serving of, 78, 89, 321 (n. 27)

Washington, George, 225, 261, 304 (n. 8), 305 (n. 8)

Wealthy whites: and property rights, 10; conflict resolution of, 71, 318–19 (n. 15); and social order, 109; and land, 157; political power of, 226; privileging of, 259

Whig Party: and rhetoric of progress, 5, 261; and state law, 31, 266; and Regulation Movement, 46; and state development, 264; and South Carolina nullification, 266

White men: domestic authority at behest of peace, 7; as freemen, 9; individual rights of, 9, 110–11, 210, 222, 224, 229, 243–44, 254–55, 257, 258, 259, 273, 274, 275, 280, 283, 289, 290, 297, 366 (n. 5); and patriarchal authority, 9, 171, 192, 223; and localized law, 57, 58; and honor, 79, 113; and conflict resolution, 81–82; and private/public acts, 94, 95; connection to body politic, 98–99; restricted rights of, without property, 102, 226; and concerns of the peace, 109; differences among, 111, 123; testimony of, 114–15; and validation of legal subordinates' testimony, 116, 117; social ranking of, 121; dependents' knowledge of, 124; and dependents' credit, 130–31; credit of, 130–31, 193,

194; exercise of discretion, 131–32; and property ownership, 136; and possession of property, 145; control of property in themselves, 162–63; and South Carolina nullification, 210–11

White v. Fort (1824), 232–33

White women: and local court records, 5; restricted rights of, 9, 102, 225, 259, 280, 284, 285, 292; social ranking of, 72; attendance at circuit court sessions, 75; use of law, 82, 297, 328 (n. 3); credibility of, 101, 113; testimony of, 106; rape cases concerning, 116; credit of, 130, 192; and assistance for poor, 150; and real property, 159; and property rights in body, 164; and domestic violence, 180; as legal subordinates, 224, 226; and procedural rights, 251; and political elites, 281–82

Wife-beating cases. *See* Domestic violence cases

Wilentz, Sean, 224

Williams, Lewis, 266

Willrich, Michael, 287

Wilson, Jesse, 280

Wilson, John Lyde, 52

Witnesses: elites as, 71; and magistrates' hearings, 87–88; and information, 112; credit of, 112, 128, 129; and individuals' credit, 120, 130

Women: as legal subordinates, 26–27, 72, 245, 281, 302 (n. 2); and social rankings, 72, 101–2; fights among, 85–86, 183; and equity law, 105, 329 (n. 8); credit of, 112, 128, 171, 181, 184, 185, 186; and individuals' credit, 123–24; testimony of, 129; and possession of produced food, 145, 340 (n. 17); domestic tools of, 154–55, 343 (n. 29), 344 (n. 30); property claims of, 155–56, 167; husbands' property rights in bodies of, 162, 164, 166; and patriarchal authority, 171; and family land, 174–75, 348 (n. 8); economic contributions of, 178–79, 350–51 (n. 18); violence against, 183–84, 353 (n. 30). *See also* African

American women; Enslaved women; Free black women; White women

Women's property rights: Bay on, 34; Blackstone on, 104, 162, 329 (n. 6); claims of, 138, 247–48, 249; and land, 158, 159, 160–61, 178, 344 (n. 36), 345 (nn. 37, 41); and marriage, 172–73; and divorce, 173–74

Women's rights, 224, 249, 280–81, 284, 293, 373 (n. 11)

Woodruff, James, 64, 65, 100, 101–2, 109, 122, 123, 129

Workmen's tools, as property, 153–54

Written sources, and private/public acts, 94

Wyatt-Brown, Bertram, 319 (n. 20)